The Complete Air Fryer Cookbook

1201 RECIPES THAT WILL ALLOW YOU TO GET THE MOST OUT OF YOUR APPLIANCE AND TO COOK HEALTHY AND DELICIOUS MEALS EASILY AND QUICKLY

[Nellie L. Redford]

Legal & Disclaimer

The information contained in this book and its contents is not designed to replace or take the place of any form of medical or professional advice; and is not meant to replace the need for independent medical, financial, legal or other professional advice or services, as may be required. The content and information in this book has been provided for educational and entertainment purposes only.

The content and information contained in this book has been compiled from sources deemed reliable, and it is accurate to the best of the Author's knowledge, information and belief. However, the Author cannot guarantee its accuracy and validity and cannot be held liable for any errors and/or omissions. Further, changes are periodically made to this book as and when needed. Where appropriate and/or necessary, you must consult a professional (including but not limited to your doctor, attorney, financial advisor or such other professional advisor) before using any of the suggested remedies, techniques, or information in this book.

Upon using the contents and information contained in this book, you agree to hold harmless the Author from and against any damages, costs, and expenses, including any legal fees potentially resulting from the application of any of the information provided by this book. This disclaimer applies to any loss, damages or injury caused by the use and application, whether directly or indirectly, of any advice or information presented, whether for breach of contract, tort, negligence, personal injury, criminal intent, or under any other cause of action.

You agree to accept all risks of using the information presented inside this book.

You agree that by continuing to read this book, where appropriate and/or necessary, you shall consult a professional (including but not limited to your doctor, attorney, or financial advisor or such other advisor as needed) before using any of the suggested remedies, techniques, or information in this book.

TABLE OF CONTENTS

INTRODUCTION

Thank you for purchasing the book *'The Complete Air Fryer Cookbook'*.

A lot of people across the world love fried food and will do just about anything to get their hands on it. People who hate cooking too manage to quickly fry these foods out of their freezer and satiate their taste buds. However, it's no surprise that these fried foods come with a host of health-related issues, thanks to the copious amounts of oil they soak in while getting fried.

To satiate your taste buds for fried foods without the health-related side effects, you could use an air fryer. This technology uses way less oil compared to traditional deep-frying and is a much healthier but equally tasty option.

This book contains 1201 air fried food recipes that will make your mouth water. You will find that you can eat French fries and any other fried foods without feeling any guilt at all. There are recipes for desserts in the book too! The recipes shared here will leave you craving for more. So, without any further delay, let's get cooking.

CONVERSION TABLES

Cooking Volume Measurement Conversion Chart

Cup	Fluid oz	Tablespoon	Teaspoon	Milliliter
1 cup	8 oz	16 Tbsp	48 tsp	237 ml
¾ cup	6 oz	12 Tbsp	36 tsp	177 ml
²/₃ cup	5 oz	11 Tbsp	32 tsp	158 ml
½ cup	4 oz	8 Tbsp	24 tsp	118 ml
¹/₃ cup	3 oz	5 Tbsp	16 tsp	79 ml
¼ cup	2 oz	4 Tbsp	12 tsp	59 ml
¹/₈ cup	1 oz	2 Tbsp	6 tsp	30 ml
¹/₁₆ cup	.5 oz	1 Tbsp	3 tsp	15 ml

Temperature Conversions

Fahrenheit	Celsius	Gas Mark	Description
225	107	1/4	Very Low
250	121	1/2	Very Low
275	135	1	Low
300	149	2	Low
325	163	3	Moderate
350	177	4	Moderate
375	190	5	Moderately Hot
400	204	6	Moderately Hot
425	218	7	Hot
450	238	8	Hot
475	246	9	Very Hot

Pounds to Kilograms conversion table

Pounds (lb)	Kilograms (kg)	Kilograms+Grams (kg+g)
1 lb	0.454 kg	0 kg 454 g
2 lb	0.907 kg	0 kg 907 g
3 lb	1.361 kg	1 kg 361 g
4 lb	1.814 kg	1 kg 814 g

BREAKFAST RECIPES

1. Tasty Baked Eggs

Prep.Time: 10 min - **Cooking Time:** 20 min - **Servings:** 4

Ingredients:
- ✓ 4 eggs
- ✓ 1 pound baby spinach, torn
- ✓ 7 ounces ham, chopped
- ✓ 4 tablespoons milk
- ✓ 1 tablespoon olive oil
- ✓ Cooking spray
- ✓ Salt and black pepper to the taste

Directions:
1. Heat up a pan with the oil over medium heat, add baby spinach, stir cook for a couple of minutes and take off heat.
2. Grease 4 ramekins with cooking spray and divide baby spinach and ham in each.
3. Crack an egg in each ramekin, also divide milk, season with salt and pepper, place ramekins in preheated air fryer at 350 degrees F and bake for 20 minutes.
4. Serve baked eggs for breakfast.

Nutrition: calories 321 - Fat 6 - Fiber 8 - Carbs 15 - Protein 12

2. Air Fried Sandwich

Prep.Time: 10 min - **Cooking Time:** 6 min - **Servings:** 2

Ingredients:
- ✓ 2 English muffins, halved
- ✓ 2 eggs
- ✓ 2 bacon strips
- ✓ Salt and black pepper to the taste

Directions:
1. Crack eggs in your air fryer, add bacon on top, cover and cook at 392 degrees F for 6 minutes.
2. Heat up your English muffin halves in your microwave for a few seconds, divide eggs on 2 halves, add bacon on top, season with salt and pepper, cover with the other 2 English muffins and serve for breakfast.

Nutrition: calories 261 - Fat 5 - Fiber 8 - Carbs 12 - Protein 4

3. Breakfast Egg Bowls

Prep.Time: 10 min - **Cooking Time:** 20 minutes - **Servings:** 4

Ingredients:
- ✓ 4 dinner rolls, tops cut off and insides scooped out
- ✓ 4 tablespoons heavy cream
- ✓ 4 eggs
- ✓ 4 tablespoons mixed chives and parsley
- ✓ Salt and black pepper to the taste
- ✓ 4 tablespoons parmesan, grated

Directions:
1. Arrange dinner rolls on a baking sheet and crack an egg in each.
2. Divide heavy cream, mixed herbs in each roll and season with salt and pepper.
3. Sprinkle parmesan on top of your rolls, place them in your air fryer and cook at 350 degrees F for 20 minutes.
4. Divide your bread bowls on plates and serve for breakfast.

Nutrition: calories 238 - Fat 4 - Fiber 7 - Carbs 14 - Protein 7

4. Rustic Breakfast

Prep.Time: 10 min - **Cooking Time:** 13 min - **Servings:** 4

Ingredients:
- ✓ 7 ounces baby spinach
- ✓ 8 chestnuts mushrooms, halved
- ✓ 8 tomatoes, halved
- ✓ 1 garlic clove, minced
- ✓ 4 chipolatas
- ✓ 4 bacon slices, chopped
- ✓ Salt and black pepper to the taste
- ✓ 4 eggs
- ✓ Cooking spray

Directions:
1. Grease a cooking pan with the oil and add tomatoes, garlic and mushrooms.
2. Add bacon and chipolatas, also add spinach and crack eggs at the end.
3. Season with salt and pepper, place pan in the cooking basket of your air fryer and cook for 13 minutes at 350 degrees F.
4. Divide among plates and serve for breakfast.

Nutrition: calories 312 - Fat 6 - Fiber 8 - Carbs 15 - Protein 5

5. Delicious Breakfast Soufflé

Prep.Time: 10 min - **Cooking Time:** 8 min - **Servings:** 4

Ingredients:
- ✓ 4 eggs, whisked
- ✓ 4 tablespoons heavy cream
- ✓ A pinch of red chili pepper, crushed
- ✓ 2 tablespoons parsley, chopped
- ✓ 2 tablespoons chives, chopped
- ✓ Salt and black pepper to the taste

Directions:
1. In a bowl, mix eggs with salt, pepper, heavy cream, red chili pepper, parsley and chives, stir well and divide into 4 soufflé dishes.
2. Arrange dishes in your air fryer and cook soufflés at 350 degrees F for 8 minutes.
3. Serve them hot.

Nutrition: calories 300 - Fat 7 - Fiber 9 - Carbs 15 - Protein 6

6. Egg Muffins

Prep.Time: 10 min - **Cooking Time:** 15 min - **Servings:** 4

Ingredients:
- ✓ 1 egg
- ✓ 2 tablespoons olive oil
- ✓ 3 tablespoons milk
- ✓ 3.5 ounces white flour
- ✓ 1 tablespoon baking powder
- ✓ 2 ounces parmesan, grated
- ✓ A splash of Worcestershire sauce

Directions:
1. In a bowl, mix egg with flour, oil, baking powder, milk, Worcestershire and parmesan, whisk well and divide into 4 silicon muffin cups.
2. Arrange cups in your air fryer's cooking basket, cover and cook at 392, degrees F for 15 minutes.
3. Serve warm for breakfast.

Nutrition: calories 251 - Fat 6 - Fiber 8 - Carbs 9 - Protein 3

7. Polenta Bites

Prep.Time: 10 min - **Cooking Time:** 20 min - **Servings:** 4

Ingredients:
For the polenta:
- ✓ 1 tablespoon butter
- ✓ 1 cup cornmeal
- ✓ 3 cups water
- ✓ Salt and black pepper to the taste

For the polenta bites:
- ✓ 2 tablespoons powdered sugar
- ✓ Cooking spray

Directions:
1. In a pan, mix water with cornmeal, butter, salt and pepper, stir, bring to a boil over medium heat, cook for 10 minutes, take off heat, whisk one more time and keep in the fridge until it's cold.
2. Scoop 1 tablespoon of polenta, shape a ball and place on a working surface.
3. Repeat with the rest of the polenta, arrange all the balls in the cooking basket of your air fryer, spray them with cooking spray, cover and cook at 380 degrees F for 8 minutes.
4. Arrange polenta bites on plates, sprinkle sugar all over and serve for breakfast

Nutrition: calories 231 - Fat 7 - Fiber 8 - Carbs 12 - Protein 4

8. Oatmeal Casserole

Prep.Time: 10 min - **Cooking Time:** 20 min - **Servings:** 8

Ingredients:
- ✓ 2 cups rolled oats
- ✓ 1 teaspoon baking powder
- ✓ 1/3 cup brown sugar
- ✓ 1 teaspoon cinnamon powder
- ✓ ½ cup chocolate chips
- ✓ 2/3 cup blueberries
- ✓ 1 banana, peeled and mashed
- ✓ 2 cups milk
- ✓ 1 eggs
- ✓ 2 tablespoons butter
- ✓ 1 teaspoon vanilla extract
- ✓ Cooking spray

Directions:
1. In a bowl, mix sugar with baking powder, cinnamon, chocolate chips, blueberries and banana and stir.
2. In a separate bowl, mix eggs with vanilla extract and butter and stir.
3. Heat up your air fryer at 320 degrees F, grease with cooking spray and add oats on the bottom.
4. Add cinnamon mix and eggs mix, toss and cook for 20 minutes.
5. Stir one more time, divide into bowls and serve for breakfast.

Nutrition: calories 300 - Fat 4 - Fiber 7 - Carbs 12 - Protein 10

9. Delicious Breakfast Potatoes

Prep.Time: 10 min - **Cooking Time:** 35 min - **Servings:** 4

Ingredients:
- ✓ 2 tablespoons olive oil
- ✓ 3 potatoes, cubed
- ✓ 1 yellow onion, chopped
- ✓ 1 red bell pepper, chopped
- ✓ Salt and black pepper to the taste
- ✓ 1 teaspoon garlic powder
- ✓ 1 teaspoon sweet paprika
- ✓ 1 teaspoon onion powder

Directions:
1. Grease your air fryer's basket with olive oil, add potatoes, toss and season with salt and pepper.
2. Add onion, bell pepper, garlic powder, paprika and onion powder, toss well, cover and cook at 370 degrees F for 30 minutes.
3. Divide potatoes mix on plates and serve for breakfast.

Nutrition: calories 214 - Fat 6 - Fiber 8 - Carbs 15 - Protein 4

10. Tasty Hash

Prep.Time: 10 min - **Cooking Time:** 15 min - **Servings:** 6

Ingredients:
- ✓ 16 ounces hash browns
- ✓ ¼ cup olive oil
- ✓ ½ teaspoon paprika
- ✓ ½ teaspoon garlic powder
- ✓ Salt and black pepper to the taste
- ✓ 1 egg, whisked
- ✓ 2 tablespoon chives, chopped
- ✓ 1 cup cheddar, shredded

Directions:
1. Add oil to your air fryer, heat it up at 350 degrees F and add hash browns.
2. Also add paprika, garlic powder, salt, pepper and egg, toss and cook for 15 minutes.
3. Add cheddar and chives, toss, divide among plates and serve.

Nutrition: calories 213 - Fat 7 - Fiber 8 - Carbs 12 - Protein 4

11. Cheese Air Fried Bake

Prep.Time: 10 min - **Cooking Time:** 20 min - **Servings:** 4

Ingredients:
- ✓ 4 bacon slices, cooked and crumbled
- ✓ 2 cups milk
- ✓ 2 and ½ cups cheddar cheese, shredded
- ✓ 1 pound breakfast sausage, casings removed and chopped
- ✓ 2 eggs
- ✓ ½ teaspoon onion powder
- ✓ Salt and black pepper to the taste
- ✓ 3 tablespoons parsley, chopped
- ✓ Cooking spray

Directions:
1. In a bowl, mix eggs with milk, cheese, onion powder, salt, pepper and parsley and whisk well.
2. Grease your air fryer with cooking spray, heat it up at 320 degrees F and add bacon and sausage.
3. Add eggs mix, spread and cook for 20 minutes.
4. Divide among plates and serve.

Nutrition: calories 214 - Fat 5 - Fiber 8 - Carbs 12 - Protein 12

12. Asparagus Frittata

Prep.Time: 10 min - **Cooking Time:** 5 min - **Servings:** 2

Ingredients:
- ✓ 4 eggs, whisked
- ✓ 2 tablespoons parmesan, grated
- ✓ 4 tablespoons milk
- ✓ Salt and black pepper to the taste
- ✓ 10 asparagus tips, steamed
- ✓ Cooking spray

Directions:
1. In a bowl, mix eggs with parmesan, milk, salt and pepper and whisk well.
2. Heat up your air fryer at 400 degrees F and grease with cooking spray.
3. Add asparagus, add eggs mix, toss a bit and cook for 5 minutes.
4. Divide frittata on plates and serve for breakfast

Nutrition: calories 312 - Fat 5 - Fiber 8 - Carbs 14 - Protein 2

13. Scrambled Eggs

Prep.Time: 10 min - Cooking Time: 10 min - Servings: 2

Ingredients:
- ✓ 2 eggs
- ✓ 2 tablespoons butter
- ✓ Salt and black pepper to the taste
- ✓ 1 red bell pepper, chopped
- ✓ A pinch of sweet paprika

Directions:
1. In a bowl, mix eggs with salt, pepper, paprika and red bell pepper and whisk well.
2. Heat up your air fryer at 140 degrees F, add butter and melt it.
3. Add eggs mix, stir and cook for 10 minutes.
4. Divide scrambled eggs on plates and serve for breakfast.

Nutrition: calories 200 - Fat 4 - Fiber 7 - Carbs 10 - Protein 3

14. Spanish Omelet

Prep.Time: 10 min - Cooking Time: 10 min - Servings: 4

Ingredients:
- ✓ 3 eggs
- ✓ ½ chorizo, chopped
- ✓ 1 potato, peeled and cubed
- ✓ ½ cup corn
- ✓ 1 tablespoon olive oil
- ✓ 1 tablespoon parsley, chopped
- ✓ 1 tablespoon feta cheese, crumbled
- ✓ Salt and black pepper to the taste

Directions:
1. Heat up your air fryer at 350 degrees F and add oil.
2. Add chorizo and potatoes, stir and brown them for a few seconds.
3. In a bowl, mix eggs with corn, parsley, cheese, salt and pepper and whisk.
4. Pour this over chorizo and potatoes, spread and cook for 5 minutes.
5. Divide omelet on plates and serve for breakfast.

Nutrition: calories 300 - Fat 6 - Fiber 9 - Carbs 12 - Protein 6

15. Smoked Air Fried Tofu Breakfast

Prep.Time: 10 min - Cooking Time: 12 minutes - Servings: 2

Ingredients:
- ✓ 1 tofu block, pressed and cubed
- ✓ Salt and black pepper to the taste
- ✓ 1 tablespoon smoked paprika
- ✓ ¼ cup cornstarch
- ✓ Cooking spray

Directions:
1. Grease your air fryer's basket with cooking spray and heat the fryer at 370 degrees F.
2. In a bowl, mix tofu with salt, pepper, smoked paprika and cornstarch and toss well.
3. Add tofu to you air fryer's basket and cook for 12 minutes shaking the fryer every 4 minutes.
4. Divide into bowls and serve for breakfast.

Nutrition: calories 172 - Fat 4 - Fiber 7 - Carbs 12 - Protein 4

16. Bell Peppers Frittata

Prep.Time: 10 min - Cooking Time: 20 min - Servings: 4

Ingredients:
- ✓ 2 tablespoons olive oil
- ✓ ½ pounds chicken sausage, casings removed and chopped
- ✓ 1 sweet onion, chopped
- ✓ 1 red bell pepper, chopped
- ✓ 1 orange bell pepper, chopped
- ✓ 1 green bell pepper, chopped
- ✓ Salt and black pepper to the taste
- ✓ 8 eggs, whisked
- ✓ ½ cup mozzarella cheese, shredded
- ✓ 2 teaspoons oregano, chopped

Directions:
1. Add 1 tablespoon oil to your air fryer, add sausage, heat up at 320 degrees F and brown for 1 minute.
2. Add the rest of the oil, onion, red bell pepper, orange and green one, stir and cook for 2 minutes more.
3. Add oregano, salt, pepper and eggs, stir and cook for 15 minutes.
4. Add mozzarella, leave frittata aside for a few minutes, divide among plates and serve.

Nutrition: calories 212 - Fat 4 - Fiber 6 - Carbs 8 - Protein 12

17. Cheesy Breakfast Bread

Prep.Time: 10 min - Cooking Time: 8 min - Servings: 3

Ingredients:
- ✓ 6 bread slices
- ✓ 5 tablespoons butter, melted
- ✓ 3 garlic cloves, minced
- ✓ 6 teaspoons sun dried tomato pesto
- ✓ 1 cup mozzarella cheese, grated

Directions:
1. Arrange bread slices on a working surface.
2. Spread butter all over, divide tomato paste, garlic and top with grated cheese.
3. Add bread slices to your heated air fryer and cook them at 350 degrees F for 8 minutes.
4. Divide among plates and serve for breakfast

Nutrition: calories 187 - Fat 5 - Fiber 6 - Carbs 8 - Protein 3

18. Breakfast Doughnuts

Prep.Time: 10 min - Cooking Time: 18 min - Servings: 6

Ingredients:
- ✓ 4 tablespoons butter, soft
- ✓ 1 and ½ teaspoon baking powder
- ✓ 2 an ¼ cups white flour
- ✓ ½ cup sugar
- ✓ 1/3 cup caster sugar
- ✓ 1 teaspoon cinnamon powder
- ✓ 2 egg yolks
- ✓ ½ cup sour cream

Directions:
1. In a bowl, mix 2 tablespoons butter with simple sugar and egg yolks and whisk well.
2. Add half of the sour cream and stir.
3. In another bowls, mix flour with baking powder, stir and also add to eggs mix.
4. Stir well until you obtain a dough, transfer it to a floured working surface, roll it out and cut big circles with smaller ones in the middle.
5. Brush doughnuts with the rest of the butter, heat up your air fryer at 360 degrees F, place doughnuts inside and cook them for 8 minutes.
6. In a bowl, mix cinnamon with caster sugar and stir.
7. Arrange doughnuts on plates and dip them in cinnamon and sugar before serving.

Nutrition: calories 182 - Fat 3 - Fiber 7 - Carbs 8 - Protein 3

19. Garlic Potatoes with Bacon

Prep.Time: 10 min - Cooking Time: 20 min - Servings: 4

Ingredients:
- ✓ 4 potatoes, peeled and cut into medium cubes
- ✓ 6 garlic cloves, minced
- ✓ 4 bacon slices, chopped
- ✓ 2 rosemary springs, chopped
- ✓ 1 tablespoon olive oil
- ✓ Salt and black pepper to the taste
- ✓ 2 eggs, whisked

Directions:
1. In your air fryer's pan, mix oil with potatoes, garlic, bacon, rosemary, salt, pepper and eggs and whisk.
2. Cook potatoes at 400 degrees F for 20 minutes, divide everything on plates and serve for breakfast.

Nutrition: calories 211 - Fat 3 - Fiber 5 - Carbs 8 - Protein 5

20. Rice, Almonds and Raisins Pudding

Prep.Time: 5 min - Cooking Time: 8 min - Servings: 4

Ingredients:
- ✓ 1 cup brown rice
- ✓ ½ cup coconut chips
- ✓ 1 cup milk
- ✓ 2 cups water
- ✓ ½ cup maple syrup
- ✓ ¼ cup raisins
- ✓ ¼ cup almonds
- ✓ A pinch of cinnamon powder

Directions:
1. Put the rice in a pan that fits your air fryer, add the water, heat up on the stove over medium high heat, cook until rice is soft and drain.
2. Add milk, coconut chips, almonds, raisins, cinnamon and maple syrup, stir well, introduce in your air fryer and cook at 360 degrees F for 8 minutes.
3. Divide rice pudding in bowls and serve.

Nutrition: calories 251 - Fat 6 - Fiber 8 - Carbs 39 - Protein 12

21. Shrimp Sandwiches

Prep.Time: 10 min - Cooking Time: 5 minutes - Servings: 4

Ingredients:
- ✓ 1 and ¼ cups cheddar, shredded
- ✓ 6 ounces canned tiny shrimp, drained
- ✓ 3 tablespoons mayonnaise
- ✓ 2 tablespoons green onions, chopped
- ✓ 4 whole wheat bread slices
- ✓ 2 tablespoons butter, soft

Directions:
1. In a bowl, mix shrimp with cheese, green onion and mayo and stir well.
2. Spread this on half of the bread slices, top with the other bread slices, cut into halves diagonally and spread butter on top.
3. Place sandwiches in your air fryer and cook at 350 degrees F for 5 minutes.
4. Divide shrimp sandwiches on plates and serve them for breakfast.

Nutrition: calories 162 - Fat 3 - Fiber 7 - Carbs 12 - Protein 4

22. Delicious Potato Hash

Prep.Time: 10 min - Cooking Time: 25 min - Servings: 4

Ingredients:
- ✓ 1 and ½ potatoes, cubed
- ✓ 1 yellow onion, chopped
- ✓ 2 teaspoons olive oil
- ✓ 1 green bell pepper, chopped
- ✓ Salt and black pepper to the taste
- ✓ ½ teaspoon thyme, dried
- ✓ 2 eggs

Directions:
1. Heat up your air fryer at 350 degrees F, add oil, heat it up, add onion, bell pepper, salt and pepper, stir and cook for 5 minutes.
2. Add potatoes, thyme and eggs, stir, cover and cook at 360 degrees F for 20 minutes.
3. Divide among plates and serve for breakfast.

Nutrition: calories 214 - Fat 4 - Fiber 7 - Carbs 12 - Protein 7

23. Mushroom Oatmeal

Prep.Time: 10 min - Cooking Time: 20 min - Servings: 4

Ingredients:
- ✓ 1 small yellow onion, chopped
- ✓ 1 cup steel cut oats
- ✓ 2 garlic cloves, minced
- ✓ 2 tablespoons butter
- ✓ ½ cup water
- ✓ 14 ounces canned chicken stock
- ✓ 3 thyme springs, chopped
- ✓ 2 tablespoons extra virgin olive oil
- ✓ ½ cup gouda cheese, grated
- ✓ 8 ounces mushroom, sliced
- ✓ Salt and black pepper to the taste

Directions:
1. Heat up a pan that fits your air fryer with the butter over medium heat, add onions and garlic, stir and cook for 4 minutes.
2. Add oats, water, salt, pepper, stock and thyme, stir, introduce in your air fryer and cook at 360 degrees F for 16 minutes.
3. Meanwhile, heat up a pan with the olive oil over medium heat, add mushrooms, cook them for 3 minutes, add to oatmeal and cheese, stir, divide into bowls and serve for breakfast

Nutrition: calories 284 - Fat 8 - Fiber 8 - Carbs 20 - Protein 17

24. Turkey Burrito

Prep.Time: 10 min - Cooking Time: 10 min - Servings: 2

Ingredients:
- ✓ 4 slices turkey breast already cooked
- ✓ ½ red bell pepper, sliced
- ✓ 2 eggs
- ✓ 1 small avocado, peeled, pitted and sliced
- ✓ 2 tablespoons salsa
- ✓ Salt and black pepper to the taste
- ✓ 1/8 cup mozzarella cheese, grated
- ✓ Tortillas for serving

Directions:
1. In a bowl, whisk eggs with salt and pepper to the taste, pour them in a pan and place it in the air fryer's basket.
2. Cook at 400 degrees F for 5 minutes, take pan out of the fryer and transfer eggs to a plate.
3. Arrange tortillas on a working surface, divide eggs on them, also divide turkey meat, bell pepper, cheese, salsa and avocado.
4. Roll your burritos and place them in your air fryer after you've lined it with some tin foil.
5. Heat up the burritos at 300 degrees F for 3 minutes, divide them on plates and serve.

Nutrition: calories 349 - Fat 23 - Fiber 11 - Carbs 20 - Protein 21

25. Tomato and Bacon Breakfast

Prep.Time: 10 min - **Cooking Time:** 30 min - **Servings:** 6

Ingredients:
- ✓ 1 pound white bread, cubed
- ✓ 1 pound smoked bacon, cooked and chopped
- ✓ ¼ cup olive oil
- ✓ 1 yellow onion, chopped
- ✓ 28 ounces canned tomatoes, chopped
- ✓ ½ teaspoon red pepper, crushed
- ✓ ½ pound cheddar, shredded
- ✓ 2 tablespoons chives, chopped
- ✓ ½ pound Monterey jack, shredded
- ✓ 2 tablespoons stock
- ✓ Salt and black pepper to the taste
- ✓ 8 eggs, whisked

Directions:
1. Add the oil to your air fryer and heat it up at 350 degrees F.
2. Add bread, bacon, onion, tomatoes, red pepper and stock and stir.
3. Add eggs, cheddar and Monterey jack and cook everything for 20 minutes.
4. Divide among plates, sprinkle chives and serve.

Nutrition: calories 231 - Fat 5 - Fiber 7 - Carbs 12 - Protein 4

26. Blackberry French Toast

Prep.Time: 10 min - **Cooking Time:** 20 min - **Servings:** 6

Ingredients:
- ✓ 1 cup blackberry jam, warm
- ✓ 12 ounces bread loaf, cubed
- ✓ 8 ounces cream cheese, cubed
- ✓ 4 eggs
- ✓ 1 teaspoon cinnamon powder
- ✓ 2 cups half and half
- ✓ ½ cup brown sugar
- ✓ 1 teaspoon vanilla extract
- ✓ Cooking spray

Directions:
1. Grease your air fryer with cooking spray and heat it up at 300 degrees F.
2. Add blueberry jam on the bottom, layer half of the bread cubes, then add cream cheese and top with the rest of the bread.
3. In a bowl, mix eggs with half and half, cinnamon, sugar and vanilla, whisk well and add over bread mix.
4. Cook for 20 minutes, divide among plates and serve for breakfast.

Nutrition: calories 215 - Fat 6 - Fiber 9 - Carbs 16 - Protein 6

27. Ham Breakfast Pie

Prep.Time: 10 min - **Cooking Time:** 25 minutes - **Servings:** 6

Ingredients:
- ✓ 16 ounces crescent rolls dough
- ✓ 2 eggs, whisked
- ✓ 2 cups cheddar cheese, grated
- ✓ 1 tablespoon parmesan, grated
- ✓ 2 cups ham, cooked and chopped
- ✓ Salt and black pepper to the taste
- ✓ Cooking spray

Directions:
1. Grease your air fryer's pan with cooking spray and press half of the crescent rolls dough on the bottom.
2. In a bowl, mix eggs with cheddar cheese, parmesan, salt and pepper, whisk well and add over dough.
3. Spread ham, cut the rest of the crescent rolls dough in strips, arrange them over ham and cook at 300 degrees F for 25 minutes.
4. Slice pie and serve for breakfast.

Nutrition: calories 400 - Fat 27 - Fiber 7 - Carbs 22 - Protein 16

28. Air Fried Tomato Breakfast Quiche

Prep.Time: 10 min - **Cooking Time:** 30 min - **Servings:** 1

Ingredients:
- ✓ 2 tablespoons yellow onion, chopped
- ✓ 2 eggs
- ✓ ¼ cup milk
- ✓ ½ cup gouda cheese, shredded
- ✓ ¼ cup tomatoes, chopped
- ✓ Salt and black pepper to the taste
- ✓ Cooking spray

Directions:
1. Grease a ramekin with cooking spray.
2. Crack eggs, add onion, milk, cheese, tomatoes, salt and pepper and stir.
3. Add this in your air fryer's pan and cook at 340 degrees F for 30 minutes.
4. Serve hot.

Nutrition: calories 241 - Fat 6 - Fiber 8 - Carbs 14 - Protein 6

29. Fast Eggs and Tomatoes

Prep.Time: 5 min - **Cooking Time:** 10 min - **Servings:** 4

Ingredients:
- ✓ 4 eggs
- ✓ 2 ounces milk
- ✓ 2 tablespoons parmesan, grated
- ✓ Salt and black pepper to the taste
- ✓ 8 cherry tomatoes, halved
- ✓ Cooking spray

Directions:
1. Grease your air fryer with cooking spray and heat it up at 200 degrees F.
2. In a bowl, mix eggs with cheese, milk, salt and pepper and whisk.
3. Add this mix to your air fryer and cook for 6 minutes.
4. Add tomatoes, cook your scrambled eggs for 3 minutes, divide among plates and serve.

Nutrition: calories 200 - Fat 4 - Fiber 7 - Carbs 12 - Protein 3

30. Egg White Omelet

Prep.Time: 10 min - **Cooking Time:** 15 min - **Servings:** 4

Ingredients:
- ✓ 1 cup egg whites
- ✓ ¼ cup tomato, chopped
- ✓ 2 tablespoons skim milk
- ✓ ¼ cup mushrooms, chopped
- ✓ 2 tablespoons chives, chopped
- ✓ Salt and black pepper to the taste

Directions:
1. In a bowl, mix egg whites with tomato, milk, mushrooms, chives, salt and pepper, whisk well and pour into your air fryer's pan.
2. Cook at 320 degrees F for 15 minutes, cool omelet down, slice, divide among plates and serve.

Nutrition: calories 100 - Fat 3 - Fiber 6 - Carbs 7 - Protein 4

31. Artichoke Frittata

Prep.Time: 10 min - **Cooking Time:** 15 min - **Servings:** 6

Ingredients:
- ✓ 3 canned artichokes hearts, drained and chopped
- ✓ 2 tablespoons olive oil
- ✓ ½ teaspoon oregano, dried
- ✓ Salt and black pepper to the taste
- ✓ 6 eggs, whisked

Directions:
1. In a bowl, mix artichokes with oregano, salt, pepper and eggs and whisk well.
2. Add the oil to your air fryer's pan, add eggs mix and cook at 320 degrees F for 15 minutes.
3. Divide frittata on plates and serve for breakfast.

Nutrition: calories 136 - Fat 6 - Fiber 6 - Carbs 9 - Protein 4

32. Cheese Sandwich

Prep.Time: 10 min - **Cooking Time:** 8 min - **Servings:** 1

Ingredients:
- ✓ 2 bread slices
- ✓ 2 teaspoons butter
- ✓ 2 cheddar cheese slices
- ✓ A pinch of sweet paprika

Directions:
5. 1. Spread butter on bread slices, add cheddar cheese on one, sprinkle paprika, top with the other bread slices, cut into 2 halves, arrange them in your air fryer and cook at 370 degrees F for 8 minutes, flipping them once, arrange on a plate and serve.

Nutrition: calories 130 - Fat 3 - Fiber 5 - Carbs 9 - Protein 3

33. Creamy Breakfast Tofu

Prep.Time: 15 min - **Cooking Time:** 20 minutes - **Servings:** 4

Ingredients:
- ✓ 1 block firm tofu, pressed and cubed
- ✓ 1 teaspoon rice vinegar
- ✓ 2 tablespoons soy sauce
- ✓ 2 teaspoons sesame oil
- ✓ 1 tablespoon potato starch
- ✓ 1 cup Greek yogurt

Directions:
1. In a bowl, mix tofu cubes with vinegar, soy sauce and oil, toss, and leave aside for 15 minutes.
2. Dip tofu cubes in potato starch, toss, transfer to your air fryer, heat up at 370 degrees F and cook for 20 minutes shaking halfway.
3. Divide into bowls and serve for breakfast with some Greek yogurt on the side.

Nutrition: calories 110 - Fat 4 - Fiber 5 - Carbs 8 - Protein 4

34. Ham Rolls

Prep.Time: 10 min - **Cooking Time:** 10 min - **Servings:** 4

Ingredients:
- ✓ 1 sheet puff pastry
- ✓ 4 handful gruyere cheese, grated
- ✓ 4 teaspoons mustard
- ✓ 8 ham slices, chopped

Directions:
1. Roll out puff pastry on a working surface, divide cheese, ham and mustard, roll tight and cut into medium rounds.
2. Place all rolls in air fryer and cook for 10 minutes at 370 degrees F.
3. Divide rolls on plates and serve for breakfast.

Nutrition: calories 182 - Fat 4 - Fiber 7 - Carbs 9 - Protein 8

35. Spinach Breakfast Parcels

Prep.Time: 10 min - **Cooking Time:** 4 min - **Servings:** 2

Ingredients:
- ✓ 4 sheets filo pastry
- ✓ 1 pound baby spinach leaves, roughly chopped
- ✓ ½ pound ricotta cheese
- ✓ 2 tablespoons pine nuts
- ✓ 1 eggs, whisked
- ✓ Zest from 1 lemon, grated
- ✓ Greek yogurt for serving
- ✓ Salt and black pepper to the taste

Directions:
1. In a bowl, mix spinach with cheese, egg, lemon zest, salt, pepper and pine nuts and stir.
2. Arrange filo sheets on a working surface, divide spinach mix, fold diagonally to shape your parcels and place them in your preheated air fryer at 400 degrees F.
3. Bake parcels for 4 minutes, divide them on plates and serve them with Greek yogurt on the side.

Nutrition: calories 182 - Fat 4 - Fiber 8 - Carbs 9 - Protein 5

36. Raspberry Rolls

Prep.Time: 30 min - **Cooking Time:** 20 min - **Servings:** 6

Ingredients:
- ✓ 1 cup milk
- ✓ 4 tablespoons butter
- ✓ 3 and ¼ cups flour
- ✓ 2 teaspoons yeast
- ✓ ¼ cup sugar
- ✓ 1 egg

For the filling:
- ✓ 8 ounces cream cheese, soft
- ✓ 12 ounces raspberries
- ✓ 1 teaspoons vanilla extract
- ✓ 5 tablespoons sugar
- ✓ 1 tablespoon cornstarch
- ✓ Zest from 1 lemon, grated

Directions:
1. In a bowl, mix flour with sugar and yeast and stir.
2. Add milk and egg, stir until you obtain a dough, leave it aside to rise for 30 minutes, transfer dough to a working surface and roll well.
3. In a bowl, mix cream cheese with sugar, vanilla and lemon zest, stir well and spread over dough.
4. In another bowl, mix raspberries with cornstarch, stir and spread over cream cheese mix.
5. Roll your dough, cut into medium pieces, place them in your air fryer, spray them with cooking spray and cook them at 350 degrees F for 30 minutes.
6. Serve your rolls for breakfast.

Nutrition: calories 261 - Fat 5 - Fiber 8 - Carbs 9 - Protein 6

37. Cinnamon and Cream Cheese Oats

Prep.Time: 10 min - Cooking Time: 25 min - Servings: 4

Ingredients:
- ✓ 1 cup steel oats
- ✓ 3 cups milk
- ✓ 1 tablespoon butter
- ✓ ¾ cup raisins
- ✓ 1 teaspoon cinnamon powder
- ✓ ¼ cup brown sugar
- ✓ 2 tablespoons white sugar
- ✓ 2 ounces cream cheese, soft

Directions:
1. Heat up a pan that fits your air fryer with the butter over medium heat, add oats, stir and toast them for 3 minutes.
2. Add milk and raisins, stir, introduce in your air fryer and cook at 350 degrees F for 20 minutes.
3. Meanwhile, in a bowl, mix cinnamon with brown sugar and stir.
4. In a second bowl, mix white sugar with cream cheese and whisk.
5. Divide oats into bowls and top each with cinnamon and cream cheese.

Nutrition: calories 152 - Fat 6 - Fiber 6 - Carbs 25 - Protein 7

38. Tofu Scramble

Prep.Time: 5 min - Cooking Time: 30 min - Servings: 4

Ingredients:
- ✓ 2 tablespoons soy sauce
- ✓ 1 tofu block, cubed
- ✓ 1 teaspoon turmeric, ground
- ✓ 2 tablespoons extra virgin olive oil
- ✓ 4 cups broccoli florets
- ✓ ½ teaspoon onion powder
- ✓ ½ teaspoon garlic powder
- ✓ 2 and ½ cup red potatoes, cubed
- ✓ ½ cup yellow onion, chopped
- ✓ Salt and black pepper to the taste

Directions:
1. Mix tofu with 1 tablespoon oil, salt, pepper, soy sauce, garlic powder, onion powder, turmeric and onion in a bowl, stir and leave aside.
2. In a separate bowl, combine potatoes with the rest of the oil, a pinch of salt and pepper and toss to coat.
3. Put potatoes in your air fryer at 350 degrees F and bake for 15 minutes, shaking once.
4. Add tofu and its marinade to your air fryer and bake for 15 minutes.
5. Add broccoli to the fryer and cook everything for 5 minutes more.
6. Serve right away.

Nutrition: calories 140 - Fat 4 - Fiber 3 - Carbs 10 - Protein 14

39. Dates and Millet Pudding

Prep.Time: 10 min - Cooking Time: 15 minutes - Servings: 4

Ingredients:
- ✓ 14 ounces milk
- ✓ 7 ounces water
- ✓ 2/3 cup millet
- ✓ 4 dates, pitted
- ✓ Honey for serving

Directions:
1. Put the millet in a pan that fits your air fryer, add dates, milk and water, stir, introduce in your air fryer and cook at 360 degrees F for 15 minutes.
2. Divide among plates, drizzle honey on top and serve for breakfast.

Nutrition: calories 231 - Fat 6 - Fiber 6 - Carbs 18 - Protein 6

40. Tasty Cinnamon Toast

Prep.Time: 10 min - Cooking Time: 5 min - Servings: 6

Ingredients:
- ✓ 1 stick butter, soft
- ✓ 12 bread slices
- ✓ ½ cup sugar
- ✓ 1 and ½ teaspoon vanilla extract
- ✓ 1 and ½ teaspoon cinnamon powder

Directions:
1. In a bowl, mix soft butter with sugar, vanilla and cinnamon and whisk well.
2. Spread this on bread slices, place them in your air fryer and cook at 400 degrees F for 5 minutes,
3. Divide among plates and serve for breakfast.

Nutrition: calories 221 - Fat 4 - Fiber 7 - Carbs 12 - Protein 8

41. Biscuits Casserole

Prep.Time: 10 min - Cooking Time: 15 min - Servings: 8

Ingredients:
- ✓ 12 ounces biscuits, quartered
- ✓ 3 tablespoons flour
- ✓ ½ pound sausage, chopped
- ✓ A pinch of salt and black pepper
- ✓ 2 and ½ cups milk
- ✓ Cooking spray

Directions:
1. Grease your air fryer with cooking spray and heat it over 350 degrees F.
2. Add biscuits on the bottom and mix with sausage.
3. Add flour, milk, salt and pepper, toss a bit and cook for 15 minutes.
4. Divide among plates and serve for breakfast.

Nutrition: calories 321 - Fat 4 - Fiber 7 - Carbs 12 - Protein 5

42. Delicious Tofu and Mushrooms

Prep.Time: 10 min - Cooking Time: 10 min - Servings: 2

Ingredients:
- ✓ 1 tofu block, pressed and cut into medium pieces
- ✓ 1 cup panko bread crumbs
- ✓ Salt and black pepper to the taste
- ✓ ½ tablespoons flour
- ✓ 1 egg
- ✓ 1 tablespoon mushrooms, minced

Directions:
1. In a bowl, mix egg with mushrooms, flour, salt and pepper and whisk well.
2. Dip tofu pieces in egg mix, then dredge them in panko bread crumbs, place them in your air fryer and cook at 350 degrees F for 10 minutes.
3. Serve them for breakfast right away.

Nutrition: calories 142 - Fat 4 - Fiber 6 - Carbs 8 - Protein 3

43. Breakfast Mushroom Quiche

Prep.Time: 10 min - **Cooking Time:** 10 min - **Servings:** 4

Ingredients:
- ✓ 1 tablespoon flour
- ✓ 1 tablespoon butter, soft
- ✓ 9 inch pie dough
- ✓ 2 button mushrooms, chopped
- ✓ 2 tablespoons ham, chopped
- ✓ 3 eggs
- ✓ 1 small yellow onion, chopped
- ✓ 1/3 cup heavy cream
- ✓ A pinch of nutmeg, ground
- ✓ Salt and black pepper to the taste
- ✓ ½ teaspoon thyme, dried
- ✓ ¼ cup Swiss cheese, grated

Directions:
1. Dust a working surface with the flour and roll the pie dough.
2. Press in on the bottom of the pie pan your air fryer has.
3. In a bowl, mix butter with mushrooms, ham, onion, eggs, heavy cream, salt, pepper, thyme and nutmeg and whisk well.
4. Add this over pie crust, spread, sprinkle Swiss cheese all over and place pie pan in your air fryer.
5. Cook your quiche at 400 degrees F for 10 minutes.
6. Slice and serve for breakfast.

Nutrition: calories 212 - Fat 4 - Fiber 6 - Carbs 7 - Protein 7

44. Breakfast Veggie Mix

Prep.Time: 10 min - **Cooking Time:** 25 min - **Servings:** 6

Ingredients:
- ✓ 1 yellow onion, sliced
- ✓ 1 red bell pepper, chopped
- ✓ 1 gold potato, chopped
- ✓ 2 tablespoons olive oil
- ✓ 8 ounces brie, trimmed and cubed
- ✓ 12 ounces sourdough bread, cubed
- ✓ 4 ounces parmesan, grated
- ✓ 8 eggs
- ✓ 2 tablespoons mustard
- ✓ 3 cups milk
- ✓ Salt and black pepper to the taste

Directions:
1. Heat up your air fryer at 350 degrees F, add oil, onion, potato and bell pepper and cook for 5 minutes.
2. In a bowl, mix eggs with milk, salt, pepper and mustard and whisk well.
3. Add bread and brie to your air fryer, add half of the eggs mix and add half of the parmesan as well.
4. Add the rest of the bread and parmesan, toss just a little bit and cook for 20 minutes.
5. Divide among plates and serve for breakfast.

Nutrition: calories 231 - Fat 5 - Fiber 10 - Carbs 20 - Protein 12

45. Special Corn Flakes Breakfast Casserole

Prep.Time: 10 min - **Cooking Time:** 8 minutes - **Servings:** 5

Ingredients:
- ✓ 1/3 cup milk
- ✓ 3 teaspoons sugar
- ✓ 2 eggs, whisked
- ✓ ¼ teaspoon nutmeg, ground
- ✓ ¼ cup blueberries
- ✓ 4 tablespoons cream cheese, whipped
- ✓ 1 and ½ cups corn flakes, crumbled
- ✓ 5 bread slices

Directions:
1. In a bowl, mix eggs with sugar, nutmeg and milk and whisk well.
2. In another bowl, mix cream cheese with blueberries and whisk well.
3. Put corn flakes in a third bowl.
4. Spread blueberry mix on each bread slice, then dip in eggs mix and dredge in corn flakes at the end.
5. Place bread in your air fryer's basket, heat up at 400 degrees F and bake for 8 minutes.
6. Divide among plates and serve for breakfast.

Nutrition: calories 300 - Fat 5 - Fiber 7 - Carbs 16 - Protein 4

46. Walnuts and Pear Oatmeal

Prep.Time: 5 min - **Cooking Time:** 12 min - **Servings:** 4

Ingredients:
- ✓ 1 cup water
- ✓ 1 tablespoon butter, soft
- ✓ ¼ cups brown sugar
- ✓ ½ teaspoon cinnamon powder
- ✓ 1 cup rolled oats
- ✓ ½ cup walnuts, chopped
- ✓ 2 cups pear, peeled and chopped
- ✓ ½ cup raisins

Directions:
1. In a heat proof dish that fits your air fryer, mix milk with sugar, butter, oats, cinnamon, raisins, pears and walnuts, stir, introduce in your fryer and cook at 360 degrees F for 12 minutes.
2. Divide into bowls and serve.

Nutrition: calories 230 - Fat 6 - Fiber 11 - Carbs 20 - Protein 5

47. Espresso Oatmeal

Prep.Time: 10 min - **Cooking Time:** 17 min - **Servings:** 4

Ingredients:
- ✓ 1 cup milk
- ✓ 1 cup steel cut oats
- ✓ 2 and ½ cups water
- ✓ 2 tablespoons sugar
- ✓ 1 teaspoon espresso powder
- ✓ 2 teaspoons vanilla extract

Directions:
1. In a pan that fits your air fryer, mix oats with water, sugar, milk and espresso powder, stir, introduce in your air fryer and cook at 360 degrees F for 17 minutes.
2. Add vanilla extract, stir, leave everything aside for 5 minutes, divide into bowls and serve for breakfast.

Nutrition: calories 261 - Fat 7 - Fiber 6 - Carbs 39 - Protein 6

48. Potato and Leek Frittata

Prep.Time: 10 min - **Cooking Time:** 18 min - **Servings:** 4

Ingredients:
- ✓ 2 gold potatoes, boiled, peeled and chopped
- ✓ 2 tablespoons butter
- ✓ 2 leeks, sliced
- ✓ Salt and black pepper to the taste
- ✓ ¼ cup whole milk
- ✓ 10 eggs, whisked
- ✓ 5 ounces fromage blanc, crumbled

Directions:
1. Heat up a pan that fits your air fryer with the butter over medium heat, add leeks, stir and cook for 4 minutes.
2. Add potatoes, salt, pepper, eggs, cheese and milk, whisk well, cook for 1 minute more, introduce in your air fryer and cook at 350 degrees F for 13 minutes.
3. Slice frittata, divide among plates and serve.

Nutrition: calories 271 - Fat 6 - Fiber 8 - Carbs 12 - Protein 6

49. Shrimp Frittata

Prep.Time: 10 min - **Cooking Time:** 15 min - **Servings:** 4

Ingredients:
- ✓ 4 eggs
- ✓ ½ teaspoon basil, dried
- ✓ Cooking spray
- ✓ Salt and black pepper to the taste
- ✓ ½ cup rice, cooked
- ✓ ½ cup shrimp, cooked, peeled, deveined and chopped
- ✓ ½ cup baby spinach, chopped
- ✓ ½ cup Monterey jack cheese, grated

Directions:
1. In a bowl, mix eggs with salt, pepper and basil and whisk.
2. Grease your air fryer's pan with cooking spray and add rice, shrimp and spinach.
3. Add eggs mix, sprinkle cheese all over and cook in your air fryer at 350 degrees F for 10 minutes.
4. Divide among plates and serve for breakfast.

Nutrition: calories 162 - Fat 6 - Fiber 5 - Carbs 8 - Protein 4

50. Tuna Sandwiches

Prep.Time: 10 min - **Cooking Time:** 5 min - **Servings:** 4

Ingredients:
- ✓ 16 ounces canned tuna, drained
- ✓ ¼ cup mayonnaise
- ✓ 2 tablespoons mustard
- ✓ 1 tablespoons lemon juice
- ✓ 2 green onions, chopped
- ✓ 3 English muffins, halved
- ✓ 3 tablespoons butter
- ✓ 6 provolone cheese

Directions:
1. In a bowl, mix tuna with mayo, lemon juice, mustard and green onions and stir.
2. Grease muffin halves with the butter, place them in preheated air fryer and bake them at 350 degrees F for 4 minutes.
3. Spread tuna mix on muffin halves, top each with provolone cheese, return sandwiches to air fryer and cook them for 4 minutes, divide among plates and serve for breakfast right away.

Nutrition: calories 182 - Fat 4 - Fiber 7 - Carbs 8 - Protein 6

51. Breakfast Fish Tacos

Prep.Time: 10 min - **Cooking Time:** 13 minutes - **Servings:** 4

Ingredients:
- ✓ 4 big tortillas
- ✓ 1 red bell pepper, chopped
- ✓ 1 yellow onion, chopped
- ✓ 1 cup corn
- ✓ 4 white fish fillets, skinless and boneless
- ✓ ½ cup salsa
- ✓ A handful mixed romaine lettuce, spinach and radicchio
- ✓ 4 tablespoon parmesan, grated

Directions:
1. Put fish fillets in your air fryer and cook at 350 degrees F for 6 minutes.
2. Meanwhile, heat up a pan over medium high heat, add bell pepper, onion and corn, stir and cook for 1-2 minutes.
3. Arrange tortillas on a working surface, divide fish fillets, spread salsa over them, divide mixed veggies and mixed greens and spread parmesan on each at the end.
4. Roll your tacos, place them in preheated air fryer and cook at 350 degrees F for 6 minutes more.
5. Divide fish tacos on plates and serve for breakfast.

Nutrition: calories 200 - Fat 3 - Fiber 7 - Carbs 9 - Protein 5

52. Amazing Breakfast Burger

Prep.Time: 10 min - **Cooking Time:** 45 min - **Servings:** 4

Ingredients:
- ✓ 1 pound beef, ground
- ✓ 1 yellow onion, chopped
- ✓ 1 teaspoon tomato puree
- ✓ 1 teaspoon garlic, minced
- ✓ 1 teaspoon mustard
- ✓ 1 teaspoon basil, dried
- ✓ 1 teaspoon parsley, chopped
- ✓ 1 tablespoon cheddar cheese, grated
- ✓ Salt and black pepper to the taste
- ✓ 4 bread buns, for serving

Directions:
1. In a bowl, mix beef with onion, tomato puree, garlic, mustard, basil, parsley, cheese, salt and pepper, stir well and shape 4 burgers out of this mix.
2. Heat up your air fryer at 400 degrees F, add burgers and cook them for 25 minutes.
3. Reduce temperature to 350 degrees F and bake burgers for 20 minutes more.
4. Arrange them on bread buns and serve for a quick breakfast.

Nutrition: calories 234 - Fat 5 - Fiber 8 - Carbs 12 - Protein 4

53. Long Beans Omelet

Prep.Time: 10 min - **Cooking Time:** 10 min - **Servings:** 3

Ingredients:
- ✓ ½ teaspoon soy sauce
- ✓ 1 tablespoon olive oil
- ✓ 3 eggs, whisked
- ✓ A pinch of salt and black pepper
- ✓ 4 garlic cloves, minced
- ✓ 4 long beans, trimmed and sliced

Directions:
1. In a bowl, mix eggs with a pinch of salt, black pepper and soy sauce and whisk well.
2. Heat up your air fryer at 320 degrees F, add oil and garlic, stir and brown for 1 minute.
3. Add long beans and eggs mix, spread and cook for 10 minutes.
4. Divide omelet on plates and serve for breakfast.

Nutrition: calories 200 - Fat 3 - Fiber 7 - Carbs 9 - Protein 3

54. Veggie Burritos

Prep.Time: 10 min - **Cooking Time:** 10 min - **Servings:** 4

Ingredients:
- ✓ 2 tablespoons cashew butter
- ✓ 2 tablespoons tamari
- ✓ 2 tablespoons water
- ✓ 2 tablespoons liquid smoke
- ✓ 4 rice papers
- ✓ ½ cup sweet potatoes, steamed and cubed
- ✓ ½ small broccoli head, florets separated and steamed
- ✓ 7 asparagus stalks
- ✓ 8 roasted red peppers, chopped
- ✓ A handful kale, chopped

Directions:
1. In a bowl, mix cashew butter with water, tamari and liquid smoke and whisk well.
2. Wet rice papers and arrange them on a working surface.
3. Divide sweet potatoes, broccoli, asparagus, red peppers and kale, wrap burritos and dip each in cashew mix.
4. Arrange burritos in your air fryer and cook them at 350 degrees F for 10 minutes.
5. Divide veggie burritos on plates d serve.

Nutrition: calories 172 - Fat 4 - Fiber 7 - Carbs 8 - Protein 3

55. Breakfast Pea Tortilla

Prep.Time: 10 min - **Cooking Time:** 7 min - **Servings:** 8

Ingredients:
- ✓ ½ pound baby peas
- ✓ 4 tablespoons butter
- ✓ 1 and ½ cup yogurt
- ✓ 8 eggs
- ✓ ½ cup mint, chopped
- ✓ Salt and black pepper to the taste

Directions:
1. Heat up a pan that fits your air fryer with the butter over medium heat, add peas, stir and cook for a couple of minutes.
2. Meanwhile, in a bowl, mix half of the yogurt with salt, pepper, eggs and mint and whisk well.
3. Pour this over the peas, toss, introduce in your air fryer and cook at 350 degrees F for 7 minutes.
4. Spread the rest of the yogurt over your tortilla and serve

Nutrition: calories 192 - Fat 5 - Fiber 4 - Carbs 8 - Protein 7

56. Onion Frittata

Prep.Time: 10 min - **Cooking Time:** 20 min - **Servings:** 6

Ingredients:
- ✓ 10 eggs, whisked
- ✓ 1 tablespoon olive oil
- ✓ 1 pound small potatoes, chopped
- ✓ 2 yellow onions, chopped
- ✓ Salt and black pepper to the taste
- ✓ 1 ounce cheddar cheese, grated
- ✓ ½ cup sour cream

Directions:
1. In a large bowl, mix eggs with potatoes, onions, salt, pepper, cheese and sour cream and whisk well.
2. Grease your air fryer's pan with the oil, add eggs mix, place in air fryer and cook for 20 minutes at 320 degrees F.
3. Slice frittata, divide among plates and serve for breakfast.

Nutrition: calories 231 - Fat 5 - Fiber 7 - Carbs 8 - Protein 4

57. Cherries Risotto

Prep.Time: 10 min - **Cooking Time:** 12 minutes - **Servings:** 4

Ingredients:
- ✓ 1 and ½ cups Arborio rice
- ✓ 1 and ½ teaspoons cinnamon powder
- ✓ 1/3 cup brown sugar
- ✓ A pinch of salt
- ✓ 2 tablespoons butter
- ✓ 2 apples, cored and sliced
- ✓ 1 cup apple juice
- ✓ 3 cups milk
- ✓ ½ cup cherries, dried

Directions:
1. Heat up a pan that fist your air fryer with the butter over medium heat, add rice, stir and cook for 4-5 minutes.
2. Add sugar, apples, apple juice, milk, cinnamon and cherries, stir, introduce in your air fryer and cook at 350 degrees F for 8 minutes.
3. Divide into bowls and serve for breakfast.

Nutrition: calories 162 - Fat 12 - Fiber 6 - Carbs 23 - Protein 8

58. Buttermilk Breakfast Biscuits

Prep.Time: 10 min - **Cooking Time:** 8 min - **Servings:** 4

Ingredients:
- ✓ 1 and ¼ cup white flour
- ✓ ½ cup self-rising flour
- ✓ ¼ teaspoon baking soda
- ✓ ½ teaspoon baking powder
- ✓ 1 teaspoon sugar
- ✓ 4 tablespoons butter, cold and cubed+ 1 tablespoon melted butter
- ✓ ¾ cup buttermilk
- ✓ Maple syrup for serving

Directions:
1. In a bowl, mix white flour with self-rising flour, baking soda, baking powder and sugar and stir.
2. Add cold butter and stir using your hands.
3. Add buttermilk, stir until you obtain a dough and transfer to a floured working surface.
4. Roll your dough and cut 10 pieces using a round cutter.
5. Arrange biscuits in your air fryer's cake pan, brush them with melted butter and cook at 400 degrees F for 8 min.
6. Serve them for breakfast with some maple syrup on top.

Nutrition: calories 192 - Fat 6 - Fiber 9 - Carbs 12 - Protein 3

59. Breakfast Bread Rolls

Prep.Time: 10 min - **Cooking Time:** 12 min - **Servings:** 4

Ingredients:
- ✓ 5 potatoes, boiled, peeled and mashed
- ✓ 8 bread slices, white parts only
- ✓ 1 coriander bunch, chopped
- ✓ 2 green chilies, chopped
- ✓ 2 small yellow onions, chopped
- ✓ ½ teaspoon turmeric powder
- ✓ 2 curry leaf springs
- ✓ ½ teaspoon mustard seeds
- ✓ 2 tablespoons olive oil
- ✓ Salt and black pepper to the taste

Directions:
1. Heat up a pan with 1 teaspoon oil, add mustard seeds, onions, curry leaves and turmeric, stir and cook for a few seconds.
2. Add mashed potatoes, salt, pepper, coriander and chilies, stir well, take off heat and cool it down.
3. Divide potatoes mix into 8 parts and shape ovals using your wet hands.
4. Wet bread slices with water, press in order to drain excess water and keep one slice in your palm.
5. Add a potato oval over bread slice and wrap it around it.
6. Repeat with the rest of the potato mix and bread.
7. Heat up your air fryer at 400 degrees F, add the rest of the oil, add bread rolls, cook them for 12 minutes.

Nutrition: calories 261 - Fat 6 - Fiber 9 - Carbs 12 - Protein 7

60. Breakfast Bread Pudding

Prep.Time: 10 min - **Cooking Time:** 22 min - **Servings:** 4

Ingredients:
- ✓ ½ pound white bread, cubed
- ✓ ¾ cup milk
- ✓ ¾ cup water
- ✓ 2 teaspoons cornstarch
- ✓ ½ cup apple, peeled, cored and roughly chopped
- ✓ 5 tablespoons honey
- ✓ 1 teaspoon vanilla extract
- ✓ 2 teaspoons cinnamon powder
- ✓ 1 and 1/3 cup flour
- ✓ 3/5 cup brown sugar
- ✓ 3 ounces soft butter

Directions:
1. In a bowl, mix bread with apple, milk with water, honey, cinnamon, vanilla and cornstarch and whisk well.
2. In a separate bowl, mix flour with sugar and butter and stir until you obtain a crumbled mixture.
3. Press half of the crumble mix on the bottom of your air fryer, add bread and apple mix, add the rest of the crumble and cook everything at 350 degrees F for 22 minutes.
4. Divide bread pudding on plates and serve.

Nutrition: calories 261 - Fat 7 - Fiber 7 - Carbs 8 - Protein 5

61. Creamy Eggs

Prep.Time: 10 min - **Cooking Time:** 12 min - **Servings:** 4

Ingredients:
- ✓ 2 teaspoons butter, soft
- ✓ 2 ham slices
- ✓ 4 eggs
- ✓ 2 tablespoons heavy cream
- ✓ Salt and black pepper to the taste
- ✓ 3 tablespoons parmesan, grated
- ✓ 2 teaspoons chives, chopped
- ✓ A pinch of smoked paprika

Directions:
1. Grease your air fryer's pan with the butter, line it with the ham and add it to your air fryer's basket.
2. In a bowl, mix 1 egg with heavy cream, salt and pepper, whisk well and add over ham.
3. Crack the rest of the eggs in the pan, sprinkle parmesan and cook your mix for 12 minutes at 320 degrees F.
4. Sprinkle paprika and chives all over, divide among plates and serve for breakfast.

Nutrition: calories 263 - Fat 5 - Fiber 8 - Carbs 12 - Protein 5

62. Delicious Potato Frittata

Prep.Time: 10 min - **Cooking Time:** 20 min - **Servings:** 6

Ingredients:
- ✓ 6 ounces jarred roasted red bell peppers, chopped
- ✓ 12 eggs, whisked
- ✓ ½ cup parmesan, grated
- ✓ 3 garlic cloves, minced
- ✓ 2 tablespoons parsley, chopped
- ✓ Salt and black pepper to the taste
- ✓ 2 tablespoons chives, chopped
- ✓ 16 potato wedges
- ✓ 6 tablespoons ricotta cheese
- ✓ Cooking spray

Directions:
1. In a bowl, mix eggs with red peppers, garlic, parsley, salt, pepper and ricotta and whisk well.
2. Heat up your air fryer at 300 degrees F and grease it with cooking spray.
3. Add half of the potato wedges on the bottom and sprinkle half of the parmesan all over.
4. Add half of the egg mix, add the rest of the potatoes and the rest of the parmesan.
5. Add the rest of the eggs mix, sprinkle chives and cook for 20 minutes.
6. Divide among plates and serve for breakfast.

Nutrition: calories 312 - Fat 6 - Fiber 9 - Carbs 16 - Protein 5

63. Breakfast Broccoli Quiche

Prep.Time: 10 min - **Cooking Time:** 20 minutes - **Servings:** 2

Ingredients:
- ✓ 1 broccoli head, florets separated and steamed
- ✓ 1 tomato, chopped
- ✓ 3 carrots, chopped and steamed
- ✓ 2 ounces cheddar cheese, grated
- ✓ 2 eggs
- ✓ 2 ounces milk
- ✓ 1 teaspoon parsley, chopped
- ✓ 1 teaspoon thyme, chopped
- ✓ Salt and black pepper to the taste

Directions:
1. In a bowl, mix eggs with milk, parsley, thyme, salt and pepper and whisk well.
2. Put broccoli, carrots and tomato in your air fryer.
3. Add eggs mix on top, spread cheddar cheese, cover and cook at 350 degrees F for 20 minutes.
4. Divide among plates and serve for breakfast.

Nutrition: calories 214 - Fat 4 - Fiber 7 - Carbs 12 - Protein 3

64. Smoked Sausage Breakfast Mix

Prep.Time: 10 min - **Cooking Time:** 30 min - **Servings:** 4

Ingredients:
- ✓ 1 and ½ pounds smoked sausage, chopped and browned
- ✓ A pinch of salt and black pepper
- ✓ 1 and ½ cups grits
- ✓ 4 and ½ cups water
- ✓ 16 ounces cheddar cheese, shredded
- ✓ 1 cup milk
- ✓ ¼ teaspoon garlic powder
- ✓ 1 and ½ teaspoons thyme, chopped
- ✓ Cooking spray
- ✓ 4 eggs, whisked

Directions:
1. Put the water in a pot, bring to a boil over medium heat, add grits, stir, cover, cook for 5 minutes and take off heat.
2. Add cheese, stir until it melts and mix with milk, thyme, salt, pepper, garlic powder and eggs and whisk really well.
3. Heat up your air fryer at 300 degrees F, grease with cooking spray and add browned sausage.
4. Add grits mix, spread and cook for 25 minutes.
5. Divide among plates and serve for breakfast.

Nutrition: calories 321 - Fat 6 - Fiber 7 - Carbs 17 - Protein 4

65. French Beans and Egg Breakfast Mix

Prep.Time: 10 min - **Cooking Time:** 10 min - **Servings:** 3

Ingredients:
- ✓ 2 eggs, whisked
- ✓ ½ teaspoon soy sauce
- ✓ 1 tablespoon olive oil
- ✓ 4 garlic cloves, minced
- ✓ 3 ounces French beans, trimmed and sliced diagonally
- ✓ Salt and white pepper to the taste

Directions:
1. In a bowl, mix eggs with soy sauce, salt and pepper and whisk well.
2. Heat up your air fryer at 320 degrees F, add oil and heat it up as well.
3. Add garlic and brown for 1 minute.
4. Add French beans and egg mix, toss and cook for 10 minutes.
5. Divide among plates and serve for breakfast.

Nutrition: calories 182 - Fat 3 - Fiber 6 - Carbs 8 - Protein 3

66. Sausage, Eggs and Cheese Mix

Prep.Time: 10 min - **Cooking Time:** 20 min - **Servings:** 4

Ingredients:
- ✓ 10 ounces sausages, cooked and crumbled
- ✓ 1 cup cheddar cheese, shredded
- ✓ 1 cup mozzarella cheese, shredded
- ✓ 8 eggs, whisked
- ✓ 1 cup milk
- ✓ Salt and black pepper to the taste
- ✓ Cooking spray

Directions:
1. In a bowl, mix sausages with cheese, mozzarella, eggs, milk, salt and pepper and whisk well.
2. Heat up your air fryer at 380 degrees F, spray cooking oil, add eggs and sausage mix and cook for 20 minutes.
3. Divide among plates and serve.

Nutrition: calories 320 - Fat 6 - Fiber 8 - Carbs 12 - Protein 5

67. Eggs Casserole

Prep.Time: 10 min - **Cooking Time:** 25 min - **Servings:** 6

Ingredients:
- ✓ 1 pound turkey, ground
- ✓ 1 tablespoon olive oil
- ✓ ½ teaspoon chili powder
- ✓ 12 eggs
- ✓ 1 sweet potato, cubed
- ✓ 1 cup baby spinach
- ✓ Salt and black pepper to the taste
- ✓ 2 tomatoes, chopped for serving

Directions:
1. In a bowl, mix eggs with salt, pepper, chili powder, potato, spinach, turkey and sweet potato and whisk well.
2. Heat up your air fryer at 350 degrees F, add oil and heat it up.
3. Add eggs mix, spread into your air fryer, cover and cook for 25 minutes.
4. Divide among plates and serve for breakfast.

Nutrition: calories 300 - Fat 5 - Fiber 8 - Carbs 13 - Protein 6

68. Ham Breakfast

Prep.Time: 10 min - **Cooking Time:** 15 min - **Servings:** 6

Ingredients:
- ✓ 6 cups French bread, cubed
- ✓ 4 ounces green chilies, chopped
- ✓ 10 ounces ham, cubed
- ✓ 4 ounces cheddar cheese, shredded
- ✓ 2 cups milk
- ✓ 5 eggs
- ✓ 1 tablespoon mustard
- ✓ Salt and black pepper to the taste
- ✓ Cooking spray

Directions:
1. Heat up your air fryer at 350 degrees F and grease it with cooking spray.
2. In a bowl, mix eggs with milk, cheese, mustard, salt and pepper and stir.
3. Add bread cubes in your air fryer and mix with chilies and ham.
4. Add eggs mix, spread and cook for 15 minutes.
5. Divide among plates and serve.

Nutrition: calories 200 - Fat 5 - Fiber 6 - Carbs 12 - Protein 14

69. Sweet Breakfast Casserole

Prep.Time: 10 min - **Cooking Time:** 30 minutes - **Servings:** 4

Ingredients:
- ✓ 3 tablespoons brown sugar
- ✓ 4 tablespoons butter
- ✓ 2 tablespoons white sugar
- ✓ ½ teaspoon cinnamon powder
- ✓ ½ cup flour

For the casserole:
- ✓ 2 eggs
- ✓ 2 tablespoons white sugar
- ✓ 2 and ½ cups white flour
- ✓ 1 teaspoon baking soda
- ✓ 1 teaspoon baking powder
- ✓ 2 eggs
- ✓ ½ cup milk
- ✓ 2 cups buttermilk
- ✓ 4 tablespoons butter
- ✓ Zest from 1 lemon, grated
- ✓ 1 and 2/3 cup blueberries

Directions:
1. In a bowl, mix eggs with 2 tablespoons white sugar, 2 and ½ cups white flour, baking powder, baking soda, 2 eggs, milk, buttermilk, 4 tablespoons butter, lemon zest and blueberries, stir and pour into a pan that fits your air fryer.
2. In another bowls, mix 3 tablespoons brown sugar with 2 tablespoons white sugar, 4 tablespoons butter, ½ cup flour and cinnamon, stir until you obtain a crumble and spread over blueberries mix.
3. Place in preheated air fryer and bake at 300 degrees F for 30 minutes.
4. Divide among plates and serve for breakfast.

Nutrition: calories 214 - Fat 5 - Fiber 8 - Carbs 12 - Protein 5

70. Creamy Hash Browns

Prep.Time: 10 min - **Cooking Time:** 20 min - **Servings:** 6

Ingredients:
- ✓ 2 pounds hash browns
- ✓ 1 cup whole milk
- ✓ 8 bacon slices, chopped
- ✓ 9 ounces cream cheese
- ✓ 1 yellow onion, chopped
- ✓ 1 cup cheddar cheese, shredded
- ✓ 6 green onions, chopped
- ✓ Salt and black pepper to the taste
- ✓ 6 eggs
- ✓ Cooking spray

Directions:
1. Heat up your air fryer at 350 degrees F and grease it with cooking spray.
2. In a bowl, mix eggs with milk, cream cheese, cheddar cheese, bacon, onion, salt and pepper and whisk well.
3. Add hash browns to your air fryer, add eggs mix over them and cook for 20 minutes.
4. Divide among plates and serve.

Nutrition: calories 261 - Fat 6 - Fiber 9 - Carbs 8 - Protein 12

71. Extra Crunchy Breakfast Casserole

Prep.Time: 2 min - **Cooking Time:** 30 min - **Servings:** 4

Ingredients:
- ✓ 4 eggs
- ✓ 6 ounces of raw sweet sausage, remove from the casings
- ✓ ½ cup bread crumbs
- ✓ 1 cup shredded cheddar cheese
- ✓ Pinch salt and pepper

Directions:
1. Preheat the air-fryer to 350°F. Cook the raw sausage for 10 minutes on medium-to-high heat, breaking it up with a wooden spoon to prevent clumping. Remove and set aside.
2. Beat the eggs in a mixing bowl, until light and fluffy. Stir in half of the bread crumbs, half of the cheese, the cooked sausage meat, salt and pepper. Pour into a baking dish and sprinkle the remaining bread crumbs and shredded cheese on top.
3. Place the baking dish in the air-fryer basket, set the timer for 20 minutes. Remove, serve and enjoy.

72. Wheat & Seed Bread

Prep.Time: 70 min - **Cooking Time:** 18 min - **Servings:** 4

Ingredients:
- ✓ 3½ ounces of flour
- ✓ 1 teaspoon of yeast
- ✓ 1 teaspoon of salt
- ✓ 3½ ounces of wheat flour
- ✓ ¼ cup of pumpkin seeds

Directions:
1. Mix the wheat flour, yeast, salt, seeds and the plain flour together in a large bowl. Stir in ¾ cup of lukewarm water, and keep stirring until dough becomes soft.
2. Knead for another 5 minutes until the dough becomes elastic and smooth. Mold into a ball and cover with a plastic bag. Set aside for 30 minutes for it to rise.
3. Heat your air-fryer to 392°F.
4. Transfer the dough into a small pizza pan and place in the air-fryer. Bake for 18 minutes until golden. Remove and place on a wire rack to cool.

73. Parmesan & Pesto Twists

Prep.Time: 10 min - **Cooking Time:** 25 minutes - **Servings:** 4

Ingredients:
- ✓ 12 ounces of packed butter puff pastry
- ✓ 1.8 ounces of cream cheese
- ✓ 3 teaspoons of flour
- ✓ ¼ cup of basil pesto
- ✓ 1 egg, whisked
- ✓ 1.8 ounces of grated Parmesan cheese

Directions:
1. Preheat your air-fryer to 460°F.
2. Spread flour on a surface lightly and roll the butter puff pastry into a rectangular shape.
3. Divide into 2 from the middle and spread the pesto and cream cheese on one half and place the other half on top.
4. Cut the sandwich into 2 from the middle, then cut each rectangular piece into 0.4" thick strips.
5. Twist the strips, pull slightly to make longer. Using a pastry brush, coat the twists with the egg and sprinkle with parmesan cheese.
6. Put into Air-fryer until it is risen and golden for about 25 minutes

74. Croissant With Ham, Mushroom And Egg

Prep.Time: 5 min - **Cooking Time:** 8 min - **Servings:** 1

Ingredients:
- ✓ 1 store-bought Croissant
- ✓ slices honey shaved ham
- ✓ 4 honey cherry tomato, halved
- ✓ 4 small button mushroom, quartered
- ✓ 1 Egg
- ✓ 1.8 oz shredded cheddar cheese
- ✓ Handful salad greens
- ✓ 1/2 Rosemary Sprig, roughly chopped (optional)

Directions:
1. Grease a baking dish lightly with butter.
2. Arrange the ingredients in two layers, placing the cheese in the middle and top layer. Create a space in the center of the ham mixture, break egg in it.
3. Sprinkle some black pepper, salt and rosemary over the mixture and place on the Air-fryer basket along with the croissant.
4. Baked in preheated 325°F temperature for 8 minutes. (Take out the croissant from the air-fryer basket after 4 minutes).
5. Serve croissant and cheesy baked egg on plate along with some salad greens.

75. Air Fried French Toast

Prep.Time: 4 min - **Cooking Time:** 6 min - **Servings:** 4

Ingredients:
- ✓ 2 slices of sourdough bread
- ✓ 3 eggs
- ✓ 1 tablespoon of butter
- ✓ 1 teaspoon of liquid vanilla
- ✓ 3 teaspoons of honey
- ✓ 2 tablespoons of Greek yogurt Berries

Directions:
1. Preheat the air fryer to 356°F.
2. Pour the vanilla in the eggs and whisk to mix. Spread the butter on all sides of the bread and soak in the eggs to absorb.
3. Put the bread into the air fryer basket and cook for 3 minutes Turn the bread over and cook for another 3 minutes.
4. Transfer to a place, top with yogurt and berries with a sprinkle of honey

76. Oatmeal Muffins

Prep.Time: 5 min - **Cooking Time:** 15 min - **Servings:** 3

Ingredients:
- ✓ 2 Eggs
- ✓ 3½ ounce oats
- ✓ 3 ounce butter, melted
- ✓ 1/2 cup flour
- ✓ 1/4 teaspoon vanilla essence
- ✓ 1/2 cup icing sugar Pinch baking powder
- ✓ 1 tablespoon raisins
- ✓ Cooking spray

Directions:
1. Combine sugar and butter until soft. Whisk together the eggs and vanilla essence. Add it to the sugar/butter mix until soft peaks forms.
2. Combine flour, raisins, baking powder and oats in a separate bowl. Add it to the mixed ingredients.
3. Grease the muffin molds lightly with cooking spray and fill with the batter mixture. Preheat the Air Fryer at 350°F.
4. Place the muffin molds into the air fryer tray. Let it cook for 12 minutes. Cool, serve and enjoy!

77. French Toast Delight

Prep.Time: 5 min - **Cooking Time:** 6 min - **Servings:** 2

Ingredients:
- ✓ 4 bread slices
- ✓ 2 tablespoons butter
- ✓ 1/2 teaspoon cinnamon
- ✓ 2 Eggs
- ✓ Pinch salt
- ✓ Pinch ground cloves
- ✓ Pinch Nutmeg Icing sugar and maple syrup, to serve

Directions:
1. Preheat Air-Fryer to 350°F. Whisk together eggs, cloves, cinnamon, nutmeg, cloves and salt in a bowl. Butter sides of each bread slice and cut into strips.
2. Soak the buttered bread strips in the egg mixture one after the other, and arrange in the tray. (Cook in two batches, if necessary).
3. Cook 2 minutes and then remove the strips. Lightly coat bread strips with cooking spray on both sides. Place back the tray into the air fryer and cook another 4 minutes, checking to ensure they are cooking evenly.
4. Remove bread from Air Fryer once it's golden brown. Sprinkle with icing sugar and drizzle with maple syrup.

78. Garlic And Cheese Bread Rolls

Prep.Time: 10 min - **Cooking Time:** 5 min - **Servings:** 2

Ingredients:
- ✓ 8 tablespoons of grated cheese
- ✓ 6 teaspoons of melted butter
- ✓ Garlic
- ✓ bread spice mix
- ✓ 2 bread rolls

Directions:
1. Slice the bread rolls from top in a crisscross pattern but not cut through at the bottom.
2. Put all the cheese into the slits and brush the tops of the bread rolls with melted butter. Sprinkle the garlic mix on the rolls.
3. Heat the air fryer to 350°F. Place the rolls into the basket and cook until cheese is melted for about 5 minutes.

79. Milky Semolina Cutlets

Prep.Time: 45 min - **Cooking Time:** 15 minutes - **Servings:** 2

Ingredients:
- ✓ 3 tablespoons of vegetable oil
- ✓ 1 cup of semolina
- ✓ 12 ounces of mixed vegetables (any of your choice), chopped
- ✓ 2½ pounds of milk
- ✓ ½ teaspoon salt
- ✓ ½ teaspoon black pepper, ground

Directions:
1. Pour the milk into a sauce pan and heat. Add the mixed vegetables and allow it to cook until they are soft for about 3 minutes.
2. Add the pepper and salt and then the semolina. Cook until the mixture thicken; this will take about 10 minutes.
3. Grease a flat plate with oil; spread the semolina mixture on it. Refrigerate for about 4 hours until it is firm.
4. Heat the air-fryer to 350°F.
5. Remove from the refrigerator and cut into flat round shapes. Brush the cutlets with oil and place them into the air-fryer.
6. Cook for 10 minutes. Serve while hot with any sauce of your choice.

80. Thai Style Omelette

Prep.Time: 5 min - **Cooking Time:** 10 min - **Servings:** 2

Ingredients:
- ✓ 3½ oz minced pork
- ✓ 2 Eggs
- ✓ 1 cup onion, chopped
- ✓ 1 tablespoon fish salt

Directions:
1. Beat the eggs until it is light and fluffy. Preheat the Air-Fryer to 280°F.
2. In a bowl, add together all the ingredients. Pour the mixture into the Air-Fryer tray.
3. Remove after 10 minutes or once omelet is golden brown. Cut and serve.

81. Rarebit Air-Fried Egg

Prep.Time: 5 min - **Cooking Time:** 5 min - **Servings:** 4

Ingredients:
- ✓ 4 Slices Sourdough
- ✓ 4 Eggs
- ✓ 1/3 cup ale
- ✓ 1½ cups cheddar, grated
- ✓ 1 teaspoon mustard powder
- ✓ 1/2 teaspoon paprika
- ✓ Black Pepper to taste
- ✓ 2 teaspoon Worcestershire Sauce

Directions:
1. Fry eggs, sunny side up and set to one side. Preheat Air Fryer to 350°F.
2. In a bowl, add together the cheddar, ale, paprika, mustard powder, and Worcestershire sauce.
3. Spread just one side of each slice of sourdough with the cheddar mixture. Place the bread slices into the Air-Fryer tray. Cook for about 3 minutes until slightly browned.
4. Top the rarebits with fried eggs and season with pepper to taste

82. Breakfast Sandwich

Prep.Time: 5 min - **Cooking Time:** 7 min - **Servings:** 1

Ingredients:
- ✓ 2 Bacon Slices
- ✓ 1 Egg
- ✓ 1 English muffin
- ✓ Salt & Pepper to taste

Directions:
1. Beat the egg into a soufflé cup and add salt and pepper to taste.
2. Heat the air fryer to 390°F and place the soufflé cup, English muffin and bacon into the tray.
3. Cook all the ingredients for 6-10 minutes. Assemble sandwich and enjoy.

83. Apple-Cinnamon Empanadas

Prep.Time: 15 min - **Cooking Time:** 30 min - **Servings:** 4

Ingredients:
- ✓ 2-3 baking apples, peeled & chopped
- ✓ 2 teaspoons of cinnamon
- ✓ 1/4 cup white sugar
- ✓ 1 tablespoon brown sugar
- ✓ 1 tablespoon of water
- ✓ ½ tablespoon cornstarch
- ✓ ¼ teaspoon of vanilla extract
- ✓ 2 tablespoons of margarine or butter
- ✓ 4 pre-made empanada dough shells (Goya)

Directions:
1. In a bowl, add together white sugar, brown sugar, cornstarch and cinnamon; set aside. Put the chopped apples in a pot and place on a stovetop.
2. Add the combined dry ingredients to the apples, then add the water, vanilla extract, and butter; stirring well to mix.
3. Cover pot and cook on high heat. Once it starts boiling, lower heat and simmer, until the apples are soft. Remove from the heat and cool.
4. Lay the empanada shells on a clean counter. Ladle the apple mixture into each of the shells, being careful to prevent spillage over the edges. Fold shells to fully cover apple mixture, seal edges with water, pressing down to secure with a fork.
5. Cover the air fryer basket with tin foil but leave the edges uncovered so that air can circulate through the basket. Place the empanadas shells in the foil-lined air fryer basket, set temperature at 350°F and timer for 15 minutes.
6. Halfway through, slide the frying basket out and flip the empanadas using a spatula. Remove when golden, and serve directly from the basket onto plates. Eat up while they're hot, and enjoy

84. Light Blueberry Muffins

Prep.Time: 15 min - **Cooking Time:** 15 min - **Servings:** 12

Ingredients:
- ✓ 1 cup of fresh, ripe blueberries, rinsed
- ✓ 1½ cups all-purpose flour
- ✓ ½ cup of white sugar
- ✓ 2 teaspoons of baking powder
- ✓ 1/3 cup of vegetable oil
- ✓ 1 medium-sized egg
- ✓ ½ teaspoon of salt
- ✓ ¼ cup unsweetened yogurt
- ✓ 1 tablespoon brown sugar
- ✓ 2 teaspoons vanilla extract

Directions:
1. Lightly coat the blueberries with flour, shake, and set aside. Combine the baking powder, sugar, flour, and salt in a large bowl, stirring well to evenly combine.
2. In a smaller bowl, whisk together the egg, oil, yogurt, and vanilla extract until evenly combined. Pour it into the larger bowl containing the dry ingredients and mix well with a whisk or fork.
3. Add the blueberries, using a wooden spoon or spatula to gently fold in. Arrange muffin cups on the baking tin and place on the air-fryer basket, (do two batches). Spoon the batter into the muffin tins, filling up about ¾ of the way.
4. Now sprinkle brown sugar onto them. Set to 350°F for 10 minutes. Remove. (Muffins are ready when an inserted toothpick in the center comes out dry. Otherwise, return basket and reset the air fryer to 320°F and 2 minutes cooking time.)
5. Let your muffins cool for a while then enjoy!

85. Corn Kernel Fritters

Prep.Time: 5 min - **Cooking Time:** 5 minutes - **Servings:** 1

Ingredients:
- ✓ 1 Egg
- ✓ 1 cup corn kernels
- ✓ 3/4 cup milk
- ✓ 1 cup flour
- ✓ 1½ teaspoons baking powder
- ✓ 1/2 teaspoons salt
- ✓ 1/4 teaspoons pepper
- ✓ 2 tablespoons butter, melted

Directions:
1. Preheat Air Fryer to 375°F. In a bowl, combine flour, baking powder, salt and pepper.
2. In another bowl, whisk together egg, milk, and butter and add to the dry ingredients, stirring well. Fold in the corn and leave for 5 minutes to allow the batter sit well.
3. Now, form batter into small rounded fritters. Place the fritters on a tray and let it freeze for 5 minutes in order to retain the shape.
4. Finally, place the fritters into the Air Fryer tray, set timer for 4-5 minutes. Serve and enjoy with yoghurt or salsa dip

86. Apple Oat Sunrise Fritters

Prep.Time: 10 min - **Cooking Time:** 5 min - **Servings:** 2

Ingredients:
- ✓ 2 Apples, peeled, cored & sliced into rings
- ✓ 1/2 cup + 2 tablespoons sugar
- ✓ 1½ teaspoons ground cinnamon, divided
- ✓ 1/2 cup rice flour
- ✓ 2 tablespoons cornstarch
- ✓ 1 teaspoon baking powder
- ✓ 1/2 cup club soda
- ✓ 1 cup oats
- ✓ 1 Egg
- ✓ 3/4 teaspoon kosher salt

Directions:
1. Combine 1 teaspoon of cinnamon and 1/2 cup sugar in a shallow bowl, whisking well. Next, preheat the Air Fryer to 350°F.
2. In a food processor, pulse the oats to a coarse powder. Remove to a large bowl and add in the rice flour, baking powder, cornstarch, salt, cinnamon and the rest of the sugar, whisking well.
3. Add in the egg and club soda, whisking in more soda, a little at a time, until the mixture is like pancake batter.
4. Dip the apple rings into the batter then place into the Air Fryer tray, one set at a time. Cook until golden brown and crisp for about 4 minutes.
5. Serve fritters sprinkled with the reserved cinnamon sugar.

87. Cinnamon Buns
Prep.Time: 10 min - Cooking Time: 10 min - Servings: 4

Ingredients:
- ✓ 8 oz. container crescent rolls, refrigerated
- ✓ 1 tbsp. ground cinnamon
- ✓ 2 oz. raisins
- ✓ 1/3 cup butter
- ✓ 2 tbsp. sugar, granulated
- ✓ 1/3 cup pecans, chopped
- ✓ cooking spray (olive oil)
- ✓ maple syrup – 2 tbsp.
- ✓ 1/3 cup brown sugar

Directions:
1. In a saucepan, dissolve the butter completely. Transfer to a dish and blend the maple syrup and brown sugar.
2. Layer one 8-inch pan with the olive oil spray.
3. Distribute the sugar into the pan and empty the raisins and pecans inside, stirring to incorporate.
4. In a glass dish, whisk the sugar and ground cinnamon.
5. Open the can of crescent rolls and place on a cutting board.
6. Slice the entire log of dough into eight individual pieces.
7. Cover the top and bottom of the dough pieces in cinnamon and sugar, and transfer the pan to the air fryer.
8. Adjust the settings to air crisp at 345° F for 5 minutes.
9. Turn over the individual buns and steam for another 5 minutes.
10. Take the pan out and move the buns to a serving plate.
11. Drizzle the remaining sugar liquid on the buns and serve immediately.

88. French Toast Sticks
Prep.Time: 10 min - Cooking Time: 8 min - Servings: 4

Ingredients:
- ✓ 1 tbsp. ground cinnamon
- ✓ 4 tbsp. butter
- ✓ 1 cup milk
- ✓ 5 large eggs
- ✓ 1/4 cup sugar, confectioner
- ✓ 12 slices Texas toast
- ✓ 1 tsp. vanilla extract

Directions:
1. In a hot saucepan, liquefy the butter completely.
2. Meanwhile, cut the bread into 3 separate pieces.
3. Using a glass dish, blend the vanilla extract, melted butter, milk, and eggs thoroughly.
4. In an additional glass dish, combine the sugar and ground cinnamon.
5. Dunk each slice of bread into the wet mixture and cover with the sugar mixture completely.
6. Transfer to a dish and blend the maple syrup and brown sugar.
7. Move to the air fryer basket and fry for approximately 8 minutes while setting at 350°F.
8. Remove the sticks from the air fryer and wait for approximately 5 minutes before serving.

89. Egg and Cheese Veggie Cups
Prep.Time: 30 min - Cooking Time: 15 minutes - Servings: 4

Ingredients:
- ✓ cooking spray (olive oil)
- ✓ large eggs - 4
- ✓ 1/4 tsp. salt
- ✓ 2 oz. half & half

Ingredients:
- ✓ Salt – ¼ tsp.
- ✓ 1 slice toast

Directions:
1. Set the air fryer to the temperature of 300° F to heat.
2. Liberally spray 4 glass or ceramic ramekin dishes.
3. In a glass dish, blend the half & half, salt, cilantro, eggs, pepper and 4 oz. of the shredded cheese until combined.
4. Evenly distribute the mixture to the greased dishes.
5. Move the dishes to the basket in the air fryer for 12 minutes.
6. Once the time has passed, sprinkle the remaining 4 oz. of shredded cheese on top of each of the dishes.
7. Adjust the temperature to 400° F and broil for an additional 2 minutes.
8. Serve immediately and enjoy!

90. Egg in a Hole
Prep.Time: 5 min - Cooking Time: 10 min - Servings: 4

Ingredients:
- ✓ Salt – ¼ tsp.
- ✓ 1 slice toast
- ✓ 1 large egg
- ✓ 1/8 tsp. pepper
- ✓ cooking spray (olive oil)

Directions:

1. Liberally spray the pan inside the air fryer with cooking spray.
2. Remove the middle of the slice of bread with a small cookie cutter and move to the pan.
3. Break the egg and put into the middle of the slice of bread.
4. Set the air fryer to heat at 330°F and cook for 6 minutes.
5. Use a metal spatula to turn the bread over and steam for an additional 4 minutes.
6. Serve hot and enjoy

91. Ham and Cheese Omelet

Prep.Time: 10 min - **Cooking Time:** 10 min - **Servings:** 4

Ingredients:
- ✓ Salt - 1/4 tsp.
- ✓ Milk – 2 oz.
- ✓ cheddar cheese - 1/4 cup, shredded
- ✓ 6 tsp. ham, diced
- ✓ 1/3 tsp. thyme seasoning
- ✓ 2 tbsp. bell pepper, diced
- ✓ 6 tsp. mushrooms
- ✓ 2 large eggs
- ✓ 1/3 tsp. oregano seasoning
- ✓ 2 tbsp. onions, diced
- ✓ 1/3 tsp. paprika seasoning
- ✓ cooking spray (olive oil)

Directions:
1. Cover a 3x6-inch pan with olive oil spray.
2. Whisk the milk, salt, and eggs until blended in a glass dish.
3. Combine the diced ham, bell pepper, mushrooms, and, onions and stir until merged.
4. Transfer to the greased pan and move to the air fryer basket.
5. Adjust the temperature of the air fryer to 350°F and heat for approximately 5 minutes.
6. In a glass dish, combine the thyme, oregano, and paprika seasons.
7. Open the lid and sprinkle the seasonings evenly over the top. Then dust with the shredded cheese.
8. Steam for an additional 5 minutes. Use a rubber scraper to place between the omelet and the pan to lift up. Move to a serving plate and serve while hot.

92. Home Fries

Prep.Time: 5 min - **Cooking Time:** 25 min - **Servings:** 2

Ingredients:
- ✓ 1 tsp. salt
- ✓ 3 russet potatoes, cubed
- ✓ 1 tsp. chili powder
- ✓ 3 tbsp. of paprika seasoning
- ✓ olive oil - 2 tbsp.
- ✓ pepper - 1/2 tsp.
- ✓ garlic powder - 3 tbsp

Directions:
1. Adjust the air fryer temperature to 400°F to heat.
2. Prepare the potatoes by scrubbing and chopping into cubes.
3. Using a glass dish, combine the cubed potatoes with paprika, olive oil, chili powder, and garlic powder until integrated.
4. In a single layer, assemble the potatoes in the air fryer basket. Fry for approximately 25 minutes.
5. Open the lid about every 10 minutes to toss the potatoes for it to be cooked fully.
6. Remove from the basket, distribute to a serving dish then serve immediately.

93. Hard-Boiled Eggs

Prep.Time: 5 min - **Cooking Time:** 16 minutes - **Servings:** 4

Ingredients:
- ✓ 6 large eggs, cold
- ✓ 4 cups of ice water

Directions:
1. Adjust the temperature of the air fryer to 250°F and insert the wire accessory into the basket.
2. Place the refrigerated eggs into the wire rack and heat for 16 minutes.
3. Remove the eggs to a dish of ice water.
4. Once cooled, peel the eggs and serve immediately

94. Loaded Hash Browns

Prep.Time: 30 min - **Cooking Time:** 20 min - **Servings:** 4

Ingredients:
- ✓ 2 garlic cloves, chopped
- ✓ 3 russet potatoes
- ✓ 2 oz. onions, chopped
- ✓ 1/4 cup red peppers, chopped
- ✓ 2 tsp. olive oil
- ✓ 1/4 tsp. salt
- ✓ 2 oz. cup green peppers, chopped
- ✓ 1 tsp. paprika seasoning
- ✓ 6 cups cold water
- ✓ 1/8 tsp. pepper

Directions:
1. Scrub the potatoes and remove the skins with a knife or vegetable peeler.
2. Use a cheese grater to shred the potatoes completely with the largest holes available. Transfer the potatoes to a glass dish.
3. Empty the cold water into the dish and saturate for approximately 20 minutes.
4. Empty the potatoes and remove the moisture thoroughly.
5. Set the temperature of the air fryer to heat at 400°F.
6. In an additional glass dish, blend the potatoes, olive oil, salt, garlic powder, paprika powder, and pepper until completely covered.
7. Transfer the potatoes to the air fryer basket and steam for 10 minutes.
8. Open the lid and combine the onion, garlic, and peppers to the basket. Toss ingredients to incorporate.
9. Heat for an additional 10 minutes and take out of the basket.
10. Wait for approximately 5 minutes before serving.

95. Maple-Glazed Bacon

Prep.Time: 10 min - **Cooking Time:** 8 min - **Servings:** 4

Ingredients:
- ✓ brown sugar - 3 tbsp.
- ✓ water - 2 tbsp.
- ✓ 8 slices bacon
- ✓ maple syrup - 2 tbsp

Directions:
1. Adjust the air fryer to heat at 400°F. Remove the basket and cover the base with baking paper.
2. Empty the water into the base of the fryer while preheating.
3. In a glass dish, whisk the 2 tbsp. of maple syrup and the 3 tbsp. brown sugar together.
4. Place the wire rack into the basket and arrange the bacon into a single layer.
5. Spread the sugar glaze on the bacon until completely covered.
6. Put the basket into the air fryer and steam for 8 minutes.
7. Move the bacon from the basket and wait about 5 minutes before serving hot.

96. Sausage Patties

Prep.Time: 25 min - **Cooking Time:** 20 min - **Servings:** 4

Ingredients:
- ✓ onion powder - 1/2 tsp.
- ✓ 11 oz. of sausage, ground and cold
- ✓ red chili flakes - 1/2 tsp.
- ✓ thyme seasoning - 1/4 tsp.
- ✓ salt - 1/8 tsp.
- ✓ paprika seasoning - 1/4 tsp.
- ✓ garlic - 1 1/2 tsp., minced
- ✓ brown sugar - 1 tsp.
- ✓ cayenne pepper - 1/4 tsp.
- ✓ Tabasco sauce - 1 tsp.
- ✓ Pepper - 1/8 tsp.

Directions:
1. Cover a baking tray with baking lining and place into the air fryer basket.
2. Mix by hand the cold ground sausage with all the listed seasonings, Tabasco sauce, and brown sugar.
3. Divide the meat into 6 sections and create individual patties.
4. Move the patties to the basket in a single layer and adjust the air fryer to heat at 370° F.
5. Heat for 10 minutes and turn the patties to the other side.
6. Continue to broil for 10 additional minutes.
7. Remove from basket to a serving platter and enjoy.

97. Sausage, Egg, and Cheese Biscuits

Prep.Time: 30 min - **Cooking Time:** 16 minutes - **Servings:** 8

Ingredients:
- ✓ pepper - 1/8 tsp.
- ✓ 10.2 oz. can biscuits, flaky
- ✓ 1/8 tsp. salt
- ✓ 1 1/2 tsp. vegetable oil
- ✓ 2oz. sharp cheddar cheese, cubed in 10 pieces
- ✓ 1 1/2 large eggs
- ✓ 1/8 lb. sausage, ground
- ✓ 1 1/2 tsp. water
- ✓ cooking spray (olive oil)

Directions:
1. Create an 8-inch circle of baking lining and set on the base of the basket of the air fryer. Cover with cooking spray. Set a separate piece of baking lining to the side.
2. Using a hot skillet, empty the oil and brown the sausage for approximately 4 minutes while breaking into small pieces with a wooden spatula.
3. Whip 2 of the eggs in a dish and blend with pepper and salt.
4. Remove the browned meat with a slotted ladle to a separate glass dish.
5. Adjust the temperature to medium. Empty the egg mixture and heat for about 60 seconds then combine with the cooked sausage dish and mix completely.
6. In the meantime, section the biscuit pastry into 5 pieces and transfer to the sheet of the baking lining.
7. Compress each into a thin circle and spoon a generous tablespoon of the meat and eggs into the middle.
8. Set a cube of cheese on the filling and enclose completely by pinching the sides of the pastry.
9. In a glass dish, combine the water and remaining egg until smooth.
10. Apply the egg wash to each of the biscuits, covering entirely.
11. Transfer to the basket with the pinched sides on the baking lining.
12. Adjust the temperature to 325°F and heat for 10 minutes.
13. Carefully flip the biscuits carefully and continue steaming for 6 minutes more.
14. Remove the biscuits to a plate and enjoy!

98. Savory Bagel Bites

Prep.Time: 10 min - **Cooking Time:** 9 min - **Servings:** 4

Ingredients:
- ✓ 1 cup self-rising flour
- ✓ 8 oz. Greek yogurt
- ✓ 1/2 cup cream cheese, whipped
- ✓ cooking spray (olive oil)

Directions:
1. In a food blender, whip the yogurt and flour until it thickens into a dough for about 2 minutes.
2. Cover the base of the pan with cooking spray.
3. Create equal sized balls of the dough and move to the greased pan.
4. Shut the air fryer top and adjust the temperature to 325°F for about 5 minutes.
5. Turn the balls over and reset at the same temperature on the air crisp setting for 4 minutes.
6. Remove the balls from the basket and let it cool for approximately 10 minutes.
7. Poke a little hole into the sides of the bagels.
8. Pack the whipped cream cheese inside the holes using a pastry bag and serve immediately.

99. Stuffed Baked Avocado

Prep.Time: 5 min - **Cooking Time:** 14 min - **Servings:** 2

Ingredients:
- ✓ Two eggs, preferably large
- ✓ Salt - 1/4 tsp.
- ✓ 1 avocado, large
- ✓ parsley seasoning - 3 tsp.
- ✓ cheddar - 2 oz., shredded
- ✓ Pepper - 1/8 tsp.

Directions:
1. Set the air fryer to the temperature of 400°F.
2. Pit the avocado by slicing in half and break the eggs into the hollow of the avocado.
3. Sprinkle the pepper, parsley, and salt on top of the whole of the avocados.
4. Move the avocado halves into the basket and heat for approximately 14 minutes.
5. Remove to a serving plate and dust with the shredded cheese before serving.

100. Air Fried Mushroom Frittata

Prep.Time: 10min - **Cooking Time:** 12 min - **Servings:** 2

Ingredients:
- ✓ 4 egg whites
- ✓ 1/3 cup mushrooms, sliced
- ✓ 1 large tomato, sliced
- ✓ ¼ cup finely chopped chives
- ✓ 2 tbsp. milk
- ✓ Salt and freshly ground black pepper to taste

Directions:
1. Start by setting your air fryer toast oven to 320 F.
2. Beat the egg whites and milk in a large bowl. Add in the fresh ingredients and mix until well combined then set the bowl aside.
3. Lightly grease your air fryer toast oven's frying pan and transfer the egg mixture into the pan.
4. Cook in the fryer for about 10 -12 minutes or until done to desire.

101. Sweet Potato Toast

Prep.Time: 10 min - **Cooking Time:** 30 minutes - **Servings:** 2

Ingredients:
- ✓ Salt - 1/4 tsp.
- ✓ paprika seasoning - 1/8 tsp.
- ✓ avocado oil - 4 tsp.
- ✓ garlic powder - 1/8 tsp.
- ✓ 1 sweet potato
- ✓ onion powder - 1/8 tsp.
- ✓ pepper - 1/4 tsp.
- ✓ oregano seasoning - 1/8 tsp.

Directions:
1. Heat the air fryer to the temperature of 380°F.
2. Cut the ends off the sweet potato and discard. Divide into 4 even pieces lengthwise.
3. Whisk the avocado oil and all of the seasonings until combined thoroughly.
4. Brush the spices on top of the slices of sweet potato.
5. Transfer the slices to the air fryer basket and fry for 15 minutes.
6. Turn the sweet potato pieces over and steam once again for 15 more minutes.
7. Remove to a serving plate and enhance with your preferred toppings.

102. Banana Croquette

Prep.Time: 10 min - **Cooking Time:** 25 min - **Servings:** 2

Ingredients:
- ✓ 2 cups sliced banana
- ✓ 3 onions chopped
- ✓ 5 green chilies-roughly chopped
- ✓ 1 ½ tbsp. ginger paste
- ✓ 1 ½ tsp. garlic paste
- ✓ 1 ½ tsp. salt
- ✓ 3 tsp. lemon juice
- ✓ 2 tsp. garam masala
- ✓ 4 tbsp. chopped coriander
- ✓ 3 tbsp. cream
- ✓ 3 tbsp. chopped capsicum
- ✓ 3 eggs
- ✓ 2 ½ tbsp. white sesame seeds

Directions:
1. Grind the ingredients except for the egg and form a smooth paste. Coat the banana in the paste. Now, beat the eggs and add a little salt to it.
2. Dip the coated bananas in the egg mixture and then transfer to the sesame seeds and coat the vegetables well. Place the vegetables on a stick.
3. Pre heat the Air fryer at 160 degrees Fahrenheit for around 5 minutes. Place the sticks in the basket and let them cook for another 25 minutes at the same temperature. Turn the sticks over in between the cooking process to get a uniform cook.

103. Tomato Mushroom Frittata

Prep.Time: 15 min - **Cooking Time:** 15 min - **Servings:** 2

Ingredients:
- ✓ skim milk - 2 tbsp.
- ✓ pepper - 1/8 tsp.
- ✓ chives - 2 tbsp., chopped
- ✓ tomato - 1/4 cup, sliced
- ✓ egg whites - 8 oz.
- ✓ mushrooms - 1/4 cup, sliced

Directions:
1. Adjust the temperature of the air fryer to 320°F.
2. Using a glass dish, blend the tomato, egg whites, mushrooms and milk until combined.
3. Incorporate the seasonings of chives and pepper into the mixture.
4. Empty into the skillet and warm for about 15 minutes.
5. Serve immediately and enjoy while hot.

104. Masala Galette

Prep.Time: 10 min - **Cooking Time:** 25 min - **Servings:** 2

Ingredients:
- ✓ 2 tbsp. garam masala
- ✓ 2 medium potatoes boiled and mashed
- ✓ 1 ½ cup coarsely crushed peanuts
- ✓ 3 tsp. ginger finely chopped
- ✓ 1-2 tbsp. fresh coriander leaves
- ✓ 2 or 3 green chilies finely chopped
- ✓ 1 ½ tbsp. lemon juice
- ✓ Salt and pepper to taste

Directions:
1. Mix the ingredients in a clean bowl.
2. Mold this mixture into round and flat galettes.
3. Wet the galettes slightly with water. Coat each galette with the crushed peanuts.
4. Pre heat the Air Fryer at 160 degrees Fahrenheit for 5 minutes. Place the galettes in the fry basket and let them cook for another 25 minutes at the same temperature. Keep rolling them over to get a uniform cook.
5. Serve either with mint chutney or ketchup.

105. Simple Cooked Egg - KETO

Prep.Time: 10 min - **Cooking Time:** 8-15 min - **Servings:** 3-6

Ingredients:
- ✓ 6 large eggs

Directions:
1. Preheat your air fryer 300-degree F.
2. Put the eggs in a single layer in your air fryer basket carefully.
3. Bake for at least 8 minutes for a slightly runny yolk. Or 12 to 15 minutes for a firmer yolk.
4. Using tongs remove the eggs from the air fryer carefully.
5. Then take a bowl of very cold water and immediately place them in it.
6. Let the eggs stand in the cold water for 5 minutes, then gently crack the shell under water.
7. After that, let the eggs stand for another minute or two, then peel and eat.
8. Enjoy!

106. Ham and Quiche in A Cup - KETO

Prep.Time: 15 min - **Cooking Time:** 15 min - **Servings:** 2-4

Ingredients:
- ✓ 5 whole eggs
- ✓ 2 and ¼ ounces ham
- ✓ 1 cup milk
- ✓ 1/8 teaspoon pepper
- ✓ 1 and ½ cup Swiss cheese
- ✓ ¼ teaspoon salt
- ✓ ¼ cup Green onion
- ✓ ½ teaspoon thyme

Directions:
1. Pre-heat your Fryer to 350-degree F.
2. Crack your eggs in a bowl and beat it well.
3. Add thyme onion, salt, Swiss cheese pepper, milk to the beaten eggs.
4. Prepare your baking forms for muffins and place ham slices in each baking form.
5. Cover the ham with egg mixture.
6. Transfer to Air Fryer and bake for 15 minutes.
7. Serve and enjoy!

107. Morning Sausage Bowl - KETO

Prep.Time: 10 min - **Cooking Time:** 12-13 minutes - **Servings:** 2-4

Ingredients:
- ✓ 8 chestnut mushrooms
- ✓ 8 tomatoes, halved
- ✓ 1 garlic clove, crushed
- ✓ 4 rashers smoked back bacon
- ✓ 7 ounces baby leaf spinach
- ✓ 4 whole eggs
- ✓ Chipotle as needed

Directions:
1. Pre-heat your Air Fryer to 392 degrees F
2. Take the Air Fryer cooking basket and add mushrooms, tomatoes and garlic
3. Spray with oil and season well
4. Add bacon, chipotle to the Air Fryer and cook for 10 minutes
5. Take a microwave proof bowl and add spinach, heat until wilt
6. Add wilt spinach into the microwave proof bowl
7. Crack the eggs the bowl and Air Fry for 2-3 minutes at 320 degrees F
8. Serve cooked eggs with bacon, enjoy!

108. Simple Baked Eggs - KETO

Prep.Time: 20 min - **Cooking Time:** 7 min - **Servings:** 2

Ingredients:
- ✓ 2 whole eggs
- ✓ 2 tablespoons milk
- ✓ 1 teaspoons parmesan cheese
- ✓ 1 tomato, chopped
- ✓ Salt and pepper to taste
- ✓ 1 bacon slice
- ✓ Parsley, chopped

Directions:
1. Pre-heat your Fryer to 350-degree Fahrenheit for about 3 minutes.
2. Cut up the bacon into small portions and divide them amongst ramekins.
3. Dice up tomatoes and divide them amongst ramekins as well.
4. Crack an egg into the dishes and add 1 tablespoon of milk into the dishes.
5. Season the ramekins with pepper and salt.
6. Sprinkle ½ a teaspoon of parmesan and transfer the ramekins to your cooking basket.
7. Cook for 7 minutes and serve with a garnish of parsley.
8. Enjoy!

109. Healthy Green Beans

Prep.Time: 10 min - **Cooking Time:** 10 min - **Servings:** 2

Ingredients:
- ✓ 2 cups green beans, cut in half
- ✓ 2 tbsp olive oil
- ✓ 1 tbsp shawarma spice
- ✓ 1/2 tsp salt

Directions:
1. Add beans, olive oil, salt, and shawarma into the bowl and toss well.
2. Place beans into the air fryer basket for 10 minutes at 370 F/ 187 C. Shake air fryer basket halfway through.
3. Serve and enjoy.

110. Lemon Garlic Shrimp

Prep.Time: 10 min - **Cooking Time:** 5-8 min - **Servings:** 2

Ingredients:
- ✓ 1 lb shrimp, peeled
- ✓ 1/4 cup parsley, chopped
- ✓ 1/4 tsp red pepper flakes
- ✓ 1 lemon juice
- ✓ 1 lemon zest
- ✓ 4 garlic cloves, minced
- ✓ 1 tbsp olive oil
- ✓ 1/4 tsp sea salt

Directions:
1. Preheat the air fryer to 400 F/ 204 C.
2. Add all ingredients into the bowl and toss well to coat.
3. Add shrimp to air fryer basket and cook for 5-8 minutes. Shake basket halfway through.
4. Serve and enjoy.

LUNCH RECIPES

1. Lunch Egg Rolls

Prep.Time: 10 min - **Cooking Time:** 15 min - **Servings:** 4

Ingredients:
- ✓ ½ cup mushrooms, chopped
- ✓ ½ cup carrots, grated
- ✓ ½ cup zucchini, grated
- ✓ 2 green onions, chopped
- ✓ 2 tablespoons soy sauce
- ✓ 8 egg roll wrappers
- ✓ 1 eggs, whisked
- ✓ 1 tablespoon cornstarch

Directions:
9. In a bowl, mix carrots with mushrooms, zucchini, green onions and soy sauce and stir well.
10. Arrange egg roll wrappers on a working surface, divide veggie mix on each and roll well.
11. In a bowl, mix cornstarch with egg, whisk well and brush eggs rolls with this mix.
12. Seal edges, place all rolls in your preheated air fryer and cook them at 370 degrees F for 15 minutes.
13. Arrange them on a platter and serve them for lunch.

Nutrition: calories 172 - Fat 6 - Fiber 6 - Carbs 8 - Protein 7

2. Tasty Cheeseburgers

Prep.Time: 10 min - **Cooking Time:** 20 min - **Servings:** 2

Ingredients:
- ✓ 12 ounces lean beef, ground
- ✓ 4 teaspoons ketchup
- ✓ 3 tablespoons yellow onion, chopped
- ✓ 2 teaspoons mustard
- ✓ Salt and black pepper to the taste
- ✓ 4 cheddar cheese slices
- ✓ 2 burger buns, halved

Directions:
8. In a bowl, mix beef with onion, ketchup, mustard, salt and pepper, stir well and shape 4 patties out of this mix.
9. Divide cheese on 2 patties and top with the other 2 patties.
10. Place them in preheated air fryer at 370 degrees F and fry them for 20 minutes.
11. Divide cheeseburger on 2 bun halves, top with the other 2 and serve for lunch.

Nutrition: calories 261 - Fat 6 - Fiber 10 - Carbs 20 - Protein 6

3. Chicken Sandwiches

Prep.Time: 10 min - **Cooking Time:** 10 minutes - **Servings:** 4

Ingredients:
- ✓ 2 chicken breasts, skinless, boneless and cubed
- ✓ 1 red onion, chopped
- ✓ 1 red bell pepper, sliced
- ✓ ½ cup Italian seasoning
- ✓ ½ teaspoon thyme, dried
- ✓ 2 cups butter lettuce, torn
- ✓ 4 pita pockets
- ✓ 1 cup cherry tomatoes, halved
- ✓ 1 tablespoon olive oil

Directions:
9. In your air fryer, mix chicken with onion, bell pepper, Italian seasoning and oil, toss and cook at 380 degrees F for 10 minutes.
10. Transfer chicken mix to a bowl, add thyme, butter lettuce and cherry tomatoes, toss well, stuff pita pockets with this mix and serve for lunch.

Nutrition: calories 126 - Fat 4 - Fiber 8 - Carbs 14 - Protein 4

4. Chinese Pork Lunch Mix

Prep.Time: 10 min - **Cooking Time:** 12 min - **Servings:** 4

Ingredients:
- ✓ 2 eggs
- ✓ 2 pounds pork, cut into medium cubes
- ✓ 1 cup cornstarch
- ✓ 1 teaspoon sesame oil
- ✓ Salt and black pepper to the taste
- ✓ A pinch of Chinese five spice
- ✓ 3 tablespoons canola oil
- ✓ Sweet tomato sauce for serving

Directions:
9. In a bowl, mix five spice with salt, pepper and cornstarch and stir.
10. In another bowl, mix eggs with sesame oil and whisk well.
11. Dredge pork cubes in cornstarch mix, then dip in eggs mix and place them in your air fryer which you've greased with the canola oil.
12. Cook at 340 degrees F for 12 minutes, shaking the fryer once.
13. Serve pork for lunch with the sweet tomato sauce on the side.

Nutrition: calories 320 - Fat 8 - Fiber 12 - Carbs 20 - Protein 5

5. Fish And Chips

Prep.Time: 10 min - **Cooking Time:** 12 min - **Servings:** 2

Ingredients:
- ✓ 2 medium cod fillets, skinless and boneless
- ✓ Salt and black pepper to the taste
- ✓ ¼ cup buttermilk
- ✓ 3 cups kettle chips, cooked

Directions:
4. In a bowl, mix fish with salt, pepper and buttermilk, toss and leave aside for 5 minutes.
5. Put chips in your food processor, crush them and spread them on a plate.
6. Add fish and press well on all sides.
7. Transfer fish to your air fryer's basket and cook at 400 degrees F for 12 minutes.
8. Serve hot for lunch.

Nutrition: calories 271 - Fat 7 - Fiber 9 - Carbs 14 - Protein 4

6. Easy Hot Dogs

Prep.Time: 10 min - **Cooking Time:** 7 min - **Servings:** 2

Ingredients:
- ✓ 2 hot dog buns
- ✓ 2 hot dogs
- ✓ 1 tablespoon Dijon mustard
- ✓ 2 tablespoons cheddar cheese, grated

Directions:
5. Put hot dogs in preheated air fryer and cook them at 390 degrees F for 5 minutes.
6. Divide hot dogs into hot dog buns, spread mustard and cheese, return everything to your air fryer and cook for 2 minutes more at 390 degrees F.
7. Serve for lunch.

Nutrition: calories 211 - Fat 3 - Fiber 8 - Carbs 12 - Protein 4

7. Lentils Fritters

Prep.Time: 10 min - **Cooking Time:** 10 min - **Servings:** 2

Ingredients:

- ✓ 1 cup yellow lentils, soaked in water for 1 hour and drained
- ✓ 1 hot chili pepper, chopped
- ✓ 1 inch ginger piece, grated
- ✓ ½ teaspoon turmeric powder
- ✓ 1 teaspoon garam masala
- ✓ 1 teaspoon baking powder
- ✓ Salt and black pepper to the taste
- ✓ 2 teaspoons olive oil
- ✓ 1/3 cup water
- ✓ ½ cup cilantro, chopped
- ✓ 1 and ½ cup spinach, chopped
- ✓ 4 garlic cloves, minced
- ✓ ¾ cup red onion, chopped
- ✓ Mint chutney for serving

Directions:

1. In your blender, mix lentils with chili pepper, ginger, turmeric, garam masala, baking powder, salt, pepper, olive oil, water, cilantro, spinach, onion and garlic, blend well and shape medium balls out of this mix.
2. Place them all in your preheated air fryer at 400 degrees F and cook for 10 minutes.
3. Serve your veggie fritters with a side salad for lunch.

Nutrition: calories 142 - Fat 2 - Fiber 8 - Carbs 12 - Protein 4

8. Italian Eggplant Sandwich

Prep.Time: 10min - **Cooking Time:** 6 min - **Servings:** 2

Ingredients:

- ✓ 1 eggplant, sliced
- ✓ 2 teaspoons parsley, dried
- ✓ Salt and black pepper to the taste
- ✓ ½ cup breadcrumbs
- ✓ ½ teaspoon Italian seasoning
- ✓ ½ teaspoon garlic powder
- ✓ ½ teaspoon onion powder
- ✓ 2 tablespoons milk
- ✓ 4 bread slices
- ✓ Cooking spray
- ✓ ½ cup mayonnaise
- ✓ ¾ cup tomato sauce
- ✓ 2 cups mozzarella cheese, grated

Directions:

1. Season eggplant slices with salt and pepper, leave aside for 10 minutes and then pat dry them well.
2. In a bowl, mix parsley with breadcrumbs, Italian seasoning, onion and garlic powder, salt and black pepper and stir.
3. In another bowl, mix milk with mayo and whisk well.
4. Brush eggplant slices with mayo mix, dip them in breadcrumbs, place them in your air fryer's basket, spray with cooking oil and cook them at 400 degrees F for 15 minutes, flipping them after 8 minutes.
5. Brush each bread slice with olive oil and arrange 2 on a working surface.
6. Add mozzarella and parmesan on each, add baked eggplant slices, spread tomato sauce and basil and top with the other bread slices, greased side down.
7. Divide sandwiches on plates, cut them in halves and serve for lunch.

Nutrition: calories 324 - Fat 16 - Fiber 4 - Carbs 39 - Protein 12

9. Meatballs Sandwich

Prep.Time: 10 min - **Cooking Time:** 22 minutes - **Servings:** 4

Ingredients:

- ✓ 3 baguettes, sliced more than halfway through
- ✓ 14 ounces beef, ground
- ✓ 7 ounces tomato sauce
- ✓ 1 small onion, chopped
- ✓ 1 egg, whisked
- ✓ 1 tablespoon bread crumbs
- ✓ 2 tablespoons cheddar cheese, grated
- ✓ 1 tablespoon oregano, chopped
- ✓ 1 tablespoon olive oil
- ✓ Salt and black pepper to the taste
- ✓ 1 teaspoon thyme, dried
- ✓ 1 teaspoon basil, dried

Directions:

1. In a bowl, combine meat with salt, pepper, onion, breadcrumbs, egg, cheese, oregano, thyme and basil, stir, shape medium meatballs and add them to your air fryer after you've greased it with the oil.
2. Cook them at 375 degrees F for 12 minutes, flipping them halfway.
3. Add tomato sauce, cook meatballs for 10 minutes more and arrange them on sliced baguettes.
4. Serve them right away.

Nutrition: calories 380 - Fat 5 - Fiber 6 - Carbs 34 - Protein 20

10. Zucchini Casserole

Prep.Time: 10 min - **Cooking Time:** 16 min - **Servings:** 8

Ingredients:

- ✓ 1 cup veggie stock
- ✓ 2 tablespoons olive oil
- ✓ 2 sweet potatoes, peeled and cut into medium wedges
- ✓ 8 zucchinis, cut into medium wedges
- ✓ 2 yellow onions, chopped
- ✓ 1 cup coconut milk
- ✓ Salt and black pepper to the taste
- ✓ 1 tablespoon soy sauce
- ✓ ¼ teaspoon thyme, dried
- ✓ ¼ teaspoon rosemary, dried
- ✓ 4 tablespoons dill, chopped
- ✓ ½ teaspoon basil, chopped

Directions:

1. Heat up a pan that fits your air fryer with the oil over medium heat, add onion, stir and cook for 2 minutes.
2. Add zucchinis, thyme, rosemary, basil, potato, salt, pepper, stock, milk, soy sauce and dill, stir, introduce in your air fryer, cook at 360 degrees F for 14 minutes, divide among plates and serve right away.

Nutrition: calories 133 - Fat 3 - Fiber 4 - Carbs 10 - Protein 5

11. Chicken and Zucchini Lunch Mix

Prep.Time: 10 min - **Cooking Time:** 20 min - **Servings:** 4

Ingredients:
- ✓ 4 zucchinis, cut with a spiralizer
- ✓ 1 pound chicken breasts, skinless, boneless and cubed
- ✓ 2 garlic cloves, minced
- ✓ 1 teaspoon olive oil
- ✓ Salt and black pepper to the taste
- ✓ 2 cups cherry tomatoes, halved
- ✓ ½ cup almonds, chopped

For the pesto:
- ✓ 2 cups basil
- ✓ 2 cups kale, chopped
- ✓ 1 tablespoon lemon juice
- ✓ 1 garlic clove
- ✓ ¾ cup pine nuts
- ✓ ½ cup olive oil
- ✓ A pinch of salt

Directions:
1. In your food processor, mix basil with kale, lemon juice, garlic, pine nuts, oil and a pinch of salt, pulse really well and leave aside.
2. Heat up a pan that fits your air fryer with the oil over medium heat, add garlic, stir and cook for 1 minute.
3. Add chicken, salt, pepper, stir, almonds, zucchini noodles, garlic, cherry tomatoes and the pesto you've made at the beginning, stir gently, introduce in preheated air fryer and cook at 360 degrees F for 17 minutes.
4. Divide among plates and serve for lunch.

Nutrition: calories 344 - Fat 8 - Fiber 7 - Carbs 12 - Protein 16

12. Special Lunch Seafood Stew

Prep.Time: 10 min - **Cooking Time:** 20 min - **Servings:** 4

Ingredients:
- ✓ 5 ounces white rice
- ✓ 2 ounces peas
- ✓ 1 red bell pepper, chopped
- ✓ 14 ounces white wine
- ✓ 3 ounces water
- ✓ 2 ounces squid pieces
- ✓ 7 ounces mussels
- ✓ 3 ounces sea bass fillet, skinless, boneless and chopped
- ✓ 6 scallops
- ✓ 3.5 ounces clams
- ✓ 4 shrimp
- ✓ 4 crayfish
- ✓ Salt and black pepper to the taste
- ✓ 1 tablespoon olive oil

Directions:
1. In your air fryer's pan, mix sea bass with shrimp, mussels, scallops, crayfish, clams and squid.
2. Add the oil, salt and pepper and toss to coat.
3. In a bowl, mix peas salt, pepper, bell pepper and rice and stir.
4. Add this over seafood, also add wine and water, place pan in your air fryer and cook at 400 degrees F for 20 minutes, stirring halfway.
5. Divide into bowls and serve for lunch.

Nutrition: calories 300 - Fat 12 - Fiber 2 - Carbs 23 - Protein 25

13. Succulent Lunch Turkey Breast

Prep.Time: 10 min - **Cooking Time:** 47 minutes - **Servings:** 4

Ingredients:
- ✓ 1 big turkey breast
- ✓ 2 teaspoons olive oil
- ✓ ½ teaspoon smoked paprika
- ✓ 1 teaspoon thyme, dried
- ✓ ½ teaspoon sage, dried
- ✓ Salt and black pepper to the taste
- ✓ 2 tablespoons mustard
- ✓ ¼ cup maple syrup
- ✓ 1 tablespoon butter, soft

Directions:
1. Brush turkey breast with the olive oil, season with salt, pepper, thyme, paprika and sage, rub, place in your air fryer's basket and fry at 350 degrees F for 25 minutes.
2. Flip turkey, cook for 10 minutes more, flip one more time and cook for another 10 minutes.
3. Meanwhile, heat up a pan with the butter over medium heat, add mustard and maple syrup, stir well, cook for a couple of minutes and take off heat.
4. Slice turkey breast, divide among plates and serve with the maple glaze drizzled on top.

Nutrition: calories 280 - Fat 2 - Fiber 7 - Carbs 16 - Protein 14

14. Japanese Chicken Mix

Prep.Time: 10 min - **Cooking Time:** 8 min - **Servings:** 2

Ingredients:
- ✓ 2 chicken thighs, skinless and boneless
- ✓ 2 ginger slices, chopped
- ✓ 3 garlic cloves, minced
- ✓ ¼ cup soy sauce
- ✓ ¼ cup mirin
- ✓ 1/8 cup sake
- ✓ ½ teaspoon sesame oil
- ✓ 1/8 cup water
- ✓ 2 tablespoons sugar
- ✓ 1 tablespoon cornstarch mixed with 2 tablespoons water
- ✓ Sesame seeds for serving

Directions:
1. In a bowl, mix chicken thighs with ginger, garlic, soy sauce, mirin, sake, oil, water, sugar and cornstarch, toss well, transfer to preheated air fryer and cook at 360 degrees F for 8 minutes.
2. Divide among plates, sprinkle sesame seeds on top and serve with a side salad for lunch.

Nutrition: calories 300 - Fat 7 - Fiber 9 - Carbs 17 - Protein 10

15. Scallops and Dill

Prep.Time: 10 min - **Cooking Time:** 5 min - **Servings:** 4

Ingredients:
- ✓ 1 pound sea scallops
- ✓ 1 tablespoon lemon juice
- ✓ 1 teaspoon dill, chopped
- ✓ 2 teaspoons olive oil
- ✓ Salt and black pepper to the taste

Directions:
1. In your air fryer, mix scallops with dill, oil, salt, pepper and lemon juice, cover and cook at 360 degrees F for 5 minutes.
2. Discard unopened ones, divide scallops and dill sauce on plates and serve for lunch.

Nutrition: calories 152 - Fat 4 - Fiber 7 - Carbs 19 - Protein 4

16. Turkish Koftas

Prep.Time: 10 min - **Cooking Time:** 15 min - **Servings:** 2

Ingredients:
- ✓ 1 leek, chopped
- ✓ 2 tablespoons feta cheese, crumbled
- ✓ ½ pound lean beef, minced
- ✓ 1 tablespoon cumin, ground
- ✓ 1 tablespoon mint, chopped
- ✓ 1 tablespoon parsley, chopped
- ✓ 1 teaspoon garlic, minced
- ✓ Salt and black pepper to the taste

Directions:
1. In a bowl, mix beef with leek, cheese, cumin, mint, parsley, garlic, salt and pepper, stir well, shape your koftas and place them on sticks.
2. Add koftas to your preheated air fryer at 360 degrees F and cook them for 15 minutes.
3. Serve them with a side salad for lunch.

Nutrition: calories 281 - Fat 7 - Fiber 8 - Carbs 17 - Protein 6

17. Sago Galette

Prep.Time: 10 min - **Cooking Time:** 25 min - **Servings:** 2

Ingredients:
- ✓ 2 cup sago soaked
- ✓ 1 ½ cup coarsely crushed peanuts
- ✓ 3 tsp. ginger finely chopped
- ✓ 1-2 tbsp. fresh coriander leaves
- ✓ 2 or 3 green chilies finely chopped
- ✓ 1 ½ tbsp. lemon juice
- ✓ Salt and pepper to taste

Directions:
1. Wash the soaked sago and mix it with the rest of the ingredients in a clean bowl.
2. Mold this mixture into round and flat galettes.
3. Wet the galettes slightly with water. Coat each galette with the crushed peanuts.
4. Pre heat the Air Fryer at 160 degrees Fahrenheit for 5 minutes. Place the galettes in the fry basket and let them cook for another 25 minutes at the same temperature. Keep rolling them over to get a uniform cook. Serve either with mint chutney or ketchup.

18. Delicious Beef Cubes

Prep.Time: 10 min - **Cooking Time:** 12 min - **Servings:** 4

Ingredients:
- ✓ 1 pound sirloin, cubed
- ✓ 16 ounces jarred pasta sauce
- ✓ 1 and ½ cups bread crumbs
- ✓ 2 tablespoons olive oil
- ✓ ½ teaspoon marjoram, dried
- ✓ White rice, already cooked for serving

Directions:
1. In a bowl, mix beef cubes with pasta sauce and toss well.
2. In another bowl, mix bread crumbs with marjoram and oil and stir well.
3. Dip beef cubes in this mix, place them in your air fryer and cook at 360 degrees F for 12 minutes.
4. Divide among plates and serve with white rice on the side.

Nutrition: calories 271 - Fat 6 - Fiber 9 - Carbs 18 - Protein 12

19. Lunch Chicken Salad

Prep.Time: 10 min - **Cooking Time:** 20 minutes - **Servings:** 4

Ingredients:
- ✓ 2 ears of corn, hulled
- ✓ 1 pound chicken tenders, boneless
- ✓ Olive oil as needed
- ✓ Salt and black pepper to the taste
- ✓ 1 teaspoon sweet paprika
- ✓ 1 tablespoon brown sugar
- ✓ ½ teaspoon garlic powder
- ✓ ½ iceberg lettuce head, cut into medium strips
- ✓ ½ romaine lettuce head, cut into medium strips
- ✓ 1 cup canned black beans, drained
- ✓ 1 cup cheddar cheese, shredded
- ✓ 3 tablespoons cilantro, chopped
- ✓ 4 green onions, chopped
- ✓ 12 cherry tomatoes, sliced
- ✓ ¼ cup ranch dressing
- ✓ 3 tablespoons BBQ sauce

Directions:
1. Put corn in your air fryer, drizzle some oil, toss, cook at 400 degrees F for 10 minutes, transfer to a plate and leave aside for now.
2. Put chicken in your air fryer's basket, add salt, pepper, brown sugar, paprika and garlic powder, toss, drizzle some more oil, cook at 400 degrees F for 10 minutes, flipping them halfway, transfer tenders to a cutting board and chop them.
3. Cur kernels off the cob, transfer corn to a bowl, add chicken, iceberg lettuce, romaine lettuce, black beans, cheese, cilantro, tomatoes, onions, bbq sauce and ranch dressing, toss well and serve for lunch.

Nutrition: calories 372 - Fat 6 - Fiber 9 - Carbs 17 - Protein 6

20. Philadelphia Chicken Lunch

Prep.Time: 10 min - **Cooking Time:** 30 min - **Servings:** 4

Ingredients:
- ✓ 1 teaspoon olive oil
- ✓ 1 yellow onion, sliced
- ✓ 2 chicken breasts, skinless, boneless and sliced
- ✓ Salt and black pepper to the taste
- ✓ 1 tablespoon Worcestershire sauce
- ✓ 14 ounces pizza dough
- ✓ 1 and ½ cups cheddar cheese, grated
- ✓ ½ cup jarred cheese sauce

Directions:
1. Preheat your air fryer at 400 degrees F, add half of the oil and onions and fry them for 8 minutes, stirring once.
2. Add chicken pieces, Worcestershire sauce, salt and pepper, toss, air fry for 8 minutes more, stirring once and transfer everything to a bowl.
3. Roll pizza dough on a working surface and shape a rectangle.
4. Spread half of the cheese all over, add chicken and onion mix and top with cheese sauce.
5. Roll your dough and shape into a U.
6. Place your roll in your air fryer's basket, brush with the rest of the oil and cook at 370 degrees for 12 minutes, flipping the roll halfway.
7. Slice your roll when it's warm and serve for lunch.

Nutrition: calories 300 - Fat 8 - Fiber 17 - Carbs 20 - Protein 6

21. Pasta Salad

Prep.Time: 10 min - Cooking Time: 12 min - Servings: 6

Ingredients:
- ✓ 1 zucchini, sliced in half and roughly chopped
- ✓ 1 orange bell pepper, roughly chopped
- ✓ 1 green bell pepper, roughly chopped
- ✓ 1 red onion, roughly chopped
- ✓ 4 ounces brown mushrooms, halved
- ✓ Salt and black pepper to the taste
- ✓ 1 teaspoon Italian seasoning
- ✓ 1 pound penne rigate, already cooked
- ✓ 1 cup cherry tomatoes, halved
- ✓ ½ cup kalamata olive, pitted and halved
- ✓ ¼ cup olive oil
- ✓ 3 tablespoons balsamic vinegar
- ✓ 2 tablespoons basil, chopped

Directions:
1. In a bowl, mix zucchini with mushrooms, orange bell pepper, green bell pepper, red onion, salt, pepper, Italian seasoning and oil, toss well, transfer to preheated air fryer at 380 degrees F and cook them for 12 minutes.
2. In a large salad bowl, mix pasta with cooked veggies, cherry tomatoes, olives, vinegar and basil, toss and serve for lunch.

Nutrition: calories 200 - Fat 5 - Fiber 8 - Carbs 10 - Protein 6

22. Coconut and Chicken Casserole

Prep.Time: 10 min - Cooking Time: 25 min - Servings: 4

Ingredients:
- ✓ 4 lime leaves, torn
- ✓ 1 cup veggie stock
- ✓ 1 lemongrass stalk, chopped
- ✓ 1 inch piece, grated
- ✓ 1 pound chicken breast, skinless, boneless and cut into thin strips
- ✓ 8 ounces mushrooms, chopped
- ✓ 4 Thai chilies, chopped
- ✓ 4 tablespoons fish sauce
- ✓ 6 ounces coconut milk
- ✓ ¼ cup lime juice
- ✓ ¼ cup cilantro, chopped
- ✓ Salt and black pepper to the taste

Directions:
1. Put stock into a pan that fits your air fryer, bring to a simmer over medium heat, add lemongrass, ginger and lime leaves, stir and cook for 10 minutes.
2. Strain soup, return to pan, add chicken, mushrooms, milk, chilies, fish sauce, lime juice, cilantro, salt and pepper, stir, introduce in your air fryer and cook at 360 degrees F for 15 minutes.
3. Divide into bowls and serve.

Nutrition: calories 150 - Fat 4 - Fiber 4 - Carbs 6 - Protein 7

23. Bacon Pudding

Prep.Time: 10 min - Cooking Time: 30 minutes - Servings: 6

Ingredients:
- ✓ 4 bacon strips, cooked and chopped
- ✓ 1 tablespoon butter, soft
- ✓ 2 cups corn
- ✓ 1 yellow onion, chopped
- ✓ ¼ cup celery, chopped
- ✓ ½ cup red bell pepper, chopped
- ✓ 1 teaspoon thyme, chopped
- ✓ 2 teaspoons garlic, minced
- ✓ Salt and black pepper to the taste
- ✓ ½ cup heavy cream
- ✓ 1 and ½ cups milk
- ✓ 3 eggs, whisked
- ✓ 3 cups bread, cubed
- ✓ 4 tablespoons parmesan, grated
- ✓ Cooking spray

Directions:
1. Grease your air fryer's pan with coking spray.
2. In a bowl, mix bacon with butter, corn, onion, bell pepper, celery, thyme, garlic, salt, pepper, milk, heavy cream, eggs and bread cubes, toss, pour into greased pan and sprinkle cheese all over
3. Add this to your preheated air fryer at 320 degrees and cook for 30 minutes.
4. Divide among plates and serve warm for a quick lunch.

Nutrition: calories 276 - Fat 10 - Fiber 2 - Carbs 20 - Protein 10

24. Chicken, Beans, Corn and Quinoa Casserole

Prep.Time: 10 min - Cooking Time: 30 min - Servings: 8

Ingredients:
- ✓ 1 cup quinoa, already cooked
- ✓ 3 cups chicken breast, cooked and shredded
- ✓ 14 ounces canned black beans
- ✓ 12 ounces corn
- ✓ ½ cup cilantro, chopped
- ✓ 6 kale leaves, chopped
- ✓ ½ cup green onions, chopped
- ✓ 1 cup clean tomato sauce
- ✓ 1 cup clean salsa
- ✓ 2 teaspoons chili powder
- ✓ 2 teaspoons cumin, ground
- ✓ 3 cups mozzarella cheese, shredded
- ✓ 1 tablespoon garlic powder
- ✓ Cooking spray
- ✓ 2 jalapeno peppers, chopped

Directions:
1. Spray a baking dish that fits your air fryer with cooking spray, add quinoa, chicken, black beans, corn, cilantro, kale, green onions, tomato sauce, salsa, chili powder, cumin, garlic powder, jalapenos and mozzarella, toss, introduce in your fryer and cook at 350 degrees F for 17 minutes.
2. Slice and serve warm for lunch.

Nutrition: calories 365 - Fat 12 - Fiber 6 - Carbs 22 - Protein 26

25. Bacon and Garlic Pizzas

Prep.Time: 10 min - **Cooking Time:** 10 min - **Servings:** 4

Ingredients:
- ✓ 4 dinner rolls, frozen
- ✓ 4 garlic cloves minced
- ✓ ½ teaspoon oregano dried
- ✓ ½ teaspoon garlic powder
- ✓ 1 cup tomato sauce
- ✓ 8 bacon slices, cooked and chopped
- ✓ 1 and ¼ cups cheddar cheese, grated
- ✓ Cooking spray

Directions:
1. Place dinner rolls on a working surface and press them to obtain 4 ovals.
2. Spray each oval with cooking spray, transfer them to your air fryer and cook them at 370 degrees F for 2 minutes.
3. Spread tomato sauce on each oval, divide garlic, sprinkle oregano and garlic powder and top with bacon and cheese.
4. Return pizzas to your heated air fryer and cook them at 370 degrees F for 8 minutes more.
5. Serve them warm for lunch.

Nutrition: calories 217 - Fat 5 - Fiber 8 - Carbs 12 - Protein 4

26. Veg Momos

Prep.Time: 10 min - **Cooking Time:** 20 min - **Servings:** 2

Ingredients:
For dough:
- ✓ 1 ½ cup all-purpose flour
- ✓ ½ tsp. salt or to taste
- ✓ 5 tbsp. water
For filling:
- ✓ 2 cup carrots grated
- ✓ 2 cup cabbage grated
- ✓ 2 tbsp. oil
- ✓ 2 tsp. ginger-garlic paste
- ✓ 2 tsp. soya sauce
- ✓ 2 tsp. vinegar

Directions:
1. Knead the dough and cover it with plastic wrap and set aside. Next, cook the ingredients for the filling and try to ensure that the vegetables are covered well with the sauce.
2. Roll the dough and cut it into a square. Place the filling in the center. Now, wrap the dough to cover the filling and pinch the edges together.
3. Pre heat the Air fryer at 200° F for 5 minutes. Place the gnocchis in the fry basket and close it. Let them cook at the same temperature for another 20 minutes. Recommended sides are chili sauce or ketchup.

27. Lunch Potato Salad

Prep.Time: 10 min - **Cooking Time:** 25 minutes - **Servings:** 4

Ingredients:
- ✓ 2 pound red potatoes, halved
- ✓ 2 tablespoons olive oil
- ✓ Salt and black pepper to the taste
- ✓ 2 green onions, chopped
- ✓ 1 red bell pepper, chopped
- ✓ 1/3 cup lemon juice
- ✓ 3 tablespoons mustard

Directions:
1. On your air fryer's basket, mix potatoes with half of the olive oil, salt and pepper and cook at 350 degrees F for 25 minutes shaking the fryer once.
2. In a bowl, mix onions with bell pepper and roasted potatoes and toss.
3. In a small bowl, mix lemon juice with the rest of the oil and mustard and whisk really well.
4. Add this to potato salad, toss well and serve for lunch.

Nutrition: calories 211 - Fat 6 - Fiber 8 - Carbs 12 - Protein 4

28. Beef Lunch Meatballs

Prep.Time: 10 min - **Cooking Time:** 15 min - **Servings:** 4

Ingredients:
- ✓ ½ pound beef, ground
- ✓ ½ pound Italian sausage, chopped
- ✓ ½ teaspoon garlic powder
- ✓ ½ teaspoon onion powder
- ✓ Salt and black pepper to the taste
- ✓ ½ cup cheddar cheese, grated
- ✓ Mashed potatoes for serving

Directions:
1. In a bowl, mix beef with sausage, garlic powder, onion powder, salt, pepper and cheese, stir well and shape 16 meatballs out of this mix.
2. Place meatballs in your air fryer and cook them at 370 degrees F for 15 minutes.
3. Serve your meatballs with some mashed potatoes on the side.

Nutrition: calories 333 - Fat 23 - Fiber 1 - Carbs 8 - Protein 20

29. Prosciutto Sandwich

Prep.Time: 10 min - **Cooking Time:** 5 min - **Servings:** 1

Ingredients:
- ✓ 2 bread slices
- ✓ 2 mozzarella slices
- ✓ 2 tomato slices
- ✓ 2 prosciutto slices
- ✓ 2 basil leaves
- ✓ 1 teaspoon olive oil
- ✓ A pinch of salt and black pepper

Directions:
1. Arrange mozzarella and prosciutto on a bread slice.
2. Season with salt and pepper, place in your air fryer and cook at 400 degrees F for 5 minutes.
3. Drizzle oil over prosciutto, add tomato and basil, cover with the other bread slice, cut sandwich in half and serve.

Nutrition: calories 172 - Fat 3 - Fiber 7 - Carbs 9 - Protein 5

30. Hash Brown Toasts

Prep.Time: 10 min - **Cooking Time:** 7 min - **Servings:** 4

Ingredients:
- ✓ 4 hash brown patties, frozen
- ✓ 1 tablespoon olive oil
- ✓ ¼ cup cherry tomatoes, chopped
- ✓ 3 tablespoons mozzarella, shredded
- ✓ 2 tablespoons parmesan, grated
- ✓ 1 tablespoon balsamic vinegar
- ✓ 1 tablespoon basil, chopped

Directions:
1. Put hash brown patties in your air fryer, drizzle the oil over them and cook them at 400 degrees F for 7 minutes.
2. In a bowl, mix tomatoes with mozzarella, parmesan, vinegar and basil and stir well.
3. Divide hash brown patties on plates, top each with tomatoes mix and serve for lunch.

Nutrition: calories 199 - Fat 3 - Fiber 8 - Carbs 12 - Protein 4

31. Lunch Fajitas

Prep.Time: 10 min - **Cooking Time:** 10 min - **Servings:** 4

Ingredients:
- ✓ 1 teaspoon garlic powder
- ✓ ¼ teaspoon cumin, ground
- ✓ ½ teaspoon chili powder
- ✓ Salt and black pepper to the taste
- ✓ ¼ teaspoon coriander, ground
- ✓ 1 pound chicken breasts, cut into strips
- ✓ 1 red bell pepper, sliced
- ✓ 1 green bell pepper, sliced
- ✓ 1 yellow onion, chopped
- ✓ 1 tablespoon lime juice
- ✓ Cooking spray
- ✓ 4 tortillas, warmed up
- ✓ Salsa for serving
- ✓ Sour cream for serving
- ✓ 1 cup lettuce leaves, torn for serving

Directions:
1. In a bowl, mix chicken with garlic powder, cumin, chili, salt, pepper, coriander, lime juice, red bell pepper, green bell pepper and onion, toss, leave aside for 10 minutes, transfer to your air fryer and drizzle some cooking spray all over.
2. Toss and cook at 400 degrees F for 10 minutes.
3. Arrange tortillas on a working surface, divide chicken mix, also add salsa, sour cream and lettuce, wrap and serve for lunch.

Nutrition: calories 317 - Fat 6 - Fiber 8 - Carbs 14 - Protein 4

32. Turkey Burgers

Prep.Time: 10 min - **Cooking Time:** 8 min - **Servings:** 4

Ingredients:
- ✓ 1 pound turkey meat, ground
- ✓ 1 shallot, minced
- ✓ A drizzle of olive oil
- ✓ 1 small jalapeno pepper, minced
- ✓ 2 teaspoons lime juice
- ✓ Zest from 1 lime, grated
- ✓ Salt and black pepper to the taste
- ✓ 1 teaspoon cumin, ground
- ✓ 1 teaspoon sweet paprika
- ✓ Guacamole for serving

Directions:
1. In a bowl, mix turkey meat with salt, pepper, cumin, paprika, shallot, jalapeno, lime juice and zest, stir well, shape burgers from this mix, drizzle the oil over them, introduce in preheated air fryer and cook them at 370 degrees F for 8 minutes on each side.
2. Divide among plates and serve with guacamole on top.

Nutrition: calories 200 - Fat 12 - Fiber 0 - Carbs 0 - Protein 12

33. Chicken Pie

Prep.Time: 10 min - **Cooking Time:** 16 minutes - **Servings:** 4

Ingredients:
- ✓ 2 chicken thighs, boneless, skinless and cubed
- ✓ 1 carrot, chopped
- ✓ 1 yellow onion, chopped
- ✓ 2 potatoes, chopped
- ✓ 2 mushrooms, chopped
- ✓ 1 teaspoon soy sauce
- ✓ Salt and black pepper to the taste
- ✓ 1 teaspoon Italian seasoning
- ✓ ½ teaspoon garlic powder
- ✓ 1 teaspoon Worcestershire sauce
- ✓ 1 tablespoon flour
- ✓ 1 tablespoon milk
- ✓ 2 puff pastry sheets
- ✓ 1 tablespoon butter, melted

Directions:
1. Heat up a pan over medium high heat, add potatoes, carrots and onion, stir and cook for 2 minutes.
2. Add chicken and mushrooms, salt, soy sauce, pepper, Italian seasoning, garlic powder, Worcestershire sauce, flour and milk, stir really well and take off heat.
3. Place 1 puff pastry sheet on the bottom of your air fryer's pan and trim edge excess.
4. Add chicken mix, top with the other puff pastry sheet, trim excess as well and brush pie with butter.
5. Place in your air fryer and cook at 360 degrees F for 6 minutes.
6. Leave pie to cool down, slice and serve for breakfast.

Nutrition: calories 300 - Fat 5 - Fiber 7 - Carbs 14 - Protein 7

34. Chicken and Corn Casserole

Prep.Time: 10 min - **Cooking Time:** 30 min - **Servings:** 6

Ingredients:
- ✓ 1 cup clean chicken stock
- ✓ 2 teaspoons garlic powder
- ✓ Salt and black pepper to the taste
- ✓ 6 ounces canned coconut milk
- ✓ 1 and ½ cups green lentils
- ✓ 2 pounds chicken breasts, skinless, boneless and cubed
- ✓ 1/3 cup cilantro, chopped
- ✓ 3 cups corn
- ✓ 3 handfuls spinach
- ✓ 3 green onions, chopped

Directions:
1. In a pan that fits your air fryer, mix stock with coconut milk, salt, pepper, garlic powder, chicken and lentils.
2. Add corn, green onions, cilantro and spinach, stir well, introduce in your air fryer and cook at 350 degrees F for 30 minutes.

Nutrition: calories 345 - Fat 12 - Fiber 10 - Carbs 20 - Protein 44

35. Veggie Toast

Prep.Time: 10 min - **Cooking Time:** 15 min - **Servings:** 4

Ingredients:
- ✓ 1 red bell pepper, cut into thin strips
- ✓ 1 cup cremini mushrooms, sliced
- ✓ 1 yellow squash, chopped
- ✓ 2 green onions, sliced
- ✓ 1 tablespoon olive oil
- ✓ 4 bread slices
- ✓ 2 tablespoons butter, soft
- ✓ ½ cup goat cheese, crumbled

Directions:
1. In a bowl, mix red bell pepper with mushrooms, squash, green onions and oil, toss, transfer to your air fryer, cook them at 350 degrees F for 10 minutes, shaking the fryer once and transfer them to a bowl.
2. Spread butter on bread slices, place them in air fryer and cook them at 350 degrees F for 5 minutes.
3. Divide veggie mix on each bread slice, top with crumbled cheese and serve for lunch.

Nutrition: calories 152 - Fat 3 - Fiber 4 - Carbs 7 - Protein 2

36. Lunch Shrimp Croquettes

Prep.Time: 10 min - **Cooking Time:** 8 min - **Servings:** 4

Ingredients:
- ✓ 2/3 pound shrimp, cooked, peeled, deveined and chopped
- ✓ 1 and ½ cups bread crumbs
- ✓ 1 egg, whisked
- ✓ 2 tablespoons lemon juice
- ✓ 3 green onions, chopped
- ✓ ½ teaspoon basil, dried
- ✓ Salt and black pepper to the taste
- ✓ 2 tablespoons olive oil

Directions:
1. In a bowl, mix half of the bread crumbs with egg and lemon juice and stir well.
2. Add green onions, basil, salt, pepper and shrimp and stir really well.
3. In a separate bowl, mix the rest of the bread crumbs with the oil and toss well.
4. Shape round balls out of shrimp mix, dredge them in bread crumbs, place them in preheated air fryer and cook the for 8 minutes at 400 degrees F.
5. Serve them with a dip for lunch.

Nutrition: calories 142 - Fat 4 - Fiber 6 - Carbs 9 - Protein 4

37. Lunch Gnocchi

Prep.Time: 10 min - **Cooking Time:** 17 minutes - **Servings:** 4

Ingredients:
- ✓ 1 yellow onion, chopped
- ✓ 1 tablespoon olive oil
- ✓ 3 garlic cloves, minced
- ✓ 16 ounces gnocchi
- ✓ ¼ cup parmesan, grated
- ✓ 8 ounces spinach pesto

Directions:
1. Grease your air fryer's pan with olive oil, add gnocchi, onion and garlic, toss, put pan in your air fryer and cook at 400 degrees F for 10 minutes.
2. Add pesto, toss and cook for 7 minutes more at 350 degrees F.
3. Divide among plates and serve for lunch.

Nutrition: calories 200 - Fat 4 - Fiber 4 - Carbs 12 - Protein 4

38. Lunch Special Pancake

Prep.Time: 10 min - **Cooking Time:** 10 min - **Servings:** 2

Ingredients:
- ✓ 1 tablespoon butter
- ✓ 3 eggs, whisked
- ✓ ½ cup flour
- ✓ ½ cup milk
- ✓ 1 cup salsa
- ✓ 1 cup small shrimp, peeled and deveined

Directions:
1. Preheat your air fryer at 400 degrees F, add fryer's pan, add 1 tablespoon butter and melt it.
2. In a bowl, mix eggs with flour and milk, whisk well and pour into air fryer's pan, spread, cook at 350 degrees for 12 minutes and transfer to a plate.
3. In a bowl, mix shrimp with salsa, stir and serve your pancake with this on the side.

Nutrition: calories 200 - Fat 6 - Fiber 8 - Carbs 12 - Protein 4

39. Squash Fritters

Prep.Time: 10 min - **Cooking Time:** 7 min - **Servings:** 4

Ingredients:
- ✓ 3 ounces cream cheese
- ✓ 1 egg, whisked
- ✓ ½ teaspoon oregano, dried
- ✓ A pinch of salt and black pepper
- ✓ 1 yellow summer squash, grated
- ✓ 1/3 cup carrot, grated
- ✓ 2/3 cup bread crumbs
- ✓ 2 tablespoons olive oil

Directions:
1. In a bowl, mix cream cheese with salt, pepper, oregano, egg, breadcrumbs, carrot and squash and stir well.
2. Shape medium patties out of this mix and brush them with the oil.
3. Place squash patties in your air fryer and cook them at 400 degrees F for 7 minutes.
4. Serve them for lunch.

Nutrition: calories 200 - Fat 4 - Fiber 7 - Carbs 8 - Protein 6

40. Fresh Chicken Mix

Prep.Time: 10 min - **Cooking Time:** 22 min - **Servings:** 4

Ingredients:
- ✓ 2 chicken breasts, skinless, boneless and cubed
- ✓ 8 button mushrooms, sliced
- ✓ 1 red bell pepper, chopped
- ✓ 1 tablespoon olive oil
- ✓ ½ teaspoon thyme, dried
- ✓ 10 ounces alfredo sauce
- ✓ 6 bread slices
- ✓ 2 tablespoons butter, soft

Directions:
1. In your air fryer, mix chicken with mushrooms, bell pepper and oil, toss to coat well and cook at 350 degrees F for 15 minutes.
2. Transfer chicken mix to a bowl, add thyme and Alfredo sauce, toss, return to air fryer and cook at 350 degrees F for 4 minutes more.
3. Spread butter on bread slices, add it to the fryer, butter side up and cook for 4 minutes more.
4. Arrange toasted bread slices on a platter, top each with chicken mix and serve for lunch.

Nutrition: calories 172 - Fat 4 - Fiber 9 - Carbs 12 - Protein 4

41. Cottage Cheese Pops

Prep.Time: 15 min - Cooking Time: 20 min - Servings: 2

Ingredients:
- ✓ 1 cup cottage cheese cut into 2" cubes
- ✓ 1 ½ tsp. garlic paste
- ✓ Salt and pepper to taste
- ✓ 1 tsp. dry oregano
- ✓ 1 tsp. dry basil
- ✓ ½ cup hung curd
- ✓ 1 tsp. lemon juice
- ✓ 1 tsp. red chili flakes

Directions:
1. Cut the cottage cheese into thick and long rectangular pieces.
2. Add the rest of the ingredients into a separate bowl and mix them well to get a consistent mixture.
3. Dip the cottage cheese pieces in the above mixture and leave them aside for some time.
4. Pre heat the Air fryer at 180° C for around 5 minutes. Place the coated cottage cheese pieces in the fry basket and close it properly. Let them cook at the same temperature for 20 more minutes. Keep turning them over in the basket so that they are cooked properly. Serve with tomato ketchup.

42. Meatballs and Tomato Sauce

Prep.Time: 10 min - Cooking Time: 15 min - Servings: 4

Ingredients:
- ✓ 1 pound lean beef, ground
- ✓ 3 green onions, chopped
- ✓ 2 garlic cloves, minced
- ✓ 1 egg yolk
- ✓ ¼ cup bread crumbs
- ✓ Salt and black pepper to the taste
- ✓ 1 tablespoon olive oil
- ✓ 16 ounces tomato sauce
- ✓ 2 tablespoons mustard

Directions:
1. In a bowl, mix beef with onion, garlic, egg yolk, bread crumbs, salt and pepper, stir well and shape medium meatballs out of this mix.
2. Grease meatballs with the oil, place them in your air fryer and cook them at 400 degrees F for 10 minutes.
3. In a bowl, mix tomato sauce with mustard, whisk, add over meatballs, toss them and cook at 400 degrees F for 5 minutes more.
4. Divide meatballs and sauce on plates and serve for lunch.

Nutrition: calories 300 - Fat 8 - Fiber 9 - Carbs 16 - Protein 5

43. Macaroni and Cheese

Prep.Time: 10 min - Cooking Time: 30 minutes - Servings: 3

Ingredients:
- ✓ 1 and ½ cups favorite macaroni
- ✓ Cooking spray
- ✓ ½ cup heavy cream
- ✓ 1 cup chicken stock
- ✓ ¾ cup cheddar cheese, shredded
- ✓ ½ cup mozzarella cheese, shredded
- ✓ ¼ cup parmesan, shredded
- ✓ Salt and black pepper to the taste

Directions:
1. Spray a pan with cooking spray, add macaroni, heavy cream, stock, cheddar cheese, mozzarella and parmesan but also salt and pepper, toss well, place pan in your air fryer's basket and cook for 30 minutes.
2. Divide among plates and serve for lunch.

Nutrition: calories 341 - Fat 7 - Fiber 8 - Carbs 18 - Protein 4

44. Corn Casserole

Prep.Time: 10 min - Cooking Time: 15 min - Servings: 4

Ingredients:
- ✓ 2 cups corn
- ✓ 3 tablespoons flour
- ✓ 1 egg
- ✓ ¼ cup milk
- ✓ ½ cup light cream
- ✓ ½ cup Swiss cheese, grated
- ✓ 2 tablespoons butter
- ✓ Salt and black pepper to the taste
- ✓ Cooking spray

Directions:
1. In a bowl, mix corn with flour, egg, milk, light cream, cheese, salt, pepper and butter and stir well.
2. Grease your air fryer's pan with cooking spray, pour cream mix, spread and cook at 320 degrees F for 15 minutes.
3. Serve warm for lunch.

Nutrition: calories 281 - Fat 7 - Fiber 8 - Carbs 9 - Protein 6

45. Sweet and Sour Sausage Mix

Prep.Time: 10min - Cooking Time: 8 min - Servings: 4

Ingredients:
- ✓ 1 pound sausages, sliced
- ✓ 1 red bell pepper, cut into strips
- ✓ ½ cup yellow onion, chopped
- ✓ 3 tablespoons brown sugar
- ✓ 1/3 cup ketchup
- ✓ 2 tablespoons mustard
- ✓ 2 tablespoons apple cider vinegar
- ✓ ½ cup chicken stock

Directions:
1. In a bowl, mix sugar with ketchup, mustard, stock and vinegar and whisk well.
2. In your air fryer's pan, mix sausage slices with bell pepper, onion and sweet and sour mix, toss and cook at 350 degrees F for 10 minutes.
3. Divide into bowls and serve for lunch.

Nutrition: calories 162 - Fat 6 - Fiber 9 - Carbs 12 - Protein 6

46. Hot Bacon Sandwiches

Prep.Time: 10 min - Cooking Time: 7 min - Servings: 4

Ingredients:
- ✓ 1/3 cup bbq sauce
- ✓ 2 tablespoons honey
- ✓ 8 bacon slices, cooked and cut into thirds
- ✓ 1 red bell pepper, sliced
- ✓ 1 yellow bell pepper, sliced
- ✓ 3 pita pockets, halved
- ✓ 1 and ¼ cup butter lettuce leaves, torn
- ✓ 2 tomatoes, sliced

Directions:
1. In a bowl, mix bbq sauce with honey and whisk well.
2. Brush bacon and all bell peppers with some of this mix, place them in your air fryer and cook at 350 degrees F for 4 minutes.
3. Shake fryer and cook them for 2 minutes more.
4. Stuff pita pockets with bacon mix, also stuff with tomatoes and lettuce, spread the rest of the bbq sauce and serve for lunch.

Nutrition: calories 186 - Fat 6 - Fiber 9 - Carbs 14 - Protein 4

47. Tuna and Zucchini Tortillas

Prep.Time: 10 min - **Cooking Time:** 10 min - **Servings:** 4

Ingredients:
- ✓ 4 corn tortillas
- ✓ 4 tablespoons butter, soft
- ✓ 6 ounces canned tuna, drained
- ✓ 1 cup zucchini, shredded
- ✓ 1/3 cup mayonnaise
- ✓ 2 tablespoons mustard
- ✓ 1 cup cheddar cheese, grated

Directions:
1. Spread butter on tortillas, place them in your air fryer's basket and cook them at 400 degrees F for 3 minutes.
2. Meanwhile, in a bowl, mix tuna with zucchini, mayo and mustard and stir.
3. Divide this mix on each tortilla, top with cheese, roll tortillas, place them in your air fryer's basket again and cook them at 400 degrees F for 4 minutes more.
4. Serve for lunch.

Nutrition: calories 162 - Fat 4 - Fiber 8 - Carbs 9 - Protein 4

48. Stuffed Meatballs

Prep.Time: 10 min - **Cooking Time:** 10 min - **Servings:** 4

Ingredients:
- ✓ 1/3 cup bread crumbs
- ✓ 3 tablespoons milk
- ✓ 1 tablespoon ketchup
- ✓ 1 egg
- ✓ ½ teaspoon marjoram, dried
- ✓ Salt and black pepper to the taste
- ✓ 1 pound lean beef, ground
- ✓ 20 cheddar cheese cubes
- ✓ 1 tablespoon olive oil

Directions:
1. In a bowl, mix bread crumbs with ketchup, milk, marjoram, salt, pepper and egg and whisk well.
2. Add beef, stir and shape 20 meatballs out of this mix.
3. Shape each meatball around a cheese cube, drizzle the oil over them and rub.
4. Place all meatballs in your preheated air fryer and cook at 390 degrees F for 10 minutes.
5. Serve them for lunch with a side salad.

Nutrition: calories 200 - Fat 5 - Fiber 8 - Carbs 12 - Protein 5

49. Quick Lunch Pizzas

Prep.Time: 10 min - **Cooking Time:** 7 minutes - **Servings:** 4

Ingredients:
- ✓ 4 pitas
- ✓ 1 tablespoon olive oil
- ✓ ¾ cup pizza sauce
- ✓ 4 ounces jarred mushrooms, sliced
- ✓ ½ teaspoon basil, dried
- ✓ 2 green onions, chopped
- ✓ 2 cup mozzarella, grated
- ✓ 1 cup grape tomatoes, sliced

Directions:
1. Spread pizza sauce on each pita bread, sprinkle green onions and basil, divide mushrooms and top with cheese.
2. Arrange pita pizzas in your air fryer and cook them at 400 degrees F for 7 minutes.
3. Top each pizza with tomato slices, divide among plates and serve.

Nutrition: calories 200 - Fat 4 - Fiber 6 - Carbs 7 - Protein 3

50. Steaks and Cabbage

Prep.Time: 10 min - **Cooking Time:** 10 min - **Servings:** 4

Ingredients:
- ✓ ½ pound sirloin steak, cut into strips
- ✓ 2 teaspoons cornstarch
- ✓ 1 tablespoon peanut oil
- ✓ 2 cups green cabbage, chopped
- ✓ 1 yellow bell pepper, chopped
- ✓ 2 green onions, chopped
- ✓ 2 garlic cloves, minced
- ✓ Salt and black pepper to the taste

Directions:
1. In a bowl, mix cabbage with salt, pepper and peanut oil, toss, transfer to air fryer's basket, cook at 370 degrees F for 4 minutes and transfer to a bowl.
2. Add steak strips to your air fryer, also add green onions, bell pepper, garlic, salt and pepper, toss and cook for 5 minutes.
3. Add over cabbage, toss, divide among plates and serve for lunch.

Nutrition: calories 282 - Fat 6 - Fiber 8 - Carbs 14 - Protein 6

51. Stuffed Mushrooms

Prep.Time: 10 min - **Cooking Time:** 20 min - **Servings:** 4

Ingredients:
- ✓ 4 big Portobello mushroom caps
- ✓ 1 tablespoon olive oil
- ✓ ¼ cup ricotta cheese
- ✓ 5 tablespoons parmesan, grated
- ✓ 1 cup spinach, torn
- ✓ 1/3 cup bread crumbs
- ✓ ¼ teaspoon rosemary, chopped

Directions:
1. Rub mushrooms caps with the oil, place them in your air fryer's basket and cook them at 350 degrees F for 2 minutes.
2. Meanwhile, in a bowl, mix half of the parmesan with ricotta, spinach, rosemary and bread crumbs and stir well.
3. Stuff mushrooms with this mix, sprinkle the rest of the parmesan on top, place them in your air fryer's basket again and cook at 350 degrees F for 10 minutes.
4. Divide them on plates and serve with a side salad for lunch.

Nutrition: calories 152 - Fat 4 - Fiber 7 - Carbs 9 - Protein 5

52. Mint Galette

Prep.Time: 10 min - **Cooking Time:** 25 min - **Servings:** 2-4

Ingredients:
- ✓ 2 cups mint leaves (Sliced fine)
- ✓ 2 medium potatoes boiled and mashed
- ✓ 1 ½ cup coarsely crushed peanuts
- ✓ 3 tsp. ginger finely chopped
- ✓ 1-2 tbsp. fresh coriander leaves
- ✓ 2 or 3 green chilies finely chopped
- ✓ 1 ½ tbsp. lemon juice
- ✓ Salt and pepper to taste

Directions:
1. Mix the sliced mint leaves with the rest of the ingredients in a clean bowl.
2. Mold this mixture into round and flat galettes.
3. Wet the galettes slightly with water. Coat each galette with the crushed peanuts.
4. Pre heat the Air Fryer at 160 degrees Fahrenheit for 5 minutes. Place the galettes in the fry basket and let them cook for another 25 minutes at the same temperature. Keep rolling them over to get a uniform cook. Serve either with mint chutney or ketchup.

53. Lunch Pork and Potatoes

Prep.Time: 10 min - Cooking Time: 25 min - Servings: 2

Ingredients:
- ✓ 2 pounds pork loin
- ✓ Salt and black pepper to the taste
- ✓ 2 red potatoes, cut into medium wedges
- ✓ ½ teaspoon garlic powder
- ✓ ½ teaspoon red pepper flakes
- ✓ 1 teaspoon parsley, dried
- ✓ A drizzle of balsamic vinegar

Directions:
1. In your air fryer's pan, mix pork with potatoes, salt, pepper, garlic powder, pepper flakes, parsley and vinegar, toss and cook at 390 degrees F for 25 minutes.
2. Slice pork, divide it and potatoes on plates and serve for lunch.

Nutrition: calories 400 - Fat 15 - Fiber 7 - Carbs 27 - Protein 20

54. Beef Stew

Prep.Time: 10 min - Cooking Time: 20 min - Servings: 4

Ingredients:
- ✓ 2 pounds beef meat, cut into medium chunks
- ✓ 2 carrots, chopped
- ✓ 4 potatoes, chopped
- ✓ Salt and black pepper to the taste
- ✓ 1 quart veggie stock
- ✓ ½ teaspoon smoked paprika
- ✓ A handful thyme, chopped

Directions:
1. In a dish that fits your air fryer, mix beef with carrots, potatoes, stock, salt, pepper, paprika and thyme, stir, place in air fryer's basket and cook at 375 degrees F for 20 minutes.
2. Divide into bowls and serve right away for lunch.

Nutrition: calories 260 - Fat 5 - Fiber 8 - Carbs 20 - Protein 22

55. Turkey Cakes

Prep.Time: 10 min - Cooking Time: 10 minutes - Servings: 4

Ingredients:
- ✓ 6 mushrooms, chopped
- ✓ 1 teaspoon garlic powder
- ✓ 1 teaspoon onion powder
- ✓ Salt and black pepper to the taste
- ✓ 1 and ¼ pounds turkey meat, ground
- ✓ Cooking spray
- ✓ Tomato sauce for serving

Directions:
1. In your blender, mix mushrooms with salt and pepper, pulse well and transfer to a bowl.
2. Add turkey, onion powder, garlic powder, salt and pepper, stir and shape cakes out of this mix.
3. Spray them with cooking spray, transfer them to your air fryer and cook at 320 degrees F for 10 minutes.
4. Serve them with tomato sauce on the side and a tasty side salad.

Nutrition: calories 202 - Fat 6 - Fiber 3 - Carbs 17 - Protein 10

56. Rustic Breakfast

Prep.Time: 10 min - Cooking Time: 5 min - Servings: 4

Ingredients:
- ✓ 1 cup carrots, grated
- ✓ 1 cup red cabbage, shredded
- ✓ A pinch of salt and black pepper
- ✓ A handful cilantro, chopped
- ✓ 1 small cucumber, chopped
- ✓ Juice from 1 lime
- ✓ 2 teaspoons red curry paste
- ✓ 12 big shrimp, cooked, peeled and deveined

Directions:
1. In a pan that fits your, mix cabbage with carrots, cucumber and shrimp, toss, introduce in your air fryer and cook at 360 degrees F for 5 minutes.
2. Add salt, pepper, cilantro, lime juice and red curry paste, toss again, divide among plates and serve right away.

Nutrition: calories 172 - Fat 5 - Fiber 7 - Carbs 8 - Protein 5

57. Cheese Ravioli and Marinara Sauce

Prep.Time: 10 min - Cooking Time: 8 min - Servings: 6

Ingredients:
- ✓ 20 ounces cheese ravioli
- ✓ 10 ounces marinara sauce
- ✓ 1 tablespoon olive oil
- ✓ 1 cup buttermilk
- ✓ 2 cups bread crumbs
- ✓ ¼ cup parmesan, grated

Directions:
1. Put buttermilk in a bowl and breadcrumbs in another bowl.
2. Dip ravioli in buttermilk, then in breadcrumbs and place them in your air fryer on a baking sheet.
3. Drizzle olive oil over them, cook at 400 degrees F for 5 minutes, divide them on plates, sprinkle parmesan on top and serve for lunch.

Nutrition: calories 270 - Fat 12 - Fiber 6 - Carbs 30 - Protein 15

58. Egg Muffins

Prep.Time: 10 min - Cooking Time: 50 min - Servings: 6

Ingredients:
- ✓ 3 big sweet potatoes, pricked with a fork
- ✓ 1 cup chicken stock
- ✓ Salt and black pepper to the taste
- ✓ A pinch of cayenne pepper
- ✓ ¼ teaspoon nutmeg, ground
- ✓ 1/3 cup coconut cream

Directions:
1. Place sweet potatoes in your air fryer, cook them at 350 degrees F for 40 minutes, cool them down, peel, roughly chop and transfer to a pan that fits your air fryer.
2. Add stock, salt, pepper, cayenne and coconut cream, toss, introduce in your air fryer and cook at 360 degrees F for 10 minutes more.
3. Divide casserole into bowls and serve.

Nutrition: calories 245 - Fat 4 - Fiber 5 - Carbs 10 - Protein 6

59. Salmon and Asparagus

Prep.Time: 10 min - **Cooking Time:** 23 min - **Servings:** 4

Ingredients:
- ✓ 1 pound asparagus, trimmed
- ✓ 1 tablespoon olive oil
- ✓ A pinch of sweet paprika
- ✓ Salt and black pepper to the taste
- ✓ A pinch of garlic powder
- ✓ A pinch of cayenne pepper
- ✓ 1 red bell pepper, cut into halves
- ✓ 4 ounces smoked salmon

Directions:
1. Put asparagus spears and bell pepper on a lined baking sheet that fits your air fryer, add salt, pepper, garlic powder, paprika, olive oil, cayenne pepper, toss to coat, introduce in the fryer, cook at 390 degrees F for 8 minutes, flip and cook for 8 minutes more.
2. Add salmon, cook for 5 minutes, more, divide everything on plates and serve.

Nutrition: calories 90 - Fat 1 - Fiber 1 - Carbs 1.2 - Protein 4

60. Cabbage Fritters

Prep.Time: 10 min - **Cooking Time:** 25 min - **Servings:** 2

Ingredients:
- ✓ 2 tbsp. garam masala
- ✓ 2 cups cabbage
- ✓ 1 ½ cup coarsely crushed peanuts
- ✓ 3 tsp. ginger finely chopped
- ✓ 1-2 tbsp. fresh coriander leaves
- ✓ 2 or 3 green chilies finely chopped
- ✓ 1 ½ tbsp. lemon juice
- ✓ Salt and pepper to taste

Directions:
1. Mix the ingredients in a clean bowl.
2. Mold this mixture into round and flat fritters.
3. Wet the fritters slightly with water. Coat each fritters with the crushed peanuts.
4. Pre heat the Air Fryer at 160 degrees Fahrenheit for 5 minutes. Place the fritters in the fry basket and let them cook for another 25 minutes at the same temperature. Keep rolling them over to get a uniform cook.
5. Serve either with mint chutney or ketchup.

61. Easy Chicken Lunch

Prep.Time: 10 min - **Cooking Time:** 20 minutes - **Servings:** 6

Ingredients:
- ✓ 1 bunch kale, chopped
- ✓ Salt and black pepper to the taste
- ✓ ¼ cup chicken stock
- ✓ 1 cup chicken, shredded
- ✓ 3 carrots, chopped
- ✓ 1 cup shiitake mushrooms, roughly sliced

Directions:
1. In a blender, mix stock with kale, pulse a few times and pour into a pan that fits your air fryer.
2. Add chicken, mushrooms, carrots, salt and pepper to the taste, toss, introduce in your air fryer and cook at 350 degrees F for 18 minutes.

Nutrition: calories 180 - Fat 7 - Fiber 2 - Carbs 10 - Protein 5

62. Cottage cheese Patties

Prep.Time: 10 min - **Cooking Time:** 12 min - **Servings:** 2

Ingredients:
- ✓ 1 cup grated cottage cheese
- ✓ A pinch of salt to taste
- ✓ ¼ tsp. ginger finely chopped
- ✓ 1 green chili finely chopped
- ✓ 1 tsp. lemon juice
- ✓ 1 tbsp. fresh coriander leaves
- ✓ ¼ tsp. red chili powder
- ✓ ¼ tsp. cumin powder

Directions:
1. Mix the ingredients together and ensure that the flavors are right. You will now make round patties with the mixture and roll them out well.
2. Pre heat the Air Fryer at 250 Fahrenheit for 5 minutes. Open the basket of the Fryer and arrange the patties in the basket. Close it carefully. Keep the fryer at 150 degrees for around 10 or 12 minutes. In between the cooking process, turn the patties over to get a uniform cook.
3. Serve hot with mint chutney.

63. Onion Galette

Prep.Time: 10 min - **Cooking Time:** 25 min - **Servings:** 2

Ingredients:
- ✓ 2 tbsp. garam masala
- ✓ 2 medium onions (Cut long)
- ✓ 1 ½ cup coarsely crushed peanuts
- ✓ 3 tsp. ginger finely chopped
- ✓ 1-2 tbsp. fresh coriander leaves
- ✓ 2 or 3 green chilies finely chopped
- ✓ 1 ½ tbsp. lemon juice
- ✓ Salt and pepper to taste

Directions:
1. Mix the ingredients in a clean bowl.
2. Mold this mixture into round and flat galettes.
3. Wet the galettes slightly with water. Coat each galette with the crushed peanuts.
4. Pre heat the Air Fryer at 160 degrees Fahrenheit for 5 minutes. Place the galettes in the fry basket and let them cook for another 25 minutes at the same temperature. Keep rolling them over to get a uniform cook.
5. Serve either with mint chutney or ketchup.

64. Cheese and Garlic French Fries

Prep.Time: 10 min - **Cooking Time:** 25 min - **Servings:** 2

Ingredients:
- ✓ 2 medium sized potatoes peeled and cut into thick pieces lengthwise

Ingredients for the marinade:
- ✓ 1 tbsp. olive oil
- ✓ 1 tsp. mixed herbs
- ✓ ½ tsp. red chili flakes
- ✓ A pinch of salt to taste
- ✓ 1 cup molten cheese
- ✓ 2 tsp. garlic powder
- ✓ 1 tbsp. lemon juice

Directions:
1. Boil the potatoes and blanch them. Cut the potato into fingers. Mix the ingredients for the marinade and add the potato fingers to it making sure that they are coated well.
2. Pre heat the Air Fryer for around 5 minutes at 300 Fahrenheit. Take out the basket of the fryer and place the potato fingers in them. Close the basket. Now keep the fryer at 200 Fahrenheit for 20 or 25 minutes. In between the process, toss the fries twice or thrice so that they get cooked properly.

65. Pineapple Kebab

Prep.Time: 10 min - Cooking Time: 25 min - Servings: 4

Ingredients:
- 2 cups cubed pineapples
- 3 onions chopped
- 5 green chilies-roughly chopped
- 1 ½ tbsp. ginger paste
- 1 ½ tsp. garlic paste
- 1 ½ tsp. salt
- 3 tsp. lemon juice
- 2 tsp. garam masala
- 4 tbsp. chopped coriander
- 3 tbsp. cream
- 3 tbsp. chopped capsicum
- 3 eggs
- 2 ½ tbsp. white sesame seeds

Directions:
1. Grind the ingredients except for the egg and form a smooth paste. Coat the pineapples in the paste. Now, beat the eggs and add a little salt to it.
2. Dip the coated vegetables in the egg mixture and then transfer to the sesame seeds and coat the pineapples well. Place the vegetables on a stick.
3. Pre heat the Air fryer at 160 degrees Fahrenheit for around 5 minutes. Place the sticks in the basket and let them cook for another 25 minutes at the same temperature. Turn the sticks over in between the cooking process to get a uniform cook.

66. Cauliflower Kebab

Prep.Time: 10 min - Cooking Time: 25 min - Servings: 4

Ingredients:
- 2 cups cauliflower florets
- 3 onions chopped
- 5 green chilies-roughly chopped
- 1 ½ tbsp. ginger paste
- 1 ½ tsp. garlic paste
- 1 ½ tsp. salt
- 3 tsp. lemon juice
- 2 tsp. garam masala
- 3 eggs
- 2 ½ tbsp. white sesame seeds

Directions:
1. Grind the ingredients except for the egg and form a smooth paste. Coat the florets in the paste. Now, beat the eggs and add a little salt to it.
2. Dip the coated florets in the egg mixture and then transfer to the sesame seeds and coat the florets well. Place the vegetables on a stick.
3. Pre heat the Air fryer at 160 degrees Fahrenheit for around 5 minutes. Place the sticks in the basket and let them cook for another 25 minutes at the same temperature. Turn the sticks over in between the cooking process to get a uniform cook.

67. Apricot Kebab

Prep.Time: 10 min - Cooking Time: 25 minutes - Servings: 4

Ingredients:
- 2 cups fresh apricots
- 3 onions chopped
- 5 green chilies-roughly chopped
- 1 ½ tbsp. ginger paste
- 1 ½ tsp. garlic paste
- 3 tsp. lemon juice
- 2 tsp. garam masala
- 3 eggs
- 2 ½ tbsp. white sesame seeds

Directions:
1. Grind the ingredients except for the egg and form a smooth paste. Coat the apricots in the paste. Now, beat the eggs and add a little salt to it.
2. Dip the coated apricots in the egg mixture and then transfer to the sesame seeds and coat the apricots well. Place the vegetables on a stick.
3. Pre heat the Air fryer at 160 degrees Fahrenheit for around 5 minutes. Place the sticks in the basket and let them cook for another 25 minutes at the same temperature. Turn the sticks over in between the cooking process to get a uniform cook.

68. Broccoli Tikka

Prep.Time: 10 min - Cooking Time: 25 min - Servings: 2

Ingredients:
- 2 cups broccoli florets
- 3 onions chopped
- 5 green chilies-roughly chopped
- 1 ½ tbsp. ginger paste
- 1 ½ tsp. garlic paste
- 1 ½ tsp. salt
- 3 tsp. lemon juice
- 2 tsp. garam masala
- 3 eggs
- 2 ½ tbsp. white sesame seeds

Directions:
1. Grind the ingredients except for the egg and form a smooth paste. Coat the florets in the paste. Now, beat the eggs and add a little salt to it.
2. Dip the coated florets in the egg mixture and then transfer to the sesame seeds and coat the florets well. Place the vegetables on a stick.
3. Pre heat the Air fryer at 160 degrees Fahrenheit for around 5 minutes. Place the sticks in the basket and let them cook for another 25 minutes at the same temperature. Turn the sticks over in between the cooking process to get a uniform cook.

69. French Bean Toast

Prep.Time: 10min - Cooking Time: 20 min - Servings: 2

Ingredients:
- Bread slices (brown or white)
- 1 egg white for every 2 slices
- 1 tsp. sugar for every 2 slices
- Crushed cornflakes
- 2 cups baked beans

Directions:
1. Put two slices together and cut them along the diagonal.
2. In a bowl, whisk the egg whites and add some sugar.
3. Dip the bread triangles into this mixture and then coat them with the crushed cornflakes.
4. Pre heat the Air Fryer at 180° C for 4 minutes. Place the coated bread triangles in the fry basket and close it. Let them cook at the same temperature for another 20 minutes at least. Halfway through the process, turn the triangles over so that you get a uniform cook. Top with baked beans and serve.

70. Potato Flat Cakes

Prep.Time: 10 min - Cooking Time: 25 min - Servings: 2

Ingredients:
- 2 tbsp. garam masala
- 2 cups sliced potato
- 3 tsp. ginger finely chopped
- 1-2 tbsp. fresh coriander leaves
- 2 or 3 green chilies finely chopped
- 1 ½ tbsp. lemon juice
- Salt and pepper to taste

Directions:
1. Mix the ingredients in a clean bowl and add water to it. Make sure that the paste is not too watery but is enough to apply on the potato slices.
2. Pre heat the Air Fryer at 160 degrees Fahrenheit for 5 minutes. Place the galettes in the fry basket and let them cook for another 25 minutes at the same temperature. Keep rolling them over to get a uniform cook. Serve either with mint chutney or ketchup.

44

71. Potato Wedges

Prep.Time: 10 min - **Cooking Time:** 25 min - **Servings:** 2

Ingredients:
- ✓ 2 medium sized potatoes (Cut into wedges)

Ingredients for the marinade:
- ✓ 1 tbsp. olive oil
- ✓ 1 tsp. mixed herbs
- ✓ ½ tsp. red chili flakes
- ✓ A pinch of salt to taste
- ✓ 1 tbsp. lemon juice

Directions:
1. Boil the potatoes and blanch them. Mix the ingredients for the marinade and add the potato fingers to it making sure that they are coated well.
2. Pre heat the Air Fryer for around 5 minutes at 300 Fahrenheit. Take out the basket of the fryer and place the potato fingers in them. Close the basket. Now keep the fryer at 200 Fahrenheit for 20 or 25 minutes. In between the process, toss the fries twice or thrice so that they get cooked properly.

72. Masala Potato Wedges

Prep.Time: 10 min - **Cooking Time:** 25 min - **Servings:** 2

Ingredients:
- ✓ 2 medium sized potatoes (Cut into wedges)
- ✓ Ingredients for the marinade:
- ✓ 1 tbsp. olive oil
- ✓ 1 tsp. garam masala
- ✓ 1 tsp. mixed herbs
- ✓ ½ tsp. red chili flakes
- ✓ A pinch of salt to taste
- ✓ 1 tbsp. lemon juice

Directions:
1. Boil the potatoes and blanch them. Mix the ingredients for the marinade and add the potato fingers to it making sure that they are coated well.
2. Pre heat the Air Fryer for around 5 minutes at 300 Fahrenheit. Take out the basket of the fryer and place the potato fingers in them. Close the basket. Now keep the fryer at 200 Fahrenheit for 20 or 25 minutes. In between the process, toss the fries twice or thrice so that they get cooked properly.

73. Potato Kebab

Prep.Time: 10 min - **Cooking Time:** 30 minutes - **Servings:** 2

Ingredients:
- ✓ 2 cups sliced potato
- ✓ Half inch ginger grated or one and a half tsp. of ginger-garlic paste
- ✓ 1-2 green chilies chopped finely
- ✓ ¼ tsp. red chili powder
- ✓ A pinch of salt to taste
- ✓ ½ tsp. roasted cumin powder
- ✓ 2 tsp. coriander powder
- ✓ 1 ½ tbsp. chopped coriander
- ✓ ½ tsp. dried mango powder
- ✓ 1 cup dry breadcrumbs
- ✓ ¼ tsp. black salt
- ✓ 1-2 tbsp. all-purpose flour for coating purposes
- ✓ 1-2 tbsp. mint (finely chopped)
- ✓ 1 onion that has been finely chopped
- ✓ ½ cup milk

Directions:
1. Take the potato slices and add the grated ginger and the cut green chilies. Grind this mixture until it becomes a thick paste. Keep adding water as and when required. Now add the onions, mint, the breadcrumbs and all the various masalas required. Mix this well until you get a soft dough. Now take small balls of this mixture (about the size of a lemon) and mold them into the shape of flat and round kebabs.
2. Here is where the milk comes into play. Pour a very small amount of milk onto each kebab to wet it. Now roll the kebab in the dry breadcrumbs.
3. Pre heat the Air Fryer for 5 minutes at 300 Fahrenheit. Take out the basket. Arrange the kebabs in the basket leaving gaps between them so that no two kebabs are touching each other. Keep the fryer at 340 Fahrenheit for around half an hour. Half way through the cooking process, turn the kebabs over so that they can be cooked properly. Recommended sides for this dish are mint chutney, tomato ketchup or yoghurt chutney

74. Mushroom Tikka

Prep.Time: 10 min - **Cooking Time:** 30 min - **Servings:** 2

Ingredients:
- ✓ 2 cups sliced mushrooms
- ✓ 1 big capsicum (Cut this capsicum into big cubes)
- ✓ 1 onion (Cut it into quarters. Now separate the layers carefully.)
- ✓ 5 tbsp. gram flour
- ✓ A pinch of salt to taste

For chutney:
- ✓ 2 cup fresh green coriander
- ✓ ½ cup mint leaves
- ✓ 4 tsp. fennel
- ✓ 2 tbsp. ginger-garlic paste
- ✓ 1 small onion
- ✓ 6-7 flakes garlic (optional)
- ✓ Salt to taste
- ✓ 3 tbsp. lemon juice

Directions:
1. Take a clean and dry container. Put into it the coriander, mint, fennel, and ginger, onion/garlic, salt and lemon juice. Mix them. Pour the mixture into a grinder and blend until you get a thick paste.
2. Slit the mushroom almost till the end and leave them aside. Now stuff all the pieces with the paste and set aside.
3. Take the chutney and add to it the gram flour and some salt. Mix them together properly. Rub this mixture all over the stuffed mushroom.
4. Now, to the leftover chutney, add the capsicum and onions. Apply the chutney generously on each of the pieces of capsicum and onion. Now take satay sticks and arrange the cottage cheese pieces and vegetables on separate sticks.
5. Pre heat the Air Fryer at 290 Fahrenheit for around 5 minutes. Open the basket. Arrange the satay sticks properly. Close the basket. Keep the sticks with the mushroom at 180 degrees for around half an hour while the sticks with the vegetables are to be kept at the same temperature for only 7 minutes. Turn the sticks in between so that one side does not get burnt and also to provide a uniform cook.

75. Potato Club Sandwich

Prep.Time: 10 min - Cooking Time: 15 min - Servings: 1

Ingredients:
- ✓ 2 slices of white bread
- ✓ 1 tbsp. softened butter
- ✓ 1 cup mashed potato
- ✓ 1 small capsicum

For Barbeque Sauce:
- ✓ ¼ tbsp. Worcestershire sauce
- ✓ ½ tsp. olive oil
- ✓ ½ flake garlic crushed
- ✓ ¼ cup chopped onion
- ✓ ¼ tbsp. red chili sauce
- ✓ ½ cup water

Directions:
1. Take the slices of bread and remove the edges. Now cut the slices horizontally.
2. Cook the ingredients for the sauce and wait till it thickens. Now, add the potato to the sauce and stir till it obtains the flavors. Roast the capsicum and peel the skin off. Cut the capsicum into slices. Apply the sauce on the slices.
3. Pre-heat the Air Fryer for 5 minutes at 300 Fahrenheit. Open the basket of the Fryer and place the prepared sandwiches in it such that no two sandwiches are touching each other. Now keep the fryer at 250 degrees for around 15 minutes. Turn the sandwiches in between the cooking process to cook both slices.

76. Lamb Pops

Prep.Time: 10 min - Cooking Time: 20 min - Servings: 1

Ingredients:
- ✓ 1 cup cubed lamb
- ✓ 1 ½ tsp. garlic paste
- ✓ Salt and pepper to taste
- ✓ 1 tsp. dry oregano
- ✓ 1 tsp. dry basil
- ✓ ½ cup hung curd
- ✓ 1 tsp. lemon juice
- ✓ 1 tsp. red chili flakes

Directions:
1. Add the ingredients into a separate bowl and mix them well to get a consistent mixture.
2. Dip the lamb pieces in the above mixture and leave them aside for some time.
3. Pre heat the Air fryer at 180° C for around 5 minutes. Place the coated lamb pieces in the fry basket and close it properly. Let them cook at the same temperature for 20 more minutes. Keep turning them over in the basket so that they are cooked properly.
4. Serve with tomato ketchup.

77. Cheesy Potato Wedges

Prep.Time: 10 min - Cooking Time: 25 minutes - Servings: 2

Ingredients:
- ✓ 2 medium sized potatoes (Cut into wedges)

Ingredients for the marinade:
- ✓ 1 tbsp. olive oil
- ✓ 1 tsp. mixed herbs
- ✓ ½ tsp. red chili flakes
- ✓ A pinch of salt to taste
- ✓ 1 tbsp. lemon juice
- ✓ 1 cup molten cheese

Directions:
1. Boil the potatoes and blanch them. Mix the ingredients for the marinade and add the potato fingers to it making sure that they are coated well.
2. Pre heat the Air Fryer for around 5 minutes at 300 Fahrenheit. Take out the basket of the fryer and place the potato fingers in them. Close the basket. Now keep the fryer at 200 Fahrenheit for 20 or 25 minutes. In between the process, toss the fries twice or thrice so that they get cooked properly.
3. Garnish with cheese and serve

78. Palak Galette

Prep.Time: 10 min - Cooking Time: 25 min - Servings: 2-4

Ingredients:
- ✓ 2 tbsp. garam masala
- ✓ 2 cups palak leaves
- ✓ 1 ½ cup coarsely crushed peanuts
- ✓ 3 tsp. ginger finely chopped
- ✓ 1-2 tbsp. fresh coriander leaves
- ✓ 2 or 3 green chilies finely chopped
- ✓ 1 ½ tbsp. lemon juice
- ✓ Salt and pepper to taste

Directions:
1. Mix the ingredients in a clean bowl.
2. Mold this mixture into round and flat galettes.
3. Wet the galettes slightly with water. Coat each galette with the crushed peanuts.
4. Pre heat the Air Fryer at 160 degrees Fahrenheit for 5 minutes. Place the galettes in the fry basket and let them cook for another 25 minutes at the same temperature. Keep rolling them over to get a uniform cook. Serve either with mint chutney or ketchup.

79. Mixed Vegetable Patties

Prep.Time: 15 min - Cooking Time: 12 min - Servings: 2

Ingredients:
- ✓ 1 cup grated mixed vegetables
- ✓ A pinch of salt to taste
- ✓ ¼ tsp. ginger finely chopped
- ✓ 1 green chili finely chopped
- ✓ 1 tsp. lemon juice
- ✓ 1 tbsp. fresh coriander leaves
- ✓ ¼ tsp. red chili powder
- ✓ ¼ tsp. cumin powder

Directions:
1. Mix the ingredients together and ensure that the flavors are right. You will now make round patties with the mixture and roll them out well.
2. Pre heat the Air Fryer at 250 Fahrenheit for 5 minutes. Open the basket of the Fryer and arrange the patties in the basket. Close it carefully. Keep the fryer at 150 degrees for around 10 or 12 minutes. In between the cooking process, turn the patties over to get a uniform cook. Serve hot with mint chutney.
3. Top with chicken and serve.

80. Beef French toast

Prep.Time: 10 min - Cooking Time: 20 min - Servings: 1

Ingredients:
- ✓ Bread slices (brown or white)
- ✓ 1 egg white for every 2 slices
- ✓ 1 tsp sugar for every 2 slices
- ✓ ½ lb. sliced beef

Directions:
1. Put two slices together and cut them along the diagonal.
2. In a bowl, whisk the egg whites and add some sugar.
3. Dip the bread triangles into this mixture. Cook the beef now.
4. Pre heat the Air Fryer at 180° C for 4 minutes. Place the coated bread triangles in the fry basket and close it. Let them cook at the same temperature for another 20 minutes at least. Halfway through the process, turn the triangles over so that you get a uniform cook.
5. Top with beef and serve.

81. Bacon and Garlic

Prep.Time: 10 min - **Cooking Time:** 15 min - **Servings:** 2

Ingredients:
- ✓ 6 slices bacon
- ✓ 2 cup dry breadcrumbs
- ✓ 2 tsp. oregano
- ✓ 2 tsp. red chili flakes
- ✓ 2 tsp. garlic paste

Marinade:
- ✓ 1 ½ tbsp. ginger-garlic paste
- ✓ 4 tbsp. lemon juice
- ✓ 2 tsp. salt
- ✓ 1 tsp. red chili powder
- ✓ 6 tbsp. corn flour
- ✓ 4 eggs

Directions:
1. Mix all the ingredients for the marinade and put the bacon slices inside and let it rest overnight.
2. Mix the breadcrumbs, oregano and red chili flakes well and place the marinated fingers on this mixture. Cover it with plastic wrap and leave it till right before you serve to cook.
3. Pre heat the Air fryer at 160 degrees Fahrenheit for 5 minutes. Place the fingers in the fry basket and close it. Let them cook at the same temperature for another 15 minutes or so. Toss the fingers well so that they are cooked uniformly.
4. Drizzle the garlic paste and serve.

82. Pheasant Tikka

Prep.Time: 10 min - **Cooking Time:** 40 min - **Servings:** 2

Ingredients:
- ✓ 2 cups sliced pheasant
- ✓ 1 big capsicum (Cut this capsicum into big cubes)
- ✓ 1 onion (Cut it into quarters. Now separate the layers carefully.)
- ✓ 5 tbsp. gram flour
- ✓ A pinch of salt to taste

For the filling:
- ✓ 2 cup fresh green coriander
- ✓ ½ cup mint leaves
- ✓ 4 tsp. fennel
- ✓ 2 tbsp. ginger-garlic paste
- ✓ 1 small onion
- ✓ 6-7 flakes garlic (optional)
- ✓ Salt to taste
- ✓ 3 tbsp. lemon juice

Directions:
1. You will first need to make the chutney. Add the ingredients to a blender and make a thick paste. Slit the pieces of pheasant and stuff half the paste into the cavity obtained.
2. Take the remaining paste and add it to the gram flour and salt. Toss the pieces of pheasant in this mixture and set aside.
3. Apply a little bit of the mixture on the capsicum and onion. Place these on a stick along with the pheasant pieces.
4. Pre heat the Air Fryer at 290 Fahrenheit for around 5 minutes. Open the basket. Arrange the satay sticks properly. Close the basket. Keep the sticks with the mutton at 180 degrees for around half an hour while the sticks with the vegetables are to be kept at the same temperature for only 7 minutes. Turn the sticks in between so that one side does not get burnt and also to provide a uniform cook.

83. Pheasant Chili

Prep.Time: 10 min - **Cooking Time:** 15 minutes - **Servings:** 2

Ingredients:
- ✓ 1 lb. cubed pheasant
- ✓ 2 ½ tsp. ginger-garlic paste
- ✓ 1 tsp. red chili sauce
- ✓ ¼ tsp. salt
- ✓ ¼ tsp. red chili powder/black pepper
- ✓ A few drops of edible orange food coloring

For sauce:
- ✓ 2 tbsp. olive oil

- ✓ 1 ½ tsp. ginger garlic paste
- ✓ ½ tbsp. red chili sauce
- ✓ 2 tbsp. tomato ketchup
- ✓ 2 tsp. soya sauce
- ✓ 1-2 tbsp. honey
- ✓ ¼ tsp. Ajinomoto
- ✓ 1-2 tsp. red chili flakes

Directions:
1. Mix all the ingredients for the marinade and put the pheasant cubes inside and let it rest overnight.
2. Mix the breadcrumbs, oregano and red chili flakes well and place the marinated fingers on this mixture. Cover it with plastic wrap and leave it till right before you serve to cook.
3. Pre heat the Air fryer at 160 degrees Fahrenheit for 5 minutes. Place the fingers in the fry basket and close it. Let them cook at the same temperature for another 15 minutes or so. Toss the fingers well so that they are cooked uniformly.

84. Carp Fritters

Prep.Time: 10 min - **Cooking Time:** 25 min - **Servings:** 4

Ingredients:
- ✓ 10 carp filets
- ✓ 3 onions chopped
- ✓ 5 green chilies-roughly chopped
- ✓ 1 ½ tbsp. ginger paste
- ✓ 1 ½ tsp. garlic paste

- ✓ 1 ½ tsp. salt
- ✓ 3 tsp. lemon juice
- ✓ 2 tsp. garam masala
- ✓ 3 eggs
- ✓ 2 ½ tbsp. white sesame seeds

Directions:
1. Grind the ingredients except for the egg and form a smooth paste. Coat the filets in the paste. Now, beat the eggs and add a little salt to it.
2. Dip the coated filets in the egg mixture and then transfer to the sesame seeds and coat the florets well. Place the vegetables on a stick.
3. Pre heat the Air fryer at 160 degrees Fahrenheit for around 5 minutes. Place the sticks in the basket and let them cook for another 25 minutes at the same temperature. Turn the sticks over in between the cooking process to get a uniform cook.

85. Beef Flat Cakes

Prep.Time: 10 min - Cooking Time: 25 min - Servings: 1

Ingredients:
- ✓ 2 tbsp. garam masala
- ✓ 1 lb. sliced beef steak
- ✓ 3 tsp ginger finely chopped
- ✓ 1-2 tbsp. fresh coriander leaves
- ✓ 2 or 3 green chilies finely chopped
- ✓ 1 ½ tbsp. lemon juice
- ✓ Salt and pepper to taste

Directions:
1. Mix the ingredients in a clean bowl and add water to it. Make sure that the paste is not too watery but is enough to apply on the sides of the steak.
2. Pre heat the Air Fryer at 160 degrees Fahrenheit for 5 minutes. Place the galettes in the fry basket and let them cook for another 25 minutes at the same temperature. Keep rolling them over to get a uniform cook. Serve either with mint chutney or ketchup.

86. Clams Galette

Prep.Time: 10 min - Cooking Time: 25 min - Servings: 2

Ingredients:
- ✓ 2 tbsp. garam masala
- ✓ 1 lb. minced clam
- ✓ 3 tsp ginger finely chopped
- ✓ 1-2 tbsp. fresh coriander leaves
- ✓ 2 or 3 green chilies finely chopped
- ✓ 1 ½ tbsp. lemon juice
- ✓ Salt and pepper to taste

Directions:
1. Mix the ingredients in a clean bowl.
2. Mold this mixture into round and flat galettes.
3. Wet the galettes slightly with water.
4. Pre heat the Air Fryer at 160 degrees Fahrenheit for 5 minutes. Place the galettes in the fry basket and let them cook for another 25 minutes at the same temperature. Keep rolling them over to get a uniform cook.
5. Serve either with mint chutney or ketchup.

87. Chili Calamari

Prep.Time: 10 min - Cooking Time: 15 minutes - Servings: 2

Ingredients:
- ✓ 1 lb. calamari
- ✓ 2 ½ tsp. ginger-garlic paste
- ✓ 1 tsp. red chili sauce
- ✓ ¼ tsp. salt
- ✓ ¼ tsp. red chili powder/black pepper
- ✓ A few drops of edible orange food coloring
- ✓ 1 ½ tsp. ginger garlic paste
- ✓ ½ tbsp. red chili sauce
- ✓ 2 tbsp. tomato ketchup
- ✓ 2 tsp. soya sauce
- ✓ 1-2 tbsp. honey
- ✓ ¼ tsp. Ajinomoto
- ✓ 1-2 tsp. red chili flakes

For sauce:
- ✓ 2 tbsp. olive oil

Directions:
1. Mix all the ingredients for the marinade and put the calamari inside and let it rest overnight.
2. Mix the breadcrumbs, oregano and red chili flakes well and place the marinated fingers on this mixture. Cover it with plastic wrap and leave it till right before you serve to cook.
3. Pre heat the Air fryer at 160 degrees Fahrenheit for 5 minutes. Place the fingers in the fry basket and close it. Let them cook at the same temperature for another 15 minutes or so. Toss the fingers well so that they are cooked uniformly.

88. Ham Club Sandwich

Prep.Time: 10 min - Cooking Time: 15 min - Servings: 1

Ingredients:
- ✓ 2 slices of white bread
- ✓ 1 tbsp. softened butter
- ✓ 1 lb. ham (Sliced)
- ✓ 1 small capsicum

For Barbeque Sauce:
- ✓ ¼ tbsp. Worcestershire sauce
- ✓ ½ tsp. olive oil
- ✓ ½ flake garlic crushed
- ✓ ¼ tsp. mustard powder
- ✓ ¼ cup chopped onion
- ✓ ½ tbsp. sugar
- ✓ 1 tbsp. tomato ketchup
- ✓ ¼ tbsp. red chili sauce
- ✓ ½ cup water.
- ✓ A pinch of salt and black pepper to taste

Directions:
1. Take the slices of bread and remove the edges. Now cut the slices horizontally.
2. Cook the ingredients for the sauce and wait till it thickens. Now, add the ham slices to the sauce and stir till it obtains the flavors. Roast the capsicum and peel the skin off. Cut the capsicum into slices. Mix the ingredients together and apply it to the bread slices.
3. Pre-heat the Air Fryer for 5 minutes at 300 Fahrenheit. Open the basket of the Fryer and place the prepared sandwiches in it such that no two sandwiches are touching each other. Now keep the fryer at 250 degrees for around 15 minutes. Turn the sandwiches in between the cooking process to cook both slices.
4. Serve the sandwiches with tomato ketchup or mint chutney.

89. Ham And Eggs

Prep.Time: 10 min - Cooking Time: 20 min - Servings: 1

Ingredients:
- ✓ Bread slices (brown or white)
- ✓ 1 egg white for every 2 slices
- ✓ 1 tsp sugar for every 2 slices
- ✓ ½ lb. sliced ham

Directions:
1. Put two slices together and cut them along the diagonal.
2. In a bowl, whisk the egg whites and add some sugar.
3. Dip the bread triangles into this mixture. Cook the chicken now. Pre heat the Air Fryer at 180° C for 4 minutes. Place the coated bread triangles in the fry basket and close it. Let them cook at the same temperature for another 20 minutes at least. Halfway through the process, turn the triangles over so that you get a uniform cook. Top with ham and serve.

90. Ham Flat cakes

Prep.Time: 10 min - Cooking Time: 25 min - Servings: 1

Ingredients:
- ✓ 2 tbsp. garam masala
- ✓ 1 lb. thinly sliced ham
- ✓ 3 tsp ginger chopped
- ✓ 1-2 tbsp. fresh coriander leaves
- ✓ 2 or 3 green chilies finely chopped
- ✓ 1 ½ tbsp. lemon juice
- ✓ Salt and pepper to taste

Directions:
1. Mix the ingredients in a clean bowl and add water to it. Make sure that the paste is not too watery but is enough to apply on the sides of the ham slices.
2. Pre heat the Air Fryer at 160 degrees Fahrenheit for 5 minutes. Place the galettes in the fry basket and let them cook for another 25 minutes at the same temperature.
3. Keep rolling them over to get a uniform cook.
4. Serve either with mint chutney or ketchup.

91. Carp Flat Cakes

Prep.Time: 10 min - **Cooking Time:** 25 min - **Servings:** 2

Ingredients:
- ✓ 2 tbsp. garam masala
- ✓ 1 lb. fileted carp
- ✓ 3 tsp ginger finely chopped
- ✓ 1-2 tbsp. fresh coriander leaves
- ✓ 2 or 3 green chilies finely chopped
- ✓ 1 ½ tbsp. lemon juice
- ✓ Salt and pepper to taste

Directions:
1. Mix the ingredients in a clean bowl and add water to it. Make sure that the paste is not too watery but is enough to apply on the sides of the carp filets.
2. Pre heat the Air Fryer at 160 degrees Fahrenheit for 5 minutes. Place the galettes in the fry basket and let them cook for another 25 minutes at the same temperature.
3. Keep rolling them over to get a uniform cook.
4. Serve either with mint chutney or ketchup.

92. Mutton Wontons

Prep.Time: 10 min - **Cooking Time:** 20 min - **Servings:** 2

Ingredients:
For Dough:
- ✓ 1 ½ cup all-purpose flour
- ✓ ½ tsp. salt
- ✓ 5 tbsp. water
For filling:
- ✓ 2 cups minced mutton
- ✓ 2 tbsp. oil
- ✓ 2 tsp. ginger-garlic paste
- ✓ 2 tsp. soya sauce
- ✓ 2 tsp. vinegar

Directions:
1. Knead the dough and cover it with plastic wrap and set aside. Next, cook the ingredients for the filling and try to ensure that the mutton is covered well with the sauce.
2. Roll the dough and place the filling in the center. Now, wrap the dough to cover the filling and pinch the edges together.
3. Pre heat the Air fryer at 200° F for 5 minutes. Place the wontons in the fry basket and close it. Let them cook at the same temperature for another 20 minutes. Recommended sides are chili sauce or ketchup.

93. Prawn Galette

Prep.Time: 10 min - **Cooking Time:** 25 minutes - **Servings:** 2

Ingredients:
- ✓ 2 tbsp. garam masala
- ✓ 1 lb. minced prawn
- ✓ 3 tsp ginger finely chopped
- ✓ 1-2 tbsp. fresh coriander leaves
- ✓ 2 or 3 green chilies finely chopped
- ✓ 1 ½ tbsp. lemon juice
- ✓ Salt and pepper to taste

Directions:
1. Mix the ingredients in a clean bowl.
2. Mold this mixture into round and flat galettes.
3. Wet the galettes slightly with water.
4. Pre heat the Air Fryer at 160 degrees Fahrenheit for 5 minutes. Place the galettes in the fry basket and let them cook for another 25 minutes at the same temperature. Keep rolling them over to get a uniform cook.
5. Serve either with mint chutney or ketchup.

94. Pork fritters

Prep.Time: 10 min - **Cooking Time:** 25 min - **Servings:** 2

Ingredients:
- ✓ 2 tbsp. garam masala
- ✓ 1 lb. sliced pork
- ✓ 3 tsp ginger finely chopped
- ✓ 1-2 tbsp. fresh coriander leaves
- ✓ 2 or 3 green chilies finely chopped
- ✓ 1 ½ tbsp. lemon juice
- ✓ Salt and pepper to taste

Directions:
1. Mix the ingredients in a clean bowl.
2. Wet the galettes slightly with water.
3. Pre heat the Air Fryer at 160 degrees Fahrenheit for 5 minutes. Place the galettes in the fry basket and let them cook for another 25 minutes at the same temperature. Keep rolling them over to get a uniform cook.
4. Serve either with mint chutney or ketchup.

95. Lamb Toast

Prep.Time: 10 min - **Cooking Time:** 20 min - **Servings:** 1

Ingredients:
- ✓ Bread slices (brown or white)
- ✓ 1 egg white for every 2 slices
- ✓ 1 tsp sugar for every 2 slices
- ✓ ½ lb. sliced lamb

Directions:
1. Put two slices together and cut them along the diagonal.
2. In a bowl, whisk the egg whites and add some sugar.
3. Dip the bread triangles into this mixture. Cook the lamb now.
4. Pre heat the Air Fryer at 180° C for 4 minutes. Place the coated bread triangles in the fry basket and close it. Let them cook at the same temperature for another 20 minutes at least. Halfway through the process, turn the triangles over so that you get a uniform cook. Top with lamb and serve.

96. Cornflakes French Toast

Prep.Time: 10 min - **Cooking Time:** 20 min - **Servings:** 1

Ingredients:
- ✓ Bread slices (brown or white)
- ✓ 1 egg white for every 2 slices
- ✓ 1 tsp. sugar for every 2 slices
- ✓ Crushed cornflakes

Directions:
1. Put two slices together and cut them along the diagonal.
2. In a bowl, whisk the egg whites and add some sugar.
3. Dip the bread triangles into this mixture and then coat them with the crushed cornflakes.
4. Pre heat the Air Fryer at 180° C for 4 minutes. Place the coated bread triangles in the fry basket and close it. Let them cook at the same temperature for another 20 minutes at least. Halfway through the process, turn the triangles over so that you get a uniform cook.
5. Serve these slices with chocolate sauce.

97. Cottage Cheese Sticks

Prep.Time: 15 min - Cooking Time: 20 min - Servings: 2

Ingredients:
- ✓ 2 cups cottage cheese
- ✓ 1 big lemon-juiced
- ✓ 1 tbsp. ginger-garlic paste
- ✓ For seasoning, use salt and red chili powder in small amounts
- ✓ ½ tsp. carom
- ✓ One or two papadums
- ✓ 4 or 5 tbsp. corn flour
- ✓ 1 cup of water

Directions:
1. Take the cottage cheese. Cut it into long pieces.
2. Now, make a mixture of lemon juice, red chili powder, salt, ginger garlic paste and carom to use as a marinade. Let the cottage cheese pieces marinate in the mixture for some time and then roll them in dry corn flour. Leave them aside for around 20 minutes.
3. Take the papadum into a pan and roast them. Once they are cooked, crush them into very small pieces. Now take another container and pour around 100 ml of water into it. Dissolve 2 tbsp. of corn flour in this water. Dip the cottage cheese pieces in this solution of corn flour and roll them on to the pieces of crushed papadum so that the papadum sticks to the cottage cheese.
4. Pre heat the Air Fryer for 10 minutes at 290 Fahrenheit. Then open the basket of the fryer and place the cottage cheese pieces inside it. Close the basket properly. Let the fryer stay at 160 degrees for another 20 minutes. Halfway through, open the basket and toss the cottage cheese around a bit to allow for uniform cooking. Once they are done, you can serve it either with ketchup or mint chutney. Another recommended side is mint chutney.

98. Pizza

Prep.Time: 10 min - Cooking Time: 10 min - Servings: 1

Ingredients:
- ✓ One pizza base
- ✓ Grated pizza cheese (mozzarella cheese preferably) for topping
- ✓ Use cooking oil for brushing and topping purposes

Ingredients for topping:
- ✓ 2 onions chopped
- ✓ 2 capsicums chopped
- ✓ 2 tomatoes that have been deseeded and chopped
- ✓ 1 tbsp. (optional) mushrooms/corns
- ✓ 2 tsp. pizza seasoning
- ✓ Some cottage cheese that has been cut into small cubes (optional)

Directions:
1. Put the pizza base in a pre-heated Air fryer for around 5 minutes. (Pre heated to 340 Fahrenheit).
2. Take out the base. Pour some pizza sauce on top of the base at the center. Using a spoon spread the sauce over the base making sure that you leave some gap around the circumference. Grate some mozzarella cheese and sprinkle it over the sauce layer.
3. Take all the vegetables mentioned in the ingredient list above and mix them in a bowl. Add some oil and seasoning. Also add some salt and pepper according to taste. Mix them properly. Put this topping over the layer of cheese on the pizza. Now sprinkle some more grated cheese and pizza seasoning on top of this layer.
4. Pre heat the Air Fryer at 250 Fahrenheit for around 5 minutes. Open the fry basket and place the pizza inside. Close the basket and keep the fryer at 170 degrees for another 10 minutes. If you feel that it is undercooked you may put it at the same temperature for another 2 minutes or so.

99. Potato Club Sandwich

Prep.Time: 10 min - Cooking Time: 15 minutes - Servings: 1

Ingredients:
- ✓ 2 slices of white bread
- ✓ 1 tbsp. softened butter
- ✓ 1 cup boiled potato
- ✓ 1 small capsicum

For Barbeque Sauce:
- ✓ ¼ tbsp. Worcestershire sauce
- ✓ ½ tsp. olive oil
- ✓ ½ flake garlic crushed
- ✓ ¼ cup chopped onion
- ✓ ¼ tbsp. red chili sauce

Directions:
1. Take the slices of bread and remove the edges. Now cut the slices horizontally.
2. Cook the ingredients for the sauce and wait till it thickens. Now, add the potato to the sauce and stir till it obtains the flavors. Roast the capsicum and peel the skin off. Cut the capsicum into slices. Mix the ingredients together and apply it to the bread slices.
3. Pre-heat the Air Fryer for 5 minutes at 300 Fahrenheit. Open the basket of the Fryer and place the prepared sandwiches in it such that no two sandwiches are touching each other. Now keep the fryer at 250 degrees for around 15 minutes. Turn the sandwiches in between the cooking process to cook both slices. Serve the sandwiches with tomato ketchup or mint chutney.

100. Vegetable Pie

Prep.Time: 20 min - Cooking Time: 15 min - Servings: 2

Ingredients:
- ✓ 1 cup plain flour
- ✓ 1 tbsp. unsalted butter
- ✓ 4 tsp. powdered sugar
- ✓ 2 cups cold milk

For filling:
- ✓ ½ cup roasted nuts
- ✓ 2 cups roasted vegetables
- ✓ 2 tbsp. sugar
- ✓ ½ tsp. cinnamon
- ✓ 2 tsp. lemon juice

Directions:
1. In a large bowl, mix the flour, butter and sugar with your fingers. The mixture should resemble breadcrumbs. Knead the dough using the cold milk and wrap it and leave it to cool for ten minutes.
2. Now, roll the dough out and cut into two circles. Press the dough into the pie tins and prick on all sides using a fork.
3. Cook the ingredients for the filling on a low flame and pour into the tin. Cover the pie tin with the second round.
4. Preheat the fryer to 300 Fahrenheit for five minutes. You will need to place the tin in the basket and cover it. When the pastry has turned golden brown, you will need to remove the tin and let it cool. Cut into slices and serve with a dollop of cream.

101. Chili Cottage Cheese

Prep.Time: 10 min - **Cooking Time:** 20 min - **Servings:** 2

Ingredients:

For cottage cheese:
- ✓ 2 cups cubed cottage cheese
- ✓ 2 ½ tsp. ginger-garlic paste
- ✓ 1 tsp. red chili sauce
- ✓ ¼ tsp. salt
- ✓ ¼ tsp. red chili powder/black pepper
- ✓ A few drops of edible orange food coloring

For sauce:
- ✓ 2 tbsp. olive oil
- ✓ 1 capsicum. Cut into thin and long pieces (lengthwise).
- ✓ 2 small onions. Cut them into halves.

- ✓ 1 ½ tsp. ginger garlic paste
- ✓ ½ tbsp. red chili sauce.
- ✓ 2 tbsp. tomato ketchup.
- ✓ 1 ½ tbsp. sweet chili sauce.
- ✓ 2 tsp. vinegar.
- ✓ 2 tsp. soya sauce.
- ✓ A few drops of edible red food coloring.
- ✓ 1-2 tbsp. honey.
- ✓ ¼ tsp. Ajinomoto.
- ✓ A pinch of black pepper powder.
- ✓ 1-2 tsp. red chili flakes.
- ✓ For the garnish, use the greens of spring onions and sesame seeds

Directions:
1. Create the mix for the cottage cheese cubes and coat the chicken well with it.
2. Pre heat the Air fryer at 250 Fahrenheit for 5 minutes or so. Open the basket of the Fryer. Place the fingers inside the basket. Now let the fryer stay at 290 Fahrenheit for another 20 minutes. Keep tossing the fingers periodically through the cook to get a uniform cook.
3. Add the ingredients to the sauce and cook it with the vegetables till it thickens. Add the fingers to the sauce and cook till the flavors have blended.

102. Zucchini Samosa

Prep.Time: 15 min - **Cooking Time:** 35 min - **Servings:** 2

Ingredients:

For wrappers:
- ✓ 2 tbsp. unsalted butter
- ✓ 1 ½ cup all-purpose flour
- ✓ A pinch of salt to taste
- ✓ Add as much water as required to make the dough stiff and firm

For filling:
- ✓ 3 medium zucchinis (mashed)
- ✓ ¼ cup boiled peas
- ✓ 1 tsp. powdered ginger
- ✓ 1 or 2 green chilies that are finely chopped or mashed

- ✓ ½ tsp. cumin
- ✓ 1 tsp. coarsely crushed coriander
- ✓ 1 dry red chili broken into pieces
- ✓ A small amount of salt (to taste)
- ✓ ½ tsp. dried mango powder
- ✓ ½ tsp. red chili power.
- ✓ 1-2 tbsp. coriander

Directions:
1. Mix the dough for the outer covering and make it stiff and smooth. Leave it to rest in a container while making the filling.
2. Cook the ingredients in a pan and stir them well to make a thick paste. Roll the paste out.
3. Roll the dough into balls and flatten them. Cut them in halves and add the filling. Use water to help you fold the edges to create the shape of a cone. Pre-heat the Air Fryer for around 5 to 6 minutes at 300 Fahrenheit. Place all the samosas in the fry basket and close the basket properly. Keep the Air Fryer at 200 degrees for another 20 to 25 minutes. Around the halfway point, open the basket and turn the samosas over for uniform cooking.
4. After this, fry at 250 degrees for around 10 minutes in order to give them the desired golden brown color.
5. Serve hot. Recommended sides are tamarind or mint chutney.

103. Cauliflower Galette

Prep.Time: 10 min - **Cooking Time:** 25 minutes - **Servings:** 2

Ingredients:
- ✓ 2 tbsp. garam masala
- ✓ 2 cups cauliflower
- ✓ 1 ½ cup coarsely crushed peanuts
- ✓ 3 tsp. ginger finely chopped

- ✓ 1-2 tbsp. fresh coriander leaves
- ✓ 2 or 3 green chilies finely chopped
- ✓ 1 ½ tbsp. lemon juice
- ✓ Salt and pepper to taste

Directions:
1. Mix the ingredients in a clean bowl.
2. Mold this mixture into round and flat galettes.
3. Wet the galettes slightly with water. Coat each galette with the crushed peanuts.
4. Pre heat the Air Fryer at 160 degrees Fahrenheit for 5 minutes. Place the galettes in the fry basket and let them cook for another 25 minutes at the same temperature. Keep rolling them over to get a uniform cook. Serve either with mint chutney or ketchup.

104. Vegetable Dumpling

Prep.Time: 15 min - **Cooking Time:** 20 min - **Servings:** 2

Ingredients:

For dough:
- ✓ 1 ½ cup all-purpose flour
- ✓ ½ tsp. salt or to taste
- ✓ 5 tbsp. water

For filling:
- ✓ 2 cup carrots grated

- ✓ 2 cup cabbage grated
- ✓ 2 tbsp. oil
- ✓ 2 tsp. ginger-garlic paste
- ✓ 2 tsp. soya sauce
- ✓ 2 tsp. vinegar

Directions:
1. Knead the dough and cover it with plastic wrap and set aside. Next, cook the ingredients for the filling and try to ensure that the vegetables are covered well with the sauce.
2. Roll the dough and place the filling in the center. Now, wrap the dough to cover the filling and pinch the edges together.
3. Pre heat the Air fryer at 200° F for 5 minutes. Place the dumplings in the fry basket and close it. Let them cook at the same temperature for another 20 minutes. Recommended sides are chili sauce or ketchup.

105. Bottle Gourd Flat Cakes

Prep.Time: 10 min - **Cooking Time:** 25 min - **Servings:** 2

Ingredients:
- ✓ 2 tbsp. garam masala
- ✓ 2 cups sliced bottle gourd
- ✓ 3 tsp. ginger finely chopped
- ✓ 1-2 tbsp. fresh coriander leaves
- ✓ 2 or 3 green chilies finely chopped
- ✓ 1 ½ tbsp. lemon juice
- ✓ Salt and pepper to taste

Directions:
1. Mix the ingredients in a clean bowl and add water to it. Make sure that the paste is not too watery but is enough to apply on the bottle gourd slices.
2. Pre heat the Air Fryer at 160 degrees Fahrenheit for 5 minutes. Place the galettes in the fry basket and let them cook for another 25 minutes at the same temperature. Keep rolling them over to get a uniform cook.
3. Serve either with mint chutney or ketchup.

106. Bitter Gourd Flat Cakes

Prep.Time: 10 min - **Cooking Time:** 25 min - **Servings:** 2

Ingredients:
- ✓ 2 tbsp. garam masala
- ✓ 2 cups sliced bitter gourd
- ✓ 3 tsp. ginger finely chopped
- ✓ 1-2 tbsp. fresh coriander leaves
- ✓ 2 or 3 green chilies finely chopped
- ✓ 1 ½ tbsp. lemon juice
- ✓ Salt and pepper to taste

Directions:
1. Mix the ingredients in a clean bowl and add water to it. Make sure that the paste is not too watery but is enough to apply on the bitter gourd slices.
2. Pre heat the Air Fryer at 160 degrees Fahrenheit for 5 minutes. Place the galettes in the fry basket and let them cook for another 25 minutes at the same temperature. Keep rolling them over to get a uniform cook.
3. Serve either with mint chutney or ketchup.

107. Snake Gourd Flat Cakes

Prep.Time: 10 min - **Cooking Time:** 25 minutes - **Servings:** 2

Ingredients:
- ✓ 2 tbsp. garam masala
- ✓ 2 cups sliced snake gourd
- ✓ 3 tsp. ginger finely chopped
- ✓ 1-2 tbsp. fresh coriander leaves
- ✓ 2 or 3 green chilies finely chopped
- ✓ 1 ½ tbsp. lemon juice
- ✓ Salt and pepper to taste

Directions:
1. Mix the ingredients in a clean bowl and add water to it. Make sure that the paste is not too watery but is enough to apply on the snake gourd slices.
2. Pre heat the Air Fryer at 160 degrees Fahrenheit for 5 minutes. Place the galettes in the fry basket and let them cook for another 25 minutes at the same temperature. Keep rolling them over to get a uniform cook.
3. Serve either with mint chutney or ketchup.

108. Pumpkin Galette

Prep.Time: 10 min - **Cooking Time:** 25 min - **Servings:** 2

Ingredients:
- ✓ 2 tbsp. garam masala
- ✓ 1 cup sliced pumpkin
- ✓ 3 tsp. ginger finely chopped
- ✓ 1-2 tbsp. fresh coriander leaves
- ✓ 2 or 3 green chilies finely chopped
- ✓ 1 ½ tbsp. lemon juice
- ✓ Salt and pepper to taste

Directions:
1. Mix the ingredients in a clean bowl.
2. Mold this mixture into round and flat galettes.
3. Wet the galettes slightly with water.
4. Pre heat the Air Fryer at 160 degrees Fahrenheit for 5 minutes. Place the galettes in the fry basket and let them cook for another 25 minutes at the same temperature. Keep rolling them over to get a uniform cook.
5. Serve either with mint chutney or ketchup.

109. Cabbage Flat Cakes

Prep.Time: 10 min - **Cooking Time:** 25 min - **Servings:** 2

Ingredients:
- ✓ 2 tbsp. garam masala
- ✓ 2 cups halved cabbage leaves
- ✓ 3 tsp. ginger finely chopped
- ✓ 1-2 tbsp. fresh coriander leaves
- ✓ 2 or 3 green chilies finely chopped
- ✓ 1 ½ tbsp. lemon juice
- ✓ Salt and pepper to taste

Directions:
1. Mix the ingredients in a clean bowl and add water to it. Make sure that the paste is not too watery but is enough to apply on the cabbage.
2. Pre heat the Air Fryer at 160 degrees Fahrenheit for 5 minutes. Place the galettes in the fry basket and let them cook for another 25 minutes at the same temperature. Keep rolling them over to get a uniform cook.
3. Serve either with mint chutney or ketchup.

110. Radish Flat Cakes

Prep.Time: 10 min - **Cooking Time:** 25 min - **Servings:** 2

Ingredients:
- ✓ 2 tbsp. garam masala
- ✓ 2 cups sliced radish
- ✓ 3 tsp. ginger finely chopped
- ✓ 1-2 tbsp. fresh coriander leaves
- ✓ 2 or 3 green chilies finely chopped
- ✓ 1 ½ tbsp. lemon juice
- ✓ Salt and pepper to taste

Directions:
1. Mix the ingredients in a clean bowl and add water to it. Make sure that the paste is not too watery but is enough to apply on the radish.
2. Pre heat the Air Fryer at 160 degrees Fahrenheit for 5 minutes. Place the galettes in the fry basket and let them cook for another 25 minutes at the same temperature. Keep rolling them over to get a uniform cook.
3. Serve either with mint chutney or ketchup.

111. Potato Samosa

Prep.Time: 15 min - Cooking Time: 35 min - Servings: 2

Ingredients:

For wrappers:
- ✓ 2 tbsp. unsalted butter
- ✓ 1 ½ cup all-purpose flour
- ✓ A pinch of salt to taste
- ✓ Add as much water as required to make the dough stiff and firm

For filling:
- ✓ 2-3 big potatoes boiled and mashed
- ✓ ¼ cup boiled peas
- ✓ 1 tsp. powdered ginger
- ✓ 1 or 2 green chilies that are finely chopped or mashed

- ✓ ½ tsp. cumin
- ✓ 1 tsp. coarsely crushed coriander
- ✓ 1 dry red chili broken into pieces
- ✓ A small amount of salt (to taste)
- ✓ ½ tsp. dried mango powder
- ✓ ½ tsp. red chili power.
- ✓ 1-2 tbsp. coriander

Directions:

1. Mix the dough for the outer covering and make it stiff and smooth. Leave it to rest in a container while making the filling.
2. Cook the ingredients in a pan and stir them well to make a thick paste. Roll the paste out.
3. Roll the dough into balls and flatten them. Cut them in halves and add the filling. Use water to help you fold the edges to create the shape of a cone.
4. Pre-heat the Air Fryer for around 5 to 6 minutes at 300 Fahrenheit. Place all the samosas in the fry basket and close the basket properly. Keep the Air Fryer at 200 degrees for another 20 to 25 minutes. Around the halfway point, open the basket and turn the samosas over for uniform cooking. After this, fry at 250 degrees for around 10 minutes in order to give them the desired golden brown color.
5. Serve hot. Recommended sides are tamarind or mint chutney.

112. Vegetable Kebab

Prep.Time: 10 min - Cooking Time: 25 min - Servings: 2

Ingredients:
- ✓ 2 cups mixed vegetables
- ✓ 3 onions chopped
- ✓ 5 green chilies-roughly chopped
- ✓ 1 ½ tbsp. ginger paste
- ✓ 1 ½ tsp. garlic paste
- ✓ 1 ½ tsp. salt
- ✓ 3 tsp. lemon juice
- ✓ 2 tsp. garam masala

- ✓ 4 tbsp. chopped coriander
- ✓ 3 tbsp. cream
- ✓ 3 tbsp. chopped capsicum
- ✓ 3 eggs
- ✓ 2 ½ tbsp. white sesame seeds

Directions:

1. Grind the ingredients except for the egg and form a smooth paste. Coat the vegetables in the paste. Now, beat the eggs and add a little salt to it.
2. Dip the coated vegetables in the egg mixture and then transfer to the sesame seeds and coat the vegetables well. Place the vegetables on a stick.
3. Pre heat the Air fryer at 160 degrees Fahrenheit for around 5 minutes. Place the sticks in the basket and let them cook for another 25 minutes at the same temperature. Turn the sticks over in between the cooking process to get a uniform cook.

113. Cottage Cheese Momos

Prep.Time: 10 min - Cooking Time: 20 minutes - Servings: 2

Ingredients:

For dough:
- ✓ 1 ½ cup all-purpose flour
- ✓ ½ tsp. salt
- ✓ 5 tbsp. water

For filling:
- ✓ 2 cups crumbled cottage cheese
- ✓ 2 tbsp. oil
- ✓ 2 tsp. ginger-garlic paste
- ✓ 2 tsp. soya sauce
- ✓ 2 tsp. vinegar

Directions:

1. Knead the dough and cover it with plastic wrap and set aside. Next, cook the ingredients for the filling and try to ensure that the cottage cheese is covered well with the sauce.
2. Roll the dough and cut it into a square. Place the filling in the center. Now, wrap the dough to cover the filling and pinch the edges together.
3. Pre heat the Air fryer at 200° F for 5 minutes. Place the gnocchis in the fry basket and close it. Let them cook at the same temperature for another 20 minutes. Recommended sides are chili sauce or ketchup.

114. Beef Steak Fingers

Prep.Time: 10 min - Cooking Time: 15 min - Servings: 2

Ingredients:
- ✓ 1 lb. boneless beef steak cut into fingers
- ✓ 2 cup dry breadcrumbs
- ✓ 2 tsp. oregano
- ✓ 2 tsp. red chili flakes

Marinade:
- ✓ 1 ½ tbsp. ginger-garlic paste

- ✓ 4 tbsp. lemon juice
- ✓ 2 tsp. salt
- ✓ 1 tsp. pepper powder
- ✓ 1 tsp. red chili powder
- ✓ 6 tbsp. corn flour
- ✓ 4 eggs

Directions:

1. Mix all the ingredients for the marinade and put the beef fingers inside and let it rest overnight.
2. Mix the breadcrumbs, oregano and red chili flakes well and place the marinated fingers on this mixture. Cover it with plastic wrap and leave it till right before you serve to cook.
3. Pre heat the Air fryer at 160 degrees Fahrenheit for 5 minutes. Place the fingers in the fry basket and close it. Let them cook at the same temperature for another 15 minutes or so. Toss the fingers well so that they are cooked uniformly.

115. Fish Club Sandwich

Prep.Time: 10 min - Cooking Time: 15 min - Servings: 1

Ingredients:
- ✓ 2 slices of white bread
- ✓ 1 tbsp. softened butter
- ✓ 1 tin tuna
- ✓ 1 small capsicum

For Barbeque Sauce:
- ✓ ¼ tbsp. Worcestershire sauce
- ✓ ½ tsp. olive oil
- ✓ ½ flake garlic crushed
- ✓ ¼ cup chopped onion
- ✓ ¼ tsp. mustard powder
- ✓ ½ tbsp. sugar
- ✓ ¼ tbsp. red chili sauce
- ✓ 1 tbsp. tomato ketchup
- ✓ ½ cup water.
- ✓ A pinch of salt and black pepper to taste

Directions:
1. Take the slices of bread and remove the edges. Now cut the slices horizontally.
2. Cook the ingredients for the sauce and wait till it thickens. Now, add the fish to the sauce and stir till it obtains the flavors. Roast the capsicum and peel the skin off. Cut the capsicum into slices. Mix the ingredients together and apply it to the bread slices.
3. Pre-heat the Air Fryer for 5 minutes at 300 Fahrenheit. Open the basket of the Fryer and place the prepared sandwiches in it such that no two sandwiches are touching each other. Now keep the fryer at 250 degrees for around 15 minutes. Turn the sandwiches in between the cooking process to cook both slices.
4. Serve the sandwiches with tomato ketchup or mint chutney.

116. Veal Club Sandwich

Prep.Time: 10 min - Cooking Time: 15 min - Servings: 1

Ingredients:
- ✓ 2 slices of white bread
- ✓ 1 tbsp. softened butter
- ✓ ½ lb. cubed veal
- ✓ 1 small capsicum

For Barbeque Sauce:
- ✓ ¼ tbsp. Worcestershire sauce
- ✓ ½ tsp. olive oil
- ✓ ½ flake garlic crushed
- ✓ ¼ cup chopped onion
- ✓ ¼ tsp. mustard powder
- ✓ ½ tbsp. sugar
- ✓ ¼ tbsp. red chili sauce
- ✓ ½ cup water

Directions:
1. Take the slices of bread and remove the edges. Now cut the slices horizontally.
2. Cook the ingredients for the sauce and wait till it thickens. Now, add the veal to the sauce and stir till it obtains the flavors. Roast the capsicum and peel the skin off. Cut the capsicum into slices. Mix the ingredients together and apply it to the bread slices.
3. Pre-heat the Air Fryer for 5 minutes at 300 Fahrenheit. Open the basket of the Fryer and place the prepared sandwiches in it such that no two sandwiches are touching each other. Now keep the fryer at 250 degrees for around 15 minutes. Turn the sandwiches in between the cooking process to cook both slices.
4. Serve the sandwiches with tomato ketchup or mint chutney.

117. Lamb Chili

Prep.Time: 20 min - Cooking Time: 15 minutes - Servings: 4

Ingredients:
- ✓ 1 lb. lamb (Cut into cubes)
- ✓ 2 ½ tsp. ginger-garlic paste
- ✓ 1 tsp. red chili sauce
- ✓ ¼ tsp. salt
- ✓ ¼ tsp. red chili powder/black pepper
- ✓ A few drops of edible orange food coloring

For sauce:
- ✓ 2 tbsp. olive oil
- ✓ 1 ½ tsp. ginger garlic paste
- ✓ ½ tbsp. red chili sauce
- ✓ 2 tbsp. tomato ketchup
- ✓ 2 tsp. soya sauce
- ✓ 1-2 tbsp. honey
- ✓ ¼ tsp. Ajinomoto
- ✓ 1-2 tsp. red chili flakes

Directions:
1. Mix all the ingredients for the marinade and put the lamb cubes inside and let it rest overnight.
2. Mix the breadcrumbs, oregano and red chili flakes well and place the marinated fingers on this mixture. Cover it with plastic wrap and leave it till right before you serve to cook.
3. Pre heat the Air fryer at 160 degrees Fahrenheit for 5 minutes. Place the fingers in the fry basket and close it. Let them cook at the same temperature for another 15 minutes or so. Toss the fingers well so that they are cooked uniformly.

118. Cottage Cheese Club Sandwich

Prep.Time: 10 min - Cooking Time: 15 min - Servings: 1

Ingredients:
- ✓ 2 slices of white bread
- ✓ 1 tbsp. softened butter
- ✓ 1 cup sliced cottage cheese
- ✓ 1 small capsicum

For Barbeque Sauce:
- ✓ ¼ tbsp. Worcestershire sauce
- ✓ ½ tsp. olive oil
- ✓ ½ flake garlic crushed
- ✓ ¼ cup chopped onion
- ✓ ¼ tbsp. red chili sauce

Directions:
1. Take the slices of bread and remove the edges. Now cut the slices horizontally.
2. Cook the ingredients for the sauce and wait till it thickens. Now, add the cottage cheese to the sauce and stir till it obtains the flavors. Roast the capsicum and peel the skin off. Cut the capsicum into slices. Mix the ingredients together and apply it to the bread slices.
3. Pre-heat the Air Fryer for 5 minutes at 300 Fahrenheit. Open the basket of the Fryer and place the prepared sandwiches in it such that no two sandwiches are touching each other. Now keep the fryer at 250 degrees for around 15 minutes. Turn the sandwiches in between the cooking process to cook both slices.
4. Serve the sandwiches with tomato ketchup or mint chutney.

119. Turkey Burger Cutlets

Prep.Time: 10 min - **Cooking Time:** 12 min - **Servings:** 2

Ingredients:
- ½ lb. minced turkey
- ½ cup breadcrumbs
- A pinch of salt to taste
- ¼ tsp. ginger finely chopped
- 1 green chili finely chopped
- 1 tsp. lemon juice
- 1 tbsp. fresh coriander leaves. Chop them finely
- ¼ tsp. red chili powder
- ½ cup of boiled peas
- ¼ tsp. cumin powder
- ¼ tsp. dried mango powder

Directions:
1. Take a container and into it pour all the masalas, onions, green chilies, peas, coriander leaves, lemon juice, ginger and 1-2 tbsp. breadcrumbs. Add the minced turkey as well. Mix all the ingredients well.
2. Mold the mixture into round Cutlets. Press them gently. Now roll them out carefully.
3. Pre heat the Air Fryer at 250 Fahrenheit for 5 minutes. Open the basket of the Fryer and arrange the Cutlets in the basket. Close it carefully. Keep the fryer at 150 degrees for around 10 or 12 minutes. In between the cooking process, turn the Cutlets over to get a uniform cook.
4. Serve hot with mint chutney.

120. Okra Kebab

Prep.Time: 15 min - **Cooking Time:** 25 min - **Servings:** 2

Ingredients:
- 2 cups sliced okra
- 3 onions chopped
- 5 green chilies-roughly chopped
- 1 ½ tbsp. ginger paste
- 1 ½ tsp. garlic paste
- 1 ½ tsp. salt
- 3 tsp. lemon juice
- 2 tsp. garam masala
- 4 tbsp. chopped coriander
- 3 tbsp. cream
- 3 tbsp. chopped capsicum
- 3 eggs
- 2 ½ tbsp. white sesame seeds

Directions:
1. Grind the ingredients except for the egg and form a smooth paste. Coat the okra in the paste. Now, beat the eggs and add a little salt to it.
2. Dip the coated vegetables in the egg mixture and then transfer to the sesame seeds and coat the okra well. Place the vegetables on a stick.
3. Pre heat the Air fryer at 160 degrees Fahrenheit for around 5 minutes. Place the sticks in the basket and let them cook for another 25 minutes at the same temperature. Turn the sticks over in between the cooking process to get a uniform cook.

121. Chicken Tikka

Prep.Time: 15 min - **Cooking Time:** 40 minutes - **Servings:** 2

Ingredients:
- 2 cups sliced chicken
- 1 big capsicum (Cut this capsicum into big cubes)
- 1 onion (Cut it into quarters. Now separate the layers carefully.)
- 5 tbsp. gram flour
- A pinch of salt to taste

For the filling:
- 2 cup fresh green coriander
- ½ cup mint leaves
- 4 tsp. fennel
- 2 tbsp. ginger-garlic paste
- 1 small onion
- 6-7 flakes garlic (optional)
- Salt to taste
- 3 tbsp. lemon juice

Directions:
1. You will first need to make the chutney. Add the ingredients to a blender and make a thick paste. Slit the pieces of chicken and stuff half the paste into the cavity obtained.
2. Take the remaining paste and add it to the gram flour and salt. Toss the pieces of chicken in this mixture and set aside.
3. Apply a little bit of the mixture on the capsicum and onion. Place these on a stick along with the chicken pieces.
4. Pre heat the Air Fryer at 290 Fahrenheit for around 5 minutes. Open the basket. Arrange the satay sticks properly. Close the basket. Keep the sticks with the chicken at 180 degrees for around half an hour while the sticks with the vegetables are to be kept at the same temperature for only 7 minutes. Turn the sticks in between so that one side does not get burnt and also to provide a uniform cook.

122. Pork Tandoor

Prep.Time: 15 min - **Cooking Time:** 40 min - **Servings:** 2

Ingredients:
- 2 cups sliced pork belly
- 1 big capsicum (Cut this capsicum into big cubes)
- 1 onion (Cut it into quarters. Now separate the layers carefully.)
- 5 tbsp. gram flour
- A pinch of salt to taste

For the filling:
- 2 cup fresh green coriander
- ½ cup mint leaves
- 4 tsp. fennel
- 2 tbsp. ginger-garlic paste
- 1 small onion
- 6-7 flakes garlic (optional)
- Salt to taste
- 3 tbsp. lemon juice

Directions:
1. You will first need to make the chutney. Add the ingredients to a blender and make a thick paste. Slit the pieces of pork and stuff half the paste into the cavity obtained.
2. Take the remaining paste and add it to the gram flour and salt. Toss the pieces of Pork in this mixture and set aside.
3. Apply a little bit of the mixture on the capsicum and onion. Place these on a stick along with the pork pieces.
4. Pre heat the Air Fryer at 290 Fahrenheit for around 5 minutes. Open the basket. Arrange the satay sticks properly. Close the basket. Keep the sticks with the pork at 180 degrees for around half an hour while the sticks with the vegetables are to be kept at the same temperature for only 7 minutes. Turn the sticks in between so that one side does not get burnt and also to provide a uniform cook.

123. Mixed Vegetable Pancakes

Prep.Time: 15 min - **Cooking Time:** 10/15 min - **Servings:** 2

Ingredients:
- ✓ 2 cups shredded vegetables
- ✓ 1 ½ cups almond flour
- ✓ 3 eggs
- ✓ 2 tsp. dried basil
- ✓ 2 tsp. dried parsley
- ✓ Salt and Pepper to taste
- ✓ 3 tbsp. Butter

Directions:
1. Preheat the air fryer to 250 Fahrenheit.
2. In a small bowl, mix the ingredients together. Ensure that the mixture is smooth and well balanced.
3. Take a pancake mold and grease it with butter. Add the batter to the mold and place it in the air fryer basket.
4. Cook till both the sides of the pancake have browned on both sides and serve with maple syrup.

124. Green Chili Flat Cakes

Prep.Time: 10 min - **Cooking Time:** 25 min - **Servings:** 2

Ingredients:
- ✓ 2 tbsp. garam masala
- ✓ 10–12 green chilies
- ✓ 3 tsp. ginger finely chopped
- ✓ 1-2 tbsp. fresh coriander leaves
- ✓ 2 or 3 green chilies finely chopped
- ✓ 1 ½ tbsp. lemon juice
- ✓ Salt and pepper to taste

Directions:
1. Mix the ingredients in a clean bowl and add water to it. Make sure that the paste is not too watery but is enough to apply to the green chilies.
2. Pre heat the Air Fryer at 160 degrees Fahrenheit for 5 minutes. Place the galettes in the fry basket and let them cook for another 25 minutes at the same temperature. Keep rolling them over to get a uniform cook.
3. Serve either with mint chutney or ketchup.

125. Prawn Wontons

Prep.Time: 15 min - **Cooking Time:** 20 minutes - **Servings:** 2

Ingredients:
- ✓ 1 ½ cup all-purpose flour
- ✓ ½ tsp. salt
- ✓ 5 tbsp. water

For filling:
- ✓ 2 cups minced prawn
- ✓ 2 tbsp. oil
- ✓ 2 tsp. ginger-garlic paste
- ✓ 2 tsp. soya sauce
- ✓ 2 tsp. vinegar

Directions:
1. Knead the dough and cover it with plastic wrap and set aside. Next, cook the ingredients for the filling and try to ensure that the prawn is covered well with the sauce.
2. Roll the dough and place the filling in the center. Now, wrap the dough to cover the filling and pinch the edges together.
3. Pre heat the Air fryer at 200° F for 5 minutes. Place the wontons in the fry basket and close it. Let them cook at the same temperature for another 20 minutes. Recommended sides are chili sauce or ketchup.

126. Mushroom Galette

Prep.Time: 10 min - **Cooking Time:** 25 min - **Servings:** 2

Ingredients:
- ✓ 2 tbsp. garam masala
- ✓ 2 cups sliced mushrooms
- ✓ 1 ½ cup coarsely crushed peanuts
- ✓ 3 tsp. ginger finely chopped
- ✓ 1-2 tbsp. fresh coriander leaves
- ✓ 2 or 3 green chilies finely chopped
- ✓ 1 ½ tbsp. lemon juice
- ✓ Salt and pepper to taste

Directions:
1. Mix the ingredients in a clean bowl.
2. Mold this mixture into round and flat galettes.
3. Wet the galettes slightly with water. Coat each galette with the crushed peanuts.
4. Pre heat the Air Fryer at 160 degrees Fahrenheit for 5 minutes. Place the galettes in the fry basket and let them cook for another 25 minutes at the same temperature. Keep rolling them over to get a uniform cook. Serve either with mint chutney or ketchup.

127. Mutton Galette

Prep.Time: 10 min - **Cooking Time:** 25 min - **Servings:** 2

Ingredients:
- ✓ 2 tbsp. garam masala
- ✓ 1 lb. minced mutton
- ✓ 3 tsp ginger finely chopped
- ✓ 1-2 tbsp. fresh coriander leaves
- ✓ 2 or 3 green chilies finely chopped
- ✓ 1 ½ tbsp. lemon juice
- ✓ Salt and pepper to taste

Directions:
1. Mix the ingredients in a clean bowl.
2. Mold this mixture into round and flat galettes.
3. Wet the galettes slightly with water.
4. Pre heat the Air Fryer at 160 degrees Fahrenheit for 5 minutes. Place the galettes in the fry basket and let them cook for another 25 minutes at the same temperature. Keep rolling them over to get a uniform cook.
5. Serve either with mint chutney or ketchup.

128. Salmon Fritters

Prep.Time: 15 min - **Cooking Time:** 25 min - **Servings:** 4

Ingredients:
- ✓ 2 tbsp. garam masala
- ✓ 1 lb. fileted Salmon
- ✓ 3 tsp ginger finely chopped
- ✓ 1-2 tbsp. fresh coriander leaves
- ✓ 2 or 3 green chilies finely chopped
- ✓ 1 ½ tbsp. lemon juice
- ✓ Salt and pepper to taste

Directions:
1. Mix the ingredients in a clean bowl.
2. Mold this mixture into round and flat galettes.
3. Wet the galettes slightly with water.
4. Pre heat the Air Fryer at 160 degrees Fahrenheit for 5 minutes. Place the galettes in the fry basket and let them cook for another 25 minutes at the same temperature. Keep rolling them over to get a uniform cook.
5. Serve either with mint chutney or ketchup.

129. Prawn Momos

Prep.Time: 10 min - **Cooking Time:** 20 min - **Servings:** 2

Ingredients:

For dough:
- ✓ 1 ½ cup all-purpose flour
- ✓ ½ tsp. salt
- ✓ 5 tbsp. water

For filling:
- ✓ 2 cups minced prawn
- ✓ 2 tbsp. oil
- ✓ 2 tsp. ginger-garlic paste
- ✓ 2 tsp. soya sauce
- ✓ 2 tsp. vinegar

Directions:
1. Knead the dough and cover it with plastic wrap and set aside. Next, cook the ingredients for the filling and try to ensure that the prawn is covered well with the sauce.
2. Roll the dough and cut it into a square. Place the filling in the center. Now, wrap the dough to cover the filling and pinch the edges together.
3. Pre heat the Air fryer at 200° F for 5 minutes. Place the wontons in the fry basket and close it. Let them cook at the same temperature for another 20 minutes. Recommended sides are chili sauce or ketchup.

130. Black Gram Galette

Prep.Time: 10 min - **Cooking Time:** 25 min - **Servings:** 2

Ingredients:
- ✓ 2 cup black gram
- ✓ 2 medium potatoes boiled and mashed
- ✓ 1 ½ cup coarsely crushed peanuts
- ✓ 3 tsp. ginger finely chopped
- ✓ 1-2 tbsp. fresh coriander leaves
- ✓ 2 or 3 green chilies finely chopped
- ✓ 1 ½ tbsp. lemon juice
- ✓ Salt and pepper to taste

Directions:
1. Mix the ingredients in a clean bowl.
2. Mold this mixture into round and flat galettes.
3. Wet the galettes slightly with water.
4. Pre heat the Air Fryer at 160 degrees Fahrenheit for 5 minutes. Place the galettes in the fry basket and let them cook for another 25 minutes at the same temperature. Keep rolling them over to get a uniform cook.
5. Serve either with mint chutney or ketchup.

131. Cottage Cheese Flat Cakes

Prep.Time: 10 min - **Cooking Time:** 25 minutes - **Servings:** 2

Ingredients:
- ✓ 2 tbsp. garam masala
- ✓ 2 cups sliced cottage cheese
- ✓ 3 tsp. ginger finely chopped
- ✓ 1-2 tbsp. fresh coriander leaves
- ✓ 2 or 3 green chilies finely chopped
- ✓ 1 ½ tbsp. lemon juice
- ✓ Salt and pepper to taste

Directions:
1. Mix the ingredients in a clean bowl and add water to it. Make sure that the paste is not too watery but is enough to apply on the cottage cheese slices.
2. Pre heat the Air Fryer at 160 degrees Fahrenheit for 5 minutes. Place the galettes in the fry basket and let them cook for another 25 minutes at the same temperature.
3. Keep rolling them over to get a uniform cook.
4. Serve either with mint chutney or ketchup.

132. Snake gourd galette

Prep.Time: 10 min - **Cooking Time:** 25 min - **Servings:** 2

Ingredients:
- ✓ 2 tbsp. garam masala
- ✓ 1 cup sliced snake gourd
- ✓ 1 ½ cup coarsely crushed peanuts
- ✓ 3 tsp. ginger finely chopped
- ✓ 1-2 tbsp. fresh coriander leaves
- ✓ 2 or 3 green chilies finely chopped
- ✓ 1 ½ tbsp. lemon juice
- ✓ Salt and pepper to taste

Directions:
1. Mix the ingredients in a clean bowl.
2. Mold this mixture into round and flat galettes.
3. Wet the galettes slightly with water. Coat each galette with the crushed peanuts.
4. Pre heat the Air Fryer at 160 degrees Fahrenheit for 5 minutes. Place the galettes in the fry basket and let them cook for another 25 minutes at the same temperature. Keep rolling them over to get a uniform cook.
5. Serve either with mint chutney or ketchup.

133. White Lentil Galette

Prep.Time: 10 min - **Cooking Time:** 25 min - **Servings:** 2

Ingredients:
- ✓ 2 cup white lentil soaked
- ✓ 3 tsp. ginger finely chopped
- ✓ 1-2 tbsp. fresh coriander leaves
- ✓ 2 or 3 green chilies finely chopped
- ✓ 1 ½ tbsp. lemon juice
- ✓ Salt and pepper to taste

Directions:
1. Wash the soaked lentils and mix it with the rest of the ingredients in a clean bowl.
2. Mold this mixture into round and flat galettes.
3. Wet the galettes slightly with water.
4. Pre heat the Air Fryer at 160 degrees Fahrenheit for 5 minutes. Place the galettes in the fry basket and let them cook for another 25 minutes at the same temperature. Keep rolling them over to get a uniform cook.
5. Serve either with mint chutney or ketchup.

134. Mushroom Pops

Prep.Time: 10 min - **Cooking Time:** 20 min - **Servings:** 2

Ingredients:
- ✓ 1 cup whole mushrooms
- ✓ 1 ½ tsp. garlic paste
- ✓ Salt and pepper to taste
- ✓ 1 tsp. dry oregano
- ✓ 1 tsp. dry basil
- ✓ 1 tsp. lemon juice
- ✓ 1 tsp. red chili flakes

Directions:
1. Add the ingredients into a separate bowl and mix them well to get a consistent mixture.
2. Dip the mushrooms in the above mixture and leave them aside for some time.
3. Pre heat the Air fryer at 180° C for around 5 minutes. Place the coated cottage cheese pieces in the fry basket and close it properly. Let them cook at the same temperature for 20 more minutes. Keep turning them over in the basket so that they are cooked properly. Serve with tomato ketchup.

135. Burger Cutlet

Prep.Time: 15 min - Cooking Time: 12 min - Servings: 1

Ingredients:
- ✓ 1 large potato boiled and mashed
- ✓ ½ cup breadcrumbs
- ✓ A pinch of salt to taste
- ✓ ¼ tsp. ginger finely chopped
- ✓ 1 green chili finely chopped
- ✓ 1 tsp. lemon juice
- ✓ 1 tbsp. fresh coriander leaves. Chop them finely
- ✓ ¼ tsp. red chili powder
- ✓ ½ cup of boiled peas
- ✓ ¼ tsp. cumin powder
- ✓ ¼ tsp. dried mango powder

Directions:
1. Mix the ingredients together and ensure that the flavors are right. You will now make round cutlets with the mixture and roll them out well.
2. Pre heat the Air Fryer at 250 Fahrenheit for 5 minutes. Open the basket of the Fryer and arrange the cutlets in the basket. Close it carefully. Keep the fryer at 150 degrees for around 10 or 12 minutes. In between the cooking process, turn the cutlets over to get a uniform cook.
3. Serve hot with mint chutney.

136. Cheese French Fries

Prep.Time: 20 min - Cooking Time: 25 min - Servings: 2

Ingredients:
- ✓ 2 medium sized potatoes peeled and cut into thick pieces lengthwise
- *Ingredients for the marinade:*
- ✓ 1 tbsp. olive oil
- ✓ 1 tsp. mixed herbs
- ✓ ½ tsp. red chili flakes
- ✓ A pinch of salt to taste
- ✓ 1 tbsp. lemon juice
- *For the garnish:*
- ✓ 1 cup melted cheddar cheese (You could put this into a piping bag and create a pattern of it on the fries.)

Directions:
1. Take all the ingredients mentioned under the heading "For the marinade" and mix them well.
2. Now pour into a container 3 cups of water. Add a pinch of salt into this water. Bring it to the boil. Now blanch the pieces of potato for around 5 minutes. Drain the water using a sieve. Dry the potato pieces on a towel and then place them on another dry towel. Coat these potato fingers with the marinade made in the previous step.
3. Pre heat the Air Fryer for around 5 minutes at 300 Fahrenheit. Take out the basket of the fryer and place the potato fingers in them. Close the basket. Now keep the fryer at 220 Fahrenheit for 20 or 25 minutes. In between the process, toss the fries twice or thrice so that they get cooked properly.
4. Towards the end of the cooking process (the last 2 minutes or so), sprinkle the cut coriander leaves on the fries. Add the melted cheddar cheese over the fries and serve hot.

137. Veal Patties

Prep.Time: 15 min - Cooking Time: 12 minutes - Servings: 2

Ingredients:
- ✓ ½ lb. minced veal
- ✓ ½ cup breadcrumbs
- ✓ A pinch of salt to taste
- ✓ ¼ tsp. ginger finely chopped
- ✓ 1 green chili finely chopped
- ✓ 1 tsp. lemon juice
- ✓ 1 tbsp. fresh coriander leaves. Chop them finely
- ✓ ¼ tsp. red chili powder
- ✓ ½ cup of boiled peas
- ✓ ¼ tsp. cumin powder
- ✓ ¼ tsp. dried mango powder

Directions:
1. Take a container and into it pour all the masalas, onions, green chilies, peas, coriander leaves, lemon juice, and ginger and 1-2 tbsp. breadcrumbs. Add the minced veal as well. Mix all the ingredients well.
2. Mold the mixture into round patties. Press them gently. Now roll them out carefully.
3. Pre heat the Air Fryer at 250 Fahrenheit for 5 minutes. Open the basket of the Fryer and arrange the patties in the basket. Close it carefully. Keep the fryer at 150 degrees for around 10 or 12 minutes. In between the cooking process, turn the patties over to get a uniform cook.
4. Serve hot with mint chutney.

138. Lamb Barbecue Club Sandwich

Prep.Time: 15 min - Cooking Time: 15 min - Servings: 1

Ingredients:
- ✓ 2 slices of white bread
- ✓ 1 tbsp. softened butter
- ✓ ½ lb. cut lamb (Get the meat cut into cubes)
- ✓ 1 small capsicum
- ✓ For Barbeque Sauce:
- ✓ ¼ tbsp. Worcestershire sauce
- ✓ ½ tsp. olive oil
- ✓ ½ flake garlic crushed
- ✓ ¼ cup chopped onion
- ✓ ½ tbsp. sugar
- ✓ ¼ tbsp. red chili sauce

Directions:
1. Take the slices of bread and remove the edges. Now cut the slices horizontally.
2. Cook the ingredients for the sauce and wait till it thickens. Now, add the lamb to the sauce and stir till it obtains the flavors. Roast the capsicum and peel the skin off. Cut the capsicum into slices. Mix the ingredients together and apply it to the bread slices.
3. Pre-heat the Air Fryer for 5 minutes at 300 Fahrenheit. Open the basket of the Fryer and place the prepared sandwiches in it such that no two sandwiches are touching each other. Now keep the fryer at 250 degrees for around 15 minutes. Turn the sandwiches in between the cooking process to cook both slices.
4. Serve the sandwiches with tomato ketchup or mint chutney.

139. Caribou Finger

Prep.Time: 20 min - **Cooking Time:** 15 min - **Servings:** 2

Ingredients:

- ✓ 1 lb. boneless caribou cut into fingers
- ✓ 2 cup dry breadcrumbs
- ✓ 2 tsp. oregano
- ✓ 2 tsp. red chili flakes

Marinade:

- ✓ 1 ½ tbsp. ginger-garlic paste
- ✓ 4 tbsp. lemon juice
- ✓ 2 tsp. salt
- ✓ 1 tsp. pepper powder
- ✓ 1 tsp. red chili powder
- ✓ 6 tbsp. corn flour
- ✓ 4 eggs

Directions:

1. Mix all the ingredients for the marinade and put the caribou fingers inside and let it rest overnight.
2. Mix the breadcrumbs, oregano and red chili flakes well and place the marinated fingers on this mixture. Cover it with plastic wrap and leave it till right before you serve to cook.
3. Pre heat the Air fryer at 160 degrees Fahrenheit for 5 minutes. Place the fingers in the fry basket and close it. Let them cook at the same temperature for another 15 minutes or so. Toss the fingers well so that they are cooked uniformly.

140. Duck Liver Fries

Prep.Time: 20 min - **Cooking Time:** 25 min - **Servings:** 2

Ingredients:

- ✓ 1 lb. duck liver (Cut in to long fingers)

Ingredients for the marinade:

- ✓ 1 tbsp. olive oil
- ✓ 1 tsp. mixed herbs
- ✓ ½ tsp. red chili flakes
- ✓ A pinch of salt to taste
- ✓ 1 tbsp. lemon juice

For the garnish:

- ✓ 1 cup melted cheddar cheese

Directions:

1. Take all the ingredients mentioned under the heading "For the marinade" and mix them well.
2. Cook the duck liver fingers and soak them in the marinade.
3. Pre heat the Air Fryer for around 5 minutes at 300 Fahrenheit. Take out the basket of the fryer and place the chicken fingers in them. Close the basket. Now keep the fryer at 220 Fahrenheit for 20 or 25 minutes. In between the process, toss the fries twice or thrice so that they get cooked properly.
4. Towards the end of the cooking process (the last 2 minutes or so), sprinkle the cut coriander leaves on the fries. Add the melted cheddar cheese over the fries and serve hot.

141. Pork Burger Cutlets

Prep.Time: 20 min - **Cooking Time:** 12 minutes - **Servings:** 2

Ingredients:

- ✓ ½ lb. pork (Make sure that you mince the pork fine)
- ✓ ½ cup breadcrumbs
- ✓ A pinch of salt to taste
- ✓ ¼ tsp. ginger finely chopped
- ✓ 1 green chili finely chopped
- ✓ 1 tsp. lemon juice
- ✓ 1 tbsp. fresh coriander leaves. Chop them finely
- ✓ ¼ tsp. red chili powder
- ✓ ½ cup of boiled peas
- ✓ ¼ tsp. cumin powder
- ✓ ¼ tsp. dried mango powder

Directions:

1. Take a container and into it pour all the masalas, onions, green chilies, peas, coriander leaves, lemon juice, and ginger and 1-2 tbsp. breadcrumbs. Add the minced pork as well. Mix all the ingredients well.
2. Mold the mixture into round Cutlets. Press them gently. Now roll them out carefully.
3. Pre heat the Air Fryer at 250 Fahrenheit for 5 minutes. Open the basket of the Fryer and arrange the Cutlets in the basket. Close it carefully. Keep the fryer at 150 degrees for around 10 or 12 minutes. In between the cooking process, turn the Cutlets over to get a uniform cook.
4. Serve hot with mint chutney.

142. Fish Fingers

Prep.Time: 20 min - **Cooking Time:** 25 min - **Servings:** 2

Ingredients:

- ✓ ½ lb. firm white fish fillet cut into fingers
- ✓ 1 tbsp. lemon juice
- ✓ 2 cups of dry breadcrumbs
- ✓ 1 cup oil for frying

Marinade:

- ✓ 1 ½ tbsp. ginger-garlic paste
- ✓ 3 tbsp. lemon juice
- ✓ 2 tsp salt
- ✓ 1 ½ tsp pepper powder
- ✓ 1 tsp red chili flakes or to taste
- ✓ 3 eggs
- ✓ 5 tbsp. corn flour
- ✓ 2 tsp tomato ketchup

Directions:

1. Rub a little lemon juice on the fingers and set aside. Wash the fish after an hour and pat dry. Make the marinade and transfer the fingers into the marinade. Leave them on a plate to dry for fifteen minutes. Now cover the fingers with the crumbs and set aside to dry for fifteen minutes.
2. Pre heat the Air Fryer at 160 degrees Fahrenheit for 5 minutes or so. Keep the fish in the fry basket now and close it properly. Let the fingers cook at the same temperature for another 25 minutes. In between the cooking process, toss the fish once in a while to avoid burning the food.
3. Serve either with tomato ketchup or chili sauce. Mint chutney also works well with the fish.

143. Fish Kebab

Prep.Time: 70 min - **Cooking Time:** 25 min - **Servings:** 2

Ingredients:
- ✓ 1 lb. boneless fish roughly chopped
- ✓ 3 onions chopped
- ✓ 5 green chilies-roughly chopped
- ✓ 1 ½ tbsp. ginger paste
- ✓ 1 ½ tsp garlic paste
- ✓ 1 ½ tsp salt
- ✓ 3 tsp lemon juice
- ✓ 2 tsp garam masala
- ✓ 4 tbsp. chopped coriander
- ✓ 3 tbsp. cream
- ✓ 2 tbsp. coriander powder
- ✓ 4 tbsp. fresh mint chopped
- ✓ 3 tbsp. chopped capsicum
- ✓ 3 eggs
- ✓ 2 ½ tbsp. white sesame seeds

Directions:
1. Take all the ingredients mentioned under the first heading and mix them in a bowl. Grind them thoroughly to make a smooth paste.
2. Take the eggs in a different bowl and beat them. Add a pinch of salt and leave them aside.
3. Take a flat plate and in it mix the sesame seeds and breadcrumbs.
4. Mold the fish mixture into small balls and flatten them into round and flat kebabs.
5. Dip these kebabs in the egg and salt mixture and then in the mixture of breadcrumbs and sesame seeds. Leave these kebabs in the fridge for an hour or so to set.
6. Pre heat the Air fryer at 160 degrees Fahrenheit for around 5 minutes. Place the kebabs in the basket and let them cook for another 25 minutes at the same temperature. Turn the kebabs over in between the cooking process to get a uniform cook.
7. Serve the kebabs with mint chutney.

144. Chinese Chili

Prep.Time: 15 min - **Cooking Time:** 15 min - **Servings:** 2

Ingredients:

For chicken fingers:
- ✓ 1 lb. chicken (Cut into cubes)
- ✓ 2 ½ tsp. ginger-garlic paste
- ✓ 1 tsp. red chili sauce
- ✓ ¼ tsp. salt
- ✓ ¼ tsp. red chili powder/black pepper
- ✓ A few drops of edible orange food coloring

For sauce:
- ✓ 2 tbsp. olive oil
- ✓ 1 ½ tsp. ginger garlic paste
- ✓ ½ tbsp. red chili sauce
- ✓ 2 tbsp. tomato ketchup
- ✓ 2 tsp. soya sauce
- ✓ 1-2 tbsp. honey
- ✓ ¼ tsp. Ajinomoto
- ✓ 1-2 tsp. red chili flakes

Directions:
1. Mix all the ingredients for the marinade and put the chicken cubes inside and let it rest overnight.
2. Mix the breadcrumbs, oregano and red chili flakes well and place the marinated fingers on this mixture. Cover it with plastic wrap and leave it till right before you serve to cook.
3. Pre heat the Air fryer at 160 degrees Fahrenheit for 5 minutes. Place the fingers in the fry basket and close it. Let them cook at the same temperature for another 15 minutes or so. Toss the fingers well so that they are cooked uniformly.

145. Cauliflower Momos

Prep.Time: 10 min - **Cooking Time:** 20 minutes - **Servings:** 2

Ingredients:
- ✓ 1 ½ cup all-purpose flour
- ✓ ½ tsp. salt
- ✓ 5 tbsp. water

For filling:
- ✓ 2 cups grated cauliflower
- ✓ 2 tbsp. oil
- ✓ 2 tsp. ginger-garlic paste
- ✓ 2 tsp. soya sauce
- ✓ 2 tsp. vinegar

Directions:
1. Knead the dough and cover it with plastic wrap and set aside. Next, cook the ingredients for the filling and try to ensure that the cauliflower is covered well with the sauce.
2. Roll the dough and cut it into a square. Place the filling in the center. Now, wrap the dough to cover the filling and pinch the edges together.
3. Pre heat the Air fryer at 200° F for 5 minutes. Place the gnocchis in the fry basket and close it. Let them cook at the same temperature for another 20 minutes. Recommended sides are chili sauce or ketchup.

146. Cottage Cheese Kebab

Prep.Time: 70 min - **Cooking Time:** 25 min - **Servings:** 2

Ingredients:
- ✓ 2 cups cubed cottage cheese
- ✓ 3 onions chopped
- ✓ 5 green chilies-roughly chopped
- ✓ 1 ½ tbsp. ginger paste
- ✓ 1 ½ tsp. garlic paste
- ✓ 1 ½ tsp. salt
- ✓ 3 tsp. lemon juice
- ✓ 2 tbsp. coriander powder
- ✓ 3 tbsp. chopped capsicum
- ✓ 2 tbsp. peanut flour
- ✓ 3 eggs

Directions:
1. Coat the cottage cheese cubes with the corn flour and mix the other ingredients in a bowl. Make the mixture into a smooth paste and coat the cheese cubes with the mixture. Beat the eggs in a bowl and add a little salt to them.
2. Dip the cubes in the egg mixture and coat them with sesame seeds and leave them in the refrigerator for an hour.
3. Pre heat the Air fryer at 290 Fahrenheit for around 5 minutes. Place the kebabs in the basket and let them cook for another 25 minutes at the same temperature. Turn the kebabs over in between the cooking process to get a uniform cook.
4. Serve the kebabs with mint chutney.

147. Bacon Cheddar Chicken Fingers

Prep.Time: 10 min - **Cooking Time:** 10 min - **Servings:** 2

Ingredients:

For the chicken fingers:
- ✓ 1 lb. chicken tenders, about 8 pieces
- ✓ cooking spray (canola oil)
- ✓ cheddar cheese - 1 cup, shredded
- ✓ Two eggs, large
- ✓ 1/3 cup bacon bits
- ✓ 2 tbsp. water

For the breading:
- ✓ 1 tsp. of onion powder
- ✓ panko bread crumbs - 2 cups
- ✓ black pepper - 1 tsp., freshly ground
- ✓ paprika - 2 tbsp.
- ✓ garlic powder - 1 tsp.
- ✓ salt - 2 tsp

Directions:
1. Set the air fryer to the temperature of 360°F.
2. In a glass dish, whip the water and eggs until combined.
3. Use a zip lock bag, shake the garlic powder, salt, breadcrumbs, cayenne, onion powder, and pepper together.
4. Immerse the chicken into the eggs and shake in the ziplock bag until fully covered.
5. Dip again in the egg mixture and back into the seasonings until a thick coating is present.
6. Remove the tenders from the bag and set in the frying pan in the basket. Do them in batches if need to not over pack the pan.
7. Apply the canola oil spray to the top of the tenders and heat for 6 minutes.
8. Flip the tenders to the other side. Steam for another 4 minutes.
9. Blend the bacon bits and shredded cheese in a dish.
10. Evenly dust the bacon and cheese onto the hot tenders and fry for 2 more minutes.
11. Remove and serve while hot.

148. Battered Cod

Prep.Time: 15 min - **Cooking Time:** 14 min - **Servings:** 2

Ingredients:
- ✓ Cod - 20 oz.
- ✓ Salt - 1/4 tsp.
- ✓ all-purpose flour - 8 oz.
- ✓ parsley seasoning - 1 tbsp.
- ✓ cornstarch - 3 tsp.
- ✓ garlic powder - 1/2 tsp.
- ✓ Two eggs, preferably large
- ✓ onion powder - 1/2 tsp.

Directions:
1. Whip the eggs in a glass dish until smooth and set to the side.
2. In a separate dish, blend the cornstarch, salt, almond flour, garlic powder, parsley, and onion powder, whisking to remove any lumpiness.
3. Immerse the pieces of cods into the egg and then into the spiced flour, covering completely.
4. Transfer to the fryer basket in a single layer.
5. Heat the fish for 7 minutes at a temperature of 350°F. Turn the cod over and steam for an additional 7 minutes.

149. Beef Kabobs

Prep.Time: 60 min - **Cooking Time:** 15 minutes - **Servings:** 1

Ingredients:
- ✓ low-fat sour cream - 1/3 cup
- ✓ one bell pepper
- ✓ 16 oz. of beef chuck ribs, boneless
- ✓ soy sauce - 2 tbsp.
- ✓ 6-inch skewers - 8
- ✓ Pepper - 1/4 tsp.
- ✓ medium onion - 1/2

Directions:
1. Slice the ribs into sections about 1-inch wide
2. In a lidded tub, combine the soy sauce, ribs and sour cream making sure the meat is fully covered.
3. Refrigerate for half an hour at least, if not overnight.
4. Immerse the wooden skewers for approximately 10 minutes in water.
5. Set the temperature of the air fryer to 400°F.
6. Slice the onion and bell pepper in 1-inch sections.
7. Remove the meat from the marinade, draining well.
8. Layer the onions, beef and bell peppers on the skewers and dust with pepper.
9. Heat for 10 minutes, ensuring you spin the skewers 5 minutes into cooking time.
10. Serve while hot and enjoy.

150. Cheese Dogs

Prep.Time: 10 min - **Cooking Time:** 7 min - **Servings:** 4

Ingredients:
- ✓ 4 hotdogs
- ✓ 1/4 cup your choice of cheese, grated
- ✓ 4 hotdog buns

Directions:
1. Adjust the air fryer to heat at a temperature of 390°F for approximately 5 minutes.
2. Set the hot dogs in the basket and broil for 5 minutes.
3. Remove and create the hot dog with the bun and cheese as desired and move back to the basket for another 2 minutes.
4. Remove and enjoy while hot.

151. Cheeseburger Patties

Prep.Time: 10 min - Cooking Time: 13 min - Servings: 2

Ingredients:

- ✓ garlic - 1/2 clove, minced
- ✓ ground beef - 1 1/3 cup
- ✓ onion - 4 oz., diced
- ✓ Worcestershire sauce - 2 tbsp.
- ✓ one egg, large
- ✓ panko breadcrumbs - 2 oz.
- ✓ cayenne pepper - 1/8 tsp.
- ✓ cooking spray (olive oil)
- ✓ salt - 1/4 tsp.
- ✓ 4 slices of cheese of your choice
- ✓ 1/8 tsp. pepper

Directions:

1. Using a big glass dish, combine the diced onion, pepper, minced garlic, cayenne pepper, breadcrumbs, and salt until incorporated.
2. Blend the ground beef, Worcestershire sauce, and egg and integrate thoroughly by hand.
3. Form the meat into 4 individual patties and move to the air fryer basket.
4. Coat the patties with cooking spray.
5. Adjust the temperature for 375°F and heat for 8 minutes.
6. Turn the burgers over and steam for an additional 2 minutes.
7. Cover with a slice of cheese and continue cooking for approximately 3 minutes.
8. Enjoy as is or place on a bun with your favorite toppings.

152. Chicken Cordon Bleu

Prep.Time: 20 min - Cooking Time: 16 min - Servings: 2

Ingredients:

- ✓ Pepper - 1/4 tsp.
- ✓ chicken paillards - 4
- ✓ salt - 1/4 tsp.
- ✓ Swiss cheese - 8 slices
- ✓ all-purpose flour - 1/2 cup
- ✓ parmesan cheese - 2/3 cup, grated
- ✓ panko breadcrumbs - 1 1/2 cup
- ✓ ham - 8 slices
- ✓ two eggs, large
- ✓ Dijon mustard - 2 tbsp.
- ✓ 8 toothpicks
- ✓ grapeseed oil spray

Directions:

1. On a section of baking lining, brush the Dijon mustard on each chicken paillard and sprinkle with pepper and salt
2. Layer 1 cheese, 2 slices of the ham and then the additional slice of cheese on each of the pieces of chicken.
3. Rotate the chicken beginning with the longer side to create a roll. Fasten in place with two toothpicks.
4. Whip the egg in one dish, empty the flour into a second dish and blend the parmesan cheese and breadcrumbs into a third.
5. Immerse one chicken first in flour, secondly immerse in the egg and then roll the chicken completely in the breadcrumbs. Press the cheese and breadcrumbs into the chicken to secure and place onto a plate.
6. Repeat for the other pieces of chicken.
7. Apply the grapeseed oil spray to each section of chicken and transfer to the air fryer basket after 5 minutes.
8. Set the air fryer temperature to heat at 350°.
9. Grill for 8 minutes and carefully turn the chicken to the other side. Heat for an additional 8 minutes.
10. Remove to a serving dish and wait approximately 5 minutes before serving hot.

153. Grilled Cheese Sandwich

Prep.Time: 5 min - Cooking Time: 5 minutes - Servings: 1

Ingredients:

- ✓ 2 slices bread, softened
- ✓ 1 tsp. butter
- ✓ 2 slices cheddar cheese

Directions:

1. Set the air fryer at a temperature of 350°F.
2. Apply 1/2 teaspoon of the softened butter to one side of the slice of bread. Repeat for the remaining bread.
3. Create the sandwich by putting the cheese in between the non-buttered sides of bread.
4. Transfer to the hot air fryer and set for 5 minutes. Flip the sandwich at the halfway point and remove.
5. Serve immediately and enjoy

154. Italian Meatballs

Prep.Time: 20 min - Cooking Time: 16 min - Servings: 2

Ingredients:

- ✓ one egg, large
- ✓ ground beef - 16 oz.
- ✓ pepper - 1/8 tsp.
- ✓ oregano seasoning - 1/2 tsp.
- ✓ bread crumbs - 1 1/4 cup
- ✓ garlic - 1/2 clove, chopped
- ✓ parsley - 1 oz., chopped
- ✓ salt - 1/4 tsp.
- ✓ Parmigiano-Reggiano cheese - 1 oz. cup, grated
- ✓ cooking spray (avocado oil)

Directions:

1. Whisk the oregano, breadcrumbs, chopped garlic, salt, chopped parsley, pepper, and grated Parmigiano-Reggiano cheese until combined.
2. Blend the ground beef and egg into the mixture using your hands. Incorporate the ingredients thoroughly.
3. Divide the meat into 12 sections and roll into rounds.
4. Coat the inside of the basket with avocado oil spray to grease.
5. Adjust the temperature to 350°F and heat for approximately 12 minutes.
6. Roll the meatballs over and steam for another 4 minutes and remove to a serving plate.
7. Enjoy as is or combine with your favorite pasta or sauce.

155. Loaded Baked Potatoes

Prep.Time: 20 min - **Cooking Time:** 8 min - **Servings:** 2

Ingredients:
- ✓ 1/3 cup milk
- ✓ 2 oz. sour cream
- ✓ 1/3 cup white cheddar, grated
- ✓ 2 oz. Parmesan cheese, grated
- ✓ 1/8 tsp. garlic salt
- ✓ 6 oz. ham, diced
- ✓ 2 medium russet potatoes
- ✓ 4 oz. sharp cheddar, shredded
- ✓ 1/8 cup. green onion, diced

Directions:
1. Puncture the potatoes deeply with a fork a few time and microwave for approximately 5 minutes. Flip them to the other side and nuke for an additional 5 minutes. The potatoes should be soft.
2. Use oven mitts to remove from the microwave and cut them in halves.
3. Spoon out the insides of the potatoes to about a quarter-inch from the skins and distribute the potato flesh to a glass bowl.
4. Combine the parmesan, garlic salt, sour cream, and white cheddar cheese to the potato dish and incorporate fully.
5. Distribute the mixture back to the emptied potato skins. Create a small hollow in the middle by pressing with a spoon.
6. Divide the ham evenly between the potatoes and place the ham inside the hollow.
7. Position the potatoes in the fryer and set the air fryer to the temperature of 300°F.
8. Heat for 8 minutes and then sprinkle the cheddar cheese on top of each potato.
9. Melt the cheese for two more minutes than serve with diced onions on top.

156. Southern Style Fried Chicken

Prep.Time: 10 min - **Cooking Time:** 18 min - **Servings:** 4

Ingredients:
- ✓ Italian seasoning - 1 tsp.
- ✓ chicken legs or breasts - 2 lbs.
- ✓ Buttermilk - 2 tbsp.
- ✓ paprika seasoning - 1 1/2tsp.
- ✓ cornstarch - 2 oz.
- ✓ onion powder - 1 tsp.
- ✓ hot sauce - 3 tsp.
- ✓ pepper - 1 1/2 tsp.
- ✓ 2 large eggs
- ✓ 1 cup self-rising flour
- ✓ 2 tsp. salt
- ✓ cooking spray (olive oil)
- ✓ 1/4 cup water
- ✓ garlic powder - 1 1/2tsp.

Directions:
1. Clean the chicken by washing thoroughly and pat dry with paper towels.
2. Use a glass dish to blend the pepper, paprika, garlic powder, onion powder, salt, and Italian seasoning.
3. Rub approximately 1 tablespoon of the spices into the pieces of chicken to cover entirely.
4. Blend the cornstarch, flour, and spices by shaking in a large ziplock bag.
5. In a separate dish, combine the eggs, hot sauce, water, and milk until integrated.
6. Completely cover the spiced chicken in the flour and then immerse in the eggs.
7. Coat in the flour for a second time and set on a tray for approximately 15 minutes.
8. Before transferring the chicken to the air fryer, spray liberally with olive oil and space the pieces out, frying a separate batch if required.
9. Adjust the temperature to 350° F for approximately 18 minutes.
10. Take the chicken out and set on a plate. Wait about 5 minutes before serving.

157. Pepperoni Pizza

Prep.Time: 5 min - **Cooking Time:** 6 min - **Servings:** 1

Ingredients:
- ✓ 1 mini naan flatbread
- ✓ 2 tbsp. pizza sauce
- ✓ 7 slices mini pepperoni
- ✓ 1 tbsp. olive oil
- ✓ 2 tbsp. mozzarella cheese, shredded

Directions:
6. Prepare the naan flatbread by brushed the olive oil on the top.
7. Layer the naan with pizza sauce, mozzarella cheese, and pepperoni.
8. Transfer to the frying basket and set the air fryer to the temperature of 375°F.
9. Heat for approximately 6 minutes and enjoy immediately.

158. Tuna Patties

Prep.Time: 10 min - **Cooking Time:** 12 min - **Servings:** 2

Ingredients:
- ✓ garlic powder - 1 tsp.
- ✓ tuna - 2 cans, in water
- ✓ dill seasoning - 1 tsp.
- ✓ all-purpose flour - 4 tsp.
- ✓ salt - 1/4 tsp.
- ✓ mayonnaise - 4 tsp.
- ✓ lemon juice - 2 tbsp.
- ✓ onion powder - 1/2 tsp.
- ✓ pepper - 1/4 tsp.

Directions:
1. Set the temperature of the air fryer to 400°F.
2. Combine the almond flour, mayonnaise, salt, onion powder, dill, garlic powder and pepper using a food blender for approximately 30 seconds until incorporated.
3. Empty the canned tuna and lemon juice into the blender and pulse for an additional 30 seconds until integrated fully.
4. Divide evenly into 4 sections and create patties by hand.
5. Transfer to the fryer basket in a single layer and heat for approximately 12 minutes.

159. Stuffed Bell Peppers

Prep.Time: 15 min - Cooking Time: 18 min - Servings: 2

Ingredients:
- ✓ medium onion - 1/2, chopped
- ✓ cheddar cheese - 4 oz., shredded
- ✓ pepper - 1/2 tsp.
- ✓ ground beef - 8 oz.
- ✓ olive oil - 1 tsp.
- ✓ tomato sauce - 4 oz.
- ✓ Worcestershire sauce - 1 tsp.
- ✓ medium green peppers - 2, stems and seeds discarded
- ✓ salt - 1 tsp., separated
- ✓ water - 4 cups
- ✓ garlic - 1 clove, minced

Directions:
1. Boil the water in pot steam the green peppers with the tops and seeds removed with 1/2 teaspoon of the salt. Move from the burner after approximately 3 minutes and drain.
2. Pat the peppers with paper towels to properly dry.
3. In a hot frying pan, melt the olive oil and toss the garlic and onion for approximately 2 minutes until browned. Drain thoroughly.
4. Set the air fryer temperature to 400°F to warm up.
5. Using a glass dish, blend the beef along with Worcestershire sauce, 2 ounces of tomato sauce, salt, vegetables, 2 ounces of cheddar cheese and pepper until fully incorporated.
6. Spoon the mixture evenly into the peppers and drizzle the remaining 2 ounces of tomato sauce on top. Then dust with the remaining 2 ounces of cheddar cheese.
7. Assemble the peppers in the basket of the air fryer and heat fully for approximately 18 minutes. The meat should be fully cooked before removing.
8. Place on a platter and serve immediately.

160. Ham and Cheese Sandwich

Prep.Time: 20 min - Cooking Time: 17 min - Servings: 2

Ingredients:
- ✓ 2 eggs
- ✓ 4 slices of bread of choice
- ✓ 4 slices turkey
- ✓ 4 slices ham
- ✓ 6 tbsp. half and half cream
- ✓ 2 tsp. melted butter
- ✓ 4 slices Swiss cheese
- ✓ ¼ tsp. pure vanilla extract
- ✓ Powdered sugar and raspberry jam for serving

Directions:
1. Mix the eggs, vanilla and cream in a bowl and set aside.
2. Make a sandwich with the bread layered with cheese slice, turkey, ham, cheese slice and the top slice of bread to make two sandwiches. Gently press on the sandwiches to somewhat flatten them.
3. Set your air fryer toast oven to 350 degrees F.
4. Spread out kitchen aluminum foil and cut it about the same size as the sandwich and spread the melted butter on the surface of the foil.
5. Dip the sandwich in the egg mixture and let it soak for about 20 seconds on each side. Repeat this for the other sandwich. Place the soaked sandwiches on the prepared foil sheets then place on the basket in your fryer.
6. Cook for 12 minutes then flip the sandwiches and brush with the remaining butter and cook for another 5 minutes or until well browned.
7. Place the cooked sandwiched on a plate and top with the powdered sugar and serve with a small bowl of raspberry jam. Enjoy!

161. Mushroom Sticks

Prep.Time: 10 min - Cooking Time: 25 minutes - Servings: 2

Ingredients:
- ✓ 2 cups whole mushrooms
- ✓ 1 big lemon-juiced
- ✓ 1 tbsp. ginger-garlic paste
- ✓ For seasoning, use salt and red chili powder in small amounts
- ✓ ½ tsp. carom
- ✓ One or two papadums
- ✓ 4 or 5 tbsp. corn flour
- ✓ 1 cup of water

Directions:
1. Make a mixture of lemon juice, red chili powder, salt, ginger garlic paste and carom to use as a marinade. Let the cottage cheese pieces marinate in the mixture for some time and then roll them in dry corn flour. Leave them aside for around 20 minutes.
2. Take the papadum into a pan and roast them. Once they are cooked, crush them into very small pieces. Now take another container and pour around 100 ml of water into it. Dissolve 2 tbsp. of corn flour in this water. Dip the cottage cheese pieces in this solution of corn flour and roll them on to the pieces of crushed papadum so that the papadum sticks to the cottage cheese.
3. Pre heat the Air Fryer for 10 minutes at 290 Fahrenheit. Then open the basket of the fryer and place the cottage cheese pieces inside it. Close the basket properly. Let the fryer stay at 160 degrees for another 20 minutes. Halfway through, open the basket and toss the cottage cheese around a bit to allow for uniform cooking. Once they are done, you can serve it either with ketchup or mint chutney. Another recommended side is mint chutney.

162. Mushroom Wonton

Prep.Time: 15 min - Cooking Time: 20 min - Servings: 2

Ingredients:
- ✓ 1 ½ cup all-purpose flour
- ✓ ½ tsp. salt or to taste
- ✓ 5 tbsp. water
- *For filling:*
- ✓ 2 cups cubed mushroom
- ✓ 2 tbsp. oil
- ✓ 2 tsp. ginger-garlic paste
- ✓ 2 tsp. soya sauce
- ✓ 2 tsp. vinegar

Directions:
1. Knead the dough and cover it with plastic wrap and set aside. Next, cook the ingredients for the filling and try to ensure that the mushroom is covered well with the sauce.
2. Roll the dough and place the filling in the center. Now, wrap the dough to cover the filling and pinch the edges together.
3. Pre heat the Air fryer at 200° F for 5 minutes. Place the dumplings in the fry basket and close it. Let them cook at the same temperature for another 20 minutes. Recommended sides are chili sauce or ketchup.

163. Asparagus Flat Cakes

Prep.Time: 15 min - **Cooking Time:** 25 min - **Servings:** 2

Ingredients:
- ✓ 2 tbsp. garam masala
- ✓ 2 cups sliced asparagus
- ✓ 3 tsp. ginger finely chopped
- ✓ 1-2 tbsp. fresh coriander leaves
- ✓ 2 or 3 green chilies finely chopped
- ✓ 1 ½ tbsp. lemon juice
- ✓ Salt and pepper to taste

Directions:
1. Mix the ingredients in a clean bowl and add water to it. Make sure that the paste is not too watery but is enough to apply on the asparagus.
2. Pre heat the Air Fryer at 160 degrees Fahrenheit for 5 minutes. Place the galettes in the fry basket and let them cook for another 25 minutes at the same temperature. Keep rolling them over to get a uniform cook. Serve either with mint chutney or ketchup.

164. Mushroom Patties

Prep.Time: 15 min - **Cooking Time:** 12 min - **Servings:** 2

Ingredients:
- ✓ 1 cup minced mushroom
- ✓ A pinch of salt to taste
- ✓ ¼ tsp. ginger finely chopped
- ✓ 1 green chili finely chopped
- ✓ 1 tsp. lemon juice
- ✓ 1 tbsp. fresh coriander leaves
- ✓ ¼ tsp. red chili powder
- ✓ ¼ tsp. cumin powder

Directions:
1. Mix the ingredients together and ensure that the flavors are right. You will now make round patties with the mixture and roll them out well.
2. Pre heat the Air Fryer at 250 Fahrenheit for 5 minutes. Open the basket of the Fryer and arrange the patties in the basket. Close it carefully. Keep the fryer at 150 degrees for around 10 or 12 minutes. In between the cooking process, turn the patties over to get a uniform cook. Serve hot with mint chutney.

165. Asparagus Galette

Prep.Time: 10 min - **Cooking Time:** 25 minutes - **Servings:** 2

Ingredients:
- ✓ 2 cups minced asparagus
- ✓ 3 tsp. ginger finely chopped
- ✓ 1-2 tbsp. fresh coriander leaves
- ✓ 2 or 3 green chilies finely chopped
- ✓ 1 ½ tbsp. lemon juice
- ✓ Salt and pepper to taste

Directions:
1. Mix the ingredients in a clean bowl.
2. Mold this mixture into round and flat galettes.
3. Wet the galettes slightly with water.
4. Pre heat the Air Fryer at 160 degrees Fahrenheit for 5 minutes. Place the galettes in the fry basket and let them cook for another 25 minutes at the same temperature. Keep rolling them over to get a uniform cook. Serve either with mint chutney or ketchup.

166. Amaranthus Galette

Prep.Time: 10 min - **Cooking Time:** 25 min - **Servings:** 2

Ingredients:
- ✓ 2 cups minced amaranthus
- ✓ 3 tsp. ginger finely chopped
- ✓ 1-2 tbsp. fresh coriander leaves
- ✓ 2 or 3 green chilies finely chopped
- ✓ 1 ½ tbsp. lemon juice
- ✓ Salt and pepper to taste

Directions:
1. Mix the ingredients in a clean bowl.
2. Mold this mixture into round and flat galettes.
3. Wet the galettes slightly with water.
4. Pre heat the Air Fryer at 160 degrees Fahrenheit for 5 minutes. Place the galettes in the fry basket and let them cook for another 25 minutes at the same temperature. Keep rolling them over to get a uniform cook. Serve either with mint chutney or ketchup.

167. Colacasia Gnocchis

Prep.Time: 15 min - **Cooking Time:** 20 min - **Servings:** 2

Ingredients:

For dough:
- ✓ 1 ½ cup all-purpose flour
- ✓ ½ tsp. salt
- ✓ 5 tbsp. water

For filling:
- ✓ 2 cups minced colacasia
- ✓ 2 tbsp. oil
- ✓ 2 tsp. ginger-garlic paste
- ✓ 2 tsp. soya sauce
- ✓ 2 tsp. vinegar

Directions:
1. Knead the dough and cover it with plastic wrap and set aside. Next, cook the ingredients for the filling and try to ensure that the colacasia is covered well with the sauce.
2. Roll the dough and place the filling in the center. Now, wrap the dough to cover the filling and pinch the edges together.
3. Pre heat the Air fryer at 200° F for 5 minutes. Place the gnocchis in the fry basket and close it. Let them cook at the same temperature for another 20 minutes. Recommended sides are chili sauce or ketchup.

168. Yam Galette

Prep.Time: 10 min - **Cooking Time:** 25 min - **Servings:** 2

Ingredients:
- ✓ 2 cups minced yam
- ✓ 3 tsp. ginger finely chopped
- ✓ 1-2 tbsp. fresh coriander leaves
- ✓ 2 or 3 green chilies finely chopped
- ✓ 1 ½ tbsp. lemon juice
- ✓ Salt and pepper to taste

Directions:
1. Mix the ingredients in a clean bowl.
2. Mold this mixture into round and flat galettes.
3. Wet the galettes slightly with water.
4. Pre heat the Air Fryer at 160 degrees Fahrenheit for 5 minutes. Place the galettes in the fry basket and let them cook for another 25 minutes at the same temperature. Keep rolling them over to get a uniform cook. Serve either with mint chutney or ketchup.

169. Okra Flat Cakes

Prep.Time: 10 min - Cooking Time: 25 min - Servings: 2

Ingredients:
- ✓ 2 tbsp. garam masala
- ✓ 2 cups sliced okra
- ✓ 3 tsp. ginger finely chopped
- ✓ 1-2 tbsp. fresh coriander leaves
- ✓ 2 or 3 green chilies finely chopped
- ✓ 1 ½ tbsp. lemon juice
- ✓ Salt and pepper to taste

Directions:
1. Mix the ingredients in a clean bowl and add water to it. Make sure that the paste is not too watery but is enough to apply on the okra.
2. Pre heat the Air Fryer at 160 degrees Fahrenheit for 5 minutes. Place the galettes in the fry basket and let them cook for another 25 minutes at the same temperature. Keep rolling them over to get a uniform cook. Serve either with mint chutney or ketchup.

170. Gherkins Flat Cakes

Prep.Time: 10 min - Cooking Time: 25 min - Servings: 2

Ingredients:
- ✓ 2 tbsp. garam masala
- ✓ 2 cups sliced gherkins
- ✓ 3 tsp. ginger finely chopped
- ✓ 1-2 tbsp. fresh coriander leaves
- ✓ 2 or 3 green chilies finely chopped
- ✓ 1 ½ tbsp. lemon juice
- ✓ Salt and pepper to taste

Directions:
1. Mix the ingredients in a clean bowl and add water to it. Make sure that the paste is not too watery but is enough to apply on the gherkin.
2. Pre heat the Air Fryer at 160 degrees Fahrenheit for 5 minutes. Place the galettes in the fry basket and let them cook for another 25 minutes at the same temperature. Keep rolling them over to get a uniform cook. Serve either with mint chutney or ketchup.

171. Fenugreek Galette

Prep.Time: 10 min - Cooking Time: 25 minutes - Servings: 2

Ingredients:
- ✓ 2 cups fenugreek
- ✓ 2 medium potatoes boiled and mashed
- ✓ 3 tsp. ginger finely chopped
- ✓ 1-2 tbsp. fresh coriander leaves
- ✓ 2 or 3 green chilies finely chopped
- ✓ 1 ½ tbsp. lemon juice
- ✓ Salt and pepper to taste

Directions:
1. Mix the ingredients in a clean bowl.
2. Mold this mixture into round and flat galettes.
3. Wet the galettes slightly with water.
4. Pre heat the Air Fryer at 160 degrees Fahrenheit for 5 minutes. Place the galettes in the fry basket and let them cook for another 25 minutes at the same temperature. Keep rolling them over to get a uniform cook. Serve either with mint chutney or ketchup.

172. Vegetable Skewer

Prep.Time: 10 min - Cooking Time: 25 min - Servings: 2

Ingredients:
- ✓ 2 cups mixed vegetables
- ✓ 3 onions chopped
- ✓ 5 green chilies
- ✓ 1 ½ tbsp. ginger paste
- ✓ 1 ½ tsp. garlic paste
- ✓ 1 ½ tsp. salt
- ✓ 3 tbsp. cream
- ✓ 3 eggs
- ✓ 2 ½ tbsp. white sesame seeds

Directions:
1. Grind the ingredients except for the egg and form a smooth paste. Coat the vegetables in the paste. Now, beat the eggs and add a little salt to it.
2. Dip the coated vegetables in the egg mixture and then transfer to the sesame seeds and coat the vegetables well. Place the vegetables on a stick.
3. Pre heat the Air fryer at 160 degrees Fahrenheit for around 5 minutes. Place the sticks in the basket and let them cook for another 25 minutes at the same temperature. Turn the sticks over in between the cooking process to get a uniform cook.

173. Aloo Patties

Prep.Time: 10 min - Cooking Time: 12 min - Servings: 2

Ingredients:
- ✓ 1 cup mashed potato
- ✓ A pinch of salt to taste
- ✓ ¼ tsp. ginger finely chopped
- ✓ 1 green chili finely chopped
- ✓ 1 tsp. lemon juice
- ✓ 1 tbsp. fresh coriander leaves
- ✓ ¼ tsp. red chili powder
- ✓ ¼ tsp. cumin powder

Directions:
1. Mix the ingredients together and ensure that the flavors are right. You will now make round patties with the mixture and roll them out well.
2. Pre heat the Air Fryer at 250 Fahrenheit for 5 minutes. Open the basket of the Fryer and arrange the patties in the basket. Close it carefully. Keep the fryer at 150 degrees for around 10 or 12 minutes. In between the cooking process, turn the patties over to get a uniform cook. Serve hot with mint chutney.

174. Broccoli Momos

Prep.Time: 10 min - Cooking Time: 20 min - Servings: 2

Ingredients:

For dough:
- ✓ 1 ½ cup all-purpose flour
- ✓ ½ tsp. salt
- ✓ 5 tbsp. water

For filling:
- ✓ 2 cups grated broccoli
- ✓ 2 tbsp. oil
- ✓ 2 tsp. ginger-garlic paste
- ✓ 2 tsp. soya sauce
- ✓ 2 tsp. vinegar

Directions:
1. Knead the dough and cover it with plastic wrap and set aside. Next, cook the ingredients for the filling and try to ensure that the broccoli is covered well with the sauce.
2. Roll the dough and cut it into a square. Place the filling in the center. Now, wrap the dough to cover the filling and pinch the edges together.
3. Pre heat the Air fryer at 200° F for 5 minutes. Place the gnocchis in the fry basket and close it. Let them cook at the same temperature for another 20 minutes. Recommended sides are chili sauce or ketchup.

175. Cottage Cheese Croquette
Prep.Time: 15 min - **Cooking Time:** 15 min - **Servings:** 2

Ingredients:
- ✓ 2 packets cottage cheese cubed

1st Marinade:
- ✓ 3 tbsp. vinegar or lemon juice
- ✓ 2 or 3 tsp. paprika
- ✓ 1 tsp. black pepper
- ✓ 1 tsp. salt
- ✓ 3 tsp. ginger-garlic paste

2nd Marinade:
- ✓ 1 cup yogurt
- ✓ 4 tsp. tandoori masala
- ✓ 2 tbsp. dry fenugreek leaves
- ✓ 1 tsp. black salt
- ✓ 1 tsp. chat masala
- ✓ 1 tsp. garam masala powder
- ✓ 1 tsp. red chili powder
- ✓ 1 tsp. salt
- ✓ 3 drops of red color

Directions:
1. Make the first marinade and soak the cubed cottage cheese in it for four hours. While this is happening, make the second marinade and soak the cottage cheese in it overnight to let the flavors blend.
2. Pre heat the Air fryer at 160 degrees Fahrenheit for 5 minutes. Place the fingers in the fry basket and close it. Let them cook at the same temperature for another 15 minutes or so. Toss the fingers well so that they are cooked uniformly. Serve them with mint chutney.

176. Aloo Tikka
Prep.Time: 30 min - **Cooking Time:** 40 min - **Servings:** 2-4

Ingredients:
- ✓ 4 medium potatoes (cut them into cubes)
- ✓ 1 big capsicum (Cut this capsicum into big cubes)
- ✓ 1 onion (Cut it into quarters. Now separate the layers carefully.)
- ✓ 5 tbsp. gram flour
- ✓ A pinch of salt to taste

For chutney:
- ✓ 2 cup fresh green coriander
- ✓ ½ cup mint leaves
- ✓ 4 tsp. fennel
- ✓ 2 tbsp. ginger-garlic paste
- ✓ 1 small onion
- ✓ 6-7 flakes garlic (optional)
- ✓ Salt to taste
- ✓ 3 tbsp. lemon juice

Directions:
1. Take a clean and dry container. Put into it the coriander, mint, fennel, and ginger, onion/garlic, salt and lemon juice. Mix them. Pour the mixture into a grinder and blend until you get a thick paste.
2. Now move on to the potato pieces. Slit these pieces almost till the end and leave them aside. Now stuff all the pieces with the paste that was obtained from the previous step. Now leave the stuffed potato aside.
3. Take the chutney and add to it the gram flour and some salt. Mix them together properly. Rub this mixture all over the stuffed potato pieces. Now leave the cottage cheese aside.
4. Now, to the leftover chutney, add the capsicum and onions. Apply the chutney generously on each of the pieces of capsicum and onion. Now take satay sticks and arrange the potato pieces and vegetables on separate sticks.
5. Pre heat the Air Fryer at 290 Fahrenheit for around 5 minutes. Open the basket. Arrange the satay sticks properly. Close the basket. Keep the sticks with the cottage cheese at 180 degrees for around half an hour while the sticks with the vegetables are to be kept at the same temperature for only 7 minutes. Turn the sticks in between so that one side does not get burnt and also to provide a uniform cook.

177. Garlic Toast with Cheese
Prep.Time: 20 min - **Cooking Time:** 10 minutes - **Servings:** 2-4

Ingredients:
- ✓ Take some French bread and cut it into slices

Garlic butter:
- ✓ 2 tbsp. softened butter
- ✓ 4-5 flakes crushed garlic
- ✓ A pinch of salt to taste
- ✓ ½ tsp. black pepper powder

Topping:
- ✓ ¾ cup grated cheese
- ✓ 2 tsp. of oregano seasoning
- ✓ Some red chili flakes to sprinkle on top
- ✓ 1 tbsp. olive oil (Optional)

Directions:
1. Take a clean and dry container. Place all the ingredients mentioned under the heading "Garlic Butter" into it and mix properly to obtain garlic butter.
2. On each slice of the French bread, spread some of this garlic butter. Sprinkle some cheese on top of the layer of butter. Pour some oil if wanted. Sprinkle some chili flakes and some oregano.
3. Pre heat the Air Fryer at 240 Fahrenheit for around 5 minutes. Open the fry basket and place the bread in it making sure that no two slices touch each other. Close the basket and continue to cook the bread at 160 degrees for another 10 minutes to toast the bread well.

178. Masala French Fries
Prep.Time: 10 min - **Cooking Time:** 25 min - **Servings:** 2

Ingredients:
- ✓ 2 medium sized potatoes peeled and cut into thick pieces lengthwise

Ingredients for the marinade:
- ✓ 1 tbsp. olive oil
- ✓ 1 tsp. mixed herbs
- ✓ ½ tsp. red chili flakes
- ✓ A pinch of salt to taste
- ✓ 1 tbsp. lemon juice

Directions:
1. Boil the potatoes and blanch them. Cut the potato into fingers. Mix the ingredients for the marinade and add the potato fingers to it making sure that they are coated well.
2. Pre heat the Air Fryer for around 5 minutes at 300 Fahrenheit. Take out the basket of the fryer and place the potato fingers in them. Close the basket. Now keep the fryer at 200 Fahrenheit for 20 or 25 minutes. In between the process, toss the fries twice or thrice so that they get cooked properly.

179. Baked Macaroni Pasta
Prep.Time: 20 min - **Cooking Time:** 10 min - **Servings:** 2

Ingredients:
- ✓ 1 cup pasta
- ✓ 7 cups of boiling water
- ✓ 1 ½ tbsp. olive oil
- ✓ A pinch of salt

For tossing pasta:
- ✓ 1 ½ tbsp. olive oil
- ✓ ½ cup carrot small pieces
- ✓ Salt and pepper to taste
- ✓ ½ tsp. oregano
- ✓ ½ tsp. basil

For white sauce:
- ✓ 2 tbsp. olive oil
- ✓ 2 tbsp. all-purpose flour
- ✓ 2 cups of milk
- ✓ 1 tsp. dried oregano
- ✓ ½ tsp. dried basil
- ✓ ½ tsp. dried parsley
- ✓ Salt and pepper to taste

Directions:
1. Boil the pasta and sieve it when done. You will need to toss the pasta in the ingredients mentioned above and set aside.
2. For the sauce, add the ingredients to a pan and bring the ingredients to a boil. Stir the sauce and continue to simmer to make a thicker sauce. Add the pasta to the sauce and transfer this into a glass bowl garnished with cheese.
3. Pre heat the Air Fryer at 160 degrees for 5 minutes. Place the bowl in the basket and close it. Let it continue to cook at the same temperature for 10 minutes more. Keep stirring the pasta in between.

180. Macaroni Samosa
Prep.Time: 20 min - **Cooking Time:** 35 min - **Servings:** 2

Ingredients:
For wrappers:
- ✓ 1 cup all-purpose flour
- ✓ 2 tbsp. unsalted butter
- ✓ A pinch of salt to taste
- ✓ Take the amount of water sufficient enough to make a stiff dough

For filling:
- ✓ 3 cups boiled macaroni
- ✓ 2 onion sliced
- ✓ 2 capsicum sliced
- ✓ 2 carrot sliced
- ✓ 2 cabbage sliced
- ✓ 2 tbsp. soya sauce
- ✓ 2 tsp. vinegar
- ✓ 2 tbsp. ginger finely chopped
- ✓ 2 tbsp. garlic finely chopped
- ✓ 2 tbsp. green chilies finely chopped
- ✓ 2 tbsp. ginger-garlic paste
- ✓ Some salt and pepper to taste
- ✓ 2 tbsp. olive oil
- ✓ ½ tsp. ajinomoto

Directions:
1. Mix the dough for the outer covering and make it stiff and smooth. Leave it to rest in a container while making the filling.
2. Cook the ingredients in a pan and stir them well to make a thick paste. Roll the paste out.
3. Roll the dough into balls and flatten them. Cut them in halves and add the filling. Use water to help you fold the edges to create the shape of a cone.
4. Pre-heat the Air Fryer for around 5 to 6 minutes at 300 Fahrenheit. Place all the samosas in the fry basket and close the basket properly. Keep the Air Fryer at 200 degrees for another 20 to 25 minutes. Around the halfway point, open the basket and turn the samosas over for uniform cooking. After this, fry at 250 degrees for around 10 minutes in order to give them the desired golden brown color. Serve hot. Recommended sides are tamarind or mint chutney.

181. Stuffed Capsicum Baskets
Prep.Time: 20 min - **Cooking Time:** 20 minutes - **Servings:** 2

Ingredients:
For baskets:
- ✓ 3-4 long capsicum
- ✓ ½ tsp. salt
- ✓ ½ tsp. pepper powder

For filling:
- ✓ 1 medium onion finely chopped
- ✓ 1 green chili finely chopped
- ✓ 2 or 3 large potatoes boiled and mashed
- ✓ 1 ½ tbsp. chopped coriander leaves
- ✓ 1 tsp. fenugreek
- ✓ 1 tsp. dried mango powder
- ✓ 1 tsp. cumin powder
- ✓ Salt and pepper to taste

For topping:
- ✓ 3 tbsp. grated cheese
- ✓ 1 tsp. red chili flakes
- ✓ ½ tsp. oregano
- ✓ ½ tsp. basil
- ✓ ½ tsp. parsley

Directions:
1. Take all the ingredients under the heading "Filling" and mix them together in a bowl.
2. Remove the stem of the capsicum. Cut off the caps. Remove the seeds as well. Sprinkle some salt and pepper on the inside of the capsicums. Leave them aside for some time.
3. Now fill the hollowed out capsicums with the filling prepared but leave a small space at the top. Sprinkle grated cheese and also add the seasoning. Pre heat the Air Fryer at 140 degrees Fahrenheit for 5 minutes. Put the capsicums in the fry basket and close it. Let them cook at the same temperature for another 20 minutes. Turn them over in between to prevent over cooking.

182. Barbeque Corn Sandwich
Prep.Time: 15 min - **Cooking Time:** 15 min - **Servings:** 1

Ingredients:
- ✓ 2 slices of white bread
- ✓ 1 tbsp. softened butter
- ✓ 1 cup sweet corn kernels
- ✓ 1 small capsicum

For Barbeque Sauce:
- ✓ ¼ tbsp. Worcestershire sauce
- ✓ ½ tsp. olive oil
- ✓ ½ flake garlic crushed
- ✓ ¼ cup chopped onion
- ✓ ¼ tbsp. red chili sauce
- ✓ ½ cup water

Directions:
1. Take the slices of bread and remove the edges. Now cut the slices horizontally.
2. Cook the ingredients for the sauce and wait till it thickens. Now, add the corn to the sauce and stir till it obtains the flavors. Roast the capsicum and peel the skin off. Cut the capsicum into slices. Apply the sauce on the slices.
3. Pre-heat the Air Fryer for 5 minutes at 300 Fahrenheit. Open the basket of the Fryer and place the prepared sandwiches in it such that no two sandwiches are touching each other. Now keep the fryer at 250 degrees for around 15 minutes. Turn the sandwiches in between the cooking process to cook both slices. Serve the sandwiches with tomato ketchup or mint chutney.

183. Roasted Garlic Bacon And Potatoes

Prep.Time: 5 min - **Cooking Time:** 25 min - **Servings:** 4

Ingredients:
- ✓ 4 medium sized potatoes, peeled and cut into 2
- ✓ 4 strips of streaky bacon
- ✓ 2 sprigs of rosemary
- ✓ 6 cloves of garlic, smashed, unpeeled
- ✓ 3 teaspoons of vegetable oil

Directions:
1. Preheat Air-fryer to 390°F.
2. Put the smashed garlic, bacon, potatoes, rosemary and then the oil in a bowl. Stir thoroughly.
3. Place into air-fryer basket and roast until golden for about 25 minutes.

184. Meat, Corn And Potato Barbecue

Prep.Time: 3 min - **Cooking Time:** 27 min - **Servings:** 4

Ingredients:
- ✓ 2 pork belly bacon slices
- ✓ 2 sausages
- ✓ 1 corn on the cob
- ✓ 1 mealy potato
- ✓ 2 spare ribs
- ✓ 2 shasliks
- ✓ Salt and pepper to taste
- ✓ Barbecue sauce

Directions:
1. Heat the air-fryer to 392°F. Put the potato in it and cook for 15 minutes.
2. Put in the corn and meat-shasliks, pork bacons, sausages and spare ribs and grill for 12 minutes.
3. Remove and sprinkle with salt and pepper. Serve with barbecue sauce and vegetable salad.

185. Pork Chops With Pineapple-Jalapeno Salsa

Prep.Time: 20 min - **Cooking Time:** 20 minutes - **Servings:** 3

Ingredients:
- ✓ 3 pieces of Pork Chops (roughly 10 ounces each)
- ✓ 2 tablespoon of finely chopped parsley
- ✓ 1 tablespoon of ground Coriander
- ✓ ¾ cup of olive oil
- ✓ 1 tablespoon of finely chopped rosemary
- ✓ 4 ounces of tomatoes, diced
- ✓ 2 cloves of garlic, chopped
- ✓ 4 ounces of pineapple, diced
- ✓ 8 Jalapenos
- ✓ 3 teaspoons of Dijon Mustard
- ✓ 1½ teaspoons of sugar
- ✓ 4 ounces of lemon juice
- ✓ 3 tablespoons of finely chopped Cilantro
- ✓ 2½ teaspoons of salt

Directions:
1. Put the rosemary, sugar, mustard, coriander, ¼ cup of olive oil, 1 tablespoon of cilantro, 1 ½ teaspoons of salt and 1 table spoon of parsley into a mixing bowl and mix thoroughly. Add the pork chops and stir.
2. Pour the marinade into a re-sealable plastic bag and place in a refrigerator for about 3 hours.
3. Heat your air-fryer to 390°F.
4. Put the jalapenos in a bowl and toss with 1 teaspoon of oil to coat them evenly. Transfer the jalapenos into the air-fryer and cook for about 7 minutes. Remove from fryer and set aside to cool.
5. When cooled, peel, remove the seeds, and chop the jalapenos into fine pieces and transfer to a mixing bowl. Add the pineapple, tomatoes, garlic, and lemon juice, the rest of the oil, parsley, cilantro and salt. Stir and set the salsa aside.
6. Remove the pork chops from the fridge and leave to stand for 30 minutes at room temperature before cooking.
7. Place the chops in the air-fryer and roast at 390°F for about 12 minutes. The pork chops are properly cooked when the internal temperature is 140°F

186. Japanese Fried Pork Chops

Prep.Time: 5 min - **Cooking Time:** 30 min - **Servings:** 1

Ingredients:
- ✓ 1 tablespoon of oil
- ✓ 2 packets of pork loin well pounded
- ✓ 1 egg
- ✓ Bread crumbs Flour
- ✓ 1 teaspoon black pepper
- 1 teaspoon salt

Directions:
1. Preheat the air fryer to 390F. Rub the pork with salt and pepper and leave for 30 minutes to marinate.
2. Beat the egg in a bowl; place bread crumbs and flour and plates. Now coat the pork with egg, then the flour and then the breadcrumbs.
3. Place pork in the air fryer cook for 15 minutes. Serve and Enjoy

187. Cheesy Bacon Stuffed Potatoes

Prep.Time: 15 min - **Cooking Time:** 36 min - **Servings:** 4

Ingredients:
- ✓ 4 medium sized potatoes, peeled and halved
- ✓ 1 small onion, chopped
- ✓ 2 rashers of bacon
- ✓ 4 ounces of cheese, grated
- ✓ 2 tablespoons of olive oil

Directions:
1. Heat air-fryer to 356°F
2. Using a brush, coat the potatoes with oil and cook for 10 minutes in air fryer. Repeat this 2 more times until potatoes are well baked.
3. Put the onions and bacon into a skillet and sauté gently on medium heat. Stir and remove from heat. Add 2 ounces of the cheese and stir.
4. Scrape out some of the cooked potatoes from the center and fill with the stuffing. Top with remaining cheese.
5. Place stuffed potatoes back into the air fryer and cook until the cheese melts for 6 minutes.

188. Air-fried Roast Pork

Prep.Time: 4 hours - **Cooking Time:** 55 min - **Servings:** 4

Ingredients:
- ✓ 2 lb pork belly, washed and pat dry
- ✓ 1 teaspoon salt
- ✓ 1.5 teaspoon rosemary

For Dry Rub:
- ✓ 2 teaspoon garlic and onion seasoning
- ✓ 1 teaspoon white pepper
- ✓ 1.5 teaspoon five-spice powder

For Rubbing Only:
- ✓ 2 tablespoons lemon juice
- ✓ About 1/2 a teaspoon
- ✓ salt

Directions:
1. Place the washed pork on a steamer rack over a plate. Blanch the pork belly with boiled water for 12 minutes. Pat dry and air-dry for 3 hours.
2. Meanwhile, combine all ingredients of the dry rub except the lemon.
3. After 3 hours, use a fork to poke holes all over the pork belly skin. Do not make it too deep; about 5mm deep is just fine. Flip pork and make 3 to 4 straight cuts into it, about 0.5 inches deep.
4. Now, massage the dry rub mixture over the meat part. Flip pork and rub salt on the skin surface. Squeeze the lemon juice over.
5. Preheat air-fryer at 160°F for 5 minutes. Cook pork belly for 30 minutes. Increase temperature to 180°F and keep air-frying for 25 minutes.
6. Cut meat and enjoy.

189. BBQ Pork Strips

Prep.Time: 4 hours - **Cooking Time:** 55 minutes - **Servings:** 4

Ingredients:
- ✓ 16 packets pork loin chops
- ✓ 1 tsp balsamic vinegar
- ✓ 2 tbsp soy sauce
- ✓ 2 tbsp honey
- ✓ 1 clove garlic, finely chopped
- ✓ 1/4 tsp ground ginger or 1/2 tsp freshly grated ginger
- ✓ Freshly ground pepper

Directions:
1. Tenderize the chops and season with pepper.
2. Prepare the marinade by combining the honey, balsamic vinegar and soy sauce in a bowl. Add the ginger and garlic into the mixture and stir thoroughly to mix. Set to one side.
3. Combine pork chops and the marinade mixture and le it marinate for 2 hours or overnight.
4. Preheat the Air-fryer at 350°F for 5 minutes.
5. Finally, air-baked the chops in the baking tray along with the marinade juice for 5-8 minutes per side until it well-cooked and golden brown.

190. Mushroom Pasta

Prep.Time: 15 min - **Cooking Time:** 10 min - **Servings:** 2

Ingredients:
- ✓ 1 cup pasta
- ✓ 1 ½ tbsp. olive oil
- ✓ A pinch of salt

For tossing pasta:
- ✓ 1 ½ tbsp. olive oil
- ✓ Salt and pepper to taste
- ✓ ½ tsp. oregano
- ✓ ½ tsp. basil

For sauce:
- ✓ 2 tbsp. olive oil
- ✓ 2 cups sliced mushroom
- ✓ 2 tbsp. all-purpose flour
- ✓ 2 cups of milk
- ✓ 1 tsp. dried oregano
- ✓ ½ tsp. dried basil
- ✓ ½ tsp. dried parsley
- ✓ Salt and pepper to taste

Directions:
1. Boil the pasta and sieve it when done. You will need to toss the pasta in the ingredients mentioned above and set aside.
2. For the sauce, add the ingredients to a pan and bring the ingredients to a boil. Stir the sauce and continue to simmer to make a thicker sauce. Add the pasta to the sauce and transfer this into a glass bowl garnished with cheese.
3. Pre heat the Air Fryer at 160 degrees for 5 minutes. Place the bowl in the basket and close it. Let it continue to cook at the same temperature for 10 minutes more. Keep stirring the pasta in between.

191. Cottage Cheese and Mushroom Burritos

Prep.Time: 30 min - **Cooking Time:** 15 min - **Servings:** 2-4

Ingredients:

Refried beans:
- ✓ ½ cup red kidney beans (soaked overnight)
- ✓ ½ small onion chopped
- ✓ 1 tbsp. olive oil
- ✓ 2 tbsp. tomato puree
- ✓ ¼ tsp. red chili powder
- ✓ 1 tsp. of salt to taste
- ✓ 4-5 flour tortillas

Vegetable Filling:
- ✓ ½ cup mushrooms thinly sliced
- ✓ 1 cup cottage cheese cut in to long and slightly thick fingers
- ✓ A pinch of salt to taste
- ✓ ½ tsp. red chili flakes
- ✓ 1 tsp. freshly ground peppercorns
- ✓ ½ cup pickled jalapenos

Salad:
- ✓ 1-2 lettuce leaves shredded.
- ✓ 1 or 2 spring onions chopped finely. Also cut the greens.
- ✓ Take one tomato. Remove the seeds and chop it into small pieces.
- ✓ 1 green chili chopped.
- ✓ 1 cup of cheddar cheese grated.

To serve:
- ✓ 1 cup boiled rice (not necessary).
- ✓ A few flour tortillas to put the filing in

Directions:

1. Cook the beans along with the onion and garlic and mash them finely.
2. Now, make the sauce you will need for the burrito. Ensure that you create a slightly thick sauce.
3. For the filling, you will need to cook the ingredients well in a pan and ensure that the vegetables have browned on the outside.
4. To make the salad, toss the ingredients together.
5. Place the tortilla and add a layer of sauce, followed by the beans and the filling at the center. Before you roll it, you will need to place the salad on top of the filling.
6. Pre-heat the Air Fryer for around 5 minutes at 200 Fahrenheit. Open the fry basket and keep the burritos inside. Close the basket properly. Let the Air Fryer remain at 200 Fahrenheit for another 15 minutes or so. Halfway through, remove the basket and turn all the burritos over in order to get a uniform cook.

192. Cheese and Mushroom Kebab

Prep.Time: 20 min - **Cooking Time:** 30 min - **Servings:** 2-4

Ingredients:
- ✓ 2 cups sliced mushrooms
- ✓ 1-2 green chilies chopped finely
- ✓ ¼ tsp. red chili powder
- ✓ A pinch of salt to taste
- ✓ ½ tsp. dried mango powder
- ✓ ¼ tsp. black salt
- ✓ 1-2 tbsp. all-purpose flour for coating purposes
- ✓ 1-2 tbsp. mint
- ✓ 1 cup molten cheese
- ✓ 1 onion that has been finely chopped
- ✓ ½ cup milk

Directions:

1. Take the mushroom slices and add the grated ginger and the cut green chilies. Grind this mixture until it becomes a thick paste. Keep adding water as and when required. Now add the onions, mint, the breadcrumbs and all the various masalas required. Mix this well until you get a soft dough. Now take small balls of this mixture (about the size of a lemon) and mold them into the shape of flat and round kebabs.
2. Here is where the milk comes into play. Pour a very small amount of milk onto each kebab to wet it. Now roll the kebab in the dry breadcrumbs.
3. Pre heat the Air Fryer for 5 minutes at 300 Fahrenheit. Take out the basket. Arrange the kebabs in the basket leaving gaps between them so that no two kebabs are touching each other. Keep the fryer at 340 Fahrenheit for around half an hour. Half way through the cooking process, turn the kebabs over so that they can be cooked properly. Recommended sides for this dish are mint chutney, tomato ketchup or yoghurt chutney.

193. Mushroom Club Sandwich

Prep.Time: 15 min - **Cooking Time:** 15 minutes - **Servings:** 1

Ingredients:
- ✓ 2 slices of white bread
- ✓ 1 tbsp. softened butter
- ✓ 1 cup minced mushroom
- ✓ 1 small capsicum

For Barbeque Sauce:
- ✓ ¼ tbsp. Worcestershire sauce
- ✓ ½ tsp. olive oil
- ✓ ½ flake garlic crushed
- ✓ ¼ cup chopped onion
- ✓ ¼ tbsp. red chili sauce
- ✓ ½ cup water

Directions:

1. Take the slices of bread and remove the edges. Now cut the slices horizontally.
2. Cook the ingredients for the sauce and wait till it thickens. Now, add the mushroom to the sauce and stir till it obtains the flavors. Roast the capsicum and peel the skin off. Cut the capsicum into slices. Apply the sauce on the slices.
3. Pre-heat the Air Fryer for 5 minutes at 300 Fahrenheit. Open the basket of the Fryer and place the prepared sandwiches in it such that no two sandwiches are touching each other. Now keep the fryer at 250 degrees for around 15 minutes. Turn the sandwiches in between the cooking process to cook both slices. Serve the sandwiches with tomato ketchup or mint chutney.

194. Asparagus Kebab

Prep.Time: 20 min - **Cooking Time:** 25 min - **Servings:** 4

Ingredients:
- ✓ 2 cups sliced asparagus
- ✓ 3 onions chopped
- ✓ 5 green chilies-roughly chopped
- ✓ 1 ½ tbsp. ginger paste
- ✓ 1 ½ tsp. garlic paste
- ✓ 1 ½ tsp. salt
- ✓ 3 tsp. lemon juice
- ✓ 2 tsp. garam masala
- ✓ 3 eggs
- ✓ 2 ½ tbsp. white sesame seeds

Directions:

1. Grind the ingredients except for the egg and form a smooth paste. Coat the asparagus in the paste. Now, beat the eggs and add a little salt to it.
2. Dip the coated apricots in the egg mixture and then transfer to the sesame seeds and coat the asparagus. Place the vegetables on a stick.
3. Pre heat the Air fryer at 160 degrees Fahrenheit for around 5 minutes. Place the sticks in the basket and let them cook for another 25 minutes at the same temperature. Turn the sticks over in between the cooking process to get a uniform cook.

195. Cottage Cheese Samosa

Prep.Time: 30 min - **Cooking Time:** 35 min - **Servings:** 2-4

Ingredients:

For wrappers:
- ✓ 2 tbsp. unsalted butter
- ✓ 1 ½ cup all-purpose flour
- ✓ A pinch of salt to taste
- ✓ Water

For filling:
- ✓ 2 cups mashed cottage cheese
- ✓ ¼ cup boiled peas
- ✓ 1 tsp. powdered ginger
- ✓ 1 or 2 green chilies that are finely chopped or mashed

- ✓ ½ tsp. cumin
- ✓ 1 tsp. coarsely crushed coriander
- ✓ 1 dry red chili broken into pieces
- ✓ A small amount of salt (to taste)
- ✓ ½ tsp. dried mango powder
- ✓ ½ tsp. red chili power
- ✓ 1-2 tbsp. coriander

Directions:

1. Mix the dough for the outer covering and make it stiff and smooth. Leave it to rest in a container while making the filling.
2. Cook the ingredients in a pan and stir them well to make a thick paste. Roll the paste out.
3. Roll the dough into balls and flatten them. Cut them in halves and add the filling. Use water to help you fold the edges to create the shape of a cone.
4. Pre-heat the Air Fryer for around 5 to 6 minutes at 300 Fahrenheit. Place all the samosas in the fry basket and close the basket properly. Keep the Air Fryer at 200 degrees for another 20 to 25 minutes. Around the halfway point, open the basket and turn the samosas over for uniform cooking. After this, fry at 250 degrees for around 10 minutes in order to give them the desired golden brown color. Serve hot. Recommended sides are tamarind or mint chutney.

196. Tuna Sandwich

Prep.Time: 15 min - **Cooking Time:** 15 min - **Servings:** 1

Ingredients:
- ✓ 2 slices of white bread
- ✓ 1 tbsp. softened butter
- ✓ 1 tin tuna
- ✓ 1 small capsicum

For Barbeque Sauce:
- ✓ ¼ tbsp. Worcestershire sauce
- ✓ ½ tsp. olive oil
- ✓ ¼ tsp. mustard powder

- ✓ ½ flake garlic crushed
- ✓ ¼ cup chopped onion
- ✓ ½ tbsp. sugar
- ✓ 1 tbsp. tomato ketchup
- ✓ ½ cup water.
- ✓ ¼ tbsp. red chili sauce
- ✓ A pinch of salt and black pepper to taste

Directions:

1. Take the slices of bread and remove the edges. Now cut the slices horizontally.
2. Cook the ingredients for the sauce and wait till it thickens. Now, add the lamb to the sauce and stir till it obtains the flavors. Roast the capsicum and peel the skin off. Cut the capsicum into slices. Mix the ingredients together and apply it to the bread slices.
3. Pre-heat the Air Fryer for 5 minutes at 300 Fahrenheit. Open the basket of the Fryer and place the prepared sandwiches in it such that no two sandwiches are touching each other. Now keep the fryer at 250 degrees for around 15 minutes. Turn the sandwiches in between the cooking process to cook both slices.
4. Serve the sandwiches with tomato ketchup or mint chutney.

197. Yam Kebab

Prep.Time: 20 min - **Cooking Time:** 25 minutes - **Servings:** 2-4

Ingredients:
- ✓ 2 cups sliced yam
- ✓ 3 onions chopped
- ✓ 5 green chilies-roughly chopped
- ✓ 1 ½ tbsp. ginger paste
- ✓ 1 ½ tsp. garlic paste
- ✓ 1 ½ tsp. salt
- ✓ 3 tsp. lemon juice

- ✓ 2 tsp. garam masala
- ✓ 4 tbsp. chopped coriander
- ✓ 3 tbsp. cream
- ✓ 3 tbsp. chopped capsicum
- ✓ 3 eggs
- ✓ 2 ½ tbsp. white sesame seeds

Directions:

1. Grind the ingredients except for the egg and form a smooth paste. Coat the yam in the paste. Now, beat the eggs and add a little salt to it.
2. Dip the coated vegetables in the egg mixture and then transfer to the sesame seeds and coat the yam well. Place the vegetables on a stick.
3. Pre heat the Air fryer at 160 degrees Fahrenheit for around 5 minutes. Place the sticks in the basket and let them cook for another 25 minutes at the same temperature. Turn the sticks over in between the cooking process to get a uniform cook.

198. Oyster Club Sandwich

Prep.Time: 15 min - **Cooking Time:** 15 min - **Servings:** 1

Ingredients:
- ✓ 2 slices of white bread
- ✓ 1 tbsp. softened butter
- ✓ ½ lb. shelled oyster
- ✓ 1 small capsicum

For Barbeque Sauce:
- ✓ ¼ tbsp. Worcestershire sauce
- ✓ ½ tsp. olive oil
- ✓ ½ flake garlic crushed

- ✓ ¼ cup chopped onion
- ✓ ¼ tsp. mustard powder
- ✓ 1 tbsp. tomato ketchup
- ✓ ½ tbsp. sugar
- ✓ ¼ tbsp. red chili sauce
- ✓ ½ cup water.
- ✓ A pinch of salt and black pepper to taste

Directions:

1. Take the slices of bread and remove the edges. Now cut the slices horizontally.
2. Cook the ingredients for the sauce and wait till it thickens. Now, add the oyster to the sauce and stir till it obtains the flavors. Roast the capsicum and peel the skin off. Cut the capsicum into slices. Mix the ingredients together and apply it to the bread slices.
3. Pre-heat the Air Fryer for 5 minutes at 300 Fahrenheit. Open the basket of the Fryer and place the prepared sandwiches in it such that no two sandwiches are touching each other. Now keep the fryer at 250 degrees for around 15 minutes. Turn the sandwiches in between the cooking process to cook both slices. Serve the sandwiches with tomato ketchup or mint chutney.

199. Seafood Pizza

Prep.Time: 15 min - **Cooking Time:** 10-12 min - **Servings:** 1

Ingredients:
- ✓ One pizza base
- ✓ Grated pizza cheese (mozzarella cheese preferably) for topping
- ✓ Some pizza topping sauce
- ✓ Use cooking oil for brushing and topping purposes

Ingredients for topping:
- ✓ 2 onions chopped
- ✓ 2 cups mixed seafood
- ✓ 2 capsicums chopped
- ✓ 2 tomatoes that have been deseeded and chopped
- ✓ 1 tbsp. (optional) mushrooms/corns
- ✓ 2 tsp. pizza seasoning
- ✓ Some cottage cheese that has been cut into small cubes (optional)

Directions:
1. Put the pizza base in a pre-heated Air fryer for around 5 minutes. (Pre heated to 340 Fahrenheit).
2. Take out the base. Pour some pizza sauce on top of the base at the center. Using a spoon spread the sauce over the base making sure that you leave some gap around the circumference. Grate some mozzarella cheese and sprinkle it over the sauce layer.
3. Take all the vegetables and the seafood and mix them in a bowl. Add some oil and seasoning. Also add some salt and pepper according to taste. Mix them properly. Put this topping over the layer of cheese on the pizza. Now sprinkle some more grated cheese and pizza seasoning on top of this layer.
4. Pre heat the Air Fryer at 250 Fahrenheit for around 5 minutes. Open the fry basket and place the pizza inside. Close the basket and keep the fryer at 170 degrees for another 10 minutes. If you feel that it is undercooked you may put it at the same temperature for another 2 minutes or so.

200. Morning Paneer Pizza - KETO

Prep.Time: 20 min - **Cooking Time:** 3-5 min - **Servings:** 1-2

Ingredients:
- ✓ 7 and ¼ ounces Paneer
- ✓ ¼ onion
- ✓ 1 cube cheese
- ✓ ½ carrot
- ✓ Salt and pepper to taste
- ✓ ¼ tomato
- ✓ 1 capsicum
- ✓ 1 teaspoon corn

Directions:
1. Pre-heat your fryer to 360-degree F.
2. Wash and dry your paneer.
3. Mix flour with water and make and knead to make nice dough.
4. Add paneer to the dough and knead again.
5. Take a bowl and make a filling of onion, tomato and carrot.
6. Add capsicum, salt and pepper to the mixture.
7. Transfer the mixture to your kneaded dough and spread carefully.
8. Transfer the prepared pizza to your Air Fryer and bake for 3 minutes.
9. Serve and enjoy with a garnish of your favorite herbs.

201. Cheesed Up Omelette - KETO

Prep.Time: 5 min - **Cooking Time:** 13 minutes - **Servings:** 2

Ingredients:
- ✓ 2 eggs
- ✓ Pepper
- ✓ Grated Cheddar
- ✓ Onion
- ✓ Coconut Amino

Directions:
1. Preheat your Air Fryer up to 340-degree F
2. Clean and chop onion
3. Take a plate and cover with 2 teaspoons amino
4. Transfer into the Air Fryer and cook for 8 minutes
5. Beat eggs and add pepper with salt
6. Pour the egg mixture on onions and cook the mix in your Air Fryer for 3 minutes more
7. Add cheddar cheese and bake for 2 minutes more
8. Serve with fresh basil leaves

202. Japanese Omelette - KETO

Prep.Time: 15 min - **Cooking Time:** 10 min - **Servings:** 2

Ingredients:
- ✓ 1 small Japanese tofu
- ✓ 3 eggs
- ✓ Pepper
- ✓ 1 teaspoon coriander
- ✓ 1 teaspoon cumin
- ✓ 2 tablespoons coconut amino
- ✓ 2 tablespoons green onion
- ✓ Olive oil

Directions:
1. Preheat your Air Fryer up to 400-degree F
2. Clean and chop onion
3. Beat eggs and add with amino, pepper, oil, salt and mix
4. Take special baking forms and cut tofu into cubes and place in the baking forms
5. Add egg mixture
6. Transfer into the Air Fryer and cook for 10 minutes
7. Serve with fresh herbs

203. Spiced Up Air Fried Buffalo Wings - KETO

Prep.Time: 10 min - **Cooking Time:** 30 min - **Servings:** 2

Ingredients:
- ✓ 4 pounds chicken wings
- ✓ ½ cup cayenne pepper sauce
- ✓ ½ cup coconut oil
- ✓ 1 tablespoon Worcestershire sauce
- ✓ 1 teaspoon salt

Directions:
1. Take a mixing cup and add cayenne pepper sauce, coconut oil, Worcestershire sauce and salt
2. Mix well and keep it on the side
3. Pat the chicken dry and transfer to your fryer
4. Cook for 25 minutes at 380-degree F, making sure to shake the basket once
5. Increase the temperature to 400-degree F and cook for 5 minutes more
6. Remove them and dump into a large sized mixing bowl
7. Add the prepared sauce and toss well
8. Serve with celery sticks and enjoy!

204. Creamy Onion Chicken - KETO

Prep.Time: 10 min - **Cooking Time:** 55 min - **Servings:** 4

Ingredients:
- ✓ 4 chicken breasts
- ✓ 1 and ½ cup onion soup mix
- ✓ 1 cup mushroom soup
- ✓ ½ cup cream

Directions:
1. Pre-heat your Fryer to 400-degree F.
2. Take a frying pan and place it over low heat.
3. Add mushrooms, onion mix and cream.
4. Heat up the mixture for 1 minute.
5. Pour the warm mixture over chicken and let it sit for 25 minutes.
6. Transfer your marinade chicken to Air Fryer cooking basket and cook for 30 minutes.
7. Serve with remaining cream and enjoy!

205. Crunchy Mustard Chicken - KETO

Prep.Time: 10 min - **Cooking Time:** 40 minutes - **Servings:** 4

Ingredients:
- ✓ 12 chicken wings
- ✓ 2 tbsp water
- ✓ 1 tbsp sazon seasoning
- ✓ 1 tbsp adobo seasoning
- ✓ 1 tsp salt

Directions:
1. Pre-heat your Air Fryer to 350-degree F
2. Take a bowl and add garlic, salt, cloves, almond meal, pepper, olive oil, melted butter and lemon zest
3. Take another bowl and mix mustard and wine
4. Place chicken slices in the wine mixture and then in the crumb mixture
5. Transfer prepared chicken to your Air Fryer cooking basket and cook for 40 minutes.
6. Serve and enjoy!

206. Caprese Chicken with Balsamic Sauce - KETO

Prep.Time: 10 min - **Cooking Time:** 20 min - **Servings:** 2

Ingredients:
- ✓ 6 chicken breasts
- ✓ 6 basil leaves
- ✓ ¼ cup balsamic vinegar
- ✓ 6 slices tomato
- ✓ 1 tablespoon butter
- ✓ 6 slices mozzarella cheese

Directions:
1. Pre-heat your Fryer to 400-degree F.
2. Take a frying pan and place it over medium heat, add butter and balsamic vinegar and let it melt.
3. Cover the chicken meat with the marinade.
4. Transfer chicken to your Air Fryer cooking basket and cook for 20 minutes.
5. Cover cooked chicken with basil, tomato slices and cheese.
6. Serve and enjoy!

207. Hearty Green Beans – KETO

Prep.Time: 10 min - **Cooking Time:** 10-12 min - **Servings:** 2

Ingredients:
- ✓ 1-pound green beans, washed and de-stemmed
- ✓ 1 lemon
- ✓ Pinch of salt
- ✓ ¼ teaspoon oil

Directions:
1. Add beans to your Air Fryer cooking basket
2. Squeeze a few drops of lemon
3. Season with salt and pepper
4. Drizzle olive oil on top
5. Cook for 10-12 minutes at 400 degrees F
6. Once done, serve and enjoy!

208. Roasted Up Brussels - KETO

Prep.Time: 15 min - **Cooking Time:** 15 min - **Servings:** 2

Ingredients:
- ✓ 1 block Brussels sprouts
- ✓ ½ teaspoon garlic
- ✓ 2 teaspoons olive oil
- ✓ ½ teaspoon pepper
- ✓ Salt as needed

Directions:
1. Pre-heat your Fryer to 390-degree F.
2. Remove leaves off the chokes, leaving only the head.
3. Wash and dry the sprouts well.
4. Make a mixture of olive oil, salt and pepper with garlic.
5. Cover sprouts with marinade and let them rest for 5 minutes.
6. Transfer coated sprouts to Air Fryer and cook for 15 minutes.
7. Serve and enjoy!

209. Roasted Brussels and Pine Nuts - KETO

Prep.Time: 2 hours - **Cooking Time:** 15 min - **Servings:** 3-4

Ingredients:
- ✓ 15 ounces Brussels sprouts
- ✓ 1 tablespoon olive oil
- ✓ 1 and ¾ ounces raisins, drained
- ✓ Juice of 1 orange
- ✓ 1 and ¾ ounces toasted pine nuts

Directions:
1. Take a pot of boiling water and add sprouts and boil them for 4 minutes.
2. Transfer the sprouts to cold water and drain them well.
3. Place them in a freezer and cool them.
4. Take your raisins and soak them in orange juice for 20 minutes.
5. Pre-heat your Air Fryer to a temperature of 392F.
6. Take a pan and pour oil and stir the sprouts.
7. Take the sprouts and transfer them to your Air Fryer.
8. Roast for 15 minutes.
9. Serve the sprouts with pine nuts, orange juice and raisins!

210. Low Calorie Beets Dish - KETO

Prep.Time: 15 min - **Cooking Time:** 10 min - **Servings:** 2-4

Ingredients:
- ✓ 4 whole beets
- ✓ 1 tablespoon balsamic vinegar
- ✓ 1 tablespoon olive oil
- ✓ Salt and pepper to taste
- ✓ 2 springs rosemary

Directions:
1. Wash your beets and peel them
2. Cut beets into cubes
3. Take a bowl and mix in rosemary, pepper, salt, vinegar
4. Cover beets with the prepared sauce
5. Coat the beets with olive oil
6. Pre-heat your Fryer to 400-degree F
7. Transfer beets to Air Fryer cooking basket and cook for 10 minutes
8. Serve with your cheese sauce and enjoy!

211. Parmesan Cabbage Wedges - KETO

Prep.Time: 10 min - **Cooking Time:** 20 minutes - **Servings:** 2

Ingredients:
- ✓ ½ a head cabbage
- ✓ 2 cups parmesan
- ✓ 4 tbsp melted butter
- ✓ Salt and pepper to taste

Directions:
1. Pre-heat your Air Fryer to 380-degree F.
2. Take a bowl and add melted butter and season with salt and pepper.
3. Cover cabbages with your melted butter.
4. Coat cabbages with parmesan.
5. Transfer the coated cabbages to your Air Fryer and bake for 20 minutes.
6. Serve with cheesy sauce and enjoy!

212. Extreme Zucchini Fries

Prep.Time: 10 min - **Cooking Time:** 20 min - **Servings:** 2

Ingredients:
- ✓ 3 medium zucchinis, sliced
- ✓ 2 egg whites
- ✓ ½ cup seasoned almond meal
- ✓ 2 tablespoons grated parmesan cheese
- ✓ Cooking spray as needed
- ✓ ¼ teaspoon garlic powder
- ✓ Salt and pepper to taste

Directions:
1. Pre-heat your Fryer to 425-degree F.
2. Take the Air Fryer cooking basket and place a cooling rack.
3. Coat the rack with cooking spray.
4. Take a bowl and add egg whites, beat it well and season with some pepper and salt.
5. Take another bowl and add garlic powder, cheese and almond meal
6. Take the Zucchini sticks and dredge them in the egg and finally breadcrumbs.
7. Transfer the Zucchini to your cooking basket and spray a bit of oil.
8. Bake for 20 minutes and serve with Ranch sauce.
9. Enjoy!

POULTRY RECIPES

1. Healthy Chicken Popcorn

Prep.Time: 10 min - Cooking Time: 15 min - Servings: 2

Ingredients:
- ✓ 1 lb chicken breast, skinless, boneless, and cut into 1-inch pieces
- ✓ 1 egg, lightly beaten
- ✓ ½ tbsp Tabasco sauce
- ✓ 1 cup buttermilk
- ✓ 1 tsp baking powder
- ✓ 1 cup all-purpose flour
- ✓ ½ tsp pepper
- ✓ 1 tsp salt

Directions:
10. Season chicken pieces with pepper and salt.
11. In a medium bowl, mix together all-purpose flour and baking powder.
12. In another mixing bowl, mix together egg, buttermilk, and Tabasco sauce.
13. Coat chicken with flour mixture then dip chicken into the egg mixture then again coat with flour mixture.
14. Place coated chicken pieces on instant vortex air fryer tray. Spray coated chicken pieces with cooking spray.
15. Air fry chicken popcorn at 400 F for 10 minutes. Turn chicken popcorn to another side and air fry for 5 minutes more.
16. Serve and enjoy.

2. Delicious Rotisserie Chicken

Prep.Time: 10 min - Cooking Time: 50 min - Servings: 6

Ingredients:
- ✓ 3 lbs whole chicken
- ✓ ¾ tsp garlic powder
- ✓ ¼ cup olive oil
- ✓ 2 cups buttermilk
- ✓ Pepper
- ✓ Salt

Directions:
9. Mix together garlic powder, olive oil, buttermilk, pepper, and salt in a large zip-lock bag.
10. Add whole chicken in bag. Seal bag and marinate the chicken overnight.
11. Remove marinated chicken from bag and season with pepper and salt.
12. Place marinated chicken on the rotisserie spit and inset into the instant vortex air fryer oven.
13. Air fry chicken to 380 F for 50 minutes or until the internal temperature of chicken reaches 165 F.
14. Serve and enjoy.

3. Cuban Chicken Wings

Prep.Time: 10 min - Cooking Time: 35 minutes - Servings: 2

Ingredients:
- ✓ 12 chicken wings
- ✓ 2 tbsp water
- ✓ 1 tbsp sazon seasoning
- ✓ 1 tbsp adobo seasoning
- ✓ 1 tsp salt

Directions:
7. Place chicken wings in a large mixing bowl.
8. Add remaining ingredients over chicken and toss until chicken is well coated.
9. Add chicken into the rotisserie basket and place basket into the instant vortex air fryer.
10. Air fry chicken at 375 F for 35 minutes.
11. Serve and enjoy.

4. Tasty Lemon Chicken

Prep.Time: 10 min - Cooking Time: 8 min - Servings: 2

Ingredients:
- ✓ 1 lb chicken breasts, skinless and boneless
- ✓ 2 tbsp fresh lemon juice
- ✓ 1 tsp garlic, minced
- ✓ 3 tbsp butter, melted
- ✓ 1 tsp Italian seasoning
- ✓ 1 tbsp olive oil
- ✓ ½ tsp pepper
- ✓ 1 tsp salt

Directions:
10. In a mixing bowl, mix together lemon juice, garlic, butter, Italian seasoning, olive oil, pepper, and salt.
11. Add chicken to the mixing bowl and coat well.
12. Spray instant vortex air fryer tray with cooking spray.
13. Place chicken on tray and air fry at 400 F for 4 minutes.
14. Turn chicken to the other side and cook for 4 minutes more.
15. Serve and enjoy.

5. Herbed Turkey Breast

Prep.Time: 10 min - Cooking Time: 50 min - Servings: 6

Ingredients:
- ✓ 3 lbs turkey breast
- ✓ 3 garlic cloves, minced
- ✓ 1 tbsp fresh sage leaves, chopped
- ✓ 1 tbsp rosemary leaves, chopped
- ✓ 1 tbsp fresh thyme
- ✓ 3 tbsp butter
- ✓ 1 tsp lemon zest, grated
- ✓ ½ tsp pepper
- ✓ 1 tsp kosher salt

Directions:
7. In a bowl, mix together butter, garlic, sage, rosemary, thyme, lemon zest, pepper, and salt.
8. Rub the butter mixture all over the turkey breast.
9. Place turkey breast into the bottom rack of instant vortex air fryer and cook at 350 F for 20 minutes.
10. Turn turkey breast to the other side and cook for 30 minutes more or until the internal temperature of turkey breast reaches 160 F.
11. Slice and serve.

6. Cheesy Chicken

Prep.Time: 15 min - Cooking Time: 13 min - Servings: 2

Ingredients:
- ✓ ½ cup Italian breadcrumbs
- ✓ 2 tbsp grated Parmesan cheese
- ✓ 1 tbsp butter, melted
- ✓ 4 chicken thighs
- ✓ ½ cup marinara sauce
- ✓ ½ cup shredded Monterrey Jack cheese

Directions:
8. Spray the frying basket with cooking spray. In a bowl, mix the crumbs and Parmesan cheese. Pour the butter into another bowl. Brush the thighs with butter. Dip each one into the crumbs mixture, until well-coated.
9. Arrange two chicken thighs in the air fryer, and lightly spray with cooking oil. Cook for 5 minutes at 380 F. Flip over, top with a few tbsp of marinara sauce and shredded Monterrey Jack cheese.
10. Cook for 4 minutes. Repeat with the remaining thighs.

7. Picante Chicken Wings

Prep.Time: 70 min - Cooking Time: 32 min - Servings: 4

Ingredients:

- ✓ 2 lb chicken wings
- ✓ 1 tbsp olive oil
- ✓ 3 cloves garlic, minced
- ✓ 1 tbsp chili powder
- ✓ ½ tbsp cinnamon powder
- ✓ ½ tsp allspice
- ✓ 1 habanero pepper, seeded
- ✓ 1 tbsp soy sauce
- ✓ ½ tbsp white pepper
- ✓ ¼ cup red wine vinegar
- ✓ 3 tbsp lime juice
- ✓ 2 scallions, chopped
- ✓ ½ tbsp grated ginger
- ✓ ½ tbsp chopped fresh thyme
- ✓ ⅓ tbsp sugar
- ✓ ½ tbsp salt

Directions:

1. In a bowl, add the olive oil, soy sauce, garlic, habanero pepper, allspice, cinnamon powder, cayenne pepper, white pepper, salt, sugar, thyme, ginger, scallions, lime juice, and red wine vinegar; mix well.
2. Add the chicken wings to the marinade mixture and coat it well with the mixture. Cover the bowl with cling film and refrigerate the chicken to marinate for 1 hour.
3. Preheat the Air Fryer oven to 400 F.
4. Remove the chicken from the fridge, drain all the liquid, and pat each wing dry using a paper towel. Place half of the wings in the basket and cook for 16 minutes. Shake halfway through. Remove onto a serving platter and repeat the cooking process for the remaining wings. Serve with blue cheese dip or ranch dressing.

8. Buttered Stuffed Chicken

Prep.Time: 10 min - Cooking Time: 40 min - Servings: 2

Ingredients:

- ✓ 1 small chicken
- ✓ 1 ½ tbsp olive oil
- ✓ Salt and black pepper to taste
- ✓ 1 cup breadcrumbs
- ✓ ⅓ cup chopped sage
- ✓ ⅓ cup chopped thyme
- ✓ 2 cloves garlic, crushed
- ✓ 1 brown onion, chopped
- ✓ 3 tbsp butter
- ✓ 2 eggs, beaten

Directions:

1. Rinse the chicken gently, pat dry with a paper towel and remove any excess fat with a knife; set aside.
2. On a stove top, place a pan. Add butter, garlic and onion and sauté to brown. Add eggs, sage, thyme, pepper, and salt. Mix well.
3. Cook for 20 seconds and turn the heat off. Stuff the chicken with the mixture into the cavity.
4. Then, tie the legs of the spatchcock with a butcher's twine and brush with olive oil. Rub the top and sides of the chicken generously with salt and pepper. Preheat the Air Fryer oven to 390 F.
5. Place the spatchcock into the frying basket and roast for 25 minutes.
6. Turn the chicken over and continue cooking for 10-15 minutes more; check throughout the cooking time to ensure it doesn't dry or overcooks.
7. Remove onto a chopping board and wrap it with aluminum foil; let rest for 10 minutes. Serve with a side of steamed broccoli.

9. Whole Chicken with Pancetta and Lemon

Prep.Time: 30 min - Cooking Time: 30 minutes - Servings: 4

Ingredients:

- ✓ 1 small whole chicken
- ✓ 1 lemon
- ✓ 4 slices pancetta, roughly chopped
- ✓ 1 onion, chopped
- ✓ 1 sprig fresh thyme
- ✓ Olive oil
- ✓ Salt and black pepper

Directions:

1. In a bowl, mix pancetta, onion, thyme, salt, and black pepper. Pat dry the chicken with. Insert the pancetta mixture into chicken's cavity and press tight.
2. Put in the whole lemon, and rub the top and sides of the chicken with salt and black pepper. Spray the frying basket with olive oil and arrange the chicken inside.
3. Cook for 30 minutes on 400 F, turning once halfway through.

10. Chicken Drumsticks with Coconut Cream

Prep.Time: 20 min - Cooking Time: 6 min - Servings: 2

Ingredients:

- ✓ 4 chicken drumsticks, boneless, skinless
- ✓ 2 tbsp green curry paste
- ✓ 3 tbsp coconut cream
- ✓ Salt and black pepper
- ✓ ½ fresh jalapeno chili, finely chopped
- ✓ A handful of fresh parsley, roughly chopped

Directions:

1. In a bowl, add drumsticks, paste, cream, salt, black pepper and jalapeno; coat the chicken well.
2. Arrange the drumsticks in the frying basket and cook for 6 minutes at 400 F, flipping once halfway through. Serve with fresh cilantro.

11. Maple Chicken Breasts with Rosemary

Prep.Time: 10min - Cooking Time: 20 min - Servings: 2

Ingredients:
- ✓ 2 tbsp Dijon mustard
- ✓ 1 tbsp maple syrup
- ✓ 2 tsp minced fresh rosemary
- ✓ Salt and black pepper to taste
- ✓ 2 chicken breasts, boneless, skinless

Directions:
1. In a bowl, mix mustard, maple syrup, rosemary, salt, and pepper. Rub mixture onto chicken. Spray generously the air fryer basket generously with cooking spray.
2. Arrange the breasts inside the frying basket and cook for 20 minutes, turning once halfway through.

12. Juicy Chicken Breasts

Prep.Time: 20 min - Cooking Time: 15 min - Servings: 2

Ingredients:
- ✓ 2 chicken breasts
- ✓ Salt and black pepper to taste
- ✓ 1 cup flour
- ✓ 3 eggs
- ✓ ½ cup apple cider vinegar
- ✓ ½ tbsp ginger paste
- ✓ ½ tbsp garlic paste
- ✓ 1 tbsp sugar
- ✓ 2 red chilies, minced
- ✓ 2 tbsp tomato puree
- ✓ 1 red pepper
- ✓ 1 green pepper
- ✓ 1 tbsp paprika
- ✓ 4 tbsp water

Directions:
1. Preheat the Air Fryer oven to 350 F. Put the chicken breasts on a clean flat surface. Cut them in cubes. Pour the flour in a bowl, crack the eggs in, add the salt and pepper; whisk. Put the chicken in the flour mixture; mix to coat.
2. Place the chicken in the frying basket, spray with cooking spray, and fry for 8 minutes. Pull out the basket, shake to toss, and spray again with cooking spray. Keep cooking for 7 minutes or until golden and crispy.
3. Remove the chicken to a plate. Put the red, yellow, and green peppers on a chopping board. Using a knife, cut open and deseed them; cut the flesh in long strips.
4. In a bowl, add the water, apple cider vinegar, sugar, ginger and garlic puree, red chili, tomato puree, and smoked paprika; mix with a fork.
5. Place a skillet over medium heat on a stovetop and spray with cooking spray. Add the chicken and pepper strips. Stir and cook until the peppers are sweaty but still crunchy.
6. Pour the chili mixture on the chicken, stir, and bring to simmer for 10 minutes; turn off the heat. Dish the chicken chili sauce into a serving bowl and serve.

13. Garlic Chicken Skewers

Prep.Time: 15 min - Cooking Time: 20 minutes - Servings: 3

Ingredients:
- ✓ 3 chicken breasts
- ✓ Salt to season
- ✓ 1 tbsp chili powder
- ✓ ¼ cup maple syrup
- ✓ ½ cup soy sauce
- ✓ 2 red peppers
- ✓ 1 green pepper
- ✓ 7 mushrooms
- ✓ 2 tbsp sesame seeds
- ✓ 1 garlic clove
- ✓ 2 tbsp olive oil
- ✓ Zest and juice from 1 lime
- ✓ A pinch of salt
- ✓ ¼ cup fresh parsley, chopped

Directions:
1. Put the chicken breasts on a clean flat surface and cut them in 2-inch cubes with a knife. Add them to a bowl, along with the chili powder, salt, maple syrup, soy sauce, sesame seeds, and spray them with cooking spray.
2. Toss to coat and set aside. Place the peppers on the chopping board. Use a knife to open, deseed and cut in cubes.
3. Likewise, cut the mushrooms in halves. Start stacking up the ingredients - stick 1 red pepper, then green, a chicken cube, and a mushroom half.
4. Repeat the arrangement until the skewer is full. Repeat the process until all the ingredients are used. Preheat the Air Fryer oven to 330 F.
5. Brush the kabobs with soy sauce mixture and place them into the fryer basket. Grease with cooking spray and grill for 20 minutes; flip halfway through.
6. Meanwhile, mix all salsa verde ingredients in your food processor and blend until you obtain a chunky paste.
7. Remove the kabobs when ready and serve with a side of salsa verde.

14. Flavorful Chicken Drumsticks

Prep.Time: 10 min - Cooking Time: 30 min - Servings: 4

Ingredients:
- ✓ 8 chicken drumsticks
- ✓ ¼ tsp cayenne pepper
- ✓ 1 tbsp onion powder
- ✓ 1 tbsp garlic powder
- ✓ 1 ½ tbsp honey
- ✓ 1 ½ tbsp fresh lemon juice
- ✓ 1 tbsp Worcestershire sauce
- ✓ ¼ cup soy sauce, low-sodium
- ✓ 1 tbsp sesame oil
- ✓ 2 tbsp olive oil
- ✓ ½ tsp kosher salt

Directions:
1. Add all ingredients except chicken in a large mixing bowl and mix well.
2. Add chicken drumsticks to the bowl and mix until well coated.
3. Place chicken drumsticks on the instant vortex air fryer rack air fry at 400 F for 15 minutes.
4. Turn chicken drumsticks to another side and cook for 15 minutes more.
5. Serve and enjoy.

15. Creamy Coconut Chicken

Prep.Time: 120 min - **Cooking Time:** 25 min - **Servings:** 4

Ingredients:
- ✓ 4 big chicken legs
- ✓ 5 teaspoons turmeric powder
- ✓ 2 tablespoons ginger, grated
- ✓ Salt and black pepper to the taste
- ✓ 4 tablespoons coconut cream

Directions:
1. In a bowl, mix cream with turmeric, ginger, salt and pepper, whisk, add chicken pieces, toss them well and leave aside for 2 hours.
2. Transfer chicken to your preheated air fryer, cook at 370 degrees F for 25 minutes, divide among plates and serve with a side salad.

Nutrition: calories 300 - Fat 4 - Fiber 12 - Carbs 22 - Protein 20

16. Chinese Chicken Wings

Prep.Time: 120 min - **Cooking Time:** 15 min - **Servings:** 6

Ingredients:
- ✓ 16 chicken wings
- ✓ 2 tablespoons honey
- ✓ 2 tablespoons soy sauce
- ✓ Salt and black pepper to the taste
- ✓ ¼ teaspoon white pepper
- ✓ 3 tablespoons lime juice

Directions:
1. In a bowl, mix honey with soy sauce, salt, black and white pepper and lime juice, whisk well, add chicken pieces, toss to coat and keep in the fridge for 2 hours.
2. Transfer chicken to your air fryer, cook at 370 degrees F for 6 minutes on each side, increase heat to 400 degrees F and cook for 3 minutes more.
3. Serve hot.

Nutrition: calories 372 - Fat 9 - Fiber 10 - Carbs 37 - Protein 24

17. Herbed Chicken

Prep.Time: 30 min - **Cooking Time:** 40 minutes - **Servings:** 4

Ingredients:
- ✓ 1 whole chicken
- ✓ Salt and black pepper to the taste
- ✓ 1 teaspoon garlic powder
- ✓ 1 teaspoon onion powder
- ✓ ½ teaspoon thyme, dried
- ✓ 1 teaspoon rosemary, dried
- ✓ 1 tablespoon lemon juice
- ✓ 2 tablespoons olive oil

Directions:
1. Season chicken with salt and pepper, rub with thyme, rosemary, garlic powder and onion powder, rub with lemon juice and olive oil and leave aside for 30 minutes.
2. Put chicken in your air fryer and cook at 360 degrees F for 20 minutes on each side.
3. Leave chicken aside to cool down, carve and serve.

Nutrition: calories 390 - Fat 10 - Fiber 5 - Carbs 22 - Protein 20

18. Chicken Parmesan

Prep.Time: 10 min - **Cooking Time:** 15 min - **Servings:** 4

Ingredients:
- ✓ 2 cups panko bread crumbs
- ✓ ¼ cup parmesan, grated
- ✓ ½ teaspoon garlic powder
- ✓ 2 cups white flour
- ✓ 1 egg, whisked
- ✓ 1 and ½ pounds chicken cutlets, skinless and boneless
- ✓ Salt and black pepper to the taste
- ✓ 1 cup mozzarella, grated
- ✓ 2 cups tomato sauce
- ✓ 3 tablespoons basil, chopped

Directions:
1. In a bowl, mix panko with parmesan and garlic powder and stir.
2. Put flour in a second bowl and the egg in a third.
3. Season chicken with salt and pepper, dip in flour, then in egg mix and in panko.
4. Put chicken pieces in your air fryer and cook them at 360 degrees F for 3 minutes on each side.
5. Transfer chicken to a baking dish that fits your air fryer, add tomato sauce and top with mozzarella, introduce in your air fryer and cook at 375 degrees F for 7 minutes.
6. Divide among plates, sprinkle basil on top and serve.

Nutrition: calories 304 - Fat 12 - Fiber 11 - Carbs 22 - Protein 15

19. Mexican Chicken

Prep.Time: 10 min - **Cooking Time:** 20 min - **Servings:** 4

Ingredients:
- ✓ 16 ounces salsa verde
- ✓ 1 tablespoon olive oil
- ✓ Salt and black pepper to the taste
- ✓ 1 pound chicken breast, boneless and skinless
- ✓ 1 and ½ cup Monterey Jack cheese, grated
- ✓ ¼ cup cilantro, chopped
- ✓ 1 teaspoon garlic powder

Directions:
1. Pour salsa verde in a baking dish that fits your air fryer, season chicken with salt, pepper, garlic powder, brush with olive oil and place it over your salsa verde.
2. Introduce in your air fryer and cook at 380 degrees F for 20 minutes.
3. Sprinkle cheese on top and cook for 2 minutes more.
4. Divide among plates and serve hot.

Nutrition: calories 340 - Fat 18 - Fiber 14 - Carbs 32 - Protein 18

20. Honey Duck Breasts

Prep.Time: 10 min - **Cooking Time:** 22 min - **Servings:** 2

Ingredients:
- ✓ 1 smoked duck breast, halved
- ✓ 1 teaspoon honey
- ✓ 1 teaspoon tomato paste
- ✓ 1 tablespoon mustard
- ✓ ½ teaspoon apple vinegar

Directions:
1. In a bowl, mix honey with tomato paste, mustard and vinegar, whisk well, add duck breast pieces, toss to coat well, transfer to your air fryer and cook at 370 degrees F for 15 minutes.
2. Take duck breast out of the fryer, add to honey mix, toss again, return to air fryer and cook at 370 degrees F for 6 minutes more.
3. Divide among plates and serve with a side salad.

Nutrition: calories 274 - Fat 11 - Fiber 13 - Carbs 22 - Protein 13

21. Creamy Chicken, Rice and Peas

Prep.Time: 10 min - Cooking Time: 30 min - Servings: 4

Ingredients:
- ✓ 1 pound chicken breasts, skinless, boneless and cut into quarters
- ✓ 1 cup white rice, already cooked
- ✓ Salt and black pepper to the taste
- ✓ 1 tablespoon olive oil
- ✓ 3 garlic cloves, minced
- ✓ 1 yellow onion, chopped
- ✓ ½ cup white wine
- ✓ ¼ cup heavy cream
- ✓ 1 cup chicken stock
- ✓ ¼ cup parsley, chopped
- ✓ 2 cups peas, frozen
- ✓ 1 and ½ cups parmesan, grated

Directions:
1. Season chicken breasts with salt and pepper, drizzle half of the oil over them, rub well, put in your air fryer's basket and cook them at 360 degrees F for 6 minutes.
2. Heat up a pan with the rest of the oil over medium high heat, add garlic, onion, wine, stock, salt, pepper and heavy cream, stir, bring to a simmer and cook for 9 minutes.
3. Transfer chicken breasts to a heat proof dish that fits your air fryer, add peas, rice and cream mix over them, toss, sprinkle parmesan and parsley all over, place in your air fryer and cook at 420 degrees F for 10 minutes.
4. Divide among plates and serve hot.

Nutrition: calories 313 - Fat 12 - Fiber 14 - Carbs 27 - Protein 44

22. Italian Chicken

Prep.Time: 10 min - Cooking Time: 16 min - Servings: 4

Ingredients:
- ✓ 5 chicken thighs
- ✓ 1 tablespoon olive oil
- ✓ 2 garlic cloves, minced
- ✓ 1 tablespoon thyme, chopped
- ✓ ½ cup heavy cream
- ✓ ¾ cup chicken stock
- ✓ 1 teaspoon red pepper flakes, crushed
- ✓ ¼ cup parmesan, grated
- ✓ ½ cup sun dried tomatoes
- ✓ 2 tablespoons basil, chopped
- ✓ Salt and black pepper to the taste

Directions:
1. Season chicken with salt and pepper, rub with half of the oil, place in your preheated air fryer at 350 degrees F and cook for 4 minutes.
2. Meanwhile, heat up a pan with the rest of the oil over medium high heat, add thyme garlic, pepper flakes, sun dried tomatoes, heavy cream, stock, parmesan, salt and pepper, stir, bring to a simmer, take off heat and transfer to a dish that fits your air fryer.
3. Add chicken thighs on top, introduce in your air fryer and cook at 320 degrees F for 12 minutes.
4. Divide among plates and serve with basil sprinkled on top.

Nutrition: calories 272 - Fat 9 - Fiber 12 - Carbs 37 - Protein 23

23. Chinese Duck Legs

Prep.Time: 10 min - Cooking Time: 36 minutes - Servings: 2

Ingredients:
- ✓ 2 duck legs
- ✓ 2 dried chilies, chopped
- ✓ 1 tablespoon olive oil
- ✓ 2 star anise
- ✓ 1 bunch spring onions, chopped
- ✓ 4 ginger slices
- ✓ 1 tablespoon oyster sauce
- ✓ 1 tablespoon soy sauce
- ✓ 1 teaspoon sesame oil
- ✓ 14 ounces water
- ✓ 1 tablespoon rice wine

Directions:
1. Heat up a pan with the oil over medium high heat, add chili, star anise, sesame oil, rice wine, ginger, oyster sauce, soy sauce and water, stir and cook for 6 minutes.
2. Add spring onions and duck legs, toss to coat, transfer to a pan that fits your air fryer, put in your air fryer and cook at 370 degrees F for 30 minutes.
3. Divide among plates and serve.

Nutrition: calories 300 - Fat 12 - Fiber 12 - Carbs 26 - Protein 18

24. Chinese Stuffed Chicken

Prep.Time: 10 min - Cooking Time: 35 min - Servings: 8

Ingredients:
- ✓ 1 whole chicken
- ✓ 10 wolfberries
- ✓ 2 red chilies, chopped
- ✓ 4 ginger slices
- ✓ 1 yam, cubed
- ✓ 1 teaspoon soy sauce
- ✓ Salt and white pepper to the taste
- ✓ 3 teaspoons sesame oil

Directions:
1. Season chicken with salt, pepper, rub with soy sauce and sesame oil and stuff with wolfberries, yam cubes, chilies and ginger.
2. Place in your air fryer, cook at 400 degrees F for 20 minutes and then at 360 degrees F for 15 minutes.
3. Carve chicken, divide among plates and serve.

Nutrition: calories 320 - Fat 12 - Fiber 17 - Carbs 22 - Protein 12

25. Chicken and Asparagus

Prep.Time: 10 min - Cooking Time: 20 min - Servings: 4

Ingredients:
- ✓ 8 chicken wings, halved
- ✓ 8 asparagus spears
- ✓ Salt and black pepper to the taste
- ✓ 1 tablespoon rosemary, chopped
- ✓ 1 teaspoon cumin, ground

Directions:
1. Pat dry chicken wings, season with salt, pepper, cumin and rosemary, put them in your air fryer's basket and cook at 360 degrees F for 20 minutes.
2. Meanwhile, heat up a pan over medium heat, add asparagus, add water to cover, steam for a few minutes, transfer to a bowl filled with ice water, drain and arrange on plates.
3. Add chicken wings on the side and serve.

Nutrition: calories 270 - Fat 8 - Fiber 12 - Carbs 24 - Protein 22

26. Chicken Cacciatore

Prep.Time: 10 min - Cooking Time: 20 min - Servings: 4

Ingredients:
- ✓ Salt and black pepper to the taste
- ✓ 8 chicken drumsticks, bone-in
- ✓ 1 bay leaf
- ✓ 1 teaspoon garlic powder
- ✓ 1 yellow onion, chopped
- ✓ 28 ounces canned tomatoes and juice, crushed
- ✓ 1 teaspoon oregano, dried
- ✓ ½ cup black olives, pitted and sliced

Directions:
1. In a heat proof dish that fits your air fryer, mix chicken with salt, pepper, garlic powder, bay leaf, onion, tomatoes and juice, oregano and olives, toss, introduce in your preheated air fryer and cook at 365 degrees F for 20 minutes.
2. Divide among plates and serve.

Nutrition: calories 300 - Fat 12 - Fiber 8 - Carbs 20 - Protein 24

27. Chicken Salad

Prep.Time: 10 min - Cooking Time: 10 min - Servings: 4

Ingredients:

- ✓ 1 pound chicken breast, boneless, skinless and halved
- ✓ Cooking spray
- ✓ Salt and black pepper to the taste
- ✓ ½ cup feta cheese, cubed
- ✓ 2 tablespoons lemon juice
- ✓ 1 and ½ teaspoons mustard
- ✓ 1 tablespoon olive oil
- ✓ 1 and ½ teaspoons red wine vinegar
- ✓ ½ teaspoon anchovies, minced
- ✓ ¾ teaspoon garlic, minced
- ✓ 1 tablespoon water
- ✓ 8 cups lettuce leaves, cut into strips
- ✓ 4 tablespoons parmesan, grated

Directions:

1. Spray chicken breasts with cooking oil, season with salt and pepper, introduce in your air fryer's basket and cook at 370 degrees F for 10 minutes, flipping halfway.
2. Transfer chicken breasts to a cutting board, shred using 2 forks, put in a salad bowl and mix with lettuce leaves.
3. In your blender, mix feta cheese with lemon juice, olive oil, mustard, vinegar, garlic, anchovies, water and half of the parmesan and blend very well.
4. Add this over chicken mix, toss, sprinkle the rest of the parmesan and serve.

Nutrition: calories 312 - Fat 6 - Fiber 16 - Carbs 22 - Protein 26

28. Chicken and Lentils Casserole

Prep.Time: 10 min - Cooking Time: 60 min - Servings: 8

Ingredients:

- ✓ 1 and ½ cups green lentils
- ✓ 3 cups chicken stock
- ✓ 2 pound chicken breasts, skinless, boneless and chopped
- ✓ Salt and cayenne pepper to the taste
- ✓ 3 teaspoons cumin, ground
- ✓ Cooking spray
- ✓ 5 garlic cloves, minced
- ✓ 1 yellow onion, chopped
- ✓ 2 red bell peppers, chopped
- ✓ 14 ounces canned tomatoes, chopped
- ✓ 2 cups corn
- ✓ 2 cups Cheddar cheese, shredded
- ✓ 2 tablespoons jalapeno pepper, chopped
- ✓ 1 tablespoon garlic powder
- ✓ 1 cup cilantro, chopped

Directions:

1. Put the stock in a pot, add some salt, add lentils, stir, bring to a boil over medium heat, cover and simmer for 35 minutes.
2. Meanwhile, spray chicken pieces with some cooking spray, season with salt, cayenne pepper and 1 teaspoon cumin, put them in your air fryer's basket and cook them at 370 degrees for 6 minutes, flipping half way.
3. Transfer chicken to a heat proof dish that fits your air fryer, add bell peppers, garlic, tomatoes, onion, salt, cayenne and 1 teaspoon cumin.
4. Drain lentils and add them to the chicken mix as well.
5. Add jalapeno pepper, garlic powder, the rest of the cumin, corn, half of the cheese and half of the cilantro, introduce in your air fryer and cook at 320 degrees F for 25 minutes.
6. Sprinkle the rest of the cheese and the remaining cilantro, divide chicken casserole on plates and serve.

Nutrition: calories 344 - Fat 11 - Fiber 12 - Carbs 22 - Protein 33

29. Chicken Thighs and Apple Mix

Prep.Time: 12 hours - Cooking Time: 30 minutes - Servings: 4

Ingredients:

- ✓ 8 chicken thighs, bone in and skin on
- ✓ Salt and black pepper to the taste
- ✓ 1 tablespoon apple cider vinegar
- ✓ 3 tablespoons onion, chopped
- ✓ 1 tablespoon ginger, grated
- ✓ ½ teaspoon thyme, dried
- ✓ 3 apples, cored and cut into quarters
- ✓ ¾ cup apple juice
- ✓ ½ cup maple syrup

Directions:

1. In a bowl, mix chicken with salt, pepper, vinegar, onion, ginger, thyme, apple juice and maple syrup, toss well, cover and keep in the fridge for 12 hours.
2. Transfer this whole mix to a baking dish that fits your air fryer, add apple pieces, place in your air fryer and cook at 350 degrees F for 30 minutes.
3. Divide among plates and serve warm.

Nutrition: calories 314 - Fat 8 - Fiber 11 - Carbs 34 - Protein 22

30. Chicken Breasts and Tomatoes Sauce

Prep.Time: 10 min - Cooking Time: 20 min - Servings: 4

Ingredients:

- ✓ 1 red onion, chopped
- ✓ 4 chicken breasts, skinless and boneless
- ✓ ¼ cup balsamic vinegar
- ✓ 14 ounces canned tomatoes, chopped
- ✓ Salt and black pepper to the taste
- ✓ ¼ cup parmesan, grated
- ✓ ¼ teaspoon garlic powder
- ✓ Cooking spray

Directions:

1. Spray a baking dish that fits your air fryer with cooking oil, add chicken, season with salt, pepper, balsamic vinegar, garlic powder, tomatoes and cheese, toss, introduce in your air fryer and cook at 400 degrees F for 20 minutes.
2. Divide among plates and serve hot.

Nutrition: calories 250 - Fat 12 - Fiber 12 - Carbs 19 - Protein 28

31. Chicken and Creamy Mushrooms

Prep.Time: 10 min - **Cooking Time:** 30 min - **Servings:** 8

Ingredients:
- ✓ 8 chicken thighs
- ✓ Salt and black pepper to the taste
- ✓ 8 ounces cremini mushrooms, halved
- ✓ 3 garlic cloves, minced
- ✓ 3 tablespoons butter, melted
- ✓ 1 cup chicken stock
- ✓ ¼ cup heavy cream
- ✓ ½ teaspoon basil, dried
- ✓ ½ teaspoon thyme, dried
- ✓ ½ teaspoon oregano, dried
- ✓ 1 tablespoon mustard
- ✓ ¼ cup parmesan, grated

Directions:
1. Rub chicken pieces with 2 tablespoons butter, season with salt and pepper, put in your air fryer's basket, cook at 370 degrees F for 5 minutes and leave aside in a bowl for now.
2. Meanwhile, heat up a pan with the rest of the butter over medium high heat, add mushrooms and garlic, stir and cook for 5 minutes.
3. Add salt, pepper, stock, oregano, thyme and basil, stir well and transfer to a heat proof dish that fits your air fryer.
4. Add chicken, toss everything, put in your air fryer and cook at 370 degrees F for 20 minutes.
5. Add mustard, parmesan and heavy cream, toss everything again, cook for 5 minutes more, divide among plates and serve.

Nutrition: calories 340 - Fat 10 - Fiber 13 - Carbs 22 - Protein 12

32. Easy Chicken Thighs and Baby Potatoes

Prep.Time: 10 min - **Cooking Time:** 30 min - **Servings:** 4

Ingredients:
- ✓ 8 chicken thighs
- ✓ 2 tablespoons olive oil
- ✓ 1 pound baby potatoes, halved
- ✓ 2 teaspoons oregano, dried
- ✓ 2 teaspoons rosemary, dried
- ✓ ½ teaspoon sweet paprika
- ✓ Salt and black pepper to the taste
- ✓ 2 garlic cloves, minced
- ✓ 1 red onion, chopped
- ✓ 2 teaspoons thyme, chopped

Directions:
1. In a bowl, mix chicken thighs with potatoes, salt, pepper, thyme, paprika, onion, rosemary, garlic, oregano and oil.
2. Toss to coat, spread everything in a heat proof dish that fits your air fryer and cook at 400 degrees F for 30 minutes, shaking halfway.
3. Divide among plates and serve.

Nutrition: calories 364 - Fat 14 - Fiber 13 - Carbs 21 - Protein 34

33. Chicken and Green Onions Sauce

Prep.Time: 10 min - **Cooking Time:** 16 minutes - **Servings:** 4

Ingredients:
- ✓ 10 green onions, roughly chopped
- ✓ 1 inch piece ginger root, chopped
- ✓ 4 garlic cloves, minced
- ✓ 2 tablespoons fish sauce
- ✓ 3 tablespoons soy sauce
- ✓ 1 teaspoon Chinese five spice
- ✓ 10 chicken drumsticks
- ✓ 1 cup coconut milk
- ✓ Salt and black pepper to the taste
- ✓ 1 teaspoon butter, melted
- ✓ ¼ cup cilantro, chopped
- ✓ 1 tablespoon lime juice

Directions:
1. In your food processor, mix green onions with ginger, garlic, soy sauce, fish sauce, five spice, salt, pepper, butter and coconut milk and pulse well.
2. In a bowl, mix chicken with green onions mix, toss well, transfer everything to a pan that fits your air fryer and cook at 370 degrees F for 16 minutes, shaking the fryer once.
3. Divide among plates, sprinkle cilantro on top, drizzle lime juice and serve with a side salad.

Nutrition: calories 321 - Fat 12 - Fiber 12 - Carbs 22 - Protein 20

34. Chicken Wings and Mint Sauce

Prep.Time: 20 min - **Cooking Time:** 16 min - **Servings:** 6

Ingredients:
- ✓ 18 chicken wings, halved
- ✓ 1 tablespoon turmeric powder
- ✓ 1 tablespoon cumin, ground
- ✓ 1 tablespoon ginger, grated
- ✓ 1 tablespoon coriander, ground
- ✓ 1 tablespoon sweet paprika
- ✓ Salt and black pepper to the taste
- ✓ 2 tablespoons olive oil

For the mint sauce:
- ✓ Juice from ½ lime
- ✓ 1 cup mint leaves
- ✓ 1 small ginger piece, chopped
- ✓ ¾ cup cilantro
- ✓ 1 tablespoon olive oil
- ✓ 1 tablespoon water
- ✓ Salt and black pepper to the taste
- ✓ 1 Serrano pepper, chopped

Directions:
1. In a bowl, mix 1 tablespoon ginger with cumin, coriander, paprika, turmeric, salt, pepper, cayenne and 2 tablespoons oil and stir well.
2. Add chicken wings pieces to this mix, toss to coat well and keep in the fridge for 10 minutes.
3. Transfer chicken to your air fryer's basket and cook at 370 degrees F for 16 minutes, flipping them halfway.
4. In your blender, mix mint with cilantro, 1 small ginger pieces, juice from ½ lime, 1 tablespoon olive oil, salt, pepper, water and Serrano pepper and blend very well.
5. Divide chicken wings on plates, drizzle mint sauce all over and serve.

Nutrition: calories 300 - Fat 15 - Fiber 11 - Carbs 27 - Protein 16

35. Fall Air Fried Chicken Mix

Prep.Time: 10 min - Cooking Time: 20 min - Servings: 8

Ingredients:
- ✓ 3 pounds chicken breasts, skinless and boneless
- ✓ 1 yellow onion, chopped
- ✓ 1 garlic clove, minced
- ✓ Salt and black pepper to the taste
- ✓ 10 white mushrooms, halved
- ✓ 1 tablespoon olive oil
- ✓ 1 red bell pepper, chopped
- ✓ 1 green bell pepper
- ✓ 2 tablespoons mozzarella cheese, shredded
- ✓ Cooking spray

Directions:
1. Season chicken with salt and pepper, rub with garlic, spray with cooking spray, place in your preheated air fryer and cook at 390 degrees F for 12 minutes.
2. Meanwhile, heat up a pan with the oil over medium heat, add onion, stir and sauté for 2 minutes.
3. Add mushrooms, garlic and bell peppers, stir and cook for 8 minutes.
4. Divide chicken on plates, add mushroom mix on the side, sprinkle cheese while chicken is still hot and serve right away.

Nutrition: calories 305 - Fat 12 - Fiber 11 - Carbs 26 - Protein 32

36. Chicken and Parsley Sauce

Prep.Time: 30 min - Cooking Time: 25 min - Servings: 6

Ingredients:
- ✓ 1 cup parsley, chopped
- ✓ 1 teaspoon oregano, dried
- ✓ ½ cup olive oil
- ✓ ¼ cup red wine
- ✓ 4 garlic cloves
- ✓ A pinch of salt
- ✓ A drizzle of maple syrup
- ✓ 12 chicken thighs

Directions:
1. In your food processor, mix parsley with oregano, garlic, salt, oil, wine and maple syrup and pulse really well.
2. In a bowl, mix chicken with parsley sauce, toss well and keep in the fridge for 30 minutes.
3. Drain chicken, transfer to your air fryer's basket and cook at 380 degrees F for 25 minutes, flipping chicken once.
4. Divide chicken on plates, drizzle parsley sauce all over and serve.

Nutrition: calories 354 - Fat 10 - Fiber 12 - Carbs 22 - Protein 17

37. Duck Breasts with Endives

Prep.Time: 10 min - Cooking Time: 25 minutes - Servings: 4

Ingredients:
- ✓ 2 duck breasts
- ✓ Salt and black pepper to the taste
- ✓ 1 tablespoon sugar
- ✓ 1 tablespoon olive oil
- ✓ 6 endives, julienned
- ✓ 2 tablespoons cranberries
- ✓ 8 ounces white wine
- ✓ 1 tablespoons garlic, minced
- ✓ 2 tablespoons heavy cream

Directions:
1. Score duck breasts and season them with salt and pepper, put in preheated air fryer and cook at 350 degrees F for 20 minutes, flipping them halfway.
2. Meanwhile, heat up a pan with the oil over medium heat, add sugar and endives, stir and cook for 2 minutes.
3. Add salt, pepper, wine, garlic, cream and cranberries, stir and cook for 3 minutes.
4. Divide duck breasts on plates, drizzle the endives sauce all over and serve.

Nutrition: calories 400 - Fat 12 - Fiber 32 - Carbs 29 - Protein 28

38. Easy Duck Breasts

Prep.Time: 10 min - Cooking Time: 40 min - Servings: 6

Ingredients:
- ✓ 6 duck breasts, halved
- ✓ Salt and black pepper to the taste
- ✓ 3 tablespoons flour
- ✓ 6 tablespoons butter, melted
- ✓ 2 cups chicken stock
- ✓ ½ cup white wine
- ✓ ¼ cup parsley, chopped
- ✓ 2 cups mushrooms, chopped

Directions:
1. Season duck breasts with salt and pepper, place them in a bowl, add melted butter, toss and transfer to another bowl.
2. Combine melted butter with flour, wine, salt, pepper and chicken stock and stir well.
3. Arrange duck breasts in a baking dish that fits your air fryer, pour the sauce over them, add parsley and mushrooms, introduce in your air fryer and cook at 350 degrees F for 40 minutes.
4. Divide among plates and serve.

Nutrition: calories 320 - Fat 28 - Fiber 12 - Carbs 12 - Protein 42

39. Lemon Chicken

Prep.Time: 10 min - Cooking Time: 30 min - Servings: 6

Ingredients:
- ✓ 1 whole chicken, cut into medium pieces
- ✓ 1 tablespoon olive oil
- ✓ Salt and black pepper to the taste
- ✓ Juice from 2 lemons
- ✓ Zest from 2 lemons, grated

Directions:
1. Season chicken with salt, pepper, rub with oil and lemon zest, drizzle lemon juice, put in your air fryer and cook at 350 degrees F for 30 minutes, flipping chicken pieces halfway.
2. Divide among plates and serve with a side salad.

Nutrition: calories 334 - Fat 24 - Fiber 12 - Carbs 26 - Protein 20

40. Duck and Veggies

Prep.Time: 10 min - Cooking Time: 20 min - Servings: 8

Ingredients:
- ✓ 1 duck, chopped in medium pieces
- ✓ 3 cucumbers, chopped
- ✓ 3 tablespoon white wine
- ✓ 2 carrots, chopped
- ✓ 1 cup chicken stock
- ✓ 1 small ginger piece, grated
- ✓ Salt and black pepper to the taste

Directions:
1. In a pan that fits your air fryer, mix duck pieces with cucumbers, wine, carrots, ginger, stock, salt and pepper, toss, introduce in your air fryer and cook at 370 degrees F for 20 minutes.
2. Divide everything on plates and serve.

Nutrition: calories 200 - Fat 10 - Fiber 8 - Carbs 20 - Protein 22

41. Chicken and Apricot Sauce

Prep.Time: 10 min - Cooking Time: 20 min - Servings: 4

Ingredients:
- ✓ 1 whole chicken, cut into medium pieces
- ✓ Salt and black pepper to the taste
- ✓ 1 tablespoon olive oil
- ✓ ½ teaspoon smoked paprika
- ✓ ¼ cup white wine
- ✓ ½ teaspoon marjoram, dried
- ✓ ¼ cup chicken stock
- ✓ 2 tablespoons white vinegar
- ✓ ¼ cup apricot preserves
- ✓ 1 and ½ teaspoon ginger, grated
- ✓ 2 tablespoons honey

Directions:
1. Season chicken with salt, pepper, marjoram and paprika, toss to coat, add oil, rub well, place in your air fryer and cook at 360 degrees F for 10 minutes.
2. Transfer chicken to a pan that fits your air fryer, add stock, wine, vinegar, ginger, apricot preserves and honey, toss, put in your air fryer and cook at 360 degrees F for 10 minutes more.
3. Divide chicken and apricot sauce on plates and serve.

Nutrition: calories 200 - Fat 7 - Fiber 19 - Carbs 20 - Protein 14

42. Chicken and Cauliflower Rice Mix

Prep.Time: 10 min - Cooking Time: 20 min - Servings: 6

Ingredients:
- ✓ 3 bacon slices, chopped
- ✓ 3 carrots, chopped
- ✓ 3 pounds chicken thighs, boneless and skinless
- ✓ 2 bay leaves
- ✓ ¼ cup red wine vinegar
- ✓ 4 garlic cloves, minced
- ✓ Salt and black pepper to the taste
- ✓ 4 tablespoons olive oil
- ✓ 1 tablespoon garlic powder
- ✓ 1 tablespoon Italian seasoning
- ✓ 24 ounces cauliflower rice
- ✓ 1 teaspoon turmeric powder
- ✓ 1 cup beef stock

Directions:
1. Heat up a pan that fits your air fryer over medium high heat, add bacon, carrots, onion and garlic, stir and cook for 8 minutes.
2. Add chicken, oil, vinegar, turmeric, garlic powder, Italian seasoning and bay leaves, stir, introduce in your air fryer and cook at 360 degrees F for 12 minutes.
3. Add cauliflower rice and stock, stir, cook for 6 minutes more, divide among plates and serve.

Nutrition: calories 340 - Fat 12 - Fiber 12 - Carbs 16 - Protein 8

43. Greek Chicken

Prep.Time: 10 min - Cooking Time: 15 minutes - Servings: 4

Ingredients:
- ✓ 2 tablespoons olive oil
- ✓ Juice from 1 lemon
- ✓ 1 teaspoon oregano, dried
- ✓ 3 garlic cloves, minced
- ✓ 1 pound chicken thighs
- ✓ Salt and black pepper to the taste
- ✓ ½ pound asparagus, trimmed
- ✓ 1 zucchini, roughly chopped
- ✓ 1 lemon sliced

Directions:
1. In a heat proof dish that fits your air fryer, mix chicken pieces with oil, lemon juice, oregano, garlic, salt, pepper, asparagus, zucchini and lemon slices, toss, introduce in preheated air fryer and cook at 380 degrees F for 15 minutes.
2. Divide everything on plates and serve.

Nutrition: calories 300 - Fat 8 - Fiber 12 - Carbs 20 - Protein 18

44. Easy Duck Breasts

Prep.Time: 10 min - Cooking Time: 15 min - Servings: 4

Ingredients:
- ✓ 4 duck breasts, skinless and boneless
- ✓ 4 garlic heads, peeled, tops cut off and quartered
- ✓ 2 tablespoons lemon juice
- ✓ Salt and black pepper to the taste
- ✓ ½ teaspoon lemon pepper
- ✓ 1 and ½ tablespoon olive oil

Directions:
1. In a bowl, mix duck breasts with garlic, lemon juice, salt, pepper, lemon pepper and olive oil and toss everything.
2. Transfer duck and garlic to your air fryer and cook at 350 degrees F for 15 minutes.
3. Divide duck breasts and garlic on plates and serve.

Nutrition: calories 200 - Fat 7 - Fiber 1 - Carbs 11 - Protein 17

45. Chicken and Radish Mix

Prep.Time: 10 min - Cooking Time: 30 min - Servings: 4

Ingredients:
- ✓ 4 chicken things, bone-in
- ✓ Salt and black pepper to the taste
- ✓ 1 tablespoon olive oil
- ✓ 1 cup chicken stock
- ✓ 6 radishes, halved
- ✓ 1 teaspoon sugar
- ✓ 3 carrots, cut into thin sticks
- ✓ 2 tablespoon chives, chopped

Directions:
1. Heat up a pan that fits your air fryer over medium heat, add stock, carrots, sugar and radishes, stir gently, reduce heat to medium, cover pot partly and simmer for 20 minutes.
2. Rub chicken with olive oil, season with salt and pepper, put in your air fryer and cook at 350 degrees F for 4 minutes.
3. Add chicken to radish mix, toss, introduce everything in your air fryer, cook for 4 minutes more, divide among plates and serve.

Nutrition: calories 237 - Fat 10 - Fiber 4 - Carbs 19 - Protein 29

46. Duck and Tea Sauce

Prep.Time: 10 min - Cooking Time: 20 min - Servings: 4

Ingredients:
- ✓ 2 duck breast halves, boneless
- ✓ 2 and ¼ cup chicken stock
- ✓ ¾ cup shallot, chopped
- ✓ 1 and ½ cup orange juice
- ✓ Salt and black pepper to the taste
- ✓ 3 teaspoons earl gray tea leaves
- ✓ 3 tablespoons butter, melted
- ✓ 1 tablespoon honey

Directions:
1. Season duck breast halves with salt and pepper, put in preheated air fryer and cook at 360 degrees F for 10 minutes.
2. Meanwhile, heat up a pan with the butter over medium heat, add shallot, stir and cook for 2-3 minutes.
3. Add stock, stir and cook for another minute.
4. Add orange juice, tea leaves and honey, stir, cook for 2-3 minutes more and strain into a bowl.
5. Divide duck on plates, drizzle tea sauce all over and serve.

Nutrition: calories 228 - Fat 11 - Fiber 2 - Carbs 20 - Protein 12

47. Duck and Cherries

Prep.Time: 10 min - **Cooking Time:** 20 min - **Servings:** 4

Ingredients:
- ½ cup sugar
- ¼ cup honey
- 1/3 cup balsamic vinegar
- 1 teaspoon garlic, minced
- 1 tbsp ginger, grated
- 1 teaspoon cumin, ground
- ½ teaspoon clove, ground
- ½ tsp cinnamon powder
- 4 sage leaves, chopped
- 1 jalapeno, chopped
- 2 cups rhubarb, sliced
- ½ cup yellow onion, chopped
- 2 cups cherries, pitted
- 4 duck breasts, boneless, skin on and scored
- Salt and black pepper to the taste

Directions:
1. Season duck breast with salt and pepper, put in your air fryer and cook at 350 degrees F for 5 minutes on each side.
2. Meanwhile, heat up a pan over medium heat, add sugar, honey, vinegar, garlic, ginger, cumin, clove, cinnamon, sage, jalapeno, rhubarb, onion and cherries, stir, bring to a simmer and cook for 10 minutes.
3. Add duck breasts, toss well, divide everything on plates and serve.

Nutrition: calories 456 - Fat 13 - Fiber 14 - Carbs 64 - Protein 31

48. Duck Breast with Fig Sauce

Prep.Time: 10 min - **Cooking Time:** 20 min - **Servings:** 4

Ingredients:
- 2 duck breasts, skin on, halved
- 1 tablespoon olive oil
- ½ tsp thyme, chopped
- ½ teaspoon garlic powder
- ¼ tsp sweet paprika
- Salt and black pepper to the taste
- 1 cup beef stock
- 3 tablespoons butter, melted
- 1 shallot, chopped
- ½ cup port wine
- 4 tablespoons fig preserves
- 1 tablespoon white flour

Directions:
1. Season duck breasts with salt and pepper, drizzle half of the melted butter, rub well, put in your air fryer's basket and cook at 350 degrees F for 5 minutes on each side.
2. Meanwhile, heat up a pan with the olive oil and the rest of the butter over medium high heat, add shallot, stir and cook for 2 minutes.
3. Add thyme, garlic powder, paprika, stock, salt, pepper, wine and figs, stir and cook for 7-8 minutes.
4. Add flour, stir well, cook until sauce thickens a bit and take off heat.
5. Divide duck breasts on plates, drizzle figs sauce all over and serve.

Nutrition: calories 246 - Fat 12 - Fiber 4 - Carbs 22 - Protein 3

49. Chicken Tenders and Flavored Sauce

Prep.Time: 10 min - **Cooking Time:** 10 minutes - **Servings:** 6

Ingredients:
- 1 teaspoon chili powder
- 2 teaspoon garlic powder
- 1 teaspoon onion powder
- 1 teaspoon sweet paprika
- Salt and black pepper to the taste
- 2 tablespoons butter
- 2 tablespoons olive oil
- 2 pounds chicken tenders
- 2 tablespoons cornstarch
- ½ cup chicken stock
- 2 cups heavy cream
- 2 tablespoons water
- 2 tablespoons parsley, chopped

Directions:
1. In a bowl, mix garlic powder with onion powder, chili, salt, pepper and paprika, stir, add chicken and toss.
2. Rub chicken tenders with oil, place in your air fryer and cook at 360 degrees F for 10 minutes.
3. Meanwhile, heat up a pan with the butter over medium high heat, add cornstarch, stock, cream, water and parsley, stir, cover and cook for 10 minutes.
4. Divide chicken on plates, drizzle sauce all over and serve.

Nutrition: calories 351 - Fat 12 - Fiber 9 - Carbs 20 - Protein 17

50. Chicken and Black Olives Sauce

Prep.Time: 10 min - **Cooking Time:** 8 min - **Servings:** 2

Ingredients:
- 1 chicken breast cut into 4 pieces
- 2 tablespoons olive oil
- 3 garlic cloves, minced

For the sauce:
- 1 cup black olives, pitted
- Salt and black pepper to the taste
- 2 tablespoons olive oil
- ¼ cup parsley, chopped
- 1 tablespoons lemon juice

Directions:
1. In your food processor, mix olives with salt, pepper, 2 tablespoons olive oil, lemon juice and parsley, blend very well and transfer to a bowl.
2. Season chicken with salt and pepper, rub with the oil and garlic, place in your preheated air fryer and cook at 370 degrees F for 8 minutes.
3. Divide chicken on plates, top with olives sauce and serve.

Nutrition: calories 270 - Fat 12 - Fiber 12 - Carbs 23 - Protein 22

51. Chicken and Capers

Prep.Time: 10 min - **Cooking Time:** 20 min - **Servings:** 2

Ingredients:
- 4 chicken thighs
- 3 tablespoons capers
- 4 garlic cloves, minced
- 3 tablespoons butter, melted
- Salt and black pepper to the taste
- ½ cup chicken stock
- 1 lemon, sliced
- 4 green onions, chopped

Directions:
1. Brush chicken with butter, sprinkle salt and pepper to the taste, place them in a baking dish that fits your air fryer.
2. Also add capers, garlic, chicken stock and lemon slices, toss to coat, introduce in your air fryer and cook at 370 degrees F for 20 minutes, shaking halfway.
3. Sprinkle green onions, divide among plates and serve.

Nutrition: calories 200 - Fat 9 - Fiber 10 - Carbs 17 - Protein 7

52. Turkey, Peas and Mushrooms Casserole

Prep.Time: 10 min - **Cooking Time:** 20 min - **Servings:** 4

Ingredients:
- 2 pounds turkey breasts, skinless, boneless
- Salt and black pepper to the taste
- 1 yellow onion, chopped
- 1 celery stalk, chopped
- ½ cup peas
- 1 cup chicken stock
- 1 cup cream of mushrooms soup
- 1 cup bread cubes

Directions:
1. In a pan that fits your air fryer, mix turkey with salt, pepper, onion, celery, peas and stock, introduce in your air fryer and cook at 360 degrees F for 15 minutes.
2. Add bread cubes and cream of mushroom soup, stir toss and cook at 360 degrees F for 5 minutes more.
3. Divide among plates and serve hot.

Nutrition: calories 271 - Fat 9 - Fiber 9 - Carbs 16 - Protein 7

53. Tasty Chicken Thighs

Prep.Time: 10 min - Cooking Time: 20 min - Servings: 6

Ingredients:
- ✓ 2 and ½ pounds chicken thighs
- ✓ Salt and black pepper to the taste
- ✓ 5 green onions, chopped
- ✓ 2 tbsp sesame oil
- ✓ 1 tablespoon sherry wine
- ✓ ½ teaspoon white vinegar
- ✓ 1 tablespoon soy sauce
- ✓ ¼ teaspoon sugar

Directions:
1. Season chicken with salt and pepper, rub with half of the sesame oil, add to your air fryer and cook at 360 degrees F for 20 minutes.
2. Meanwhile, heat up a pan with the rest of the oil over medium high heat, add green onions, sherry wine, vinegar, soy sauce and sugar, toss, cover and cook for 10 minutes
3. Shred chicken using 2 forks divide among plates, drizzle sauce all over and serve.

Nutrition: calories 321 - Fat 8 - Fiber 12 - Carbs 36 - Protein 24

54. Chicken and Chestnuts Mix

Prep.Time: 10 min - Cooking Time: 12 min - Servings: 2

Ingredients:
- ✓ ½ pound chicken pieces
- ✓ 1 small yellow onion, chopped
- ✓ 2 tsp garlic, minced
- ✓ A pinch of ginger, grated
- ✓ A pinch of allspice, ground
- ✓ 4 tbsp water chestnuts
- ✓ 2 tablespoons soy sauce
- ✓ 2 tablespoons chicken stock
- ✓ 2 tablespoons balsamic vinegar
- ✓ 2 tortillas for serving

Directions:
1. In a pan that fits your air fryer, mix chicken meat with onion, garlic, ginger, allspice, chestnuts, soy sauce, stock and vinegar, stir, transfer to your air fryer and cook at 360 degrees F for 12 minutes.
2. Divide everything on plates and serve.

Nutrition: calories 301 - Fat 12 - Fiber 7 - Carbs 24 - Protein 12

55. Cider Glazed Chicken

Prep.Time: 10 min - Cooking Time: 14 minutes - Servings: 4

Ingredients:
- ✓ 1 sweet potato, cubed
- ✓ 2 apples, cored and sliced
- ✓ 1 tablespoon olive oil
- ✓ 1 tablespoon rosemary, chopped
- ✓ Salt and black pepper to the taste
- ✓ 6 chicken thighs, bone in and skin on
- ✓ 2/3 cup apple cider
- ✓ 1 tablespoon mustard
- ✓ 2 tablespoons honey
- ✓ 1 tablespoon butter

Directions:
1. Heat up a pan that fits your air fryer with half of the oil over medium high heat, add cider, honey, butter and mustard, whisk well, bring to a simmer, take off heat, add chicken and toss really well.
2. In a bowl, mix potato cubes with rosemary, apples, salt, pepper and the rest of the oil, toss well and add to chicken mix.
3. Place pan in your air fryer and cook at 390 degrees F for 14 minutes.
4. Divide everything on plates and serve.

Nutrition: calories 241 - Fat 7 - Fiber 12 - Carbs 28 - Protein 22

56. Veggie Stuffed Chicken Breasts

Prep.Time: 10 min - Cooking Time: 15 min - Servings: 4

Ingredients:
- ✓ 4 chicken breasts, skinless and boneless
- ✓ 2 tablespoons olive oil
- ✓ Salt and black pepper to the taste
- ✓ 1 zucchini, chopped
- ✓ 1 tsp Italian seasoning
- ✓ 2 yellow bell peppers, chopped
- ✓ 3 tomatoes, chopped
- ✓ 1 red onion, chopped
- ✓ 1 cup mozzarella, shredded

Directions:
1. Mix a slit on each chicken breast creating a pocket, season with salt and pepper and rub them with olive oil.
2. In a bowl, mix zucchini with Italian seasoning, bell peppers, tomatoes and onion and stir.
3. Stuff chicken breasts with this mix, sprinkle mozzarella over them, place them in your air fryer's basket and cook at 350 degrees F for 15 minutes.
4. Divide among plates and serve.

Nutrition: calories 300 - Fat 12 - Fiber 7 - Carbs 22 - Protein 18

57. Duck Breasts and Raspberry Sauce

Prep.Time: 10 min - Cooking Time: 15 min - Servings: 4

Ingredients:
- ✓ 2 duck breasts, skin on and scored
- ✓ Salt and black pepper to the taste
- ✓ Cooking spray
- ✓ ½ teaspoon cinnamon powder
- ✓ ½ cup raspberries
- ✓ 1 tablespoon sugar
- ✓ 1 teaspoon red wine vinegar
- ✓ ½ cup water

Directions:
1. Season duck breasts with salt and pepper, spray them with cooking spray, put in preheated air fryer skin side down and cook at 350 degrees F for 10 minutes.
2. Heat up a pan with the water over medium heat, add raspberries, cinnamon, sugar and wine, stir, bring to a simmer, transfer to your blender, puree and return to pan.
3. Add air fryer duck breasts to pan as well, toss to coat, divide among plates and serve right away.

Nutrition: calories 456 - Fat 22 - Fiber 4 - Carbs 14 - Protein 45

58. Chicken Breasts with Passion Fruit Sauce

Prep.Time: 10 min - Cooking Time: 10 min - Servings: 4

Ingredients:
- ✓ 4 chicken breasts
- ✓ Salt and black pepper to the taste
- ✓ 4 passion fruits, halved, deseeded and pulp reserved
- ✓ 1 tablespoon whiskey
- ✓ 2 star anise
- ✓ 2 ounces maple syrup
- ✓ 1 bunch chives, chopped

Directions:
1. Heat up a pan with the passion fruit pulp over medium heat, add whiskey, star anise, maple syrup and chives, stir well, simmer for 5-6 minutes and take off heat.
2. Season chicken with salt and pepper, put in preheated air fryer and cook at 360 degrees F for 10 minutes, flipping halfway.
3. Divide chicken on plates, heat up the sauce a bit, drizzle it over chicken and serve.

Nutrition: calories 374 - Fat 8 - Fiber 22 - Carbs 34 - Protein 37

86

59. Chicken Breasts and BBQ Chili Sauce

Prep.Time: 10 min - **Cooking Time:** 20 min - **Servings:** 6

Ingredients:
- ✓ 2 cups chili sauce
- ✓ 2 cups ketchup
- ✓ 1 cup pear jelly
- ✓ ¼ cup honey
- ✓ ½ teaspoon liquid smoke
- ✓ 1 teaspoon chili powder
- ✓ 1 teaspoon mustard powder
- ✓ 1 teaspoon sweet paprika
- ✓ Salt and black pepper to the taste
- ✓ 1 teaspoon garlic powder
- ✓ 6 chicken breasts, skinless and boneless

Directions:
1. Season chicken breasts with salt and pepper, put in preheated air fryer and cook at 350 degrees F for 10 minutes.
2. Meanwhile, heat up a pan with the chili sauce over medium heat, add ketchup, pear jelly, honey, liquid smoke, chili powder, mustard powder, sweet paprika, salt, pepper and the garlic powder, stir, bring to a simmer and cook for 10 minutes.
3. Add air fried chicken breasts, toss well, divide among plates and serve.

Nutrition: calories 473 - Fat 13 - Fiber 7 - Carbs 39 - Protein 33

60. Duck Breasts And Mango Mix

Prep.Time: 60 min - **Cooking Time:** 10 min - **Servings:** 4

Ingredients:
- ✓ 4 duck breasts
- ✓ 1 and ½ tablespoons lemongrass, chopped
- ✓ 3 tablespoons lemon juice
- ✓ 2 tablespoons olive oil
- ✓ Salt and black pepper to the taste
- ✓ 3 garlic cloves, minced

For the mango mix:
- ✓ 1 mango, peeled and chopped
- ✓ 1 tablespoon coriander, chopped
- ✓ 1 red onion, chopped
- ✓ 1 tablespoon sweet chili sauce
- ✓ 1 and ½ tablespoon lemon juice
- ✓ 1 teaspoon ginger, grated
- ✓ ¾ teaspoon sugar

Directions:
1. In a bowl, mix duck breasts with salt, pepper, lemongrass, 3 tablespoons lemon juice, olive oil and garlic, toss well, keep in the fridge for 1 hour, transfer to your air fryer and cook at 360 degrees F for 10 minutes, flipping once.
2. Meanwhile, in a bowl, mix mango with coriander, onion, chili sauce, lemon juice, ginger and sugar and toss well.
3. Divide duck on plates, add mango mix on the side and serve.

Nutrition: calories 465 - Fat 11 - Fiber 4 - Carbs 29 - Protein 38

61. Marinated Duck Breasts

Prep.Time: 1 day - **Cooking Time:** 15 minutes - **Servings:** 2

Ingredients:
- ✓ 2 duck breasts
- ✓ 1 cup white wine
- ✓ ¼ cup soy sauce
- ✓ 2 garlic cloves, minced
- ✓ 6 tarragon springs
- ✓ Salt and black pepper to the taste
- ✓ 1 tablespoon butter
- ✓ ¼ cup sherry wine

Directions:
1. In a bowl, mix duck breasts with white wine, soy sauce, garlic, tarragon, salt and pepper, toss well and keep in the fridge for 1 day.
2. Transfer duck breasts to your preheated air fryer at 350 degrees F and cook for 10 minutes, flipping halfway.
3. Meanwhile, pour the marinade in a pan, heat up over medium heat, add butter and sherry, stir, bring to a simmer, cook for 5 minutes and take off heat.
4. Divide duck breasts on plates, drizzle sauce all over and serve.

Nutrition: calories 475 - Fat 12 - Fiber 3 - Carbs 10 - Protein 48

62. Chicken and Peaches

Prep.Time: 10 min - **Cooking Time:** 30 min - **Servings:** 6

Ingredients:
- ✓ 1 whole chicken, cut into medium pieces
- ✓ ¾ cup water
- ✓ 1/3 cup honey
- ✓ Salt and black pepper to the taste
- ✓ ¼ cup olive oil
- ✓ 4 peaches, halved

Directions:
1. Put the water in a pot, bring to a simmer over medium heat, add honey, whisk really well and leave aside.
2. Rub chicken pieces with the oil, season with salt and pepper, place in your air fryer's basket and cook at 350 degrees F for 10 minutes.
3. Brush chicken with some of the honey mix, cook for 6 minutes more, flip again, brush one more time with the honey mix and cook for 7 minutes more.
4. Divide chicken pieces on plates and keep warm.
5. Brush peaches with what's left of the honey marinade, place them in your air fryer and cook them for 3 minutes.
6. Divide among plates next to chicken pieces and serve.

Nutrition: calories 430 - Fat 14 - Fiber 3 - Carbs 15 - Protein 20

63. Tea Glazed Chicken
Prep.Time: 10 min - **Cooking Time:** 30 min - **Servings:** 6

Ingredients:
- ✓ ½ cup apricot preserves
- ✓ ½ cup pineapple preserves
- ✓ 6 chicken legs
- ✓ 1 cup hot water
- ✓ 6 black tea bags
- ✓ 1 tablespoon soy sauce
- ✓ 1 onion, chopped
- ✓ ¼ teaspoon red pepper flakes
- ✓ 1 tablespoon olive oil
- ✓ Salt and black pepper to the taste
- ✓ 6 chicken legs

Directions:
1. Put the hot water in a bowl, add tea bags, leave aside covered for 10 minutes, discard bags at the end and transfer tea to another bowl.
2. Add soy sauce, pepper flakes, apricot and pineapple preserves, whisk really well and take off heat.
3. Season chicken with salt and pepper, rub with oil, put in your air fryer and cook at 350 degrees F for 5 minutes.
4. Spread onion on the bottom of a baking dish that fits your air fryer, add chicken pieces, drizzle the tea glaze on top, introduce in your air fryer and cook at 320 degrees F for 25 minutes.
5. Divide everything on plates and serve.

Nutrition: calories 298 - Fat 14 - Fiber 1 - Carbs 14 - Protein 30

64. Quick Creamy Chicken Casserole
Prep.Time: 10 min - **Cooking Time:** 12 min - **Servings:** 4

Ingredients:
- ✓ 10 ounces spinach, chopped
- ✓ 4 tablespoons butter
- ✓ 3 tablespoons flour
- ✓ 1 and ½ cups milk
- ✓ ½ cup parmesan, grated
- ✓ ½ cup heavy cream
- ✓ Salt and black pepper to the taste
- ✓ 2 cup chicken breasts, skinless, boneless and cubed
- ✓ 1 cup bread crumbs

Directions:
1. Heat up a pan with the butter over medium heat, add flour and stir well.
2. Add milk, heavy cream and parmesan, stir well, cook for 1-2 minutes more and take off heat.
3. In a pan that fits your air fryer, spread chicken and spinach.
4. Add salt and pepper and toss.
5. Add cream mix and spread, sprinkle bread crumbs on top, introduce in your air fryer and cook at 350 for 12 minutes.
6. Divide chicken and spinach mix on plates and serve.

Nutrition: calories 321 - Fat 9 - Fiber 12 - Carbs 22 - Protein 17

65. Duck Breasts with Red Wine and Orange Sauce
Prep.Time: 10 min - **Cooking Time:** 35 minutes - **Servings:** 4

Ingredients:
- ✓ ½ cup honey
- ✓ 2 cups orange juice
- ✓ 4 cups red wine
- ✓ 2 tbsp. sherry vinegar
- ✓ 2 cups chicken stock
- ✓ 2 tsp. pumpkin pie spice
- ✓ 2 tbsp. butter
- ✓ 2 duck breasts, skin on and halved
- ✓ 2 tbsp. olive oil
- ✓ Salt and black pepper to the taste

Directions:
1. Heat up a pan with the orange juice over medium heat, add honey, stir well and cook for 10 minutes.
2. Add wine, vinegar, stock, pie spice and butter, stir well, cook for 10 minutes more and take off heat.
3. Season duck breasts with salt and pepper, rub with olive oil, place in preheated air fryer at 370 degrees F and cook for 7 minutes on each side.
4. Divide duck breasts on plates, drizzle wine and orange juice all over and serve right away.

Nutrition: calories 300 - Fat 8 - Fiber 12 - Carbs 24 - Protein 11

66. Chicken and Spinach Salad
Prep.Time: 10 min - **Cooking Time:** 12 min - **Servings:** 2

Ingredients:
- ✓ 2 tsp. parsley, dried
- ✓ 2 chicken breasts, skinless and boneless
- ✓ ½ tsp. onion powder
- ✓ 2 tsp. sweet paprika
- ✓ ½ cup lemon juice
- ✓ Salt and black pepper to the taste
- ✓ 5 cups baby spinach
- ✓ 8 strawberries, sliced
- ✓ 1 small red onion, sliced
- ✓ 2 tbsp. balsamic vinegar
- ✓ 1 avocado, pitted, peeled and chopped
- ✓ ¼ cup olive oil
- ✓ 1 tbsp. tarragon, chopped

Directions:
1. Put chicken in a bowl, add lemon juice, parsley, onion powder and paprika and toss.
2. Transfer chicken to your air fryer and cook at 360 degrees F for 12 minutes.
3. In a bowl, mix spinach, onion, strawberries and avocado and toss.
4. In another bowl, mix oil with vinegar, salt, pepper and tarragon, whisk well, add to the salad and toss.
5. Divide chicken on plates, add spinach salad on the side and serve.

Nutrition: calories 240 - Fat 5 - Fiber 13 - Carbs 25 - Protein 22

67. Pepperoni Chicken
Prep.Time: 10 min - **Cooking Time:** 22 min - **Servings:** 6

Ingredients:
- ✓ 14 ounces tomato paste
- ✓ 1 tablespoon olive oil
- ✓ 4 medium chicken breasts, skinless and boneless
- ✓ Salt and black pepper to the taste
- ✓ 1 teaspoon oregano, dried
- ✓ 6 ounces mozzarella, sliced
- ✓ 1 teaspoon garlic powder
- ✓ 2 ounces pepperoni, sliced

Directions:
1. In a bowl, mix chicken with salt, pepper, garlic powder and oregano and toss.
2. Put chicken in your air fryer, cook at 350 degrees F for 6 minutes and transfer to a pan that fits your air fryer.
3. Add mozzarella slices on top, spread tomato paste, top with pepperoni slices, introduce in your air fryer and cook at 350 degrees F for 15 minutes more.
4. Divide among plates and serve.

Nutrition: calories 320 - Fat 10 - Fiber 16 - Carbs 23 - Protein 27

68. Chicken and Garlic Sauce
Prep.Time: 10 min - **Cooking Time:** 20 min - **Servings:** 4

Ingredients:
- ✓ 1 tablespoon butter, melted
- ✓ 4 chicken breasts, skin on and bone-in
- ✓ 1 tablespoon olive oil
- ✓ Salt and black pepper to the taste
- ✓ 40 garlic cloves, peeled and chopped
- ✓ 2 thyme springs
- ✓ ¼ cup chicken stock
- ✓ 2 tablespoons parsley, chopped
- ✓ ¼ cup dry white wine

Directions:
1. Season chicken breasts with salt and pepper, rub with the oil, place in your air fryer, cook at 360 degrees F for 4 minutes on each side and transfer to a heat proof dish that fits your air fryer.
2. Add melted butter, garlic, thyme, stock, wine and parsley, toss, introduce in your air fryer and cook at 350 degrees F for 15 minutes more.
3. Divide everything on plates and serve.

Nutrition: calories 227 - Fat 9 - Fiber 13 - Carbs 22 - Protein 12

69. Turkey Quarters and Veggies

Prep.Time: 10 min - **Cooking Time:** 34 min - **Servings:** 4

Ingredients:
- ✓ 1 yellow onion, chopped
- ✓ 1 carrot, chopped
- ✓ 3 garlic cloves, minced
- ✓ 2 pounds turkey quarters
- ✓ 1 celery stalk, chopped
- ✓ 1 cup chicken stock
- ✓ 2 tablespoons olive oil
- ✓ 2 bay leaves
- ✓ ½ tsp rosemary, dried
- ✓ ½ teaspoon sage, dried
- ✓ ½ teaspoon thyme, dried
- ✓ Salt and black pepper to the taste

Directions:
1. Rub turkey quarters with salt, pepper, half of the oil, thyme, sage, rosemary and thyme, put in your air fryer and cook at 360 degrees F for 20 minutes.
2. In a pan that fits your air fryer, mix onion with carrot, garlic, celery, the rest of the oil, stock, bay leaves, salt and pepper and toss.
3. Add turkey, introduce everything in your air fryer and cook at 360 degrees F for 14 minutes more.
4. Divide everything on plates and serve.

Nutrition: calories 362 - Fat 12 - Fiber 16 - Carbs 22 - Protein 17

70. Chicken and Creamy Veggie Mix

Prep.Time: 10 min - **Cooking Time:** 30 min - **Servings:** 6

Ingredients:
- ✓ 2 cups whipping cream
- ✓ 40 ounces chicken pieces, boneless and skinless
- ✓ 3 tbsp. butter, melted
- ✓ ½ cup yellow onion, chopped
- ✓ ¾ cup red peppers, chopped
- ✓ 29 ounces chicken stock
- ✓ Salt and black pepper to the taste
- ✓ 1 bay leaf
- ✓ 8 ounces mushrooms, chopped
- ✓ 17 ounces asparagus, trimmed
- ✓ 3 tsp. thyme, chopped

Directions:
1. Heat up a pan with the butter over medium heat, add onion and peppers, stir and cook for 3 minutes.
2. Add stock, bay leaf, salt and pepper, bring to a boil and simmer for 10 minutes.
3. Add asparagus, mushrooms, chicken, cream, thyme, salt and pepper to the taste, stir, introduce in your air fryer and cook at 360 degrees F for 15 minutes.
4. Divide chicken and veggie mix on plates and serve.

Nutrition: calories 360 - Fat 27 - Fiber 13 - Carbs 24 - Protein 47

71. Cheese Crusted Chicken

Prep.Time: 10 min - **Cooking Time:** 15 minutes - **Servings:** 4

Ingredients:
- ✓ 4 bacon slices, cooked and crumbled
- ✓ 4 chicken breasts, skinless and boneless
- ✓ 1 tablespoon water
- ✓ ½ cup avocado oil
- ✓ 1 egg, whisked
- ✓ Salt and black pepper to the taste
- ✓ 1 cup asiago cheese, shredded
- ✓ ¼ teaspoon garlic powder
- ✓ 1 cup parmesan cheese, grated

Directions:
1. In a bowl, mix parmesan with garlic, salt and pepper and stir.
2. In another bowl, mix egg with water and whisk well.
3. Season chicken with salt and pepper and dip each pieces into egg and then into cheese mix.
4. Add chicken to your air fryer and cook at 320 degrees F for 15 minutes.
5. Divide chicken on plates, sprinkle bacon and asiago cheese on top and serve.

Nutrition: calories 400 - Fat 22 - Fiber 12 - Carbs 32 - Protein 47

72. Chicken and Simple Coconut Sauce

Prep.Time: 10 min - **Cooking Time:** 12 min - **Servings:** 6

Ingredients:
- ✓ 1 tablespoon olive oil
- ✓ 3 and ½ pounds chicken breasts
- ✓ 1 cup chicken stock
- ✓ 1 and ¼ cups yellow onion, chopped
- ✓ 1 tablespoon lime juice
- ✓ ¼ cup coconut milk
- ✓ 2 tsp sweet paprika
- ✓ 1 tsp red pepper flakes
- ✓ 2 tablespoons green onions, chopped
- ✓ Salt and black pepper to the taste

Directions:
1. Heat up a pan that fits your air fryer with the oil over medium high heat, add onions, stir and cook for 4 minutes.
2. Add stock, coconut milk, pepper flakes, paprika, lime juice, salt and pepper and stir well.
3. Add chicken to the pan, add more salt and pepper, toss, introduce in your air fryer and cook at 360 degrees F for 12 minutes.
4. Divide chicken and sauce on plates and serve.

Nutrition: calories 320 - Fat 13 - Fiber 13 - Carbs 32 - Protein 23

73. Air Fried Japanese Duck Breasts

Prep.Time: 10 min - **Cooking Time:** 20 min - **Servings:** 6

Ingredients:
- ✓ 6 duck breasts, boneless
- ✓ 4 tablespoons soy sauce
- ✓ 1 and ½ teaspoon five spice powder
- ✓ 2 tablespoons honey
- ✓ Salt and black pepper to the taste
- ✓ 20 ounces chicken stock
- ✓ 4 ginger slices
- ✓ 4 tablespoons hoisin sauce
- ✓ 1 teaspoon sesame oil

Directions:
1. In a bowl, mix five spice powder with soy sauce, salt, pepper and honey, whisk, add duck breasts, toss to coat and leave aside for now.
2. Heat up a pan with the stock over medium high heat, hoisin sauce, ginger and sesame oil, stir well, cook for 2-3 minutes more, take off heat and leave aside.
3. Put duck breasts in your air fryer and cook them at 400 degrees F for 15 minutes.
4. Divide among plates, drizzle hoisin and ginger sauce all over them and serve.

Nutrition: calories 336 - Fat 12 - Fiber 1 - Carbs 25 - Protein 33

74. Duck and Plum Sauce

Prep.Time: 10 min - **Cooking Time:** 32 min - **Servings:** 2

Ingredients:
- ✓ 2 duck breasts
- ✓ 1 tablespoon butter, melted
- ✓ 1 star anise
- ✓ 1 tablespoon olive oil
- ✓ 1 shallot, chopped
- ✓ 9 ounces red plumps, stoned, cut into small wedges
- ✓ 2 tablespoons sugar
- ✓ 2 tablespoons red wine
- ✓ 1 cup beef stock

Directions:
1. Heat up a pan with the olive oil over medium heat, add shallot, stir and cook for 5 minutes,
2. Add sugar and plums, stir and cook until sugar dissolves.
3. Add stock and wine, stir, cook for 15 minutes, take off heat and keep warm for now.
4. Score duck breasts, season with salt and pepper, rub with melted butter, transfer to a heat proof dish that fits your air fryer, add star anise and plum sauce, introduce in your air fryer and cook at 360 degrees F for 12 minutes.
5. Divide everything on plates and serve.

Nutrition: calories 400 - Fat 25 - Fiber 12 - Carbs 29 - Protein 44

75. Cheese Chicken Fries
Prep.Time: 10 min - Cooking Time: 25 min - Servings: 2

Ingredients:
- ✓ 1 lb. chicken (Cut in to long fingers)
- ✓ A pinch of salt to taste
- ✓ 1 tbsp. lemon juice

Ingredients for the marinade:
- ✓ 1 tbsp. olive oil
- ✓ 1 tsp. mixed herbs
- ✓ ½ tsp. red chili flakes

For the garnish:
- ✓ 1 cup melted cheddar cheese

Directions:
1. Take all the ingredients mentioned under the heading "For the marinade" and mix them well.
2. Cook the chicken fingers and soak them in the marinade.
3. Pre heat the Air Fryer for around 5 minutes at 300 Fahrenheit. Take out the basket of the fryer and place the chicken fingers in them. Close the basket. Now keep the fryer at 220 Fahrenheit for 20 or 25 minutes. In between the process, toss the fries twice or thrice so that they get cooked properly.
4. Towards the end of the cooking process (the last 2 minutes or so), sprinkle the cut coriander leaves on the fries. Add the melted cheddar cheese over the fries and serve hot.

76. Chicken Pizza
Prep.Time: 10 min - Cooking Time: 15-17 min - Servings: 1

Ingredients:
- ✓ One pizza base
- ✓ Grated pizza cheese (mozzarella cheese preferably) for topping
- ✓ Some pizza topping sauce
- ✓ Use cooking oil for brushing and topping purposes

Ingredients for topping:
- ✓ 2 onions chopped
- ✓ ½ lb. chicken (Cut the chicken into tiny pieces)
- ✓ 2 capsicums chopped
- ✓ 2 tomatoes that have been deseeded and chopped
- ✓ 1 tbsp. (optional) mushrooms/corns
- ✓ 2 tsp. pizza seasoning
- ✓ Some cottage cheese that has been cut into small cubes (optional)

Directions:
1. Put the pizza base in a pre-heated Air fryer for around 5 minutes. (Pre heated to 340 Fahrenheit).
2. Take out the base. Pour some pizza sauce on top of the base at the center. Using a spoon spread the sauce over the base making sure that you leave some gap around the circumference. Grate some mozzarella cheese and sprinkle it over the sauce layer.
3. Take all the vegetables and the chicken mentioned in the ingredient list above and mix them in a bowl. Add some oil and seasoning. Also add some salt and pepper according to taste. Mix them properly. Put this topping over the layer of cheese on the pizza. Now sprinkle some more grated cheese and pizza seasoning on top of this layer.
4. Pre heat the Air Fryer at 250 Fahrenheit for around 5 minutes. Open the fry basket and place the pizza inside. Close the basket and keep the fryer at 170 degrees for another 10 minutes. If you feel that it is undercooked you may put it at the same temperature for another 2 minutes or so.

77. Chicken Fingers
Prep.Time: 12 hours - Cooking Time: 15 minutes - Servings: 2

Ingredients:
- ✓ 1 lb. boneless chicken breast cut into fingers
- ✓ 2 cup dry breadcrumbs
- ✓ 2 tsp. oregano
- ✓ 2 tsp. red chili flakes

Marinade:
- ✓ 1 ½ tbsp. ginger-garlic paste
- ✓ 4 tbsp. lemon juice
- ✓ 2 tsp. salt
- ✓ 1 tsp. pepper powder
- ✓ 1 tsp. red chili powder
- ✓ 6 tbsp. corn flour
- ✓ 4 eggs

Directions:
1. Mix all the ingredients for the marinade and put the chicken fingers inside and let it rest overnight.
2. Mix the breadcrumbs, oregano and red chili flakes well and place the marinated fingers on this mixture. Cover it with plastic wrap and leave it till right before you serve to cook.
3. Pre heat the Air fryer at 160 degrees Fahrenheit for 5 minutes. Place the fingers in the fry basket and close it. Let them cook at the same temperature for another 15 minutes or so. Toss the fingers well so that they are cooked uniformly.

78. Chicken Croquette
Prep.Time: 16 hours - Cooking Time: 15 min - Servings: 4-6

Ingredients:
- ✓ 2 lb. boneless chicken cut into 1½" pieces

1st Marinade:
- ✓ 3 tbsp. vinegar or lemon juice
- ✓ 2 or 3 tsp. paprika
- ✓ 1 tsp. black pepper
- ✓ 1 tsp. salt
- ✓ 3 tsp. ginger-garlic paste

2nd Marinade:
- ✓ 1 cup yogurt
- ✓ 4 tsp. tandoori masala
- ✓ 2 tbsp. dry fenugreek leaves
- ✓ 1 tsp. black salt
- ✓ 1 tsp. chat masala
- ✓ 1 tsp. garam masala powder
- ✓ 1 tsp. red chili powder
- ✓ 1 tsp. salt
- ✓ 3 drops of red color

Directions:
1. Make the first marinade and soak the cut chicken in it for four hours. While this is happening, make the second marinade and soak the chicken in it overnight to let the flavors blend.
2. Pre heat the Air fryer at 160 degrees Fahrenheit for 5 minutes. Place the fingers in the fry basket and close it. Let them cook at the same temperature for another 15 minutes or so. Toss the fingers well so that they are cooked uniformly. Serve them with mint chutney.

79. Chicken Samosa
Prep.Time: 20 min - **Cooking Time:** 35 min - **Servings:** 2-4

Ingredients:
For wrappers:
- ✓ 2 tbsp. unsalted butter
- ✓ 1 ½ cup all-purpose flour
- ✓ A pinch of salt to taste
- ✓ Add as much water as required to make the dough stiff and firm

For filling:
- ✓ 1 lb. chicken (Remove the chicken from the bone and cut it into pieces)
- ✓ ¼ cup boiled peas
- ✓ 1 tsp. powdered ginger
- ✓ 1 or 2 green chilies that are finely chopped or mashed
- ✓ ½ tsp. cumin
- ✓ 1 tsp. coarsely crushed coriander
- ✓ 1 dry red chili broken into pieces
- ✓ A small amount of salt (to taste)
- ✓ ½ tsp. dried mango powder
- ✓ ½ tsp. red chili power.
- ✓ 1-2 tbsp. coriander

Directions:
1. You will first need to make the outer covering. In a large bowl, add the flour, butter and enough water to knead it into dough that is stiff. Transfer this to a container and leave it to rest for five minutes.
2. Place a pan on medium flame and add the oil. Roast the mustard seeds and once roasted, add the coriander seeds and the chopped dry red chilies. Add all the dry ingredients for the filling and mix the ingredients well. Add a little water and continue to stir the ingredients.
3. Make small balls out of the dough and roll them out. Cut the rolled out dough into halves and apply a little water on the edges to help you fold the halves into a cone. Add the filling to the cone and close up the samosa.
4. Pre-heat the Air Fryer for around 5 to 6 minutes at 300 Fahrenheit. Place all the samosas in the fry basket and close the basket properly. Keep the Air Fryer at 200 degrees for another 20 to 25 minutes. Around the halfway point, open the basket and turn the samosas over for uniform cooking. After this, fry at 250 degrees for around 10 minutes in order to give them the desired golden brown color. Serve hot. Recommended sides are tamarind or mint chutney.

80. Chicken Burritos
Prep.Time: 2 hours - **Cooking Time:** 15 min - **Servings:** 2-4

Ingredients:
- ✓ ½ lb. chicken (You will need to cut the chicken into small pieces)
- ✓ ½ small onion chopped
- ✓ 1 tbsp. olive oil
- ✓ 2 tbsp. tomato puree
- ✓ ¼ tsp. red chili powder
- ✓ 1 tsp. of salt to taste
- ✓ 4-5 flour tortillas

Filling:
- ✓ 1 tbsp. Olive oil
- ✓ 1 medium onion finely sliced
- ✓ 3 flakes garlic crushed
- ✓ 1 tsp. white wine
- ✓ A pinch of salt to taste
- ✓ ½ tsp. red chili flakes
- ✓ 2 carrots (Cut in to long thin slices)

Salad:
- ✓ 1-2 lettuce leaves shredded.
- ✓ 1 or 2 spring onions chopped finely. Also cut the greens.
- ✓ Take one tomato. Remove the seeds and chop it into small pieces.
- ✓ 1 green chili chopped.
- ✓ 1 cup of cheddar cheese grated.

To serve:
- ✓ 1 cup boiled rice (not necessary).
- ✓ A few flour tortillas to put the filing in

Directions:
1. Cook the chicken, onions and garlic in two cups of water. You will need to cook till the chicken pieces have turned very soft. Now, mash the beans very fine.
2. In a pan, add oil and a few more onions to the pan and cook till the onions have turned translucent. Add the tomato puree and the cooked chicken and stir. Add the chili powder and salt to the pan and continue to cook till you get a thick paste. Set it aside.
3. For the filling, you will need to sauté the onions and garlic in oil. Add the French beans and the chopped carrots. You will need to stir-fry for a few minutes and add the remaining ingredients for the filling. Cook for another ten minutes and take the pan off the flame. Mix it well and add the jalapenos.
4. To make the salad, toss the ingredients together.
5. Place a tortilla and add a layer of the French beans to it. Cover the edges using the chicken paste. Put the filling in the center of the tortilla along with the salad and some boiled rice. Roll up the tortilla using the chicken sauce to help you hold it together.
6. Pre-heat the Air Fryer for around 5 minutes at 200 Fahrenheit. Open the fry basket and keep the burritos inside. Close the basket properly. Let the Air Fryer remain at 200 Fahrenheit for another 15 minutes or so. Halfway through, remove the basket and turn all the burritos over in order to get a uniform cook. You can either serve the burritos as they are or you can cut them into pieces so that they are easier to eat. Recommended sides are salsa or some salad.

81. Tandoori Chicken
Prep.Time: 20 min - **Cooking Time:** 40 min - **Servings:** 2-4

Ingredients:
- ✓ 1 lb. chicken (Cut the chicken into cubes of one inch each. Make sure that they have been deboned well)
- ✓ 1 big capsicum (Cut this capsicum into big cubes)
- ✓ 1 onion (Cut it into quarters. Now separate the layers carefully.)
- ✓ 5 tbsp. gram flour
- ✓ A pinch of salt to taste

For chutney:
- ✓ 2 cup fresh green coriander
- ✓ ½ cup mint leaves
- ✓ 4 tsp. fennel
- ✓ 2 tbsp. ginger-garlic paste
- ✓ 1 small onion
- ✓ 6-7 flakes garlic (optional)
- ✓ Salt to taste
- ✓ 3 tbsp. lemon juice

Directions:
1. You will first need to make the chutney. Add the ingredients to a blender and make a thick paste. Slit the pieces of chicken and stuff half the paste into the cavity obtained.
2. Take the remaining paste and add it to the gram flour and salt. Toss the pieces of chicken in this mixture and set aside.
3. Apply a little bit of the mixture on the capsicum and onion. Place these on a stick along with the chicken pieces.
4. Pre heat the Air Fryer at 290 Fahrenheit for around 5 minutes. Open the basket. Arrange the satay sticks properly. Close the basket. Keep the sticks with the chicken at 180 degrees for around half an hour while the sticks with the vegetables are to be kept at the same temperature for only 7 minutes. Turn the sticks in between so that one side does not get burnt and also to provide a uniform cook.

82. Honey Chili Chicken
Prep.Time: 10 min - **Cooking Time:** 20 min - **Servings:** 2-4

Ingredients:
For chicken fingers:
- ✓ 1 lb. chicken (Cut the chicken into slices)
- ✓ 2 ½ tsp. ginger-garlic paste
- ✓ 1 tsp. red chili sauce
- ✓ ¼ tsp. salt
- ✓ ¼ tsp. red chili powder/black pepper
- ✓ A few drops of edible orange food coloring

For sauce:
- ✓ 2 tbsp. olive oil
- ✓ 1 capsicum (Cut in to long pieces)
- ✓ 2 small onions. Cut them into halves
- ✓ 1 ½ tsp. ginger garlic paste
- ✓ ½ tbsp. red chili sauce
- ✓ 2 tbsp. tomato ketchup
- ✓ 1 ½ tbsp. sweet chili sauce
- ✓ 2 tsp. soya sauce
- ✓ 2 tsp. vinegar
- ✓ 1-2 tbsp. honey
- ✓ A pinch of black pepper
- ✓ 2 tsp. red chili flakes

Directions:
1. Create the mix for the chicken fingers and coat the chicken well with it.
2. Pre heat the Air fryer at 250 Fahrenheit for 5 minutes or so. Open the basket of the Fryer. Place the fingers inside the basket. Now let the fryer stay at 290 Fahrenheit for another 20 minutes. Keep tossing the fingers periodically through the cook to get a uniform cook.
3. Add the ingredients to the sauce and cook it with the vegetables till it thickens. Add the chicken fingers to the sauce and cook till the flavors have blended.

83. Quail Tikka
Prep.Time: 20 min - **Cooking Time:** 40 minutes - **Servings:** 2

Ingredients:
- ✓ 2 cups sliced quail
- ✓ 1 big capsicum (Cut this capsicum into big cubes)
- ✓ 1 onion (Cut it into quarters. Now separate the layers carefully.)
- ✓ 5 tbsp. gram flour
- ✓ A pinch of salt to taste

For the filling:
- ✓ 2 cup fresh green coriander
- ✓ ½ cup mint leaves
- ✓ 4 tsp. fennel
- ✓ 2 tbsp. ginger-garlic paste
- ✓ 1 small onion
- ✓ 6-7 flakes garlic (optional)
- ✓ Salt to taste
- ✓ 3 tbsp. lemon juice

Directions:
1. You will first need to make the chutney. Add the ingredients to a blender and make a thick paste. Slit the pieces of quail and stuff half the paste into the cavity obtained.
2. Take the remaining paste and add it to the gram flour and salt. Toss the pieces of quail in this mixture and set aside.
3. Apply a little bit of the mixture on the capsicum and onion. Place these on a stick along with the quail pieces.
4. Pre heat the Air Fryer at 290 Fahrenheit for around 5 minutes. Open the basket. Arrange the satay sticks properly. Close the basket. Keep the sticks with the quail at 180 degrees for around half an hour while the sticks with the vegetables are to be kept at the same temperature for only 7 minutes. Turn the sticks in between so that one side does not get burnt and also to provide a uniform cook.

84. Turkey Wontons
Prep.Time: 15 min - **Cooking Time:** 20 min - **Servings:** 2

Ingredients:
For dough:
- ✓ 1 ½ cup all-purpose flour
- ✓ ½ tsp. salt
- ✓ 5 tbsp. water

For filling:
- ✓ 2 cups minced turkey
- ✓ 2 tbsp. oil
- ✓ 2 tsp. ginger-garlic paste
- ✓ 2 tsp. soya sauce
- ✓ 2 tsp. vinegar

Directions:
1. Knead the dough and cover it with plastic wrap and set aside. Next, cook the ingredients for the filling and try to ensure that the turkey is covered well with the sauce.
2. Roll the dough and place the filling in the center. Now, wrap the dough to cover the filling and pinch the edges together.
3. Pre heat the Air fryer at 200° F for 5 minutes. Place the wontons in the fry basket and close it. Let them cook at the same temperature for another 20 minutes. Recommended sides are chili sauce or ketchup.

85. Quail Samosa

Prep.Time: 45 min - **Cooking Time:** 35 min - **Servings:** 2-4

Ingredients:

For wrappers:
- ✓ 2 tbsp. unsalted butter
- ✓ 1 ½ cup all-purpose flour
- ✓ A pinch of salt to taste
- ✓ Add as much water as required to make the dough stiff and firm

For filling:
- ✓ 1 lb. quail
- ✓ ¼ cup boiled peas
- ✓ 1 tsp. powdered ginger
- ✓ 1 or 2 green chilies that are finely chopped or mashed
- ✓ ½ tsp. cumin
- ✓ 1 tsp. coarsely crushed coriander
- ✓ 1 dry red chili broken into pieces
- ✓ A small amount of salt (to taste)
- ✓ ½ tsp. dried mango powder
- ✓ ½ tsp. red chili power.
- ✓ 1-2 tbsp. coriander

Directions:

1. You will first need to make the outer covering. In a large bowl, add the flour, butter and enough water to knead it into dough that is stiff. Transfer this to a container and leave it to rest for five minutes.
2. Place a pan on medium flame and add the oil. Roast the mustard seeds and once roasted, add the coriander seeds and the chopped dry red chilies. Add all the dry ingredients for the filling and mix the ingredients well. Add a little water and continue to stir the ingredients.
3. Make small balls out of the dough and roll them out. Cut the rolled out dough into halves and apply a little water on the edges to help you fold the halves into a cone. Add the filling to the cone and close up the samosa.
4. Pre-heat the Air Fryer for around 5 to 6 minutes at 300 Fahrenheit. Place all the samosas in the fry basket and close the basket properly. Keep the Air Fryer at 200 degrees for another 20 to 25 minutes. Around the halfway point, open the basket and turn the samosas over for uniform cooking. After this, fry at 250 degrees for around 10 minutes in order to give them the desired golden brown color. Serve hot. Recommended sides are tamarind or mint chutney.

86. Quail Chili

Prep.Time: 12 hours - **Cooking Time:** 15 min - **Servings:** 6

Ingredients:
- ✓ 1 lb. quail (Cut into cubes)
- ✓ 2 ½ tsp. ginger-garlic paste
- ✓ 1 tsp. red chili sauce
- ✓ ¼ tsp. salt
- ✓ ¼ tsp. red chili powder/black pepper
- ✓ A few drops of edible orange food coloring

For sauce:
- ✓ 2 tbsp. olive oil
- ✓ 1 ½ tsp. ginger garlic paste
- ✓ ½ tbsp. red chili sauce
- ✓ 2 tbsp. tomato ketchup
- ✓ 2 tsp. soya sauce
- ✓ 1-2 tbsp. honey
- ✓ ¼ tsp. Ajinomoto
- ✓ 1-2 tsp. red chili flakes

Directions:

1. Mix all the ingredients for the marinade and put the quail cubes inside and let it rest overnight.
2. Mix the breadcrumbs, oregano and red chili flakes well and place the marinated fingers on this mixture. Cover it with plastic wrap and leave it till right before you serve to cook.
3. Pre heat the Air fryer at 160 degrees Fahrenheit for 5 minutes. Place the fingers in the fry basket and close it. Let them cook at the same temperature for another 15 minutes or so. Toss the fingers well so that they are cooked uniformly.

87. Duck fingers

Prep.Time: 12 hours - **Cooking Time:** 15 minutes - **Servings:** 2-4

Ingredients:
- ✓ 1 lb. boneless duck (Cut into fingers)
- ✓ 2 cup dry breadcrumbs
- ✓ 2 tsp. oregano
- ✓ 2 tsp. red chili flakes

Marinade:
- ✓ 1 ½ tbsp. ginger-garlic paste
- ✓ 4 tbsp. lemon juice
- ✓ 2 tsp. salt
- ✓ 1 tsp. pepper powder
- ✓ 1 tsp. red chili powder
- ✓ 6 tbsp. corn flour
- ✓ 4 eggs

Directions:

1. Mix all the ingredients for the marinade and put the duck fingers inside and let it rest overnight.
2. Mix the breadcrumbs, oregano and red chili flakes well and place the marinated fingers on this mixture. Cover it with plastic wrap and leave it till right before you serve to cook.
3. Pre heat the Air fryer at 160 degrees Fahrenheit for 5 minutes. Place the fingers in the fry basket and close it. Let them cook at the same temperature for another 15 minutes or so. Toss the fingers well so that they are cooked uniformly.

88. Squab Cutlet

Prep.Time: 16 hours - **Cooking Time:** 15 min - **Servings:** 4

Ingredients:
- ✓ 2 lb. boneless squab cut into slices

1st Marinade:
- ✓ 3 tbsp. vinegar or lemon juice
- ✓ 2 or 3 tsp. paprika
- ✓ 1 tsp. black pepper
- ✓ 1 tsp. salt
- ✓ 3 tsp. ginger-garlic paste

2nd Marinade:
- ✓ 1 cup yogurt
- ✓ 4 tsp. tandoori masala
- ✓ 2 tbsp. dry fenugreek leaves
- ✓ 1 tsp. black salt
- ✓ 1 tsp. chat masala
- ✓ 1 tsp. garam masala powder
- ✓ 1 tsp. red chili powder
- ✓ 1 tsp. salt
- ✓ 3 drops of red color

Directions:

1. Make the first marinade and soak the cut squab in it for four hours. While this is happening, make the second marinade and soak the squab in it overnight to let the flavors blend.
2. Pre heat the Air fryer at 160 degrees Fahrenheit for 5 minutes. Place the fingers in the fry basket and close it. Let them cook at the same temperature for another 15 minutes or so. Toss the fingers well so that they are cooked uniformly. Serve them with mint chutney.

89. Poultry Samosa

Prep.Time: 45 min - **Cooking Time:** 35 min - **Servings:** 2-4

Ingredients:

For wrappers:
- ✓ 2 tbsp. unsalted butter
- ✓ 1 ½ cup all-purpose flour
- ✓ A pinch of salt to taste
- ✓ Water to knead the dough

For filling:
- ✓ 1 lb. mixed minced poultry (squab, chicken, duck, pheasant, turkey)
- ✓ ¼ cup boiled peas
- ✓ 1 tsp. powdered ginger
- ✓ 1 or 2 green chilies that are finely chopped or mashed
- ✓ ½ tsp. cumin
- ✓ 1 tsp. coarsely crushed coriander
- ✓ 1 dry red chili broken into pieces
- ✓ A small amount of salt (to taste)
- ✓ ½ tsp. dried mango powder
- ✓ ½ tsp. red chili power.
- ✓ 1-2 tbsp. coriander

Directions:

1. You will first need to make the outer covering. In a large bowl, add the flour, butter and enough water to knead it into dough that is stiff. Transfer this to a container and leave it to rest for five minutes.
2. Place a pan on medium flame and add the oil. Roast the mustard seeds and once roasted, add the coriander seeds and the chopped dry red chilies. Add all the dry ingredients for the filling and mix the ingredients well. Add a little water and continue to stir the ingredients.
3. Make small balls out of the dough and roll them out. Cut the rolled out dough into halves and apply a little water on the edges to help you fold the halves into a cone. Add the filling to the cone and close up the samosa.
4. Pre-heat the Air Fryer for around 5 to 6 minutes at 300 Fahrenheit. Place all the samosas in the fry basket and close the basket properly. Keep the Air Fryer at 200 degrees for another 20 to 25 minutes. Around the halfway point, open the basket and turn the samosas over for uniform cooking. After this, fry at 250 degrees for around 10 minutes in order to give them the desired golden brown color. Serve hot. Recommended sides are tamarind or mint chutney.

90. Squab fingers

Prep.Time: 30 min - **Cooking Time:** 25 min - **Servings:** 2

Ingredients:
- ✓ ½ lb. squab fingers
- ✓ 2 cups of dry breadcrumbs
- ✓ 1 cup oil for frying

Marinade:
- ✓ 1 ½ tbsp. ginger-garlic paste
- ✓ 3 tbsp. lemon juice
- ✓ 2 tsp salt
- ✓ 1 ½ tsp pepper powder
- ✓ 1 tsp red chili flakes or to taste
- ✓ 3 eggs
- ✓ 5 tbsp. corn flour
- ✓ 2 tsp tomato ketchup

Directions:

1. Make the marinade and transfer the fingers into the marinade. Leave them on a plate to dry for fifteen minutes. Now cover the fingers with the crumbs and set aside to dry for fifteen minutes.
2. Pre heat the Air Fryer at 160 degrees Fahrenheit for 5 minutes or so. Keep the fish in the fry basket now and close it properly. Let the fingers cook at the same temperature for another 25 minutes. In between the cooking process, toss the fish once in a while to avoid burning the food. Serve either with tomato ketchup or chili sauce. Mint chutney also works well with the fish.

91. Spicy Garlic Chicken Nuggets

Prep.Time: 20 min - **Cooking Time:** 20 minutes - **Servings:** 2

Ingredients:
- ✓ 1 eggs, whisked
- ✓ 2 chicken breast halves, boneless, skinless
- ✓ ½ pound of flour
- ✓ 3 tablespoons of garlic powder
- ✓ 1 tablespoon of black pepper
- ✓ 1 teaspoon of salt

Directions:

1. Mix the garlic, salt, pepper and flour in a shallow dish. Put the whisked egg in a separate bowl.
2. Preheat the air-fryer at 356°F.
3. Cut the chicken into small pieces and dip them into the eggs and then coat with the flour mixture. Shake off any excess flour coating and place the chicken in a plate.
4. Put the chicken pieces into the air-fryer and cook until golden for 20 minutes. Shake the chicken halfway through.

92. Onion And Parsley Turkey Rolls

Prep.Time: 15 min - **Cooking Time:** 40 min - **Servings:** 4

Ingredients:
- ✓ 1 pound of turkey breast fillets
- ✓ 6 teaspoons of olive oil
- ✓ 1 teaspoon of cinnamon
- ✓ 1 clove of garlic, crushed
- ✓ 1 small sized onion, finely chopped
- ✓ 1 teaspoon of salt
- ✓ 1½ ounces of parsley, finely chopped
- ✓ 1½ tsp. of ground cumin
- ✓ ½ tsp. of ground chili

Directions:

1. Place the turkey fillets on a chopping board with the smaller side facing you and cut through horizontally up to about 2/3 of the length. Fold open the slit and cut through again to form a long strip of meat.
2. Mix the chili, garlic, cumin, pepper, cinnamon and salt together in a large bowl. Stir in the olive oil. Remove 1 tablespoon of the mixture and set aside in a small bowl.
3. Add the parsley and onion to the mixture in the large bowl and stir.
4. Heat your air-fryer to 356°F.
5. Spread the herb mixture on the surface of the meat and roll firmly beginning from the shorter end. Tie the roll with a string at about an inch interval. Coat the outside of the meat rolls with the spice mixture that was set aside.
6. Place in the air fryer and cook for 40 minutes

93. Crispy Chicken Fillets

Prep.Time: 10 min - Cooking Time: 15 min - Servings: 3

Ingredients:
- ✓ 12 ounces of chicken fillets
- ✓ 1 tsp. of ground black pepper
- ✓ 2 tbsp. of vegetable oil
- ✓ 8 tbsp. of breadcrumbs
- ✓ 4 ounces of flour
- ✓ 2 eggs, whisked
- ✓ ½ teaspoon salt

Directions:
1. Heat your Air-fryer up to 330°F.
2. Add the salt, pepper and oil to the breadcrumbs then mix thoroughly.
3. Put the flour and egg into shallow bowls. Place the chicken in the flour, shake off excess and then dip into the whisked eggs and then coat evenly with breadcrumbs pressing to ensure that the breadcrumbs stick.
4. Shake off excess and place into the basket of the air fryer. Cook for 10 minutes and then increase heat to 390°F. Finally, cook for another 5 minutes until golden.

94. Sweet Potatoes & Creamy Crisp Chicken Air fry

Prep.Time: 15 min - Cooking Time: 40 min - Servings: 2

Ingredients:
- ✓ ¼ cup of flour, seasoned with salt and pepper
- ✓ 1 cup of buttermilk
- ✓ 1 teaspoon of garlic, finely chopped
- ✓ 1 egg, whisked
- ✓ 2 (5-ounce) chicken breast
- ✓ ½ teaspoon of pepper
- ✓ 7 ounces of breadcrumbs
- ✓ 2 medium sized sweet potatoes
- ✓ 3 teaspoons of smoked paprika
- ✓ 3 teaspoons of vegetable oil
- ✓ Salt and pepper to taste

Directions:
1. Put the pepper, garlic and buttermilk into the bowl of chicken breasts, cover and leave to marinate in the fridge overnight.
2. Preheat the air fryer to 374°F for about 3 minutes.
3. Rub off the marinade from the chicken and dip the chicken into the seasoned flour, then into the egg and lastly the breadcrumbs. Ensure the coating sticks firmly to the chicken.
4. Fry the chicken in the air fryer for 20 minutes until well cooked. Remove from the fryer.
5. Peel the sweet potatoes and slice into chips, 1cm thick. Add the oil and paprika to the chips and toss.
6. Place the chips into the fryer and fry for 20 minutes at 374°F. Shake at about 6 minutes intervals. Season chips with salt and pepper when ready.

95. Mushroom & Chicken Noodles With Glasswort And Sesame

Prep.Time: 30 min - Cooking Time: 17 minutes - Servings: 4

Ingredients:
- ✓ 14 ounces of chicken thigh fillets, cut to pieces
- ✓ 14 ounces of noodles, cooked
- ✓ 2 cloves of garlic
- ✓ 2/3 cup of chestnut mushrooms
- ✓ 2/3 cup of shiitake mushrooms
- ✓ 1/4 cup of soy sauce
- ✓ 6 teaspoons of sesame oil
- ✓ 3 teaspoons of sesame seeds
- ✓ 7 ounces of glasswort
- ✓ 5.3 ounces of bean sprouts
- ✓ 1 teaspoon sambal
- ✓ 1 medium sized onion, thinly sliced Krupuk

Directions:
1. Mix the soy sauce, garlic and sambal to form a marinade and soak the chicken pieces in it to absorb.
2. Add 3 teaspoons of oil to the cooked noodles.
3. Heat the air-fryer to 392°F. Place the chicken pieces in the fryer basket and sprinkle with oil. Cook for 6 minutes, shaking at intervals.
4. Add the onion, mushrooms, glasswort and bean sprouts. Cook for another 5 minutes. Put in the noodles and cook further for 5 minutes. Finally, add the krupuk at the last minute.
5. Remove from the air-fryer and sprinkle with sesame seed.

96. Prawn Chicken Drumettes

Prep.Time: 15 min - Cooking Time: 15 min - Servings: 3

Ingredients:
- ✓ 10½ ounces of chicken drumettes
- ✓ 1 teaspoon of sesame oil
- ✓ 1 teaspoon of ginger juice
- ✓ 6 teaspoons of vegetable oil
- ✓ ¾ teaspoon of sugar
- ✓ 3 teaspoons of prawn paste
- ✓ ½ teaspoon of Shaoxing wine

Directions:
1. Mix the sesame oil, ginger juice, sugar, prawn paste and Shaoxing wine together to form the marinade. Soak the chicken in the marinade for an hour or overnight in the refrigerator.
2. Preheat your air-fryer for 5 minutes at 356°F.
3. Brush the chicken lightly with vegetable oil and arrange in a single layer in the fryer basket. Cook for 8 minutes, turn the chicken over and cook for another 7 minutes until golden.

97. Asian Popcorn Chicken

Prep.Time: 30 min - Cooking Time: 15 min - Servings: 2

Ingredients:
- 1 lbs. chicken breast chicken thigh, boneless
- 1 clove garlic, medium, minced
- 1 tbsp. soy sauce
- 2 green onions, minced
- ¼ tsp. of pepper
- ¼ tsp. of chili pepper
- ¼ t tsp. of five spice
- ½ tsp. of sweet potato starch or corn starch
- 1 cup sweet potato starch/corn starch
- 1 egg
- ¼ cup water
- Breadcrumbs

Directions:
1. Wash the chicken and dice. Put the washed and minced green onions and garlic in a medium bowl. Add the chili pepper, five spice powder, pepper, soy sauce and starch, mixing well.
2. Place chicken into the bowl and ensure the pieces are fully coated on all the sides. Leave the chicken to marinate in the bowl for at least 30 minutes or overnight if you like.
3. Preheat the air fryer to 390F. Beat 1 egg with water in a small ball, add starch and mix thoroughly.
4. Coat the chicken with the starch, pressing with hands, so it does not fall off. Place in the air fryer and cook for 12 minutes. Served, tossed with salt and pepper.

98. Herbal Chicken With Purple Sweet Potato

Prep.Time: 5 min - Cooking Time: 22 min - Servings: 2

Ingredients:
- 1/2 portion of chicken, halved
- 1 teaspoon olive
- 1 tablespoon herbs chicken spices, (Seahs Emperor)
- Handful of purple sweet potato, brushed clean and pat dry
- Handful of salad green

Directions:
1. Trim the chicken then rinse and pat dry. Marinate with olive oil and herb chicken spices for 1 hour or overnight in the refrigerator.
2. Place the sweet potato in the air-fryer basket, set temperature to 350°F and cook for 10 minutes.
3. Arrange the marinated chicken on the air-fryer basket and cook another 12 minutes.
4. During the last 4 to 5 minutes, check the color of the chicken to make sure they are nicely brown then keep cooking.
5. Leave the food for 1-2 minutes in the air-fryer before removing and serving with salad greens.

99. Tasty And Spicy Chicken Jerks

Prep.Time: 38 min - Cooking Time: 18 minutes - Servings: 5

Ingredients:
- 6 tsp. of vegetable oil
- 1 tsp. of white pepper
- 3 tsp. of chopped fresh thyme
- 6 cloves of garlic, finely diced
- 1 tsp. of cinnamon
- 4 green onions
- 2½ ounces of lime juice
- 3 tsp. of grated ginger
- 1 habanera pepper, finely chopped
- 1 tsp. cayenne pepper
- 6 tsp. of sugar
- 30 chicken wings
- 8 tbsp. of red wine vinegar
- 6 tsp. of soy sauce
- 1 tsp. of salt

Directions:
1. Add up all the ingredients in a large bowl, ensuring that the chicken is well covered with the spices and seasonings. Pour into a large re-sealable bag and leave to marinate in a refrigerator for 2-24 hours.
2. Heat your Air fryer to 390°F.
3. Remove the chicken wings from bag, discard the liquid and dry the wings with a disposable paper towel.
4. Put the wings into the fryer basket and fry for 18 minutes. Shake the chicken halfway through. Serve with ranch dressing.

100. Honey & Sauce Chicken Wings

Prep.Time: 40 min - Cooking Time: 25 min - Servings: 6-8

Ingredients:
- 1½ ounces of honey
- 1 pack of 21 pieces of chicken wings
- 1½ ounces of canola oil
- 1 teaspoon of light soy sauce
- 3 teaspoons of oyster sauce
- 3 teaspoons of dark soy sauce
- ½ teaspoon of pepper
- Huo Tiao Chinese Wine

Directions:
1. Wash the chicken and dry with kitchen paper towels 2. Mix the soy sauces, oyster sauce, oil, pepper, Huo Tiao wine and honey together to form the marinate.
2. Put the mixture and wings in a re-sealable bag and marinate for 30 min or longer. . Line the air fryer basket with aluminum foil and place the chicken in a single layer.
3. Heat the air-fryer to 392°F. Air fry the chicken for 15 min, turn the chicken and cook for another 10 min until golden brown. Repeat until they are cooked

101. Delicious Spicy Drumsticks

Prep.Time: 2 min - Cooking Time: 18 minutes - Servings: 4

Ingredients:
- 4 chicken drumsticks
- 6 teaspoons of Montreal chicken spices
- 6 teaspoons of ground black pepper
- 1 teaspoon of olive oil
- 1 teaspoon of salt
- 6 teaspoons of chicken seasoning (your choice)

Directions:
1. Mix all the spices and seasonings in a bowl. Brush the chicken with olive oil.
2. Rub the spices on the chicken. Ensure the spices stick firmly to the drumsticks.
3. Heat your air-fryer to 200°F for 3 minutes. Put the chicken into the fryer and cook for 10 minutes.
4. Turn down the heat to 150°F and cook again for 8 minutes cheese on top and serve.

102. Air Fryer Turkey Breast

Prep.Time: 5 min - Cooking Time: 55 min - Servings: 10

Ingredients:
- 4 pound turkey breast, on the bone with skin (ribs removed)
- 1 tablespoon olive oil
- 2 teaspoons kosher
- 1/2 tablespoon dry turkey or poultry seasoning, I used Bell's which has not salt

Directions:
1. Rub 1/2 tablespoon of oil all over the turkey breast. Season both sides with salt and turkey seasoning then rub in the remaining half tablespoon of oil over the skin side.
2. Preheat the air fryer 350F and cook skin side down 20 minutes, turn over and cook until the internal temperature is 160F using an instant-read thermometer about 30 to 40 minutes more depending on the size of your breast. Let is rest 10 minutes before carving

103. Honey Lime Air-fried Chicken

Prep.Time: 6 hours 40 min - **Cooking Time:** 15 min - **Servings:** 4

Ingredients:
- ✓ 16 mid joint chicken wings; washed & pat dry

Marinate:
- ✓ 2 tablespoons good quality honey
- ✓ 2 tablespoons light soya sauce
- ✓ 1/4 teaspoon white pepper powder
- ✓ 1/2 teaspoon sea salt
- ✓ 1/2 black pepper, crushed
- ✓ 2 tablespoons lime/ lemon juice

Directions:
1. Combine all the marinate ingredients into a glass dish, add the mid wings, mix thoroughly, refrigerate for 6 h.
2. 30 minutes before air-frying, remove to rest in room temperature.
3. Air fry for 6 minutes with a temperature of 350° F. Flip over and cook for another 6 minutes and flip again to air fry for 3 minutes with a temperature of 400° F.
4. Cool for 5 min and serve with a wedge of lemon or lime.

104. Jerk Chicken Wings

Prep.Time: 15 min - **Cooking Time:** 30 min - **Servings:** 5

Ingredients:
- ✓ 2 tablespoons olive oil
- ✓ 3 pounds chicken wings
- ✓ 2 tablespoons soy sauce
- ✓ 6 cloves garlic, chopped finely
- ✓ 1 habanero pepper, seeds and ribs removed, finely chopped
- ✓ 1 teaspoon cinnamon
- ✓ 1 tablespoon allspice
- ✓ 1 teaspoon cayenne pepper
- ✓ 1 teaspoon salt
- ✓ 1 teaspoon white pepper
- ✓ 2 tablespoons brown sugar
- ✓ 1 tablespoon fresh ginger, grated
- ✓ 1 tablespoon fresh thyme, finely chopped
- ✓ 5 tablespoons lime juice
- ✓ 4 scallions, finely chopped
- ✓ ½ cup red wine vinegar

Directions:
1. Add together all the ingredients in a large bowl, coating the chicken well with these seasonings and marinade.
2. Remove to a re-sealable bag and place in the refrigerator for 2-24 hours.
3. Preheat the Air-fryer to 390°F. Take out the wings from the bag then drain out all liquid. Pat dry wings completely with a paper towel.
4. Put the wings in the cooking basket, cook for 16 to18 minutes, while shaking halfway through.
5. Once cooked, serve with ranch dressing or blue cheese dipping.

105. Gluten-Free Air Fried Chicken

Prep.Time: 10 min - **Cooking Time:** 25 minutes - **Servings:** 2

Ingredients:
- ✓ 6 chicken drumsticks, rinse and pat dry with a paper towel
- ✓ 1 tsp ginger
- ✓ 1 tsp onion powder
- ✓ 1 tsp garlic powder
- ✓ 1 tsp paprika
- ✓ 1 cup buttermilk
- ✓ ¼ cup brown sugar
- ✓ ½ cup breadcrumbs
- ✓ 1 cup all-purpose flour
- ✓ ½ tsp pepper
- ✓ 1 tsp salt

Directions:
1. Preheat the instant vortex air fryer using bake mode at 390 F.
2. Add breadcrumbs, spices, and flour into the zip-lock bag and mix well.
3. In a bowl, mix together chicken and buttermilk and let sit for 2 minutes.
4. Now put a single piece of chicken into the zip-lock bag and shake it until chicken is evenly coated with breadcrumb mixture. Do this same with remaining chicken pieces.
5. Spray coated chicken with cooking spray.
6. Place chicken into the bottom tray of instant vortex air fryer and bake for 25 minutes.
7. Serve and enjoy.

106. Parmesan Garlic Chicken Wings – version 1

Prep.Time: 10 min - **Cooking Time:** 21 min - **Servings:** 2

Ingredients:
- ✓ 1 lb chicken wings
- ✓ 1 tsp parsley
- ✓ 2 tbsp garlic, minced
- ✓ ¾ cup parmesan cheese, grated
- ✓ 1 tbsp butter, melted
- ✓ ¼ tsp pepper
- ✓ 1 tsp salt

Directions:
1. Arrange chicken wings on instant vortex air fryer tray and air fry at 400 F for 7 minutes.
2. Turn chicken wings to the other side and air fry for 7 minutes more.
3. Turn chicken wings again and air fry for another 7 minutes.
4. In a mixing bowl, mix together cheese, butter, parsley, garlic, pepper, and salt.
5. Once chicken wings are done then transfer in mixing bowl and toss well with cheese mixture until well coated.
6. Serve and enjoy.

107. Turkey Fritters

Prep.Time: 10 min - **Cooking Time:** 25 min - **Servings:** 2

Ingredients:
- ✓ 2 tbsp. garam masala
- ✓ 1 lb. minced turkey
- ✓ 3 tsp ginger finely chopped
- ✓ 1-2 tbsp. fresh coriander leaves
- ✓ 2 or 3 green chilies finely chopped
- ✓ 1 ½ tbsp. lemon juice
- ✓ Salt and pepper to taste

Directions:
1. Mix the ingredients in a clean bowl.
2. Mold this mixture into round and flat galettes.
3. Wet the galettes slightly with water.
4. Pre heat the Air Fryer at 160 degrees Fahrenheit for 5 minutes. Place the galettes in the fry basket and let them cook for another 25 minutes at the same temperature. Keep rolling them over to get a uniform cook.
5. Serve either with mint chutney or ketchup.

108. Chicken Galette

Prep.Time: 10 min - **Cooking Time:** 25 min - **Servings:** 2

Ingredients:
- ✓ 2 tbsp. garam masala
- ✓ 1 lb. minced chicken
- ✓ 3 tsp ginger finely chopped
- ✓ 1-2 tbsp. fresh coriander leaves
- ✓ 2 or 3 green chilies finely chopped
- ✓ 1 ½ tbsp. lemon juice
- ✓ Salt and pepper to taste

Directions:
1. Mix the ingredients in a clean bowl.
2. Mold this mixture into round and flat galettes.
3. Wet the galettes slightly with water.
4. Pre heat the Air Fryer at 160 degrees Fahrenheit for 5 minutes. Place the galettes in the fry basket and let them cook for another 25 minutes at the same temperature. Keep rolling them over to get a uniform cook.
5. Serve either with mint chutney or ketchup.

109. Chicken and Eggs

Prep.Time: 10 min - **Cooking Time:** 20 min - **Servings:** 1

Ingredients:
- ✓ Bread slices (brown or white)
- ✓ 1 egg white for every 2 slices
- ✓ 1 tsp sugar for every 2 slices
- ✓ ½ lb. sliced chicken

Directions:
1. Put two slices together and cut them along the diagonal.
2. In a bowl, whisk the egg whites and add some sugar.
3. Dip the bread triangles into this mixture. Cook the chicken now.
4. Pre heat the Air Fryer at 180° C for 4 minutes. Place the coated bread triangles in the fry basket and close it. Let them cook at the same temperature for another 20 minutes at least. Halfway through the process, turn the triangles over so that you get a uniform cook.
5. Top with chicken and serve.

110. Duck Poppers

Prep.Time: 10 min - **Cooking Time:** 20 min - **Servings:** 1-2

Ingredients:
- ✓ 1 cup cubed duck
- ✓ 1 ½ tsp. garlic paste
- ✓ Salt and pepper to taste
- ✓ 1 tsp. dry oregano
- ✓ 1 tsp. dry basil
- ✓ ½ cup hung curd
- ✓ 1 tsp. lemon juice
- ✓ 1 tsp. red chili flakes

Directions:
1. Add the ingredients into a separate bowl and mix them well to get a consistent mixture.
2. Dip the duck pieces in the above mixture and leave them aside for some time.
3. Pre heat the Air fryer at 180° C for around 5 minutes. Place the coated duck pieces in the fry basket and close it properly. Let them cook at the same temperature for 20 more minutes. Keep turning them over in the basket so that they are cooked properly.
4. Serve with tomato ketchup.

111. Creamy Chicken Stew

Prep.Time: 10 min - **Cooking Time:** 25 min - **Servings:** 4

Ingredients:
- ✓ 1 and ½ cups canned cream of celery soup
- ✓ 6 chicken tenders
- ✓ Salt and black pepper to the taste
- ✓ 2 potatoes, chopped
- ✓ 1 bay leaf
- ✓ 1 thyme spring, chopped
- ✓ 1 tablespoon milk
- ✓ 1 egg yolk
- ✓ ½ cup heavy cream

Directions:
1. In a bowl, mix chicken with cream of celery, potatoes, heavy cream, bay leaf, thyme, salt and pepper, toss, pour into your air fryer's pan and cook at 320 degrees F for 25 minutes.
2. Leave your stew to cool down a bit, discard bay leaf, divide among plates and serve right away.

Nutrition: calories 300 - Fat 11 - Fiber 2 - Carbs 23 - Protein 14

112. Buttermilk Chicken

Prep.Time: 10 min - **Cooking Time:** 18 min - **Servings:** 4

Ingredients:
- ✓ 1 and ½ pounds chicken thighs
- ✓ 2 cups buttermilk
- ✓ Salt and black pepper to the taste
- ✓ A pinch of cayenne pepper
- ✓ 2 cups white flour
- ✓ 1 tablespoon baking powder
- ✓ 1 tablespoon sweet paprika
- ✓ 1 tablespoon garlic powder

Directions:
1. In a bowl, mix chicken thighs with buttermilk, salt, pepper and cayenne, toss and leave aside for 6 hours.
2. In a separate bowl, mix flour with paprika, baking powder and garlic powder and stir,
3. Drain chicken thighs, dredge them in flour mix, arrange them in your air fryer and cook at 360 degrees F for 8 minutes.
4. Flip chicken pieces, cook them for 10 minutes more, arrange on a platter and serve for lunch.

Nutrition: calories 200 - Fat 3 - Fiber 9 - Carbs 14 - Protein 4

113. Delicious Chicken Wings

Prep.Time: 10 min - Cooking Time: 45 min - Servings: 4

Ingredients:
- ✓ 3 pounds chicken wings
- ✓ ½ cup butter
- ✓ 1 tablespoon old bay seasoning
- ✓ ¾ cup potato starch
- ✓ 1 teaspoon lemon juice
- ✓ Lemon wedges for serving

Directions:
1. In a bowl, mix starch with old bay seasoning and chicken wings and toss well.
2. Place chicken wings in your air fryer's basket and cook them at 360 degrees F for 35 minutes shaking the fryer from time to time.
3. Increase temperature to 400 degrees F, cook chicken wings for 10 minutes more and divide them on plates.
4. Heat up a pan over medium heat, add butter and melt it.
5. Add lemon juice, stir well, take off heat and drizzle over chicken wings.
6. Serve them for lunch with lemon wedges on the side.

Nutrition: calories 271 - Fat 6 - Fiber 8 - Carbs 18 - Protein 18

114. Chicken Kabobs

Prep.Time: 10 min - Cooking Time: 20 min - Servings: 2

Ingredients:
- ✓ 3 orange bell peppers, cut into squares
- ✓ ¼ cup honey
- ✓ 1/3 cup soy sauce
- ✓ Salt and black pepper to the taste
- ✓ Cooking spray
- ✓ 6 mushrooms, halved
- ✓ 2 chicken breasts, skinless, boneless and roughly cubed

Directions:
1. In a bowl, mix chicken with salt, pepper, honey, say sauce and some cooking spray and toss well.
2. Thread chicken, bell peppers and mushrooms on skewers, place them in your air fryer and cook at 338 degrees F for 20 minutes.
3. Divide among plates and serve for lunch.

Nutrition: calories 261 - Fat 7 - Fiber 9 - Carbs 12 - Protein 6

115. Q1

Prep.Time: 10 min - Cooking Time: 25 min - Servings: 6

Ingredients:
- ✓ 6 chicken drumsticks, rinse and pat dry with a paper towel
- ✓ 1 tsp ginger
- ✓ 1 tsp onion powder
- ✓ 1 tsp garlic powder
- ✓ 1 tsp paprika
- ✓ 1 cup buttermilk
- ✓ ¼ cup brown sugar
- ✓ ½ cup breadcrumbs
- ✓ 1 cup all-purpose flour
- ✓ ½ tsp pepper
- ✓ 1 tsp salt

Directions:
1. Preheat the instant vortex air fryer using bake mode at 390 F.
2. Add breadcrumbs, spices, and flour into the zip-lock bag and mix well.
3. In a bowl, mix together chicken and buttermilk and let it sit for 2 minutes.
4. Now put a single piece of chicken into the zip-lock bag and shake it until chicken is evenly coated with breadcrumb mixture. Do this same with remaining chicken pieces.
5. Spray coated chicken with cooking spray.
6. Place chicken into the bottom tray of instant vortex air fryer and bake for 25 minutes.
7. Serve and enjoy.

116. Parmesan Garlic Chicken Wings – version 2

Prep.Time: 10 min - Cooking Time: 21 min - Servings: 2

Ingredients:
- ✓ 1 lb chicken wings
- ✓ 1 tsp parsley
- ✓ 2 tbsp garlic, minced
- ✓ ¾ cup parmesan cheese, grated
- ✓ 1 tbsp butter, melted
- ✓ ¼ tsp pepper
- ✓ 1 tsp salt

Directions:
1. Arrange chicken wings on instant vortex air fryer tray and air fry at 400 F for 7 minutes.
2. Turn chicken wings to the other side and air fry for 7 minutes more.
3. Turn chicken wings again and air fry for another 7 minutes.
4. In a mixing bowl, mix together cheese, butter, parsley, garlic, pepper, and salt.
5. Once chicken wings are done then transfer in mixing bowl and toss well with cheese mixture until well coated.
6. Serve and enjoy.

117. Delicious Rotisserie Chicken

Prep.Time: 10 min - Cooking Time: 50 min - Servings: 4

Ingredients:
- ✓ 3 lbs whole chicken
- ✓ ¾ tsp garlic powder
- ✓ ¼ cup olive oil
- ✓ 2 cups buttermilk
- ✓ Pepper
- ✓ Salt

Directions:
1. Mix together garlic powder, olive oil, buttermilk, pepper, and salt in a large zip-lock bag.
2. Add whole chicken in bag. Seal bag and marinate the chicken overnight.
3. Remove marinated chicken from bag and season with pepper and salt.
4. Place marinated chicken on the rotisserie spit and inset into the instant vortex air fryer oven.
5. Air fry chicken to 380 F for 50 minutes or until the internal temperature of chicken reaches 165 F.
6. Serve and enjoy.

118. Cuban Chicken Wings

Prep.Time: 10 min - Cooking Time: 35 min - Servings: 4-6

Ingredients:
- ✓ 12 chicken wings
- ✓ 2 tbsp water
- ✓ 1 tbsp sazon seasoning
- ✓ 1 tbsp adobo seasoning
- ✓ 1 tsp salt

Directions:
1. Place chicken wings in a large mixing bowl.
2. Add remaining ingredients over chicken and toss until chicken is well coated.
3. Add chicken into the rotisserie basket and place basket into the instant vortex air fryer.
4. Air fry chicken at 375 F for 35 minutes.
5. Serve and enjoy.

119. Healthy Chicken Popcorn

Prep.Time: 10 min - **Cooking Time:** 10 min - **Servings:** 2

Ingredients:
- ✓ 1 lb chicken breast, skinless, boneless, and cut into 1-inch pieces
- ✓ 1 egg, lightly beaten
- ✓ ½ tbsp Tabasco sauce
- ✓ 1 cup buttermilk
- ✓ 1 tsp baking powder
- ✓ 1 cup all-purpose flour
- ✓ ½ tsp pepper
- ✓ 1 tsp salt

Directions:
1. Season chicken pieces with pepper and salt.
2. In a medium bowl, mix together all-purpose flour and baking powder.
3. In another mixing bowl, mix together egg, buttermilk, and Tabasco sauce.
4. Coat chicken with flour mixture then dip chicken into the egg mixture then again coat with flour mixture.
5. Place coated chicken pieces on instant vortex air fryer tray. Spray coated chicken pieces with cooking spray.
6. Air fry chicken popcorn at 400 F for 5 minutes. Turn chicken popcorn to another side and air fry for 5 minutes more.
7. Serve and enjoy.

120. Tasty Lemon Chicken

Prep.Time: 10 min - **Cooking Time:** 8 min - **Servings:** 2

Ingredients:
- ✓ 1 lb chicken breasts, skinless and boneless
- ✓ 2 tbsp fresh lemon juice
- ✓ 1 tsp garlic, minced
- ✓ 3 tbsp butter, melted
- ✓ 1 tsp Italian seasoning
- ✓ 1 tbsp olive oil
- ✓ ½ tsp pepper
- ✓ 1 tsp salt

Directions:
1. In a mixing bowl, mix together lemon juice, garlic, butter, Italian seasoning, olive oil, pepper, and salt.
2. Add chicken to the mixing bowl and coat well.
3. Spray instant vortex air fryer tray with cooking spray.
4. Place chicken on tray and air fry at 400 F for 4 minutes.
5. Turn chicken to the other side and cook for 4 minutes more.
6. Serve and enjoy.

Nutrition: calories 261 - Fat 7 - Fiber 9 - Carbs 12 - Protein 6

121. Herbed Turkey Breast

Prep.Time: 10 min - **Cooking Time:** 50 min - **Servings:** 6

Ingredients:
- ✓ 3 lbs turkey breast
- ✓ 3 garlic cloves, minced
- ✓ 1 tbsp fresh sage leaves, chopped
- ✓ 1 tbsp rosemary leaves, chopped
- ✓ 1 tbsp fresh thyme
- ✓ 3 tbsp butter
- ✓ 1 tsp lemon zest, grated
- ✓ ½ tsp pepper
- ✓ 1 tsp kosher salt

Directions:
1. In a bowl, mix together butter, garlic, sage, rosemary, thyme, lemon zest, pepper, and salt.
2. Rub the butter mixture all over the turkey breast.
3. Place turkey breast into the bottom rack of instant vortex air fryer and cook at 350 F for 20 minutes.
4. Turn turkey breast to the other side and cook for 30 minutes more or until the internal temperature of turkey breast reaches 160 F.
5. Slice and serve.

122. Cheesy Chicken

Prep.Time: 20 min - **Cooking Time:** 9 min - **Servings:** 2-4

Ingredients:
- ✓ ½ cup Italian breadcrumbs
- ✓ 2 tbsp grated Parmesan cheese
- ✓ 1 tbsp butter, melted
- ✓ 4 chicken thighs
- ✓ ½ cup marinara sauce
- ✓ ½ cup shredded Monterrey Jack cheese

Directions:
1. Spray the frying basket with cooking spray. In a bowl, mix the crumbs and Parmesan cheese. Pour the butter into another bowl. Brush the thighs with butter. Dip each one into the crumbs mixture, until well-coated.
2. Arrange two chicken thighs in the air fryer, and lightly spray with cooking oil. Cook for 5 minutes at 380 F. Flip over, top with a few tbsp of marinara sauce and shredded Monterrey Jack cheese.
3. Cook for 4 minutes. Repeat with the remaining thighs.

123. Maple Chicken Breasts with Rosemary

Prep.Time: 10 min - **Cooking Time:** 20 min - **Servings:** 2

Ingredients:
- ✓ 2 tbsp Dijon mustard
- ✓ 1 tbsp maple syrup
- ✓ 2 tsp minced fresh rosemary
- ✓ Salt and black pepper to taste
- ✓ 2 chicken breasts, boneless, skinless

Directions:
1. In a bowl, mix mustard, maple syrup, rosemary, salt, and pepper. Rub mixture onto chicken. Spray generously the air fryer basket generously with cooking spray.
2. Arrange the breasts inside the frying basket and cook for 20 minutes, turning once halfway through.

124. Whole Chicken with Pancetta and Lemon

Prep.Time: 30 min - **Cooking Time:** 30 min - **Servings:** 2

Ingredients:
- ✓ 1 small whole chicken
- ✓ 1 lemon
- ✓ 4 slices pancetta, roughly chopped
- ✓ 1 onion, chopped
- ✓ 1 sprig fresh thyme
- ✓ Olive oil
- ✓ Salt and black pepper

Directions:
1. In a bowl, mix pancetta, onion, thyme, salt, and black pepper. Pat dry the chicken with. Insert the pancetta mixture into chicken's cavity and press tight.
2. Put in the whole lemon, and rub the top and sides of the chicken with salt and black pepper. Spray the frying basket with olive oil and arrange the chicken inside.
3. Cook for 30 minutes on 400 F, turning once halfway through.

125. Picante Chicken Wings

Prep.Time: 1 hour 10 min - **Cooking Time:** 32 min - **Servings:** 4

Ingredients:
- ✓ 2 lb chicken wings
- ✓ 1 tbsp olive oil
- ✓ 3 cloves garlic, minced
- ✓ 1 tbsp chili powder
- ✓ ½ tbsp cinnamon powder
- ✓ ½ tsp allspice
- ✓ 1 habanero pepper, seeded
- ✓ 1 tbsp soy sauce
- ✓ ½ tbsp white pepper
- ✓ ¼ cup red wine vinegar
- ✓ 3 tbsp lime juice
- ✓ 2 scallions, chopped
- ✓ ½ tbsp grated ginger
- ✓ ½ tbsp chopped fresh thyme
- ✓ ⅓ tbsp sugar
- ✓ ½ tbsp salt

Directions:
1. In a bowl, add the olive oil, soy sauce, garlic, habanero pepper, allspice, cinnamon powder, cayenne pepper, white pepper, salt, sugar, thyme, ginger, scallions, lime juice, and red wine vinegar; mix well.
2. Add the chicken wings to the marinade mixture and coat it well with the mixture. Cover the bowl with cling film and refrigerate the chicken to marinate for 1 hour.
3. Preheat the Air Fryer oven to 400 F.
4. Remove the chicken from the fridge, drain all the liquid, and pat each wing dry using a paper towel. Place half of the wings in the basket and cook for 16 minutes. Shake halfway through. Remove onto a serving platter and repeat the cooking process for the remaining wings. Serve with blue cheese dip or ranch dressing.

126. Buttered Stuffed Chicken

Prep.Time: 10 min - **Cooking Time:** 40 min - **Servings:** 2-4

Ingredients:
- ✓ 1 small chicken
- ✓ 1 ½ tbsp olive oil
- ✓ Salt and black pepper to taste
- ✓ 1 cup breadcrumbs
- ✓ ⅓ cup chopped sage
- ✓ ⅓ cup chopped thyme
- ✓ 2 cloves garlic, crushed
- ✓ 1 brown onion, chopped
- ✓ 3 tbsp butter
- ✓ 2 eggs, beaten

Directions:
1. Rinse the chicken gently, pat dry with a paper towel and remove any excess fat with a knife; set aside.
2. On a stove top, place a pan. Add butter, garlic and onion and sauté to brown. Add eggs, sage, thyme, pepper, and salt. Mix well.
3. Cook for 20 seconds and turn the heat off. Stuff the chicken with the mixture into the cavity.
4. Then, tie the legs of the spatchcock with a butcher's twine and brush with olive oil. Rub the top and sides of the chicken generously with salt and pepper. Preheat the Air Fryer oven to 390 F.
5. Place the spatchcock into the frying basket and roast for 25 minutes.
6. Turn the chicken over and continue cooking for 10-15 minutes more; check throughout the cooking time to ensure it doesn't dry or overcooks.
7. Remove onto a chopping board and wrap it with aluminum foil; let rest for 10 minutes. Serve with a side of steamed broccoli.

127. Chicken Drumsticks with Coconut Cream

Prep.Time: 20 min - **Cooking Time:** 6 min - **Servings:** 4

Ingredients:
- ✓ 4 chicken drumsticks, boneless, skinless
- ✓ 2 tbsp green curry paste
- ✓ 3 tbsp coconut cream
- ✓ Salt and black pepper
- ✓ ½ fresh jalapeno chili, finely chopped
- ✓ A handful of fresh parsley, roughly chopped

Directions:
1. In a bowl, add drumsticks, paste, cream, salt, black pepper and jalapeno; coat the chicken well.
2. Arrange the drumsticks in the frying basket and cook for 6 minutes at 400 F, flipping once halfway through. Serve with fresh cilantro.

128. Flavorful Chicken Drumsticks

Prep.Time: 10 min - **Cooking Time:** 30 min - **Servings:** 4

Ingredients:
- ✓ 8 chicken drumsticks
- ✓ ¼ tsp cayenne pepper
- ✓ 1 tbsp onion powder
- ✓ 1 tbsp garlic powder
- ✓ 1 ½ tbsp honey
- ✓ 1 ½ tbsp fresh lemon juice
- ✓ 1 tbsp Worcestershire sauce
- ✓ ¼ cup soy sauce, low-sodium
- ✓ 1 tbsp sesame oil
- ✓ 2 tbsp olive oil
- ✓ ½ tsp kosher salt

Directions:
1. Add all ingredients except chicken in a large mixing bowl and mix well.
2. Add chicken drumsticks to the bowl and mix until well coated.
3. Place chicken drumsticks on the instant vortex air fryer rack air fry at 400 F for 15 minutes.
4. Turn chicken drumsticks to another side and cook for 15 minutes more.
5. Serve and enjoy.

129. Garlic Chicken Skewers

Prep.Time: 15 min - Cooking Time: 20 min - Servings: 3

Ingredients:
- 3 chicken breasts
- Salt to season
- 1 tbsp chili powder
- ¼ cup maple syrup
- ½ cup soy sauce
- 2 red peppers
- 1 green pepper
- 7 mushrooms
- 2 tbsp sesame seeds
- 1 garlic clove
- 2 tbsp olive oil
- Zest and juice from 1 lime
- A pinch of salt
- ¼ cup fresh parsley, chopped

Directions:
1. Put the chicken breasts on a clean flat surface and cut them in 2-inch cubes with a knife. Add them to a bowl, along with the chili powder, salt, maple syrup, soy sauce, sesame seeds, and spray them with cooking spray.
2. Toss to coat and set aside. Place the peppers on the chopping board. Use a knife to open, deseed and cut in cubes.
3. Likewise, cut the mushrooms in halves. Start stacking up the ingredients - stick 1 red pepper, then green, a chicken cube, and a mushroom half.
4. Repeat the arrangement until the skewer is full. Repeat the process until all the ingredients are used. Preheat the Air Fryer oven to 330 F.
5. Brush the kabobs with soy sauce mixture and place them into the fryer basket. Grease with cooking spray and grill for 20 minutes; flip halfway through.
6. Meanwhile, mix all salsa verde ingredients in your food processor and blend until you obtain a chunky paste.
7. Remove the kabobs when ready and serve with a side of salsa verde.

130. Juicy Chicken Breasts

Prep.Time: 10 min - Cooking Time: 25 min - Servings: 2

Ingredients:
- 2 chicken breasts
- Salt and black pepper to taste
- 1 cup flour
- 3 eggs
- ½ cup apple cider vinegar
- ½ tbsp ginger paste
- ½ tbsp garlic paste
- 1 tbsp sugar
- 2 red chilies, minced
- 2 tbsp tomato puree
- 1 red pepper
- 1 green pepper
- 1 tbsp paprika
- 4 tbsp water

Directions:
1. Preheat the Air Fryer oven to 350 F. Put the chicken breasts on a clean flat surface. Cut them in cubes. Pour the flour in a bowl, crack the eggs in, add the salt and pepper; whisk. Put the chicken in the flour mixture; mix to coat.
2. Place the chicken in the frying basket, spray with cooking spray, and fry for 8 minutes. Pull out the basket, shake to toss, and spray again with cooking spray. Keep cooking for 7 minutes or until golden and crispy.
3. Remove the chicken to a plate. Put the red, yellow, and green peppers on a chopping board. Using a knife, cut open and deseed them; cut the flesh in long strips.
4. In a bowl, add the water, apple cider vinegar, sugar, ginger and garlic puree, red chili, tomato puree, and smoked paprika; mix with a fork.
5. Place a skillet over medium heat on a stovetop and spray with cooking spray. Add the chicken and pepper strips. Stir and cook until the peppers are sweaty but still crunchy.
6. Pour the chili mixture on the chicken, stir, and bring to simmer for 10 minutes; turn off the heat. Dish the chicken chili sauce into a serving bowl and serve.

131. Grilled Hawaiian Chicken

Prep.Time: 15 min - Cooking Time: 15 min - Servings: 4

Ingredients:
- 4 chicken breasts
- 2 garlic cloves
- ½ cup ketchup, Keto-friendly
- ½ teaspoon ginger
- ½ cup coconut amino
- 2 tablespoons red wine vinegar
- ½ cup pineapple juice
- 2 tablespoons apple cider vinegar

Directions:
1. Pre-heat your Air Fryer to 360-degree F.
2. Take a bowl and mix in ketchup, pineapple juice, cider vinegar, ginger.
3. Take a frying and place it over low heat, add sauce and let it heat up.
4. Cover chicken with the amino and vinegar, pour hot sauce on top.
5. Let the chicken sit for 15 minutes to marinade.
6. Transfer chicken to your Air Fryer and bake for 15 minutes.
7. Serve and enjoy!

132. Baked Coconut Chicken

Prep.Time: 10 min - Cooking Time: 12-14 min - Servings: 2

Ingredients:
- 2 large eggs
- 2 teaspoons garlic powder
- 1 teaspoon salt
- 1/2 teaspoon ground black pepper
- ¾ cup coconut amino
- ¾ cup shredded coconut
- 1-pound chicken tenders
- Cooking spray

Directions:
1. Pre-heat your fryer to 400-degree Fahrenheit.
2. Take a large sized baking sheet and spray it with cooking spray.
3. Take a wide dish and add garlic powder, eggs, pepper and salt.
4. Whisk well until everything is combined.
5. Add the almond meal and coconut and mix well.
6. Take your chicken tenders and dip them in egg followed by dipping in the coconut mix.
7. Shake off any excess.
8. Transfer them to your fryer and spray the tenders with a bit of oil.
9. Cook for 12-14 minutes until you have a nice golden-brown texture.

133. Lemon Pepper Chicken - KETO

Prep.Time: 15 min - **Cooking Time:** 15 min - **Servings:** 1-2

Ingredients:

- ✓ 1 chicken breast
- ✓ 2 lemon, juiced and rind reserved
- ✓ 1 tablespoon chicken seasoning
- ✓ 1 teaspoon garlic puree
- ✓ Handful of peppercorns
- ✓ Salt and pepper to taste

Directions:

1. Pre-heat your fryer to 352-degree F.
2. Take a large sized sheet of silver foil and work on top, add all of the seasoning alongside the lemon rind.
3. Lay out the chicken breast onto a chopping board and trim any fat and little bones.
4. Season each side with the pepper and salt.
5. Rub the chicken seasoning on both sides well.
6. Place on your silver foil sheet and rub.
7. Seal it up tightly.
8. Slap it with rolling pin and flatten it.
9. Place it in your fryer and cook for 15 minutes until the center is fully cooked.
10. Serve and enjoy!

134. Chicken and Sage Scallops

Prep.Time: 10 min - **Cooking Time:** 5 min - **Servings:** 4

Ingredients:

- ✓ 4 skinless chicken breasts
- ✓ 2 and ½ ounces almond meal
- ✓ 1-ounce parmesan, grated
- ✓ 6 sage leaves, chopped
- ✓ 1 and ¾ ounces almond flour
- ✓ 2 eggs, beaten

Directions:

1. Take cling paper and wrap chicken with cling wrap
2. Beat into ½ cm thickness using a rolling pin
3. Take separate bowls add parmesan, sage, almond meal, flour and beaten eggs into the different bowls
4. Take chicken and dredge into flour, eggs, bread crumbs and finally parmesan
5. Pre-heat your Fryer to 392 degrees F
6. Take the basket out and spray chicken with oil on both sides
7. Cook chicken for 5 minutes each side until golden
8. Serve and enjoy!

135. Cool Cheese Dredged Chicken

Prep.Time: 10 min - **Cooking Time:** 10 minutes - **Servings:** 2-4

Ingredients:

- ✓ 2-piece (6 ounces each) chicken breast, fat trimmed and sliced up in half
- ✓ 6 tablespoons seasoned breadcrumbs
- ✓ 2 tablespoons parmesan, grated
- ✓ 1 tablespoon melted butter
- ✓ 2 tablespoons low-fat mozzarella cheese
- ✓ ½ cup marinara sauce
- ✓ Cooking spray as needed

Directions:

1. Pre-heat your Air Fryer to 390-degree Fahrenheit for about 9 minutes
2. Take the cooking basket and spray it evenly with cooking spray
3. Take a small bowl and add breadcrumbs and parmesan cheese
4. Mix them well
5. Take another bowl and add the butter, melt it in your microwave
6. Brush the chicken pieces with the butter and dredge them into the breadcrumb mix
7. Once the fryer is ready, place 2 pieces of your prepared chicken breast and spray the top a bit of oil
8. Cook for about 7 minutes
9. Turn them over and top them up with 1 tablespoon of Marinara and 1 and a ½ tablespoon of shredded mozzarella
10. Cook for 3 minutes more until the cheese has completely melted
11. Keep the cooked breasts on the side and repeat with the remaining pieces

SIDE DISH RECIPES

1. Potato Wedges

Prep.Time: 10 min - **Cooking Time:** 25 min - **Servings: 4**

Ingredients:
- ✓ 2 potatoes, cut into wedges
- ✓ 1 tablespoon olive oil
- ✓ Salt and black pepper to the taste
- ✓ 3 tablespoons sour cream
- ✓ 2 tablespoons sweet chili sauce

Directions:
11. In a bowl, mix potato wedges with oil, salt and pepper, toss well, add to air fryer's basket and cook at 360 degrees F for 25 minutes, flipping them once.
12. Divide potato wedges on plates, drizzle sour cream and chili sauce all over and serve them as a side dish.

Nutrition: calories 171 - Fat 8 - Fiber 9 - Carbs 18 - Protein 7

2. Brussels Sprouts Side Dish

Prep.Time: 10 min - **Cooking Time:** 15 min - **Servings: 4**

Ingredients:
- ✓ 1 pound Brussels sprouts, trimmed and halved
- ✓ Salt and black pepper to the taste
- ✓ 6 teaspoons olive oil
- ✓ ½ teaspoon thyme, chopped
- ✓ ½ cup mayonnaise
- ✓ 2 tablespoons roasted garlic, crushed

Directions:
9. In your air fryer, mix Brussels sprouts with salt, pepper and oil, toss well and cook them at 390 degrees F for 15 minutes.
10. Meanwhile, in a bowl, mix thyme with mayo and garlic and whisk well.
11. Divide Brussels sprouts on plates, drizzle garlic sauce all over and serve as a side dish.

Nutrition: calories 172 - Fat 6 - Fiber 8 - Carbs 12 - Protein 6

3. Mushroom Side Dish

Prep.Time: 10 min - **Cooking Time:** 8 minutes - **Servings: 4**

Ingredients:
- ✓ 10 button mushrooms, stems removed
- ✓ 1 tablespoon Italian seasoning
- ✓ Salt and black pepper to the taste
- ✓ 2 tablespoons cheddar cheese, grated
- ✓ 1 tablespoon olive oil
- ✓ 2 tablespoons mozzarella, grated
- ✓ 1 tablespoon dill, chopped

Directions:
12. In a bowl, mix mushrooms with Italian seasoning, salt, pepper, oil and dill and rub well.
13. Arrange mushrooms in your air fryer's basket, sprinkle mozzarella and cheddar in each and cook them at 360 degrees F for 8 minutes.
14. Divide them on plates and serve them as a side dish.

Nutrition: calories 241 - Fat 7 - Fiber 8 - Carbs 14 - Protein 6

4. Roasted Pumpkin

Prep.Time: 10 min - **Cooking Time:** 12 min - **Servings: 4**

Ingredients:
- ✓ 1 and ½ pound pumpkin, deseeded, sliced and roughly chopped
- ✓ 3 garlic cloves, minced
- ✓ 1 tablespoon olive oil
- ✓ A pinch of sea salt
- ✓ A pinch of brown sugar
- ✓ A pinch of nutmeg, ground
- ✓ A pinch of cinnamon powder

Directions:
4. In your air fryer's basket, mix pumpkin with garlic, oil, salt, brown sugar, cinnamon and nutmeg, toss well, cover and cook at 370 degrees F for 12 minutes.
5. Divide among plates and serve as a side dish.

Nutrition: calories 200 - Fat 5 - Fiber 4 - Carbs 7 - Protein 4

5. Sweet Potato Fries

Prep.Time: 10 min - **Cooking Time:** 20 min - **Servings: 2**

Ingredients:
- ✓ 2 sweet potatoes, peeled and cut into medium fries
- ✓ Salt and black pepper to the taste
- ✓ 2 tablespoons olive oil
- ✓ ½ teaspoon curry powder
- ✓ ¼ teaspoon coriander, ground
- ✓ ¼ cup ketchup
- ✓ 2 tablespoons mayonnaise
- ✓ ½ teaspoon cumin, ground
- ✓ A pinch of ginger powder
- ✓ A pinch of cinnamon powder

Directions:
5. In your air fryer's basket, mix sweet potato fries with salt, pepper, coriander, curry powder and oil, toss well and cook at 370 degrees F for 20 minutes, flipping them once.
6. Meanwhile, in a bowl, mix ketchup with mayo, cumin, ginger and cinnamon and whisk well.
7. Divide fries on plates, drizzle ketchup mix over them and serve as a side dish.

Nutrition: calories 200 - Fat 5 – Fiber 8 - Carbs 9 - Protein 7

6. Zucchini Fries

Prep.Time: 10 min - **Cooking Time:** 12 min - **Servings: 4**

Ingredients:
- ✓ 1 zucchini, cut into medium sticks
- ✓ A drizzle of olive oil
- ✓ Salt and black pepper to the taste
- ✓ 2 eggs, whisked
- ✓ 1 cup bread crumbs
- ✓ ½ cup flour

Directions:
6. Put flour in a bowl and mix with salt and pepper and stir.
7. Put breadcrumbs in another bowl.
8. In a third bowl mix eggs with a pinch of salt and pepper.
9. Dredge zucchini fries in flour, then in eggs and in bread crumbs at the end.
10. Grease your air fryer with some olive oil, heat up at 400 degrees F, add zucchini fries and cook them for 12 minutes.
11. Serve them as a side dish.

Nutrition: calories 172 - Fat 3 - Fiber 3 - Carbs 7 - Protein 3

7. Delicious Roasted Carrots

Prep.Time: 10 min - Cooking Time: 20 min - Servings: 4

Ingredients:
- ✓ 1 pound baby carrots
- ✓ 2 teaspoons olive oil
- ✓ 1 teaspoon herbs de Provence
- ✓ 4 tablespoons orange juice

Directions:
1. In your air fryer's basket, mix carrots with herbs de Provence, oil and orange juice, toss and cook at 320 degrees F for 20 minutes.
2. Divide among plates and serve as a side dish.

Nutrition: calories 112 - Fat 2 - Fiber 3 - Carbs 4 - Protein 3

8. Green Beans Side Dish

Prep.Time: 10 min - Cooking Time: 25 min - Servings: 4

Ingredients:
- ✓ 1 and ½ pounds green beans, trimmed and steamed for 2 minutes
- ✓ Salt and black pepper to the taste
- ✓ ½ pound shallots, chopped
- ✓ ¼ cup almonds, toasted
- ✓ 2 tablespoons olive oil

Directions:
1. In your air fryer's basket, mix green beans with salt, pepper, shallots, almonds and oil, toss well and cook at 400 degrees F for 25 minutes.
2. Divide among plates and serve as a side dish.

Nutrition: calories 152 - Fat 3 - Fiber 6 - Carbs 7 - Protein 4

9. Creamy Air Fried Potato Side Dish

Prep.Time: 10 min - Cooking Time: 1 hour and 20 minutes - Servings: 2

Ingredients:
- ✓ 1 big potato
- ✓ 2 bacon strips, cooked and chopped
- ✓ 1 teaspoon olive oil
- ✓ 1/3 cup cheddar cheese, shredded
- ✓ 1 tablespoon green onions, chopped
- ✓ Salt and black pepper to the taste
- ✓ 1 tablespoon butter
- ✓ 2 tablespoons heavy cream

Directions:
1. Rub potato with oil, season with salt and pepper, place in preheated air fryer and cook at 400 degrees F for 30 minutes.
2. Flip potato, cook for 30 minutes more, transfer to a cutting board, cool it down, slice in half lengthwise and scoop pulp in a bowl.
3. Add bacon, cheese, butter, heavy cream, green onions, salt and pepper, stir well and stuff potato skins with this mix.
4. Return potatoes to your air fryer and cook them at 400 degrees F for 20 minutes.
5. Divide among plates and serve as a side dish.

Nutrition: calories 172 - Fat 5 - Fiber 7 - Carbs 9 - Protein 4

10. Garlic Potatoes

Prep.Time: 10 min - Cooking Time: 20 min - Servings: 6

Ingredients:
- ✓ 2 tablespoons parsley, chopped
- ✓ 5 garlic cloves, minced
- ✓ ½ teaspoon basil, dried
- ✓ ½ teaspoon oregano, dried
- ✓ 3 pounds red potatoes, halved
- ✓ 1 teaspoon thyme, dried
- ✓ 2 tablespoons olive oil
- ✓ Salt and black pepper to the taste
- ✓ 2 tablespoons butter
- ✓ 1/3 cup parmesan, grated spray

Directions:
1. In a bowl, mix potato halves with parsley, garlic, basil, oregano, thyme, salt, pepper, oil and butter, toss really well and transfer to your air fryer's basket.
2. Cover and cook at 400 degrees F for 20 minutes, flipping them once.
3. Sprinkle parmesan on top, divide potatoes on plates and serve as a side dish.

Nutrition: calories 162 - Fat 5 - Fiber 5 - Carbs 7 - Protein 5

11. Mushrooms and Sour Cream

Prep.Time: 10 min - Cooking Time: 10 min - Servings: 6

Ingredients:
- ✓ 2 bacon strips, chopped
- ✓ 1 yellow onion, chopped
- ✓ 1 green bell pepper, chopped
- ✓ 24 mushrooms, stems removed
- ✓ 1 carrot, grated
- ✓ ½ cup sour cream
- ✓ 1 cup cheddar cheese, grated
- ✓ Salt and black pepper to the taste

Directions:
1. Heat up a pan over medium high heat, add bacon, onion, bell pepper and carrot, stir and cook for 1 minute.
2. Add salt, pepper and sour cream, stir cook for 1 minute more, take off heat and cool down.
3. Stuff mushrooms with this mix, sprinkle cheese on top and cook at 360 degrees F for 8 minutes.
4. Divide among plates and serve as a side dish.

Nutrition: calories 211 - Fat 4 - Fiber 7 - Carbs 8 - Protein 3

12. Fried Tomatoes

Prep.Time: 10 min - Cooking Time: 5 min - Servings: 4

Ingredients:
- ✓ 2 green tomatoes, sliced
- ✓ Salt and black pepper to the taste
- ✓ ½ cup flour
- ✓ 1 cup buttermilk
- ✓ 1 cup panko bread crumbs
- ✓ ½ tablespoon Creole seasoning
- ✓ Cooking spray

Directions:
1. Season tomato slices with salt and pepper.
2. Put flour in a bowl, buttermilk in another and panko crumbs and Creole seasoning in a third one.
3. Dredge tomato slices in flour, then in buttermilk and panko bread crumbs, place them in your air fryer's basket greased with cooking spray and cook them at 400 degrees F for 5 minutes.
4. Divide among plates and serve as a side dish.

Nutrition: calories 124 - Fat 5 - Fiber 7 - Carbs 9 - Protein 4

13. Corn with Lime and Cheese

Prep.Time: 10 min - Cooking Time: 15 min - Servings: 2

Ingredients:
- ✓ 2 corns on the cob, husks removed
- ✓ A drizzle of olive oil
- ✓ ½ cup feta cheese, grated
- ✓ 2 teaspoons sweet paprika
- ✓ Juice from 2 limes

Directions:
1. Rub corn with oil and paprika, place in your air fryer and cook at 400 degrees F for 15 minutes, flipping once.
2. Divide corn on plates, sprinkle cheese on top, drizzle lime juice and serve as a side dish.

Nutrition: calories 200 - Fat 5 - Fiber 2 - Carbs 6 - Protein 6

14. Brussels Sprouts and Pomegran. Seeds Side Dish

Prep.Time: 5 min - Cooking Time: 10 min - Servings: 4

Ingredients:
- ✓ 1 pound Brussels sprouts, trimmed and halved
- ✓ Salt and black pepper to the taste
- ✓ 1 cup pomegranate seeds
- ✓ ¼ cup pine nuts, toasted
- ✓ 1 tablespoons olive oil
- ✓ 2 tablespoons veggie stock

Directions:
1. In a heat proof dish that fits your air fryer, mix Brussels sprouts with salt, pepper, pomegranate seeds, pine nuts, oil and stock, stir, place in your air fryer's basket and cook at 390 degrees F for 10 minutes.
2. Divide among plates and serve as a side dish.

Nutrition: calories 152 - Fat 4 - Fiber 7 - Carbs 12 - Protein 3

15. Parmesan Mushrooms

Prep.Time: 10 min - Cooking Time: 15 minutes - Servings: 3

Ingredients:
- ✓ 9 button mushroom caps
- ✓ 3 cream cracker slices, crumbled
- ✓ 1 egg white
- ✓ 2 tablespoons parmesan, grated
- ✓ 1 teaspoon Italian seasoning
- ✓ A pinch of salt and black pepper
- ✓ 1 tablespoon butter, melted

Directions:
1. In a bowl, mix crackers with egg white, parmesan, Italian seasoning, butter, salt and pepper, stir well and stuff mushrooms with this mix.
2. Arrange mushrooms in your air fryer's basket and cook them at 360 degrees F for 15 minutes.
3. Divide among plates and serve as a side dish.

Nutrition: calories 124 - Fat 4 - Fiber 4 - Carbs 7 - Protein 3

16. Roasted Parsnips

Prep.Time: 10 min - Cooking Time: 40 min - Servings: 6

Ingredients:
- ✓ 2 pounds parsnips, peeled and cut into medium chunks
- ✓ 2 tablespoons maple syrup
- ✓
- ✓ 1 tablespoon parsley flakes, dried
- ✓ 1 tablespoon olive oil

Directions:
1. Preheat your air fryer at 360 degrees F, add oil and heat it up as well.
2. Add parsnips, parsley flakes and maple syrup, toss and cook them for 40 minutes.
3. Divide among plates and serve as a side dish.

Nutrition: calories 124 - Fat 3 - Fiber 3 - Carbs 7 - Protein 4

17. Hasselback Potatoes

Prep.Time: 10 min - Cooking Time: 20 min - Servings: 2

Ingredients:
- ✓ 2 potatoes, peeled and thinly sliced almost all the way horizontally
- ✓ 2 tablespoons olive oil
- ✓ 1 teaspoon garlic, minced
- ✓ Salt and black pepper to the taste
- ✓
- ✓ ½ teaspoon oregano, dried
- ✓ ½ teaspoon basil, dried
- ✓ ½ teaspoon sweet paprika

Directions:
1. In a bowl, mix oil with garlic, salt, pepper, oregano, basil and paprika and whisk really well.
2. Rub potatoes with this mix, place them in your air fryer's basket and fry them at 360 degrees F for 20 minutes.
3. Divide them on plates and serve as a side dish.

Nutrition: calories 172 - Fat 6 - Fiber 6 - Carbs 9 - Protein 6

18. Carrots and Rhubarb

Prep.Time: 10 min - Cooking Time: 40 min - Servings: 4

Ingredients:
- ✓ 1 pound baby carrots
- ✓ 2 teaspoons walnut oil
- ✓ 1 pound rhubarb, roughly chopped
- ✓ 1 orange, peeled, cut into medium segments and zest grated
- ✓ ½ cup walnuts, halved
- ✓ ½ teaspoon stevia

Directions:
1. Put the oil in your air fryer, add carrots, toss and fry them at 380 degrees F for 20 minutes.
2. Add rhubarb, orange zest, stevia and walnuts, toss and cook for 20 minutes more.
3. Add orange segments, toss and serve as a side dish.

Nutrition: calories 172 - Fat 2 - Fiber 3 - Carbs 4 - Protein 4

19. Onion Rings Side Dish

Prep.Time: 10 min - Cooking Time: 10 min - Servings: 3

Ingredients:
- ✓ 1 onion cut into medium slices and rings separated
- ✓ 1 and ¼ cups white flour
- ✓ A pinch of salt
- ✓ 1 egg
- ✓ 1 cup milk
- ✓ 1 teaspoon baking powder
- ✓ ¾ cup bread crumbs

Directions:
1. In a bowl, mix flour with salt and baking powder, stir, dredge onion rings in this mix and place them on a separate plate.
2. Add milk and egg to flour mix and whisk well.
3. Dip onion rings in this mix, dredge them in breadcrumbs, put them in your air fryer's basket and cook them at 360 degrees F for 10 minutes.
4. Divide among plates and serve as a side dish for a steak.

Nutrition: calories 140 - Fat 8 - Fiber 20 - Carbs 12 - Protein 3

20. Simple Potato Chips

Prep.Time: 30 min - Cooking Time: 30 min - Servings: 4

Ingredients:
- ✓ 4 potatoes, scrubbed, peeled into thin chips, soaked in water for 30 minutes, drained and pat dried
- ✓ Salt the taste
- ✓ 1 tablespoon olive oil
- ✓ 2 teaspoons rosemary, chopped
- ✓

Directions:
1. In a bowl, mix potato chips with salt and oil toss to coat, place them in your air fryer's basket and cook at 330 degrees F for 30 minutes.
2. Divide among plates, sprinkle rosemary all over and serve as a side dish.

Nutrition: calories 200 - Fat 4 - Fiber 4 - Carbs 14 – Protein 5

21. Herbed Tomatoes

Prep.Time: 10 min - Cooking Time: 15 minutes - Servings: 4

Ingredients:
- ✓ 4 big tomatoes, halved and insides scooped out
- ✓ Salt and black pepper to the taste
- ✓ 1 tablespoon olive oil
- ✓ 2 garlic cloves, minced
- ✓ ½ teaspoon thyme, chopped

Directions:
1. In your air fryer, mix tomatoes with salt, pepper, oil, garlic and thyme, toss and cook at 390 degrees F for 15 minutes.
2. Divide among plates and serve them as a side dish

Nutrition: calories 112 - Fat 1 - Fiber 3 - Carbs 4 - Protein 4

22. Zucchini Croquettes

Prep.Time: 10 min - Cooking Time: 10 min - Servings: 4

Ingredients:
- ✓ 1 carrot, grated
- ✓ 1 zucchini, grated
- ✓ 2 slices of bread, crumbled
- ✓ 1 egg
- ✓ Salt and black pepper to the taste
- ✓ ½ teaspoon sweet paprika
- ✓ 1 teaspoon garlic, minced
- ✓ 2 tablespoons parmesan cheese, grated
- ✓ 1 tablespoon corn flour

Directions:
1. Put zucchini in a bowl, add salt, leave aside for 10 minutes, squeeze excess water and transfer them to another bowl.
2. Add carrots, salt, pepper, paprika, garlic, flour, parmesan, egg and bread crumbs, stir well, shape 8 croquettes, place them in your air fryer and cook at 360 degrees F for 10 minutes.
3. Divide among plates and serve as a side dish.

Nutrition: calories 100 - Fat 3 - Fiber 1 - Carbs 7 - Protein 4

23. Rice and Sausage Side Dish

Prep.Time: 10 min - Cooking Time: 20 min - Servings: 4

Ingredients:
- ✓ 2 cups white rice, already boiled
- ✓ 1 tablespoon butter
- ✓ Salt and black pepper to the taste
- ✓ 4 garlic cloves, minced
- ✓ 1 pork sausage, chopped
- ✓
- ✓ 2 tablespoons carrot, chopped
- ✓ 3 tablespoons cheddar cheese, grated
- ✓ 2 tablespoons mozzarella cheese, shredded

Directions:
1. Heat up your air fryer at 350 degrees F, add butter, melt it, add garlic, stir and brown for 2 minutes.
2. Add sausage, salt, pepper, carrots and rice, stir and cook at 350 degrees F for 10 minutes.
3. Add cheddar and mozzarella, toss, divide among plates and serve as a side dish.

Nutrition: calories 240 - Fat 12 - Fiber 5 - Carbs 20 - Protein 13

24. Roasted Eggplant

Prep.Time: 10 min - Cooking Time: 20 min - Servings: 6

Ingredients:
- ✓ 1 and ½ pounds eggplant, cubed
- ✓ 1 tablespoon olive oil
- ✓ 1 teaspoon garlic powder
- ✓ 1 teaspoon onion powder
- ✓ 1 teaspoon sumac
- ✓ 2 teaspoons za'atar
- ✓ Juice from ½ lemon
- ✓ 2 bay leaves

Directions:
1. In your air fryer, mix eggplant cubes with oil, garlic powder, onion powder, sumac, za'atar, lemon juice and bay leaves, toss and cook at 370 degrees F for 20 minutes.
2. Divide among plates and serve as a side dish.

Nutrition: calories 172 - Fat 4 - Fiber 7 - Carbs 12 - Protein 3

25. Tortilla Chips

Prep.Time: 10 min - **Cooking Time: 6 min** - **Servings:** 4

Ingredients:
- ✓ 8 corn tortillas, cut into triangles
- ✓ Salt and black pepper to the taste
- ✓ 1 tablespoon olive oil
- ✓ A pinch of garlic powder
- ✓ A pinch of sweet paprika

Directions:
1. In a bowl, mix tortilla chips with oil, add salt, pepper, garlic powder and paprika, toss well, place them in your air fryer's basket and cook them at 400 degrees F for 6 minutes.
2. Serve them as a side for a fish dish.

Nutrition: calories 53 - Fat 1 - Fiber 1 - Carbs 6 - Protein 4

26. Eggplant Side Dish

Prep.Time: 10 min - **Cooking Time: 10 min** - **Servings:** 4

Ingredients:
- ✓ 8 baby eggplants, scooped in the center and pulp reserved
- ✓ Salt and black pepper to the taste
- ✓ A pinch of oregano, dried
- ✓ 1 green bell pepper, chopped
- ✓ 1 tablespoon tomato paste
- ✓ 1 bunch coriander, chopped
- ✓ ½ teaspoon garlic powder
- ✓ 1 tablespoon olive oil
- ✓ 1 yellow onion, chopped
- ✓ 1 tomato chopped

Directions:
1. Heat up a pan with the oil over medium heat, add onion, stir and cook for 1 minute.
2. Add salt, pepper, eggplant pulp, oregano, green bell pepper, tomato paste, garlic power, coriander and tomato, stir, cook for 1-2 minutes more, take off heat and cool down.
3. Stuff eggplants with this mix, place them in your air fryer's basket and cook at 360 degrees F for 8 minutes.
4. Divide eggplants on plates and serve them as a side dish.

Nutrition: calories 200 - Fat 3 - Fiber 7 - Carbs 12 - Protein 4

27. Creamy Endives

Prep.Time: 10 min - **Cooking Time: 10 minutes** - **Servings:** 6

Ingredients:
- ✓ 6 endives, trimmed and halved
- ✓ 1 teaspoon garlic powder
- ✓ ½ cup Greek yogurt
- ✓ ½ teaspoon curry powder
- ✓ Salt and black pepper to the taste
- ✓ 3 tablespoons lemon juice

Directions:
1. In a bowl, mix endives with garlic powder, yogurt, curry powder, salt, pepper and lemon juice, toss, leave aside for 10 minutes and transfer to your preheated air fryer at 350 degrees F.
2. Cook endives for 10 minutes, divide them on plates and serve as a side dish.

Nutrition: calories 100 - Fat 2 - Fiber 2 - Carbs 7 - Protein 4

28. Eggplant Fries

Prep.Time: 10 min - **Cooking Time: 5 min** - **Servings:** 4

Ingredients:
- ✓ Cooking spray
- ✓ 1 eggplant, peeled and cut into medium fries
- ✓ 2 tablespoons milk
- ✓ 1 egg, whisked
- ✓ 2 cups panko bread crumbs
- ✓ ½ cup Italian cheese, shredded
- ✓ A pinch of salt and black pepper to the taste

Directions:
1. In a bowl, mix egg with milk, salt and pepper and whisk well.
2. In another bowl, mix panko with cheese and stir.
3. Dip eggplant fries in egg mix, then coat in panko mix, place them in your air fryer greased with cooking spray and cook at 400 degrees F for 5 minutes.
4. Divide among plates and serve as a side dish.

Nutrition: calories 162 – Fat56 - Fiber 5 - Carbs 7 - Protein 6

29. Cauliflower Cakes

Prep.Time: 10 min - **Cooking Time: 10 min** - **Servings:** 6

Ingredients:
- ✓ 3 and ½ cups cauliflower rice
- ✓ 2 eggs
- ✓ ¼ cup white flour
- ✓ ½ cup parmesan, grated
- ✓ Salt and black pepper to the taste
- ✓ Cooking spray

Directions:
1. In a bowl, mix cauliflower rice with salt and pepper, stir and squeeze excess water.
2. Transfer cauliflower to another bowl, add eggs, salt, pepper, flour and parmesan, stir really well and shape your cakes.
3. Grease your air fryer with cooking spray, heat it up at 400 degrees, add cauliflower cakes and cook them for 10 minutes flipping them halfway.
4. Divide cakes on plates and serve as a side dish.

Nutrition: calories 125 - Fat 2 - Fiber 6 - Carbs 6 - Protein 3

30. Roasted Peppers

Prep.Time: 10 min - **Cooking Time: 20 min** - **Servings:** 4

Ingredients:
- ✓ 1 tablespoon sweet paprika
- ✓ 1 tablespoon olive oil
- ✓ 4 red bell peppers, cut into medium strips
- ✓ 4 green bell peppers, cut into medium strips
- ✓ 4 yellow bell peppers, cut into medium strips
- ✓ 1 yellow onion, chopped
- ✓ Salt and black pepper to the taste

Directions:
1. In your air fryer, mix red bell peppers with green and yellow ones.
2. Add paprika, oil, onion, salt and pepper, toss and cook at 350 degrees F for 20 minutes.
3. Divide among plates and serve as a side dish

Nutrition: calories 142 - Fat 4 - Fiber 4 - Carbs 7 - Protein 4

31. Creamy Brussels Sprouts

Prep.Time: 10 min - **Cooking Time:** 25 min - **Servings:** 8

Ingredients:
- ✓ 3 pounds Brussels sprouts, halved
- ✓ A drizzle of olive oil
- ✓ 1 pound bacon, chopped
- ✓ Salt and black pepper to the taste
- ✓ 4 tablespoons butter
- ✓ 3 shallots, chopped
- ✓ 1 cup milk
- ✓ 2 cups heavy cream
- ✓ ¼ teaspoon nutmeg, ground
- ✓ 3 tablespoons prepared hors

Directions:
1. Preheated you air fryer at 370 degrees F, add oil, bacon, salt and pepper and Brussels sprouts and toss.
2. Add butter, shallots, heavy cream, milk, nutmeg and horseradish, toss again and cook for 25 minutes.
3. Divide among plates and serve as a side dish.

Nutrition: calories 214 - Fat 5 - Fiber 8 - Carbs 12 - Protein 5

32. Vermouth Mushrooms

Prep.Time: 10 min - **Cooking Time:** 25 min - **Servings:** 4

Ingredients:
- ✓ 1 tablespoon olive oil
- ✓ 2 pounds white mushrooms
- ✓ 2 tablespoons white vermouth
- ✓ 2 teaspoons herbs de Provence
- ✓ 2 garlic cloves, minced

Directions:
1. In your air fryer, mix oil with mushrooms, herbs de Provence and garlic, toss and cook at 350 degrees F for 20 minutes.
2. Add vermouth, toss and cook for 5 minutes more.
3. Divide among plates and serve as a side dish.

Nutrition: calories 121 - Fat 2 - Fiber 5 - Carbs 7 - Protein 4

33. Glazed Beets

Prep.Time: 10 min - **Cooking Time:** 40 minutes - **Servings:** 8

Ingredients:
- ✓ 3 pounds small beets, trimmed
- ✓ 4 tablespoons maple syrup
- ✓ 1 tablespoon duck fat

Directions:
1. Heat up your air fryer at 360 degrees F, add duck fat and heat it up.
2. Add beets and maple syrup, toss and cook for 40 minutes.
3. Divide among plates and serve as a side dish.

Nutrition: calories 121 - Fat 3 - Fiber 2 - Carbs 3 - Protein 4

34. Delicious Air Fried Broccoli

Prep.Time: 10 min - **Cooking Time:** 20 min - **Servings:** 4

Ingredients:
- ✓ 1 tablespoon duck fat
- ✓ 1 broccoli head, florets separated
- ✓ 3 garlic cloves, minced
- ✓ Juice from ½ lemon
- ✓ 1 tablespoon sesame seeds

Directions:
1. Heat up your air fryer at 350 degrees F, add duck fat and heat as well.
2. Add broccoli, garlic, lemon juice and sesame seeds, toss and cook for 20 minutes.
3. Divide among plates and serve as a side dish.

Nutrition: calories 132 - Fat 3 - Fiber 3 - Carbs 6 - Protein 4

35. Potatoes Patties

Prep.Time: 10 min - **Cooking Time:** 8 min - **Servings:** 4

Ingredients:
- ✓ 4 potatoes, cubed, boiled and mashed
- ✓ 1 cup parmesan, grated
- ✓ Salt and black pepper to the taste
- ✓ A pinch of nutmeg
- ✓ 2 egg yolks
- ✓ 2 tablespoons white flour
- ✓ 3 tablespoons chives, chopped

For the breading:
- ✓ ¼ cup white flour
- ✓ 3 tablespoons vegetable oil
- ✓ 2 eggs, whisked
- ✓ ¼ cup bread crumbs

Directions:
1. In a bowl, mix mashed potatoes with egg yolks, salt, pepper, nutmeg, parmesan, chives and 2 tablespoons flour, stir well, shape medium cakes and place them on a plate.
2. In another bowl, mix vegetable oil with bread crumbs and stir.
3. Put whisked eggs in a third bowl and ¼ cup flour in a forth one.
4. Dip cakes in flour, then in eggs and in breadcrumbs at the end, place them in your air fryer's basket, cook them at 390 degrees F for 8 minutes, divide among plates and serve as a side dish.

Nutrition: calories 140 - Fat 3 - Fiber 4 - Carbs 17 - Protein 4

36. Avocado Fries

Prep.Time: 10 min - **Cooking Time:** 10 min - **Servings:** 4

Ingredients:
- ✓ 1 avocado, pitted, peeled, sliced and cut into medium fries
- ✓ Salt and black pepper to the taste
- ✓ ½ cup panko bread crumbs
- ✓ 1 tablespoon lemon juice
- ✓ 1 egg, whisked
- ✓ 1 tablespoon olive oil

Directions:
1. In a bowl, mix panko with salt and pepper and stir.
2. In another bowl, mix egg with a pinch of salt and whisk.
3. In a third bowl, mix avocado fries with lemon juice and oil and toss.
4. Dip fries in egg, then in panko, place them in your air fryer's basket and cook at 390 degrees F for 10 minutes, shaking halfway.
5. Divide among plates and serve as a side dish.

Nutrition: calories 130 - Fat 11 - Fiber 3 - Carbs 16 - Protein 4

37. Creamy Potatoes

Prep.Time: 10 min - Cooking Time: 20 min - Servings: 4

Ingredients:
- ✓ 1 an ½ pounds potatoes, peeled and cubed
- ✓ 2 tablespoons olive oil
- ✓ Salt and black pepper to the taste
- ✓ 1 tablespoon hot paprika
- ✓ 1 cup Greek yogurt

Directions:
1. Put potatoes in a bowl, add water to cover, leave aside for 10 minutes, drain, pat dry them, transfer to another bowl, add salt, pepper, paprika and half of the oil and toss them well.
2. Put potatoes in your air fryer's basket and cook at 360 degrees F for 20 minutes.
3. In a bowl, mix yogurt with salt, pepper and the rest of the oil and whisk.
4. Divide potatoes on plates, drizzle yogurt dressing all over, toss them and serve as a side dish.

Nutrition: calories 170 - Fat 3 - Fiber 5 - Carbs 20 - Protein 5

38. Air Fried Creamy Cabbage

Prep.Time: 10 min - Cooking Time: 20 min - Servings: 4

Ingredients:
- ✓ 1 green cabbage head, chopped
- ✓ 1 yellow onion, chopped
- ✓ Salt and black pepper to the taste
- ✓ 4 bacon slices, chopped
- ✓ 1 cup whipped cream
- ✓ 2 tablespoons cornstarch

Directions:
1. Put cabbage, bacon and onion in your air fryer.
2. In a bowl, mix cornstarch with cream, salt and pepper, stir and add over cabbage.
3. Toss, cook at 400 degrees F for 20 minutes, divide among plates and serve as a side dish.

Nutrition: calories 208 - Fat 10 – Fiber 3 - Carbs 16 - Protein 5

39. Cauliflower Rice

Prep.Time: 10 min - Cooking Time: 40 minutes - Servings: 8

Ingredients:
- ✓ 1 tablespoon peanut oil
- ✓ 1 tablespoon sesame oil
- ✓ 4 tablespoons soy sauce
- ✓ 3 garlic cloves, minced
- ✓ 1 tablespoon ginger, grated
- ✓ Juice from ½ lemon
- ✓ 1 cauliflower head, riced
- ✓ 9 ounces water chestnuts, drained
- ✓ ¾ cup peas
- ✓ 15 ounces mushrooms, chopped
- ✓ 1 egg, whisked

Directions:
1. In your air fryer, mix cauliflower rice with peanut oil, sesame oil, soy sauce, garlic, ginger and lemon juice, stir, cover and cook at 350 degrees F for 20 minutes.
2. Add chestnuts, peas, mushrooms and egg, toss and cook at 360 degrees F for 20 minutes more.
3. Divide among plates and serve for breakfast.

Nutrition: calories 142 - Fat 3 - Fiber 2 - Carbs 6 - Protein 4

40. Greek Veggie Side Dish

Prep.Time: 10 min - Cooking Time: 45 min - Servings: 4

Ingredients:
- ✓ 1 eggplant, sliced
- ✓ 1 zucchini, sliced
- ✓ 2 red bell peppers, chopped
- ✓ 2 garlic cloves, minced
- ✓ 3 tablespoons olive oil
- ✓ 1 bay leaf
- ✓ 1 thyme spring, chopped
- ✓ 2 onions, chopped
- ✓ 4 tomatoes, cut into quarters
- ✓ Salt and black pepper to the taste

Directions:
1. In your air fryer's pan, mix eggplant slices with zucchini ones, bell peppers, garlic, oil, bay leaf, thyme, onions, tomatoes, salt and pepper, toss and cook them at 300 degrees F for 35 minutes.
2. Divide among plates and serve as a side dish

Nutrition: calories 200 - Fat 1 - Fiber 3 - Carbs 7 - Protein 6

41. Mushroom Cakes

Prep.Time: 10 min - Cooking Time: 8 min - Servings: 8

Ingredients:
- ✓ 4 ounces mushrooms, chopped
- ✓ 1 yellow onion, chopped
- ✓ Salt and black pepper to the taste
- ✓ ½ teaspoon nutmeg, ground
- ✓ 2 tablespoons olive oil

Ingredients:
- ✓ 4 parsnips, cut into medium sticks
- ✓ 2 sweet potatoes cut into medium sticks
- ✓ 4 mixed carrots cut into medium sticks
- ✓ Salt and black pepper to the taste

Directions:
1. Heat up a pan with the butter over medium high heat, add onion and mushrooms, stir, cook for 3 minutes, add flour, stir well again and take off heat.
2. Add milk gradually, salt, pepper and nutmeg, stir and leave aside to cool down completely.
3. In a bowl, mix oil with bread crumbs and whisk.
4. Take spoonfuls of the mushroom filling, add to breadcrumbs mix, coat well, shape patties out of this mix, place them in your air fryer's basket and cook at 400 degrees F for 8 minutes.
5. Divide among plates and serve as a side for a steak.

Nutrition: calories 192 - Fat 2 - Fiber 1 - Carbs 16 - Protein 6

42. Veggie Fries

Prep.Time: 10 min - Cooking Time: 30 min - Servings: 4

Ingredients:
- ✓ 4 parsnips, cut into medium sticks
- ✓ 2 sweet potatoes cut into medium sticks
- ✓ 4 mixed carrots cut into medium sticks
- ✓ Salt and black pepper to the taste
- ✓ 3.5 ounces white flour
- ✓ 1 tablespoon baking powder
- ✓ 2 ounces parmesan, grated
- ✓ A splash of Worcestershire sauce

Directions:
3. Put veggie fries in a bowl, add oil, garlic powder, salt, pepper, flour and rosemary and toss to coat.
4. Put sweet potatoes in your preheated air fryer, cook them for 10 minutes at 350 degrees F and transfer them to a platter.
5. Put parsnip fries in your air fryer, cook for 5 minutes and transfer over potato fries.
6. Put carrot fries in your air fryer, cook for 15 minutes at 350 degrees F and transfer to the platter with the other fries.
7. Divide veggie fries on plates and serve them as a side dish.

Nutrition: calories 100 - Fat 0 - Fiber 4 - Carbs 7 - Protein 4

43. Cajun Onion Wedges

Prep.Time: 10 min - Cooking Time: 15 min - Servings: 4

Ingredients:
- ✓ 2 big white onions, cut into wedges
- ✓ Salt and black pepper to the taste
- ✓ 2 eggs
- ✓ ¼ cup milk
- ✓ 1/3 cup panko
- ✓ A drizzle of olive oil
- ✓ 1 and ½ teaspoon paprika
- ✓ 1 teaspoon garlic powder
- ✓ ½ teaspoon Cajun seasoning

Directions:
1. In a bowl, mix panko with Cajun seasoning and oil and stir.
2. In another bowl, mix egg with milk, salt and pepper and stir.
3. Sprinkle onion wedges with paprika and garlic powder, dip them in egg mix, then in bread crumbs mix, place in your air fryer's basket, cook at 360 degrees F for 10 minutes, flip and cook for 5 minutes more.
4. Divide among plates and serve as a side dish.

Nutrition: calories 200 - Fat 2 - Fiber 2 - Carbs 14 - Protein 7

44. Buffalo Cauliflower Snack

Prep.Time: 10 min - Cooking Time: 15 min - Servings: 4

Ingredients:
- ✓ 4 cups cauliflower florets
- ✓ 1 cup panko bread crumbs
- ✓ ¼ cup butter, melted
- ¼ cup buffalo sauce
- ✓ Mayonnaise for serving

Directions:
1. In a bowl, mix buffalo sauce with butter and whisk well.
2. Dip cauliflower florets in this mix and coat them in panko bread crumbs.
3. Place them in your air fryer's basket and cook at 350 degrees F for 15 minutes.
4. Arrange them on a platter and serve with mayo on the side.

Nutrition: calories 241 - Fat 4 - Fiber 7 - Carbs 8 - Protein 4

45. Creamy Roasted Peppers Side Dish

Prep.Time: 10 min - Cooking Time: 10 minutes - Servings: 4

Ingredients:
- ✓ 1 tablespoon lemon juice
- ✓ 1 red bell pepper
- ✓ 1 green bell pepper
- ✓ 1 yellow bell pepper
- ✓ 1 lettuce head, cut into strips
- ✓ 1 ounce rocket leaves
- ✓ Salt and black pepper to the taste
- ✓ 3 tablespoons Greek yogurt
- ✓ 2 tablespoons olive oil

Directions:
1. Place bell peppers in your air fryer's basket, cook at 400 degrees F for 10 minutes, transfer to a bowl, leave aside for 10 minutes, peel them, discard seeds, cut them in strips, transfer to a larger bowl, add rocket leaves and lettuce strips and toss.
2. In a bowl, mix oil with lemon juice, yogurt, salt and pepper and whisk well.
3. Add this over bell peppers mix, toss to coat, divide among plates and serve as a side salad.

Nutrition: calories 170 - Fat 1 - Fiber 1 - Carbs 2 - Protein 6

46. Flavored Cauliflower Side Dish

Prep.Time: 10 min - Cooking Time: 10 min - Servings: 4

Ingredients:
- ✓ 12 cauliflower florets, steamed
- ✓ Salt and black pepper to the taste
- ✓ ¼ teaspoon turmeric powder
- ✓ 1 and ½ teaspoon red chili powder
- ✓ 1 tablespoon ginger, grated
- ✓ 2 teaspoons lemon juice
- ✓ 3 tablespoons white flour
- ✓ 2 tablespoons water
- ✓ Cooking spray
- ✓ ½ teaspoon corn flour

Directions:
1. In a bowl, mix chili powder with turmeric powder, ginger paste, salt, pepper, lemon juice, white flour, corn flour and water, stir, add cauliflower, toss well and transfer them to your air fryer's basket.
2. Coat them with cooking spray, cook them at 400 degrees F for 10 minutes, divide among plates and serve as a side dish.

Nutrition: calories 70 - Fat 1 - Fiber 2 - Carbs 12 - Protein 3

47. Crispy Radish Chips

Prep.Time: 10 min - Cooking Time: 10 min - Servings: 4

Ingredients:
- ✓ Cooking spray
- ✓ 15 radishes, sliced
- ✓ Salt and black pepper to the taste
- ✓ 1 tablespoon chives, chopped

Directions:
1. Arrange radish slices in your air fryer's basket, spray them with cooking oil, season with salt and black pepper to the taste, cook them at 350 degrees F for 10 minutes, flipping them halfway, transfer to bowls and serve with chives sprinkled on top

Nutrition: calories 80 - Fat 1 - Fiber 1- Carbs 1 - Protein 1

48. Zucchini Chips

Prep.Time: 10 min - Cooking Time: 1 hour - Servings: 6

Ingredients:
- ✓ 3 zucchinis, thinly sliced
- ✓ Salt and black pepper to the taste
- ✓ 2 tablespoons olive oil
- ✓ 2 tablespoons balsamic vinegar

Directions:
1. In a bowl, mix oil with vinegar, salt and pepper and whisk well.
2. Add zucchini slices, toss to coat well, introduce in your air fryer and cook at 200 degrees F for 1 hour.
3. Serve zucchini chips cold as a snack.

Nutrition: calories 40 - Fat 3 - Fiber 7 - Carbs 3 - Protein 7

49. Potato Casserole

Prep.Time: 15 min - Cooking Time: 40 min - Servings: 4

Ingredients:
- ✓ 3 pounds sweet potatoes, scrubbed
- ✓ ¼ cup milk
- ✓ ½ teaspoon nutmeg, ground
- ✓ 2 tablespoons white flour
- ✓ ¼ teaspoon allspice, ground
- ✓ Salt to the taste

For the topping:
- ✓ ½ cup almond flour
- ✓ ½ cup walnuts, soaked, drained and ground
- ✓ ¼ cup pecans, soaked, drained and ground
- ✓ ¼ cup coconut, shredded
- ✓ 1 tablespoon chia seeds
- ✓ ¼ cup sugar
- ✓ 1 teaspoon cinnamon powder
  5 tablespoons butter

Directions:
1. Place potatoes in your air fryer's basket, prick them with a fork and cook at 360 degrees F for 30 minutes.
2. Meanwhile, in a bowl, mix almond flour with pecans, walnuts, ¼ cup coconut, ¼ cup sugar, chia seeds, 1 teaspoon cinnamon and the butter and stir everything.
3. Transfer potatoes to a cutting board, cool them, peel and place them in a baking dish that fits your air fryer.
4. Add milk, flour, salt, nutmeg and allspice and stir
5. Add crumble mix you've made earlier on top, place dish in your air fryer's basket and cook at 400 degrees F for 8 minutes.
6. Divide among plates and serve as a side dish.

Nutrition: calories 162 - Fat 4 - Fiber 8 - Carbs 18 - Protein 4

50. Garlic Beet Wedges

Prep.Time: 10 min - Cooking Time: 15 min - Servings: 4

Ingredients:
- ✓ 4 beets, washed, peeled and cut into large wedges
- ✓ 1 tablespoon olive oil
- ✓ Salt and black to the taste
- ✓
- ✓ 2 garlic cloves, minced
- ✓ 1 teaspoon lemon juice

Directions:
2. In a bowl, mix beets with oil, salt, pepper, garlic and lemon juice, toss well, transfer to your air fryer's basket and cook them at 400 degrees F for 15 minutes.
3. Divide beets wedges on plates and serve as a side dish.

Nutrition: calories 182 - Fat 6 - Fiber 3- Carbs 8 - Protein 2

51. Crispy Brussels Sprouts and Potatoes

Prep.Time: 10 min - Cooking Time: 8 min - Servings: 4

Ingredients:
- ✓ 1 and ½ pounds Brussels sprouts, washed and trimmed
- ✓ 1 cup new potatoes, chopped
- ✓ 1 and ½ tbsp bread crumbs
- ✓ Salt and black pepper to the taste
  1 and ½ tbsp butter

Directions:
1. Put Brussels sprouts and potatoes in your air fryer's pan, add bread crumbs, salt, pepper and butter, toss well and cook at 400 degrees F for 8 minutes.
2. Divide among plates and serve as a side dish.

Nutrition: calories 152 - Fat 3 - Fiber 7 - Carbs 17 - Protein 4

52. Chickpeas Snack

Prep.Time: 10 min - Cooking Time: 10 min - Servings: 4

Ingredients:
- ✓ 15 ounces canned chickpeas, drained
- ✓ ½ teaspoon cumin, ground
- ✓ 1 tablespoon olive oil

Directions:
1. In a bowl, mix chickpeas with oil, cumin, paprika, salt and pepper, toss to coat, place them in your fryer's basket and cook at 390 degrees F for 10 minutes.
2. Divide into bowls and serve as a snack.

Nutrition: calories 140 - Fat 1 - Fiber 6- Carbs 20 - Protein 6

53. Crab Sticks

Prep.Time: 10 min - Cooking Time: 12 min - Servings: 4

Ingredients:
- ✓ 10 crabsticks, halved
- ✓ 2 teaspoons sesame oil
- ✓ 2 teaspoons Cajun seasoning

Directions:
1. Put crab sticks in a bowl, add sesame oil and Cajun seasoning, toss, transfer them to your air fryer's basket and cook at 350 degrees F for 12 minutes.
   Arrange on a platter and serve as an appetizer

Nutrition: calories 110 - Fat 0 - Fiber 1- Carbs 4 - Protein 2

54. Cauliflower Bars

Prep.Time: 10 min - Cooking Time: 25 min - Servings: 12

Ingredients:
- ✓ 1 big cauliflower head, florets separated
- ✓ ½ cup mozzarella, shredded
- ✓ ¼ cup egg whites
- ✓ 1 tsp Italian seasoning
- ✓ Salt and black pepper to the taste

Directions:
2. Put cauliflower florets in your food processor, pulse well, spread on a lined baking sheet that fits your air fryer, introduce in the fryer and cook at 360 degrees F for 10 minutes.
3. Transfer cauliflower to a bowl, add salt, pepper, cheese, egg whites and Italian seasoning, stir really well, spread this into a rectangle pan that fits your air fryer, press well, introduce in the fryer and cook at 360 degrees F for 15 minutes more.
4. Cut into 12 bars, arrange them on a platter and serve as a snack.

Nutrition: calories 50 - Fat 1 - Fiber 2- Carbs 3 - Protein 3

55. Yellow Squash and Zucchinis Side Dish

Prep.Time: 10min - Cooking Time: 35 min - Servings: 4

Ingredients:
- ✓ 6 teaspoons olive oil
- ✓ 1 pound zucchinis, sliced
- ✓ ½ pound carrots, cubed
- ✓ 1 yellow squash, halved, deseeded and cut into chunks
- ✓ Salt and white pepper to the taste
- ✓ 1 tablespoon tarragon, chopped

Directions:
1. In your air fryer's basket, mix zucchinis with carrots, squash, salt, pepper and oil, toss well and cook at 400 degrees F for 25 minutes.
2. Divide them on plates and serve as a side dish with tarragon sprinkled on top.

Nutrition: calories 160 - Fat 2 - Fiber 1 - Carbs 5 - Protein 5

56. Coconut Cream Potatoes

Prep.Time: 10min - Cooking Time: 20 min - Servings: 4

Ingredients:
- ✓ 2 eggs, whisked
- ✓ Salt and black pepper to the taste
- ✓ 1 tablespoon cheddar cheese, grated
- ✓ 1 tablespoon flour
- ✓ 2 potatoes, sliced
- ✓ 4 ounces coconut cream

Directions:
1. Place potato slices in your air fryer's basket and cook at 360 degrees F for 10 minutes.
2. Meanwhile, in a bowl, mix eggs with coconut cream, salt, pepper and flour.
3. Arrange potatoes in your air fryer's pan, add coconut cream mix over them, sprinkle cheese, return to air fryer's basket and cook at 400 degrees F for 10 minutes more.
4. Divide among plates and serve as a side dish.

Nutrition: calories 170 - Fat 4 - Fiber 1 - Carbs 15 - Protein 17

57. Artichokes and Tarragon Sauce

Prep.Time: 10min - Cooking Time: 18 minutes - Servings: 4

Ingredients:
- ✓ 4 artichokes, trimmed
- ✓ 2 tablespoons tarragon, chopped
- ✓ 2 tablespoons chicken stock
- ✓ Lemon zest from 2 lemons, grated
- ✓ 2 tablespoons lemon juice
- ✓ 1 celery stalk, chopped
- ✓ ½ cup olive oil
- ✓ Salt to the taste

Directions:
1. In your food processor, mix tarragon, chicken stock, lemon zest, lemon juice, celery, salt and olive oil and pulse very well.
2. In a bowl, mix artichokes with tarragon and lemon sauce, toss well, transfer them to your air fryer's basket and cook at 380 degrees F for 18 minutes.
3. Divide artichokes on plates, drizzle the rest of the sauce all over and serve as a side dish.

Nutrition: calories 215 - Fat 3 - Fiber 8 - Carbs 28 - Protein 6

58. Wild Rice Pilaf

Prep.Time: 10min - Cooking Time: 25 min - Servings: 12

Ingredients:
- ✓ 1 shallot, chopped
- ✓ 1 teaspoon garlic, minced
- ✓ A drizzle of olive oil
- ✓ 1 cup farro
- ✓ ¾ cup wild rice
- ✓ 4 cups chicken stock
- ✓ Salt and black pepper to the taste
- ✓ 1 tablespoon parsley, chopped
- ✓ ½ cup hazelnuts, toasted and chopped
- ✓ ¾ cup cherries, dried
- ✓ Chopped chives for serving

Directions:
1. In a dish that fits your air fryer, mix shallot with garlic, oil, faro, wild rice, stock, salt, pepper, parsley, hazelnuts and cherries, stir, place in your air fryer's basket and cook at 350 degrees F for 25 minutes.
2. Divide among plates and serve as a side dish.

Nutrition: calories 142 - Fat 4 - Fiber 4 - Carbs 16 - Protein 4

59 Pumpkin Rice

Prep.Time: 5min - Cooking Time: 30 min - Servings: 4

Ingredients:
- ✓ 2 tablespoons olive oil
- ✓ 1 small yellow onion, chopped
- ✓ 2 garlic cloves, minced
- ✓ 12 ounces white rice
- ✓ 4 cups chicken stock
- ✓ 6 ounces pumpkin puree
- ✓ ½ teaspoon nutmeg
- ✓ 1 teaspoon thyme, chopped
- ✓ ½ teaspoon ginger, grated
- ✓ ½ teaspoon cinnamon powder
- ✓ ½ teaspoon allspice
- ✓ 4 ounces heavy cream

Directions:
1. In a dish that fits your air fryer, mix oil with onion, garlic, rice, stock, pumpkin puree, nutmeg, thyme, ginger, cinnamon, allspice and cream, stir well, place in your air fryer's basket and cook at 360 degrees F for 30 minutes.
2. Divide among plates and serve as a side dish.

Nutrition: calories 261 - Fat 6 - Fiber 7 - Carbs 29 - Protein 4

60. Fried Red Cabbage

Prep.Time: 10min - Cooking Time: 15 min - Servings: 4

Ingredients:
- ✓ 4 garlic cloves, minced
- ✓ ½ cup yellow onion, chopped
- ✓ 1 tablespoon olive oil
- ✓ 6 cups red cabbage, chopped
- ✓ 1 cup veggie stock
- ✓ 1 tablespoon apple cider vinegar
- ✓ 1 cup applesauce
- ✓ Salt and black pepper to the taste

Directions:
1. In a heat proof dish that fits your air fryer, mix cabbage with onion, garlic, oil, stock, vinegar, applesauce, salt and pepper, toss really well, place dish in your air fryer's basket and cook at 380 degrees F for 15 minutes.
2. Divide among plates and serve as a side dish

Nutrition: calories 172 - Fat 7 - Fiber 7 - Carbs 14 - Protein 5

61. Cauliflower and Broccoli Delight

Prep.Time: 10min - **Cooking Time: 7 min** - **Servings:** 4

Ingredients:
- ✓ 2 cauliflower heads, florets separated and steamed
- ✓ 1 broccoli head, florets separated and steamed
- ✓ Zest from 1 orange, grated
- ✓ Juice from 1 orange
- ✓ A pinch of hot pepper flakes
- ✓ 4 anchovies
- ✓ 1 tablespoon capers, chopped
- ✓ Salt and black pepper to the taste
- ✓ 4 tablespoons olive oil

Directions:
1. In a bowl, mix orange zest with orange juice, pepper flakes, anchovies, capers salt, pepper and olive oil and whisk well.
2. Add broccoli and cauliflower, toss well, transfer them to your air fryer's basket and cook at 400 degrees F for 7 minutes.
3. Divide among plates and serve as a side dish with some of the orange vinaigrette drizzled on top.

Nutrition: calories 300 - Fat 4 - Fiber 7 - Carbs 28 - Protein 4

62. Colored Veggie Rice

Prep.Time: 10min - **Cooking Time: 25 min** - **Servings:** 4

Ingredients:
- ✓ 2 cups basmati rice
- ✓ 1 cup mixed carrots, peas, corn and green beans
- ✓ 2 cups water
- ✓ ½ teaspoon green chili, minced
- ✓ ½ teaspoon ginger, grated
- ✓ 3 garlic cloves, minced
- ✓ 2 tablespoons butter
- ✓ 1 teaspoon cinnamon powder
- ✓ 1 tablespoon cumin seeds
- ✓ 2 bay leaves
- ✓ 3 whole cloves
- ✓ 5 black peppercorns
- ✓ 2 whole cardamoms
- ✓ 1 tablespoon sugar
- ✓ Salt to the taste

Directions:
1. Put the water in a heat proof dish that fits your air fryer, add rice, mixed veggies, green chili, grated ginger, garlic cloves, cinnamon, cloves, butter, cumin seeds, bay leaves, cardamoms, black peppercorns, salt and sugar, stir, put in your air fryer's basket and cook at 370 degrees F for 25 minutes.
2. Divide among plates and serve as a side dish.

Nutrition: calories 283 - Fat 4 - Fiber 8 - Carbs 34 - Protein 14

63. Lemony Artichokes

Prep.Time: 10min - **Cooking Time: 15 minutes** - **Servings:** 4

Ingredients:
- ✓ 2 medium artichokes, trimmed and halved
- ✓ Cooking spray
- ✓ 2 tablespoons lemon juice
- ✓ Salt and black pepper to the taste

Directions:
1. Grease your air fryer with cooking spray, add artichokes, drizzle lemon juice and sprinkle salt and black pepper and cook them at 380 degrees F for 15 minutes.
2. Divide them on plates and serve as a side dish.

Nutrition: calories 121 - Fat 3 - Fiber 6 - Carbs 9 - Protein 4

64. Beer Risotto

Prep.Time: 10min - **Cooking Time: 30 min** - **Servings:** 4

Ingredients:
- ✓ 2 tablespoons olive oil
- ✓ 2 yellow onions, chopped
- ✓ 1 cup mushrooms, sliced
- ✓ 1 teaspoon basil, dried
- ✓ 1 teaspoon oregano, dried
- ✓ 1 and ½ cups rice
- ✓ 2 cups beer
- ✓ 2 cups chicken stock
- ✓ 1 tablespoon butter
- ✓ ½ cup parmesan, grated

Directions:
1. In a dish that fits your air fryer, mix oil with onions, mushrooms, basil and oregano and stir.
2. Add rice, beer, butter, stock and butter, stir again, place in your air fryer's basket and cook at 350 degrees F for 30 minutes.
3. Divide among plates and serve with grated parmesan on top as a side dish.

Nutrition: calories 142 - Fat 4 - Fiber 4 - Carbs 6 - Protein 4

65. Barley Risotto

Prep.Time: 10min - **Cooking Time:30 min** - **Servings:** 8

Ingredients:
- ✓ 5 cups veggie stock
- ✓ 3 tablespoons olive oil
- ✓ 2 yellow onions, chopped
- ✓ 2 garlic cloves, minced
- ✓ ¾ pound barley
- ✓ 3 ounces mushrooms, sliced
- ✓ 2 ounces skim milk
- ✓ 1 teaspoon thyme, dried
- ✓ 1 teaspoon tarragon, dried
- ✓ Salt and black pepper to the taste
- ✓ 2 pounds sweet potato, peeled and chopped

Directions:
1. Put stock in a pot, add barley, stir, bring to a boil over medium heat and cook for 15 minutes.
2. Heat up your air fryer at 350 degrees F, add oil and heat it up.
3. Add barley, onions, garlic, mushrooms, milk, salt, pepper, tarragon and sweet potato, stir and cook for 15 minutes more.
4. Divide among plates and serve as a side dish.

Nutrition: calories 124 - Fat 4 - Fiber 4 - Carbs 6 - Protein 4

66. Cheddar Biscuits

Prep.Time: 10min - **Cooking Time: 20 min** - **Servings:** 8

Ingredients:
- ✓ 2 and 1/3 cup self-rising flour
- ✓ ½ cup butter+ 1 tablespoon, melted
- ✓ 2 tablespoons sugar
- ✓ ½ cup cheddar cheese, grated
- ✓ 1 and 1/3 cup buttermilk
- ✓ 1 cup flour

Directions:
1. In a bowl, mix self-rising flour with ½ cup butter, sugar, cheddar cheese and buttermilk and stir until you obtain a dough.
2. Spread 1 cup flour on a working surface, roll dough, flatten it, cut 8 circles with a cookie cutter and coat them with flour.
3. Line your air fryer's basket with tin foil, add biscuits, brush them with melted butter and cook them at 380 degrees F for 20 minutes.
4. Divide among plates and serve as a side.

Nutrition: calories 221 - Fat 3 - Fiber 8 - Carbs 12 - Protein 4

67. Bacon Brussels Sprouts

Prep.Time: 10 min - **Cooking Time:** 35 min - **Servings:** 4

Ingredients:

- ✓ 1/2 lb. bacon
- ✓ 16 oz. brussels sprouts, cut in half
- ✓ 6 tsp. avocado oil
- ✓ 1/2tsp. garlic powder
- ✓ 6 tsp. lime juice
- ✓ 1 tsp. mint leaves, garnish
- ✓ 2 oz. pistachios
- ✓ 1 1/4 tsp. salt, separated
- ✓ 5 dates, pitted and diced
- ✓ 1 tsp. basil leaves, garnish
- ✓ 4 tsp. lime juice, separated
- ✓ 1/8 tsp. pepper

Directions:

1. Brown the bacon in a frying pan for about 3 minutes and set on a plate covered with paper towels.
2. In a glass dish, coat the Brussels sprouts with 3 teaspoons of the lime juice, one teaspoon of salt, avocado oil, and garlic powder until completely covered.
3. Transfer to the air fryer basket with the temperature set to the 385°F.
4. Heat for a total of 25 minutes while tossing the Brussels sprouts approximately every 5 minutes.
5. Crumble the bacon into a glass dish and set to the side.
6. At the 15 minute mark, combine the crumbled bacon, dates and pistachios into the basket of Brussels sprouts and continue to cook for the remaining 10 minutes.
7. Remove and transfer the Brussels sprouts to a serving platter and drizzle the remaining teaspoon of lime juice over the dish.
8. Dust the remaining 1/4 teaspoon of salt and pepper over the dish and garnish with the basil and mint leaves.
9. Serve right away and enjoy.

68. Cheesy Ravioli

Prep.Time: 10 min - **Cooking Time:** 15 min - **Servings:** 4

Ingredients:

- ✓ prepackaged ravioli - 16 oz., frozen
- ✓ bread crumbs - 1 cup
- ✓ garlic powder - 3 tsp.
- ✓ parmesan cheese - 1/2 cup
- ✓ two eggs, preferably large
- ✓ Italian seasoning - 1 tbs.
- ✓ cooking spray (olive oil)

Directions:

1. Blend the parmesan cheese, Italian seasoning, garlic powder, breadcrumbs in a glass dish.
2. Whisk the eggs in another bowl and set to the side.
3. Coat the basket of the air fryer with olive oil spray.
4. Immerse the frozen ravioli pieces into the egg making sure they are covered completely.
5. Coat the ravioli in the flour and transfer to the air fryer basket when breaded.
6. Adjust the air fryer temperature to 350°F and heat for a total of 15 minutes.
7. At the 8 minute mark, toss the ravioli to ensure they will fully cook.
8. Remove and empty onto a serving plate and enjoy immediately.

69. Side Dish - Chicken Wings

Prep.Time: 10 min - **Cooking Time:** 25 minutes - **Servings:** 4-6

Ingredients:

- ✓ pepper - 1 tsp.
- ✓ chicken wings - 2 lbs.
- ✓ salt - 1 tsp.
- ✓ sauce of your choice -3/4 cup
- ✓ parsley seasoning - 1 tbsp.

Directions:

1. Using paper towels, remove the excess moisture from the chicken. Sprinkle with the pepper and salt.
2. Arrange the wings in the basket of the air fryer in a single layer so they do not touch.
3. Heat for 10 minutes at a temperature of 400°F.
4. Flip the chicken and continue to fry for an additional 10 minutes.
5. Use a meat thermometer to ensure the chicken is cooked to 160°F before removing to a glass dish.
6. Empty the sauce you have chosen over the chicken and coat the chicken completely using a rubber spatula to toss.
7. Grill the chicken once again in the air fryer at the same temperature for an additional 5 minutes.
8. Remove to a plate, sprinkle the parsley over the dish and enjoy hot!

70. Blooming Onion

Prep.Time: 20 min - **Cooking Time:** 10-15 min - **Servings:** 2

Ingredients:

- ✓ one large onion, sweet
- ✓ salt - 3 tsp.
- ✓ cayenne pepper - 1 /2 tsp.
- ✓ cooking spray (olive oil)
- ✓ garlic powder - 1 tsp.
- ✓ milk - 4 oz.
- ✓ one large egg
- ✓ all-purpose flour - 4 oz.
- ✓ olive oil - 1/2 tsp.

Directions:

1. You will need to prepare a piece of tin foil on top of a cutting board. Brush 1/2 tsp. of olive oil onto the center of the foil.
2. Slice the top half-inch of the onion off and remove the outer skin of the onion entirely.
3. Slice the onion in half, stopping half an inch above the root. Make a similar cut perpendicular to the first, creating 4 sections of sliced onion.
4. Continue to cut the onion using this method and finish the cuts once there are 16 sections of onion slices.
5. Adjust the air fryer temperature to 370°F to heat.
6. Whip the cayenne pepper, garlic powder, flour, and salt in a glass dish with a whisk to remove all lumpiness.
7. Using another bowl, blend the egg and milk until combined.
8. Immerse the onion slices in the eggs ensuring they are completely coated.
9. Repeat by coating completely in the seasoned flour and spoon over each section to make sure no area is missed. Shake thoroughly to remove extra flour by turning upside down.
10. Apply the cooking oil onto each section of the onion and transfer to the air fryer basket.
11. Heat for approximately 10 minutes and remove if the crust is golden. If not, cook for an additional 5 minutes.

71. Edamame

Prep.Time: 5 min - **Cooking Time:** 10 min - **Servings:** 2-4

Ingredients:
- ✓ 1 tsp. avocado oil
- ✓ 16 oz. Edamame, unshelled and frozen

Directions:
1. Drizzle the avocado oil over a dish containing the edamame and toss to coat completely.
2. Adjust the air fryer temperature to heat at 390°F for approximately 10 minutes.
3. At the 5 minute mark, stir the edamame.
4. Remove to a serving dish and enjoy while warm

72. Bok Choy Salad

Prep.Time: 5 min - **Cooking Time:** 5 min - **Servings:** 2

Ingredients:
- ✓ 1/2 tsp. sesame seeds, toasted
- ✓ 2 heads baby bok choy, halved
- ✓ 1 tbsp. toasted sesame oil
- ✓ 2 oz. shiitake mushrooms, stemmed
- ✓ 1/4 tsp. salt

Directions:
1. Adjust the temperature of the air fryer to 400°F.
2. Slice the stems off the mushrooms and chop the bok choy in halves.
3. Apply sesame oil by brushing over the mushrooms and bok choy. Dust with salt and transfer to the air fryer basket.
4. Set for 5 minutes and remove to a plate. Drizzle the sesame seeds over the dish and enjoy while hot.

73. Eggplant Parmesan

Prep.Time: 35 min - **Cooking Time:** 10 minutes - **Servings:** 2-4

Ingredients:
- ✓ eggplant - 1 1/4 lb.
- ✓ all-purpose flour - 3 tbsp.
- ✓ parsley - 1 tbsp., chopped
- ✓ bread crumbs - 4 oz.
- ✓ basil - 1 tbsp., chopped
- ✓ parmesan cheese - 3 tbsp., grated finely
- ✓ Italian seasoning - 1 tsp.
- ✓ cooking spray (olive oil)
- ✓ salt - 1/4 tsp.
- ✓ marinara sauce - 8 oz.
- ✓ mozzarella cheese - 1/4 cup, grated
- ✓ one egg white, large
- ✓ water - 1 tbsp.

Directions:
1. Slice the eggplant into half-inch rounds and sprinkle salt on either side. Transfer to a baking lining covered flat sheet and set aside for approximately 15 minutes.
2. In the meantime, blend the water, flour and egg white in a glass dish.
3. In a separate dish, toss the parmesan cheese, breadcrumbs, salt, and Italian seasoning until thoroughly integrated.
4. Adjust the temperature of the air fryer to heat at 360°F.
5. Using a fork to hold the individual eggplant slices, dunk into the dish with the egg and then the breadcrumbs, making sure not to over bread. Transfer back to the baking sheet.
6. Apply the cooking spray (olive oil) over the eggplant slices and arrange greased side down on a wire rack placed inside the air fryer basket.
7. Steam for about 8 minutes and open the lid.
8. Spread approximately a tablespoon of marinara sauce on each eggplant slice.
9. Divide the mozzarella cheese evenly and sprinkle on top of each serving of eggplant.
10. Heat for another 2 minutes and enjoy immediately while hot.

74. Fried Mushrooms

Prep.Time: 10 min - **Cooking Time:** 7 min - **Servings:** 2-4

Ingredients:
- ✓ Salt - 3/4 tbsp.
- ✓ baby portobello mushrooms - 1 lb.
- ✓ garlic powder - 3/4 tsp.
- ✓ two eggs, large
- ✓ onion powder - 3/4 tsp.
- ✓ 1 tsp. creole seasoning, separated
- ✓ cooking spray (olive oil)
- ✓ panko bread crumbs - 1 cup
- ✓ pepper - 3/4 tsp.
- ✓ all-purpose flour - 1 cup
- ✓ paprika seasoning - 3/4 tsp.

Directions:
1. Clean the portabella mushrooms by removing any dirt and slice into 4 sections.
2. In a glass dish, whip the eggs and blend with 1/4 teaspoon of the creole seasoning.
3. Empty the flour, garlic powder, salt, breadcrumbs, onion powder, pepper, paprika seasoning, and the remaining 3/4 teaspoon of the creole seasoning into a large ziplock bag. Shake until combined and set to the side.
4. Transfer the sections of mushrooms in stages to the egg mixture. Once fully coated, shake to remove the excess egg.
5. Transfer to the ziplock bag and agitate to coat the mushrooms completely in the breading.
6. Remove the mushrooms from the bag and distribute to the basket of the air fryer, leaving space in between.
7. Coat the mushrooms generously with the cooking spray. Shake the basket and spray the mushrooms on the other side with the cooking spray (olive oil).
8. Adjust the temperature of the air fryer to 400°F and heat for 3 minutes.
9. Open the lid and agitate the basket. Fry for an additional 4 minutes.
10. Transfer the mushrooms from the air fryer to a serving plate.
11. Repeat steps 6 through 10 as necessary.
12. Serve and enjoy immediately.

75. Fried Pickles

Prep.Time: 10 min - **Cooking Time:** 10 min - **Servings:** 2-4

Ingredients:
- ✓ panko bread crumbs - 1/3 cup
- ✓ jar dill pickles - 16 oz., whole
- ✓ one egg, large
- ✓ dill weed - 1/8 tsp.
- ✓ grated Parmesan - 2 tbsp.

Directions:
1. Drain the pickles from the jar and cut diagonally to be quarter-inch thick slices.
2. Transfer to a few sections of paper towels to remove all the fluid. Set to the side.
3. Whip the egg in a glass dish and set aside.
4. Use a ziplock bag to shake the parmesan, dill weed, and bread crumbs until combined.
5. Immerse the chips in small quantities into the egg and shake to remove the extra fluid.
6. Transfer to the ziplock bag and shake until the chips are fully coated.
7. Move to the air fry basket and put no more than 2 layers of pickles in the basket. Repeat steps 5 through 8 for a second batch if necessary.
8. At a temperature of 400°F, heat the pickles for 9 minutes.
9. Remove and serve immediately.

76. Fried Okra

Prep.Time: 15 min - **Cooking Time:** 8 min - **Servings:** 2-3

Ingredients:
- ✓ one large egg
- ✓ salt - 1/2 tsp.
- ✓ okra - 2 1/2 cups
- ✓ all-purpose flour - 1 cup
- ✓ paprika seasoning - 1/2 tsp.
- ✓ cooking spray (olive oil)
- ✓ pepper - 1/2 tsp.

Directions:
1. In a glass dish, whip the egg and blend with half the pepper and salt.
2. Empty the flour, paprika and the remaining 1/4 teaspoon of pepper and salt into a large ziplock bag. Shake until blended and set to the side.
3. Scrub the okra and dry using several paper towels to remove any moisture.
4. Remove both the ends of each piece of okra with a knife and discard.
5. Chop the okra into half-inch pieces.
6. Transfer the sliced okra in batches to the egg mixture. Once coated, transfer to the ziplock bag using a slotted spoon.
7. Agitate the ziplock bag to coat the okra completely in the breading.
8. Remove the okra from the bag and distribute to the basket of the air fryer.
9. Spray the okra with the olive oil.
10. Adjust the temperature of the air fryer to 400°F and heat for 4 minutes.
11. Open the lid and agitate the basket. Spray with olive oil once again. Fry for an additional 4 minutes.
12. Transfer the fried okra from the air fryer to a serving plate.
13. Serve and enjoy immediately.

77. French Fries

Prep.Time: 10 min - **Cooking Time:** 20 minutes - **Servings:** 2-3

Ingredients:
- ✓ salt - 1/4 tsp.
- ✓ olive oil - 2 tsp.
- ✓ garlic powder - 1/4 tsp.
- ✓ potatoes - 1 lb.
- ✓ pepper - 1/4 tsp.

Directions:
1. Scrub the potatoes and remove the skins with a vegetable peeler if you prefer.
2. Slice the potatoes into long quarter-inch sections and place into a glass dish.
3. Using a rubber scraper, blend the salt, olive oil, garlic powder, and pepper over the potatoes, evenly coating.
4. Evenly arrange the fries in the basket of the fryer, keeping them 2 layers or less.
5. Heat the air fryer for approximately 20 minutes at a temperature of 380°F.
6. At the 10 minute mark, toss the fries gently and continue to broil for the remaining 10 minutes.
7. Empty the basket onto a plate and serve immediately.

78. Fried Green Tomatoes

Prep.Time: 10 min - **Cooking Time:** 8 min - **Servings:** 2

Ingredients:
- ✓ Buttermilk - 1/2 cup
- ✓ Two green tomatoes, medium
- ✓ salt - 1/2 tsp., separated
- ✓ two large eggs
- ✓ pepper - 1/4 tsp.
- ✓ panko bread crumbs - 8 oz.
- ✓ cornmeal - 1 cup
- ✓ all-purpose flour - 4 oz.
- ✓ cooking spray (olive oil)

Directions:
1. Chop the tomatoes into quarter-inch slices and use paper towels to remove the moisture.
2. Dust with the pepper and 1/4 teaspoon of salt on both sides and set to the side on a plate.
3. Empty the flour into a glass dish. In an additional dish, whip the buttermilk and eggs until combined.
4. In a third dish, blend the cornmeal and breadcrumbs.
5. Adjust the temperature of the air fryer to heat at 400°F.
6. Cover the slices of tomato firstly in the flour and then the egg, removing the excess.
7. Compress the tomato slices into the breadcrumbs on either side to help the crumbs to stick properly. Dust the tomatoes with the remaining 1/4 teaspoon of salt.
8. Coat the basket of the air fryer with the cooking spray and transfer the slices inside.
9. Apply a layer of cooking spray (olive oil) to the top of the tomatoes and close the lid.
10. Set the timer for five minutes and then turn the slices over.
11. Use the cooking spray (olive oil) to apply another coat to the tomatoes and continue to fry for an additional 3 minutes.
12. Serve immediately and enjoy while hot.

117

SNACK AND APPETIZER RECIPES

1. Zucchini Cakes

Prep.Time: 10 min - **Cooking Time:** 12 min - **Servings:** 12

Ingredients:
- ✓ Cooking spray
- ✓ ½ cup dill, chopped
- ✓ 1 egg
- ✓ ½ cup whole wheat flour
- ✓ Salt and black pepper to the taste
- ✓ 1 yellow onion, chopped
- ✓ 2 garlic cloves, minced
- ✓ 3 zucchinis, grated

Directions:
1. In a bowl, mix zucchinis with garlic, onion, flour, salt, pepper, egg and dill, stir well, shape small patties out of this mix, spray them with cooking spray, place them in your air fryer's basket and cook at 370 degrees F for 6 minutes on each side.
2. Serve them as a snack right away.

Nutrition: calories 60 - Fat 1 - Fiber 2 - Carbs 6 - Protein 2

2. Pumpkin Muffins

Prep.Time: 10 min - **Cooking Time:** 15 min - **Servings:** 18

Ingredients:
- ✓ ¼ cup butter
- ✓ ¾ cup pumpkin puree
- ✓ 2 tablespoons flaxseed meal
- ✓ ¼ cup flour
- ✓ ½ cup sugar
- ✓ ½ teaspoon nutmeg, ground
- ✓ 1 teaspoon cinnamon powder
- ✓ ½ teaspoon baking soda
- ✓ 1 egg
- ✓ ½ teaspoon baking powder

Directions:
1. In a bowl, mix butter with pumpkin puree and egg and blend well.
2. Add flaxseed meal, flour, sugar, baking soda, baking powder, nutmeg and cinnamon and stir well.
3. Spoon this into a muffin pan that fits your fryer introduce in the fryer at 350 degrees F and bake for 15 minutes.
4. Serve muffins cold as a snack.

Nutrition: calories 50 - Fat 3 - Fiber 1 - Carbs 2 - Protein 2

3. Banana Chips

Prep.Time: 10 min - **Cooking Time:** 15 min - **Servings:** 4

Ingredients:
- ✓ 4 bananas, peeled and sliced
- ✓ A pinch of salt
- ✓ ½ teaspoon turmeric powder
- ✓ ½ teaspoon chaat masala
- ✓ 1 teaspoon olive oil

Directions:
1. In a bowl, mix banana slices with salt, turmeric, chaat masala and oil, toss and leave aside for 10 minutes.
2. Transfer banana slices to your preheated air fryer at 360 degrees F and cook them for 15 minutes flipping them once.
3. Serve as a snack.

Nutrition: calories 121 - Fat 1 - Fiber 2 - Carbs 3 - Protein 3

4. Sausage Balls

Prep.Time: 10 min - **Cooking Time:** 15 min - **Servings:** 9

Ingredients:
- ✓ 4 ounces sausage meat, ground
- ✓ Salt and black pepper to the taste
- ✓ 1 teaspoon sage
- ✓ ½ teaspoon garlic, minced
- ✓ 1 small onion, chopped
- ✓ 3 tablespoons breadcrumbs

Directions:
1. In a bowl, mix sausage with salt, pepper, sage, garlic, onion and breadcrumbs, stir well and shape small balls out of this mix.
2. Put them in your air fryer's basket, cook at 360 degrees F for 15 minutes, divide into bowls and serve as a snack.

Nutrition: calories 130 - Fat 7 - Fiber 1 - Carbs 13 - Protein 4

5. Honey Party Wings

Prep.Time: 1 hour 10 min- **Cooking Time:** 12 min - **Servings:** 8

Ingredients:
- ✓ 16 chicken wings, halved
- ✓ 2 tablespoons soy sauce
- ✓ 2 tablespoons honey
- ✓ Salt and black pepper to the taste
- ✓ 2 tablespoons lime juice

Directions:
1. In a bowl, mix chicken wings with soy sauce, honey, salt, pepper and lime juice, toss well and keep in the fridge for 1 hour.
2. Transfer chicken wings to your air fryer and cook them at 360 degrees F for 12 minutes, flipping them halfway.
3. Arrange them on a platter and serve as an appetizer.

Nutrition: calories 211 - Fat 4 - Fiber 7 - Carbs 14 - Protein 3

6. Air Fried Dill Pickles

Prep.Time: 10 min - **Cooking Time:** 5 min - **Servings:** 4

Ingredients:
- ✓ 16 ounces jarred dill pickles, cut into wedges and pat dried
- ✓ ½ cup white flour
- ✓ 1 egg
- ✓ ¼ cup milk
- ✓ ½ teaspoon garlic powder
- ✓ ½ teaspoon sweet paprika
- ✓ Cooking spray
- ✓ ¼ cup ranch sauce

Directions:
1. In a bowl, combine milk with egg and whisk well.
2. In a second bowl, mix flour with salt, garlic powder and paprika and stir as well
3. Dip pickles in flour, then in egg mix and again in flour and place them in your air fryer.
4. Grease them with cooking spray, cook pickle wedges at 400 degrees F for 5 minutes, transfer to a bowl and serve with ranch sauce on the side.

Nutrition: calories 109 - Fat 2 - Fiber 2 - Carbs 10 - Protein 4

7. Salmon Party Patties

Prep.Time: 10 min - **Cooking Time:** 22 min - **Servings:** 4

Ingredients:

- ✓ 3 big potatoes, boiled, drained and mashed
- ✓ 1 big salmon fillet, skinless, boneless
- ✓ 2 tablespoons parsley, chopped
- ✓ 2 tablespoon dill, chopped
- ✓ Salt and black pepper to the taste
- ✓ 1 egg
- ✓ 2 tablespoons bread crumbs
- ✓ Cooking spray

Directions:

1. Place salmon in your air fryer's basket and cook for 10 minutes at 360 degrees F.
2. Transfer salmon to a cutting board, cool it down, flake it and put it in a bowl.
3. Add mashed potatoes, salt, pepper, dill, parsley, egg and bread crumbs, stir well and shape 8 patties out of this mix.
4. Place salmon patties in your air fryer's basket, spry them with cooking oil, cook at 360 degrees F for 12 minutes, flipping them halfway, transfer them to a platter and serve as an appetizer.

Nutrition: calories 231 - Fat 3 – Fiber 7 - Carbs 14 - Protein 4

8. Spring Rolls

Prep.Time: 10 min - **Cooking Time:** 25 min - **Servings:**

Ingredients:

- ✓ 2 cups green cabbage, shredded
- ✓ 2 yellow onions, chopped
- ✓ 1 carrot, grated
- ✓ ½ chili pepper, minced
- ✓ 1 tablespoon ginger, grated
- ✓ 3 garlic cloves, minced
- ✓ 1 teaspoon sugar
- ✓ Salt and black pepper to the taste
- ✓ 1 teaspoon soy sauce
- ✓ 2 tablespoons olive oil
- ✓ 10 spring roll sheets
- ✓ 2 tablespoons corn flour
- ✓ 2 tablespoons water

Directions:

1. Heat up a pan with the oil over medium heat, add cabbage, onions, carrots, chili pepper, ginger, garlic, sugar, salt, pepper and soy sauce, stir well, cook for 2-3 minutes, take off heat and cool down.
2. Cut spring roll sheets in squares, divide cabbage mix on each and roll them.
3. In a bowl, mix corn flour with water, stir well and seal spring rolls with this mix.
4. Place spring rolls in your air fryer's basket and cook them at 360 degrees F for 10 minutes.
5. Flip roll and cook them for 10 minutes more.
6. Arrange on a platter and serve them as an appetizer.

Nutrition: calories 214 - Fat 4 - Fiber 4 - Carbs 12 - Protein 4

9. Beef Jerky Snack

Prep.Time: 2 hours - **Cooking Time:** 1 hour 30 min - **Servings:** 6

Ingredients:

- ✓ 2 cups soy sauce
- ✓ ½ cup Worcestershire sauce
- ✓ 2 tablespoons black peppercorns
- ✓ 2 tablespoons black pepper
- ✓ 2 pounds beef round, sliced

Directions:

1. In a bowl, mix soy sauce with black peppercorns, black pepper and Worcestershire sauce and whisk well.
2. Add beef slices, toss to coat and leave aside in the fridge for 6 hours.
3. Introduce beef rounds in your air fryer and cook them at 370 degrees F for 1 hour and 30 minutes.
4. Transfer to a bowl and serve cold.

Nutrition: calories 300 - Fat 12 - Fiber 4 - Carbs 3 - Protein 8

10. Bread Sticks

Prep.Time: 10 min - **Cooking Time:** 10 min - **Servings:** 2

Ingredients:

- ✓ 4 bread slices, each cut into 4 sticks
- ✓ 2 eggs
- ✓ ¼ cup milk
- ✓ 1 teaspoon cinnamon powder
- ✓ 1 tablespoon honey
- ✓ ¼ cup brown sugar
- ✓ A pinch of nutmeg

Directions:

1. In a bowl, mix eggs with milk, brown sugar, cinnamon, nutmeg and honey and whisk well.
2. Dip bread sticks in this mix, place them in your air fryer's basket and cook at 360 degrees F for 10 minutes.
3. Divide bread sticks into bowls and serve as a snack.

Nutrition: calories 140 - Fat 1 - Fiber 4 - Carbs 8 – Protein 4

11. Pesto Crackers

Prep.Time: 10 min - **Cooking Time:** 17 min - **Servings:** 6

Ingredients:
- ✓ ½ teaspoon baking powder
- ✓ Salt and black pepper to the taste
- ✓ 1 and ¼ cups flour
- ✓ ¼ teaspoon basil, dried
- ✓ 1 garlic clove, minced
- ✓ 2 tablespoons basil pesto
- ✓ 3 tablespoons butter

Directions:
1. In a bowl, mix salt, pepper, baking powder, flour, garlic, cayenne, basil, pesto and butter and stir until you obtain a dough.
2. Spread this dough on a lined baking sheet that fits your air fryer, introduce in the fryer at 325 degrees F and bake for 17 minutes.
3. Leave aside to cool down, cut crackers and serve them as a snack.

Nutrition: calories 200 - Fat 20 - Fiber 1 - Carbs 4 - Protein 7

12. Shrimp Muffins

Prep.Time: 10 min - **Cooking Time:** 26 min - **Servings:** 6

Ingredients:
- ✓ 1 spaghetti squash, peeled and halved
- ✓ 2 tablespoons mayonnaise
- ✓ 1 cup mozzarella, shredded
- ✓ 8 ounces shrimp, peeled, cooked and chopped
- ✓ 1 and ½ cups panko
- ✓ 1 teaspoon parsley flakes
- ✓ 1 garlic clove, minced
- ✓ Salt and black pepper to the taste
- ✓ Cooking spray

Directions:
1. Put squash halves in your air fryer, cook at 350 degrees F for 16 minutes, leave aside to cool down and scrape flesh into a bowl.
2. Add salt, pepper, parsley flakes, panko, shrimp, mayo and mozzarella and stir well.
3. Spray a muffin tray that fits your air fryer with cooking spray and divide squash and shrimp mix in each cup.
4. Introduce in the fryer and cook at 360 degrees F for 10 minutes.
5. Arrange muffins on a platter and serve as a snack.

Nutrition: calories 60 - Fat 2 - Fiber 0.4 - Carbs 4 - Protein 4

13. Chicken Dip

Prep.Time: 10 min - **Cooking Time:** 25 min - **Servings:** 10

Ingredients:
- ✓ 3 tablespoons butter, melted
- ✓ 1 cup yogurt
- ✓ 12 ounces cream cheese
- ✓ 2 cups chicken meat, cooked and shredded
- ✓ 2 teaspoons curry powder
- ✓ 4 scallions, chopped
- ✓ 6 ounces Monterey jack cheese, grated
- ✓ 1/3 cup raisins
- ✓ ¼ cup cilantro, chopped
- ✓ ½ cup almonds, sliced
- ✓ Salt and black pepper to the taste
- ✓ ½ cup chutney

Directions:
1. In a bowl mix cream cheese with yogurt and whisk using your mixer.
2. Add curry powder, scallions, chicken meat, raisins, cheese, cilantro, salt and pepper and stir everything.
3. Spread this into a baking dish that fist your air fryer, sprinkle almonds on top, place in your air fryer, bake at 300 degrees for 25 minutes, divide into bowls, top with chutney and serve as an appetizer.

Nutrition: calories 240 - Fat 10 - Fiber 2 - Carbs 2480 - Protein 12

14. Fish Nuggets

Prep.Time: 10 min - **Cooking Time:** 12 min - **Servings:** 4

Ingredients:
- ✓ 28 ounces fish fillets, skinless and cut into medium pieces
- ✓ Salt and black pepper to the taste
- ✓ 5 tablespoons flour
- ✓ 1 egg, whisked
- ✓ 5 tablespoons water
- ✓ 3 ounces panko bread crumbs
- ✓ 1 tablespoon garlic powder
- ✓ 1 tablespoon smoked paprika
- ✓ 4 tablespoons homemade mayonnaise
- ✓ Lemon juice from ½ lemon
- ✓ 1 teaspoon dill, dried
- ✓ Cooking spray

Directions:
1. In a bowl, mix flour with water and stir well.
2. Add egg, salt and pepper and whisk well.
3. In a second bowl, mix panko with garlic powder and paprika and stir well.
4. Dip fish pieces in flour and egg mix and then in panko mix, place them in your air fryer's basket, spray them with cooking oil and cook at 400 degrees F for 12 minutes.
5. Meanwhile, in a bowl mix mayo with dill and lemon juice and whisk well.
6. Arrange fish nuggets on a platter and serve with dill mayo on the side.

Nutrition: calories 332 - Fat 12 - Fiber 6 - Carbs 17 - Protein 15

15. Sweet Popcorn	16. Crispy Shrimp
Prep.Time: 5 min - **Cooking Time:** 10 minutes - **Servings:** 4	**Prep.Time:** 10 min - **Cooking Time:** 5 min - **Servings:** 4

15. Sweet Popcorn

Prep.Time: 5 min - **Cooking Time:** 10 minutes - **Servings:** 4

Ingredients:
- ✓ 2 tablespoons corn kernels
- ✓ 2 and ½ tablespoons butter

2 ounces brown sugar

Directions:
1. Put corn kernels in your air fryer's pan, cook at 400 degrees F for 6 minutes, transfer them to a tray, spread and leave aside for now.
2. Heat up a pan over low heat, add butter, melt it, add sugar and stir until it dissolves.
3. Add popcorn, toss to coat, take off heat and spread on the tray again.
4. Cool down, divide into bowls and serve as a snack.

Nutrition: calories 70 – Fat 0.2 - Fiber 0 - Carbs 1 - Protein 1

16. Crispy Shrimp

Prep.Time: 10 min - **Cooking Time:** 5 min - **Servings:** 4

Ingredients:
- ✓ 12 big shrimp, deveined and peeled
- ✓ 2 egg whites
- ✓ 1 cup coconut, shredded
- ✓ 1 cup panko bread crumbs
- ✓ 1 cup white flour
- ✓ Salt and black pepper to the taste

Directions:
1. In a bowl, mix panko with coconut and stir.
2. Put flour, salt and pepper in a second bowl and whisk egg whites in a third one.
3. Dip shrimp in flour, egg whites mix and coconut, place them all in your air fryer's basket, cook at 350 degrees F for 10 minutes flipping halfway.
4. Arrange on a platter and serve as an appetizer.

Nutrition: calories 140 - Fat 4 - Fiber 0 – Carbs 3 - Protein 4

17. Banana Snack

Prep.Time: 10 min - **Cooking Time:** 5 min - **Servings:** 8

Ingredients:
- ✓ 16 baking cups crust
- ✓ ¼ cup peanut butter
- ✓ ¾ cup chocolate chips
- ✓ 1 banana, peeled and sliced into 16 pieces
- ✓ 1 tablespoon vegetable oil

Directions:
1. Put chocolate chips in a small pot, heat up over low heat, stir until it melts and take off heat.
2. In a bowl, mix peanut butter with coconut oil and whisk well.
3. Spoon 1 teaspoon chocolate mix in a cup, add 1 banana slice and top with 1 teaspoon butter mix
4. Repeat with the rest of the cups, place them all into a dish that fits your air fryer, cook at 320 degrees F for 5 minutes, transfer to a freezer and keep there until you serve them as a snack.

Nutrition: calories 70 - Fat 4 - Fiber 1 - Carbs 10 - Protein 1

18. Cajun Shrimp Appetizer

Prep.Time: 10 min - **Cooking Time:** 5 min - **Servings:** 2

Ingredients:
- ✓ ½ teaspoon old bay seasoning
- ✓ 1 tablespoon olive oil
- ¼ teaspoon smoked paprika
- ✓ 20 tiger shrimp, peeled and deveined
- ✓ Salt and black pepper to the taste

Directions:
1. In a bowl, mix shrimp with oil, salt, pepper, old bay seasoning and paprika and toss to coat.
2. Place shrimp in your air fryer's basket and cook at 390 degrees F for 5 minutes.
3. Arrange them on a platter and serve as an appetizer

Nutrition: calories 162 - Fat 6 - Fiber 4 - Carbs 8 - Protein 14

19. Apple Chips

Prep.Time: 10 min - **Cooking Time:** 10 min - **Servings:** 2

Ingredients:
- ✓ 1 apple, cored and sliced
- ✓ A pinch of salt
- ✓ ½ teaspoon cinnamon powder
- ✓ 1 tablespoon white sugar

Directions:
1. In a bowl, mix apple slices with salt, sugar and cinnamon, toss, transfer to your air fryer's basket, cook for 10 minutes at 390 degrees F flipping once.
2. Divide apple chips in bowls and serve as a snack

Nutrition: calories 70- Fat 0 - Fiber 4 - Carbs 3 - Protein 1

20. Mexican Apple Snack

Prep.Time: 10 min - **Cooking Time:** 5 min - **Servings:** 4

Ingredients:
- ✓ 3 big apples, cored, peeled and cubed
- ✓ 2 teaspoons lemon juice
- ✓ ¼ cup pecans, chopped
- ✓ ½ cup dark chocolate chips
- ✓ ½ cup clean caramel sauce

Directions:
1. In a bowl, mix apples with lemon juice, stir and transfer to a pan that fits your air fryer.
2. Add chocolate chips, pecans, drizzle the caramel sauce, toss, introduce in your air fryer and cook at 320 degrees F for 5 minutes.
3. Toss gently, divide into small bowls and serve right away as a snack.

Nutrition: calories 200 - Fat 4 - Fiber 3 - Carbs 20 - Protein 3

21. Potato Spread

Prep.Time: 10 min - **Cooking Time:** 10 minutes - **Servings:** 10

Ingredients:
- ✓ 19 ounces canned garbanzo beans, drained
- ✓ 1 cup sweet potatoes, peeled and chopped
- ✓ ¼ cup tahini
- ✓ 2 tablespoons lemon juice
- ✓ 1 tablespoon olive oil
- ✓ 5 garlic cloves, minced
- ✓ ½ teaspoon cumin, ground
- ✓ 2 tablespoons water
- ✓ A pinch of salt and white pepper

Directions:
1. Put potatoes in your air fryer's basket, cook them at 360 degrees F for 15 minutes, cool them down, peel, put them in your food processor and pulse well. basket,
2. Add sesame paste, garlic, beans, lemon juice, cumin, water and oil and pulse really well.
3. Add salt and pepper, pulse again, divide into bowls and serve.

Nutrition: calories 200 - Fat 3 - Fiber 10 - Carbs 20 - Protein 11

22. Coconut Chicken Bites

Prep.Time: 10 min - **Cooking Time:** 13 min - **Servings:** 4

Ingredients:
- ✓ 2 teaspoons garlic powder
- ✓ 2 eggs
- ✓ Salt and black pepper to the taste
- ✓ ¾ cup panko bread crumbs
- ✓ ¾ cup coconut, shredded
- ✓ Cooking spray
- ✓ 8 chicken tenders

Directions:
1. In a bowl, mix eggs with salt, pepper and garlic powder and whisk well.
2. In another bowl, mix coconut with panko and stir well.
3. Dip chicken tenders in eggs mix and then coat in coconut one well.
4. Spray chicken bites with cooking spray, place them in your air fryer's basket and cook them at 350 degrees F for 10 minutes.
5. Arrange them on a platter and serve as an appetizer.

Nutrition: calories 252 - Fat 4 - Fiber 2 - Carbs 14 – Protein 24

23. Crispy Fish Sticks

Prep.Time: 10 min - **Cooking Time:** 12 min - **Servings:** 2

Ingredients:
- ✓ 4 ounces bread crumbs
- ✓ 4 tablespoons olive oil
- ✓ 1 egg, whisked
- ✓ 4 white fish filets, boneless, skinless and cut into medium sticks
- ✓ Salt and black pepper to the taste

Directions:
1. In a bowl, mix bread crumbs with oil and stir well.
2. Put egg in a second bowl, add salt and pepper and whisk well.
3. Dip fish stick in egg and them in bread crumb mix, place them in your air fryer's basket and cook at 360 degrees F for 12 minutes.
4. Arrange fish sticks on a platter and serve as an appetizer.

Nutrition: calories 160 - Fat 3 - Fiber 5 - Carbs 12 - Protein 3

24. Shrimp and Chestnut Rolls

Prep.Time: 10 min - **Cooking Time:** 15 min - **Servings:** 4

Ingredients:
- ✓ ½ pound already cooked shrimp, chopped
- ✓ 8 ounces water chestnuts, chopped
- ✓ ½ pounds shiitake mushrooms, chopped
- ✓ 2 cups cabbage, chopped
- ✓ 2 tablespoons olive oil
- ✓ 1 garlic clove, minced
- ✓ 1 teaspoon ginger, grated
- ✓ 3 scallions, chopped
- ✓ Salt and black pepper to the taste
- ✓ 1 tablespoon water
- ✓ 1 egg yolk
- ✓ 6 spring roll wrappers

Directions:
1. Heat up a pan with the oil over medium high heat, add cabbage, shrimp, chestnuts, mushrooms, garlic, ginger, scallions, salt and pepper, stir and cook for 2 minutes.
2. In a bowl, mix egg with water and stir well.
3. Arrange roll wrappers on a working surface, divide shrimp and veggie mix on them, seal edges with egg wash, place them all in your air fryer's basket, cook at 360 degrees F for 15 minutes, transfer to a platter and serve as an appetizer.

Nutrition: calories 140 - Fat 3 - Fiber 1 - Carbs 12 - Protein 3

25. Crispy Chicken Breast Sticks

Prep.Time: 10 min - **Cooking Time:** 16 min - **Servings:** 4

Ingredients:
- ¾ cup white flour
- 1 pound chicken breast, skinless, boneless and cut into medium sticks
- 1 teaspoon sweet paprika
- 1 cup panko bread crumbs
- 1 egg, whisked
- Salt and black pepper to the taste
- ½ tablespoon olive oil
- Zest from 1 lemon, grated

Directions:
1. In a bowl, mix paprika with flour, salt, pepper and lemon zest and stir.
2. Put whisked egg in another bowl and the panko breadcrumbs in a third one.
3. Dredge chicken pieces in flour, egg and panko and place them in your lined air fryer's basket, drizzle the oil over them, cook at 400 degrees F for 8 minutes, flip and cook for 8 more minutes.
4. Arrange them on a platter and serve as a snack.

Nutrition: calories 254 - Fat 4 - Fiber 7 - Carbs 20 - Protein 22

26. Seafood Appetizer

Prep.Time: 10 min - **Cooking Time:** 25 min - **Servings:** 4

Ingredients:
- ½ cup yellow onion, chopped
- 1 cup green bell pepper, chopped
- 1 cup celery, chopped
- 1 cup baby shrimp, peeled and deveined
- 1 cup crabmeat, flaked
- 1 cup homemade mayonnaise
- 1 tsp Worcestershire sauce
- Salt and black pepper to the taste
- 2 tbsp bread crumbs
- 1 tablespoon butter
- 1 teaspoon sweet paprika

Directions:
1. In a bowl, mix shrimp with crab meat, bell pepper, onion, mayo, celery, salt and pepper and stir.
2. Add Worcestershire sauce, stir again and pour everything into a baking dish that fits your air fryer.
3. Sprinkle bread crumbs and add butter, introduce in your air fryer and cook at 320 degrees F for 25 minutes, shaking halfway.
4. Divide into bowl and serve with paprika sprinkled on top as an appetizer.

Nutrition: calories 200 - Fat 1 - Fiber 2 - Carbs 5 - Protein 1

27. Salmon Meatballs

Prep.Time: 10 min - **Cooking Time:** 12 minutes - **Servings:** 4

Ingredients:
- 3 tbsp cilantro, minced
- 1 pound salmon, skinless and chopped
- 1 small yellow onion, chopped
- 1 egg white
- Salt and black pepper to the taste
- 2 garlic cloves, minced
- ½ teaspoon paprika
- ¼ cup panko
- ½ tsp. oregano, ground
- Cooking spray

Directions:
1. In your food processor, mix salmon with onion, cilantro, egg white, garlic cloves, salt, pepper, paprika and oregano and stir well.
2. Add panko, blend again and shape meatballs from this mix using your palms.
3. Place them in your air fryer's basket, spray them with cooking spray and cook at 320 degrees F for 12 minutes shaking the fryer halfway.
4. Arrange meatballs on a platter and serve them as an appetizer

Nutrition: calories 289 - Fat 12 - Fiber 3 - Carbs 22 - Protein 23

28. Empanadas

Prep.Time: 10 min - **Cooking Time:** 25 min - **Servings:** 4

Ingredients:
- 1 package empanada shells
- 1 tablespoon olive oil
- 1 pound beef meat, ground
- 1 yellow onion, chopped
- Salt and black pepper to the taste
- 2 garlic cloves, minced
- ½ tsp. cumin, ground
- ¼ cup tomato salsa
- 1 egg yolk whisked with 1 tablespoon water
- 1 green bell pepper, chopped

Directions:
1. Heat up a pan with the oil over medium high heat, add beef and brown on all sides.
2. Add onion, garlic, salt, pepper, bell pepper and tomato salsa, stir and cook for 15 minutes.
3. Divide cooked meat in empanada shells, brush them with egg wash and seal.
4. Place them in your air fryer's steamer basket and cook at 350 degrees F for 10 minutes.
5. Arrange on a platter and serve as an appetizer.

Nutrition: calories 274 - Fat 17 - Fiber 14 - Carbs 20 - Protein 7

29. Easy Chicken Wings

Prep.Time: 10 min - **Cooking Time:** 1 hour - **Servings:** 2

Ingredients:
- 16 pieces chicken wings
- Salt and black pepper to the taste
- ¼ cup butter
- ¾ cup potato starch
- ¼ cup honey
- 4 tablespoons garlic, minced

Directions:
1. In a bowl, mix chicken wings with salt, pepper and potato starch, toss well, transfer to your air fryer's basket, cook them at 380 degrees F for 25 minutes and at 400 degrees F for 5 minutes more.
2. Meanwhile, heat up a pan with the butter over medium high heat, melt it, add garlic, stir, cook for 5 minutes and then mix with salt, pepper and honey.
3. Whisk well, cook over medium heat for 20 minutes and take off heat.
4. Arrange chicken wings on a platter, drizzle honey sauce all over and serve as an appetizer.

Nutrition: calories 244 - Fat 7 - Fiber 3 - Carbs 19 - Protein 8

30. Chicken Breast Rolls

Prep.Time: 10 min - **Cooking Time:** 22 min - **Servings:** 4

Ingredients:
- 2 cups baby spinach
- 4 chicken breasts, boneless and skinless
- 1 cup sun dried tomatoes, chopped
- Salt and black pepper to the taste
- 1 and ½ tablespoons Italian seasoning
- 4 mozzarella slices
- A drizzle of olive oil

Directions:
1. Flatten chicken breasts using a meat tenderizer, divide tomatoes, mozzarella and spinach, season with salt, pepper and Italian seasoning, roll and seal them.
2. Place them in your air fryer's basket, drizzle some oil over them and cook at 375 degrees F for 17 minutes, flipping once.
3. Arrange chicken rolls on a platter and serve them as an appetizer.

Nutrition: calories 300 - Fat 1 - Fiber 4 – Carbs79 - Protein 10

31. Beef Rolls

Prep.Time: 10 min - **Cooking Time:** 14 min - **Servings:** 4

Ingredients:
- ✓ 2 pounds beef steak, opened and flattened with a meat tenderizer
- ✓ Salt and black pepper to the taste
- ✓ 1 cup baby spinach
- ✓ 3 ounces red bell pepper, roasted and chopped
- ✓ 6 slices provolone cheese
- ✓ 3 tablespoons pesto

Directions:
1. Arrange flattened beef steak on a cutting board, spread pesto all over, add cheese in a single layer, add bell peppers, spinach, salt and pepper to the taste.
2. Roll your steak, secure with toothpicks, season again with salt and pepper, place roll in your air fryer's basket and cook at 400 degrees F for 14 minutes, rotating roll halfway.
3. Leave aside to cool down, cut into 2 inch smaller rolls, arrange on a platter and serve them as an appetizer.

Nutrition: calories 230 - Fat 1 - Fiber 3 - Carbs 12 - Protein 10

32. Beef Patties

Prep.Time: 10 min - **Cooking Time:** 8 min - **Servings:** 4

Ingredients:
- ✓ 14 ounces beef, minced
- ✓ 2 tablespoons ham, cut into strips
- ✓ 1 leek, chopped
- ✓ 3 tablespoons bread crumbs
- ✓ Salt and black pepper to the taste
- ✓ ½ teaspoon nutmeg, ground

Directions:
1. In a bowl, mix beef with leek, salt, pepper, ham, breadcrumbs and nutmeg, stir well and shape small patties out of this mix.
2. Place them in your air fryer's basket, cook at 400 degrees F for 8 minutes, arrange on a platter and serve as an appetizer.

Nutrition: calories 260 - Fat 12 - Fiber 3 - Carbs 12 - Protein 21

33. Beef Party Rolls

Prep.Time: 10 min - **Cooking Time:** 15 min - **Servings:** 4

Ingredients:
- ✓ 14 ounces beef stock
- ✓ 7 ounces white wine
- ✓ 4 beef cutlets
- ✓ Salt and black pepper to the taste
- ✓ 8 sage leaves
- ✓ 4 ham slices
- ✓ 1 tablespoon butter, melted

Directions:
1. Heat up a pan with the stock over medium high heat, add wine, cook until it reduces, take off heat and divide into small bowls
2. Season cutlets with salt and pepper, cover with sage and roll each in ham slices.
3. Brush rolls with butter, place them in your air fryer's basket and cook at 400 degrees F for 15 minutes.
4. Arrange rolls on a platter and serve them with the gravy on the side.

Nutrition: calories 260 - Fat 12 - Fiber 1 – Carbs 22 - Protein 21

34. Herbed Tomatoes Appetizer

Prep.Time: 10 min - **Cooking Time:** 20 min - **Servings:** 2

Ingredients:
- ✓ 2 tomatoes, halved
- ✓ Cooking spray
- ✓ Salt and black pepper to the taste
- ✓ 1 teaspoon parsley, dried
- ✓ 1 teaspoon basil, dried
- ✓ 1 teaspoon oregano, dried
- ✓ 1 teaspoon rosemary, dried

Directions:
1. Spray tomato halves with cooking oil, season with salt, pepper, parsley, basil, oregano and rosemary over them.
2. Place them in your air fryer's basket and cook at 320 degrees F for 20 minutes.
3. Arrange them on a platter and serve as an appetizer.

Nutrition: calories 100 - Fat 1 - Fiber 1 - Carbs 4 - Protein 1

35. Greek Lamb Meatballs

Prep.Time: 10 min - **Cooking Time:** 8 min - **Servings:** 10

Ingredients:
- ✓ 4 ounces lamb meat, minced
- ✓ Salt and black pepper to the taste
- ✓ 1 slice of bread, toasted and crumbled
- ✓ 2 tablespoons feta cheese, crumbled
- ✓ ½ tablespoon lemon peel, grated
- ✓ 1 tablespoon oregano, chopped

Directions:
1. In a bowl, combine meat with bread crumbs, salt, pepper, feta, oregano and lemon peel, stir well, shape 10 meatballs and place them in you air fryer.
2. Cook at 400 degrees F for 8 minutes, arrange them on a platter and serve as an appetizer.

Nutrition: calories 234 - Fat 12 - Fiber 2 - Carbs 20 - Protein 30

36. Pork Rolls

Prep.Time: 10 min - **Cooking Time:** 40 min - **Servings:** 4

Ingredients:
- ✓ 1 15 ounces pork fillet
- ✓ ½ teaspoon chili powder
- ✓ 1 teaspoon cinnamon powder
- ✓ 1 garlic clove, minced
- ✓ Salt and black pepper to the taste
- ✓ 2 tablespoons olive oil
- ✓ 1 and ½ teaspoon cumin, ground
- ✓ 1 red onion, chopped
- ✓ 3 tablespoons parsley, chopped

Directions:
1. In a bowl, mix cinnamon with garlic, salt, pepper, chili powder, oil, onion, parsley and cumin and stir well
2. Put pork fillet on a cutting board, flatten it using a meat tenderizer. And use a meat tenderizer to flatten it.
3. Spread onion mix on pork, roll tight, cut into medium rolls, place them in your preheated air fryer at 360 degrees F and cook them for 35 minutes.
4. Arrange them on a platter and serve as an appetizer

Nutrition: calories 304 - Fat 12 - Fiber 1 - Carbs 15 - Protein 23

37. Roasted Bell Pepper Rolls

Prep.Time: 10 min - **Cooking Time:** 10 min - **Servings:** 8

Ingredients:
- ✓ 1 yellow bell pepper, halved
- ✓ 1 orange bell pepper, halved
- ✓ Salt and black pepper to the taste
- ✓ 4 ounces feta cheese, crumbled
- ✓ 1 green onion, chopped
- ✓ 2 tablespoons oregano, chopped

Directions:
1. In a bowl, mix cheese with onion, oregano, salt and pepper and whisk well.
2. Place bell pepper halves in your air fryer's basket, cook at 400 degrees F for 10 minutes, transfer to a cutting board, cool down and peel.
3. Divide cheese mix on each bell pepper half, roll, secure with toothpicks, arrange on a platter and serve as an appetizer.

Nutrition: calories 170 - Fat 1 - Fiber 2 - Carbs 8 - Protein 5

38. Cheese Sticks

Prep.Time: 1 hour 10 min - **Cooking Time:** 8 min - **Servings:** 16

Ingredients:
- ✓ 2 eggs, whisked
- ✓ Salt and black pepper to the taste
- ✓ 8 mozzarella cheese strings, cut into halves
- ✓ 1 cup parmesan, grated
- ✓ 1 tablespoon Italian seasoning
- ✓ Cooking spray
- ✓ 1 garlic clove, minced

Directions:
1. In a bowl, mix parmesan with salt, pepper, Italian seasoning and garlic and stir well.
2. Put whisked eggs in another bowl.
3. Dip mozzarella sticks in egg mixture, then in cheese mix.
4. Dip them again in egg and in parmesan mix and keep them in the freezer for 1 hour.
5. Spray cheese sticks with cooking oil, place them in your air fryer's basket and cook at 390 degrees F for 8 minutes flipping them halfway.
6. Arrange them on a platter and serve as an appetizer

Nutrition: calories 140 - Fat 5 - Fiber 1 - Carbs 3 - Protein 4

39. Olives Balls

Prep.Time: 10 min - **Cooking Time:** 4 minutes - **Servings:** 6

Ingredients:
- ✓ 8 black olives, pitted and minced
- ✓ Salt and black pepper to the taste
- ✓ 2 tablespoons sun dried tomato pesto
- ✓ 14 pepperoni slices, chopped
- ✓ 4 ounces cream cheese
- ✓ 1 tablespoons basil, chopped

Directions:
1. In a bowl, mix cream cheese with salt, pepper, basil, pepperoni, pesto and black olives, stir well and shape small balls out of this mix.
2. Place them in your air fryer's basket, cook at 350 degrees F for 4 minutes, arrange on a platter and serve as a snack.

Nutrition: calories 100 - Fat 1 - Fiber 0 - Carbs 8 - Protein 3

40. Cheesy Zucchini Snack

Prep.Time: 10 min - **Cooking Time:** 8 min - **Servings:** 4

Ingredients:
- ✓ 1 cup mozzarella, shredded
- ✓ ¼ cup tomato sauce
- ✓ 1 zucchini, sliced
- ✓ Salt and black pepper to the taste
- ✓ A pinch of cumin
- ✓ Cooking spray

Directions:
1. Arrange zucchini slices in your air fryer's basket, spray them with cooking oil, spread tomato sauce all over, them, season with salt, pepper, cumin, sprinkle mozzarella at the end and cook them at 320 degrees F for 8 minutes.
2. Arrange them on a platter and serve as a snack.

Nutrition: calories 150 - Fat 4 - Fiber 2 - Carbs 12 - Protein 4

41. Jalapeno Balls

Prep.Time: 10 min - **Cooking Time:** 4 min - **Servings:** 3

Ingredients:
- ✓ 3 bacon slices, cooked and crumbled
- ✓ 3 ounces cream cheese
- ✓ ¼ teaspoon onion powder
- ✓ Salt and black pepper to the taste
- ✓ 1 jalapeno pepper, chopped
- ✓ ½ teaspoon parsley, dried
- ✓ ¼ teaspoon garlic powder

Directions:
1. In a bowl, mix cream cheese with jalapeno pepper, onion and garlic powder, parsley, bacon salt and pepper and stir well.
2. Shape small balls out of this mix, place them in your air fryer's basket, cook at 350 degrees F for 4 minutes, arrange on a platter and serve as an appetizer.

Nutrition: calories 172 - Fat 4 - Fiber 1 - Carbs 12 - Protein 5

42. Mushrooms Appetizer

Prep.Time: 10 min - **Cooking Time:** 10 min - **Servings:** 4

Ingredients:
- ✓ ¼ cup mayonnaise
- ✓ 1 teaspoon garlic powder
- ✓ 1 small yellow onion, chopped
- ✓ 24 ounces white mushroom caps
- ✓ Salt and black pepper to the taste
- ✓ 1 teaspoon curry powder
- ✓ 4 ounces cream cheese, soft
- ✓ ¼ cup sour cream
- ✓ ½ cup Mexican cheese, shredded
- ✓ 1 cup shrimp, cooked, peeled, deveined and chopped

Directions:
1. In a bowl, mix mayo with garlic powder, onion, curry powder, cream cheese, sour cream, Mexican cheese, shrimp, salt and pepper to the taste and whisk well.
2. Stuff mushrooms with this mix, place them in your air fryer's basket and cook at 300 degrees F for 10 minutes.
3. Arrange on a platter and serve as an appetizer.

Nutrition: calories 200 - Fat 20 - Fiber 3 - Carbs 16 - Protein 14

43. Calamari and Shrimp Snack

Prep.Time: 10 min - **Cooking Time:** 20 min - **Servings:** 4

Ingredients:
- ✓ 8 ounces calamari, cut into medium rings
- ✓ 7 ounces shrimp, peeled and deveined
- ✓ 1 eggs
- ✓ 3 tablespoons white flour
- ✓ 1 tablespoon olive oil
- ✓ 2 tablespoons avocado, chopped
- ✓ 1 teaspoon tomato paste
- ✓ 1 tablespoon mayonnaise
- ✓ A splash of Worcestershire sauce
- ✓ 1 teaspoon lemon juice
- ✓ Salt and black pepper to the taste
- ✓ ½ teaspoon turmeric powder

Directions:
1. In a bowl, whisk egg with oil, add calamari rings and shrimp and toss to coat.
2. In another bowl, mix flour with salt, pepper and turmeric and stir.
3. Dredge calamari and shrimp in this mix, place them in your air fryer's basket and cook at 350 degrees F for 9 minutes, flipping them once.
4. Meanwhile, in a bowl, mix avocado with mayo and tomato paste and mash using a fork.
5. Add Worcestershire sauce, lemon juice, salt and pepper and stir well.
6. Arrange calamari and shrimp on a platter and serve with the sauce on the side.

Nutrition: calories 288 - Fat 23- Fiber 3 - Carbs 10 - Protein 15

44. Air Fried Sandwich

Prep.Time: 10 min - **Cooking Time:** 6 min - **Servings:** 2

Ingredients:
- ✓ 6 pound chicken wings, halved
- ✓ Salt and black pepper to the taste
- ✓ ½ teaspoon Italian seasoning
- ✓ 2 tablespoons butter
- ✓ ½ cup parmesan cheese, grated
- ✓ A pinch of red pepper flakes, crushed
- ✓ 1 teaspoon garlic powder
- ✓ 1 egg

Directions:
1. Arrange chicken wings in your air fryer's basket and cook at 390 degrees F and cook for 9 minutes.
2. Meanwhile, in your blender, mix butter with cheese, egg, salt, pepper, pepper flakes, garlic powder and Italian seasoning and blend very well.
3. Take chicken wings out, pour cheese sauce over them, toss to coat well and cook in your air fryer's basket at 390 degrees F for 3 minutes.
4. Serve them as an appetizer.

Nutrition: calories 204 - Fat 8 - Fiber 1 - Carbs 18 - Protein 14

45. Stuffed Peppers

Prep.Time: 10 min - **Cooking Time:** 8 min - **Servings:** 8

Ingredients:
- ✓ 8 small bell peppers, tops cut off and seeds removed
- ✓ 1 tablespoon olive oil
- ✓ Salt and black pepper to the taste
- ✓ 3.5 ounces goat cheese, cut into 8 pieces

Directions:
1. In a bowl, mix cheese with oil with salt and pepper and toss to coat.
2. Stuff each pepper with goat cheese, place them in your air fryer's basket, cook at 400 degrees F for 8 minutes, arrange on a platter and serve as an appetizer.

Nutrition: calories 120 - Fat 1 - Fiber 1 - Carbs 12 - Protein 8

46. Wrapped Shrimp

Prep.Time: 10 min - **Cooking Time:** 8 min - **Servings:** 16

Ingredients:
- ✓ 2 tablespoons olive oil
- ✓ 10 ounces already cooked shrimp, peeled and deveined
- ✓ 1 tablespoons mint, chopped
- ✓ 1/3 cup blackberries, ground
- ✓ 11 prosciutto sliced
- ✓ 1/3 cup red wine

Directions:
1. Wrap each shrimp in a prosciutto slices, drizzle the oil over them, rub well, place in your preheated air fryer at 390 degrees F and fry them for 8 minutes.
2. Meanwhile, heat up a pan with ground blackberries over medium heat, add mint and wine, stir, cook for 3 minutes and take off heat.
3. Arrange shrimp on a platter, drizzle blackberries sauce over them and serve as an appetizer.

Nutrition: calories 224 – Fat 12 - Fiber 2 - Carbs 12 - Protein 14

47. Egg White Chips

Prep.Time: 5 min - **Cooking Time:** 8 min - **Servings:** 2

Ingredients:
- ✓ ½ tablespoon water
- ✓ 2 tablespoons parmesan, shredded
- ✓ 4 eggs whites
- ✓ Salt and black pepper to the taste

Directions:
1. In a bowl, mix egg whites with salt, pepper and water and whisk well.
2. Spoon this into a muffin pan that fits your air fryer, sprinkle cheese on top, introduce in your air fryer and cook at 350 degrees F for 8 minutes.
3. Arrange egg white chips on a platter and serve as a snack.

Nutrition: calories 180 - Fat 2 - Fiber 1 - Carbs 12 - Protein 7

48. Sweet Bacon Snack

Prep.Time: 10 min - **Cooking Time:** 30 min - **Servings:** 16

Ingredients:
- ✓ ½ teaspoon cinnamon powder
- ✓ 16 bacon slices
- ✓ 1 tablespoon avocado oil
- ✓ 3 ounces dark chocolate
- ✓ 1 teaspoon maple extract

Directions:
1. Arrange bacon slices in your air fryer's basket, sprinkle cinnamon mix over them and cook them at 300 degrees F for 30 minutes.
2. Heat up a pot with the oil over medium heat, add chocolate and stir until it melts.
3. Add maple extract, stir, take off heat and leave aside to cool down a bit.
4. Take bacon strips out of the oven, leave them to cool down, dip each in chocolate mix, place them on a parchment paper and leave them to cool down completely.
5. Serve cold as a snack.

Nutrition: calories 200 - Fat 4 - Fiber 5 - Carbs 12 - Protein 3

49. Different Stuffed Peppers

Prep.Time: 10 min - **Cooking Time:** 20 min - **Servings:** 6

Ingredients:

- ✓ 1 pound mini bell peppers, halved
- ✓ Salt and black pepper to the taste
- ✓ 1 teaspoon garlic powder
- ✓ 1 teaspoon sweet paprika
- ✓ ½ teaspoon oregano, dried
- ✓ ¼ teaspoon red pepper flakes
- ✓ 1 pound beef meat, ground
- ✓ 1 and ½ cups cheddar cheese, shredded
- ✓ 1 tablespoons chili powder
- ✓ 1 teaspoon cumin, ground
- ✓ Sour cream for serving

Directions:

1. In a bowl, mix chili powder with paprika, salt, pepper, cumin, oregano, pepper flakes and garlic powder and stir.
2. Heat up a pan over medium heat, add beef, stir and brown for 10 minutes.
3. Add chili powder mix, stir, take off heat and stuff pepper halves with this mix.
4. Sprinkle cheese all over, place peppers in your air fryer's basket and cook them at 350 degrees F for 6 minutes.
5. Arrange peppers on a platter and serve them with sour cream on the side.

Nutrition: calories 170 - Fat 22 - Fiber 3 - Carbs 6 - Protein 27

50. Chicken Rolls

Prep.Time: 2 hours 10 min - **Cooking Time:** 10 min - **Servings:** 12

Ingredients:

- ✓ 4 ounces blue cheese, crumbled
- ✓ 2 cups chicken, cooked and chopped
- ✓ Salt and black pepper to the taste
- ✓ 2 green onions, chopped
- ✓ 2 celery stalks, finely chopped
- ✓ ½ cup tomato sauce
- ✓ 12 egg roll wrappers
- ✓ Cooking spray

Directions:

1. In a bowl, mix chicken meat with blue cheese, salt, pepper, green onions, celery and tomato sauce, stir well and keep in the fridge for 2 hours.
2. Place egg wrappers on a working surface, divide chicken mix on them, roll and seal edges.
3. Place rolls in your air fryer's basket, spray them with cooking oil and cook at 350 degrees F for 10 minutes, flipping them halfway.

Nutrition: calories 220 - Fat 7 - Fiber 2 - Carbs 14 - Protein 10

51. Spinach Balls

Prep.Time: 10 min - **Cooking Time:** 7 minutes - **Servings:** 3

Ingredients:

- ✓ 4 tablespoons butter, melted
- ✓ 2 eggs
- ✓ 1 cup flour
- ✓ 16 ounces spinach
- ✓ 1/3 cup feta cheese, crumbled
- ✓ ¼ teaspoon nutmeg, ground
- ✓ 1/3 cup parmesan, grated
- ✓ Salt and black pepper to the taste
- ✓ 1 tablespoon onion powder
- ✓ 3 tablespoons whipping cream
- ✓ 1 teaspoon garlic powder

Directions:

1. In your blender, mix spinach with butter, eggs, flour, feta cheese, parmesan, nutmeg, whipping cream, salt, pepper, onion and garlic pepper, blend very well and keep in the freezer for 10 minutes.
2. Shape 30 spinach balls, place them in your air fryer's basket and cook at 300 degrees F for 7 minutes.
3. Serve as a party appetizer.

Nutrition: calories 60- Fat 5 - Fiber 1 - Carbs 1 - Protein 2

52. Tasty Kale and Celery Crackers

Prep.Time: 10 min - **Cooking Time:** 20 min - **Servings:** 6

Ingredients:

- ✓ 2 cups flax seed, ground
- ✓ 2 cups flax seed, soaked overnight and drained
- ✓ 4 bunches kale, chopped
- ✓ 1 bunch basil, chopped
- ✓ ½ bunch celery, chopped
- ✓ 4 garlic cloves, minced
- ✓ 1/3 cup olive oil

Directions:

1. In your food processor mix ground flaxseed with celery, kale, basil and garlic and blend well.
2. Add oil and soaked flaxseed and blend again, spread in your air fryer's pan, cut into medium crackers and cook them at 380 degrees F for 20 minutes.
3. Divide into bowls and serve as an appetizer.

Nutrition: calories 143 - Fat 1 - Fiber 2 - Carbs 8 – Protein 4

53. Broccoli Patties

Prep.Time: 10 min - **Cooking Time:** 10 min - **Servings:** 12

Ingredients:

- ✓ 4 cups broccoli florets
- ✓ 1 and ½ cup almond flour
- ✓ 1 teaspoon paprika
- ✓ Salt and black pepper to the taste
- ✓ 2 eggs
- ✓ ¼ cup olive oil
- ✓ 2 cups cheddar cheese, grated
- ✓ 1 teaspoon garlic powder
- ✓ ½ tsp apple cider vinegar
- ✓ ½ teaspoon baking soda

Directions:

1. Put broccoli florets in your food processor, add salt and pepper, blend well and transfer to a bowl.
2. Add almond flour, salt, pepper, paprika, garlic powder, baking soda, cheese, oil, eggs and vinegar, stir well and shape 12 patties out of this mix.
3. Place them in your preheated air fryer's basket and cook at 350 degrees F for 10 minutes.
4. Arrange patties on a platter and serve as an appetizer.

Nutrition: calories 203 - Fat 12 - Fiber 2 - Carbs 14 - Protein 2

54. Tuna Cakes

Prep.Time: 10 min - **Cooking Time:** 10 min - **Servings:** 12

Ingredients:

- ✓ 15 ounces canned tuna, drain and flaked
- ✓ 3 eggs
- ✓ ½ teaspoon dill, dried
- ✓ 1 teaspoon parsley, dried
- ✓ ½ cup red onion, chopped
- ✓ 1 teaspoon garlic powder
- ✓ Salt and black pepper to the taste
- ✓ Cooking spray

Directions:

1. In a bowl, mix tuna with salt, pepper, dill, parsley, onion, garlic powder and eggs, stir well and shape medium cakes out of this mix.
2. Place tuna cakes in your air fryer's basket, spray them with cooking oil and cook at 350 degrees F for 10 minutes, flipping them halfway.
3. Arrange them on a platter and serve as an appetizer.

Nutrition: calories 140 - Fat 2 - Fiber 1 - Carbs 8 - Protein 6

55. Air Fryer Apple Slices

Prep.Time: 10 min - **Cooking Time:** 12 min - **Servings:** 1

Ingredients:
- ✓ 1 apple, core and slice ¼-inch thick
- ✓ ¼ tsp ground cinnamon
- ✓ Pinch of salt

Directions:
1. Spray air fryer oven tray with cooking spray.
2. Arrange apple slices on the tray and sprinkle with cinnamon and salt.
3. Air fry at 390 F for 10-12 minutes. Turn apple slices halfway through.
4. Serve and enjoy

56. Simple Potato Chips

Prep.Time: 10 min - **Cooking Time:** 9 min - **Servings:** 2

Ingredients:
- ✓ 2 potatoes, scrubbed and washed
- ✓ 2 tbsp olive oil
- ✓ Pepper
- ✓ Salt

Directions:
1. Slice potatoes 1 inch thick slices using a mandolin slicer.
2. Add potato slices into the mixing bowl. Add oil, pepper, and salt to the bowl and toss until potato slices are well coated.
3. Arrange potato slices on air fryer oven tray and cook at 370 F for 3 minutes.
4. Turn potato slices to the other side and air fry for 3 minutes more.
5. Again turn potato slices and air fry for 3 minutes more.
6. Serve and enjoy.

57. Crispy Baked Potato Wedges

Prep.Time: 10 min - **Cooking Time:** 12 minutes - **Servings:** 3

Ingredients:
- ✓ 6 potatoes, cut into wedges
- ✓ 2/3 cup parmesan cheese, grated
- ✓ 1 tsp paprika
- ✓ 1 tbsp garlic, minced
- ✓ ¼ cup olive oil
- ✓ Sea salt

Directions:
1. In a mixing bowl, mix together cheese, paprika, garlic, oil, and salt.
2. Add potato wedges into the bowl and toss until well coated.
3. Arrange potato wedges on air fryer oven pan and bake at 400 F for 7 minutes.
4. Turn potato wedges to the other side and cook for 5 minutes more.
5. Serve and enjoy.

58. Roasted Pecans

Prep.Time: 5 min - **Cooking Time:** 6-8 min - **Servings:** 1-2

Ingredients:
- ✓ 2 cups pecan halves
- ✓ 1 tbsp butter, melted
- ✓ Salt

Directions:
1. Preheat the instant vortex air fryer to 200 F.
2. Add pecans, butter, and salt in a mixing bowl and toss well.
3. Transfer pecans on air fryer tray and air fry for 4-6 minutes. Toss after every 2 minutes.
4. Serve and enjoy.

59. Delicious Pizza Toast

Prep.Time: 10 min - **Cooking Time:** 5 min - **Servings:** 2

Ingredients:
- ✓ 4 Texas toast slices
- ✓ 8 oz mozzarella cheese, shredded
- ✓ ½ jar pizza sauce
- ✓ 4 basil leaves

Directions:
1. Arrange toast slices on instant vortex air fryer oven drip pan and air fry at 380 F for 2 minutes.
2. After 2 minutes remove the pan from the air fryer oven.
3. Add pizza sauce, mozzarella cheese, and basil leaves on each toast slice.
4. Return pan in air fryer oven and air fry until cheese is melted.
5. Serve and enjoy.

60. Delicious Air Fried Jalapeno Poppers

Prep.Time: 10 min - **Cooking Time:** 10 min - **Servings:** 2-3

Ingredients:
- ✓ 10 jalapeno peppers, halved, deseeded
- ✓ 3/4 bread crumbs
- ✓ 1 cup cream cheese
- ✓ 1/4 cup chopped fresh parsley

Directions:
1. In a bowl, mix together cream cheese and half of the bread crumbs; stir in parsley and stuff each pepper with the mixture, pressing each pepper top with more bread crumbs to create a top coating.
2. Cook in a preheated air fryer toast oven for 10 minutes.
3. Let cool before serving.

61. Sweet Potato Fries

Prep.Time: 10 min - **Cooking Time:** 16 min - **Servings:** 1

Ingredients:
- ✓ 2 sweet potatoes, peeled and cut into fries shape
- ✓ ½ tsp chili powder
- ✓ ¼ tsp garlic powder
- ✓ ¼ tsp onion powder
- ✓ 1 tbsp olive oil
- ✓ Salt

Directions:
1. In a bowl, mix together oil, chili powder, garlic powder, onion powder, and salt.
2. Add sweet potato fries and toss until well coated.
3. Arrange sweet potato fries on instant vortex air fryer drip pan and bake at 380 F for 8 minutes.
4. Turn sweet potato fries to the other side and cook for 8 minutes more.
5. Serve and enjoy.

62. Roasted Chickpeas

Prep.Time: 10 min - **Cooking Time:** 12 min - **Servings:** 2

Ingredients:
- ✓ 15 oz can chickpeas, drained and pat dry
- ✓ 1 ½ tsp paprika
- ✓ 1 tsp garlic powder
- ✓ ½ tbsp cumin powder
- ✓ 2 tbsp olive oil

Directions:
1. Add chickpeas in the mixing bowl.
2. Add remaining ingredients on top of chickpeas and toss until well coated.
3. Arrange chickpeas on air fryer oven tray and roast at 375 F for 6 minutes.
4. Shake chickpeas and roast for 6 minutes more.
5. Serve and enjoy.

63. Jalapeno Poppers

Prep.Time: 10 min - **Cooking Time:** 6-8 min - **Servings:** 2-4

Ingredients:
- ✓ 10 jalapeno peppers, halved, remove seeds and stem
- ✓ ½ cup cheddar cheese, shredded
- ✓ ½ cup Monterey jack cheese, shredded
- ✓ ½ cup Monterey jack cheese, shredded
- ✓ 1 tsp ground cumin
- ✓ 8 oz cream cheese, softened
- ✓ 10 bacon slices, cut in half

Directions:
1. In a bowl, mix together Monterey jack cheese, cumin, and cream cheese.
2. Stuff cheese mixture into jalapeno halved.
3. Wrap each jalapeno with half bacon slice.
4. Arrange jalapeno on instant vortex air fryer oven tray and air fry at 370 F for 6-8 minutes.
5. Serve and enjoy.

64. Air Fried Chicken Wings

Prep.Time: 10 min - **Cooking Time:** 30 min - **Servings:** 2-4

Ingredients:
- ✓ 2 ½ pounds chicken wings
- ✓ ½ cup butter
- ✓ ¼ teaspoon cayenne pepper
- ✓ 1 teaspoon garlic powder
- ✓ 2 tablespoons vinegar
- ✓ ⅔ cup cayenne pepper sauce
- ✓ 1 tablespoon olive oil

Directions:
1. Preheat your air fryer toast oven to 360⬚ F. place the chicken wings in a bowl and drizzle with oil, massaging until well coated.
2. Add half of the wings to the fryer basket and cook for about 25 minutes. With the tongs, flip over the wings and cook for another 5 minutes; transfer to a bowl and repeat with the remaining wings.
3. Meanwhile, in a small pan set over medium heat, mix butter, pepper sauce, cayenne pepper, garlic powder and vinegar.
4. Stir until well combined and keep warm.
5. Pour the hot sauce over the air fried wings and toss until well coated.
6. Serve right away.

65. Mushroom Samosa

Prep.Time: 20 min - **Cooking Time:** 35 minutes - **Servings:** 4

Ingredients:

For wrappers:
- ✓ 1 cup all-purpose flour
- ✓ 2 tbsp. unsalted butter
- ✓ A pinch of salt to taste
- ✓ Take the amount of water sufficient enough to make a stiff dough

For filling:
- ✓ 3 cups whole mushrooms
- ✓ 2 onion sliced
- ✓ 2 capsicum sliced
- ✓ 2 carrot sliced
- ✓ 2 cabbage sliced
- ✓ 2 tbsp. soya sauce
- ✓ 2 tsp. vinegar
- ✓ 2 tbsp. green chilies finely chopped
- ✓ 2 tbsp. ginger-garlic paste
- ✓ Some salt and pepper to taste

Directions:
1. Mix the dough for the outer covering and make it stiff and smooth. Leave it to rest in a container while making the filling.
2. Cook the ingredients in a pan and stir them well to make a thick paste. Roll the paste out.
3. Roll the dough into balls and flatten them. Cut them in halves and add the filling. Use water to help you fold the edges to create the shape of a cone.
4. Pre-heat the Air Fryer for around 5 to 6 minutes at 300 Fahrenheit. Place all the samosas in the fry basket and close the basket properly. Keep the Air Fryer at 200 degrees for another 20 to 25 minutes. Around the halfway point, open the basket and turn the samosas over for uniform cooking.
5. After this, fry at 250 degrees for around 10 minutes in order to give them the desired golden brown color. Serve hot. Recommended sides are tamarind or mint chutney.

66. Seafood Wontons

Prep.Time: 20 min - **Cooking Time:** 20 min - **Servings:** 2-4

Ingredients:

For dough:
- ✓ 1 ½ cup all-purpose flour
- ✓ ½ tsp. salt
- ✓ 5 tbsp. water

For filling:
- ✓ 2 cups minced seafood (prawns, shrimp, oysters, scallops)
- ✓ 2 tbsp. oil
- ✓ 2 tsp. ginger-garlic paste
- ✓ 2 tsp. soya sauce
- ✓ 2 tsp. vinegar

Directions:
1. Knead the dough and cover it with plastic wrap and set aside. Next, cook the ingredients for the filling and try to ensure that the seafood is covered well with the sauce.
2. Roll the dough and place the filling in the center. Now, wrap the dough to cover the filling and pinch the edges together.
3. Pre heat the Air fryer at 200° F for 5 minutes. Place the wontons in the fry basket and close it. Let them cook at the same temperature for another 20 minutes. Recommended sides are chili sauce or ketchup.

67. Air Fried Crab Sticks

Prep.Time: 5 min - **Cooking Time:** 12 min - **Servings:** 1-2

Ingredients:
- ✓ 1 packet crabsticks, break length-wise &cut into small even pieces
- ✓ 2 teaspoon oil, to toss
- ✓ Cajun or curry seasoning powder (Optional)

Directions:
1. Preheat air-fryer at 325°F for 5 minutes. Place cut and even crabsticks in a bowl and drizzle oil over, tossing well to combine.
2. Air fry until golden brown for 12 minutes. Every few minutes, check to ensure they are cooking evenly.
3. Sprinkle with seasoning, if desired.

68. Crispy French Fries

Prep.Time: 30 min - **Cooking Time:** 30 min - **Servings:** 4

Ingredients:
- ✓ 6 teaspoons of vegetable oil
- ✓ 6 medium sized Irish potatoes

Directions:
1. Peel potatoes and slice them into 3" long strips. Soak them in water for 30 minutes, drain and then dry with paper towel.
2. Heat your air-fryer to about 360°F.
3. Pour the oil into the potato strips and toss until thoroughly mixed.
4. Put the potatoes in the fryer basket and cook until golden for 30 minutes, shaking at 10 minutes intervals.

69. Feta And Onion Bell Pepper Rolls

Prep.Time: 25 min - **Cooking Time:** 10 minutes - **Servings:** 8

Ingredients:
- ✓ 4 medium sized bell red and yellow peppers
- ✓ 2 tablespoons of finely chopped basil
- ✓ 1 green onion, thinly sliced
- ✓ 3½ ounces of feta cheese, grated
- ✓ 8 toothpicks or tapas forks

Directions:
1. Heat your air-fryer to 392°F.
2. Place the peppers into the fryer basket and air fry for 10 minutes until they are charred to an extent.
3. Mix the feta cheese, basil and green onions together in a bowl and set aside.
4. Bring out the bell peppers and cut them vertically into halves, remove skin and the seeds.
5. Put the feta-onion mixture into each pepper and roll up beginning from the thinner end. Fasten the rolls with a toothpick of a tapas fork and serve.

70. Tomato Sauced Meatballs

Prep.Time: 10 min - **Cooking Time:** 13 min - **Servings:** 3-4

Ingredients:
- ✓ ¾ pounds (12oz) ground beef
- ✓ 1 small onion, finely chopped
- ✓ 1 tablespoon fresh parsley, chopped
- ✓ ½ tablespoon fresh thyme leaves, chopped
- ✓ 1 egg
- ✓ 3 tablespoons breadcrumbs Pepper & salt to taste
- ✓ 10oz tomato sauce of choice, extra

Directions:
1. Combine all ingredients into bowl, mixing well. Make 10 to 12 balls with this mixture.
2. Now preheat the Air-fryer to 390°F. Put the meatballs in the Air-fryer basket and into the Air-fryer. Cook for 8 minutes.
3. Remove the meatballs to an oven dish, add in the tomato sauce and place the dish into the Air-fryer basket. Return the basket to the air-fryer.
4. Warm everything through with a temperature of 330°F and for 5 minutes.

71. Cheddar Bacon Croquettes

Prep.Time: 40 min - **Cooking Time:** 10 minutes - **Servings:** 6

Ingredients:
- ✓ 1 pound bacon, sliced thinly & set at room temperature
- ✓ 1 pound sharp cheddar cheese, block (cut into 6 portions of 1-inch x 1¾ - inch each)

For The Breading:
- ✓ 1 cup all-purpose flour
- ✓ 4 tablespoons olive oil
- ✓ 1 cup seasoned breadcrumbs

Directions:
1. Wrap 2 bacon pieces around each cheddar piece completely. Trim off any excess fat and then freeze the cheddar bacon bites for 5 minutes to make firm, but not to freeze.
2. Preheat Air-fryer to 390°F. Combine the breadcrumbs and oil and stir until it becomes loose and crumbly.
3. Put the cheddar block into the flour, place the eggs and then finally the breadcrumbs, pressing the coating to the croquettes to make sure it sticks.
4. (To prevent cheese from running out, double the coating by dipping twice into the egg and then the breadcrumbs)
5. Place the croquettes in the basket and cook until golden brown or for about 8 minutes.

72. Chimichurri Skirt Steak

Prep.Time: 15 min - **Cooking Time:** 20 min - **Servings:** 2

Ingredients:
- ✓ 1 pound skirt steak, cut into 2 portions of 8-ounce
- ✓ For The Chimichurri:
- ✓ ¼ cup mint, finely chopped
- ✓ 1 cup parsley, chopped finely
- ✓ 2 tablespoons oregano, chopped finely
- ✓ 1 teaspoon crushed red pepper
- ✓ 3 garlic cloves, chopped finely
- ✓ 2 teaspoons smoked paprika
- ✓ 1 tablespoon ground cumin
- ✓ 1 teaspoon cayenne pepper
- ✓ ¾ cup olive oil
- ✓ ¼ teaspoon black pepper
- ✓ 3 tablespoons red wine vinegar
- ✓ 1 teaspoon salt

Directions:
1. Combine the chimichurri ingredients in a mixing bowl.
2. Add the cut steak into a re-sealable bag, and add ¼ cup of the chimichurri.
3. Place in the refrigerator for 2-24 hours. Remove from the refrigerator and leave for 30 minutes before cooking.
4. Preheat the Air-fryer to 390°F. Pat dry steak with a paper towel. Add to the cooking basket and cook for 8 to10 minutes.
5. Serve garnished with 2 tablespoons of chimichurri.

73. Rolled Flanks

Prep.Time: 15 min - **Cooking Time:** 15 min - **Servings:** 4

Ingredients:
- ✓ 1 8-ounce can of crescent rolls
- ✓ 12 ounce package cocktail franks

Directions:
1. Drain the cocktail franks and pat dry on paper towels. Cut the dough into rectangular-shaped strips, about 1-inch x 1.5-inch.
2. Roll the cut strips around the franks, ensuring that the ends can be seen. Make them firm by placing in the freezer for 5 minutes.
3. Preheat the Air-fryer to 330°F. Take the franks out from the freezer and place in the cooking basket. Cook for 6 to8 minutes.
4. Reset the temperature to 390ºF and cook again for 3 minutes. Once it is golden brown, serve and enjoy.

74. Sage & Onion Stuffing Balls Air-Fried

Prep.Time: 3 min - **Cooking Time:** 15 min - **Servings:** 9

Ingredients:
- ✓ 3.5 oz sausage meat
- ✓ ½ small onion, peeled & diced
- ✓ 1 teaspoon sage
- ✓ ½ teaspoon garlic puree
- ✓ 3 tablespoons breadcrumbs
- ✓ Salt & pepper

Directions:
1. Combine all ingredients in a bowl and mix well.
2. Form mixture into medium sized balls and place in the Air Fryer
3. Cook at 350°F for 15 minutes. Serve and enjoy!

Note: if meat isn't firm enough, add to the number of breadcrumbs in recipe.

75. Moroccan Meatballs With Mint Yogurt

Prep.Time: 25 min - **Cooking Time:** 10 min - **Servings:** 4

Ingredients:

For The Meatballs
- ✓ 1 egg white
- ✓ 4 ounces ground turkey
- ✓ 1 pound ground lamb
- ✓ 1 tablespoon mint, finely chopped
- ✓ 1½ tablespoons parsley, finely chopped
- ✓ 1 teaspoon ground cumin
- ✓ 1 teaspoon cayenne pepper
- ✓ 1 tsp. ground coriander
- ✓ 1 teaspoon red chili paste
- ✓ ¼ cup olive oil
- ✓ 2 garlic cloves, finely chopped
- ✓ 1 teaspoon salt
- ✓ For The Mint Yogurt:
- ✓ ¼ cup sour cream
- ✓ ½ cup non-fat Greek yogurt
- ✓ ¼ cup mint, finely chopped
- ✓ 2 tablespoons buttermilk
- ✓ 1 garlic clove, finely chopped
- ✓ 2 pinches of salt

Directions:
1. Preheat the Air-fryer to 390°F. In a large mixing bowl, add together all the meatball ingredients.
2. Roll the meatballs between your hands until it is as small as a golf ball. Place the rolled meatballs into the cooking basket and set timer for 6 to 8 minutes.
3. Meanwhile, combine all the mint yoghurt ingredients to a medium mixing bowl, mixing well
4. Garnish the meatballs with fresh mint and olive and enjoy.

76. Air-Fried Calamari

Prep.Time: 10 min - **Cooking Time:** 10 min - **Servings:** 2

Ingredients:
- ✓ 1 1/2 pounds baby squid, cut hoods into rings and separate tentacles.
- ✓ 5-6 cups + 2 tablespoons vegetable oil
- ✓ 1/2 cup semolina flour
- ✓ 1/2 cup all-purpose flour
- ✓ 1/2 teaspoon Old Bay seasoning
- ✓ 1/3 cup plain cornmeal
- ✓ 1/2 teaspoon salt
- ✓ Black pepper, to taste

Directions:
1. Rinse squid well in cold water. Cut off the tentacles using one cut but keep1/4 inch of the hood so as to keep all the tentacles in one piece. For larger squid, make them bite-sized by cutting pieces in half lengthwise.
2. Add oil to a medium-sized deep pot; oil must reach 4 inches up the side of the pot. Heat the oil to 325°F. In the meantime, combine the dry mixture in a bowl and set aside.
3. With the oil heated up, dredge your squid. Squeeze off any liquid and dredge the squid in the dry mixture. (Work in batches).
4. Lower the calamari gently into the hot oil and fry back and forth. Remove after 2 to 2 1/2 minutes or golden brown. Drain on a paper-towel-lined plate (Work in batches).
5. Serve with marinara sauce and lemon wedges on the side.

77. Air-Fried Kale Chips

Prep.Time: 5 min - **Cooking Time:** 3 minutes - **Servings:** 1-2

Ingredients:
- ✓ 1 head of kale
- ✓ 1 tablespoon of olive oil
- ✓ 1 teaspoon of soya sauce

Directions:
1. Take out the center steam of the kale and tear it up into 1 1/2" pieces. Wash the pieces and dry well.
2. 2. Next, toss with the soya sauce and olive oil. Place in the air-fryer at 400° F for 2 to 3 minutes, tossing halfway through. Enjoy!

78. Bacon Wrapped Shrimp

Prep.Time: 10 min - **Cooking Time:** 25 min - **Servings:** 4

Ingredients:
- ✓ 16 pieces (1¼ pounds) tiger shrimp, peeled & deveined
- ✓ 16 slices (1 pound bacon) thinly sliced

Directions:
1. Wrap a slice of bacon around the shrimp completely. Refrigerate the wrapped shrimp for 20 minutes.
2. Preheat the Air-fryer to 390°F. Take the shrimp out from the refrigerator and place in the cooking basket.
3. Cool for 5 to 7 minutes. Drain on a paper towel and serve.

79. Air Fried Mac & Cheese Wheel

Prep.Time: 10 min - **Cooking Time:** 30 min - **Servings:** 6-8

Ingredients:
- ✓ ½ pound elbow pasta
- ✓ 2 tablespoons, plus ½ teaspoon salt
- ✓ ½ cup whole milk
- ✓ ½ cup grated Fontina cheese
- ✓ ½ cup heavy cream
- ✓ ½ cup grated Gruyere cheese
- ✓ ½ teaspoon Emeril's Original Essence
- ✓ ½ cup grated sharp cheddar cheese
- ✓ ¼ teaspoon ground black pepper
- ✓ ¼ cup bread crumbs
- ✓ ¼ teaspoon ground nutmeg
- ✓ ¼ cup finely grated Parmesan cheese
- ✓ 1 tablespoon unsalted butter, melted

Directions:
1. Add water to a large saucepan until it is three-quarters full and bring to a boil over high heat. Add 2 tablespoons salt to the water. Cook the pasta until just al dente. Remove and drain well. Place in a medium bowl.
2. Add the heavy cream, milk, Fontina, Essence, Gruyere, Cheddar, nutmeg, black pepper and the rest of 1/2 teaspoon of salt, stirring well to mix.
3. Place the pasta into the pan. In a separate, bowl, combine the bread crumbs, butter and Parmesan cheese and stir to combine. Sprinkle the mixture over the pasta and place in the Air Fryer basket.
4. Set the temperature to 350° F and the timer for 30 minutes. Remove the deep casserole pan afterwards and let the Mac & Cheese cool for about 20 minutes.
5. Invert pan over a plate and remove the pan to release. Cut the Mac & cheese into wedges and serve warm.

80. Veggie Spring Rolls

Prep.Time: 15 min - **Cooking Time:** 25 min - **Servings:** 8

Ingredients:
For Stuffing:
- ✓ 2 cups cabbage, shredded thinly
- ✓ 1 big carrot, chopped thinly
- ✓ 2 inch piece ginger, chopped finely
- ✓ 1/2 capsicum, cut thinly
- ✓ 8 garlic cloves, chopped finely
- ✓ Big pinch of sugar
- ✓ 1 tablespoon of pepper powder
- ✓ 1 teaspoon soya sauce Spring onion, to garnish
- ✓ 2 big onions, cut thinly
- ✓ Salt - as needed
- ✓ 2 tablespoons of cooking oil
- ✓ For The Sheet:
- ✓ 10 Spring roll sheet
- ✓ 2 tablespoons of corn flour Water, as needed

Directions:
1. To make the stuffing, sauté all the chopped veggies, adding salt and sugar continuously for 2 to 3 minutes. Add the pepper powder and soya sauce, mixing well. Garnish with spring onions.
2. Make a cream like paste by adding some water to the corn flour. Roll the sheets by cutting into 4 (for small sized spring rolls) and arrange them.
3. Now, place 1 tablespoon of stuffing in a corner of the sheet, roll tight so the spring roll does not become flat. In the other corner, apply the corn flour paste and stick it. Do the same with the sheets and arrange.
4. Preheat the air fryer for 5 minutes in 350°F. Brush the spring rolls with a bit of oil and place the sheets in the Air fryer basket.
5. Bake for 10 minutes at 350°F. Remove the basket and flip rolls, bake another 10 minutes. If the spring rolls color remains white, bake another 2 to 3 minutes.
6. Remove and serve hot.

81. Spicy Coconut Coated Shrimp

Prep.Time: 10 min - **Cooking Time:** 14 min - **Servings:** 4

Ingredients:
- ✓ 4 ounces of grated coconut
- ✓ 16 ounces of large sized shrimps, peeled, deveined
- ✓ 4 ounces of flour
- ✓ 2 egg whites, whisked
- ✓ 8 tablespoons of breadcrumbs
- ✓ ½ teaspoon of salt Zest of 1 small lemon
- ✓ Sweet chili sauce
- ✓ ½ teaspoon ground black pepper
- ✓ Oil spray

Directions:
1. Mix the breadcrumbs with the zest, pepper, coconut and salt in a dish and set aside. Season the flour with pepper and salt in a separate dish. Put the eggs in another dish.
2. Heat your air-fryer to 400°F.
3. Put each shrimp into the flour, the dip into the whisked eggs and lastly, coat evenly with the breadcrumb mixture.
4. Place the dredged shrimps on a plate and coat with oil using an oil spray.
5. Divide the shrimps into two batches and place the first into the air-fryer. Cook for 6 minutes until firm. Do same with the second batch. Turn down the temperature to 340°F and add the first batch to the second in the air-fryer. Air fry for 2 more minutes.
6. Best served with sweet chili sauce.

82. Bread Rolls With Crisp Potato Stuffing

Prep.Time: 20 min - **Cooking Time:** 15 min - **Servings:** 8

Ingredients:
- ✓ 8 slice bread, white part only
- ✓ 5 large potatoes
- ✓ 2 green chilies, seeded & finely chopped
- ✓ 1 small coriander bunch, finely chopped
- ✓ 1/2 teaspoon turmeric
- ✓ 2 small onions, finely chopped
- ✓ 1/2 teaspoon mustard seeds
- ✓ 2 tablespoons oil
- ✓ 2 sprigs curry leaf
- ✓ Salt to taste

Directions:
1. Add the potato, a spoon of salt and water to a pot. Boil, peel and mash the potatoes thoroughly.
2. Heat a teaspoon of oil and mustard seeds in a pan. Once they sputter, add the onions and fry until translucent and the curry leaves and add turmeric. Fry and then add the mashed potatoes and salt. Mix well and let it cool.
3. Using your palms, shape the mixture into 8 oval shapes and set aside.
4. Now, trim off the sides of the bread and wet it totally with water. Remove excess water by pressing with your palm.
5. Keeping the wet bread in your palm, place the potato and roll the bread in a spindle shape. Afterwards, seal the edges and ensure that the potato filling is wholly inside the bread.
6. Make all the rolls and brush with oil. Keep aside. Preheat the Air-fryer at 400°F for 8 minutes and brush the basket with some oil before placing the ready rolls.
7. Cook 12-13 minutes until golden crisp. Enjoy with tomato ketchup along with masala chai!

83. Asian Barbecue Satay

Prep.Time: 15 min - Cooking Time: 15 min - Servings: 3

Ingredients:
- ✓ 4 garlic cloves, chopped
- ✓ ¾ pound (12 oz) boneless skinless chicken tenders
- ✓ ½ cup pineapple juice
- ✓ ½ cup low sodium soy sauce
- ✓ ¼ cup sesame oil
- ✓ 4 scallions, chopped
- ✓ 2 teaspoons sesame seeds, toasted
- ✓ 1 tablespoon fresh ginger, grated
- ✓ 1 pinch black pepper

Directions:
1. Skewer the chicken tender, trimming any excess fat or meat.
2. Add together all the other ingredients in a large bowl. Add the skewered chicken to the bowl, combine, cover and place in the refrigerator for 2 -24hours.
3. Preheat the Air-fryer to 390°F. Pat dry chicken. Add the skewers to the basket and cook for 5 to 7minutes.

84. Toasted Seasoned Nuts

Prep.Time: 5 min - Cooking Time: 50 min - Servings: 3

Ingredients:
- ✓ ¼ teaspoon garlic cloves, ground
- ✓ ½ pound of cashews
- ✓ 4 tablespoons of sugar
- ✓ 8 ounces of pecan halves
- ✓ 1 egg white, whisked
- ✓ 1 teaspoon of salt
- ✓ ½ teaspoon of cinnamon
- ✓ ¼ teaspoon of mixed spice
- ✓ ¼ teaspoon of cayenne pepper
- ✓ 1 cup of almonds

Directions:
1. Mix the sugar, garlic, mixed spice, pepper, salt, cinnamon and egg together in a bowl.
2. Heat your air-fryer to 300°F.
3. Put the cashews, almonds and pecan, into the egg mixture and toss.
4. Coat the fryer basket with oil using a brush and pour half the nut mixture on it. Toast for 25 minutes until crunchy, stirring the nuts at intervals. Do same with the second batch of nuts.
5. Store in a sealed jar if not eaten immediately.

85. Nacho Coated Prawns

Prep.Time: 30 min - Cooking Time: 8 min - Servings: 3-4

Ingredients:
- ✓ 9 ounces of nacho chips
- ✓ 1 egg, whisked
- ✓ 18 medium sized prawns

Directions:
1. Remove the shell and veins from the prawns, wash thoroughly and wipe dry.
2. Grind the chips in a bowl until pieces are as that of breadcrumbs.
3. Dip each prawn into the egg and then coat with the chip crumbs.
4. Heat the air fryer to 356°F.
5. Put the prawns into the air fryer and cook for 8 minutes. Serve with salsa or sour cream.

86. Cheesy Mustard And Ham Rounds

Prep.Time: 35 min - Cooking Time: 10 min - Servings: 6

Ingredients:
- ✓ 2 cups of Gruyere cheese, grated
- ✓ 6 slices of ham
- ✓ 1 tablespoon of mustard
- ✓ 1 sheet of pre-rolled puff pastry

Directions:
1. Cover your work bench with flour and put the pastry on it.
2. Add the ham, mustard and cheese evenly on the pastry and roll up beginning from the shorter edge.
3. Cover with cling film and place in the freezer until firm for 30 minutes. Remove, and slice into 1cm thick small circles.
4. Heat your air-fryer to 370°F and cook the rounds in it until golden brown for 10 minutes.

87. Filo Covered Apple Pie

Prep.Time: 20 min - Cooking Time: 8 minutes - Servings: 10

Ingredients:
- ✓ 3 large apples, finely chopped
- ✓ 6 teaspoons of sugar
- ✓ 6 ounces of melted butter
- ✓ 10 sheets of filo pastry
- ✓ 2 teaspoons of cinnamon
- ✓ 2 teaspoons of flour
- ✓ ½ teaspoon cloves, ground
- ✓ ½ teaspoon nutmeg, ground
- ✓ 3 teaspoons of lemon juice

Directions:
1. Mix the apples, flour, lemon juice, cloves, cinnamon, nutmeg and sugar together in a bowl.
2. Place the filo pastry on a clean surface, unroll and brush gently with butter.
3. Spoon some apple filling and place on the filo sheets about 2" away from the base. Fold the base of the sheet and then a third of the length over the filling. Roll-up the entire filling with the filo sheet to form a triangle shape, brushing the edges with butter.
4. Coat all sides of the filo triangles with the melted butter and sprinkle some sugar on top.
5. Heat your air-fryer to 320°F and cook the apple pies in batches for 8 minutes depending on the size. Remove when they appear light brown and crisp. Serve while warm.

88. Curried Veggie Samosa

Prep.Time: 15 min - Cooking Time: 10 min - Servings: 3

Ingredients:
- ✓ 2 large potatoes, peeled, boiled in salted water and mashed
- ✓ 3 sheets puff pastry
- ✓ 1/2 cup onion, diced
- ✓ 2 garlic cloves, minced
- ✓ 2 tablespoons ginger, grated
- ✓ 1/2 cup carrot, diced
- ✓ 1/2 cup green peas
- ✓ 1 teaspoon garam masala
- ✓ 1 tablespoons curry powder
- ✓ Salt and pepper to taste

Directions:
1. Sauté the onion, carrots, garlic and ginger in a saucepan until tender and add to the mashed potatoes.
2. Add the spices and the green peas, and salt and pepper to taste.
3. Now cut the puff pastry sheets into quarters and then each of the quarters into a circular shape.
4. Place two tablespoons of filling into each pastry circle and moisten edges with water. Fold the pastry in half and seal edges well using a fork.
5. Preheat the Air Fryer to 390 degrees.
6. Working in batches, fry samosas for 5 minutes each until golden brown and crispy.

133

89. Puff Pastry Banana Rolls

Prep.Time: 10 min - **Cooking Time:** 10 min - **Servings:** 3

Ingredients:
- ✓ 2 puff pastry sheet
- ✓ 3 medium sized bananas, peeled

Directions:
1. Cut the pastry sheets into thin strips. Twine two strips to form a cord. Make as many cords as needed.
2. Wind the bananas with the cords until the entire banana is covered with the pastry.
3. Heat your air-fryer to 356°F and cook the wrapped bananas for about 10 minutes until golden.

90. Air Fried Cheeseburgers

Prep.Time: 5 min - **Cooking Time:** 10 min - **Servings:** 2

Ingredients:
- ✓ 2 slices of Cheddar Cheese
- ✓ 2 bread rolls
- ✓ ½ pound of ground beef
- ✓ ½ tsp. of black pepper, ground
- ✓ 2 tbsp. of melted butte
- ✓ 2 tsp. of salt

Directions:
1. Heat your air-fryer to 390°F.
2. Mold the ground beef to form 2 patties. Sprinkle with pepper and salt.
3. Slice the bread rolls from the center and place each patties in it.
4. Put the burgers in the cooking basket and cook for about 11 minutes. Add the cheddar cheese on the patties and cook for another 1 minute until the cheese melts.

91. Roti Prata Mini Sausage Rolls

Prep.Time: 5 min - **Cooking Time:** 15 min - **Servings:** 4

Ingredients:
- ✓ 1 packet of Roti prata
- ✓ 10 mini beef sausage

Directions:
1. Slice the prata into triangles. Roll each sausage in a prata triangle until all are well wrapped.
2. Heat your air-fryer to 356°F and place the rolls in the fryer basket. Bake them for 15 minutes until crispy, turning the rolls halfway through.

92. Grilled Cheese Delight

Prep.Time: 10 min - **Cooking Time:** 5 min - **Servings:** 2

Ingredients:
- ✓ 4 slices white bread
- ✓ ¼ cup butter, melted
- ✓ ½ cup sharp cheddar cheese

Directions:
1. Preheat the Air-fryer to 360°F. Place the butter and cheese in two separate bowls.
2. Brush the butter on both sides of bread. Place the cheese on 2 of the 4 bread pieces.
3. Put together the grilled cheese and add to the air-fryer cooking basket.
4. Cook until the cheese has melted and is golden brown or for 5 to 7 minutes.

93. Syrupy Buttered Figs With Mascarpone

Prep.Time: 10 min - **Cooking Time:** 5 minutes - **Servings:** 4

Ingredients:
- ✓ 2 tablespoons of butter
- ✓ 5.2 ounces of mascarpone
- ✓ 1 teaspoon of rose water
- ✓ 8 figs
- ✓ 1½ ounces of maple syrup
- ✓ Toasted almonds

Directions:
1. Preheat the air-fryer to 350°F.
2. Cut the top of the figs vertically and horizontally to form a cross and squeeze bottom lightly to open.
3. Put a small lump of butter into each fig and place in a dish. Drizzle the maple syrup over the figs.
4. Place the dish into the air-fryer basket and cook for 5 minutes until soft.
5. Pour the rosewater into the mascarpone and stir. Place a spoonful in each serving and sprinkle the almond on top.

94. Banana & marshmallow Relish

Prep.Time: 5 min - **Cooking Time:** 6 min - **Servings:** 4

Ingredients:
- ✓ 1½ ounces of mini marshmallows
- ✓ 1½ ounces graham cracker cereal
- ✓ 4 medium sized bananas
- ✓ 1½ ounces of mini peanut butter chips
- ✓ 1½ ounces of mini semi-sweet chocolate chips

Directions:
1. Heat your air-fryer to 400°F.
2. Using a knife, slice vertically through the inner side of the unpeeled bananas but not to the bottom, piercing the opposite skin. Open up the cut slits.
3. Fill the slits with the marshmallows, crackers, chocolate and peanut butter chips.
4. Put the filled bananas into the basket ensuring they are upright.
5. Cook for 6 minutes until the banana peel is black and the chips are toasted and melted.

95. Crunchy Sweet Potato Sticks

Prep.Time: 5 min - **Cooking Time:** 10 minutes - **Servings:** 1

Ingredients:
- ✓ 1 medium sized sweet potato
- ✓ Salt to taste
- ✓ 1 teaspoon of coconut oil
- ✓ 1 tablespoon of aioli

Directions:
1. Heat your air-fryer to 200°F.
2. Cut the sweet potato into sticks and toss in the coconut oil.
3. Place the potato sticks into the cooking basket and fry for 10 minutes until they turn crisp.
4. Add the salt and serve with aioli.

96. Corn Tortilla Chips

Prep.Time: 1 min - **Cooking Time:** 6 min - **Servings:** 3

Ingredients:
- ✓ 6 teaspoons of vegetable oil
- ✓ 8 Corn Tortillas
- ✓ Salt to taste

Directions:
1. Heat the air-fryer to 390°F.
2. Cut out shapes from the tortillas using a knife. Coat the tortillas with oil using a pastry brush.
3. Put half the tortilla into the fryer basket and cook for 3 minutes. Do same with the second batch until all the chips are ready. Add the salt and serve hot with a sauce.

97. Sweet Cinnamon Doughnuts

Prep.Time: 15 min - **Cooking Time:** 18 min - **Servings:** 9

Ingredients:
- ✓ 8 tablespoons of sugar
- ✓ 18 ounces of flour
- ✓ 8 tablespoons of sour cream
- ✓ 1 ounce of butter
- ✓ 1 teaspoon cinnamon
- ✓ 3 egg yolks
- ✓ 2.6 ounce of caster sugar
- ✓ 1 teaspoon of salt
- ✓ ¼ cup of melted butter
- ✓ ½ tablespoon of baking powder

Directions:
1. Mix the sugar and butter together in a bowl until crumbly. Add the egg yolk and mix thoroughly.
2. Sieve the baking powder, flour and salt in another bowl. Mix half of the sour cream and a third of the sifted flour together. Add the other part of the sour cream and a third of the flour till all are thoroughly combined.
3. Flour the table lightly and flatten the dough with a rolling pin to about 1cm thick. Cut out doughnut shapes from the dough.
4. Heat the air fryer to 350°F.
5. Brush all sides of the doughnuts lightly with the melted butter and place in the fryer and bake for 8 minutes.
6. Remove the doughnut from the air-fryer and brush again with melted butter then dip into a mixture of cinnamon and caster sugar.
7. Serve while it's still hot.

98. Air Fried Rosemary Chips

Prep.Time: 40 min - **Cooking Time:** 30 min - **Servings:** 4

Ingredients:
- ✓ 2 teaspoons of finely chopped rosemary
- ✓ 4 russet potatoes
- ✓ 3 teaspoons of olive oil
- ✓ ¼ teaspoon of salt

Directions:
1. Peel potatoes and slice them into thin chips. Soak them in water for 30 minutes, drain and then pat dry with paper towel.
2. Heat your air-fryer to about 330°F.
3. Pour the olive oil into the potato chips and toss until all the potatoes are coated.
4. Put the potatoes into the fryer basket and air fry for 30 minutes until golden and crisp. Shake often to during cooking to ensure the potatoes are evenly cooked.
5. Remove from fryer, add the rosemary and salt and toss to mix.

99. Air Fried Banana Chips

Prep.Time: 15 min - **Cooking Time:** 15 min - **Servings:** 4

Ingredients:
- ✓ 3 medium sized bananas, peeled
- ✓ 1 teaspoon of vegetable oil
- ✓ ½ teaspoon of Chaat masala seasoning
- ✓ ½ teaspoon of Turmeric powder
- ✓ 1 teaspoon of salt

Directions:
1. Add about 1½ cups of water to the turmeric powder and a little salt. Slice the bananas into the turmeric mixture to prevent it from getting black and to give it a yellow color. Soak the bananas for 10 minutes and then drain off and dry.
2. Heat your air-fryer to 356°F for 5 minutes.
3. Add the oil on the chips and toss lightly.
4. Fry for 15 minutes in the air-fryer.
5. Remove from fryer and add the salt and seasoning.
6. Serve immediately or preserve in an airtight container.

100. Air Fried Spring Rolls

Prep.Time: 20 min - **Cooking Time:** 24 min - **Servings:** 20

Ingredients:
- ✓ 3 teaspoon olive oil
- ✓ 1 small sized onion, diced
- ✓ 2 ounces of Asian noodles
- ✓ 1 packets of spring roll wrappers
- ✓ 3 cloves of garlic, crushed
- ✓ 8 ounces of mixed vegetables
- ✓ 1 teaspoon of soy sauce
- ✓ 7 ounces of mince
- ✓ 6 teaspoons of water

Directions:
1. Put the noodles in hot water, allowing it soak until soft; drain it, then cut into shorter length.
2. Heat the oil in a skillet then add the onion, mixed vegetables, mince and garlic. Cook the mixture until mince is soft then add soy sauce.
3. Remove from heat and mix with the noodles. Allow to stand until the noodles absorb the juices.
4. Place the spring roll wrapper, one after the other and add the noodle mixture diagonally across. Fold the pointed edge close to the filling over it, then fold the 2 side points together. Brush the last point with water, then roll over the spring roll to seal it.
5. Heat the Air-fryer to 356°F.
6. Coat each roll with oil using a pastry brush place in a single layer in air-fryer to cook for 8 minutes. Cook in batches until all rolls are cooked.

101. Zucchini Chips

Prep.Time: 10 min - **Cooking Time:** 8 min - **Servings:** 2

Ingredients:
- ✓ 1 large zucchini, cut into 1/8" slices
- ✓ 1 tbsp olive oil
- ✓ 1 tsp Cajun seasoning

Directions:
1. Place zucchini slices into the air fryer basket and drizzle with olive oil.
2. Sprinkle Cajun seasoning on top of zucchini slices.
3. Air-fry them for 187 C / 370 F for 8 minutes.
4. Turn zucchini chips to other side and cook for 8 minutes more.

102. Healthy Apple Chips

Prep.Time: 1 hour - **Cooking Time:** 8 min - **Servings:** 2

Ingredients:
- ✓ 1 large apple, slice using the slicer
- ✓ 1/4 tsp ground nutmeg
- ✓ 1/4 tsp ground cinnamon

Directions:
1. Preheat air fryer at 375 F / 190 C for 3 minutes.
2. Season apple slices with nutmeg and cinnamon.
3. Place apple slice in the air fryer basket and cook for 7-8 minutes.

FISH AND SEAFOOD RECIPES

1 Buttered Shrimp Skewers

Prep.Time: 10 min - **Cooking Time:** 6 min - **Servings:** 2

Ingredients:
- ✓ 8 shrimps, peeled and deveined
- ✓ 4 garlic cloves, minced
- ✓ Salt and black pepper to the taste
- ✓ 8 green bell pepper slices
- ✓ 1 tablespoon rosemary, chopped
- ✓ 1 tablespoon butter, melted

Directions:
5. In a bowl, mix shrimp with garlic, butter, salt, pepper, rosemary and bell pepper slices, toss to coat and leave aside for 10 minutes.
6. Arrange 2 shrimp and 2 bell pepper slices on a skewer and repeat with the rest of the shrimp and bell pepper pieces.
7. Place them all in your air fryer's basket and cook at 360 degrees F for 6 minutes.
8. Divide among plates and serve right away

Nutrition: calories 140 - Fat 61- Fiber 12 - Carbs 15 - Protein 7

2. Flavored Air Fried Salmon

Prep.Time: 1 hour - **Cooking Time:** 8 min - **Servings:** 2

Ingredients:
- ✓ 2 salmon fillets
- ✓ 2 tablespoons lemon juice
- ✓ Salt and black pepper to the taste
- ✓ ½ teaspoon garlic powder
- ✓ 1/3 cup water
- ✓ 1/3 cup soy sauce
- ✓ 3 scallions, chopped
- ✓ 1/3 cup brown sugar
- ✓ 2 tablespoons olive oil

Directions:
4. In a bowl, mix sugar with water, soy sauce, garlic powder, salt, pepper, oil and lemon juice, whisk well, add salmon fillets, toss to coat and leave aside in the fridge for 1 hour.
5. Transfer salmon fillets to the fryer's basket and cook at 360 degrees F for 8 minutes flipping them halfway.
6. Divide salmon on plates, sprinkle scallions on top and serve right away.

Nutrition: calories 300 - Fat 12 - Fiber 10 - Carbs 23 - Protein 20

3. Delicious Catfish

Prep.Time: 10 min - **Cooking Time:** 20 minutes - **Servings:** 4

Ingredients:
- ✓ 4 cat fish fillets
- ✓ Salt and black pepper to the taste
- ✓ A pinch of sweet paprika
- ✓ 1 tablespoon parsley, chopped
- ✓ 1 tablespoon lemon juice
- ✓ 1 tablespoon olive oil

Directions:
1. Season catfish fillets with salt, pepper, paprika, drizzle oil, rub well, place in your air fryer's basket and cook at 400 degrees F for 20 minutes, flipping the fish after 10 minutes.
2. Divide fish on plates, drizzle lemon juice all over, sprinkle parsley and serve.

Nutrition: calories 253 - Fat 6 - Fiber 12 - Carbs 26 - Protein 22

4. Tabasco Shrimp

Prep.Time: 10 min - **Cooking Time:** 10 min - **Servings:** 4

Ingredients:
- ✓ 1 pound shrimp, peeled and deveined
- ✓ 1 teaspoon red pepper flakes
- ✓ 2 tablespoon olive oil
- ✓ 1 teaspoon Tabasco sauce
- ✓ 2 tablespoons water
- ✓ 1 teaspoon oregano, dried
- ✓ Salt and black pepper to the taste
- ✓ ½ teaspoon parsley, dried
- ✓ ½ teaspoon smoked paprika

Directions:
1. In a bowl, mix oil with water, Tabasco sauce, pepper flakes, oregano, parsley, salt, pepper, paprika and shrimp and toss well to coat.
2. Transfer shrimp to your preheated air fryer at 370 degrees F and cook for 10 minutes shaking the fryer once.
3. Divide shrimp on plates and serve with a side salad.

Nutrition: calories 200 - Fat 5 - Fiber 6 - Carbs 13 - Protein 8

5. Lemony Saba Fish

Prep.Time: 10 min - **Cooking Time:** 8 min - **Servings:** 1

Ingredients:
- ✓ 4 Saba fish fillet, boneless
- ✓ Salt and black pepper to the taste
- ✓ 3 red chili pepper, chopped
- ✓ 2 tablespoons lemon juice
- ✓ 2 tablespoon olive oil
- ✓ 2 tablespoon garlic, minced

Directions:
1. Season fish fillets with salt and pepper and put in a bowl.
2. Add lemon juice, oil, chili and garlic toss to coat, transfer fish to your air fryer and cook at 360 degrees F for 8 minutes, flipping halfway.
3. Divide among plates and serve with some fries.

Nutrition: calories 300 - Fat 4 - Fiber 8 - Carbs 15 - Protein 15

6. Cod Steaks with Plum Sauce

Prep.Time: 10 min - **Cooking Time:** 20 min - **Servings:** 2

Ingredients:
- ✓ 2 big cod steaks
- ✓ Salt and black pepper to the taste
- ✓ ½ teaspoon garlic powder
- ✓ ½ teaspoon ginger powder
- ✓ ¼ teaspoon turmeric powder
- ✓ 1 tablespoon plum sauce
- ✓ Cooking spray

Directions:
1. Season cod steaks with salt and pepper, spray them with cooking oil, add garlic powder, ginger powder and turmeric powder and rub well.
2. Place cod steaks in your air fryer and cook at 360 degrees F for 15 minutes, flipping them after 7 minutes.
3. Heat up a pan over medium heat, add plum sauce, stir and cook for 2 minutes.
4. Divide cod steaks on plates, drizzle plum sauce all over and serve.

Nutrition: calories 250 - Fat 7 - Fiber 1 - Carbs 14 - Protein

7. Cod Fillets with Fennel and Grapes Salad

Prep.Time: 10 min - Cooking Time: 15 min - Servings: 2

Ingredients:
- ✓ 2 black cod fillets, boneless
- ✓ 1 tablespoon olive oil
- ✓ Salt and black pepper to the taste
- ✓ 1 fennel bulb, thinly sliced
- ✓ 1 cup grapes, halved
- ✓ ½ cup pecans

Directions:
1. Drizzle half of the oil over fish fillets, season with salt and pepper, rub well, place fillets in your air fryer's basket, cook for 10 minutes at 400 degrees F and transfer to a plate.
2. In a bowl, mix pecans with grapes, fennel, the rest of the oil, salt and pepper, toss to coat, add to a pan that fits your air fryer and cook at 400 degrees F for 5 minutes.
3. Divide cod on plates, add fennel and grapes mix on the side and serve.

Nutrition: calories 300 - Fat 4 - Fiber 2 - Carbs 32 - Protein 22

8. Asian Halibut

Prep.Time: 30 min - Cooking Time: 10 min - Servings: 3

Ingredients:
- ✓ 1 pound halibut steaks
- ✓ 2/3 cup soy sauce
- ✓ ¼ cup sugar
- ✓ 2 tablespoons lime juice
- ✓ ½ cup mirin
- ✓ ¼ teaspoon red pepper flakes, crushed
- ✓ ¼ cup orange juice
- ✓ ¼ teaspoon ginger, grated
- ✓ 1 garlic clove, minced

Directions:
1. Put soy sauce in a pan, heat up over medium heat, add mirin, sugar, lime and orange juice, pepper flakes, ginger and garlic, stir well, bring to a boil and take off heat.
2. Transfer half of the marinade to a bowl, add halibut, toss to coat and leave aside in the fridge for 30 minutes.
3. Transfer halibut to your air fryer and cook at 390 degrees F for 10 minutes, flipping once.
4. Divide halibut steaks on plates, drizzle the rest of the marinade all over and serve hot.

Nutrition: calories 286 - Fat 5 - Fiber 12 - Carbs 14 - Protein 23

9. Tasty Air Fried Cod

Prep.Time: 10 min - Cooking Time: 12 minutes - Servings: 4

Ingredients:
- ✓ 2 cod fish, 7 ounces each
- ✓ A drizzle of sesame oil
- ✓ Salt and black pepper to the taste
- ✓ 1 cup water
- ✓ 1 tsp dark soy sauce
- ✓ 4 tbsp light soy sauce
- ✓ 1 tablespoon sugar
- ✓ 3 tablespoons olive oil
- ✓ 4 ginger slices
- ✓ 3 spring onions, chopped
- ✓ 2 tbsp coriander, chopped

Directions:
1. Season fish with salt, pepper, drizzle sesame oil, rub well and leave aside for 10 minutes.
2. Add fish to your air fryer and cook at 356 degrees F for 12 minutes.
3. Meanwhile, heat up a pot with the water over medium heat, add dark and light soy sauce and sugar, stir, bring to a simmer and take off heat.
4. Heat up a pan with the olive oil over medium heat, add ginger and green onions, stir, cook for a few minutes and take off heat.
5. Divide fish on plates, top with ginger and green onions, drizzle soy sauce mix, sprinkle coriander and serve right away.

Nutrition: calories 300 - Fat 17 - Fiber 8 - Carbs 20 - Protein 22

10. Asian Salmon

Prep.Time: 1 hour - Cooking Time: 15 min - Servings: 2

Ingredients:
- ✓ Asian Salmon
- ✓ 1 teaspoon water
- ✓
- ✓ 6 tablespoons honey

Directions:
1. In a bowl, mix soy sauce with honey, water and mirin, whisk well, add salmon, rub well and leave aside in the fridge for 1 hour.
2. Transfer salmon to your air fryer and cook at 360 degrees F for 15 minutes, flipping them after 7 minutes.
3. Meanwhile, put the soy marinade in a pan, heat up over medium heat, whisk well, cook for 2 minutes and take off heat.
4. Divide salmon on plates, drizzle marinade all over and serve.

Nutrition: calories 300 - Fat 12 - Fiber 8 - Carbs 13 - Protein 24

11. Cod and Vinaigrette

Prep.Time: 10 min - Cooking Time: 15 min - Servings: 4

Ingredients:
- ✓ 4 cod fillets, skinless and boneless
- ✓ 12 cherry tomatoes, halved
- ✓ 8 black olives, pitted and roughly chopped
- ✓ 2 tbsp lemon juice
- ✓ Salt and black pepper to the taste
- ✓ 2 tablespoons olive oil
- ✓ Cooking spray
- ✓ 1 bunch basil, chopped

Directions:
1. Season cod with salt and pepper to the taste, place in your air fryer's basket and cook at 360 degrees F for 10 minutes, flipping after 5 minutes.
2. Meanwhile, heat up a pan with the oil over medium heat, add tomatoes, olives and lemon juice, stir, bring to a simmer, add basil, salt and pepper, stir well and take off heat.
3. Divide fish on plates and serve with the vinaigrette drizzled on top.

Nutrition: calories 300 - Fat 5 - Fiber 8 - Carbs 12 - Protein 8

12. Trout Fillet and Orange Sauce

Prep.Time: 10 min - Cooking Time: 10 min - Servings: 4

Ingredients:
- ✓ 4 trout fillets, skinless and boneless
- ✓ 4 spring onions, chopped
- ✓ 1 tablespoon olive oil
- ✓ 1 tablespoon ginger, minced
- ✓ Salt and black pepper to the taste
- ✓ Juice and zest from 1 orange

Directions:
1. Season trout fillets with salt, pepper, rub them with the olive oil, place in a pan that fits your air fryer, add ginger, green onions, orange zest and juice, toss well, place in your air fryer and cook at 360 degrees F for 10 minutes.
2. Divide fish and sauce on plates and serve right away

Nutrition: calories 239 - Fat 10 - Fiber 7 - Carbs 18 - Protein 23

13. Salmon with Capers and Mash

Prep.Time: 10 min - **Cooking Time:** 20 min - **Servings:** 4

Ingredients:
- ✓ 4 salmon fillets, skinless and boneless
- ✓ 1 tbsp capers, drained
- ✓ Salt and black pepper to the taste
- ✓ Juice from 1 lemon
- ✓ 2 teaspoons olive oil

For the potato mash:
- ✓ 2 tablespoons olive oil
- ✓ 1 tablespoon dill, dried
- ✓ 1 pound potatoes, chopped
- ✓ ½ cup milk

Directions:
1. Put potatoes in a pot, add water to cover, add some salt, bring to a boil over medium high heat, cook for 15 minutes, drain, transfer to a bowl, mash with a potato masher, add 2 tablespoons oil, dill, salt, pepper and milk, whisk well and leave aside for now.
2. Season salmon with salt and pepper, drizzle 2 teaspoons oil over them, rub, transfer to your air fryer's basket, add capers on top, cook at 360 degrees F and cook for 8 minutes. Divide salmon and capers on plates, add mashed potatoes on the side, drizzle lemon juice all over and serve.

Nutrition: calories 300 - Fat 17 - Fiber 8 - Carbs 12 - Protein 18

14. Shrimp and Crab Mix

Prep.Time: 10 min - **Cooking Time:** 25 min - **Servings:** 4

Ingredients:
- ✓ ½ cup yellow onion, chopped
- ✓ 1 cup green bell pepper, chopped
- ✓ 1 cup celery, chopped
- ✓ 1 pound shrimp, peeled and deveined
- ✓ 1 cup crabmeat, flaked
- ✓ 1 cup mayonnaise
- ✓ 1 teaspoon Worcestershire sauce
- ✓ Salt and black pepper to the taste
- ✓ 2 tbsp breadcrumbs
- ✓ 1 tbsp butter, melted
- ✓ 1 teaspoon sweet paprika

Directions:
1. In a bowl, mix shrimp with crab meat, bell pepper, onion, mayo, celery, salt, pepper and Worcestershire sauce, toss well and transfer to a pan that fits your air fryer.
2. Sprinkle bread crumbs and paprika, add melted butter, place in your air fryer and cook at 320 degrees F for 25 minutes, shaking halfway.
3. Divide among plates and serve right away.

Nutrition: calories 200 - Fat 13 - Fiber 9 - Carbs 17 - Protein 19

15. Cod Fillets and Peas

Prep.Time: 10 min - **Cooking Time:** 10 minutes - **Servings:** 4

Ingredients:
- ✓ 4 cod fillets, boneless
- ✓ 2 tbsp parsley, chopped
- ✓ 2 cups peas
- ✓ 4 tablespoons wine
- ✓ ½ tsp oregano, dried
- ✓ ½ tsp sweet paprika
- ✓ 2 garlic cloves, minced
- ✓ Salt and pepper to the taste

Directions:
1. In your food processor mix garlic with parsley, salt, pepper, oregano, paprika and wine and blend well.
2. Rub fish with half of this mix, place in your air fryer and cook at 360 degrees F for 10 minutes.
3. Meanwhile, put peas in a pot, add water to cover, add salt, bring to a boil over medium high heat, cook for 10 minutes, drain and divide among plates.
4. Also divide fish on plates, spread the rest of the herb dressing all over and serve.

Nutrition: calories 261 - Fat 8 - Fiber 12 - Carbs 20 - Protein 22

16. Thyme and Parsley Salmon

Prep.Time: 10 min - **Cooking Time:** 15 min - **Servings:** 4

Ingredients:
- ✓ 4 salmon fillets, boneless
- ✓ Juice from 1 lemon
- ✓ 1 yellow onion, chopped
- ✓ 3 tomatoes, sliced
- ✓ 4 thyme springs
- ✓ 4 parsley springs
- ✓ 3 tbsp extra virgin olive oil
- ✓ Salt and black pepper to the taste

Directions:
1. Drizzle 1 tablespoon oil in a pan that fits your air fryer,, add a layer of tomatoes, salt and pepper, drizzle 1 more tablespoon oil, add fish, season them with salt and pepper, drizzle the rest of the oil, add thyme and parsley springs, onions, lemon juice, salt and pepper, place in your air fryer's basket and cook at 360 degrees F for 12 minutes shaking once.
2. Divide everything on plates and serve right away.

Nutrition: calories 242 - Fat 9 - Fiber 12 - Carbs 20 - Protein 31

17. Creamy Salmon

Prep.Time: 10 min - **Cooking Time:** 10 min - **Servings:** 4

Ingredients:
- ✓ 4 salmon fillets, boneless
- ✓ 1 tablespoons olive oil
- ✓ Salt and black pepper to the taste
- ✓ 1/3 cup cheddar cheese, grated
- ✓ 1 and ½ teaspoon mustard
- ✓ ½ cup coconut cream

Directions:
1. Season salmon with salt and pepper, drizzle the oil and rub well. In a bowl, mix coconut cream with cheddar, mustard, salt and pepper and stir well.
2. Transfer salmon to a pan that fits your air fryer, add coconut cream mix, introduce in your air fryer and cook at 320 degrees F for 10 minutes.
3. Divide among plates and serve.

Nutrition: calories 200 - Fat 6 - Fiber 14 - Carbs 17 - Protein 20

18. Squid and Guacamole

Prep.Time: 10 min - **Cooking Time:** 6 min - **Servings:** 2

Ingredients:
- ✓ 2 medium squids, tentacles separated and tubes scored lengthwise
- ✓ 1 tablespoon olive oil
- ✓ Juice from 1 lime
- ✓ Salt and black pepper to the taste

For the guacamole:
- ✓ 2 avocados, pitted, peeled and chopped
- ✓ 1 tbsp coriander, chopped
- ✓ 2 red chilies, chopped
- ✓ 1 tomato, chopped
- ✓ 1 red onion, chopped
- ✓ Juice from 2 limes

Directions:
1. Season squid and squid tentacles with salt, pepper, drizzle the olive oil all over, put in your air fryer's basket and cook at 360 degrees F for 3 minutes on each side.
2. Transfer squid to a bowl, drizzle lime juice all over and toss. Meanwhile, put avocado in a bowl, mash with a fork, add coriander, chilies, tomato, onion and juice from 2 limes and toss.
3. Divide squid on plates, top with guacamole and serve.

Nutrition: calories 500 - Fat 43 - Fiber 6 - Carbs 7 - Protein 20

19. Seafood Casserole

Prep.Time: 10 min - **Cooking Time:** 40 min - **Servings:** 6

Ingredients:
- ✓ 6 tablespoons butter
- ✓ 2 ounces mushrooms, chopped
- ✓ 1 small green bell pepper, chopped
- ✓ 1 celery stalk, chopped
- ✓ 2 garlic cloves, minced
- ✓ 1 small yellow onion, chopped
- ✓ Salt and black pepper to the taste
- ✓ 4 tablespoons flour
- ✓ ½ cup white wine
- ✓ 1 and ½ cups milk
- ✓ ½ cup heavy cream
- ✓ 4 sea scallops, sliced
- ✓ 4 ounces haddock, skinless, boneless and cut into small pieces
- ✓ 4 ounces lobster meat, already cooked and cut into small pieces
- ✓ ½ teaspoon mustard powder
- ✓ 1 tablespoon lemon juice
- ✓ 1/3 cup bread crumbs
- ✓ Salt and black pepper to the taste
- ✓ 3 tablespoons cheddar cheese, grated
- ✓ A handful parsley, chopped
- ✓ 1 teaspoon sweet paprika

Directions:
1. Heat up a pan with 4 tablespoons butter over medium high heat, add bell pepper, mushrooms, celery, garlic, onion and wine, stir and cook for 10 minutes
2. Add flour, cream and milk, stir well and cook for 6 minutes.
3. Add lemon juice, salt, pepper, mustard powder, scallops, lobster meat and haddock, stir well, take off heat and transfer to a pan that fits your air fryer.
4. In a bowl, mix the rest of the butter with bread crumbs, paprika and cheese and sprinkle over seafood mix.
5. Transfer pan to your air fryer and cook at 360 degrees F for 16 minutes.
6. Divide among plates and serve with parsley sprinkled on top.

Nutrition: calories 270 - Fat 32 - Fiber 14 - Carbs 15 - Protein 23

20. Creamy Shrimp and Veggies

Prep.Time: 10 min - **Cooking Time:** 30 min - **Servings:** 4

Ingredients:
- ✓ 8 ounces mushrooms, chopped
- ✓ 1 asparagus bunch, cut into medium pieces
- ✓ 1 pound shrimp, peeled and deveined
- ✓ Salt and black pepper to the taste
- ✓ 1 spaghetti squash, cut into halves
- ✓ 2 tablespoons olive oil
- ✓ 2 teaspoons Italian seasoning
- ✓ 1 yellow onion, chopped
- ✓ 1 teaspoon red pepper flakes, crushed
- ✓ ¼ cup butter, melted
- ✓ 1 cup parmesan cheese, grated
- ✓ 2 garlic cloves, minced
- ✓ 1 cup heavy cream

Directions:
1. Place squash halves in you air fryer's basket, cook at 390 degrees F for 17 minutes, transfer to a cutting board, scoop insides and transfer to a bowl.
2. Put water in a pot, add some salt, bring to a boil over medium heat, add asparagus, steam for a couple of minutes, transfer to a bowl filled with ice water, drain and leave aside as well.
3. Heat up a pan that fits your air fryer with the oil over medium heat, add onions and mushrooms, stir and cook for 7 minutes.
4. Add pepper flakes, Italian seasoning, salt, pepper, squash, asparagus, shrimp, melted butter, cream, parmesan and garlic, toss and cook in your air fryer at 360 degrees F for 6 minutes.
5. Divide everything on plates and serve

Nutrition: calories 325 - Fat 6 - Fiber 50 - Carbs 14 - Protein 13

21. Salmon and Avocado Salsa

Prep.Time: 30 min - **Cooking Time:** 10 minutes - **Servings:** 4

Ingredients:
- ✓ 4 salmon fillets
- ✓ 1 tablespoon olive oil
- ✓ Salt and black pepper to the taste
- ✓ 1 teaspoon cumin, ground
- ✓ 1 teaspoon sweet paprika
- ✓ ½ teaspoon chili powder
- ✓ 1 teaspoon garlic powder

For the salsa:
- ✓ 1 small red onion, chopped
- ✓ 1 avocado, pitted, peeled and chopped
- ✓ 2 tablespoons cilantro, chopped
- ✓ Juice from 2 limes
- ✓ Salt and black pepper to the taste

Directions:
1. In a bowl, mix salt, pepper, chili powder, onion powder, paprika and cumin, stir, rub salmon with this mix, drizzle the oil, rub again, transfer to your air fryer and cook at 350 degrees F for 5 minutes on each side.
2. Meanwhile, in a bowl, mix avocado with red onion, salt, pepper, cilantro and lime juice and stir.
3. Divide fillets on plates, top with avocado salsa and serve.

Nutrition: calories 300 - Fat 14 - Fiber 4 - Carbs 18 - Protein 16

22. Italian Barramundi Fillets and Tomato Salsa

Prep.Time: 10 min - **Cooking Time:** 8 min - **Servings:** 4

Ingredients:
- ✓ 2 barramundi fillets, boneless
- ✓ 1 tablespoon olive oil+ 2 teaspoons
- ✓ 2 teaspoons Italian seasoning
- ✓ ¼ cup green olives, pitted and chopped
- ✓ ¼ cup cherry tomatoes, chopped
- ✓ ¼ cup black olives, chopped
- ✓ 1 tablespoon lemon zest
- ✓ 2 tablespoons lemon zest
- ✓ Salt and black pepper to the taste
- ✓ 2 tablespoons parsley, chopped

Directions:
1. Rub fish with salt, pepper, Italian seasoning and 2 teaspoons olive oil, transfer to your air fryer and cook at 360 degrees F for 8 minutes, flipping them halfway.
2. In a bowl, mix tomatoes with black olives, green olives, salt, pepper, lemon zest and lemon juice, parsley and 1 tablespoon olive oil and toss well
3. Divide fish on plates, add tomato salsa on top and serve.

Nutrition: calories 270 - Fat 4 - Fiber 2 - Carbs 18 - Protein 27

23. Stuffed Salmon

Prep.Time: 10 min - Cooking Time: 20 min - Servings: 2

Ingredients:
- ✓ 2 salmon fillets, skinless and boneless
- ✓ 1 tablespoon olive oil
- ✓ 5 ounces tiger shrimp, peeled, deveined and chopped
- ✓ 6 mushrooms, chopped
- ✓ 3 green onions, chopped
- ✓ 2 cups spinach, torn
- ✓ ¼ cup macadamia nuts, toasted and chopped
- ✓ Salt and black pepper to the taste

Directions:
1. Heat up a pan with half of the oil over medium high heat, add mushrooms, onions, salt and pepper, stir and cook for 4 minutes.
2. Add macadamia nuts, spinach and shrimp, stir, cook for 3 minutes and take off heat.
3. Make an incision lengthwise in each salmon fillet, season with salt and pepper, divide spinach and shrimp mix into incisions and rub with the rest of the olive oil.
4. Place in your air fryer's basket and cook at 360 degrees F and cook for 10 minutes, flipping halfway.
5. Divide stuffed salmon on plates and serve.

Nutrition: calories 290 - Fat 15 - Fiber 3 - Carbs 12 - Protein 31

24. Tuna and Chimichuri Sauce

Prep.Time: 10 min - Cooking Time: 8 min - Servings: 4

Ingredients:
- ✓ ½ cup cilantro, chopped
- ✓ 1/3 cup olive oil+ 2 tablespoons
- ✓ 1 small red onion, chopped
- ✓ 3 tablespoon balsamic vinegar
- ✓ 2 tablespoons parsley, chopped
- ✓ 2 tablespoons basil, chopped
- ✓ 1 jalapeno pepper, chopped
- ✓ 1 pound sushi tuna steak
- ✓ Salt and black pepper to the taste
- ✓ 1 teaspoon red pepper flakes
- ✓ 1 teaspoon thyme, chopped
- ✓ 3 garlic cloves, minced
- ✓ 2 avocados, pitted, peeled and sliced
- ✓ 6 ounces baby arugula

Directions:
1. In a bowl, mix 1/3 cup oil with jalapeno, vinegar, onion, cilantro, basil, garlic, parsley, pepper flakes, thyme, salt and pepper, whisk well and leave aside for now.
2. Season tuna with salt and pepper, rub with the rest of the oil, place in your air fryer and cook at 360 degrees F for 3 minutes on each side.
3. Mix arugula with half of the chimichuri mix you've made and toss to coat.
4. Divide arugula on plates, slice tuna and also divide among plates, top with the rest of the chimichuri and serve.

Nutrition: calories 276 - Fat 3 - Fiber 1 - Carbs 14 - Protein 20

25. Trout and Butter Sauce

Prep.Time: 10 min - Cooking Time: 10 minutes - Servings: 4

Ingredients:
- ✓ 4 trout fillets, boneless
- ✓ Salt and black pepper to the taste
- ✓ 3 teaspoons lemon zest, grated
- ✓ 3 tablespoons chives, chopped
- ✓ 6 tablespoons butter
- ✓ 2 tablespoons olive oil
- ✓ 2 teaspoons lemon juice

Directions:
1. Season trout with salt and pepper, drizzle the olive oil, rub, transfer to your air fryer and cook at 360 degrees F for 10 minutes, flipping once.
2. Meanwhile, heat up a pan with the butter over medium heat, add salt, pepper, chives, lemon juice and zest, whisk well, cook for 1-2 minutes and take off heat
3. Divide fish fillets on plates, drizzle butter sauce all over and serve

Nutrition: calories 300 - Fat 12 - Fiber 9 - Carbs 27 - Protein 24

26. Shrimp and Cauliflower

Prep.Time: 10 min - Cooking Time: 12 min - Servings: 2

Ingredients:
- ✓ 1 tablespoon butter
- ✓ Cooking spray
- ✓ 1 cauliflower head, riced
- ✓ 1 pound shrimp, peeled and deveined
- ✓ ¼ cup heavy cream
- ✓ 8 ounces mushrooms, roughly chopped
- ✓ A pinch of red pepper flakes
- ✓ Salt and black pepper to the taste
- ✓ 2 garlic cloves, minced
- ✓ 4 bacon slices, cooked and crumbled
- ✓ ½ cup beef stock
- ✓ 1 tablespoon parsley, finely chopped
- ✓ 1 tablespoon chives, chopped

Directions:
1. Season shrimp with salt and pepper, spray with cooking oil, place in your air fryer and cook at 360 degrees F for 7 minutes.
2. Meanwhile, heat up a pan with the butter over medium heat, add mushrooms, stir and cook for 3-4 minutes.
3. Add garlic, cauliflower rice, pepper flakes, stock, cream, chives, parsley, salt and pepper, stir, cook for a few minutes and take off heat.
4. Divide shrimp on plates, add cauliflower mix on the side, sprinkle bacon on top and serve.

Nutrition: calories 245 - Fat 7 - Fiber 4 - Carbs 6 - Protein 20

27. Tilapia and Chives Sauce

Prep.Time: 10 min - **Cooking Time:** 8 min - **Servings:** 4

Ingredients:
- ✓ 4 medium tilapia fillets
- ✓ Cooking spray
- ✓ Salt and black pepper to the taste
- ✓ 2 teaspoons honey
- ✓ ¼ cup Greek yogurt
- ✓ Juice from 1 lemon
- ✓ 2 tablespoons chives, chopped

Directions:
1. Season fish with salt and pepper, spray with cooking spray, place in preheated air fryer 350 degrees F and cook for 8 minutes, flipping halfway.
2. Meanwhile, in a bowl, mix yogurt with honey, salt, pepper, chives and lemon juice and whisk really well.
3. Divide air fryer fish on plates, drizzle yogurt sauce all over and serve right away.

Nutrition: calories 261 - Fat 8 - Fiber 18 - Carbs 24 - Protein 21

28. Salmon and Blackberry Glaze

Prep.Time: 10 min - **Cooking Time:** 33 min - **Servings:** 4

Ingredients:
- ✓ 1 cup water
- ✓ 1 inch ginger piece, grated
- ✓ Juice from ½ lemon
- ✓ 12 ounces blackberries
- ✓ 1 tablespoon olive oil
- ✓ ¼ cup sugar
- ✓ 4 medium salmon fillets, skinless
- ✓ Salt and black pepper to the taste

Directions:
1. Heat up a pot with the water over medium high heat, add ginger, lemon juice and blackberries, stir, bring to a boil, cook for 4-5 minutes, take off heat, strain into a bowl, return to pan and combine with sugar.
2. Stir this mix, bring to a simmer over medium low heat and cook for 20 minutes.
3. Leave blackberry sauce to cool down, brush salmon with it, season with salt and pepper, drizzle olive oil all over and rub fish well.
4. Place fish in your preheated air fryer at 350 degrees F and cook for 10 minutes, flipping fish fillets once.
5. Divide among plates, drizzle some of the remaining blackberry sauce all over and serve.

Nutrition: calories 312 - Fat 4 - Fiber 9 - Carbs 19 - Protein 14

29. Snapper Fillets and Veggies

Prep.Time: 10 min - **Cooking Time:** 14 minutes - **Servings:** 2

Ingredients:
- ✓ 2 red snapper fillets, boneless
- ✓ 1 tablespoon olive oil
- ✓ ½ cup red bell pepper, chopped
- ✓ ½ cup green bell pepper, chopped
- ✓ ½ cup leeks, chopped
- ✓ Salt and black pepper to the taste
- ✓ 1 teaspoon tarragon, dried
- ✓ A splash of white wine

Directions:
1. In a heat proof dish that fits your air fryer, mix fish fillets with salt, pepper, oil, green bell pepper, red bell pepper, leeks, tarragon and wine, toss well everything, introduce in preheated air fryer at 350 degrees F and cook for 14 minutes, flipping fish fillets halfway.
2. Divide fish and veggies on plates and serve warm.

Nutrition: calories 300 - Fat 12 - Fiber 8 - Carbs 29 - Protein 12

30. Mustard Salmon

Prep.Time: 10 min - **Cooking Time:** 10 min - **Servings:** 1

Ingredients:
- ✓ 1 big salmon fillet, boneless
- ✓ Salt and black pepper to the taste
- ✓ 2 tablespoons mustard
- ✓ 1 tablespoon coconut oil
- ✓ 1 tablespoon maple extract

Directions:
1. In a bowl, mix maple extract with mustard, whisk well, season salmon with salt and pepper and brush salmon with this mix.
2. Spray some cooking spray over fish, place in your air fryer and cook at 370 degrees F for 10 minutes, flipping halfway.
3. Serve with a tasty side salad.

Nutrition: calories 300 - Fat 7 - Fiber 14 - Carbs 16 - Protein 20

31. Crusted Salmon

Prep.Time: 10 min - **Cooking Time:** 10 min - **Servings:** 4

Ingredients:
- ✓ 1 cup pistachios, chopped
- ✓ 4 salmon fillets
- ✓ ¼ cup lemon juice
- ✓ 2 tablespoons honey
- ✓ 1 teaspoon dill, chopped
- ✓ Salt and black pepper to the taste
- ✓ 1 tablespoon mustard

Directions:
1. In a bowl, mix pistachios with mustard, honey, lemon juice, salt, black pepper and dill, whisk and spread over salmon.
2. Put in your air fryer and cook at 350 degrees F for 10 minutes.
3. Divide among plates and serve with a side salad.

Nutrition: calories 300 - Fat 17 - Fiber 12 - Carbs 20 - Protein 22

32. Salmon and Chives Vinaigrette

Prep.Time: 10 min - **Cooking Time:** 12 min - **Servings:** 4

Ingredients:
- ✓ 2 tablespoons dill, chopped
- ✓ 4 salmon fillets, boneless
- ✓ 2 tablespoons chives, chopped
- ✓ 1/3 cup maple syrup
- ✓ 1 tablespoon olive oil
- ✓ 3 tablespoons balsamic vinegar
- ✓ Salt and black pepper to the taste

Directions:
1. Season fish with salt and pepper, rub with the oil, place in your air fryer and cook at 350 degrees F for 8 minutes, flipping once.
2. Heat up a small pot with the vinegar over medium heat, add maple syrup, chives and dill, stir and cook for 3 minutes.
3. Divide fish on plates and serve with chives vinaigrette on top.

Nutrition: calories 270 - Fat 3 - Fiber 13 - Carbs 25 - Protein 10

33. Flavored Jamaican Salmon

Prep.Time: 10 min - **Cooking Time:** 10 min - **Servings:** 4

Ingredients:
- ✓ 2 teaspoons sriracha sauce
- ✓ 4 teaspoons sugar
- ✓ 3 scallions, chopped
- ✓ Salt and black pepper to the taste
- ✓ 2 teaspoons olive oil
- ✓ 4 teaspoons apple cider vinegar
- ✓ 3 teaspoons avocado oil
- ✓ 4 medium salmon fillets, boneless
- ✓ 4 cups baby arugula
- ✓ 2 cups cabbage, shredded
- ✓ 1 and ½ teaspoon Jamaican jerk seasoning
- ✓ ¼ cup pepitas, toasted
- ✓ 2 cups radish, julienned

Directions:
1. In a bowl, mix sriracha with sugar, whisk and transfer 2 teaspoons to another bowl.
2. Combine 2 teaspoons sriracha mix with the avocado oil, olive oil, vinegar, salt and pepper and whisk well.
3. Sprinkle jerk seasoning over salmon, rub with sriracha and sugar mix and season with salt and pepper.
4. Transfer to your air fryer and cook at 360 degrees F for 10 minutes, flipping once.
5. In a bowl, mix radishes with cabbage, arugula, salt, pepper, sriracha and vinegar mix and toss well.
6. Divide salmon and radish mix on plates, sprinkle pepitas and scallions on top and serve.

Nutrition: calories 290 - Fat 6 - Fiber 12 - Carbs 17 - Protein 10

34. Swordfish and Mango Salsa

Prep.Time: 10 min - **Cooking Time:** 6 min - **Servings:** 2

Ingredients:
- ✓ 2 medium swordfish steaks
- ✓ Salt and black pepper to the taste
- ✓ 2 teaspoons avocado oil
- ✓ 1 tablespoon cilantro, chopped
- ✓ 1 mango, chopped
- ✓ 1 avocado, pitted, peeled and chopped
- ✓ A pinch of cumin
- ✓ A pinch of onion powder
- ✓ A pinch of garlic powder
- ✓ 1 orange, peeled and sliced
- ✓ ½ tablespoon balsamic vinegar

Directions:
1. Season fish steaks with salt, pepper, garlic powder, onion powder and cumin and rub with half of the oil, place in your air fryer and cook at 360 degrees F for 6 minutes, flipping halfway.
2. Meanwhile, in a bowl, mix avocado with mango, cilantro, balsamic vinegar, salt, pepper and the rest of the oil and stir well.
3. Divide fish on plates, top with mango salsa and serve with orange slices on the side.

Nutrition: calories 200 - Fat 7 - Fiber 2 - Carbs 14 - Protein 14

35. Salmon and Lemon Relish

Prep.Time: 10 min - **Cooking Time:** 30 minutes - **Servings:** 2

Ingredients:
- ✓ 2 salmon fillets, boneless
- ✓ Salt and black pepper to the taste
- ✓ 1 tablespoon olive oil

For the relish:
- ✓ 1 tablespoon lemon juice
- ✓ 1 shallot, chopped
- ✓ 1 Meyer lemon, cut in wedges and then sliced
- ✓ 2 tablespoons parsley, chopped
- ✓ ¼ cup olive oil

Directions:
1. Season salmon with salt and pepper, rub with 1 tablespoon oil, place in your air fryer's basket and cook at 320 degrees F for 20 minutes, flipping the fish halfway.
2. Meanwhile, in a bowl, mix shallot with the lemon juice, a pinch of salt and black pepper, stir and leave aside for 10 minutes.
3. In a separate bowl, mix marinated shallot with lemon slices, salt, pepper, parsley and ¼ cup oil and whisk well.
4. Divide salmon on plates, top with lemon relish and serve.

Nutrition: calories 200 - Fat 3 - Fiber 3 - Carbs 23 - Protein 19

36. Chili Salmon

Prep.Time: 10 min - **Cooking Time:** 15 min - **Servings:** 12

Ingredients:
- ✓ 1 and ¼ cups coconut, shredded
- ✓ 1 pound salmon, cubed
- ✓ 1/3 cup flour
- ✓ A pinch of salt and black pepper
- ✓ 1 egg
- ✓ 2 tablespoons olive oil
- ✓ ¼ cup water
- ✓ 4 red chilies, chopped
- ✓ 3 garlic cloves, minced
- ✓ ¼ cup balsamic vinegar
- ✓ ½ cup honey

Directions:
1. In a bowl, mix flour with a pinch of salt and stir.
2. In another bowl, mix egg with black pepper and whisk.
3. Put coconut in a third bowl.
4. Dip salmon cubes in flour, egg and coconut, put them in your air fryer's basket, cook at 370 degrees F for 8 minutes, shaking halfway and divide among plates.
5. Heat up a pan with the water over medium high heat, add chilies, cloves, vinegar and honey, stir very well, bring to a boil, simmer for a couple of minutes, drizzle over salmon and serve.

Nutrition: calories 220 - Fat 12 - Fiber 2 - Carbs 14 - Protein 13

37. Chinese Cod

Prep.Time: 10 min - **Cooking Time:** 10 min - **Servings:** 2

Ingredients:
- ✓ 2 medium cod fillets, boneless
- ✓ 1 teaspoon peanuts, crushed
- ✓ 2 teaspoons garlic powder
- ✓ 1 tablespoon light soy sauce
- ✓ ½ teaspoon ginger, grated

Directions:
1. Put fish fillets in a heat proof dish that fits your air fryer, add garlic powder, soy sauce and ginger, toss well, put in your air fryer and cook at 350 degrees F for 10 minutes.
2. Divide fish on plates, sprinkle peanuts on top and serve.

Nutrition: calories 254 - Fat 10 - Fiber 11 - Carbs 14 - Protein 23

38. Cod with Pearl Onions

Prep.Time: 10 min - **Cooking Time:** 15 min - **Servings:** 2

Ingredients:
- ✓ 14 ounces pearl onions
- ✓ 2 medium cod fillets
- ✓ 1 tablespoon parsley, dried
- ✓ 1 teaspoon thyme, dried
- ✓ Black pepper to the taste
- ✓ 8 ounces mushrooms, sliced

Directions:
1. Put fish in a heat proof dish that fits your air fryer, add onions, parsley, mushrooms, thyme and black pepper, toss well, put in your air fryer and cook at 350 degrees F and cook for 15 minutes.
2. Divide everything on plates and serve.

Nutrition: calories 270 - Fat 14 - Fiber 8 - Carbs 14 - Protein 22

39. Hawaiian Salmon

Prep.Time: 10 min - Cooking Time: 10 min - Servings: 2

Ingredients:
- ✓ 20 ounces canned pineapple pieces and juice
- ✓ ½ teaspoon ginger, grated
- ✓ 2 teaspoons garlic powder
- ✓ 1 teaspoon onion powder
- ✓ 1 tablespoon balsamic vinegar
- ✓ 2 medium salmon fillets, boneless
- ✓ Salt and black pepper to the taste

Directions:
1. Season salmon with garlic powder, onion powder, salt and black pepper, rub well, transfer to a heat proof dish that fits your air fryer, add ginger and pineapple chunks and toss them really gently.
2. Drizzle the vinegar all over, put in your air fryer and cook at 350 degrees F for 10 minutes.
3. Divide everything on plates and serve.

Nutrition: calories 200 - Fat 8 - Fiber 12 - Carbs 17 - Protein 20

40. Marinated Salmon

Prep.Time: 60 min - Cooking Time: 20 min - Servings: 6

Ingredients:
- ✓ 1 whole salmon
- ✓ 1 tablespoon dill, chopped
- ✓ 1 tablespoon tarragon, chopped
- ✓ 1 tablespoon garlic, minced
- ✓ Juice from 2 lemons
- ✓ 1 lemon, sliced
- ✓ A pinch of salt and black pepper

Directions:
1. In a large bowl, mix fish with salt, pepper and lemon juice, toss well and keep in the fridge for 1 hour.
2. Stuff salmon with garlic and lemon slices, place in your air fryer's basket and cook at 320 degrees F for 25 minutes.
3. Divide among plates and serve with a tasty coleslaw on the side.

Nutrition: calories 300 - Fat 8 - Fiber 9 - Carbs 19 - Protein 27

41. Air Fried Branzino

Prep.Time: 10 min - Cooking Time: 10 minutes - Servings: 4

Ingredients:
- ✓ Zest from 1 lemon, grated
- ✓ Zest from 1 orange, grated
- ✓ Juice from ½ lemon
- ✓ Juice from ½ orange
- ✓ Salt and black pepper to the taste
- ✓ 4 medium branzino fillets, boneless
- ✓ ½ cup parsley, chopped
- ✓ 2 tablespoons olive oil
- ✓ A pinch of red pepper flakes, crushed

Directions:
1. In a large bowl, mix fish fillets with lemon zest, orange zest, lemon juice, orange juice, salt, pepper, oil and pepper flakes, toss really well, transfer fillets to your preheated air fryer at 350 degrees F and bake for 10 minutes, flipping fillets once.
2. Divide fish on plates, sprinkle with parsley and serve right away.

Nutrition: calories 261 - Fat 8 - Fiber 12 - Carbs 21 - Protein 12

42. Coconut Tilapia

Prep.Time: 10 min - Cooking Time: 10 min - Servings: 4

Ingredients:
- ✓ 4 medium tilapia fillets
- ✓ Salt and black pepper to the taste
- ✓ ½ cup coconut milk
- ✓ 1 teaspoon ginger, grated
- ✓ ½ cup cilantro, chopped
- ✓ 2 garlic cloves, chopped
- ✓ ½ teaspoon garam masala
- ✓ Cooking spray
- ✓ ½ jalapeno, chopped

Directions:
1. In your food processor, mix coconut milk with salt, pepper, cilantro, ginger, garlic, jalapeno and garam masala and pulse really well.
2. Spray fish with cooking spray, spread coconut mix all over, rub well, transfer to your air fryer's basket and cook at 400 degrees F for 10 minutes.
3. Divide among plates and serve hot.

Nutrition: calories 200 - Fat 5 - Fiber 6 - Carbs 25 - Protein 26

43. Spanish Salmon

Prep.Time: 10 min - Cooking Time: 15 min - Servings: 6

Ingredients:
- ✓ 2 cups bread croutons
- ✓ 3 red onions, cut into medium wedges
- ✓ ¾ cup green olives, pitted
- ✓ 3 red bell peppers, cut into medium wedges
- ✓ ½ teaspoon smoked paprika
- ✓ Salt and black pepper to the taste
- ✓ 5 tablespoons olive oil
- ✓ 6 medium salmon fillets, skinless and boneless
- ✓ 2 tablespoons parsley, chopped

Directions:
1. In a heat proof dish that fits your air fryer, mix bread croutons with onion wedges, bell pepper ones, olives, salt, pepper, paprika and 3 tablespoons olive oil, toss well, place in your air fryer and cook at 356 degrees F for 7 minutes.
2. Rub salmon with the rest of the oil, add over veggies and cook at 360 degrees F for 8 minutes.
3. Divide fish and veggie mix on plates, sprinkle parsley all over and serve.

Nutrition: calories 321 - Fat 8 - Fiber 14 - Carbs 27 - Protein 22

44. Halibut and Sun Dried Tomatoes Mix

Prep.Time: 10 min - Cooking Time: 10 min - Servings: 2

Ingredients:
- ✓ 2 medium halibut fillets
- ✓ 2 garlic cloves, minced
- ✓ 2 teaspoons olive oil
- ✓ Salt and black pepper to the taste
- ✓ 6 sun dried tomatoes, chopped
- ✓ 2 small red onions, sliced
- ✓ 1 fennel bulb, sliced
- ✓ 9 black olives, pitted and sliced
- ✓ 4 rosemary springs, chopped
- ✓ ½ teaspoon red pepper flakes, crushed

Directions:
1. Season fish with salt, pepper, rub with garlic and oil and put in a heat proof dish that fits your air fryer.
2. Add onion slices, sun dried tomatoes, fennel, olives, rosemary and sprinkle pepper flakes, transfer to your air fryer and cook at 380 degrees F for 10 minutes.
3. Divide fish and veggies on plates and serve.

Nutrition: calories 300 - Fat 12 - Fiber 9 - Carbs 18 - Protein 30

45. Roasted Cod and Prosciutto

Prep.Time: 10 min - **Cooking Time:** 10 min - **Servings:** 4

Ingredients:
- ✓ 1 tbsp parsley, chopped
- ✓ 4 medium cod filets
- ✓ ¼ cup butter, melted
- ✓ 2 garlic cloves, minced
- ✓ 2 tbsp lemon juice
- ✓ 3 tbsp prosciutto, chopped
- ✓ 1 teaspoon Dijon mustard
- ✓ 1 shallot, chopped
- ✓ Salt and black pepper to the taste

Directions:
1. In a bowl, mix mustard with butter, garlic, parsley, shallot, lemon juice, prosciutto, salt and pepper and whisk well.
2. Season fish with salt and pepper, spread prosciutto mix all over, put in your air fryer and cook at 390 degrees F for 10 minutes.
3. Divide among plates and serve.

Nutrition: calories 200 - Fat 4 - Fiber 7 - Carbs 12 - Protein 6

46. Stuffed Calamari

Prep.Time: 10 min - **Cooking Time:** 25 min - **Servings:** 4

Ingredients:
- ✓ 4 big calamari, tentacles separated and chopped and tubes reserved
- ✓ 2 tbsp parsley, chopped
- ✓ 5 ounces kale, chopped
- ✓ 2 garlic cloves, minced
- ✓ 1 red bell pepper, chopped
- ✓ 1 tablespoon olive oil
- ✓ 2 ounces canned tomato puree
- ✓ 1 yellow onion, chopped
- ✓ Salt and black pepper to the taste

Directions:
1. Heat up a pan with the oil over medium heat, add onion and garlic, stir and cook for 2 minutes.
2. Add bell pepper, tomato puree, calamari tentacles, kale, salt and pepper, stir, cook for 10 minutes and take off heat. stir and cook for 3 minutes.
3. Stuff calamari tubes with this mix, secure with toothpicks, put in your air fryer and cook at 360 degrees F for 20 minutes.
4. Divide calamari on plates, sprinkle parsley all over and serve.

Nutrition: calories 322 - Fat 10 - Fiber 14 - Carbs 14 - Protein 22

47. Salmon and Avocado Sauce

Prep.Time: 10 min - **Cooking Time:** 10 minutes - **Servings:** 4

Ingredients:
- ✓ 1 avocado, pitted, peeled and chopped
- ✓ 4 salmon fillets, boneless
- ✓ ¼ cup cilantro, chopped
- ✓ 1/3 cup coconut milk
- ✓ 1 tablespoon lime juice
- ✓ 1 tbsp lime zest, grated
- ✓ 1 teaspoon onion powder
- ✓ 1 teaspoon garlic powder
- ✓ Salt and black pepper to the taste

Directions:
1. Season salmon fillets with salt, black pepper and lime zest, rub well, put in your air fryer, cook at 350 degrees F for 9 minutes, flipping once and divide among plates.
2. In your food processor, mix avocado with cilantro, garlic powder, onion powder, lime juice, salt, pepper and coconut milk, blend well, drizzle over salmon and serve right away.

Nutrition: calories 260 - Fat 7 - Fiber 20 - Carbs 28 - Protein 18

48. Salmon and Orange Marmalade

Prep.Time: 10 min - **Cooking Time:** 15 min - **Servings:** 4

Ingredients:
- ✓ 1 pound wild salmon, skinless, boneless and cubed
- ✓ 2 lemons, sliced
- ✓ ¼ cup balsamic vinegar
- ✓ ¼ cup orange juice
- ✓ 1/3 cup orange marmalade
- ✓ A pinch of salt and black pepper

Directions:
1. Heat up a pot with the vinegar over medium heat, add marmalade and orange juice, stir, bring to a simmer, cook for 1 minute and take off heat.
2. Thread salmon cubes and lemon slices on skewers, season with salt and black pepper, brush them with half of the orange marmalade mix, arrange in your air fryer's basket and cook at 360 degrees F for 3 minutes on each side.
3. Brush skewers with the rest of the vinegar mix, divide among plates and serve right away with a side salad.

Nutrition: calories 240 - Fat 9 - Fiber 12 - Carbs 14 - Protein 10

49. Delicious Red Snapper

Prep.Time: 30 min - **Cooking Time:** 15 min - **Servings:** 4

Ingredients:
- ✓ 1 big red snapper, cleaned and scored
- ✓ Salt and black pepper
- ✓ 3 garlic cloves, minced
- ✓ 1 jalapeno, chopped
- ✓ ¼ pound okra, chopped
- ✓ 1 tablespoon butter
- ✓ 2 tablespoons olive oil
- ✓ 1 red bell pepper, chopped
- ✓ 2 tablespoons white wine
- ✓ 2 tbsp parsley, chopped

Directions:
1. In a bowl, mix jalapeno, wine with garlic, stir well and rub snapper with this mix. Season fish with salt and pepper and leave it aside for 30 minutes.
2. Meanwhile, heat up a pan with 1 tablespoon butter over medium heat, add bell pepper and okra, stir and cook for 5 minutes. Stuff red snapper's belly with this mix, also add parsley and rub with the olive oil.
3. Place in preheated air fryer and cook at 400 degrees F for 15 minutes, flipping the fish halfway.
4. Divide among plates and serve.

Nutrition: calories 261 - Fat 7 - Fiber 18 - Carbs 28 - Protein 18

50. Tasty Pollock

Prep.Time: 10 min - **Cooking Time:** 15 min - **Servings:** 6

Ingredients:
- ✓ ½ cup sour cream
- ✓ 4 Pollock fillets, boneless
- ✓ ¼ cup parmesan, grated
- ✓ 2 tablespoons butter, melted
- ✓ Salt and black pepper to the taste
- ✓ Cooking spray

Directions:
1. In a bowl, mix sour cream with butter, parmesan, salt and pepper and whisk well.
2. Spray fish with cooking spray and season with salt and pepper.
3. Spread sour cream mix on one side of each Pollock fillet, arrange them in your preheated air fryer at 320 degrees F and cook them for 15 minutes.
4. Divide Pollock fillets on plates and serve with a tasty side salad.

Nutrition: calories 300 - Fat 13 - Fiber 3 - Carbs 14 - Protein 44

51. Honey Sea Bass

Prep.Time: 10 min - **Cooking Time:** 10 min - **Servings:** 2

Ingredients:
- ✓ 2 sea bass fillets
- ✓ Zest from ½ orange, grated
- ✓ Juice from ½ orange
- ✓ A pinch of salt and black pepper
- ✓ 2 tablespoons mustard
- ✓ 2 teaspoons honey
- ✓ 2 tablespoons olive oil
- ✓ ½ pound canned lentils, drained
- ✓ A small bunch of dill, chopped
- ✓ 2 ounces watercress
- ✓ A small bunch of parsley, chopped

Directions:
1. Season fish fillets with salt and pepper, add orange zest and juice, rub with 1 tablespoon oil, with honey and mustard, rub, transfer to your air fryer and cook at 350 degrees F for 10 minutes, flipping halfway.
2. Meanwhile, put lentils in a small pot, warm it up over medium heat, add the rest of the oil, watercress, dill and parsley, stir well and divide among plates.
3. Add fish fillets and serve right away.

Nutrition: calories 212 - Fat 8 - Fiber 12 - Carbs 9 - Protein 17

52. Special Catfish Fillets

Prep.Time: 10 min - **Cooking Time:** 12 min - **Servings:** 4

Ingredients:
- ✓ 2 catfish fillets
- ✓ ½ teaspoon garlic, minced
- ✓ 2 ounces butter
- ✓ 4 ounces Worcestershire sauce
- ✓ ½ teaspoon jerk seasoning
- ✓ 1 teaspoon mustard
- ✓ 1 tablespoon balsamic vinegar
- ✓ ¾ cup catsup
- ✓ Salt and black pepper to the taste
- ✓ 1 tablespoon parsley, chopped

Directions:
1. Heat up a pan with the butter over medium heat, add Worcestershire sauce, garlic, jerk seasoning, mustard, catsup, vinegar, salt and pepper, stir well, take off heat and add fish fillets.
2. Toss well, leave aside for 10 minutes, drain fillets, transfer them to your preheated air fryer's basket at 350 degrees F and cook for 8 minutes, flipping fillets halfway.
3. Divide among plates, sprinkle parsley on top and serve right away.

Nutrition: calories 351 - Fat 8 - Fiber 16 - Carbs 27 - Protein 17

53. Delicious French Cod

Prep.Time: 10 min - **Cooking Time:** 22 minutes - **Servings:** 4

Ingredients:
- ✓ 2 tablespoons olive oil
- ✓ 1 yellow onion, chopped
- ✓ ½ cup white wine
- ✓ 2 garlic cloves, minced
- ✓ 14 ounces canned tomatoes, stewed
- ✓ 3 tablespoons parsley, chopped
- ✓ 2 pounds cod, boneless
- ✓ Salt and black pepper to the taste
- ✓ 2 tablespoons butter

Directions:
1. Heat up a pan with the oil over medium heat, add garlic and onion, stir and cook for 5 minutes.
2. Add wine, stir and cook for 1 minute more.
3. Add tomatoes, stir, bring to a boil, cook for 2 minutes, add parsley, stir again and take off heat.
4. Pour this mix into a heat proof dish that fits your air fryer, add fish, season it with salt and pepper and cook in your fryer at 350 degrees F for 14 minutes.
5. Divide fish and tomatoes mix on plates and serve.

Nutrition: calories 231 - Fat 8 - Fiber 12 - Carbs 26 - Protein 14

54. Oriental Fish

Prep.Time: 10 min - **Cooking Time:** 12 min - **Servings:** 4

Ingredients:
- ✓ 2 pounds red snapper fillets, boneless
- ✓ Salt and black pepper to the taste
- ✓ 3 garlic cloves, minced
- ✓ 1 yellow onion, chopped
- ✓ 1 tablespoon tamarind paste
- ✓ 1 tablespoon oriental sesame oil
- ✓ 1 tablespoon ginger, grated
- ✓ 2 tablespoons water
- ✓ ½ teaspoon cumin, ground
- ✓ 1 tablespoon lemon juice
- ✓ 3 tablespoons mint, chopped

Directions:
1. In your food processor, mix garlic with onion, salt, pepper, tamarind paste, sesame oil, ginger, water and cumin, pulse well and rub fish with this mix.
2. Place fish in your preheated air fryer at 320 degrees F and cook for 12 minutes, flipping fish halfway.
3. Divide fish on plates, drizzle lemon juice all over, sprinkle mint and serve right away.

Nutrition: calories 241 - Fat 8 - Fiber 16 - Carbs 17 - Protein 12

55. Cajun Air fryer toast oven Salmon

Prep.Time: 10 min - **Cooking Time:** 10 min - **Servings:** 2

Ingredients:
- ✓ 2 (6 ounce each) skin-on salmon fillets
- ✓ 1 teaspoon brown sugar
- ✓ 1 tablespoon Cajun seasoning

Directions:
1. Preheat your air fryer toast oven to 390 F.
2.
3. Spray the salmon fillets with cooking spray; mix brown sugar and Cajun seasoning in a bowl and sprinkle the fillets with the mixture until well coated.
4. Coat the fryer basket with cooking spray and place the fish inside skin side down.
5. Cook for 10 minutes and then remove to a plate to rest before serving.

56. Cajun Shrimp

Prep.Time: 20 min - **Cooking Time:** 5 min - **Servings:** 4

Ingredients:
- ✓ 1 lb shrimp
- ✓ 2 tbsp parmesan cheese, grated
- ✓ 1 tsp garlic, minced
- ✓ ½ cup breadcrumbs
- ✓ 1 tsp olive oil
- ✓ 1 tbsp Cajun seasoning

Directions:
1. In a mixing bowl, mix together parmesan cheese, garlic, breadcrumbs, olive oil, and Cajun seasoning.
2. Add shrimp and toss until well coated.
3. Arrange shrimp on instant vortex air fryer oven tray and air fry at 390 F for 5 minutes.
4. Serve and enjoy.

57. Salmon and Avocado Salad

Prep.Time: 10 min - **Cooking Time:** 20 min - **Servings:** 4

Ingredients:
- ✓ 2 medium salmon fillets
- ✓ ¼ cup melted butter
- ✓ 4 ounces mushrooms, sliced
- ✓ Sea salt and black pepper to the taste
- ✓ 12 cherry tomatoes, halved
- ✓ 2 tablespoons olive oil
- ✓ 8 ounces lettuce leaves, torn
- ✓ 1 avocado, pitted, peeled and cubed
- ✓ 1 jalapeno pepper, chopped
- ✓ 5 cilantro springs, chopped
- ✓ 2 tablespoons white wine vinegar
- ✓ 1 ounce feta cheese, crumbled

Directions:
1. Place salmon on a lined baking sheet, brush with 2 tablespoons melted butter, season with salt and pepper, broil for 15 minutes over medium heat and then keep warm.
2. Meanwhile, heat up a pan with the rest of the butter over medium heat, add mushrooms, stir and cook for a few minutes.
3. Put tomatoes in a bowl, add salt, pepper and 1 tablespoon olive oil and toss to coat.
4. In a salad bowl, mix salmon with mushrooms, lettuce, avocado, tomatoes, jalapeno and cilantro.
5. Add the rest of the oil, vinegar, salt and pepper, sprinkle cheese on top and serve.

Nutrition: calories 235 - Fat 6 - Fiber 8 - Carbs 19 - Protein 5

58. Salmon and Greek Yogurt Sauce

Prep.Time: 10 min - **Cooking Time:** 20 min - **Servings:** 2

Ingredients:
- ✓ 2 medium salmon fillets
- ✓ 1 tablespoon basil, chopped
- ✓ 6 lemon slices
- ✓ Sea salt and black pepper to the taste
- ✓ 1 cup Greek yogurt
- ✓ 2 teaspoons curry powder
- ✓ A pinch of cayenne pepper
- ✓ 1 garlic clove, minced
- ✓ ½ teaspoon cilantro, chopped
- ✓ ½ teaspoon mint, chopped

Directions:
1. Place each salmon fillet on a parchment paper piece, make 3 splits in each and stuff them with basil.
2. Season with salt and pepper, top each fillet with 3 lemon slices, fold parchment, seal edges, introduce in the oven at 400 degrees F and bake for 20 minutes.
3. Meanwhile, in a bowl, mix yogurt with cayenne pepper, salt to the taste, garlic, curry, mint and cilantro and whisk well.
4. Transfer fish to plates, drizzle the yogurt sauce you've just prepared on top and serve right away.

Nutrition: calories 242 - Fat 1 - Fiber 2 - Carbs 3 - Protein 3

59. Special Salmon

Prep.Time: 10 min - **Cooking Time:** 25 minutes - **Servings:** 4

Ingredients:
- ✓ 1 pound medium beets, sliced
- ✓ 6 tablespoons olive oil
- ✓ 1 and ½ pounds salmon fillets, skinless and boneless
- ✓ Salt and pepper to the taste
- ✓ 1 tablespoon chives, chopped
- ✓ 1 tablespoon parsley, chopped
- ✓ 1 tablespoon fresh tarragon, chopped
- ✓ 3 tablespoon shallots, chopped
- ✓ 1 tablespoon grated lemon zest
- ✓ ¼ cup lemon juice
- ✓ 4 cups mixed baby greens

Directions:
1. In a bowl, mix beets with ½ tablespoon oil and toss to coat.
2. Season them with salt and pepper, arrange them on a baking sheet, introduce in the oven at 450 degrees F and bake for 20 minutes.
3. Take beets out of the oven, add salmon on top, brush it with the rest if the oil and season with salt and pepper.
4. In a bowl, mix chives with parsley and tarragon and sprinkle 1 tablespoon of this mix over salmon.
5. Introduce in the oven again and bake for 15 minutes.
6. Meanwhile, in a boil with shallots with lemon peel, salt, pepper and lemon juice and the rest of the herbs mixture and stir gently.
7. Combine 2 tablespoons of shallots dressing with mixed greens and toss gently.
8. Take salmon out of the oven, arrange on plates, add beets and greens on the side, drizzle the rest of the shallot dressing on top and serve right away.

Nutrition: calories 312 - Fat 2 - Fiber 2 - Carbs 2 - Protein 4

60. Lemon Sole and Swiss Chard

Prep.Time: 10 min - **Cooking Time:** 14 min - **Servings:** 4

Ingredients:
- ✓ 1 teaspoon lemon zest, grated
- ✓ 4 white bread slices, quartered
- ✓ ¼ cup walnuts, chopped
- ✓ ¼ cup parmesan, grated
- ✓ 4 tablespoons olive oil
- ✓ 4 sole fillets, boneless
- ✓ Salt and black pepper to the taste
- ✓ 4 tablespoons butter
- ✓ ¼ cup lemon juice
- ✓ 3 tablespoons capers
- ✓ 2 garlic cloves, minced
- ✓ 2 bunches Swiss chard, chopped

Directions:
1. In your food processor, mix bread with walnuts, cheese and lemon zest and pulse well.
2. Add half of the olive oil, pulse really well again and leave aside for now.
3. Heat up a pan with the butter over medium heat, add lemon juice, salt, pepper and capers, stir well, add fish and toss it.
4. Transfer fish to your preheated air fryer's basket, top with bread mix you've made at the beginning and cook at 350 degrees F for 14 minutes.
5. Meanwhile, heat up another pan with the rest of the oil, add garlic, Swiss chard, salt and pepper, stir gently, cook for 2 minutes and take off heat.
6. Divide fish on plates and serve with sautéed chard on the side.

Nutrition: calories 321 - Fat 7 - Fiber 18 - Carbs 27 - Protein 12

61. Fish and Couscous

Prep.Time: 10 min - **Cooking Time:** 15 min - **Servings:** 4

Ingredients:
- ✓ 2 red onions, chopped
- ✓ Cooking spray
- ✓ 2 small fennel bulbs, cored and sliced
- ✓ ¼ cup almonds, toasted and sliced
- ✓ Salt and black pepper to the taste
- ✓ 2 and ½ pounds sea bass, gutted
- ✓ 5 teaspoons fennel seeds
- ✓ ¾ cup whole wheat couscous, cooked

Directions:
1. Season fish with salt and pepper, spray with cooking spray, place in your air fryer and cook at 350 degrees F for 10 minutes.
2. Meanwhile, spray a pan with some cooking oil and heat it up over medium heat.
3. Add fennel seeds to this pan, stir and toast them for 1 minute.
4. Add onion, salt, pepper, fennel bulbs, almonds and couscous, stir, cook for 2-3 minutes and divide among plates.
5. Add fish next to couscous mix and serve right away.

Nutrition: calories 354 - Fat 7 - Fiber 10 - Carbs 20 - Protein 30

62. Black Cod and Plum Sauce

Prep.Time: 10 min - **Cooking Time:** 15 min - **Servings:** 2

Ingredients:
- ✓ 1 egg white
- ✓ ½ cup red quinoa, already cooked
- ✓ 2 teaspoons whole wheat flour
- ✓ 4 teaspoons lemon juice
- ✓ ½ teaspoon smoked paprika
- ✓ 1 teaspoon olive oil
- ✓ 2 medium black cod fillets, skinless and boneless
- ✓ 1 red plum, pitted and chopped
- ✓ 2 teaspoons raw honey
- ✓ ¼ teaspoon black peppercorns, crushed
- ✓ 2 teaspoons parsley
- ✓ ¼ cup water

Directions:
1. In a bowl, mix 1 teaspoon lemon juice with egg white, flour and ¼ teaspoon paprika and whisk well.
2. Put quinoa in a bowl and mix it with 1/3 of egg white mix.
3. Put the fish into the bowl with the remaining egg white mix and toss to coat.
4. Dip fish in quinoa mix, coat well and leave aside for 10 minutes.
5. Heat up a pan with 1 teaspoon oil over medium heat, add peppercorns, honey and plum, stir, bring to a simmer and cook for 1 minute.
6. Add the rest of the lemon juice, the rest of the paprika and the water, stir well and simmer for 5 minutes.
7. Add parsley, stir, take sauce off heat and leave aside for now.
8. Put fish in your air fryer and cook at 380 degrees F for 10 minutes
9. Arrange fish on plates, drizzle plum sauce on top and serve.

Nutrition: calories 324 - Fat 14 - Fiber 22 - Carbs 27 - Protein 22

63. Simple Fried Catfish

Prep.Time: 25 min - **Cooking Time:** 25 minutes - **Servings:** 3

Ingredients:
- ✓ 3 medium catfish fillets
- ✓ 1 tbsp. extra virgin olive oil
- ✓ ¼ cup fish fry seasoning of choice
- ✓ 2 tbsp. finely chopped fresh parsley for serving

Directions:
1. Start by setting your air fryer toast oven to 400 degrees F.
2. Rinse the fillets under tap water and pat dry using a kitchen towel.
3. In a large Ziploc bag, pour in the fish fry seasoning and add in one fish fillet and shake well to ensure it's coated on all sides the place it on a plate. Do this for the remaining fillets.
4. Gently brush olive on all the seasoned fillets and arrange them on your air fryer toast oven's basket. (Cook in batches if they can't all fit)
5. Cook for 10 minutes then turn the fillets and cook for an additional 10 minutes or until golden brown.
6. You can cook for a further 3-5 minutes for a crispier crust.
7. Serve hot and sprinkle with the Parsley. Enjoy!

64. Shrimp Scampi

Prep.Time: 10 min - **Cooking Time:** 10 min - **Servings:** 2

Ingredients:
- ✓ 1 lb shrimp
- ✓ 1 cup breadcrumbs
- ✓ ¼ tsp onion powder
- ✓ ¼ tsp paprika
- ✓ ¼ tsp cayenne pepper
- ✓ ¼ cup white wine
- ✓ 3 garlic cloves, minced
- ✓ 8 tbsp butter
- ✓ ½ tsp salt

Directions:
1. In a bowl, mix together breadcrumbs, onion powder, paprika, cayenne pepper, and salt. Set aside.
2. Melt butter in a pan over medium heat.
3. Add white wine and garlic in melted butter and stir well.
4. Remove pan from heat. Add breadcrumbs and shrimp in melted butter mixture and stir everything well and transfer to a baking dish.
5. Air fry at 350 F for 10 minutes.
6. Serve and enjoy.

65. Coconut Coated Shrimp with Spicy Dip

Prep.Time: 10 min - **Cooking Time:** 20 min - **Servings:** 4

Ingredients:

For the coconut coated shrimp:
- ✓ 8 jumbo shrimp, shelled, deveined and thoroughly cleaned
- ✓ 1 can (225g) coconut milk
- ✓ ½ cup panko bread crumbs
- ✓ ½ cup sweetened grated coconut
- ✓ ¼ tsp. freshly ground pepper, divided
- ✓ ½ tsp. cayenne pepper, divided
- ✓ ½ tsp. sea salt, divided

For the spicy dip:
- ✓ ½ cup orange marmalade
- ✓ 1 tsp. mustard
- ✓ 1 tbsp. pure honey
- ✓ ¼ tsp. tabasco or hot sauce of choice

Directions:

1. Mix the coconut milk with part of the cayenne, salt and ground pepper in a medium bowl until well blended and set aside.
2. Next, combine the shredded coconut, bread crumbs and the remaining salt, cayenne and ground pepper.
3. Dunk the jumbo shrimp, one at a time, roll in the bread crumb mix then gently place in the basket of your air fryer toast oven. Repeat this process for all your shrimp.
4. Set your air fryer toast oven to 350 degrees F and cook for 20 minutes, turning the shrimp halfway though.
5. Meanwhile, combine all the spicy dip ingredients in a small bowl.
6. Serve hot with the marmalade dip.
7. Enjoy!

66. Cajun Shrimp

Prep.Time: 20 min - **Cooking Time:** 5 min - **Servings:** 2

Ingredients:
- ✓ 1 lb shrimp
- ✓ 2 tbsp parmesan cheese, grated
- ✓ 1 tsp garlic, minced
- ✓ ½ cup breadcrumbs
- ✓ 1 tsp olive oil
- ✓ 1 tbsp Cajun seasoning

Directions:

1. In a mixing bowl, mix together parmesan cheese, garlic, breadcrumbs, olive oil, and Cajun seasoning.
2. Add shrimp and toss until well coated.
3. Arrange shrimp on instant vortex air fryer oven tray and air fry at 390 F for 5 minutes.
4. Serve and enjoy.

67. Dijon Garlic Salmon

Prep.Time: 10 min - **Cooking Time:** 15 minutes - **Servings:** 2

Ingredients:
- ✓ 1 ½ lb salmon fillets
- ✓ ½ tbsp Dijon mustard
- ✓ 1 tbsp garlic, minced
- ✓ 2 tbsp fresh lemon juice
- ✓ 2 tbsp olive oil
- ✓ 2 tbsp fresh parsley, chopped
- ✓ 1/8 tsp pepper
- ✓ ½ tsp salt

Directions:

1. Preheat the instant vortex air fryer to 400 F.
2. In a small bowl, mix together Dijon mustard, garlic, lemon juice, olive oil, parsley, pepper, and salt.
3. Arrange salmon fillets on instant vortex air fryer oven tray.
4. Spread marinade over salmon fillets.
5. Bake salmon for 12-15 minutes.
6. Serve and enjoy.

68. Lemon Pepper Shrimp

Prep.Time: 10 min - **Cooking Time:** 8 min - **Servings:** 2

Ingredients:
- ✓ 12 oz shrimp, peeled and deveined
- ✓ ¼ tsp garlic powder
- ✓ ¼ tsp paprika
- ✓ 1 tsp lemon pepper
- ✓ 1 fresh lemon juice
- ✓ ½ tbsp olive oil

Directions:

1. In a mixing bowl, mix together garlic powder, paprika, lemon pepper, lemon juice, and olive oil.
2. Add shrimp and toss until shrimp is well coated.
3. Transfer shrimp on instant vortex air fryer tray and air fry at 400 F for 6-8 minutes or until firm.
4. Serve and enjoy.

69. Crispy Coconut Shrimp

Prep.Time: 10 min - **Cooking Time:** 12 min - **Servings:** 2

Ingredients:
- ✓ 1 lb shrimp, peeled and deveined
- ✓ ½ cup shredded coconut
- ✓ 1 cup breadcrumbs
- ✓ 2 egg whites, lightly beaten
- ✓ ½ cup flour
- ✓ Pepper
- ✓ Salt

Directions:
1. In a shallow dish, mix together flour, pepper, and salt.
2. In a second shallow dish add egg whites.
3. In a third shallow dish, mix together breadcrumbs, shredded coconut, and salt.
4. Coat shrimp with flour mixture then coat with egg mixture and finally coat with breadcrumb mixture.
5. Arrange shrimp on instant vortex air fryer tray.
6. Air fry at 400 F for 6 minutes.
7. Turn shrimp to the other side and air fry for 6 minutes more.
8. Serve and enjoy.

70. Delicious Tilapia

Prep.Time: 10 min - **Cooking Time:** 8 min - **Servings:** 4

Ingredients:
- ✓ 4 tilapia fillets
- ✓ ¼ tsp cayenne pepper
- ✓ ½ tsp cumin
- ✓ 1 tsp garlic powder
- ✓ 1 tsp dried oregano
- ✓ 2 tsp brown sugar
- ✓ 1 ½ tbsp paprika
- ✓ 1 tsp salt

Directions:
1. In a small bowl, mix together paprika, cayenne pepper, cumin, garlic powder, oregano, brown sugar, and salt and rub onto the fish fillets.
2. Spray fish fillets with cooking spray.
3. Arrange fish fillets on instant vortex air fryer tray and air fry at 400 F for 4 minutes.
4. Turn fish fillets to the other side and air fry for 4 minutes more.
5. Serve and enjoy.

71. Easy Air Fryer Scallops

Prep.Time: 10 min - **Cooking Time:** 4 minutes - **Servings:** 2

Ingredients:
- ✓ 8 scallops
- ✓ Pepper
- ✓ Salt

Directions:
1. Arrange scallops on instant vortex air fryer tray.
2. Spray scallops with cooking spray and season with pepper and salt.
3. Air fry scallops at 390 F for 2 minutes.
4. Turn scallops to the other side and air fry for 2 minutes more.
5. Serve and enjoy.

72. Flavorful Crab Cake

Prep.Time: 10 min - **Cooking Time:** 10 min - **Servings:** 4

Ingredients:
- ✓ 8 oz lump crab meat
- ✓ 1 tsp old bay seasoning
- ✓ ½ tbsp Dijon mustard
- ✓ 2 tbsp breadcrumbs
- ✓ 1 ½ tbsp mayonnaise
- ✓ 2 tbsp green onion, chopped
- ✓ ¼ cup bell pepper, chopped

Directions:
1. Add all ingredients into the mixing bowl and mix until well combined.
2. Make four even shape patties of bowl mixture and place on an instant vortex air fryer tray.
3. Lightly spray patties with a cooking spray.
4. Air fry at 370 F for 10 minutes.
5. Serve and enjoy.

73. Cajun Air Fryer Toast Oven Salmon

Prep.Time: 10 min - **Cooking Time:** 10 min - **Servings:** 2

Ingredients:
- ✓ 2 (6 ounce each) skin-on salmon fillets
- ✓ 1 teaspoon brown sugar
- ✓ 1 tablespoon Cajun seasoning

Directions:
1. Preheat your air fryer toast oven to 390 F.
2. Spray the salmon fillets with cooking spray; mix brown sugar and Cajun seasoning in a bowl and sprinkle the fillets with the mixture until well coated.
3. Coat the fryer basket with cooking spray and place the fish inside skin side down.
4. Cook for 10 minutes and then remove to a plate to rest before serving.

74. Shrimp Momos

Prep.Time: 20 min - **Cooking Time:** 20 min - **Servings:** 4

Ingredients:

For dough:
- ✓ 1 ½ cup all-purpose flour
- ✓ ½ tsp. salt
- ✓ 5 tbsp. water

For filling:
- ✓ 2 cups minced shrimp
- ✓ 2 tbsp. oil
- ✓ 2 tsp. ginger-garlic paste
- ✓ 2 tsp. soya sauce
- ✓ 2 tsp. vinegar

Directions:
1. Knead the dough and cover it with plastic wrap and set aside. Next, cook the ingredients for the filling and try to ensure that the shrimp is covered well with the sauce.
2. Roll the dough and cut it into a square. Place the filling in the center. Now, wrap the dough to cover the filling and pinch the edges together.
3. Pre heat the Air fryer at 200° F for 5 minutes. Place the wontons in the fry basket and close it. Let them cook at the same temperature for another 20 minutes. Recommended sides are chili sauce or ketchup

75. Salmon And Potato Fishcakes
Prep.Time: 63 min - **Cooking Time:** 7 min - **Servings:** 4

Ingredients:
- ✓ 14 ounces of potatoes, cooked and mashed
- ✓ 4 tablespoons of chopped parsley
- ✓ ½ pound of salmon, cooked and shredded
- ✓ ¼ cup of flour
- ✓ 1 ounce of capers
- ✓ 1 lemon zest
- ✓ Salt and pepper to taste
- ✓ Oil spray

Directions:
1. Mix the mashed potatoes with the salmon, capers, parsley and zest. Add salt and pepper and mix thoroughly.
2. Mold into cakes and coat with flour. Refrigerate for an hour until firm.
3. Preheat the air-fryer to 356°F.
4. Put the fishcakes into the air fryer basket, spray oil on them and bake for about 7 minutes.

76. Steamed Salmon & Dill Dip
Prep.Time: 15 min - **Cooking Time:** 10 min - **Servings:** 2

Ingredients:
- ✓ ¾ pound of salmon, cut in half
- ✓ 8 tablespoons of sour cream
- ✓ 2 teaspoons of olive oil
- ✓ 6 teaspoons of finely chopped dill
- ✓ 8 tablespoons of Greek Yogurt
- ✓ ¼ teaspoons of salt

Directions:
1. Heat your air-fryer to 285°F. Add a cup of cool water at the base of your air-fryer.
2. Coat each portion of the salmon with olive oil and season with salt.
3. Place into the fryer basket and cook for about 11 minutes.
4. While cooking the fish, mix the sour cream, salt, yogurt and dill in a bowl.
5. Remove the fish from the air-fryer and garnish with a pinch of dill and serve with the dill dip.

77. Air Fried Crumbed Fish
Prep.Time: 10 min - **Cooking Time:** 12 minutes - **Servings:** 2

Ingredients:
- ✓ 4 fish fillets
- ✓ 3.5 oz. breadcrumbs
- ✓ 4 tablespoons vegetable oil
- ✓ 1 egg, whisked
- ✓ 1 lemon, to serve

Directions:
1. Preheat air fryer to 350 degrees F. Combine breadcrumbs and stir well until crumbly and loose.
2. Dip the fish fillets into the egg, shake off residual then dip into breadcrumb mix, ensuring that it is thoroughly and evenly coated.
3. Lay in the air fryer gently and cook for 12 minutes. Serve with lemon.

78. Fried Fish With Onions
Prep.Time: 40 min - **Cooking Time:** 40 min - **Servings:** 2

Ingredients:
- ✓ ½ pound fish fillets, wash & cubed
- ✓ ½ onion, minced
- ✓ 1 clove garlic, minced
- ✓ 1 tablespoon oil
- ✓ 1 tablespoon chili paste
- ✓ 1½ tablespoon soy sauce
- ✓ 1 tablespoon sugar
- ✓ ¼ cup water
- ✓ 1/2 tablespoon salt
- ✓ 2 tablespoon vinegar

Directions:
1. Marinate fish cubes with salt for 30 minutes. Preheat air-fryer to 390F. Layer the fish with oil, and place in the air fryer. Cook for 15 minutes.
2. Meanwhile, add the oil, chili paste, onion and garlic to a small pan. Turn heat to medium and stir-fry for 5 minutes until the onions are translucent.
3. Remove fish from the air fryer, and place in the pan. Now add the water, soy sauce, sugar, salt and vinegar. Lower heat, cover and simmer for 10 minutes.
4. Finally, set heat to high. Remove when sauce thickens.

79. Cod Fish Nuggets
Prep.Time: 15 min - **Cooking Time:** 10 min - **Servings:** 4

Ingredients:
- ✓ 1 pound cod, cut lengthwise into strips of 1-inch by 2.5
- ✓ For The Breading:
- ✓ 1 cup all-purpose flour
- ✓ 2 tablespoons olive oil
- ✓ ¾ cup panko breadcrumbs
- ✓ 2 eggs, beaten
- ✓ 1 pinch salt

Directions:
1. Preheat the Air-fryer to 390°F. Blend the panko, breadcrumbs, olive oil and salt in a food processor.
2. Set aside the panko mixture, flour and eggs in three separate bowls.
3. Place cod pieces into the flour, the eggs and the breadcrumbs, pressing firmly to ensure that the breadcrumbs stick to the fish. Shake any excess breadcrumbs off.
4. Add the cod nuggets to the cooking basket and cook 8 to10 minutes until golden brown.

80. Teriyaki Glazed Halibut Steak
Prep.Time: 30 min - **Cooking Time:** 10-15 min - **Servings:** 3

Ingredients:
- ✓ 1 pound halibut steak
- ✓ For The Marinade:
- ✓ 2/3 cup low sodium soy sauce
- ✓ ½ cup mirin
- ✓ 2 tablespoons lime juice
- ✓ ¼ cup sugar
- ✓ ¼ cup orange juice
- ✓ ¼ teaspoon ginger ground
- ✓ ¼ teaspoon crushed red pepper flakes
- ✓ 1 each garlic clove (smashed)

Directions:
1. Place all the ingredients for the teriyaki glaze/marinade in a sauce pan. Bring to a boil and lessen by half, then let it cool.
2. When it cools, pour half of the glaze/marinade into a Ziploc bag together with the halibut then refrigerate for 30 minutes.
3. Preheat the Air fryer to 390°F. Place the marinated halibut into the Air fryer and cook 10-12 minutes. Brush some of the glaze that's left over the halibut steak.
4. Spread over white rice with basil/mint chutney.

81. Salmon And Potato Patties

Prep.Time: 10 min - **Cooking Time:** 29 min - **Servings:** 8

Ingredients:
- ✓ 7 ounces of salmon
- ✓ 1 cup of breadcrumbs
- ✓ 3 russet potatoes (about 4.7 ounce each) peeled, chopped
- ✓ 1 egg, whisked
- ✓ 4 ounces of frozen vegetables, parboiled and drained
- ✓ 1 tablespoon of finely chopped parsley
- ✓ ½ teaspoon of black pepper
- ✓ 1 teaspoon of dill
- ✓ Salt to taste
- ✓ Oil spray

Directions:
1. Put the chopped potatoes into boiling water and cook for 10-12 minutes. Drain off water completely. Mash the potatoes with a wooden mixer and place in a refrigerator to cool.
2. Heat your air fryer to 356°F for 5 minutes. Put in the salmon and grill for 5 minutes. Remove and flake the salmon using a fork.
3. Take the mashed potatoes out of the refrigerator and add the salmon, vegetables, black pepper, salt, dill and parsley and mix together. Add the whisked egg and stir.
4. Mold into 8 patties and coat the patties with the breadcrumbs. Spray the patties with oil using oil spray.
5. Place them into the air fryer and cook for about 12 minutes or until golden. You can serve with mayo and lemon with a salad

82. Coconut Coated Fish Cakes With Mango Sauce

Prep.Time: 20 min - **Cooking Time:** 14 min - **Servings:** 4

Ingredients:
- ✓ 18 ounces of white fish fillet
- ✓ 1 green onion, finely chopped
- ✓ 1 mango, peeled, cubed
- ✓ 4 tablespoons of ground coconut
- ✓ 1½ ounces of parsley, finely chopped
- ✓ 1½ teaspoons of ground fresh red chili
- ✓ 1 lime, juice and zest
- ✓ 1 egg
- ✓ 1 teaspoon of salt

Directions:
1. Add ½ ounce of parsley, ½ teaspoon of ground chili, half of the lime juice and zest to the mango cubes and mix thoroughly.
2. Using a food processor, puree the fish and add the salt, egg, and the rest of the lime zest, lime juice and chili. Stir in the green onions, 2 tablespoons of coconut and the rest of the parsley.
3. Put the rest of the coconut in a shallow dish. Mold the fish mixture into 12 round cakes. Place the cakes in the coconut to coat them.
4. Put half of the cakes into the fryer basket and bake for 7 minutes at 356°F. Remove when cakes are golden and bake the second batch of cakes.
5. Serve the cakes with the mango salsa.

83. Crab And Vegetable Croquettes

Prep.Time: 30 min - **Cooking Time:** 20 minutes - **Servings:** 6

Ingredients:
- ✓ 4 tablespoons of finely chopped bell pepper
- ✓ 4 tablespoons of mayonnaise
- ✓ 4 tablespoons of finely chopped onions
- ✓ 4 tablespoons of sour cream
- ✓ 16 ounces of lump crabmeat
- ✓ 1 teaspoon of vegetable oil
- ✓ ½ teaspoon of lemon juice
- ✓ ½ teaspoon of salt
- ✓ ½ teaspoon of finely chopped parsley
- ✓ ½ teaspoon of ground pepper
- ✓ 2 egg whites
- ✓ 6 teaspoons of finely chopped celery
- ✓ ¼ teaspoon of finely chopped tarragon
- ✓ ¼ teaspoon of finely chopped chives
- ✓ 1 cup of breadcrumbs
- ✓ 1 cup of flour

Directions:
1. Mix the onions, vegetable oil, celery and peppers in a pot and place over medium heat. Sweat for 5 minutes until translucent. Turn off heat and set aside to cool.
2. Transfer the mixture into a mixing bowl and add the crabmeat, chives, tarragon, mayonnaise, ground pepper, lemon juice, sour cream, and parsley. Mix thoroughly and mold into small balls.
3. Heat your air-fryer to 390°F.
4. Mix the breadcrumbs and salt together and set aside. Put the egg white and flour into separate bowls.
5. Put the molded balls into the flour, then dip into egg whites and finally roll them in the breadcrumbs to coat evenly.
6. Place half of the balls in the fryer basket and cook for 10 minutes until golden. Do same for the second batch until all the croquettes are cooked.

84. Battered & Crispy Fish Tacos

Prep.Time: 10 min - **Cooking Time:** 10 min - **Servings:** 2

Ingredients:
- ✓ 1 1/2 cup Flour Corn tortillas
- ✓ Peach salsa
- ✓ Cilantro
- ✓ Fresh halibut, slice into strips
- ✓ 1 can of beer
- ✓ 2 tablespoons Vegetable Oil
- ✓ 1 teaspoon baking powder
- ✓ 1 teaspoon Salt
- ✓ Cholula sauce
- ✓ Avocado Cream

Directions:
1. Lay out the corn tortillas topped with peach salsa on a plate and set aside.
2. Combine 1 cup of flour, beer and baking powder until it forms a pancake like consistency.
3. Toss the fish in the remaining flour then dip in the beer batter mixture until well coated.
4. Place on preheated air-fryer rack and cook 6-8 minutes or until golden at 200°F.
5. Place the fish on top of the salsa mixture topped with avocado cream, cilantro and Cholula sauce.
6. To Make The Avocado Cream: 1 large avocado 3/4 cup buttermilk Juice from 1/2 lime Combine in a blender until smooth.

151

85. Prawn Samosa

Prep.Time: 30 min - **Cooking Time:** 35 min - **Servings:** 2-4

Ingredients:

For wrappers:
- ✓ 2 tbsp. unsalted butter
- ✓ 1 ½ cup all-purpose flour
- ✓ A pinch of salt to taste
- ✓ Add as much water as required to make the dough stiff and firm

For filling:
- ✓ 1 lb. prawn
- ✓ ¼ cup boiled peas
- ✓ 1 tsp. powdered ginger
- ✓ 1 or 2 green chilies that are finely chopped
- ✓ ½ tsp. cumin
- ✓ 1 tsp. coarsely crushed coriander
- ✓ 1 dry red chili broken into pieces
- ✓ A small amount of salt (to taste)
- ✓ ½ tsp. dried mango powder
- ✓ ½ tsp. red chili power.
- ✓ 1-2 tbsp. coriander

Directions:

1. You will first need to make the outer covering. In a large bowl, add the flour, butter and enough water to knead it into dough that is stiff. Transfer this to a container and leave it to rest for five minutes.
2. Place a pan on medium flame and add the oil. Roast the mustard seeds and once roasted, add the coriander seeds and the chopped dry red chilies. Add all the dry ingredients for the filling and mix the ingredients well. Add a little water and continue to stir the ingredients.
3. Make small balls out of the dough and roll them out. Cut the rolled out dough into halves and apply a little water on the edges to help you fold the halves into a cone. Add the filling to the cone and close up the samosa.
4. Pre-heat the Air Fryer for around 5 to 6 minutes at 300 Fahrenheit. Place all the samosas in the fry basket and close the basket properly. Keep the Air Fryer at 200 degrees for another 20 to 25 minutes. Around the halfway point, open the basket and turn the samosas over for uniform cooking. After this, fry at 250 degrees for around 10 minutes in order to give them the desired golden brown color. Serve hot. Recommended sides are tamarind or mint chutney.

86. Salmon Tandoor

Prep.Time: 16 hours - **Cooking Time:** 15 min - **Servings:** 4

Ingredients:
- ✓ 2 lb. boneless salmon filets

1st Marinade:
- ✓ 3 tbsp. vinegar or lemon juice
- ✓ 2 or 3 tsp. paprika
- ✓ 1 tsp. black pepper
- ✓ 1 tsp. salt
- ✓ 3 tsp. ginger-garlic paste

2nd Marinade:
- ✓ 1 cup yogurt
- ✓ 4 tsp. tandoori masala
- ✓ 2 tbsp. dry fenugreek leaves
- ✓ 1 tsp. black salt
- ✓ 1 tsp. chat masala
- ✓ 1 tsp. garam masala powder
- ✓ 1 tsp. red chili powder
- ✓ 1 tsp. salt
- ✓ 3 drops of red color

Directions:

1. Make the first marinade and soak the fileted salmon in it for four hours. While this is happening, make the second marinade and soak the salmon in it overnight to let the flavors blend.
2. Pre heat the Air fryer at 160 degrees Fahrenheit for 5 minutes. Place the fingers in the fry basket and close it. Let them cook at the same temperature for another 15 minutes or so. Toss the fingers well so that they are cooked uniformly. Serve them with mint chutney.

87. Carp Croquette

Prep.Time: 20 min - **Cooking Time:** 25 minutes - **Servings:** 2-4

Ingredients:
- ✓ 1 lb. Carp filets
- ✓ 3 onions chopped
- ✓ 5 green chilies-roughly chopped
- ✓ 1 ½ tbsp. ginger paste
- ✓ 1 ½ tsp garlic paste
- ✓ 1 ½ tsp salt
- ✓ 3 tsp lemon juice
- ✓ 2 tsp garam masala
- ✓ 4 tbsp. chopped coriander
- ✓ 3 tbsp. cream
- ✓ 2 tbsp. coriander powder
- ✓ 4 tbsp. fresh mint chopped
- ✓ 3 tbsp. chopped capsicum
- ✓ 3 eggs
- ✓ 2 ½ tbsp. sesame seeds

Directions:

1. Take all the ingredients mentioned under the first heading and mix them in a bowl. Grind them thoroughly to make a smooth paste. Take the eggs in a different bowl and beat them. Add a pinch of salt and leave them aside.
2. Mold the fish mixture into small balls and flatten them into round and flat Croquettes.
3. Dip these Croquettes in the egg and salt mixture and then in the mixture of breadcrumbs and sesame seeds. Leave these Croquettes in the fridge for an hour or so to set. Pre heat the Air fryer at 160 degrees Fahrenheit for around 5 minutes. Place the Croquettes in the basket and let them cook for another 25 minutes at the same temperature. Turn the Croquettes over in between the cooking process to get a uniform cook. Serve the Croquettes with mint chutney.

88. Salmon Fries

Prep.Time: 12 hours - **Cooking Time:** 15 min - **Servings:** 2

Ingredients:
- ✓ 1 lb. boneless salmon filets
- ✓ 2 cup dry breadcrumbs
- ✓ 2 tsp. oregano
- ✓ 2 tsp. red chili flakes

Marinade:
- ✓ 1 ½ tbsp. ginger-garlic paste
- ✓ 4 tbsp. lemon juice
- ✓ 2 tsp. salt
- ✓ 1 tsp. pepper powder
- ✓ 1 tsp. red chili powder
- ✓ 6 tbsp. corn flour
- ✓ 4 eggs

Directions:

1. Mix all the ingredients for the marinade and put the salmon filets inside and let it rest overnight.
2. Mix the breadcrumbs, oregano and red chili flakes well and place the marinated fingers on this mixture. Cover it with plastic wrap and leave it till right before you serve to cook.
3. Pre heat the Air fryer at 160 degrees Fahrenheit for 5 minutes. Place the fingers in the fry basket and close it. Let them cook at the same temperature for another 15 minutes or so. Toss the fingers well so that they are cooked uniformly.

89. Cheese Carp Fries

Prep.Time: 15 min - **Cooking Time:** 25 min - **Servings:** 2

Ingredients:
- ✓ 1 lb. carp fingers
- *Ingredients for the marinade:*
- ✓ 1 tbsp. olive oil
- ✓ 1 tsp. mixed herbs
- ✓ ½ tsp. red chili flakes
- ✓ A pinch of salt to taste
- ✓ 1 tbsp. lemon juice
- *For the garnish:*
- ✓ 1 cup melted cheddar cheese

Directions:
1. Take all the ingredients mentioned under the heading "For the marinade" and mix them well.
2. Cook the carp fingers and soak them in the marinade.
3. Pre heat the Air Fryer for around 5 minutes at 300 Fahrenheit. Take out the basket of the fryer and place the carp in them. Close the basket. Now keep the fryer at 220 Fahrenheit for 20 or 25 minutes. In between the process, toss the fries twice or thrice so that they get cooked properly.
4. Towards the end of the cooking process (the last 2 minutes or so), sprinkle the melted cheddar cheese over the fries and serve hot.

90. Seafood Platter

Prep.Time: 12 hours - **Cooking Time:** 15 min - **Servings:** 2-4

Ingredients:
- *1 large plate with assorted prepared seafood 1st Marinade:*
- ✓ 3 tbsp. vinegar or lemon juice
- ✓ 2 or 3 tsp. paprika
- ✓ 1 tsp. black pepper
- ✓ 1 tsp. salt
- ✓ 3 tsp. ginger-garlic paste
- *2nd Marinade:*
- ✓ 1 cup yogurt
- ✓ 4 tsp. tandoori masala
- ✓ 2 tbsp. dry fenugreek leaves
- ✓ 1 tsp. black salt
- ✓ 1 tsp. chat masala
- ✓ 1 tsp. garam masala powder
- ✓ 1 tsp. red chili powder
- ✓ 1 tsp. salt
- ✓ 3 drops of red color

Directions:
1. Make the first marinade and soak the seafood in it for four hours. While this is happening, make the second marinade and soak the seafood in it overnight to let the flavors blend.
2. Pre heat the Air fryer at 160 degrees Fahrenheit for 5 minutes. Place the fingers in the fry basket and close it. Let them cook at the same temperature for another 15 minutes or so. Toss the fingers well so that they are cooked uniformly. Serve them with mint chutney.

91. Lobster Kebab

Prep.Time: 20 min - **Cooking Time:** 25 minutes - **Servings:** 2-4

Ingredients:
- ✓ 1 lb. lobster (Shelled and cubed)
- ✓ 3 onions chopped
- ✓ 5 green chilies-roughly chopped
- ✓ 1 ½ tbsp. ginger paste
- ✓ 1 ½ tsp garlic paste
- ✓ 1 ½ tsp salt
- ✓ 3 tsp lemon juice
- ✓ 2 tsp garam masala
- ✓ 4 tbsp. chopped coriander
- ✓ 3 tbsp. cream
- ✓ 2 tbsp. coriander powder
- ✓ 4 tbsp. fresh mint chopped
- ✓ 3 tbsp. chopped capsicum
- ✓ 3 eggs
- ✓ 2 ½ tbsp. white sesame seeds

Directions:
1. Take all the ingredients mentioned under the first heading and mix them in a bowl. Grind them thoroughly to make a smooth paste.
2. Take the eggs in a different bowl and beat them. Add a pinch of salt and leave them aside.
3. Take a flat plate and in it mix the sesame seeds and breadcrumbs.
4. Dip the lobster cubes in the egg and salt mixture and then in the mixture of breadcrumbs and sesame seeds. Leave these kebabs in the fridge for an hour or so to set.
5. Pre heat the Air fryer at 160 degrees Fahrenheit for around 5 minutes. Place the kebabs in the basket and let them cook for another 25 minutes at the same temperature. Turn the kebabs over in between the cooking process to get a uniform cook.
6. Serve the kebabs with mint chutney.

92. Herbed Healthy Salmon

Prep.Time: 10 min - **Cooking Time:** 11 minutes - **Servings:** 2

Ingredients:
- ✓ 2 salmon fillets
- ✓ 2 teaspoons garlic, minced
- ✓ 1 teaspoons olive oil
- ✓ 1 cup white wine vinegar
- ✓ 3 tablespoons coconut oil
- ✓ Salt as needed
- ✓ Dried Italian herbs

Directions:
1. Pre-heat your fryer to 350-degree Fahrenheit
2. Pat the salmon pieces dry using a kitchen towel and season with salt
3. Transfer them to your fryer and cook for 6 minutes
4. Take a saucepan and add olive oil, heat it up over medium heat
5. Add garlic to the pan and stir cook
6. Add white wine vinegar and bring the mix to a boil, cook for 5 minutes
7. Stir in coconut oil and sprinkle Italian herb seasoning
8. Serve the salmon with this sauce
9. Enjoy!

93. Lovely Garlic Flavored Prawn - KETO

Prep.Time: 15 min - **Cooking Time:** 8 min - **Servings:** 3-4

Ingredients:
- ✓ 15 fresh prawns
- ✓ 1 tablespoon olive oil
- ✓ 1 teaspoon chili powder
- ✓ 1 tablespoon black pepper
- ✓ 1 tablespoon chili sauce, Keto-Friendly
- ✓ 1 garlic clove, minced
- ✓ Salt as needed

Directions:
1. Pre-heat your Air Fryer to 356 degrees F
2. Wash prawns thoroughly and rinse them
3. Take a mixing bowl and add washed prawn, chili powder, oil, garlic, pepper, chili sauce and stir the mix
4. Transfer prawn to Air Fryer and cook for 8 minutes
5. Serve and enjoy!

94. Fennel and Cod - KETO

Prep.Time: 15 min - **Cooking Time:** 15 min - **Servings:** 2

Ingredients:
- ✓ 2 cod fillets
- ✓ Salt and pepper to taste
- ✓ 1 cup grapes, halved
- ✓ ½ cup pecans
- ✓ 1 small fennel, sliced
- ✓ 3 cups kale, shredded
- ✓ 2 teaspoons balsamic vinegar
- ✓ 2 tablespoons extra virgin olive oil

Directions:
1. Pre-heat your Fryer to 400-degree Fahrenheit and season your fillets with pepper and salt
2. Drizzle olive oil on top
3. Transfer the fillets to your cooking basket making sure that the skin side is facing down
4. Fry for 10 minutes and remove them once done
5. Make an aluminum tent and allow them to cool
6. Take a bowl and add grapes, pecans, fennels
7. Drizzle olive oil and season with salt and pepper
8. Add the mix to your cooking basket and cook for 5 minutes
9. Dress them with balsamic vinegar and add olive oil
10. Season with some additional pepper and salt it you need, enjoy!

95. Bacon and Shrimp Wrap - KETO

Prep.Time: 30 min - **Cooking Time:** 7 minutes - **Servings:** 4-8

Ingredients:
- ✓ 1 and a quarter pound of deveined shrimps
- ✓ 16 slices of 1 pound thinly sliced bacon

Directions:
1. Take your bacon slices and wrap them up around the shrimp
2. Make sure to start from the bottom and go all way to the top
3. Repeat until all the shrimps are used up
4. Transfer them to your fridge and chill for 20 minutes
5. Pre-heat your fryer to 390-degree Fahrenheit
6. Take the shrimp and transfer them to the cooking basket, cook for 5-7 minutes

96. Herbed Garlic Lobster Tails - KETO

Prep.Time: 10 min - **Cooking Time:** 10 minutes - **Servings:** 2-4

Ingredients:
- ✓ 4-ounce lobster tails
- ✓ 1 teaspoon garlic, minced
- ✓ 1 tablespoon butter
- ✓ Salt and pepper to taste
- ✓ ½ tablespoon lemon juice

Directions:
1. Take your food processor and add all the ingredients except lobster, blend well.
2. Wash your lobster and halve them using meat knife.
3. Clean the skin of lobsters.
4. Cover lobsters with marinade.
5. Pre-heat your Fryer t o380 degree F.
6. Transfer prepared lobster to Air Fryer and bake for 10 minutes.
7. Serve with some fresh herbs and enjoy!

97. Excellent Catfish - KETO

Prep.Time: 10 min - **Cooking Time:** 23 minutes - **Servings:** 4

Ingredients:
- ✓ 4 catfish fillets
- ✓ ¼ cup of seasoned fish fry
- ✓ 1 tablespoon of olive oil
- ✓ 1 tablespoon of chopped parsley

Directions:
1. Pre-heat your Fryer to 400-degree Fahrenheit
2. Take your catfish and rinse it well, pat it dry using kitchen towel
3. Take a large sized zip bag and add the fish and seasoning
4. Add a bit of olive oil and coat the fish, shake it well
5. Transfer the fillets to your Fryer and fry for 10 minutes
6. Flip it up and fry for 10 minutes more
7. Flip it for the last time and cook for 1-3 minutes
8. Top it up with parsley and enjoy!

98. Authentic Alaskan Crab Legs - KETO

Prep.Time: 10 min - **Cooking Time:** 10 minutes - **Servings:** 2

Ingredients:
- ✓ 3 pounds crab legs
- ✓ 2 cups Butter, melted
- ✓ 1 cup water
- ✓ ½ teaspoon salt

Directions:
1. Pre-heat your Fryer to 380-degree F.
2. Cover legs with water and salt.
3. Place crab legs in Air Fryer.
4. Bake for 10 minutes.
5. Melt butter and pour butter over your baked Crab Legs.
6. Enjoy!

99. Simple Grilled Fish and Cheese - KETO
Prep.Time: 10 min - **Cooking Time:** 8 minutes - **Servings:** 4

Ingredients:
- ✓ 1 bunch basil
- ✓ 2 garlic cloves
- ✓ 1 tbsp olive oil (for cooking)
- ✓ ¼ cup olive oil (extra)
- ✓ ¼ cup olive oil (extra)
- ✓ 1 tbsp parmesan cheese
- ✓ Salt and pepper to taste
- ✓ 2 tablespoons Pinenuts
- ✓ 6 ounces white fish fillet

Directions:
1. Brush the fish fillets with oil and season with some pepper and salt
2. Pre-heat your Air Fryer to a temperature of 356-degree Fahrenheit. Carefully transfer the fillets to your Air Fryer cooking basket. Cook for about 8 minutes
3. Take a small bowl and add basil, olive oil, pine nuts, garlic, parmesan cheese and blend using your hand
4. Serve this mixture with the fish!

100. Fresh Broiled Tilapia - KETO
Prep.Time: 5 min - **Cooking Time:** 10 minutes - **Servings:** 2

Ingredients:
- ✓ 1-pound tilapia fillets
- ✓ Old bay seasoning as needed
- ✓ Canola oil as needed
- ✓ Lemon pepper as needed
- ✓ Salt to taste
- ✓ Butter buds

Directions:
1. Pre-heat your Fryer to 400-degree F.
2. Cover tilapia with oil.
3. Take a bowl and mix in salt, lemon pepper, butter buds, seasoning.
4. Cover your fish with the sauce.
5. Bake fillets for 10 minutes.
6. Serve and enjoy!

101. Healthy Salmon
Prep.Time: 10 min - **Cooking Time:** 10 minutes - **Servings:** 2

Ingredients:
- ✓ 1 lb salmon
- ✓ 1/2 tsp paprika
- ✓ 1/2 tsp garlic powder
- ✓ 1/2 tsp kosher salt

Directions:
1. Preheat the air fryer to 280 F/ 137 C.
2. In a small bowl, mix together paprika, garlic powder, and salt.
3. Rub spice mixture over the salmon. Place salmon in air fryer basket skin side down and cook for 10 minutes.

102. Honey Lime Salmon
Prep.Time: 10 min - **Cooking Time:** 10 minutes - **Servings:** 2

Ingredients:
- ✓ 1 lb salmon cut in cubes
- ✓ 1 tsp paprika
- ✓ 1 tbsp sesame
- ✓ 1 tbsp honey
- ✓ 1 tbsp fresh lemon juice

Directions:
1. Preheat the air fryer to 400 F/ 204 C.
2. Add lemon juice, honey, sesame, paprika, and salt in a bowl and mix well.
3. Add salmon in a bowl and coat well. Place salmon in air fryer basket and cook for 10 minutes.

103. Buttery Lobster Tail
Prep.Time: 10 min - **Cooking Time:** 6 minutes - **Servings:** 2

Ingredients:
- ✓ 1 lb lobster tails, cut through the tail section
- ✓ 2 tbsp grass-fed butter, melted
- ✓ Pepper and Salt

Directions:
1. Preheat the air fryer to 193 C/ 380 F.
2. Brush lobster tails with melted butter and season with pepper and salt.
3. Place lobster tails in air fryer basket and cook for 6 minutes

104. Simple Air Fried Mackerel
Prep.Time: 10 min - **Cooking Time:** 20 minutes - **Servings:** 2-3

Ingredients:
- ✓ 1 1/2 lbs mackerel fish fillet
- ✓ 1/2 tsp olive oil
- ✓ Pepper and Salt

Directions:
1. Place fish fillet in a bowl and drizzle with oil and season with pepper and salt.
2. Preheat the air fryer at 392 F/ 200 C for 5 minutes.
3. Place fish fillet in air fryer basket on the grill pan and cook for 20 minutes at 356 F/ 180 C.

105. Buttery Lobster Tail
Prep.Time: 10 min - **Cooking Time:** 8-10 minutes - **Servings:** 2

Ingredients:
- ✓ 1/2 lb shrimp, peeled and deveined
- ✓ 1/4 tsp smoked paprika
- ✓ 1/2 tsp old bay seasoning
- ✓ 1/4 tsp cayenne pepper
- ✓ Pinch of salt

Directions:
1. Preheat the air fryer at 200 C/ 390 F.
2. Add all ingredients into the mixing bowl and mix until well coated.
3. Add marinated shrimp into the air fryer basket and cook for 8-10 minutes.

106. Shrimp Scampi
Prep.Time: 10 min - **Cooking Time:** 5-6 minutes - **Servings:** 2-4

Ingredients:
- ✓ 1 lb shrimp
- ✓ 2 tbsp white wine
- ✓ 1 tsp dried basil
- ✓ 1 tsp dried chives
- ✓ 2 tsp red pepper flakes
- ✓ 1 tbsp garlic, minced
- ✓ 1 tbsp fresh lemon juice
- ✓ 4 tbsp grass-fed butter

Directions:
1. Preheat the air fryer to 165 C/ 330 F.
2. Add all ingredients to the 6" pan and mix well.
3. Place shrimp pan into the air fryer and cook for 5-6 minutes.

107. Quick and Easy Fried Catfish
Prep.Time: 10 min - **Cooking Time:** 8-10 minutes - **Servings:** 2

Ingredients:
- ✓ 4 catfish fillets
- ✓ 1 tbsp parsley, chopped
- ✓ 1 tbsp olive oil
- ✓ Pepper and Salt

Directions:
1. Preheat the air fryer to 400 F/ 204 C. Season fish fillets with pepper and salt. Place seasoned fish fillet in air fryer and drizzle with oil.
2. Close air fryer basket and cook fish fillet for 10 minutes.
3. Turn fish fillet to other side and cook for 10 minutes more. Garnish with chopped parsley and serve.

108. Shrimp with Veggie
Prep.Time: 10 min - **Cooking Time:** 5-6 minutes - **Servings:** 2-4

Ingredients:
- ✓ 2 lbs shrimp, peeled and deveined
- ✓ 1 tbsp Cajun seasoning
- ✓ 1 bag frozen mixed vegetables

Directions:
1. Add vegetables and shrimp into the air fryer basket.
2. Sprinkle Cajun seasoning on top of veggies and shrimp and spray with cooking spray.
3. Cook shrimp and veggies for 10 minutes at 355 F/ 179 C.
4. Toss shrimp and veggies well and cook for 10 min more.

MEAT RECIPES

1. Crispy Lamb
Prep.Time: 10 min - Cooking Time: 30 min - Servings: 4

Ingredients:
- ✓ 1 tbsp bread crumbs
- ✓ 2 tablespoons macadamia nuts, toasted and crushed
- ✓ 1 tablespoon olive oil
- ✓ 1 garlic clove, minced
- ✓ 28 ounces rack of lamb
- ✓ Salt and black pepper to the taste
- ✓ 1 egg,
- ✓ 1 tbsp rosemary, chopped

Directions:
1. In a bowl, mix oil with garlic and stir well.
2. Season lamb with salt, pepper and brush with the oil.
3. In another bowl, mix nuts with breadcrumbs and rosemary.
4. Put the egg in a separate bowl and whisk well.
5. Dip lamb in egg, then in macadamia mix, place them in your air fryer's basket, cook at 360 degrees F and cook for 25 minutes, increase heat to 400 degrees F and cook for 5 minutes more.
6. Divide among plates and serve right away.

Nutrition: calories 230 - Fat 2 - Fiber 2 - Carbs 10 - Protein 12

2. Provencal Pork
Prep.Time: 10 min - Cooking Time: 15 min - Servings: 2

Ingredients:
- ✓ 1 red onion, sliced
- ✓ 1 yellow bell pepper, cut into strips
- ✓ 1 green bell pepper, cut into strips
- ✓ Salt and black pepper to the taste
- ✓ 2 teaspoons Provencal herbs
- ✓ ½ tablespoon mustard
- ✓ 1 tablespoon olive oil
- ✓ 7 ounces pork tenderloin

Directions:
1. In a baking dish that fits your air fryer, mix yellow bell pepper with green bell pepper, onion, salt, pepper, Provencal herbs and half of the oil and toss well.
2. Season pork with salt, pepper, mustard and the rest of the oil, toss well and add to veggies.
3. Introduce everything in your air fryer, cook at 370 degrees F for 15 minutes, divide among plates and serve.

Nutrition: calories 300 - Fat 8 - Fiber 7 - Carbs 21 - Protein 23

3. Beef Fillets with Garlic Mayo
Prep.Time: 10 min - Cooking Time: 40 minutes - Servings: 8

Ingredients:
- ✓ 1 cup mayonnaise
- ✓ 1/3 cup sour cream
- ✓ 2 garlic cloves, minced
- ✓ 3 pounds beef fillet
- ✓ 2 tbsp chives, chopped
- ✓ 2 tablespoons mustard
- ✓ 2 tablespoons mustard
- ✓ ¼ cup tarragon, chopped
- ✓ Salt and black pepper to the taste

Directions:
1. Season beef with salt and pepper to the taste, place in your air fryer, cook at 370 degrees F for 20 minutes, transfer to a plate and leave aside for a few minutes.
2. In a bowl, mix garlic with sour cream, chives, mayo, some salt and pepper, whisk and leave aside.
3. In another bowl, mix mustard with Dijon mustard and tarragon, whisk, add beef, toss, return to your air fryer and cook at 350 degrees F for 20 minutes more.
4. Divide beef on plates, spread garlic mayo on top and serve.

Nutrition: calories 400 - Fat 12 - Fiber 2 - Carbs 27 - Protein 19

4. Marinated Pork Chops and Onions
Prep.Time: 24 hours - Cooking Time: 25 min - Servings: 6

Ingredients:
- ✓ 2 pork chops
- ✓ ¼ cup olive oil
- ✓ 2 yellow onions, sliced
- ✓ 2 garlic cloves, minced
- ✓ 2 teaspoons mustard
- ✓ 1 teaspoon sweet paprika
- ✓ Salt and black pepper to the taste
- ✓ ½ tsp oregano, dried
- ✓ ½ teaspoon thyme, dried
- ✓ A pinch of cayenne pepper

Directions:
1. In a bowl, mix oil with garlic, mustard, paprika, black pepper, oregano, thyme and cayenne and whisk well.
2. Combine onions with meat and mustard mix, toss to coat, cover and keep in the fridge for 1 day.
3. Transfer meat and onions mix to a pan that fits your air fryer and cook at 360 degrees F for 25 minutes.
4. Divide everything on plates and serve.

Nutrition: calories 384 - Fat 4 - Fiber 4 - Carbs 17 - Protein 25

5. Indian Pork
Prep.Time: 35 min - Cooking Time: 10 min - Servings: 4

Ingredients:
- ✓ 1 tsp. ginger powder
- ✓ 2 tsp. chili paste
- ✓ 2 garlic cloves, minced
- ✓ 14 ounces pork chops, cubed
- ✓ 1 shallot, chopped
- ✓ 1 tsp. coriander, ground
- ✓ 7 ounces coconut milk
- ✓ 2 tbsp olive oil
- ✓ 3 ounces peanuts, ground
- ✓ 3 tbsp. soy sauce
- ✓ Salt and black pepper to the taste

Directions:
1. In a bowl, mix ginger with 1 teaspoon chili paste, half of the garlic, half of the soy sauce and half of the oil, whisk, add meat, toss and leave aside for 10 minutes.
2. Transfer meat to your air fryer's basket and cook at 400 degrees F for 12 minutes, turning halfway.
3. Meanwhile, heat up a pan with the rest of the oil over medium high heat, add shallot, the rest of the garlic, coriander, coconut milk, the rest of the peanuts, the rest of the chili paste and the rest of the soy sauce, stir and cook for 5 minutes.
4. Divide pork on plates and spread coconut mix on top.

Nutrition: calories 423 - Fat 11 - Fiber 4 - Carbs 42 - Protein 18

6. Pork with Couscous
Prep.Time: 10 min - Cooking Time: 35 min - Servings: 6

Ingredients:
- ✓ 2 and ½ pounds pork loin, boneless and trimmed
- ✓ ¾ cup chicken stock
- ✓ 2 tablespoons olive oil
- ✓ ½ tbsp sweet paprika
- ✓ 2 and ¼ tsp. sage, dried
- ✓ ½ tbsp. garlic powder
- ✓ ¼ tsp. rosemary, dried
- ✓ ¼ tsp. marjoram, dried
- ✓ 1 teaspoon basil, dried
- ✓ 1 tbsp oregano, dried
- ✓ Salt and black pepper to the taste
- ✓ 2 cups couscous, cooked

Directions:
1. In a bowl, mix oil with stock, paprika, garlic powder, sage, rosemary, thyme, marjoram, oregano, salt and pepper to the taste, whisk well, add pork loin, toss well and leave aside for 1 hour.
2. Transfer everything to a pan that fits your air fryer and cook at 370 degrees F for 35 minutes.
3. Divide among plates and serve with couscous on the side.

Nutrition: calories 310 - Fat 4 - Fiber 6 - Carbs 37 - Protein 34

7. Simple Air Fried Pork Shoulder

Prep.Time: 30 min - **Cooking Time:** 1 hour and 20 min - **Servings:** 6

Ingredients:
- ✓ 3 tablespoons garlic, minced
- ✓ 3 tablespoons olive oil
- ✓ 4 pounds pork shoulder
- ✓ Salt and black pepper to the taste

Directions:
1. In a bowl, mix olive oil with salt, pepper and oil, whisk well and brush pork shoulder with this mix.
2. Place in preheated air fryer and cook at 390 degrees F for 10 minutes.
3. Reduce heat to 300 degrees F and roast pork for 1 hour and 10 minutes.
4. Slice pork shoulder, divide among plates and serve with a side salad.

Nutrition: calories 221 - Fat 4 - Fiber 4 - Carbs 7 - Protein 10

8. Garlic Lamb Chops

Prep.Time: 10 min - **Cooking Time:** 10 min - **Servings:** 4

Ingredients:
- ✓ 3 tablespoons olive oil
- ✓ 8 lamb chops
- ✓ Salt and black pepper to the taste
- ✓ 4 garlic cloves, minced
- ✓ 1 tablespoon oregano, chopped
- ✓ 1 tablespoon coriander, chopped

Directions:
1. In a bowl, mix oregano with salt, pepper, oil, garlic and lamb chops and toss to coat.
2. Transfer lamb chops to your air fryer and cook at 400 degrees F for 10 minutes.
3. Divide lamb chops on plates and serve with a side salad.

Nutrition: calories 231 – Fat7 - Fiber 5 - Carbs 14 - Protein 23

9. Creamy Pork

Prep.Time: 10 min - **Cooking Time:** 22 minutes - **Servings:** 6

Ingredients:
- ✓ 2 pounds pork meat, boneless and cubed
- ✓ 2 yellow onions, chopped
- ✓ 1 tablespoon olive oil
- ✓ 1 garlic clove, minced
- ✓ 3 cups chicken stock
- ✓ 2 tablespoons sweet paprika
- ✓ Salt and black pepper to the taste
- ✓ 2 tablespoons white flour
- ✓ 1 and ½ cups sour cream
- ✓ 2 tablespoons dill, chopped

Directions:
1. In a pan that fits your air fryer, mix pork with salt, pepper and oil, toss, introduce in your air fryer and cook at 360 degrees F for 7 minutes.
2. Add onion, garlic, stock, paprika, flour, sour cream and dill, toss and cook at 370 degrees F for 15 minutes more.
3. Divide everything on plates and serve right away

Nutrition: calories 300 - Fat 4 - Fiber 10 - Carbs 26 - Protein 34

10. Lamb and Creamy Brussels Sprouts

Prep.Time: 10 min - **Cooking Time:** 1 hour and 10 min - **Servings:** 4

Ingredients:
- ✓ 2 pounds leg of lamb, scored
- ✓ 2 tablespoons olive oil
- ✓ 1 tablespoon rosemary, chopped
- ✓ 1 tablespoon lemon thyme, chopped
- ✓ 1 garlic clove, minced
- ✓ 1 and ½ pounds Brussels sprouts, trimmed
- ✓ 1 tablespoon butter, melted
- ✓ ½ cup sour cream
- ✓ Salt and black pepper to the taste

Directions:
1. Season leg of lamb with salt, pepper, thyme and rosemary, brush with oil, place in your air fryer's basket, cook at 300 degrees F for 1 hour, transfer to a plate and keep warm.
2. In a pan that fits your air fryer, mix Brussels sprouts with salt, pepper, garlic, butter and sour cream, toss, put in your air fryer and cook at 400 degrees F for 10 minutes.
3. Divide lamb on plates, add Brussels sprouts on the side and serve.

Nutrition: calories 440 - Fat 23 - Fiber 0 - Carbs 2 - Protein 49

11. Beef and Green Onions Marinade

Prep.Time: 10 min - **Cooking Time:** 20 min - **Servings:** 4

Ingredients:
- ✓ 1 cup green onion, chopped
- ✓ 1 cup soy sauce
- ✓ ½ cup water
- ✓ ¼ cup brown sugar
- ✓ ¼ cup sesame seeds
- ✓ 5 garlic cloves, minced
- ✓ 1 teaspoon black pepper
- ✓ 1 pound lean beef

Directions:
1. In a bowl, mix onion with soy sauce, water, sugar, garlic, sesame seeds and pepper, whisk, add meat, toss and leave aside for 10 minutes.
2. Drain beef, transfer to your preheated air fryer and cook at 390 degrees F for 20 minutes.
3. Slice, divide among plates and serve with a side salad.

Nutrition: calories 329 - Fat 8 - Fiber 12 - Carbs 26 - Protein 22

12. Lamb Roast and Potatoes

Prep.Time: 10 min - **Cooking Time:** 45 min - **Servings:** 6

Ingredients:
- ✓ 4 pounds lamb roast
- ✓ 1 spring rosemary
- ✓ 3 garlic cloves, minced
- ✓ 6 potatoes, halved
- ✓ ½ cup lamb stock
- ✓ 4 bay leaves
- ✓ Salt and black pepper to the taste

Directions:
1. Put potatoes in a dish that fits your air fryer, add lamb, garlic, rosemary spring, salt, pepper, bay leaves and stock, toss, introduce in your air fryer and cook at 360 degrees F for 45 minutes.
2. Slice lamb, divide among plates and serve with potatoes and cooking juices.

Nutrition: calories 273 - Fat 4 - Fiber 12 - Carbs 25 - Protein 29

13. Beef Brisket and Onion Sauce

Prep.Time: 10 min - **Cooking Time:** 2 hours - **Servings:** 6

Ingredients:
- ✓ 1 pound yellow onion, chopped
- ✓ 4 pounds beef brisket
- ✓ 1 pound carrot, chopped
- ✓ 8 earl grey tea bags
- ✓ ½ pound celery, chopped
- ✓ Salt and black pepper to the taste
- ✓ 4 cups water

For the sauce:
- ✓ 16 ounces canned tomatoes, chopped
- ✓ ½ pound celery, chopped
- ✓ 1 ounce garlic, minced
- ✓ 4 ounces vegetable oil
- ✓ 1 pound sweet onion, chopped
- ✓ 1 cup brown sugar
- ✓ 8 earl grey tea bags
- ✓ 1 cup white vinegar

Directions:
1. Put the water in a heat proof dish that fits your air fryer, add 1 pound onion, 1 pound carrot, ½ pound celery, salt and pepper, stir and bring to a simmer over medium high heat.
2. Add beef brisket and 8 tea bags, stir, transfer to your air fryer and cook at 300 degrees F for 1 hour and 30 minutes.
3. Meanwhile, heat up a pan with the vegetable oil over medium high heat, add 1 pound onion, stir and sauté for 10 minutes.
4. Add garlic, ½ pound celery, tomatoes, sugar, vinegar, salt, pepper and 8 tea bags, stir, bring to a simmer, cook for 10 minutes and discard tea bags.
5. Transfer beef brisket to a cutting board, slice, divide among plates, drizzle onion sauce all over and serve.

Nutrition: calories 400 - Fat 12 - Fiber 4 - Carbs 38 - Protein 34

14. Lemony Lamb Leg

Prep.Time: 10 min - **Cooking Time:** 1 hour - **Servings:** 6

Ingredients:
- ✓ 4 pounds lamb leg
- ✓ 2 tablespoons olive oil
- ✓ 2 springs rosemary, chopped
- ✓ 2 tablespoons parsley, chopped
- ✓ 2 tablespoons oregano, chopped
- ✓ Salt and black pepper to the taste
- ✓ 1 tablespoon lemon rind, grated
- ✓ 3 garlic cloves, minced
- ✓ 2 tablespoons lemon juice
- ✓ 2 pounds baby potatoes
- ✓ 1 cup beef stock

Directions:
4. Make small cuts all over lamb, insert rosemary springs and season with salt and pepper.
5. In a bowl, mix 1 tablespoon oil with oregano, parsley, garlic, lemon juice and rind, stir and rub lamb with this mix.
6. Heat up a pan that fits your air fryer with the rest of the oil over medium high heat, add potatoes, stir and cook for 3 minutes.
7. Add lamb and stock, stir, introduce in your air fryer and cook at 360 degrees F for 1 hour.
8. Divide everything on plates and serve.

Nutrition: calories 264 - Fat 4 - Fiber 12 - Carbs 27 - Protein 32

15. Creamy Lamb

Prep.Time: 1 day - **Cooking Time:** 1 hour - **Servings:** 8

Ingredients:
- ✓ 4 dinner rolls, tops cut off and insides scooped out
- ✓ 4 tablespoons heavy cream
- ✓ 4 eggs
- ✓ 4 tablespoons mixed chives and parsley
- ✓ Salt and black pepper to the taste
- ✓ 4 tablespoons parmesan, grated

Directions:
1. Arrange dinner rolls on a baking sheet and crack an egg in each.
2. Divide heavy cream, mixed herbs in each roll and season with salt and pepper.
3. Sprinkle parmesan on top of your rolls, place them in your air fryer and cook at 350 degrees F for 20 minutes.
4. Divide your bread bowls on plates and serve for breakfast.

Nutrition: calories 238 - Fat 4 - Fiber 7 - Carbs 14 - Protein 7

16. Beef Curry

Prep.Time: 10 min - **Cooking Time:** 45 min - **Servings:** 4

Ingredients:
- ✓ 2 pounds beef steak, cubed
- ✓ 2 tablespoons olive oil
- ✓ 3 potatoes, cubed
- ✓ 1 tablespoon wine mustard
- ✓ 2 and ½ tablespoons curry powder
- ✓ 2 yellow onions, chopped
- ✓ 2 garlic cloves, minced
- ✓ 10 ounces canned coconut milk
- ✓ 2 tablespoons tomato sauce
- ✓ Salt and black pepper to the taste

Directions:
1. Heat up a pan that fits your air fryer with the oil over medium high heat, add onions and garlic, stir and cook for 4 minutes.
2. Add potatoes and mustard, stir and cook for 1 minute.
3. Add beef, curry powder, salt, pepper, coconut milk and tomato sauce, stir, transfer to your air fryer and cook at 360 degrees F for 40 minutes.
4. Divide into bowls and serve.

Nutrition: calories 432 - Fat 16 – Fiber48 - Carbs 20 - Protein 27

17. Lamb Shanks and Carrots

Prep.Time: 10 min - **Cooking Time:** 45 min - **Servings:** 4

Ingredients:
- ✓ 4 lamb shanks
- ✓ 2 tbsp. olive oil
- ✓ 1 yellow onion, finely chopped
- ✓ 6 carrots, roughly chopped
- ✓ 2 garlic cloves, minced
- ✓ 2 tbsp tomato paste
- ✓ 1 tsp. oregano, dried
- ✓ 1 tomato, roughly chopped
- ✓ 2 tbsp. water
- ✓ 4 ounces red wine
- ✓ Salt and black pepper to the taste.

Directions:
1. Season lamb with salt and pepper, rub with oil, put in your air fryer and cook at 360 degrees F for 10 minutes.
2. In a pan that fits your air fryer, mix onion with carrots, garlic, tomato paste, tomato, oregano, wine and water and toss.
3. Add lamb, toss, introduce in your air fryer and cook at 370 degrees F for 35 minutes.
4. Divide everything on plates and serve

Nutrition: calories 432 - Fat 17 - Fiber 8 - Carbs 17 - Protein 43

18. Marinated Lamb and Veggies

Prep.Time: 10 min - **Cooking Time:** 30 min - **Servings:** 4

Ingredients:
- ✓ 1 carrot, chopped
- ✓ 1 onion, sliced
- ✓ ½ tbsp. olive oil
- ✓ 3 ounces bean sprouts
- ✓ 8 ounces lamb loin, sliced
- *For the marinade:*
- ✓ 1 garlic clove, minced
- ✓ ½ apple, grated
- ✓ Salt and black pepper to the taste
- ✓ 1 small yellow onion, grated
- ✓ 1 tbsp. ginger, grated
- ✓ 5 tbsp. soy sauce
- ✓ 1 tbsp. sugar
- ✓ 2 tbsp. orange juice

Directions:
1. In a bowl, mix 1 grated onion with the apple, garlic, 1 tablespoon ginger, soy sauce, orange juice, sugar and black pepper, whisk well, add lamb and leave aside for 10 minutes.
2. Heat up a pan that fits your air fryer with the olive oil over medium high heat, add 1 sliced onion, carrot and bean sprouts, stir and cook for 3 minutes.
3. Add lamb and the marinade, transfer pan to your preheated air fryer and cook at 360 degrees F for 25 minutes.
4. Divide everything into bowls and serve

Nutrition: calories 265 - Fat 3 - Fiber 7 - Carbs 18 - Protein 22

19. Air Fryer Lamb Shanks

Prep.Time: 10 min - **Cooking Time:** 45 minutes - **Servings:** 4

Ingredients:
- ✓ 4 lamb shanks
- ✓ 1 yellow onion, chopped
- ✓ 1 tbsp. olive oil
- ✓ 4 tsp. coriander seeds, crushed
- ✓ 2 tbsp. white flour
- ✓ 4 bay leaves
- ✓ 2 tsp. honey
- ✓ 5 ounces dry sherry
- ✓ 2 and ½ cups chicken stock
- ✓ Salt and pepper to the taste

Directions:
1. Season lamb shanks with salt and pepper, rub with half of the oil, put in your air fryer and cook at 360 degrees F for 10 minutes.
2. Heat up a pan that fits your air fryer with the rest of the oil over medium high heat, add onion and coriander, stir and cook for 5 minutes.
3. Add flour, sherry, stock, honey and bay leaves, salt and pepper, stir, bring to a simmer, add lamb, introduce everything in your air fryer and cook at 360 degrees F for 30 minutes.
4. Divide everything on plates and serve.

Nutrition: calories 283 - Fat 4 - Fiber 2 - Carbs 17 - Protein 26

20. Garlic and Bell Pepper Beef

Prep.Time: 30 min - **Cooking Time:** 30 min - **Servings:** 4

Ingredients:
- ✓ 11 ounces steak fillets, sliced
- ✓ 4 garlic cloves, minced
- ✓ 2 tbsp. olive oil
- ✓ 1 red bell pepper, cut into strips
- ✓ Black pepper to the taste
- ✓ 1 tablespoon sugar
- ✓ 2 tablespoons fish sauce
- ✓ 2 teaspoons corn flour
- ✓ ½ cup beef stock
- ✓ 4 green onions, sliced

Directions:
1. In a pan that fits your air fryer mix beef with oil, garlic, black pepper and bell pepper, stir, cover and keep in the fridge for 30 minutes.
2. Put the pan in your preheated air fryer and cook at 360 degrees F for 14 minutes.
3. In a bowl, mix sugar with fish sauce, stir well, pour over beef and cook at 360 degrees F for 7 minutes more.
4. Add stock mixed with corn flour and green onions, toss and cook at 370 degrees F for 7 minutes more.
5. Divide everything on plates and serve.

Nutrition: calories 343 - Fat 3 - Fiber 12 - Carbs 26 - Protein 38

21. Beef and Cabbage Mix

Prep.Time: 10 min - **Cooking Time:** 40 min - **Servings:** 6

Ingredients:
- ✓ 2 and ½ pounds beef brisket
- ✓ 1 cup beef stock
- ✓ 2 bay leaves
- ✓ 3 garlic cloves, chopped
- ✓ 4 carrots, chopped
- ✓ 1 cabbage head, cut into medium wedges
- ✓ Salt and black pepper to the taste
- ✓ 3 turnips, cut into quarters

Directions:
1. Put beef brisket and stock in a large pan that fits your air fryer, season beef with salt and pepper, add garlic and bay leaves, carrots, cabbage, potatoes and turnips, toss, introduce in your air fryer and cook at 360 degrees F and cook for 40 minutes.
2. Divide among plates and serve.

Nutrition: calories 353 - Fat 16 - Fiber 7 - Carbs 20 - Protein 24

22. Short Ribs and Special Sauce

Prep.Time: 10 min - **Cooking Time:** 36 min - **Servings:** 4

Ingredients:
- ✓ 2 and ½ pounds beef brisket
- ✓ 1 cup beef stock
- ✓ 2 bay leaves
- ✓ 3 garlic cloves, chopped
- ✓ 4 carrots, chopped
- ✓ 1 cabbage head, cut into medium wedges
- ✓ Salt and black pepper to the taste
- ✓ 3 turnips, cut into quarters

Directions:
1. Heat up a pan that fits your air fryer with the oil over medium heat, add green onions, ginger and garlic, stir and cook for 1 minute.
2. Add ribs, water, wine, soy sauce, sesame oil and pear juice, stir, introduce in your air fryer and cook at 350 degrees F for 35 minutes.
3. Divide ribs and sauce on plates and serve.

Nutrition: calories 321 - Fat 12 - Fiber 4 - Carbs 20 - Protein 14

23. Flavored Rib Eye Steak

Prep.Time: 10 min - **Cooking Time:** 20 min - **Servings:** 4

Ingredients:
- ✓ 2 pounds rib eye steak
- ✓ Salt and black pepper to the taste
- ✓ 1 tablespoons olive oil
- *For the rub:*
- ✓ 3 tablespoons sweet paprika
- ✓ 2 tablespoons onion powder
- ✓ 2 tbsp. garlic powder
- ✓ 1 tablespoon brown sugar
- ✓ 2 tablespoons oregano, dried
- ✓ 1 tablespoon cumin, ground
- ✓ 1 tablespoon rosemary, dried

Directions:
1. In a bowl, mix paprika with onion and garlic powder, sugar, oregano, rosemary, salt, pepper and cumin, stir and rub steak with this mix.
2. Season steak with salt and pepper, rub again with the oil, put in your air fryer and cook at 400 degrees F for 20 minutes, flipping them halfway.
3. Transfer steak to a cutting board, slice and serve with a side salad

Nutrition: calories 320 - Fat 8 - Fiber 7 - Carbs 22 - Protein 21

24. Mustard Marinated Beef

Prep.Time: 10 min - **Cooking Time:** 45 min - **Servings:** 6

Ingredients:
- ✓ 6 bacon strips
- ✓ 2 tablespoons butter
- ✓ 3 garlic cloves, minced
- ✓ Salt and black pepper to the taste
- ✓ 1 tablespoon horseradish
- ✓ 1 tablespoon mustard
- ✓ 3 pounds beef roast
- ✓ 1 and ¾ cup beef stock
- ✓ ¾ cup red wine

Directions:
1. In a bowl, mix butter with mustard, garlic, salt, pepper and horseradish, whisk and rub beef with this mix.
2. Arrange bacon strips on a cutting board, place beef on top, fold bacon around beef, transfer to your air fryer's basket, cook at 400 degrees F for 15 minutes and transfer to a pan that fits your fryer.
3. Add stock and wine to beef, introduce pan in your air fryer and cook at 360 degrees F for 30 minutes more.
4. Carve beef, divide among plates and serve with a side salad.

Nutrition: calories 500 - Fat 9 - Fiber4 - Carbs 29 - Protein 36

25. Beef Strips with Snow Peas and Mushrooms

Prep.Time: 10 min - **Cooking Time:** 22 minutes - **Servings:** 2

Ingredients:
- ✓ 2 beef steaks, cut into strips
- ✓ Salt and black pepper to the taste
- ✓ 7 ounces snow peas
- ✓ 8 ounces white mushrooms, halved
- ✓ 1 yellow onion, cut into rings
- ✓ 2 tablespoons soy sauce
- ✓ 1 teaspoon olive oil

Directions:
1. In a bowl, mix olive oil with soy sauce, whisk, add beef strips and toss.
2. In another bowl, mix snow peas, onion and mushrooms with salt, pepper and the oil, toss well, put in a pan that fits your air fryer and cook at 350 degrees F for 16 minutes.
3. Add beef strips to the pan as well and cook at 400 degrees F for 6 minutes more.
4. Divide everything on plates and serve.

Nutrition: calories 235 - Fat 8 - Fiber 2 - Carbs 22 - Protein 24

26. Fennel Flavored Pork Roast

Prep.Time: 10 min - **Cooking Time:** 1 hour - **Servings:** 10

Ingredients:
- ✓ 5 and ½ pounds pork loin roast, trimmed
- ✓ Salt and black pepper to the taste
- ✓ 3 garlic cloves, minced
- ✓ 2 tablespoons rosemary, chopped
- ✓ 1 teaspoon fennel, ground
- ✓ 1 tablespoon fennel seeds
- ✓ 2 teaspoons red pepper, crushed
- ✓ ¼ cup olive oil

Directions:
1. In your food processor mix garlic with fennel seeds, fennel, rosemary, red pepper, some black pepper and the olive oil and blend until you obtain a paste.
2. Spread 2 tablespoons garlic paste on pork loin, rub well, season with salt and pepper, introduce in your preheated air fryer and cook at 350 degrees F for 30 minutes.
3. Reduce heat to 300 degrees F and cook for 15 minutes more.
4. Slice pork, divide among plates and serve.

Nutrition: calories 300 - Fat 14 - Fiber 9 - Carbs 26 - Protein 22

27. Chinese Steak and Broccoli

Prep.Time: 45 min - **Cooking Time:** 12 min - **Servings:** 4

Ingredients:
- ✓ ¾ pound round steak, cut into strips
- ✓ 1 pound broccoli florets
- ✓ 1/3 cup oyster sauce
- ✓ 2 teaspoons sesame oil
- ✓ 1 teaspoon soy sauce
- ✓ 1 teaspoon sugar
- ✓ 1/3 cup sherry
- ✓ 1 tablespoon olive oil
- ✓ 1 garlic clove, minced

Directions:
1. In a bowl, mix sesame oil with oyster sauce, soy sauce, sherry and sugar, stir well, add beef, toss and leave aside for 30 minutes.
2. Transfer beef to a pan that fits your air fryer, also add broccoli, garlic and oil, toss everything and cook at 380 degrees F for 12 minutes.
3. Divide among plates and serve.

Nutrition: calories 330 - Fat 12 - Fiber 7 - Carbs 23 - Protein 23

28. Pork Chops and Mushrooms Mix

Prep.Time: 10 min - **Cooking Time:** 40 min - **Servings:** 3

Ingredients:
- ✓ 8 ounces mushrooms, sliced
- ✓ 1 teaspoon garlic powder
- ✓ 1 yellow onion, chopped
- ✓ 1 cup mayonnaise
- ✓ 3 pork chops, boneless
- ✓ 1 teaspoon nutmeg
- ✓ 1 tablespoon balsamic vinegar
- ✓ ½ cup olive oil

Directions:
1. Heat up a pan that fits your air fryer with the oil over medium heat, add mushrooms and onions, stir and cook for 4 minutes.
2. Add pork chops, nutmeg and garlic powder and brown on both sides.
3. Introduce pan your air fryer at 330 degrees F and cook for 30 minutes.
4. Add vinegar and mayo, stir, divide everything on plates and serve.

Nutrition: calories 600 - Fat 10 - Fiber 1 - Carbs 8 - Protein 30

29. Oriental Air Fried Lamb

Prep.Time: 10 min - **Cooking Time:** 42 min - **Servings:** 8

Ingredients:
- ✓ 2 and ½ pounds lamb shoulder, chopped
- ✓ 3 tablespoons honey
- ✓ 3 ounces almonds, peeled and chopped
- ✓ 9 ounces plumps, pitted
- ✓ 8 ounces veggie stock
- ✓ 2 yellow onions, chopped
- ✓ 2 garlic cloves, minced
- ✓ Salt and black pepper to the tastes
- ✓ 1 tsp. cumin powder
- ✓ 1 tsp. turmeric powder
- ✓ 1 tsp. ginger powder
- ✓ 1 tsp. cinnamon powder
- ✓ 3 tablespoons olive oil

Directions:
1. In a bowl, mix cinnamon powder with ginger, cumin, turmeric, garlic, olive oil and lamb, toss to coat, place in your preheated air fryer and cook at 350 degrees F for 8 minutes.
2. Transfer meat to a dish that fits your air fryer, add onions, stock, honey and plums, stir, introduce in your air fryer and cook at 350 degrees F for 35 minutes.
3. Divide everything on plates and serve with almond sprinkled on top.

Nutrition: calories 432 - Fat 23 - Fiber 6 - Carbs 30 - Protein 20

30. Beef Roast and Wine Sauce

Prep.Time: 10 min - **Cooking Time:** 45 min - **Servings:** 6

Ingredients:
- ✓ 3 pounds beef roast
- ✓ Salt and black pepper to the taste
- ✓ 17 ounces beef stock
- ✓ 3 ounces red wine
- ✓ ½ teaspoon chicken salt
- ✓ ½ teaspoon smoked paprika
- ✓ 1 yellow onion, chopped
- ✓ 4 garlic cloves, minced
- ✓ 3 carrots, chopped
- ✓ 5 potatoes, chopped

Directions:
1. In a bowl, mix salt, pepper, chicken salt and paprika, stir, rub beef with this mix and put it in a big pan that fits your air fryer.
2. Add onion, garlic, stock, wine, potatoes and carrots, introduce in your air fryer and cook at 360 degrees F for 45 minutes.
3. Divide everything on plates and serve.

Nutrition: calories 304 - Fat 20 - Fiber 7 - Carbs 20 - Protein 32

31. Short Ribs and Beer Sauce

Prep.Time: 15 min - **Cooking Time:** 45 minutes - **Servings:** 6

Ingredients:
- ✓ 4 pounds short ribs, cut into small pieces
- ✓ 1 yellow onion, chopped
- ✓ Salt and black pepper to the taste
- ✓ ¼ cup tomato paste
- ✓ 1 cup dark beer
- ✓ cup chicken stock
- ✓ 1 bay leaf
- ✓ 6 thyme springs, chopped
- ✓ 1 Portobello mushroom, dried

Directions:
1. Heat up a pan that fits your air fryer over medium heat, add tomato paste, onion, stock, beer, mushroom, bay leaves and thyme and bring to a simmer.
2. Add ribs, introduce in your air fryer and cook at 350 degrees F for 40 minutes.
3. Divide everything on plates and serve.

Nutrition: calories 300 - Fat 7 - Fiber 8 - Carbs 18 - Protein 23

32. Roasted Pork Belly and Apple Sauce

Prep.Time: 10 min - **Cooking Time:** 40 min - **Servings:** 6

Ingredients:
- ✓ 2 tablespoons sugar
- ✓ 1 tablespoon lemon juice
- ✓ 1 quart water
- ✓ 17 ounces apples, cored and cut into wedges
- ✓ 2 pounds pork belly, scored
- ✓ Salt and black pepper to the taste
- ✓ A drizzle of olive oil

Directions:
1. In your blender, mix water with apples, lemon juice and sugar, pulse well, transfer to a bowl, add meat, toss well, drain, put in your air fryer and cook at 400 degrees F for 40 minutes.
2. Pour the sauce in a pot, heat up over medium heat and simmer for 15 minutes.
3. Slice pork belly, divide among plates, drizzle the sauce all over and serve.

Nutrition: calories 456 - Fat 34 - Fiber 4 - Carbs 10 - Protein 25

33. Lamb and Spinach Mix

Prep.Time: 10 min - **Cooking Time:** 35 min - **Servings:** 6

Ingredients:
- ✓ 2 tbsp ginger, grated
- ✓ 2 garlic cloves, minced
- ✓ 2 tsp cardamom, ground
- ✓ 1 red onion, chopped
- ✓ 1 pound lamb meat, cubed
- ✓ 2 tsp cumin powder
- ✓ 1 teaspoon garam masala
- ✓ ½ teaspoon chili powder
- ✓ 1 teaspoon turmeric
- ✓ 2 tsp. coriander, ground
- ✓ 1 pound spinach
- ✓ 14 ounces canned tomatoes, chopped

Directions:
1. In a heat proof dish that fits your air fryer, mix lamb with spinach, tomatoes, ginger, garlic, onion, cardamom, cloves, cumin, garam masala, chili, turmeric and coriander, stir, introduce in preheated air fryer and cook at 360 degrees F for 35 minutes.
2. Divide into bowls and serve.

Nutrition: calories 160 - Fat 6 - Fiber 3 - Carbs 17 - Protein 20

34. Lamb Racks and Fennel Mix

Prep.Time: 10 min - **Cooking Time:** 16 min - **Servings:** 4

Ingredients:
- ✓ 12 ounces lamb racks
- ✓ 2 fennel bulbs, sliced
- ✓ Salt and black pepper to the taste
- ✓ 2 tablespoons olive oil
- ✓ 4 figs, cut into halves
- ✓ 1/8 cup apple cider vinegar
- ✓ 1 tablespoon brown sugar

Directions:
1. In a bowl, mix fennel with figs, vinegar, sugar and oil, toss to coat well, transfer to a baking dish that fits your air fryer, introduce in your air fryer and cook at 350 degrees F for 6 minutes.
2. Season lamb with salt and pepper, add to the baking dish with the fennel mix and air fry for 10 minutes more.
3. Divide everything on plates and serve

Nutrition: calories 240 - Fat 9 - Fiber 3 - Carbs 15 - Protein 12

35. Beef Stuffed Squash

Prep.Time: 10 min - **Cooking Time:** 40 min - **Servings:** 2

Ingredients:
- ✓ 1 spaghetti squash, pricked
- ✓ 1 pound beef, ground
- ✓ Salt and black pepper to the taste
- ✓ 3 garlic cloves, minced
- ✓ 1 yellow onion, chopped
- ✓ 1 Portobello mushroom, sliced
- ✓ 28 ounces canned tomatoes, chopped
- ✓ 1 tsp. oregano, dried
- ✓ ¼ tsp. cayenne pepper
- ✓ ½ teaspoon thyme, dried
- ✓ 1 green bell pepper, chopped

Directions:
1. Put spaghetti squash in your air fryer, cook at 350 degrees F for 20 minutes, transfer to a cutting board, and cut into halves and discard seeds.
2. Heat up a pan over medium high heat, add meat, garlic, onion and mushroom, stir and cook until meat browns.
3. Add salt, pepper, thyme, oregano, cayenne, tomatoes and green pepper, stir and cook for 10 minutes.
4. Stuff squash with this beef mix, introduce in the fryer and cook at 360 degrees F for 10 minutes.
5. Divide among plates and serve.

Nutrition: calories 260 - Fat 7 - Fiber 2 - Carbs 14 - Protein 10

36. Beef Casserole

Prep.Time: 30 min - **Cooking Time:** 35 min - **Servings:** 12

Ingredients:
- ✓ 1 tablespoon olive oil
- ✓ 2 pounds beef, ground
- ✓ 2 cups eggplant, chopped
- ✓ Salt and black pepper to the taste
- ✓ 2 teaspoons mustard
- ✓ 2 teaspoons gluten free Worcestershire sauce
- ✓ 28 ounces canned tomatoes, chopped
- ✓ 2 cups mozzarella, grated
- ✓ 16 ounces tomato sauce
- ✓ 2 tbsp. parsley, chopped
- ✓ 1 teaspoon oregano, dried

Directions:
1. In a bowl, mix eggplant with salt, pepper and oil and toss to coat.
2. In another bowl, mix beef with salt, pepper, mustard and Worcestershire sauce, stir well and spread on the bottom of a pan that fits your air fryer.
3. Add eggplant mix, tomatoes, tomato sauce, parsley, oregano and sprinkle mozzarella at the end.
4. Introduce in your air fryer and cook at 360 degrees F for 35 minutes
5. Divide among plates and serve hot.

Nutrition: calories 200 - Fat 12 - Fiber 2 - Carbs 16 - Protein 15

37. Lamb and Lemon Sauce

Prep.Time: 10 min - **Cooking Time:** 30 minutes - **Servings:** 4

Ingredients:
- ✓ 2 lamb shanks
- ✓ Salt and black pepper to the taste
- ✓ 2 garlic cloves, minced
- ✓ 4 tablespoons olive oil
- ✓ Juice from ½ lemon
- ✓ Zest from ½ lemon
- ✓ ½ teaspoon oregano, dried

Directions:
1. Season lamb with salt, pepper, rub with garlic, put in your air fryer and cook at 350 degrees F for 30 minutes.
2. Meanwhile, in a bowl, mix lemon juice with lemon zest, some salt and pepper, the olive oil and oregano and whisk very well.
3. Shred lamb, discard bone, divide among plates, drizzle the lemon dressing all over and serve.

Nutrition: calories 260 - Fat 7 - Fiber 3 - Carbs 15 - Protein 12

38. Creamy Ham and Cauliflower Mix

Prep.Time: 10 min - **Cooking Time:** 4 hours - **Servings:** 6

Ingredients:
- ✓ 8 ounces cheddar cheese, grated
- ✓ 4 cups ham, cubed
- ✓ 14 ounces chicken stock
- ✓ ½ teaspoon garlic powder
- ✓ ½ tsp. onion powder
- ✓ Salt and black pepper to the taste
- ✓ 4 garlic cloves, minced
- ✓ ¼ cup heavy cream
- ✓ 16 ounces cauliflower florets

Directions:
1. In a pot that fits your air fryer, mix ham with stock, cheese, cauliflower, garlic powder, onion powder, salt, pepper, garlic and heavy cream, stir, put in your air fryer and cook at 300 degrees F for 1 hour.
2. Divide into bowls and serve.

Nutrition: calories 320 - Fat 20 - Fiber 3 - Carbs 16 - Protein 23

39. Air Fried Sausage and Mushrooms

Prep.Time: 10 min - **Cooking Time:** 40 min - **Servings:** 6

Ingredients:
- ✓ 3 red bell peppers, chopped
- ✓ 2 pounds pork sausage, sliced
- ✓ Salt and black pepper to the taste
- ✓ 2 pounds Portobello mushrooms, sliced
- ✓ 2 sweet onions, chopped
- ✓ 1 tbsp. brown sugar
- ✓ 1 teaspoon olive oil

Directions:
1. In a baking dish that fits your air fryer, mix sausage slices with oil, salt, pepper, bell pepper, mushrooms, onion and sugar, toss, introduce in your air fryer and cook at 300 degrees F for 40 minutes.
2. Divide among plates and serve right away.

Nutrition: calories 130 - Fat 12 - Fiber 1 - Carbs 13 - Protein 18

40. Sausage and Kale

Prep.Time: 10 min - **Cooking Time:** 20 min - **Servings:** 4

Ingredients:
- ✓ 1 cup yellow onion, chopped
- ✓ 1 and ½ pound Italian pork sausage, sliced
- ✓ ½ cup red bell pepper, chopped
- ✓ Salt and black pepper to the taste
- ✓ 5 pounds kale, chopped
- ✓ 1 teaspoon garlic, minced
- ✓ ¼ cup red hot chili pepper, chopped
- ✓ 1 cup water

Directions:
1. In a pan that fits your air fryer, mix sausage with onion, bell pepper, salt, pepper, kale, garlic, water and chili pepper, toss, introduce in preheated air fryer and cook at 300 degrees F for 20 minutes.
2. Divide everything on plates and serve.

Nutrition: calories 150 - Fat 4 - Fiber 1 - Carbs 12 - Protein 14

41. Beef Patties and Mushroom Sauce

Prep.Time: 10 min - **Cooking Time:** 25 min - **Servings:** 4

Ingredients:
- ✓ 2 pounds beef, ground
- ✓ Salt and black pepper to the taste
- ✓ ½ teaspoon garlic powder
- ✓ 1 tablespoon soy sauce
- ✓ ¼ cup beef stock
- ✓ ¾ cup flour
- ✓ 1 tablespoon parsley, chopped
- ✓ 1 tablespoon onion flakes

For the sauce:
- ✓ 1 cup yellow onion, chopped
- ✓ 2 cups mushrooms, sliced
- ✓ 2 tablespoons bacon fat
- ✓ 2 tablespoons butter
- ✓ ½ teaspoon soy sauce
- ✓ ¼ cup sour cream
- ✓ ½ cup beef stock
- ✓ Salt and black pepper to the taste

Directions:
1. In a bowl, mix beef with salt, pepper, garlic powder, 1 tablespoon soy sauce, ¼ cup beef stock, flour, parsley and onion flakes, stir well, shape 6 patties, place them in your air fryer and cook at 350 degrees F for 14 minutes.
2. Meanwhile, heat up a pan with the butter and the bacon fat over medium heat, add mushrooms, stir and cook for 4 minutes.
3. Add onions, stir and cook for 4 minutes more.
4. Add ½ teaspoon soy sauce, sour cream and ½ cup stock, stir well, bring to a simmer and take off heat.
5. Divide beef patties on plates and serve with mushroom sauce on top.

Nutrition: calories 435 - Fat 23 - Fiber 4 - Carbs 6 - Protein 32

42. Greek Beef Meatballs Salad

Prep.Time: 10 min - **Cooking Time:** 10 min - **Servings:** 2

Ingredients:
- ✓ ¼ cup milk
- ✓ 17 ounces beef, ground
- ✓ 1 yellow onion, grated
- ✓ 5 bread slices, cubed
- ✓ 1 egg, whisked
- ✓ ¼ cup parsley, chopped
- ✓ Salt and black pepper to the taste
- ✓ 2 garlic cloves, minced
- ✓ ¼ cup mint, chopped
- ✓ 2 and ½ teaspoons oregano, dried
- ✓ 1 tablespoon olive oil
- ✓ Cooking spray
- ✓ 7 ounces cherry tomatoes, halved
- ✓ 1 cup baby spinach
- ✓ 1 and ½ tablespoons lemon juice
- ✓ 7 ounces Greek yogurt

Directions:
1. Put torn bread in a bowl, add milk, soak for a few minutes, squeeze and transfer to another bowl.
2. Add beef, egg, salt, pepper, oregano, mint, parsley, garlic and onion, stir and shape medium meatballs out of this mix.
3. Spray them with cooking spray, place them in your air fryer and cook at 370 degrees F for 10 minutes.
4.
5. In a salad bowl, mix spinach with cucumber and tomato.
6. Add meatballs, the oil, some salt, pepper, lemon juice and yogurt, toss and serve.

Nutrition: calories 200 - Fat 4 - Fiber 8 - Carbs 13 - Protein 27

43. Stuffed Pork Steaks

Prep.Time: 10 min - **Cooking Time:** 20 minutes - **Servings:** 4

Ingredients:
- ✓ Zest from 2 limes, grated
- ✓ Zest from 1 orange, grated
- ✓ Juice from 1 orange
- ✓ Juice from 2 limes
- ✓ 4 teaspoons garlic, minced
- ✓ ¾ cup olive oil
- ✓ 1 cup cilantro, chopped
- ✓ 1 cup mint, chopped
- ✓ 1 teaspoon oregano, dried
- ✓ Salt and black pepper to the taste
- ✓ 2 teaspoons cumin, ground
- ✓ 4 pork loin steaks
- ✓ 2 pickles, chopped
- ✓ 4 ham slices
- ✓ 6 Swiss cheese slices
- ✓ 2 tablespoons mustard

Directions:
1. In your food processor, mix lime zest and juice with orange zest and juice, garlic, oil, cilantro, mint, oregano, cumin, salt and pepper and blend well.
2. Season steaks with salt and pepper, place them into a bowl, add marinade and toss to coat.
3. Place steaks on a working surface, divide pickles, cheese, mustard and ham on them, roll and secure with toothpicks.
4. Put stuffed pork steaks in your air fryer and cook at 340 degrees F for 20 minutes.
5. Divide among plates and serve with a side salad.

Nutrition: calories 270 - Fat 7 - Fiber 2 - Carbs 13 - Protein 20

44. Creamy Lamb

Prep.Time: 1 day - **Cooking Time:** 1 hour - **Servings:** 8

Ingredients:
- ✓ 5 pounds leg of lamb
- ✓ 2 cups low fat buttermilk
- ✓ 2 tablespoons mustard
- ✓ ½ cup butter
- ✓ 2 tablespoons basil, chopped
- ✓ 2 tablespoons tomato paste
- ✓ 2 garlic cloves, minced
- ✓ Salt and black pepper to the taste
- ✓ 1 cup white wine
- ✓ 1 tablespoon cornstarch mixed with 1 tablespoon water
- ✓ ½ cup sour cream

Directions:
1. Put lamb roast in a big dish, add buttermilk, toss to coat, cover and keep in the fridge for 24 hours.
2. Pat dry lamb and put in a pan that fits your air fryer.
3. In a bowl, mix butter with tomato paste, mustard, basil, rosemary, salt, pepper and garlic, whisk well, spread over lamb, introduce everything in your air fryer and cook at 300 degrees F for 1 hour.
4. Slice lamb, divide among plates, leave aside for now and heat up cooking juices from the pan on your stove.
5. Add wine, cornstarch mix, salt, pepper and sour cream, stir, take off heat, drizzle this sauce over lamb and serve.

Nutrition: calories 287 - Fat 4 - Fiber 7 - Carbs 19 - Protein 25

45. Simple Braised Pork

Prep.Time: 40 min - **Cooking Time:** 40 min - **Servings:** 4

Ingredients:
- ✓ 2 pounds pork loin roast, boneless and cubed
- ✓ 4 tbsp. butter, melted
- ✓ Salt and black pepper to the taste
- ✓ 2 cups chicken stock
- ✓ ½ cup dry white wine
- ✓ 2 garlic cloves, minced
- ✓ 1 teaspoon thyme, chopped
- ✓ 1 thyme spring
- ✓ 1 bay leaf
- ✓ ½ yellow onion, chopped
- ✓ 2 tablespoons white flour
- ✓ ½ pound red grapes

Directions:
1. Season pork cubes with salt and pepper, rub with 2 tablespoons melted butter, put in your air fryer and cook at 370 degrees F for 8 minutes.
2. Meanwhile, heat up a pan that fits your air fryer with 2 tablespoons butter over medium high heat, add garlic and onion, stir and cook for 2 minutes.
3. Add wine, stock, salt, pepper, thyme, flour and bay leaf, stir well, bring to a simmer and take off heat.
4. Add pork cubes and grapes, toss, introduce in your air fryer and cook at 360 degrees F for 30 minutes more.
5. Divide everything on plates and serve.

Nutrition: calories 320 - Fat 4 - Fiber 5 - Carbs 29 - Protein 38

46. Lamb and Green Pesto

Prep.Time: 1 hour - **Cooking Time:** 45 min - **Servings:** 4

Ingredients:
- ✓ 1 cup parsley
- ✓ 1 cup mint
- ✓ 1 small yellow onion, roughly chopped
- ✓ 1/3 cup pistachios, chopped
- ✓ 1 tsp. lemon zest, grated
- ✓ 5 tablespoons olive oil
- ✓ Salt and black pepper to the taste
- ✓ 2 pounds lamb riblets
- ✓ ½ onion, chopped
- ✓ 5 garlic cloves, minced
- ✓ Juice from 1 orange

Directions:
1. In your food processor, mix parsley with mint, onion, pistachios, lemon zest, salt, pepper and oil and blend very well.
2. Rub lamb with this mix, place in a bowl, cover and leave in the fridge for 1 hour.
3. Transfer lamb to a baking dish that fits your air fryer, also add garlic, drizzle orange juice and cook in your air fryer at 300 degrees F for 45 minutes.
4. Divide lamb on plates and serve.

Nutrition: calories 200 - Fat 4 - Fiber 6 - Carbs 15 - Protein 7

47. Sirloin Steaks and Pico De Gallo

Prep.Time: 10 min - **Cooking Time:** 10 minutes - **Servings:** 4

Ingredients:
- ✓ 2 tablespoons chili powder
- ✓ 4 medium sirloin steaks
- ✓ 1 teaspoon cumin, ground
- ✓ ½ tablespoon sweet paprika
- ✓ 1 teaspoon onion powder
- ✓ 1 teaspoon garlic powder
- ✓ Salt and black pepper to the taste

For the Pico de Gallo:
- ✓ 1 small red onion, chopped
- ✓ 2 tomatoes, chopped
- ✓ 2 garlic cloves, minced
- ✓ 2 tablespoons lime juice
- ✓ 1 small green bell pepper, chopped
- ✓ 1 jalapeno, chopped
- ✓ ¼ cup cilantro, chopped
- ✓ ¼ teaspoon cumin, ground

Directions:
1. In a bowl, mix chili powder with a pinch of salt, black pepper, onion powder, garlic powder, paprika and 1 teaspoon cumin, stir well, season steaks with this mix, put them in your air fryer and cook at 360 degrees F for 10 minutes.
2. In a bowl, mix red onion with tomatoes, garlic, lime juice, bell pepper, jalapeno, cilantro, black pepper to the taste and ¼ teaspoon cumin and toss.
3. Top steaks with this mix and serve right away.

Nutrition: calories 200 - Fat 12 - Fiber 4 - Carbs 15 - Protein 18

48. Filet Mignon and Mushrooms Sauce

Prep.Time: 10 min - **Cooking Time:** 25 min - **Servings:** 4

Ingredients:
- ✓ 12 mushrooms, sliced
- ✓ 1 shallot, chopped
- ✓ 4 fillet mignons
- ✓ 2 garlic cloves, minced
- ✓ 2 tablespoons olive oil
- ✓ ¼ cup Dijon mustard
- ✓ ¼ cup wine
- ✓ 1 and ¼ cup coconut cream
- ✓ 2 tablespoons parsley, chopped
- ✓ Salt and black pepper to the taste

Directions:
1. Heat up a pan with the oil over medium high heat, add garlic and shallots, stir and cook for 3 minutes.
2. Add mushrooms, stir and cook for 4 minutes more.
3. Add wine, stir and cook until it evaporates.
4. Add coconut cream, mustard, parsley, a pinch of salt and black pepper to the taste, stir, cook for 6 minutes more and take off heat.
5. Season fillets with salt and pepper, put them in your air fryer and cook at 360 degrees F for 10 minutes.
6. Divide fillets on plates and serve with the mushroom sauce on top.

Nutrition: calories 340 - Fat 12 - Fiber 1 - Carbs 14 - Protein 23

49. Beef Medallions Mix

Prep.Time: 2 hours - **Cooking Time:** 10 min - **Servings:** 4

Ingredients:
- ✓ 2 teaspoons chili powder
- ✓ 1 cup tomatoes, crushed
- ✓ 4 beef medallions
- ✓ 2 teaspoons onion powder
- ✓ 2 tablespoons soy sauce
- ✓ Salt and black pepper to the taste
- ✓ 1 tablespoons hot pepper
- ✓ 2 tablespoons lime juice

Directions:
1. In a bowl, mix tomatoes with hot pepper, soy sauce, chili powder, onion powder, a pinch of salt, black pepper and lime juice and whisk well.
2. Arrange beef medallions in a dish, pour sauce over them, toss and leave them aside for 2 hours.
3. Discard tomato marinade, put beef in your preheated air fryer and cook at 360 degrees F for 10 minutes.
4. Divide steaks on plates and serve with a side salad.

Nutrition: calories 230 - Fat 4 - Fiber 1 - Carbs 13 - Protein 14

50. Pork Chops and Sage Sauce

Prep.Time: 10 min - **Cooking Time:** 15 min - **Servings:** 2

Ingredients:
- ✓ 2 pork chops
- ✓ Salt and black pepper to the taste
- ✓ 1 tablespoon olive oil
- ✓ 2 tablespoons butter
- ✓ 1 shallot, sliced
- ✓ 1 handful sage, chopped
- ✓ 1 teaspoon lemon juice

Directions:
1. Season pork chops with salt and pepper, rub with the oil, put in your air fryer and cook at 370 degrees F for 10 minutes, flipping them halfway.
2. Meanwhile, heat up a pan with the butter over medium heat, add shallot, stir and cook for 2 minutes.
3. Add sage and lemon juice, stir well, cook for a few more minutes and take off heat.
4. Divide pork chops on plates, drizzle sage sauce all over and serve.

Nutrition: calories 265 - Fat 6 - Fiber 8 - Carbs 19 - Protein 12

51. Tasty Ham and Greens

Prep.Time: 10 min - **Cooking Time:** 16 minutes - **Servings:** 8

Ingredients:
- ✓ 2 tablespoons olive oil
- ✓ 4 cups ham, chopped
- ✓ 2 tablespoons flour
- ✓ 3 cups chicken stock
- ✓ 5 ounces onion, chopped
- ✓ 16 ounces collard greens, chopped
- ✓ 14 ounces canned black eyed peas, drained
- ✓ ½ teaspoon red pepper, crushed

Directions:
1. Drizzle the oil in a pan that fits your air fryer, add ham, stock and flour and whisk.
2. Also add onion, black eyed peas, red pepper and collard greens, introduce in your air fryer and cook at 390 degrees F for 16 minutes.
3. Divide everything on plates and serve.

Nutrition: calories 322 - Fat 6 - Fiber 8 - Carbs 12 - Protein 5

52. Ham and Veggie Air Fried Mix

Prep.Time: 10 min - **Cooking Time:** 20 min - **Servings:** 6

Ingredients:
- ✓ ¼ cup butter
- ✓ ¼ cup flour
- ✓ 3 cups milk
- ✓ ½ teaspoon thyme, dried
- ✓ 2 cups ham, chopped
- ✓ 6 ounces sweet peas
- ✓ 4 ounces mushrooms, halved
- ✓ 1 cup baby carrots

Directions:
1. Heat up a large pan that fits your air fryer with the butter over medium heat, melt it, add flour and whisk well.
2. Add milk and, well again and take off heat.
3. Add thyme, ham, peas, mushrooms and baby carrots, toss, put in your air fryer and cook at 360 degrees F for 20 minutes.
4. Divide everything on plates and serve.

Nutrition: calories 311 - Fat 6 - Fiber 8 - Carbs 12 - Protein 7

53. Pork Chops and Green Beans

Prep.Time: 10 min - **Cooking Time:** 15 min - **Servings:** 4

Ingredients:
- ✓ 4 pork chops, bone in
- ✓ 2 tablespoons olive oil
- ✓ 1 tablespoon sage, chopped
- ✓ Salt and black pepper to the taste
- ✓ 16 ounces green beans
- ✓ 3 garlic cloves, minced
- ✓ 2 tablespoons parsley, chopped

Directions:
1. In a pan that fits your air fryer, mix pork chops with olive oil, sage, salt, pepper, green beans, garlic and parsley, toss, introduce in your air fryer and cook at 360 degrees F for 15 minutes.
2. Divide everything on plates and serve.

Nutrition: calories 261 - Fat 7 - Fiber 9 - Carbs 14 - Protein 20

54. Pork Chops and Roasted Peppers

Prep.Time: 10 min - **Cooking Time:** 16 min - **Servings:** 4

Ingredients:
- ✓ 3 tablespoons olive oil
- ✓ 3 tablespoons lemon juice
- ✓ 1 tablespoon smoked paprika
- ✓ 2 tablespoons thyme, chopped
- ✓ 3 garlic cloves, minced
- ✓ 4 pork chops, bone in
- ✓ Salta and black pepper to the taste
- ✓ 2 roasted bell peppers, chopped

Directions:
1. In a pan that fits your air fryer, mix pork chops with oil, lemon juice, smoked paprika, thyme, garlic, bell peppers, salt and pepper, toss well, introduce in your air fryer and cook at 400 degrees F for 16 minutes.
2. Divide pork chops and peppers mix on plates and serve right away.

Nutrition: calories 321 - Fat 6 - Fiber 8 - Carbs 14 - Protein 17

55. Balsamic Beef

Prep.Time: 10 min - **Cooking Time:** 1 hour - **Servings:** 6

Ingredients:
- ✓ 1 medium beef roast
- ✓ 1 tablespoon Worcestershire sauce
- ✓ ½ cup balsamic vinegar
- ✓ 1 cup beef stock
- ✓ 1 tablespoons honey
- ✓ 1 tablespoon soy sauce
- ✓ 4 garlic cloves, minced

Directions:
1. In a heat proof dish that fits your air fryer, mix roast with roast with Worcestershire sauce, vinegar, stock, honey, soy sauce and garlic, toss well, introduce in your air fryer and cook at 370 degrees F for 1 hour.
2. Slice roast, divide among plates, drizzle the sauce all over and serve.

Nutrition: calories 311 - Fat 7 - Fiber 12 - Carbs 20 - Protein 16

56. Coffee Flavored Steaks

Prep.Time: 10 min - **Cooking Time:** 15 min - **Servings:** 4

Ingredients:
- ✓ 1 and ½ tbsp. coffee, ground
- ✓ 4 rib eye steaks
- ✓ ½ tbsp. sweet paprika
- ✓ 2 tbsp. chili powder
- ✓ 2 tsp. garlic powder
- ✓ 2 tsp. onion powder
- ✓ ¼ tsp. ginger, ground
- ✓ ¼ tsp., coriander, ground
- ✓ A pinch of cayenne pepper
- ✓ Black pepper to the taste

Directions:
1. In a bowl, mix coffee with paprika, chili powder, garlic powder, onion powder, ginger, coriander, cayenne and black pepper, stir, rub steaks with this mix, put in preheated air fryer and cook at 360 degrees F for 15 minutes.
2. Divide steaks on plates and serve with a side salad.

Nutrition: calories 160 - Fat 10 - Fiber 8 - Carbs 14 - Protein 12

57. Mediterranean Steaks and Scallops

Prep.Time: 10 min - **Cooking Time:** 14 minutes - **Servings:** 2

Ingredients:
- ✓ 10 sea scallops
- ✓ 2 beef steaks
- ✓ 4 garlic cloves, minced
- ✓ 1 shallot, chopped
- ✓ 2 tbsp. lemon juice
- ✓ 2 tbsp. parsley, chopped
- ✓ 2 tbsp. basil, chopped
- ✓ 1 teaspoon lemon zest
- ✓ ¼ cup butter
- ✓ ¼ cup veggie stock
- ✓ Salt and black pepper to the taste

Directions:
1. Season steaks with salt and pepper, put them in your air fryer, cook at 360 degrees F for 10 minutes and transfer to a pan that fits the fryer.
2. Add shallot, garlic, butter, stock, basil, lemon juice, parsley, lemon zest and scallops, toss everything gently and cook at 360 degrees F for 4 minutes more.
3. Divide steaks and scallops on plates and serve.

Nutrition: calories 150 - Fat 2 - Fiber 2 - Carbs 14 - Protein 17

58. Beef Kabobs

Prep.Time: 10 min - **Cooking Time:** 10 min - **Servings:** 4

Ingredients:
- ✓ 2 red bell peppers, chopped
- ✓ 2 pounds sirloin steak, cut into medium pieces
- ✓ 1 red onion, chopped
- ✓ 1 zucchini, sliced
- ✓ Juice form 1 lime
- ✓ 2 tbsp. chili powder
- ✓ 2 tbsp. hot sauce
- ✓ ½ tbsp. cumin, ground
- ✓ ¼ cup olive oil
- ✓ ¼ cup salsa
- ✓ Salt and black pepper to the taste

Directions:
1. In a bowl, mix salsa with lime juice, oil, hot sauce, chili powder, cumin, salt and black pepper and whisk well.
2. Divide meat bell peppers, zucchini and onion on skewers, brush kabobs with the salsa mix you made earlier, put them in your preheated air fryer and cook them for 10 minutes at 370 degrees F flipping kabobs halfway.
3. Divide among plates and serve with a side salad.

Nutrition: calories 170 - Fat 5 - Fiber 2 - Carbs 13 - Protein 16

59. Mexican Beef Mix

Prep.Time: 10 min - **Cooking Time:** 70 min - **Servings:** 8

Ingredients:
- ✓ 2 yellow onions, chopped
- ✓ 2 tablespoons olive oil
- ✓ 2 pounds beef roast, cubed
- ✓ 2 green bell peppers, chopped
- ✓ 1 habanero pepper, chopped
- ✓ 4 jalapenos, chopped
- ✓ 14 ounces canned tomatoes, chopped
- ✓ 2 tbsp. cilantro, chopped
- ✓ 6 garlic cloves, minced
- ✓ ½ cup water
- ✓ Salt and black pepper to the taste
- ✓ 1 and ½ teaspoons cumin, ground
- ✓ ½ cup black olives, pitted and chopped
- ✓ 1 tsp. oregano, dried

Directions:
1. In a pan that fits your air fryer, combine beef with oil, green bell peppers, onions, jalapenos, habanero pepper, tomatoes, garlic, water, cilantro, oregano, cumin, salt and pepper, stir, put in your air fryer and cook at 300 degrees F for 1 hour and 10 minutes.
2. Add olives, stir, divide into bowls and serve.

Nutrition: calories 305 - Fat 14 - Fiber 4 - Carbs 18 - Protein 25

60. Burgundy Beef Mix

Prep.Time: 10 min - **Cooking Time:** 1 hour - **Servings:** 7

Ingredients:
- ✓ 2 pounds beef chuck roast, cubed
- ✓ 15 ounces canned tomatoes, chopped
- ✓ 4 carrots, chopped
- ✓ Salt and black pepper to the taste
- ✓ ½ pounds mushrooms, sliced
- ✓ 2 celery ribs, chopped
- ✓ 2 yellow onions, chopped
- ✓ 1 cup beef stock
- ✓ 1 tablespoon thyme, chopped
- ✓ ½ teaspoon mustard powder
- ✓ 3 tablespoons almond flour
- ✓ 1 cup water

Directions:
1. Heat up a heat proof pot that fits your air fryer over medium high heat, add beef, stir and brown them for a couple of minutes.
2. Add tomatoes, mushrooms, onions, carrots, celery, salt, pepper mustard, stock and thyme and stir.
3. In a bowl mix water with flour, stir well, add this to the pot, toss, introduce in your air fryer and cook at 300 degrees F for 1 hour.
4. Divide into bowls and serve.

Nutrition: calories 275 - Fat 13 - Fiber 4 - Carbs 17 - Protein 28

61. Tasty Lamb Ribs

Prep.Time: 15 min - **Cooking Time:** 40 min - **Servings:** 8

Ingredients:
- ✓ 8 lamb ribs
- ✓ 4 garlic cloves, minced
- ✓ 2 carrots, chopped
- ✓ 2 cups veggie stock
- ✓ 1 tbsp. rosemary, chopped
- ✓ 2 tbsp. extra virgin olive oil
- ✓ Salt and black pepper to the taste
- ✓ 3 tbsp. white flour

Directions:
1. Season lamb ribs with salt and pepper, rub with oil and garlic, put in preheated air fryer and cook at 360 degrees F for 10 minutes.
2. In a heat proof dish that fits your fryer, mix stock with flour and whisk well.
3. Add rosemary, carrots and lamb ribs, place in your air fryer and cook at 350 degrees F for 30 minutes.
4. Divide lamb mix on plates and serve hot.

Nutrition: calories 302 - Fat 7 - Fiber 2 - Carbs 22 - Protein 27

62. Lamb Fries

Prep.Time: 12 hours - **Cooking Time:** 15 min - **Servings:** 2

Ingredients:
- ✓ 1 lb. boneless lamb cut into fingers
- ✓ 2 cup dry breadcrumbs
- ✓ 2 tsp. oregano
- ✓ 2 tsp. red chili flakes
- *Marinade:*
- ✓ 1 ½ tbsp. ginger-garlic paste
- ✓ 4 tbsp. lemon juice
- ✓ 2 tsp. salt
- ✓ 1 tsp. pepper powder
- ✓ 1 tsp. red chili powder
- ✓ 6 tbsp. corn flour
- ✓ 4 eggs

Directions:
1. Mix all the ingredients for the marinade and put the lamb fingers inside and let it rest overnight.
2. Mix the breadcrumbs, oregano and red chili flakes well and place the marinated fingers on this mixture. Cover it with plastic wrap and leave it till right before you serve to cook.
3. Pre heat the Air fryer at 160 degrees Fahrenheit for 5 minutes. Place the fingers in the fry basket and close it. Let them cook at the same temperature for another 15 minutes or so. Toss the fingers well so that they are cooked uniformly.

63. Barbecue Pork Club Sandwich

Prep.Time: 60 min - **Cooking Time:** 15 minutes - **Servings:** 1

Ingredients:
- ✓ 2 slices of white bread
- ✓ 1 tbsp. softened butter
- ✓ ½ lb. cut pork (Get the meat cut into cubes)
- ✓ 1 small capsicum
- *For Barbeque Sauce:*
- ✓ ¼ tbsp. Worcestershire sauce
- ✓ ½ tsp. olive oil
- ✓ ½ flake garlic crushed
- ✓ ¼ cup chopped onion
- ✓ ¼ tsp. mustard powder
- ✓ ½ tbsp. sugar
- ✓ ¼ tbsp. red chili sauce
- ✓ 1 tbsp. tomato ketchup
- ✓ ½ cup water.
- ✓ A pinch of salt and black pepper to taste

Directions:
1. Take the slices of bread and remove the edges. Now cut the slices horizontally.
2. Cook the ingredients for the sauce and wait till it thickens. Now, add the pork to the sauce and stir till it obtains the flavors. Roast the capsicum and peel the skin off. Cut the capsicum into slices. Mix the ingredients together and apply it to the bread slices.
3. Pre-heat the Air Fryer for 5 minutes at 300 Fahrenheit. Open the basket of the Fryer and place the prepared sandwiches in it such that no two sandwiches are touching each other. Now keep the fryer at 250 degrees for around 15 minutes. Turn the sandwiches in between the cooking process to cook both slices. Serve the sandwiches with tomato ketchup or mint chutney.

64. Pork Kebab

Prep.Time: 70 min - **Cooking Time:** 25 min - **Servings:** 2

Ingredients:
- ✓ 1 lb. boneless pork cubed
- ✓ 3 onions chopped
- ✓ 5 green chilies-roughly chopped
- ✓ 1 ½ tbsp. ginger paste
- ✓ 1 ½ tsp. garlic paste
- ✓ 1 ½ tsp. salt
- ✓ 3 tsp. lemon juice
- ✓ 2 tsp. garam masala
- ✓ 4 tbsp. chopped coriander
- ✓ 3 tbsp. cream
- ✓ 2 tbsp. coriander powder
- ✓ 4 tbsp. fresh mint chopped
- ✓ 3 tbsp. chopped capsicum
- ✓ 3 eggs
- ✓ 2 ½ tbsp. white sesame seeds

Directions:
1. Mix the dry ingredients in a bowl. Make the mixture into a smooth paste and coat the pork cubes with the mixture. Beat the eggs in a bowl and add a little salt to them.
2. Dip the cubes in the egg mixture and coat them with sesame seeds and leave them in the refrigerator for an hour.
3. Pre heat the Air fryer at 290 Fahrenheit for around 5 minutes. Place the kebabs in the basket and let them cook for another 25 minutes at the same temperature. Turn the kebabs over in between the cooking process to get a uniform cook. Serve the kebabs with mint chutney.

65. Pork Wontons

Prep.Time: 15 min - **Cooking Time:** 20 min - **Servings:** 2

Ingredients:
For dough:
- ✓ 1 ½ cup all-purpose flour
- ✓ ½ tsp. salt
- ✓ 5 tbsp. water

For filling:
- ✓ 2 cups minced pork
- ✓ 2 tbsp. oil
- ✓ 2 tsp. ginger-garlic paste
- ✓ 2 tsp. soya sauce
- ✓ 2 tsp. vinegar

Directions:
1. Knead the dough and cover it with plastic wrap and set aside. Next, cook the ingredients for the filling and try to ensure that the pork is covered well with the sauce.
2. Roll the dough and place the filling in the center. Now, wrap the dough to cover the filling and pinch the edges together.
3. Pre heat the Air fryer at 200° F for 5 minutes. Place the wontons in the fry basket and close it. Let them cook at the same temperature for another 20 minutes. Recommended sides are chili sauce or ketchup.

66. Lamb Tikka

Prep.Time: 20 min - **Cooking Time:** 30 min - **Servings:** 2

Ingredients:
- ✓ 2 cups sliced lamb
- ✓ 1 big capsicum (Cut this capsicum into big cubes)
- ✓ 1 onion (Cut it into quarters. Now separate the layers carefully.)
- ✓ 5 tbsp. gram flour
- ✓ A pinch of salt to taste
- ✓ For the filling:
- ✓ 2 cup fresh green coriander
- ✓ ½ cup mint leaves
- ✓ 4 tsp. fennel
- ✓ 2 tbsp. ginger-garlic paste
- ✓ 1 small onion
- ✓ 6-7 flakes garlic (optional)
- ✓ Salt to taste
- ✓ 3 tbsp. lemon juice

Directions:
1. You will first need to make the chutney. Add the ingredients to a blender and make a thick paste. Slit the pieces of lamb and stuff half the paste into the cavity obtained.
2. Take the remaining paste and add it to the gram flour and salt. Toss the pieces of lamb in this mixture and set aside.
3. Apply a little bit of the mixture on the capsicum and onion. Place these on a stick along with the lamb pieces.
4. Pre heat the Air Fryer at 290 Fahrenheit for around 5 minutes. Open the basket. Arrange the satay sticks properly. Close the basket. Keep the sticks with the lamb at 180 degrees for around half an hour while the sticks with the vegetables are to be kept at the same temperature for only 7 minutes. Turn the sticks in between so that one side does not get burnt and also to provide a uniform cook.

67. Pork Sticks

Prep.Time: 12 hours - **Cooking Time:** 15 minutes - **Servings:** 2

Ingredients:
- ✓ 1 lb. boneless pork cut into fingers
- ✓ 2 cup dry breadcrumbs
- ✓ 2 tsp. oregano
- ✓ 2 tsp. red chili flakes
- ✓ Marinade:
- ✓ 1 ½ tbsp. ginger-garlic paste
- ✓ 4 tbsp. lemon juice
- ✓ 2 tsp. salt
- ✓ 1 tsp. pepper powder
- ✓ 1 tsp. red chili powder
- ✓ 6 tbsp. corn flour
- ✓ 4 eggs

Directions:
1. Mix all the ingredients for the marinade and put the pork fingers inside and let it rest overnight.
2. Mix the breadcrumbs, oregano and red chili flakes well and place the marinated fingers on this mixture. Cover it with plastic wrap and leave it till right before you serve to cook.
3. Pre heat the Air fryer at 160 degrees Fahrenheit for 5 minutes. Place the fingers in the fry basket and close it. Let them cook at the same temperature for another 15 minutes or so. Toss the fingers well so that they are cooked uniformly.

68. Lamb Skewered Momos

Prep.Time: 10 min - **Cooking Time:** 20 min - **Servings:** 2

Ingredients:
For dough:
- ✓ 1 ½ cup all-purpose flour
- ✓ ½ tsp. salt
- ✓ 5 tbsp. water

For filling:
- ✓ 2 cups minced lamb
- ✓ 2 tbsp. oil
- ✓ 2 tsp. ginger-garlic paste
- ✓ 2 tsp. soya sauce
- ✓ 2 tsp. vinegar

Directions:
1. Knead the dough and cover it with plastic wrap and set aside. Next, cook the ingredients for the filling and try to ensure that the lamb is covered well with the sauce.
2. Roll the dough and cut it into a square. Place the filling in the center. Now, wrap the dough to cover the filling and pinch the edges together.
3. Pre heat the Air fryer at 200° F for 5 minutes. Place the wontons in the fry basket and close it. Let them cook at the same temperature for another 20 minutes. Recommended sides are chili sauce or ketchup.

69. Garlic Venison

Prep.Time: 12 hours - **Cooking Time:** 15 min - **Servings:** 2

Ingredients:

- ✓ 1 lb. boneless venison cut into fingers
- ✓ 2 cup dry breadcrumbs
- ✓ 2 tsp. oregano
- ✓ 2 tsp. red chili flakes
- ✓ 2 tsp. garlic paste

Marinade:
- ✓ 1 ½ tbsp. ginger-garlic paste
- ✓ 4 tbsp. lemon juice
- ✓ 2 tsp. salt
- ✓ 1 tsp. red chili powder
- ✓ 6 tbsp. corn flour
- ✓ 4 eggs

Directions:

1. Mix all the ingredients for the marinade and put the venison fingers inside and let it rest overnight.
2. Mix the breadcrumbs, oregano and red chili flakes well and place the marinated fingers on this mixture. Cover it with plastic wrap and leave it till right before you serve to cook.
3. Pre heat the Air fryer at 160 degrees Fahrenheit for 5 minutes. Place the fingers in the fry basket and close it. Let them cook at the same temperature for another 15 minutes or so. Toss the fingers well so that they are cooked uniformly. Drizzle the garlic paste and serve.

70. Venison Wontons

Prep.Time: 15 min - **Cooking Time:** 20 min - **Servings:** 2

Ingredients:
For dough:
- ✓ 1 ½ cup all-purpose flour
- ✓ ½ tsp. salt
- ✓ 5 tbsp. water

For filling:
- ✓ 2 cups minced venison
- ✓ 2 tbsp. oil
- ✓ 2 tsp. ginger-garlic paste
- ✓ 2 tsp. soya sauce
- ✓ 2 tsp. vinegar

Directions:

1. Knead the dough and cover it with plastic wrap and set aside. Next, cook the ingredients for the filling and try to ensure that the venison is covered well with the sauce.
2. Roll the dough and place the filling in the center. Now, wrap the dough to cover the filling and pinch the edges together.
3. Pre heat the Air fryer at 200° F for 5 minutes. Place the wontons in the fry basket and close it. Let them cook at the same temperature for another 20 minutes. Recommended sides are chili sauce or ketchup.

71. Veal and Chili

Prep.Time: 12 hours - **Cooking Time:** 15 minutes - **Servings:** 2

Ingredients:

- ✓ 1 lb. veal (Cut into fingers)
- ✓ 2 ½ tsp. ginger-garlic paste
- ✓ 1 tsp. red chili sauce
- ✓ ¼ tsp. salt
- ✓ ¼ tsp. red chili powder/black pepper
- ✓ A few drops of edible orange food coloring

For sauce:
- ✓ 2 tbsp. olive oil
- ✓ 1 ½ tsp. ginger garlic paste
- ✓ ½ tbsp. red chili sauce
- ✓ 2 tbsp. tomato ketchup
- ✓ 2 tsp. soya sauce
- ✓ 1-2 tbsp. honey
- ✓ ¼ tsp. Ajinomoto
- ✓ 1-2 tsp. red chili flakes

Directions:

1. Mix all the ingredients for the marinade and put the veal fingers inside and let it rest overnight.
2. Mix the breadcrumbs, oregano and red chili flakes well and place the marinated fingers on this mixture. Cover it with plastic wrap and leave it till right before you serve to cook. Pre heat the Air fryer at 160 degrees Fahrenheit for 5 minutes. Place the fingers in the fry basket and close it. Let them cook at the same temperature for another 15 minutes or so. Toss the fingers well so that they are cooked uniformly.

72. Chili Cheese Pork

Prep.Time: 12 hours - **Cooking Time:** 15 min - **Servings:** 2

Ingredients:
For pork fingers:
- ✓ 1 lb. pork (Cut in to long strips)
- ✓ 2 ½ tsp. ginger-garlic paste
- ✓ 1 tsp. red chili sauce
- ✓ ¼ tsp. salt
- ✓ ¼ tsp. red chili powder/black pepper
- ✓ A few drops of edible orange food coloring

For sauce:
- ✓ 2 tbsp. olive oil
- ✓ 1 ½ tsp. ginger garlic paste
- ✓ ½ tbsp. red chili sauce
- ✓ 2 tbsp. tomato ketchup
- ✓ 2 tsp. soya sauce
- ✓ 1-2 tbsp. honey
- ✓ ¼ tsp. Ajinomoto
- ✓ 1-2 tsp. red chili flakes

Directions:

1. Mix all the ingredients for the marinade and put the pork fingers inside and let it rest overnight.
2. Mix the breadcrumbs, oregano and red chili flakes well and place the marinated fingers on this mixture. Cover it with plastic wrap and leave it till right before you serve to cook. Pre heat the Air fryer at 160 degrees Fahrenheit for 5 minutes. Place the fingers in the fry basket and close it. Let them cook at the same temperature for another 15 minutes or so. Toss the fingers well so that they are cooked uniformly.

73. Beef Wontons

Prep.Time: 15 min - **Cooking Time:** 20 min - **Servings:** 4

Ingredients:
For dough:
- ✓ 1 ½ cup all-purpose flour
- ✓ ½ tsp. salt
- ✓ 5 tbsp. water

For filling:
- ✓ 2 cups minced beef steak

- ✓ 2 tbsp. oil
- ✓ 2 tsp. ginger-garlic paste
- ✓ 2 tsp. soya sauce
- ✓ 2 tsp. vinegar

Directions:

1. Knead the dough and cover it with plastic wrap and set aside. Next, cook the ingredients for the filling and try to ensure that the beef is covered well with the sauce.
2. Roll the dough and place the filling in the center. Now, wrap the dough to cover the filling and pinch the edges together.
3. Pre heat the Air fryer at 200° F for 5 minutes. Place the wontons in the fry basket and close it. Let them cook at the same temperature for another 20 minutes. Recommended sides are chili sauce or ketchup.

74. Chicken Momos

Prep.Time: 20 min - **Cooking Time:** 20 min - **Servings:** 2

Ingredients:
For dough:
- ✓ 1 ½ cup all-purpose flour
- ✓ ½ tsp. salt
- ✓ 5 tbsp. water

For filling:
- ✓ 2 cups minced chicken
- ✓ 2 tbsp. oil
- ✓ 2 tsp. ginger-garlic paste
- ✓ 2 tsp. soya sauce
- ✓ 2 tsp. vinegar

Directions:

1. Knead the dough and cover it with plastic wrap and set aside. Next, cook the ingredients for the filling and try to ensure that the beef is covered well with the sauce.
2. Roll the dough and cut it into a square. Place the filling in the center. Now, wrap the dough to cover the filling and pinch the edges together.
3. Pre heat the Air fryer at 200° F for 5 minutes. Place the wontons in the fry basket and close it. Let them cook at the same temperature for another 20 minutes. Recommended sides are chili sauce or ketchup.

75. Beef steak Momos

Prep.Time: 15 min - **Cooking Time:** 20 min - **Servings:** 2

Ingredients:

For dough:
- ✓ 1 ½ cup all-purpose flour
- ✓ ½ tsp. salt
- ✓ 5 tbsp. water

For filling:
- ✓ 2 cups minced beef steak
- ✓ 2 tbsp. oil
- ✓ 2 tsp. ginger-garlic paste
- ✓ 2 tsp. soya sauce
- ✓ 2 tsp. vinegar

Directions:

1. Knead the dough and cover it with plastic wrap and set aside. Next, cook the ingredients for the filling and try to ensure that the beef is covered well with the sauce.
2. Roll the dough and cut it into a square. Place the filling in the center. Now, wrap the dough to cover the filling and pinch the edges together.
3. Pre heat the Air fryer at 200° F for 5 minutes. Place the wontons in the fry basket and close it. Let them cook at the same temperature for another 20 minutes. Recommended sides are chili sauce or ketchup.

76. Mutton Tikka

Prep.Time: 20 min - **Cooking Time:** 40 min - **Servings:** 2

Ingredients:
- ✓ 2 cups sliced mutton
- ✓ 1 big capsicum (Cut this capsicum into big cubes)
- ✓ 1 onion (Cut it into quarters. Now separate the layers carefully.)
- ✓ 5 tbsp. gram flour
- ✓ A pinch of salt to taste

For the filling:
- ✓ 2 cup fresh green coriander
- ✓ ½ cup mint leaves
- ✓ 4 tsp. fennel
- ✓ 2 tbsp. ginger-garlic paste
- ✓ 1 small onion
- ✓ 6-7 flakes garlic (optional)
- ✓ Salt to taste
- ✓ 3 tbsp. lemon juice

Directions:

1. You will first need to make the chutney. Add the ingredients to a blender and make a thick paste. Slit the pieces of mutton and stuff half the paste into the cavity obtained. Take the remaining paste and add it to the gram flour and salt. Toss the pieces of mutton in this mixture and set aside.
2. Apply a little bit of the mixture on the capsicum and onion. Place these on a stick along with the mutton pieces. Pre heat the Air Fryer at 290 Fahrenheit for around 5 minutes. Open the basket. Arrange the satay sticks properly. Close the basket. Keep the sticks with the mutton at 180 degrees for around half an hour while the sticks with the vegetables are to be kept at the same temperature for only 7 minutes. Turn the sticks in between so that one side does not get burnt and also to provide a uniform cook.

77. Lamb Kebab

Prep.Time: 12 hours - **Cooking Time:** 25 minutes - **Servings:** 2

Ingredients:
- ✓ 1 lb. of lamb
- ✓ 3 onions chopped
- ✓ 5 green chilies-roughly chopped
- ✓ 1 ½ tbsp. ginger paste
- ✓ 1 ½ tsp garlic paste
- ✓ 1 ½ tsp salt
- ✓ 3 tsp lemon juice
- ✓ 2 tsp garam masala
- ✓ 4 tbsp. chopped coriander
- ✓ 3 tbsp. cream
- ✓ 4 tbsp. fresh mint chopped
- ✓ 3 tbsp. chopped capsicum
- ✓ 3 eggs
- ✓ 2 ½ tbsp. white sesame seeds

Directions:

1. Cut the lamb into medium sized chunks. Marinate these chunks overnight in any marinade of your choice. You can use any of the marinades mentioned in this book.
2. Take all the ingredients mentioned under the first heading and mix them in a bowl. Grind them thoroughly to make a smooth paste.
3. Take the eggs in a different bowl and beat them. Add a pinch of salt and leave them aside.
4. Take a flat plate and in it mix the sesame seeds and breadcrumbs. Mold the lamb mixture into small balls and flatten them into round and flat kebabs.
5. Dip these kebabs in the egg and salt mixture and then in the mixture of breadcrumbs and sesame seeds. Leave these kebabs in the fridge for an hour or so to set.
6. Pre heat the Air fryer at 160 degrees Fahrenheit for around 5 minutes. Place the kebabs in the basket and let them cook for another 25 minutes at the same temperature. Turn the kebabs over in between the cooking process to get a uniform cook. Serve the kebabs with mint chutney.

78. Mutton Samosa

Prep.Time: 40 min - **Cooking Time:** 35 min - **Servings:** 2

Ingredients:

For wrappers:
- ✓ 2 tbsp. unsalted butter
- ✓ 1 ½ cup all-purpose flour
- ✓ A pinch of salt to taste
- ✓ Add as much water as required to make the dough stiff and firm

For filling:
- ✓ 2 cups minced mutton
- ✓ ¼ cup boiled peas
- ✓ A small amount of ginger either grated or finely chopped
- ✓ 1 or 2 green chilies that are finely chopped or mashed
- ✓ ½ tsp cumin
- ✓ 1 tsp coarsely crushed whole coriander
- ✓ 1 dry red chili broken into pieces
- ✓ A small amount of salt
- ✓ ½ tsp dried mango powder
- ✓ ½ tsp red chili power
- ✓ 1-2 tbsp. coriander

Directions:

1. You will first need to make the outer covering. In a large bowl, add the flour, butter and enough water to knead it into dough that is stiff. Transfer this to a container and leave it to rest for five minutes.
2. Place a pan on medium flame and add the oil. Roast the mustard seeds and once roasted, add the coriander seeds and the chopped dry red chilies. Add all the dry ingredients for the filling and mix the ingredients well. Add a little water and continue to stir the ingredients.
3. Make small balls out of the dough and roll them out. Cut the rolled out dough into halves and apply a little water on the edges to help you fold the halves into a cone. Add the filling to the cone and close up the samosa.
4. Pre-heat the Air Fryer for around 5 to 6 minutes at 300 Fahrenheit. Place all the samosas in the fry basket and close the basket properly. Keep the Air Fryer at 200 degrees for another 20 to 25 minutes. Around the halfway point, open the basket and turn the samosas over for uniform cooking. After this, fry at 250 degrees for around 10 minutes in order to give them the desired golden brown color. Serve hot. Recommended sides are tamarind or mint chutney.

79. Lamb Cheese Sticks

Prep. Time: 40 min - **Cooking Time:** 25 min - **Servings:** 2

Ingredients:
- ✓ 2 cups lamb (Cut the lamb into long strips)
- ✓ 1 cup cheddar cheese
- ✓ 1 big lemon-juiced
- ✓ 1 tbsp. ginger-garlic paste
- ✓ For seasoning, use salt and red chili powder in small amounts
- ✓ ½ tsp. carom
- ✓ One or two papadums
- ✓ 4 or 5 tbsp. corn flour
- ✓ 1 cup of water

Directions:
1. Make a mixture of lemon juice, red chili powder, salt, ginger garlic paste and carom to use as a marinade. Let the lamb pieces marinate in the mixture for some time and then roll them in dry corn flour. Leave them aside for around 20 minutes.
2. Take the papadum into a pan and roast them. Once they are cooked, crush them into very small pieces. Now take another container and pour around 100 ml of water into it. Dissolve 2 tbsp. of corn flour in this water. Dip the cottage cheese pieces in this solution of corn flour and roll them on to the pieces of crushed papadum so that the papadum sticks to the lamb.
3. Pre heat the Air Fryer for 10 minutes at 300 Fahrenheit. Then open the basket of the fryer and place the lamb pieces inside it. Close the basket properly. Let the fryer stay at 250 degrees for another 20 minutes. Halfway through, open the basket and toss the lamb around a bit to allow for uniform cooking. Once they are done, you can serve it either with ketchup or mint chutney. Another recommended side is mint chutney.

80. Cheesy Mutton Sticks

Prep. Time: 12 hours - **Cooking Time:** 15 min - **Servings:** 2

Ingredients:
- ✓ 1 lb. boneless mutton cut into fingers
- ✓ 2 cup dry breadcrumbs
- ✓ 2 tsp. oregano
- ✓ 2 tsp. red chili flakes
- ✓ 1 cup molten cheese

Marinade:
- ✓ 1 ½ tbsp. ginger-garlic paste
- ✓ 4 tbsp. lemon juice
- ✓ 2 tsp. salt
- ✓ 1 tsp. red chili powder
- ✓ 6 tbsp. corn flour
- ✓ 4 eggs

Directions:
1. Mix all the ingredients for the marinade and put the mutton fingers inside and let it rest overnight.
2. Mix the breadcrumbs, oregano and red chili flakes well and place the marinated fingers on this mixture. Cover it with plastic wrap and leave it till right before you serve to cook.
3. Pre heat the Air fryer at 160 degrees Fahrenheit for 5 minutes. Place the fingers in the fry basket and close it. Let them cook at the same temperature for another 15 minutes or so. Toss the fingers well so that they are cooked uniformly. Serve with molten cheese.

81. Beef Samosa

Prep. Time: 45 min - **Cooking Time:** 35 minutes - **Servings:** 2

Ingredients:
For wrappers:
- ✓ 2 tbsp. unsalted butter
- ✓ 1 ½ cup all-purpose flour
- ✓ A pinch of salt to taste
- ✓ Add as much water as required to make the dough stiff and firm

For filling:
- ✓ 2 cups minced beef
- ✓ ¼ cup boiled peas

- ✓ 1 or 2 green chilies that are finely chopped or mashed
- ✓ ½ tsp cumin
- ✓ 1 tsp coarsely crushed whole coriander
- ✓ 1 dry red chili broken into pieces
- ✓ A small amount of salt
- ✓ 1 tsp. coriander seeds

Directions:
1. You will first need to make the outer covering. In a large bowl, add the flour, butter and enough water to knead it into dough that is stiff. Transfer this to a container and leave it to rest for five minutes.
2. Place a pan on medium flame and add the oil. Roast the mustard seeds and once roasted, add the coriander seeds and the chopped dry red chilies. Add all the dry ingredients for the filling and mix the ingredients well. Add a little water and continue to stir the ingredients.
3. Make small balls out of the dough and roll them out. Cut the rolled out dough into halves and apply a little water on the edges to help you fold the halves into a cone. Add the filling to the cone and close up the samosa.
4. Pre-heat the Air Fryer for around 5 to 6 minutes at 300 Fahrenheit. Place all the samosas in the fry basket and close the basket properly. Keep the Air Fryer at 200 degrees for another 20 to 25 minutes. Around the halfway point, open the basket and turn the samosas over for uniform cooking. After this, fry at 250 degrees for around 10 minutes in order to give them the desired golden brown color. Serve hot. Recommended sides are tamarind or mint chutney.

82. Veal Tikka

Prep. Time: 20 min - **Cooking Time:** 40 min - **Servings:** 2

Ingredients:
- ✓ 2 cups sliced veal
- ✓ 1 big capsicum (Cut this capsicum into big cubes)
- ✓ 1 onion (Cut it into quarters. Now separate the layers carefully.)
- ✓ 5 tbsp. gram flour
- ✓ A pinch of salt to taste

For the filling:
- ✓ 2 cup fresh green coriander
- ✓ ½ cup mint leaves
- ✓ 4 tsp. fennel
- ✓ 2 tbsp. ginger-garlic paste
- ✓ 1 small onion
- ✓ Salt to taste
- ✓ 3 tbsp. lemon juice

Directions:
1. You will first need to make the chutney. Add the ingredients to a blender and make a thick paste. Slit the pieces of veal and stuff half the paste into the cavity obtained.
2. Take the remaining paste and add it to the gram flour and salt. Toss the pieces of veal in this mixture and set aside.
3. Apply a little bit of the mixture on the capsicum and onion. Place these on a stick along with the veal pieces.
4. Pre heat the Air Fryer at 290 Fahrenheit for around 5 minutes. Open the basket. Arrange the satay sticks properly. Close the basket. Keep the sticks with the veal at 180 degrees for around half an hour while the sticks with the vegetables are to be kept at the same temperature for only 7 minutes. Turn the sticks in between so that one side does not get burnt and also to provide a uniform cook.

83. Venison Tandoor

Prep.Time: 20 min - **Cooking Time:** 40 min - **Servings:** 2

Ingredients:
- ✓ 2 cups sliced venison
- ✓ 1 big capsicum (Cut this capsicum into big cubes)
- ✓ 1 onion (Cut it into quarters. Now separate the layers carefully.)
- ✓ 5 tbsp. gram flour
- ✓ A pinch of salt to taste

For the filling:
- ✓ 2 cup fresh green coriander
- ✓ ½ cup mint leaves
- ✓ 4 tsp. fennel
- ✓ 2 tbsp. ginger-garlic paste
- ✓ 1 small onion
- ✓ 6-7 flakes garlic (optional)
- ✓ Salt to taste
- ✓ 3 tbsp. lemon juice

Directions:
1. You will first need to make the chutney. Add the ingredients to a blender and make a thick paste. Slit the pieces of venison and stuff half the paste into the cavity obtained.
2. Take the remaining paste and add it to the gram flour and salt. Toss the pieces of venison in this mixture and set aside.
3. Apply a little bit of the mixture on the capsicum and onion. Place these on a stick along with the venison pieces.
4. Pre heat the Air Fryer at 290 Fahrenheit for around 5 minutes. Open the basket. Arrange the satay sticks properly. Close the basket. Keep the sticks with the venison at 180 degrees for around half an hour while the sticks with the vegetables are to be kept at the same temperature for only 7 minutes. Turn the sticks in between so that one side does not get burnt and also to provide a uniform cook.

84. Garlic Kangaroo

Prep.Time: 12 hours - **Cooking Time:** 15 min - **Servings:** 2

Ingredients:
- ✓ 1 lb. boneless kangaroo
- ✓ 2 cup dry breadcrumbs
- ✓ 2 tsp. oregano
- ✓ 2 tsp. red chili flakes
- ✓ 2 tsp. garlic paste

Marinade:
- ✓ 1 ½ tbsp. ginger-garlic paste
- ✓ 4 tbsp. lemon juice
- ✓ 2 tsp. salt
- ✓ 1 tsp. red chili powder
- ✓ 6 tbsp. corn flour
- ✓ 4 eggs

Directions:
1. Mix all the ingredients for the marinade and put the kangaroo fingers inside and let it rest overnight.
2. Mix the breadcrumbs, oregano and red chili flakes well and place the marinated fingers on this mixture. Cover it with plastic wrap and leave it till right before you serve to cook.
3. Pre heat the Air fryer at 160 degrees Fahrenheit for 5 minutes. Place the fingers in the fry basket and close it. Let them cook at the same temperature for another 15 minutes or so. Toss the fingers well so that they are cooked uniformly. Drizzle the garlic paste and serve.

85. Lobster Wontons

Prep.Time: 20 min - **Cooking Time:** 20 minutes - **Servings:** 2

Ingredients:
For dough:
- ✓ 1 ½ cup all-purpose flour
- ✓ ½ tsp. salt
- ✓ 5 tbsp. water

For filling:
- ✓ 2 cups minced lobster
- ✓ 2 tbsp. oil
- ✓ 2 tsp. ginger-garlic paste
- ✓ 2 tsp. soya sauce
- ✓ 2 tsp. vinegar

Directions:
1. Knead the dough and cover it with plastic wrap and set aside. Next, cook the ingredients for the filling and try to ensure that the lobster is covered well with the sauce.
2. Roll the dough and place the filling in the center. Now, wrap the dough to cover the filling and pinch the edges together.
3. Pre heat the Air fryer at 200° F for 5 minutes. Place the wontons in the fry basket and close it. Let them cook at the same temperature for another 20 minutes. Recommended sides are chili sauce or ketchup.

86. Veal Momos

Prep.Time: 20 min - **Cooking Time:** 20 min - **Servings:** 2

Ingredients:
For dough:
- ✓ 1 ½ cup all-purpose flour
- ✓ ½ tsp. salt
- ✓ 5 tbsp. water

For filling:
- ✓ 2 cups minced veal
- ✓ 2 tbsp. oil
- ✓ 2 tsp. ginger-garlic paste
- ✓ 2 tsp. soya sauce
- ✓ 2 tsp. vinegar

Directions:
1. Knead the dough and cover it with plastic wrap and set aside. Next, cook the ingredients for the filling and try to ensure that the veal is covered well with the sauce.
2. Roll the dough and cut it into a square. Place the filling in the center. Now, wrap the dough to cover the filling and pinch the edges together.
3. Pre heat the Air fryer at 200° F for 5 minutes. Place the wontons in the fry basket and close it. Let them cook at the same temperature for another 20 minutes. Recommended sides are chili sauce or ketchup.

87. Kyinkyinga

Prep.Time: 80 min - **Cooking Time:** 25 min - **Servings:** 2

Ingredients:
- ✓ 1 lb. boneless beef liver (Chop into cubes)
- ✓ 3 onions chopped
- ✓ 5 green chilies-roughly chopped
- ✓ 1 ½ tbsp. ginger paste
- ✓ 1 ½ tsp. garlic paste
- ✓ 1 ½ tsp. salt
- ✓ 3 tsp. lemon juice
- ✓ 2 tsp. garam masala
- ✓ 4 tbsp. chopped coriander
- ✓ 3 tbsp. cream
- ✓ 2 tbsp. coriander powder
- ✓ 4 tbsp. fresh mint (chopped)
- ✓ 3 tbsp. chopped capsicum
- ✓ 2 tbsp. peanut flour
- ✓ 3 eggs

Directions:
1. Mix the dry ingredients in a bowl. Make the mixture into a smooth paste and coat the beef cubes with the mixture. Beat the eggs in a bowl and add a little salt to them.
2. Dip the cubes in the egg mixture and coat them in sesame seeds and leave them in the refrigerator for 1h.
3. Pre heat the Air fryer at 290 Fahrenheit for around 5 minutes. Place the kebabs in the basket and let them cook for another 25 minutes at the same temperature. Turn the kebabs over in between the cooking process to get a uniform cook. Serve the kebabs with mint chutney.

88. Chenjeh

Prep.Time: 80 min - **Cooking Time:** 25 min - **Servings:** 4

Ingredients:
- ✓ 2 lb. mutton chopped
- ✓ 3 onions chopped
- ✓ 5 green chilies-roughly chopped
- ✓ 1 ½ tbsp. ginger paste
- ✓ 1 ½ tsp. garlic paste
- ✓ 1 ½ tsp. salt
- ✓ 3 tsp. lemon juice
- ✓ 2 tsp. garam masala
- ✓ 4 tbsp. chopped coriander
- ✓ 3 tbsp. cream
- ✓ 2 tbsp. coriander powder
- ✓ 4 tbsp. fresh mint (chopped)
- ✓ 3 tbsp. chopped capsicum
- ✓ 2 tbsp. peanut flour
- ✓ 3 eggs

Directions:
1. Mix the dry ingredients in a bowl. Make the mixture into a smooth paste and coat the mutton cubes with the mixture. Beat the eggs in a bowl and add a little salt to them.
2. Dip the cubes in the egg mixture and coat them with sesame seeds and leave them in the refrigerator for 1h.
3. Pre heat the Air fryer at 290 Fahrenheit for around 5 minutes. Place the kebabs in the basket and let them cook for another 25 minutes at the same temperature. Turn the kebabs over in between the cooking process to get a uniform cook. Serve the kebabs with mint chutney.

89. Beef Steak

Prep.Time: 16 hours - **Cooking Time:** 15 min - **Servings:** 4

Ingredients:
- ✓ 2 lb. boneless beef cut into slices

1st Marinade:
- ✓ 3 tbsp. vinegar or lemon juice
- ✓ 2 or 3 tsp. paprika
- ✓ 1 tsp. black pepper
- ✓ 1 tsp. salt
- ✓ 3 tsp. ginger-garlic paste

2nd Marinade:
- ✓ 1 cup yogurt
- ✓ 4 tsp. tandoori masala
- ✓ 2 tbsp. dry fenugreek leaves
- ✓ 1 tsp. black salt
- ✓ 1 tsp. chat masala
- ✓ 1 tsp. garam masala powder
- ✓ 1 tsp. red chili powder
- ✓ 1 tsp. salt
- ✓ 3 drops of red color

Directions:
1. Make the first marinade and soak the cut beef in it for 4 hours. Make the second marinade and soak the beef in it overnight to let the flavors blend.
2. Pre heat the Air fryer at 160 degrees Fahrenheit for 5 minutes. Place the fingers in the fry basket and close it. Let them cook at the same temperature for another 15 minutes or so. Toss the fingers well so that they are cooked uniformly. Serve them with mint chutney.

90. Lamb Chops Raita

Prep.Time: 1 hour 5 min - **Cooking Time:** 10 min - **Servings:** 4

Ingredients:
- ✓ ¼ cup of yogurt
- ✓ 4 lamp chops
- ✓ ½ tsp. of ground chili
- ✓ 2 tsp. of garam masala
- ✓ 3 tsp. of ground coriander seeds
- ✓ 1 ounce of lemon juice
- ✓ 1 tsp. of cumin seeds
- ✓ Salt to taste

Directions:
1. Mix the lemon juice, yogurt, salt and all the spices together in a bowl. Coat lamb chops using the mixture and marinate for 1h. Preheat your air-fryer to 390°F.
2. Put the lamb chops into the air-fryer basket and cook for 10 minutes.

91. Easy Air Fried Meatballs

Prep.Time: 10 min - **Cooking Time:** 8 min - **Servings:** 4

Ingredients:
- ✓ 1½ cups of ground beef
- ✓ ½ ounce of breadcrumbs
- ✓ 1 egg
- ✓ 1 small sized onion, finely chopped
- ✓ 3 tsp. of parsley, chopped
- ✓ 2 tsp. of fresh thyme, chopped
- ✓ Salt and pepper to taste

Directions:
1. Mix the onions, parsley, beef, breadcrumbs, egg, thyme, salt and pepper in a bowl. Mold the mixture into 12 balls.
2. Heat your air-fryer to 390°F and put the balls into the fryer basket. Cook the meatballs for 8 minutes.
3. Serve the meatballs with ketchup or your favorite tomato sauce.

92. Creamy Beef Rice Bake

Prep.Time: 5 min - **Cooking Time:** 25 min - **Servings:** 6

Ingredients:
- ✓ 1 beef sausage, sliced
- ✓ 4 cloves of garlic, crushed
- ✓ 6 tsp of carrot, cubed
- ✓ 1½ ounces of grated cheddar cheese
- ✓ 2 packs of rice, cooked
- ✓ 6 tsp. of grated mozzarella cheese
- ✓ ½ cup of creamy sauce
- ✓ 3 tsp. of butter
- ✓ 1½ ounces of broccoli florets

Directions:
1. Heat you air-fryer to 356°F for 5 minutes.
2. Put the butter in a baking pan and melt in the fryer for a minute. Add the garlic and sauté for 2 minutes.
3. Put in the carrots and broccoli, fry for 4 minutes and add water to aid its softening. Add the sausage and cook until slightly brown for about 3 minutes. Stir in the rice and include the creamy sauce. Stir thoroughly and level with a spoon. Spread the cheese evenly on top.
4. Place back into air-fryer and cook for about 10 minutes

93. Rack Of Lamb Roast With A Hazel Crust

Prep.Time: 10 min - **Cooking Time:** 40 min - **Servings:** 4-6

Ingredients:
- ✓ 1¾ pound rack of lamb
- ✓ 1 garlic clove, chopped
- ✓ 1 tablespoon olive oil
- ✓ Salt & pepper

Hazel Crust:
- ✓ 1 egg
- ✓ 3oz hazelnuts, unsalted and finely chopped
- ✓ 1 tbsp. homemade breadcrumbs
- ✓ 1 tbsp. chopped fresh rosemary

Directions:
1. Combine olive oil and garlic. Brush the rack of lamb with the garlic oil and season with salt and pepper 2. Preheat the Air-fryer to 220°F. Place the chopped nut into a bowl. Add the breadcrumbs and rosemary, stirring well.
2. In another bowl, whisk the egg. Now, dip the meat into the egg mixture to coat and then drain off any excess. Coat the meat with the hazel crust.
3. Transfer the coated meat in the Air-fryer basket and into the Air-fryer. Set timer for 30 minutes. Afterwards, increase the temperature to 390°F and set the timer again for 5 more minutes.
4. Remove the lamb; cover meat with aluminum foil for 10 minutes then serve and enjoy.

94. Pumpkin Wedges And Veggie-Crust Lamb Racks

Prep.Time: 10 min - **Cooking Time:** 20 min - **Servings:** 2

Ingredients:
- ✓ ¼ cup of breadcrumbs
- ✓ 1 lamb rack
- ✓ 6 teaspoons of vegetable oil
- ✓ 3 teaspoons of Dijon mustard
- ✓ 1 ounce of fresh herbs, chopped
- ✓ 1 lemon zest
- ✓ 2 tablespoons of grated parmesan cheese
- ✓ 1 small sized pumpkin, peeled and cored
- ✓ Salt and pepper to taste

Directions:
1. Preheat your air-fryer to 390°F for 3 minutes.
2. Dry the lamb using a paper towel. Make a cut on the fat with a knife to enable it leak out of the meat to reduce the calories. Rub the cuts with mustard.
3. Mix the herbs with the breadcrumbs, lemon zest, cheese, salt and pepper together. Roll the lamb over the breadcrumb mixture to form the outer layer. Season the joints and coat with oil.
4. Place into the air fryer and cook for 20 minutes until golden and the lamb well cooked. Remove and set aside.
5. Coat the pumpkin lightly with oil and season with salt and pepper.
6. Place the pumpkin wedges in the air-fryer basket in a layer and cook for 20 minutes until crisp.
7. Serve the wedges with a salad along with the lamb.

95. Crispy Meatballs

Prep.Time: 10 min - **Cooking Time:** 12 min - **Servings:** 4

Ingredients:
- ✓ 1 lb ground pork
- ✓ 1 lb ground beef
- ✓ 1 tbsp Worcestershire sauce
- ✓ ½ cup feta cheese, crumbled
- ✓ ½ cup breadcrumbs
- ✓ 2 eggs, lightly beaten
- ✓ ¼ cup fresh parsley, chopped
- ✓ 1 tbsp garlic, minced
- ✓ 1 onion, chopped
- ✓ ¼ tsp pepper
- ✓ 1 tsp salt

Directions:
1. Add all ingredients into the mixing bowl and mix until well combined.
2. Spray air fryer oven tray pan with cooking spray.
3. Make small balls from meat mixture and arrange on a pan and air fry t 400 F for 10-12 minutes.
4. Serve and enjoy.

96. Lemon Garlic Lamb Chops

Prep.Time: 10 min - **Cooking Time:** 6 min - **Servings:** 3

Ingredients:
- ✓ 6 lamb loin chops
- ✓ 2 tbsp fresh lemon juice
- ✓ 1 ½ tbsp lemon zest
- ✓ 1 tbsp dried rosemary
- ✓ 1 tbsp olive oil
- ✓ 1 tbsp garlic, minced
- ✓ Pepper
- ✓ Salt

Directions:
1. Add lamb chops in a mixing bowl.
2. Add remaining ingredients on top of lamb chops and coat well.
3. Arrange lamb chops on air fryer oven tray and air fry at 400 F for 3 minutes.
4. Turn lamb chops to another side and air fry for 3 minutes more.
5. Serve and enjoy.

97. Flavorful Steak

Prep.Time: 10 min - **Cooking Time:** 18 min - **Servings:** 2

Ingredients:
- ✓ 2 steaks, rinsed and pat dry
- ✓ ½ tsp garlic powder
- ✓ 1 tsp olive oil
- ✓ Pepper
- ✓ Salt

Directions:
1. Rub steaks with olive oil and season with garlic powder, pepper, and salt.
2. Preheat the instant vortex air fryer oven to 400 F.
3. Place steaks on air fryer oven pan and air fry for 10-18 minutes. Turn halfway through.
4. Serve and enjoy.

98. Honey Mustard Pork Tenderloin

Prep.Time: 10 min - **Cooking Time:** 26 min - **Servings:** 2

Ingredients:
- ✓ 1 lb pork tenderloin
- ✓ 1 tsp sriracha sauce
- ✓ 1 tbsp garlic, minced
- ✓ 2 tbsp soy sauce
- ✓ 1 ½ tbsp honey
- ✓ ¾ tbsp Dijon mustard
- ✓ 1 tbsp mustard

Directions:
1. Add sriracha sauce, garlic, soy sauce, honey, Dijon mustard, and mustard into the large zip-lock bag and mix well.
2. Add pork tenderloin into the bag. Seal bag and place in the refrigerator for overnight.
3. Preheat the instant vortex air fryer oven to 380 F.
4. Spray instant vortex air fryer tray with cooking spray then place marinated pork tenderloin on a tray and air fry for 26 minutes. Turn pork tenderloin after every 5 minutes.
5. Slice and serve.

99. Easy Rosemary Lamb Chops

Prep.Time: 10 min - **Cooking Time:** 6 min - **Servings:** 4

Ingredients:
- ✓ 4 lamb chops
- ✓ 2 tbsp dried rosemary
- ✓ ¼ cup fresh lemon juice
- ✓ Pepper
- ✓ Salt

Directions:
1. In a small bowl, mix together lemon juice, rosemary, pepper, and salt.
2. Brush lemon juice rosemary mixture over lamb chops.
3. Place lamb chops on air fryer oven tray and air fry at 400 F for 3 minutes.
4. Turn lamb chops to the other side and cook for 3 minutes more. Serve and enjoy.

100. BBQ Pork Ribs

Prep.Time: 10 min - **Cooking Time:** 12 min - **Servings:** 2

Ingredients:
- ✓ 1 slab baby back pork ribs, cut into pieces
- ✓ ½ cup BBQ sauce
- ✓ ½ tsp paprika
- ✓ Salt

Directions:
1. Add pork ribs in a mixing bowl.
2. Add BBQ sauce, paprika, and salt over pork ribs and coat well and set aside for 30 minutes.
3. Preheat the instant vortex air fryer oven to 350 F.
4. Arrange marinated pork ribs on instant vortex air fryer oven pan and cook for 10-12 minutes. Turn halfway through. Serve and enjoy.

101. Crispy Meatballs

Prep.Time: 10 min - **Cooking Time:** 9 min - **Servings:** 2

Ingredients:
- ✓ 1 lb sirloin steak, cut into bite-size pieces
- ✓ 1 tbsp steak seasoning
- ✓ 1 tbsp olive oil
- ✓ Pepper
- ✓ Salt

Directions:
1. Preheat the instant vortex air fryer oven to 390 F.
2. Add steak pieces into the large mixing bowl. Add steak seasoning, oil, pepper, and salt over steak pieces and toss until well coated.
3. Transfer steak pieces on instant vortex air fryer pan and air fry for 5 minutes.
4. Turn steak pieces to the other side and cook for 4 minutes more. Serve and enjoy.

102. Herb Butter Rib-eye Steak

Prep.Time: 10 min - **Cooking Time:** 14 min - **Servings:** 4

Ingredients:
- ✓ 2 lbs rib eye steak, bone-in
- ✓ 1 tsp fresh rosemary, chopped
- ✓ 1 tsp fresh thyme, chopped
- ✓ 1 tsp fresh chives
- ✓ 2 tsp fresh parsley, chopped
- ✓ 1 tsp garlic, minced
- ✓ ¼ cup butter softened
- ✓ Pepper
- ✓ Salt

Directions:
1. In a small bowl, combine together butter and herbs.
2. Rub herb butter on rib-eye steak and place it in the refrigerator for 30 minutes.
3. Place marinated steak on instant vortex air fryer oven pan and cook at 400 F for 12-14 minutes.
4. Serve and enjoy.

103. Greek Lamb Chops

Prep.Time: 10 min - **Cooking Time:** 10 min - **Servings:** 4

Ingredients:
- ✓ 2 lbs lamb chops
- ✓ 2 tsp garlic, minced
- ✓ 1 ½ tsp dried oregano
- ✓ ¼ cup fresh lemon juice
- ✓ ¼ cup olive oil
- ✓ ½ tsp pepper
- ✓ 1 tsp salt

Directions:
1. Add lamb chops in a mixing bowl. Add remaining ingredients over the lamb chops and coat well.
2. Arrange lamb chops on the air fryer oven tray and cook at 400 F for 5 minutes.
3. Turn lamb chops and cook for 5 minutes more.
4. Serve and enjoy.

104. Easy Beef Roast

Prep.Time: 10 min - **Cooking Time:** 45 min - **Servings:** 4

Ingredients:
- ✓ 2 ½ lbs beef roast
- ✓ 2 tbsp Italian seasoning

Directions:
1. Arrange roast on the rotisserie spite.
2. Rub roast with Italian seasoning then insert into the instant vortex air fryer oven.
3. Air fry at 350 F for 45 minutes or until the internal temperature of the roast reaches to 145 F.
4. Slice and serve.

105. Juicy Pork Chops

Prep.Time: 10 min - **Cooking Time:** 16 min - **Servings:** 4

Ingredients:
- ✓ 4 pork chops, boneless
- ✓ 2 tsp olive oil
- ✓ ½ tsp celery seed
- ✓ ½ tsp parsley

Ingredients:
- ✓ ½ tsp granulated onion
- ✓ ½ tsp granulated garlic
- ✓ ¼ tsp sugar
- ✓ ½ tsp salt

Directions:
1. In a small bowl, mix together oil, celery seed, parsley, granulated onion, granulated garlic, sugar, and salt.
2. Rub seasoning mixture all over the pork chops.
3. Place pork chops on the air fryer oven pan and cook at 350 F for 8 minutes.
4. Turn pork chops to other side and cook for 8 minutes more. Serve and enjoy.

106. Chicken Wontons

Prep.Time: 20 min - **Cooking Time:** 20 min - **Servings:** 2

Ingredients:
For dough:
- ✓ 1 ½ cup all-purpose flour
- ✓ ½ tsp. salt
- ✓ 5 tbsp. water

For filling:
- ✓ 2 cups minced chicken
- ✓ 2 tbsp. oil
- ✓ 2 tsp. ginger-garlic paste
- ✓ 2 tsp. soya sauce
- ✓ 2 tsp. vinegar

Directions:
1. Knead the dough and cover it with plastic wrap and set aside. Next, cook the ingredients for the filling and try to ensure that the chicken is covered well with the sauce.
2. Roll the dough and place the filling in the center. Wrap the dough to cover the filling and pinch the edges together.
3. Pre heat the Air fryer at 200° F for 5 minutes. Place the wontons in the fry basket and close it. Let them cook at the same temperature for another 20 minutes. Recommended sides are chili sauce or ketchup.

107. Mutton Fingers

Prep. Time: 12 hours - **Cooking Time:** 15 min - **Servings:** 2-3

Ingredients:
- ✓ 1 lb. boneless mutton cut into fingers
- ✓ 2 cup dry breadcrumbs
- ✓ 2 tsp. oregano
- ✓ 2 tsp. red chili flakes

Marinade:
- ✓ 1 ½ tbsp. ginger-garlic paste
- ✓ 4 tbsp. lemon juice
- ✓ 2 tsp. salt
- ✓ 1 tsp. pepper powder
- ✓ 1 tsp. red chili powder
- ✓ 6 tbsp. corn flour
- ✓ 4 eggs

Directions:
1. Mix all the ingredients for the marinade and put the mutton fingers inside and let it rest overnight.
2. Mix the breadcrumbs, oregano and red chili flakes well and place the marinated fingers on this mixture. Cover it with plastic wrap and leave it till right before you serve to cook.
3. Pre heat the Air fryer at 160 degrees Fahrenheit for 5 minutes. Place the fingers in the fry basket and close it. Let them cook at the same temperature for another 15 minutes or so. Toss the fingers well so that they are cooked uniformly.

108. Juicy Kebab

Prep. Time: 1 hour 20 min - **Cooking Time:** 25 min - **Servings:** 4-6

Ingredients:
- ✓ 2 lb. chicken breasts cubed
- ✓ 3 onions chopped
- ✓ 5 green chilies-roughly chopped
- ✓ 1 ½ tbsp. ginger paste
- ✓ 1 ½ tsp. garlic paste
- ✓ 1 ½ tsp. salt
- ✓ 3 tsp. lemon juice
- ✓ 2 tsp. garam masala
- ✓ 4 tbsp. chopped coriander
- ✓ 3 tbsp. cream
- ✓ 2 tbsp. coriander powder
- ✓ 4 tbsp. fresh mint (chopped)
- ✓ 3 tbsp. chopped capsicum
- ✓ 2 tbsp. peanut flour
- ✓ 3 eggs

Directions:
1. Mix the dry ingredients in a bowl. Make the mixture into a smooth paste and coat the chicken cubes with the mixture. Beat the eggs in a bowl and add a little salt to them.
2. Dip the cubes in the egg mixture and coat them with sesame seeds and leave them in the refrigerator for an hour.
3. Pre heat the Air fryer at 290 Fahrenheit for around 5 minutes. Place the kebabs in the basket and let them cook for another 25 minutes at the same temperature. Turn the kebabs over in between the cooking process to get a uniform cook.
4. Serve the kebabs with mint chutney

109. Delicious Vietnamese Pork Chop

Prep. Time: 10 min - **Cooking Time:** 12 min - **Servings:** 2

Ingredients:
- ✓ 2 pork chops
- ✓ 1 tbsp olive oil
- ✓ 1 tbsp fish sauce
- ✓ 1 tsp black pepper
- ✓ 3 tbsp lemongrass, chopped
- ✓ 1 tbsp shallot, chopped
- ✓ 1 tbsp garlic, chopped

Directions:
1. Add all ingredients into the mixing bowl and coat well. Place in refrigerator for 2 hours.
2. Preheat the air fryer to 400 F/ 200 C for 3 minutes.
3. Place marinated pork chops into the air fryer and cook for 7 minutes.
4. Flip pork chops to other side and cook for 5 minutes more.
5. Serve and enjoy.

110. Onion Pepper Pork Tenderloin

Prep. Time: 10 min - **Cooking Time:** 15 min - **Servings:** 2-4

Ingredients:
- ✓ 10.5 oz pork tenderloin, cut into 4 pieces
- ✓ 1/2 tbsp mustard
- ✓ 1 tbsp olive oil
- ✓ 2 tsp herb provence
- ✓ 1 onion, sliced
- ✓ 1 red bell pepper, cut into strips
- ✓ 1/4 tsp black pepper

Directions:
1. Preheat the air fryer to 392 F/ 200 C.
2. In a dish, mix together 1/2 tablespoon olive oil, herb provence, bell pepper, onion, and salt.
3. Season pork tenderloin pieces with pepper, mustard, and salt. Thinly coat with remaining olive oil and place them in the dish on top of onion and pepper mixture.
4. Place the dish in the air fryer basket and cook for 8 minutes.
5. Turn meat pieces and mix the peppers and onion and cook for 7 minutes more.
6. Serve and enjoy.

VEGETABLE RECIPES

1. Spinach Pie

Prep.Time: 10 min - **Cooking Time:** 15 min - **Servings:** 4

Ingredients:
- ✓ 7 ounces flour
- ✓ 2 tablespoons butter
- ✓ 7ounces spinach
- ✓ 1 tablespoon olive oil
- ✓ 2 eggs
- ✓ 2 tablespoons milk
- ✓ 3 ounces cottage cheese
- ✓ Salt and black pepper to the taste
- ✓ 1 yellow onion, chopped

Directions:
1. In your food processor, mix flour with butter, 1 egg, milk, salt and pepper, blend well, transfer to a bowl, knead, cover and leave for 10 minutes.
2. Heat up a pan with the oil over medium high heat, add onion and spinach, stir and cook for 2 minutes.
3. Add salt, pepper, the remaining egg and cottage cheese, stir well and take off heat.
4. Divide dough in 4 pieces, roll each piece, place on the bottom of a ramekin, add spinach filling over dough, place ramekins in your air fryer's basket and cook at 360 degrees F for 15 minutes.
5. Serve warm.

Nutrition: calories 250 - Fat 12 - Fiber 2 - Carbs 23 - Protein 12

2. Beet Salad and Parsley Dressing

Prep.Time: 10 min - **Cooking Time:** 14 min - **Servings:** 4

Ingredients:
- ✓ 4 beets
- ✓ 2 tablespoons balsamic vinegar
- ✓ A bunch of parsley, chopped
- ✓ Salt and black pepper to the taste
- ✓ 1 tablespoon extra-virgin olive oil
- ✓ 1 garlic clove, chopped
- ✓ 2 tablespoons capers

Directions:
1. Put beets in your air fryer and cook them at 360 degrees F for 14 minutes.
2. Meanwhile, in a bowl, mix parsley with garlic, salt, pepper, olive oil and capers and stir very well.
3. Transfer beets to a cutting board, leave them to cool down, peel them, slice put them in a salad bowl.
4. Add vinegar, drizzle the parsley dressing all over and serve.

Nutrition: calories 70 - Fat 2 - Fiber 6 - Carbs 6 - Protein 4

3. Balsamic Artichokes

Prep.Time: 10 min - **Cooking Time:** 7 minutes - **Servings:** 4

Ingredients:
- ✓ 4 big artichokes, trimmed
- ✓ Salt and black pepper to the taste
- ✓ 2 tablespoons lemon juice
- ✓ ¼ cup extra virgin olive oil
- ✓ 2 teaspoons balsamic vinegar
- ✓ 1 teaspoon oregano, dried
- ✓ 2 garlic cloves, minced

Directions:
1. Season artichokes with salt and pepper, rub them with half of the oil and half of the lemon juice, put them in your air fryer and cook at 360 degrees F for 7 minutes.
2. Meanwhile, in a bowl, mix the rest of the lemon juice with vinegar, the remaining oil, salt, pepper, garlic and oregano and stir very well.
3. Arrange artichokes on a platter, drizzle the balsamic vinaigrette over them and serve

Nutrition: calories 200 - Fat 3 - Fiber 6 - Carbs 12 - Protein 4

4. Brussels Sprouts and Butter Sauce

Prep.Time: 4 min - **Cooking Time:** 10 min - **Servings:** 4

Ingredients:
- ✓ 1 pound Brussels sprouts, trimmed
- ✓ Salt and black pepper to the taste
- ✓ ½ cup bacon, cooked and chopped
- ✓ 1 tablespoon mustard
- ✓ 1 tablespoon butter
- ✓ 2 tablespoons dill, finely chopped

Directions:
1. Put Brussels sprouts in your air fryer and cook them at 350 degrees F for 10 minutes.
2. Heat up a pan with the butter over medium high heat, add bacon, mustard and dill and whisk well.
3. Divide Brussels sprouts on plates, drizzle butter sauce all over and serve.

Nutrition: calories 162 - Fat 8 - Fiber 8 - Carbs 14 - Protein 5

5. Collard Greens Mix

Prep.Time: 10 min - **Cooking Time:** 10 min - **Servings:** 4

Ingredients:
- ✓ 1 bunch collard greens, trimmed
- ✓ 2 tablespoons olive oil
- ✓ 2 tablespoons tomato puree
- ✓ 1 yellow onion, chopped
- ✓ 3 garlic cloves, minced
- ✓ Salt and black pepper to the taste
- ✓ 1 tablespoon balsamic vinegar
- ✓ 1 teaspoon sugar

Directions:
1. In a dish that fits your air fryer, mix oil, garlic, vinegar, onion and tomato puree and whisk.
2. Add collard greens, salt, pepper and sugar, toss, introduce in your air fryer and cook at 320 degrees F for 10 minutes.
3. Divide collard greens mix on plates and serve.

Nutrition: calories 211 - Fat 3 - Fiber 3 - Carbs 7 - Protein 3

6. Brussels Sprouts and Tomatoes Mix

Prep.Time: 5 min - **Cooking Time:** 10 min - **Servings:** 4

Ingredients:
- ✓ 1 pound Brussels sprouts, trimmed
- ✓ Salt and black pepper to the taste
- ✓ 6 cherry tomatoes, halved
- ✓ ¼ cup green onions, chopped
- ✓ 1 tablespoon olive oil

Directions:
1. Season Brussels sprouts with salt and pepper, put them in your air fryer and cook at 350 degrees F for 10 minutes.
2. Transfer them to a bowl, add salt, pepper, cherry tomatoes, green onions and olive oil, toss well and serve.

Nutrition: calories 121 - Fat 4 - Fiber 4 - Carbs 11 - Protein 4

7. Sweet Baby Carrots Dish

Prep.Time: 10 min - **Cooking Time:** 10 min - **Servings:** 4

Ingredients:
- ✓ 2 cups baby carrots
- ✓ A pinch of salt and black pepper
- ✓ 1 tablespoon brown sugar
- ✓ ½ tablespoon butter, melted

Directions:
6. In a dish that fits your air fryer, mix baby carrots with butter, salt, pepper and sugar, toss, introduce in your air fryer and cook at 350 degrees F for 10 minutes.
7. Divide among plates and serve.

Nutrition: calories 100 - Fat 2 - Fiber 3 - Carbs 7 - Protein 4

8. Beets and Blue Cheese Salad

Prep.Time: 10 min - **Cooking Time:** 14 min - **Servings:** 6

Ingredients:
- ✓ 6 beets, peeled and quartered
- ✓ Salt and black pepper to the taste
- ✓ ¼ cup blue cheese, crumbled
- ✓ 1 tablespoon olive oil

Directions:
7. Put beets in your air fryer, cook them at 350 degrees F for 14 minutes and transfer them to a bowl.
8. Add blue cheese, salt, pepper and oil, toss and serve.

Nutrition: calories 100 - Fat 4 - Fiber 4 - Carbs 10 - Protein 5

9. Cheesy Artichokes

Prep.Time: 10 min - **Cooking Time:** 6 min - **Servings:** 6

Ingredients:
- ✓ 14 ounces canned artichoke hearts
- ✓ 8 ounces cream cheese
- ✓ 16 ounces parmesan cheese, grated
- ✓ 10 ounces spinach
- ✓ ½ cup chicken stock
- ✓ 8 ounces mozzarella, shredded
- ✓ ½ cup sour cream
- ✓ 3 garlic cloves, minced
- ✓ ½ cup mayonnaise
- ✓ 1 teaspoon onion powder

Directions:
5. In a pan that fits your air fryer, mix artichokes with stock, garlic, spinach, cream cheese, sour cream, onion powder and mayo, toss, introduce in your air fryer and cook at 350 degrees F for 6 minutes.
6. Add mozzarella and parmesan, stir well and serve.

Nutrition: calories 261 - Fat 12 - Fiber 2 - Carbs 12 - Protein 15

10. Beets and Arugula Salad

Prep.Time: 10 min - **Cooking Time:** 10 min - **Servings:** 4

Ingredients:
- ✓ 1 and ½ pounds beets, peeled and quartered
- ✓ A drizzle of olive oil
- ✓ 2 teaspoons orange zest, grated
- ✓ 2 tablespoons cider vinegar
- ✓ ½ cup orange juice
- ✓ 2 tablespoons brown sugar
- ✓ 2 scallions, chopped
- ✓ 2 teaspoons mustard
- ✓ 2 cups arugula

Directions:
5. Rub beets with the oil and orange juice, place them in your air fryer and cook at 350 degrees F for 10 minutes.
6. Transfer beet quarters to a bowl, add scallions, arugula and orange zest and toss.
7. In a separate bowl, mix sugar with mustard and vinegar, whisk well, add to salad, toss and serve.

Nutrition: calories 121 - Fat 2 - Fiber 3 - Carbs 11 - Protein 4

11. Spicy Cabbage

Prep.Time: 10 min - **Cooking Time:** 8 min - **Servings:** 4

Ingredients:
- ✓ 1 cabbage, cut into 8 wedges
- ✓ 1 tablespoon sesame seed oil
- ✓ 1 carrots, grated
- ✓ ¼ cup apple cider vinegar
- ✓ ¼ cups apple juice
- ✓ ½ teaspoon cayenne pepper
- ✓ 1 teaspoon red pepper flakes, crushed

Directions:
4. In a pan that fits your air fryer, combine cabbage with oil, carrot, vinegar, apple juice, cayenne and pepper flakes, toss, introduce in preheated air fryer and cook at 350 degrees F for 8 minutes.
5. Divide cabbage mix on plates and serve.

Nutrition: calories 100 - Fat 4 - Fiber 2 - Carbs 11 - Protein 7

12. Broccoli Salad

Prep.Time: 10 min - **Cooking Time:** 8 min - **Servings:** 4

Ingredients:
- ✓ 1 broccoli head, florets separated
- ✓ 1 tablespoon peanut oil
- ✓ 6 garlic cloves, minced
- ✓ 1 tablespoon Chinese rice wine vinegar
- ✓ Salt and black pepper to the taste
- ✓

Directions:
5. In a bowl, mix broccoli with salt, pepper and half of the oil, toss, transfer to your air fryer and cook at 350 degrees F for 8 minutes, shaking the fryer halfway.
6. Transfer broccoli to a salad bowl, add the rest of the peanut oil, garlic and rice vinegar, toss really well and serve.

Nutrition: calories 121 - Fat 3 - Fiber 4 - Carbs 4 - Protein 4

13. Beet, Tomato and Goat Cheese Mix

Prep.Time: 10 min - **Cooking Time:** 14 min - **Servings:** 8

Ingredients:
- ✓ 8 small beets, trimmed, peeled and halved
- ✓ 1 red onion, sliced
- ✓ 4 ounces goat cheese, crumbled
- ✓ 1 tablespoon balsamic vinegar
- ✓ Salt and black pepper to the taste
- ✓ 2 tablespoons sugar
- ✓ 1 pint mixed cherry tomatoes, halved
- ✓ 2 ounces pecans
- ✓ 2 tablespoons olive oil

Directions:
1. Put beets in your air fryer, season them with salt and pepper, cook at 350 degrees F for 14 minutes and transfer to a salad bowl.
2. Add onion, cherry tomatoes and pecans and toss.
3. In another bowl, mix vinegar with sugar and oil, whisk well until sugar dissolves and add to salad.
4. Also add goat cheese, toss and serve.

Nutrition: calories 124 - Fat 7 - Fiber 5 - Carbs 12 - Protein 6

14. Artichokes and Special Sauce

Prep.Time: 10 min - **Cooking Time:** 6 min - **Servings:** 2

Ingredients:
- ✓ 2 artichokes, trimmed
- ✓ A drizzle of olive oil
- ✓ 2 garlic cloves, minced
- ✓ 1 tablespoon lemon juice
- ✓ For the sauce:
- ✓ ¼ cup coconut oil
- ✓ ¼ cup extra virgin olive oil
- ✓ 3 anchovy fillets
- ✓ 3 garlic cloves

Directions:
1. In a bowl, mix artichokes with oil, 2 garlic cloves and lemon juice, toss well, transfer to your air fryer, cook at 350 degrees F for 6 minutes and divide among plates.
2. In your food processor, mix coconut oil with anchovy, 3 garlic cloves and olive oil, blend very well, drizzle over artichokes and serve.

Nutrition: calories 261 - Fat 4 - Fiber 7 - Carbs 20 - Protein 12

15. Cheesy Brussels Sprouts

Prep.Time: 10 min - **Cooking Time:** 8 minutes - **Servings:** 4

Ingredients:
- ✓ 1 pound Brussels sprouts, washed
- ✓ Juice of 1 lemon
- ✓ Salt and black pepper to the taste
- ✓ 2 tablespoons butter
- ✓ 3 tablespoons parmesan, grated

Directions:
1. Put Brussels sprouts in your air fryer, cook them at 350 degrees F for 8 minutes and transfer them to a bowl.
2. Heat up a pan with the butter over medium heat, add lemon juice, salt and pepper, whisk well and add to Brussels sprouts.
3. Add parmesan, toss until parmesan melts and serve.

Nutrition: calories 152 - Fat 6 - Fiber 6 - Carbs 8 - Protein 12

16. Collard Greens and Turkey Wings

Prep.Time: 10 min - **Cooking Time:** 20 min - **Servings:** 6

Ingredients:
- ✓ 1 sweet onion, chopped
- ✓ 2 smoked turkey wings
- ✓ 2 tbsp. olive oil
- ✓ 3 garlic cloves, minced
- ✓ 2 and ½ pounds collard greens, chopped
- ✓ Salt and black pepper to the taste
- ✓ 2 tbsp. apple cider vinegar
- ✓ 1 tbsp. brown sugar
- ✓ ½ tsp. crushed red pepper

Directions:
1. Heat up a pan that fits your air fryer with the oil over medium high heat, add onions, stir and cook for 2 minutes.
2. Add garlic, greens, vinegar, salt, pepper, crushed red pepper, sugar and smoked turkey, introduce in preheated air fryer and cook at 350 degrees F for 15 minutes.
3. Divide greens and turkey on plates and serve.

Nutrition: calories 262 - Fat 4 - Fiber 8 - Carbs 12 - Protein 4

17. Air Fried Leeks

Prep.Time: 10 min - **Cooking Time:** 7 min - **Servings:** 4

Ingredients:
- ✓ 4 leeks, washed, ends cut off and halved
- ✓ Salt and black pepper to the taste
- ✓ 1 tablespoon butter, melted
- ✓ 1 tablespoon lemon juice

Directions:
1. Rub leeks with melted butter, season with salt and pepper, put in your air fryer and cook at 350 degrees F for 7 minutes.
2. Arrange on a platter, drizzle lemon juice all over and serve

Nutrition: calories 100 - Fat 4 - Fiber 2 - Carbs 6 - Protein 2

18. Herbed Eggplant and Zucchini Mix

Prep.Time: 10 min - **Cooking Time:** 8 min - **Servings:** 4

Ingredients:
- ✓ 1 eggplant, roughly cubed
- ✓ 3 zucchinis, roughly cubed
- ✓ 2 tbsp. lemon juice
- ✓ Salt and black pepper to the taste
- ✓ 1 teaspoon thyme, dried
- ✓ 1 teaspoon oregano, dried
- ✓ 3 tablespoons olive oil

Directions:
1. Put eggplant in a dish that fits your air fryer, add zucchinis, lemon juice, salt, pepper, thyme, oregano and olive oil, toss, introduce in your air fryer and cook at 360 degrees F for 8 minutes.
2. Divide among plates and serve right away.

Nutrition: calories 152 - Fat 5 - Fiber 7 - Carbs 19 - Protein 5

19. Okra and Corn Salad

Prep.Time: 10 min - **Cooking Time:** 12 min - **Servings:** 6

Ingredients:
- ✓ 1 pound okra, trimmed
- ✓ 6 scallions, chopped
- ✓ 3 green bell peppers, chopped
- ✓ Salt and black pepper to the taste
- ✓ 2 tablespoons olive oil
- ✓ 1 teaspoon sugar
- ✓ 28 ounces canned tomatoes, chopped
- ✓ 1 cup con

Directions:
1. Heat up a pan that fits your air fryer with the oil over medium high heat, add scallions and bell peppers, stir and cook for 5 minutes.
2. Add okra, salt, pepper, sugar, tomatoes and corn, stir, introduce in your air fryer and cook at 360 degrees F for 7 minutes.
3. Divide okra mix on plates and serve warm.

Nutrition: calories 152 - Fat 4 – Fiber 3 - Carbs 18 - Protein 4

20. Indian Turnips Salad

Prep.Time: 10 min - **Cooking Time:** 12 min - **Servings:** 4

Ingredients:
- ✓ 20 ounces turnips, peeled and chopped
- ✓ 1 teaspoon garlic, minced
- ✓ 1 teaspoon ginger, grated
- ✓ 2 yellow onions, chopped
- ✓ 2 tomatoes, chopped
- ✓ 1 teaspoon cumin, ground
- ✓ 1 teaspoon coriander, ground
- ✓ 2 green chilies, chopped
- ✓ ½ teaspoon turmeric powder
- ✓ 2 tablespoons butter
- ✓ Salt and black pepper to the taste
- ✓ A handful coriander leaves, chopped

Directions:
1. Heat up a pan that fits your air fryer with the butter, melt it, add green chilies, garlic and ginger, stir and cook for 1 minute.
2. Add onions, salt, pepper, tomatoes, turmeric, cumin, ground coriander and turnips, stir, introduce in your air fryer and cook at 350 degrees F for 10 minutes.
3. Divide among plates, sprinkle fresh coriander on top and serve.

Nutrition: calories 100 - Fat 5 - Fiber 6 - Carbs 12 - Protein 4

21. Flavored Fennel

Prep.Time: 10 min - **Cooking Time:** 8 minutes - **Servings:** 4

Ingredients:
- ✓ 2 fennel bulbs, cut into quarters
- ✓ 3 tablespoons olive oil
- ✓ Salt and black pepper to the taste
- ✓ 1 garlic clove, minced
- ✓ 1 red chili pepper, chopped
- ✓ ¾ cup veggie stock
- ✓ Juice from ½ lemon
- ✓ ¼ cup white wine
- ✓ ¼ cup parmesan, grated

Directions:
1. Heat up a pan that fits your air fryer with the oil over medium high heat, add garlic and chili pepper, stir and cook for 2 minutes.
2. Add fennel, salt, pepper, stock, wine, lemon juice, and parmesan, toss to coat, introduce in your air fryer and cook at 350 degrees F for 6 minutes.
3. Divide among plates and serve right away.

Nutrition: calories 100 - Fat 4 - Fiber 8 - Carbs 4 - Protein 4

22. Crispy Potatoes and Parsley

Prep.Time: 10 min - **Cooking Time:** 10 min - **Servings:** 4

Ingredients:
- ✓ 1 pound gold potatoes, cut into wedges
- ✓ Salt and black pepper to the taste
- ✓ 2 tablespoons olive
- ✓ Juice from ½ lemon
- ✓ ¼ cup parsley leaves, chopped

Directions:
1. Rub potatoes with salt, pepper, lemon juice and olive oil, put them in your air fryer and cook at 350 degrees F for 10 minutes.
2. Divide among plates, sprinkle parsley on top and serve

Nutrition: calories 152 - Fat 3 - Fiber 7 - Carbs 17 - Protein 4

23. Collard Greens and Bacon

Prep.Time: 10 min - **Cooking Time:** 12 min - **Servings:** 4

Ingredients:
- ✓ 1 pound collard greens
- ✓ 3 bacon strips, chopped
- ✓ ¼ cup cherry tomatoes, halved
- ✓ 1 tablespoon apple cider vinegar
- ✓ 2 tablespoons chicken stock
- ✓ Salt and black pepper to the taste

Directions:
1. Heat up a pan that fits your air fryer over medium heat, add bacon, stir and cook 1-2 minutes
2. Add tomatoes, collard greens, vinegar, stock, salt and pepper, stir, introduce in your air fryer and cook at 320 degrees F for 10 minutes.
3. Divide among plates and serve.

Nutrition: calories 120 - Fat 3 - Fiber 1 - Carbs 3 - Protein 7

24. Radish Hash

Prep.Time: 10 min - **Cooking Time:** 7 min - **Servings:** 4

Ingredients:
- ✓ ½ teaspoon onion powder
- ✓ 1 pound radishes, sliced
- ✓ ½ teaspoon garlic powder
- ✓ Salt and black pepper to the taste
- ✓ 4 eggs
- ✓ 1/3 cup parmesan, grated

Directions:
1. In a bowl, mix radishes with salt, pepper, onion and garlic powder, eggs and parmesan and stir well.
2. Transfer radishes to a pan that fits your air fryer and cook at 350 degrees F for 7 minutes.
3. Divide hash on plates and serve.

Nutrition: calories 80 - Fat 5 - Fiber 2 – Carbs 59 - Protein 7

25. Simple Stuffed Tomatoes

Prep.Time: 10 min - Cooking Time: 15 min - Servings: 4

Ingredients:
- ✓ 4 tomatoes, tops cut off and pulp scooped and chopped
- ✓ Salt and black pepper to the taste
- ✓ 1 yellow onion, chopped
- ✓ 1 tablespoon butter
- ✓ 2 tbsp celery, chopped
- ✓ ½ cup mushrooms, chopped
- ✓ 1 tbsp bread crumbs
- ✓ 1 cup cottage cheese
- ✓ ¼ tsp caraway seeds
- ✓ 1 tbsp parsley, chopped

Directions:
1. Heat up a pan with the butter over medium heat, melt it, add onion and celery, stir and cook for 3 minutes.
2. Add tomato pulp and mushrooms, stir and cook for 1 minute more.
3. Add salt, pepper, crumbled bread, cheese, caraway seeds and parsley, stir, cook for 4 minutes more and take off heat.
4. Stuff tomatoes with this mix, place them in your air fryer and cook at 350 degrees F for 8 minutes.
5. Divide stuffed tomatoes on plates and serve

Nutrition: calories 143 - Fat 4 - Fiber 6 - Carbs 4 - Protein 4

26. Sesame Mustard Greens

Prep.Time: 10 min - Cooking Time: 11 min - Servings: 4

Ingredients:
- ✓ 2 garlic cloves, minced
- ✓ 1 pound mustard greens, torn
- ✓ 1 tablespoon olive oil
- ✓ ½ cup yellow onion, sliced
- ✓ Salt and black pepper to the taste
- ✓ 3 tablespoons veggie stock
- ✓ ¼ teaspoon dark sesame oil

Directions:
1. Heat up a pan that fits your air fryer with the oil over medium heat, add onions, stir and brown them for 5 minutes.
2. Add garlic, stock, greens, salt and pepper, stir, introduce in your air fryer and cook at 350 degrees F for 6 minutes.
3. Add sesame oil, toss to coat, divide among plates and serve.

Nutrition: calories 120 - Fat 3 - Fiber 1 - Carbs 3 - Protein 7

27. Swiss Chard and Sausage

Prep.Time: 10 min - Cooking Time: 20 minutes - Servings: 8

Ingredients:
- ✓ 8 cups Swiss chard, chopped
- ✓ ½ cup onion, chopped
- ✓ 1 tablespoon olive oil
- ✓ 1 garlic clove, minced
- ✓ Salt and black pepper to the taste
- ✓ 3 eggs
- ✓ 2 cups ricotta cheese
- ✓ 1 cup mozzarella, shredded
- ✓ A pinch of nutmeg
- ✓ ¼ cup parmesan, grated
- ✓ 1 pound sausage, chopped

Directions:
1. Heat up a pan that fits your air fryer with the oil over medium heat, add onions, garlic, Swiss chard, salt, pepper and nutmeg, stir, cook for 2 minutes and take off heat.
2. In a bowl, whisk eggs with mozzarella, parmesan and ricotta, stir, pour over Swiss chard mix, toss, introduce in your air fryer and cook at 320 degrees F for 17 minutes.
3. Divide among plates and serve.

Nutrition: calories 332 - Fat 13 - Fiber 3 - Carbs 14 - Protein 23

28. Indian Potatoes

Prep.Time: 10 min - Cooking Time: 12 min - Servings: 4

Ingredients:
- ✓ 1 tablespoon coriander seeds
- ✓ 1 tablespoon cumin seeds
- ✓ Salt and black pepper to the taste
- ✓ ½ teaspoon turmeric powder
- ✓ ½ tsp red chili powder
- ✓ 1 teaspoon pomegranate powder
- ✓ 1 tablespoon pickled mango, chopped
- ✓ 2 teaspoons fenugreek, dried
- ✓ 5 potatoes, boiled, peeled and cubed
- ✓ 2 tablespoons olive oil

Directions:
1. Heat up a pan that fits your air fryer with the oil over medium heat, add coriander and cumin seeds, stir and cook for 2 minutes.
2. Add salt, pepper, turmeric, chili powder, pomegranate powder, mango, fenugreek and potatoes, toss, introduce in your air fryer and cook at 360 degrees F for 10 minutes.
3. Divide among plates and serve hot.

Nutrition: calories 251 - Fat 7 - Fiber 4 - Carbs 12 - Protein 7

29. Delicious Zucchini Mix

Prep.Time: 10 min - Cooking Time: 14 min - Servings: 6

Ingredients:
- ✓ 6 zucchinis, halved and then sliced
- ✓ Salt and black pepper to the taste
- ✓ 1 tablespoon butter
- ✓ 1 tsp oregano, dried
- ✓ ½ cup yellow onion, chopped
- ✓ 3 garlic cloves, minced
- ✓ 2 ounces parmesan, grated
- ✓ ¾ cup heavy cream

Directions:
1. Heat up a pan that fits your air fryer with the butter over medium high heat, add onion, stir and cook for 4 minutes.
2. Add garlic, zucchinis, oregano, salt, pepper and heavy cream, toss, introduce in your air fryer and cook at 350 degrees F for 10 minutes.
3. Add parmesan, stir, divide among plates and serve.

Nutrition: calories 160 - Fat 4 - Fiber 2 - Carbs 8 - Protein 8

30. Broccoli and Tomatoes Air Fried Stew

Prep.Time: 10 min - Cooking Time: 20 min - Servings: 4

Ingredients:
- ✓ 1 broccoli head, florets separated
- ✓ 2 tsp coriander seeds
- ✓ 1 tablespoon olive oil
- ✓ 1 yellow onion, chopped
- ✓ Salt and black pepper to the taste
- ✓ A pinch of red pepper, crushed
- ✓ 1 small ginger piece, chopped
- ✓ 1 garlic clove, minced
- ✓ 28 ounces canned tomatoes, pureed

Directions:
1. Heat up a pan that fits your air fryer with the oil over medium heat, add onions, salt, pepper and red pepper, stir and cook for 7 minutes.
2. Add ginger, garlic, coriander seeds, tomatoes and broccoli, stir, introduce in your air fryer and cook at 360 degrees F for 12 minutes
3. Divide into bowls and serve.

Nutrition: calories 150 - Fat 4 - Fiber 2 - Carbs 7 - Protein 12

31. Swiss Chard Salad

Prep.Time: 10 min - **Cooking Time:** 13 min - **Servings:** 4

Ingredients:
- ✓ 1 bunch Swiss chard, torn
- ✓ 2 tablespoons olive oil
- ✓ 1 small yellow onion, chopped
- ✓ A pinch of red pepper flakes
- ✓ ¼ cup pine nuts, toasted
- ✓ ¼ cup raisins
- ✓ 1 tbsp balsamic vinegar
- ✓ Salt and black pepper to the taste

Directions:
1. Heat up a pan that fits your air fryer with the oil over medium heat, add chard and onions, stir and cook for 5 minutes.
2. Add salt, pepper, pepper flakes, raisins, pine nuts and vinegar, stir, introduce in your air fryer and cook at 350 degrees F for 8 minutes.
3. Divide among plates and serve.

Nutrition: calories 120 - Fat 2 - Fiber 1 - Carbs 8 - Protein 8

32. Italian Eggplant Stew

Prep.Time: 10 min - **Cooking Time:** 15 min - **Servings:** 4

Ingredients:
- ✓ 1 red onion, chopped
- ✓ 2 garlic cloves, chopped
- ✓ 1 bunch parsley, chopped
- ✓ Salt and black pepper to the taste
- ✓ 1 tsp oregano, dried
- ✓ 2 eggplants, cut into medium chunks
- ✓ 2 tablespoons olive oil
- ✓ 2 tbsp capers, chopped
- ✓ 1 handful green olives, pitted and sliced
- ✓ 5 tomatoes, chopped
- ✓ 3 tbsp herb vinegar

Directions:
1. Heat up a pan that fits your air fryer with the oil over medium heat, add eggplant, oregano, salt and pepper, stir and cook for 5 minutes.
2. Add garlic, onion, parsley, capers, olives, vinegar and tomatoes, stir, introduce in your air fryer and cook at 360 degrees F for 15 minutes.
3. Divide into bowls and serve.

Nutrition: calories 170 - Fat 13 - Fiber 3 - Carbs 5 - Protein 7

33. Garlic Tomatoes

Prep.Time: 10 min - **Cooking Time:** 15 minutes - **Servings:** 4

Ingredients:
- ✓ 4 garlic cloves, crushed
- ✓ 1 pound mixed cherry tomatoes
- ✓ 3 thyme springs, chopped
- ✓ Salt and black pepper to the taste
- ✓ ¼ cup olive oil

Directions:
1. In a bowl, mix tomatoes with salt, black pepper, garlic, olive oil and thyme, toss to coat, introduce in your air fryer and cook at 360 degrees F for 15 minutes.
2. Divide tomatoes mix on plates and serve.

Nutrition: calories 100 - Fat 0 - Fiber 1 - Carbs 1 - Protein 6

34. Flavored Air Fried Tomatoes

Prep.Time: 10 min - **Cooking Time:** 15 min - **Servings:** 8

Ingredients:
- ✓ 1 jalapeno pepper, chopped
- ✓ 4 garlic cloves, minced
- ✓ 2 pounds cherry tomatoes, halved
- ✓ Salt and black pepper to the taste
- ✓ ¼ cup olive oil
- ✓ ½ teaspoon oregano, dried
- ✓ ¼ cup basil, chopped
- ✓ ½ cup parmesan, grated

Directions:
1. In a bowl, mix tomatoes with garlic, jalapeno, season with salt, pepper and oregano and drizzle the oil, toss to coat, introduce in your air fryer and cook at 380 degrees F for 15 minutes.
2. Transfer tomatoes to a bowl, add basil and parmesan, toss and serve.

Nutrition: calories 140 - Fat 2 - Fiber 2 - Carbs 6 - Protein 8

35. Tomato and Basil Tart

Prep.Time: 10 min - **Cooking Time:** 14 min - **Servings:** 2

Ingredients:
- ✓ 1 bunch basil, chopped
- ✓ 4 eggs
- ✓ 1 garlic clove, minced
- ✓ Salt and black pepper to the taste
- ✓ ½ cup cherry tomatoes, halved
- ✓ ¼ cup cheddar cheese, grated

Directions:
1. In a bowl, mix eggs with salt, black pepper, cheese and basil and whisk well.
2. Pour this into a baking dish that fits your air fryer, arrange tomatoes on top, introduce in the fryer and cook at 320 degrees F for 14 minutes.
3. Slice and serve right away.

Nutrition: calories 140 - Fat 1 - Fiber 1 - Carbs 2 - Protein 10

36. Spanish Greens

Prep.Time: 10 min - **Cooking Time:** 8 min - **Servings:** 4

Ingredients:
- ✓ 1 apple, cored and chopped
- ✓ 1 yellow onion, sliced
- ✓ 3 tablespoons olive oil
- ✓ ¼ cup raisins
- ✓ 6 garlic cloves, chopped
- ✓ ¼ cup pine nuts, toasted
- ✓ ¼ cup balsamic vinegar
- ✓ 5 cups mixed spinach and chard
- ✓ Salt and black pepper to the taste
- ✓ A pinch of nutmeg

Directions:
1. Heat up a pan that fits your air fryer with the oil over medium high heat, add onion, stir and cook for 3 minutes.
2. Add apple, garlic, raisins, vinegar, mixed spinach and chard, nutmeg, salt and pepper, stir, introduce in preheated air fryer and cook at 350 degrees F for 5 minutes.
3. Divide among plates, sprinkle pine nuts on top and serve.

Nutrition: calories 120 - Fat 1 - Fiber 2 - Carbs 3 - Protein 6

37. Tasty Baked Eggs

Prep.Time: 10 min - **Cooking Time:** 20 min - **Servings:** 4

Ingredients:
- ✓ 4 eggs
- ✓ 1 pound baby spinach, torn
- ✓ 7 ounces ham, chopped
- ✓ 4 tablespoons milk
- ✓ 1 tablespoon olive oil
- ✓ Cooking spray
- ✓ Salt and black pepper to the taste

Directions:
4. Heat up a pan with the oil over medium heat, add baby spinach, stir cook for a couple of minutes and take off heat.
5. Grease 4 ramekins with cooking spray and divide baby spinach and ham in each.
6. Crack an egg in each ramekin, also divide milk, season with salt and pepper, place ramekins in preheated air fryer at 350 degrees F and bake for 20 minutes.
7. Serve baked eggs for breakfast.

Nutrition: calories 321 - Fat 6 - Fiber 8 - Carbs 15 - Protein 12

38. Air Fried Sandwich

Prep.Time: 10 min - **Cooking Time:** 6 min - **Servings:** 2

Ingredients:
- ✓ 2 English muffins, halved
- ✓ 2 eggs
- ✓ 2 bacon strips
- ✓ Salt and black pepper to the taste

Directions:
4. Crack eggs in your air fryer, add bacon on top, cover and cook at 392 degrees F for 6 minutes.
5. Heat up your English muffin halves in your microwave for a few seconds, divide eggs on 2 halves, add bacon on top, season with salt and pepper, cover with the other 2 English muffins and serve for breakfast.

Nutrition: calories 261 - Fat 5 - Fiber 8 - Carbs 12 - Protein 4

39. Delicious Portobello Mushrooms

Prep.Time: 10 min - **Cooking Time:** 12 minutes - **Servings:** 4

Ingredients:
- ✓ 10 basil leaves
- ✓ 1 cup baby spinach
- ✓ 3 garlic cloves, chopped
- ✓ 1 cup almonds, roughly chopped
- ✓ 1 tablespoon parsley
- ✓ ¼ cup olive oil
- ✓ 8 cherry tomatoes, halved
- ✓ Salt and black pepper to the taste
- ✓ 4 Portobello mushrooms, stems removed and chopped

Directions:
1. In your food processor, mix basil with spinach, garlic, almonds, parsley, oil, salt, black pepper to the taste and mushroom stems and blend well.
2. Stuff each mushroom with this mix, place them in your air fryer and cook at 350 degrees F for 12 minutes.
3. Divide mushrooms on plates and serve.

Nutrition: calories 145 - Fat 3 - Fiber 2 - Carbs 6 - Protein 17

40. Peppers Stuffed With Beef

Prep.Time: 10 min - **Cooking Time:** 55 min - **Servings:** 4

Ingredients:
- ✓ 1 pound beef, ground
- ✓ 1 teaspoon coriander, ground
- ✓ 1 onion, chopped
- ✓ 3 garlic cloves, minced
- ✓ 2 tablespoons olive oil
- ✓ 1 tablespoon ginger, grated
- ✓ ½ teaspoon cumin, ground
- ✓ ½ tsp. turmeric powder
- ✓ 1 tbsp. hot curry powder
- ✓ Salt and black pepper to the taste
- ✓ 1 egg
- ✓ 4 bell peppers, cut into halves and seeds removed
- ✓ 1/3 cup raisins
- ✓ 1/3 cup walnuts, chopped

Directions:
1. Heat up a pan with the oil over medium high heat, add onion, stir and cook for 4 minutes.
2. Add garlic and beef, stir and cook for 10 minutes.
3. Add coriander, ginger, cumin, curry powder, salt, pepper, turmeric, walnuts and raisins, stir take off heat and mix with the egg.
4. Stuff pepper halves with this mix, introduce them in your air fryer and cook at 320 degrees F for 20 minutes.
5. Divide among plates and serve.

Nutrition: calories 170 - Fat 4 – Fiber 3 - Carbs 7 - Protein 12

41. Zucchini Noodles Delight

Prep.Time: 10 min - **Cooking Time:** 20 min - **Servings:** 6

Ingredients:
- ✓ 2 tablespoons olive oil
- ✓ 3 zucchinis, cut with a spiralizer
- ✓ 16 ounces mushrooms, sliced
- ✓ ¼ cup sun dried tomatoes, chopped
- ✓ 1 teaspoon garlic, minced
- ✓ ½ cup cherry tomatoes, halved
- ✓ 2 cups tomatoes sauce
- ✓ 2 cups spinach, torn
- ✓ Salt and black pepper to the taste
- ✓ A handful basil, chopped

Directions:
1. Put zucchini noodles in a bowl, season salt and black pepper and leave them aside for 10 minutes.
2. Heat up a pan that fits your air fryer with the oil over medium high heat, add garlic, stir and cook for 1 minute.
3. Add mushrooms, sun dried tomatoes, cherry tomatoes, spinach, sauce and zucchini noodles, stir, introduce in your air fryer and cook at 320 degrees F for 10 minutes.
4. Divide among plates and serve with basil sprinkled on top.

Nutrition: calories 120 - Fat 1 - Fiber 1 - Carbs 2 - Protein 9

42. Sweet Potatoes Mix

Prep.Time: 10 min - **Cooking Time:** 15 min - **Servings:** 4

Ingredients:
- ✓ 3 sweet potatoes, cubed
- ✓ 4 tablespoons olive oil
- ✓ 4 garlic cloves, minced
- ✓ ½ pound bacon, chopped
- ✓ Juice from 1 lime
- ✓ Salt and black pepper to the taste
- ✓ 2 tablespoons balsamic vinegar
- ✓ A handful dill, chopped
- ✓ 2 green onions, chopped
- ✓ A pinch of cinnamon powder
- ✓ A pinch of red pepper flakes

Directions:
1. Arrange bacon and sweet potatoes in your air fryer's basket, add garlic and half of the oil, toss well and cook at 350 degrees F and bake for 15 minutes.
2. Meanwhile, in a bowl, mix vinegar with lime juice, olive oil, green onions, pepper flakes, dill, salt, pepper and cinnamon and whisk.
3. Transfer bacon and sweet potatoes to a salad bowl, add salad dressing, toss well and serve right away.

Nutrition: calories 170 - Fat 3 - Fiber 2 - Carbs 5 - Protein 12

43. Stuffed Poblano Peppers

Prep.Time: 10 min - **Cooking Time:** 15 min - **Servings:** 4

Ingredients:
- ✓ 2 teaspoons garlic, minced
- ✓ 1 white onion, chopped
- ✓ 10 poblano peppers, tops cut off and deseeded
- ✓ 1 tablespoon olive oil
- ✓ 8 ounces mushrooms, chopped
- ✓ Salt and black pepper to the taste
- ✓ ½ cup cilantro, chopped

Directions:
1. Heat up a pan with the oil over medium high heat, add onion and mushrooms, stir and cook for 5 minutes.
2. Add garlic, cilantro, salt and black pepper, stir and cook for 2 minutes.
3. Divide this mix into poblanos, introduce them in your air fryer and cook at 350 degrees F for 15 minutes.
4. Divide among plates and serve.

Nutrition: calories 150 - Fat 3 - Fiber 2 - Carbs 7 - Protein 10

44. Greek Potato Mix

Prep.Time: 10 min - **Cooking Time:** 20 min - **Servings:** 2

Ingredients:
- ✓ 2 medium potatoes, cut into wedges
- ✓ 1 yellow onion, chopped
- ✓ 2 tablespoons butter
- ✓ 1 small carrot, roughly chopped
- ✓ 1 and ½ tablespoon flour
- ✓ 1 bay leaf
- ✓ ½ cup chicken stock
- ✓ 2 tablespoons Greek yogurt
- ✓ Salt and black pepper to the taste

Directions:
1. Heat up a pan that fits your air fryer with the butter over medium high heat, add onion and carrot, stir and cook for 3-4 minutes.
2. Add potatoes, flour, chicken stock, salt, pepper and bay leaf, stir, introduce in your air fryer and cook at 320 degrees F for 16 minutes.
3. Add Greek yogurt, toss, divide among plates and serve.

Nutrition: calories 198 - Fat 3 - Fiber 2 - Carbs 6 - Protein 8

45. Green Beans and Parmesan

Prep.Time: 10 min - **Cooking Time:** 8 minutes - **Servings:** 4

Ingredients:
- ✓ 12 ounces green beans
- ✓ 2 teaspoons garlic, minced
- ✓ 2 tablespoons olive oil
- ✓ Salt and black pepper to the taste
- ✓ 1 egg, whisked
- ✓ 1/3 cup parmesan, grated

Directions:
1. In a bowl, mix oil with salt, pepper, garlic and egg and whisk well.
2. Add green beans to this mix, toss well and sprinkle parmesan all over.
3. Transfer green beans to your air fryer and cook them at 390 degrees F for 8 minutes.
4. Divide green beans on plates and serve them right away.

Nutrition: calories 120 - Fat 8 - Fiber 2 - Carbs 7 - Protein 4

46. Broccoli Hash

Prep.Time: 30 min - **Cooking Time:** 8 min - **Servings:** 2

Ingredients:
- ✓ 10 ounces mushrooms, halved
- ✓ 1 broccoli head, florets separated
- ✓ 1 garlic clove, minced
- ✓ 1 tablespoon balsamic vinegar
- ✓ 1 yellow onion, chopped
- ✓ 1 yellow onion, chopped
- ✓ 1 tablespoon olive oil
- ✓ Salt and black pepper
- ✓ 1 teaspoon basil, dried
- ✓ 1 avocado, peeled and pitted
- ✓ A pinch of red pepper flakes

Directions:
1. In a bowl, mix mushrooms with broccoli, onion, garlic and avocado.
2. In another bowl, mix vinegar, oil, salt, pepper and basil and whisk well.
3. Pour these over veggies, toss to coat, leave aside for 30 minutes, transfer to your air fryer's basket and cook at 350 degrees F for 8 minutes,
4. Divide among plates and serve with pepper flakes on top.

Nutrition: calories 182 - Fat 3 - Fiber 3 - Carbs 5 - Protein 8

47. Stuffed Baby Peppers

Prep.Time: 10 min - **Cooking Time:** 6 min - **Servings:** 4

Ingredients:
- ✓ 12 baby bell peppers, cut into halves lengthwise
- ✓ ¼ teaspoon red pepper flakes, crushed
- ✓ 1 pound shrimp, cooked, peeled and deveined
- ✓ 6 tablespoons jarred basil pesto
- ✓ Salt and black pepper to the taste
- ✓ 1 tablespoon lemon juice
- ✓ 1 tablespoon olive oil
- ✓ A handful parsley, chopped

Directions:
1. In a bowl, mix shrimp with pepper flakes, pesto, salt, black pepper, lemon juice, oil and parsley, whisk very well and stuff bell pepper halves with this mix.
2. Place them in your air fryer and cook at 320 degrees F for 6 minutes,
3. Arrange peppers on plates and serve.

Nutrition: calories 130 - Fat 2 - Fiber 1 - Carbs 3 - Protein 15

48. Air Fried Asparagus

Prep.Time: 10 min - **Cooking Time:** 15 min - **Servings:** 4

Ingredients:
- ✓ 2 pounds fresh asparagus, trimmed
- ✓ ¼ cup olive oil
- ✓ Salt and black pepper to the taste
- ✓ 1 teaspoon lemon zest
- ✓ 4 garlic cloves, minced
- ✓ ½ teaspoon oregano, dried
- ✓ ¼ teaspoon red pepper flakes
- ✓ 4 ounces feta cheese, crumbled
- ✓ 2 tablespoons parsley, finely chopped
- ✓ Juice from 1 lemon

Directions:
1. In a bowl, mix oil with lemon zest, garlic, pepper flakes and oregano and whisk.
2. Add asparagus, cheese, salt and pepper, toss, transfer to your air fryer's basket and cook at 350 degrees F for 8 minutes.
3. Divide asparagus on plates, drizzle lemon juice and sprinkle parsley on top and serve.

Nutrition: calories 162 - Fat 13 - Fiber 5 - Carbs 12 - Protein 8

49. Simple Tomatoes and Bell Pepper Sauce

Prep.Time: 10 min - Cooking Time: 15 min - Servings: 4

Ingredients:
- ✓ 2 red bell peppers, chopped
- ✓ 2 garlic cloves, minced
- ✓ 1 pound cherry tomatoes, halved
- ✓ 1 tsp rosemary, dried
- ✓ 3 bay leaves
- ✓ 2 tablespoons olive oil
- ✓ 1 tbsp balsamic vinegar
- ✓ Salt and black pepper to the taste

Directions:
1. In a bowl mix tomatoes with garlic, salt, black pepper, rosemary, bay leaves, half of the oil and half of the vinegar, toss to coat, introduce in your air fryer and roast them at 320 degrees F for 15 minutes.
2. Meanwhile, in your food processor, mix bell peppers with a pinch of sea salt, black pepper, the rest of the oil and the rest of the vinegar and blend very well.
3. Divide roasted tomatoes on plates, drizzle the bell peppers sauce over them and serve.

Nutrition: calories 123 - Fat 1 - Fiber 1 - Carbs 8 - Protein 10

50. Eggplant and Garlic Sauce

Prep.Time: 10 min - Cooking Time: 10 min - Servings: 4

Ingredients:
- ✓ 2 tablespoons olive oil
- ✓ 2 garlic cloves, minced
- ✓ 3 eggplants, halved and sliced
- ✓ 1 red chili pepper, chopped
- ✓ 1 green onion stalk, chopped
- ✓ 1 tablespoon ginger, grated
- ✓ 1 tablespoon soy sauce
- ✓ 1 tablespoon balsamic vinegar

Directions:
1. Heat up a pan that fits your air fryer with the oil over medium high heat, add eggplant slices and cook for 2 minutes.
2. Add chili pepper, garlic, green onions, ginger, soy sauce and vinegar, introduce in your air fryer and cook at 320 degrees F for 7 minutes.
3. Divide among plates and serve.

Nutrition: calories 130 - Fat 2 - Fiber 4 - Carbs 7 - Protein 9

51. Stuffed Eggplants

Prep.Time: 10 min - Cooking Time: 30 minutes - Servings: 4

Ingredients:
- ✓ 4 small eggplants, halved lengthwise
- ✓ Salt and black pepper to the taste
- ✓ 10 tbsp olive oil
- ✓ 2 and ½ pounds tomatoes, cut into halves and grated
- ✓ 1 green bell pepper, chopped
- ✓ 1 yellow onion, chopped
- ✓ 1 tbsp garlic, minced
- ✓ ½ cup cauliflower, chopped
- ✓ 1 tsp oregano, chopped
- ✓ ½ cup parsley, chopped
- ✓ 3 ounces feta cheese, crumbled

Directions:
1. Season eggplants with salt, pepper and 4 tablespoons oil, toss, put them in your air fryer and cook at 350 degrees F for 16 minutes.
2. Meanwhile, heat up a pan with 3 tablespoons oil over medium high heat, add onion, stir and cook for 5 minutes.
3. Add bell pepper, garlic and cauliflower, stir, cook for 5 minutes, take off heat, add parsley, tomato, salt, pepper, oregano and cheese and whisk everything.
4. Stuff eggplants with the veggie mix, drizzle the rest of the oil over them, put them in your air fryer and cook at 350 degrees F for 6 minutes more.
5. Divide among plates and serve right away.

Nutrition: calories 240 - Fat 4 - Fiber 2 - Carbs 19 - Protein 2

52. Eggplant Hash

Prep.Time: 20 min - Cooking Time: 10 min - Servings: 4

Ingredients:
- ✓ 1 eggplant, roughly chopped
- ✓ ½ cup olive oil
- ✓ ½ pound cherry tomatoes, halved
- ✓ 1 teaspoon Tabasco sauce
- ✓ ¼ cup basil, chopped
- ✓ ¼ cup mint, chopped
- ✓ Salt and black pepper to the taste

Directions:
1. Heat up a pan that fits your air fryer with half of the oil over medium high heat, add eggplant pieces, cook for 3 minutes, flip, cook them for 3 minutes more and transfer to a bowl.
2. Heat up the same pan with the rest of the oil over medium high heat, add tomatoes, stir and cook for 1-2 minutes.
3. Return eggplant pieces to the pan, add salt, black pepper, basil, mint and Tabasco sauce, introduce in your air fryer and cook at 320 degrees F for 6 minutes.
3. Divide among plates and serve

Nutrition: calories 120 - Fat 1 - Fiber 4 - Carbs 8 - Protein 15

53. Delicious Creamy Green Beans

Prep.Time: 10 min - Cooking Time: 15 min - Servings: 4

Ingredients:
- ✓ ½ cup heavy cream
- ✓ 1 cup mozzarella, shredded
- ✓ 2/3 cup parmesan, grated
- ✓ Salt and black pepper to the taste
- ✓ 2 pounds green beans
- ✓ 2 teaspoons lemon zest, grated
- ✓ A pinch of red pepper flakes

Directions:
1. Put the beans in a dish that fits your air fryer, add heavy cream, salt, pepper, lemon zest, pepper flakes, mozzarella and parmesan, toss, introduce in your air fryer and cook at 350 degrees F for 15 minutes.
2. Divide among plates and serve right away.

Nutrition: calories 231 - Fat 6- Fiber 7 - Carbs 8 - Protein 5

54. Balsamic Potatoes

Prep.Time: 10 min - Cooking Time: 20 min - Servings: 4

Ingredients:
- ✓ 1 and ½ pounds baby potatoes, halved
- ✓ 2 garlic cloves, chopped
- ✓ 2 red onions, chopped
- ✓ 9 ounces cherry tomatoes
- ✓ 3 tablespoons olive oil
- ✓ 1 and ½ tablespoons balsamic vinegar
- ✓ 2 thyme springs, chopped
- ✓ Salt and black pepper to the taste

Directions:
1. In your food processor, mix garlic with onions, oil, vinegar, thyme, salt and pepper and pulse really well.
2. In a bowl, mix potatoes with tomatoes and balsamic marinade, toss well, transfer to your air fryer and cook at 380 degrees F for 20 minutes.
3. Divide among plates and serve.

Nutrition: calories 301 - Fat 6 - Fiber 8 - Carbs 18 - Protein 6

55. Burritos

Prep.Time: 30 min - **Cooking Time:** 15 min - **Servings:** 2-4

Ingredients:

Refried beans:
- ½ cup red kidney beans (soaked overnight)
- ½ small onion chopped
- 1 tbsp. olive oil
- 2 tbsp. tomato puree
- ¼ tsp. red chili powder
- 1 tsp. of salt to taste
- 4-5 flour tortillas

Vegetable Filling:
- 1 tbsp. Olive oil
- 1 medium onion sliced
- 3 flakes garlic crushed
- ½ cup French beans (Slice them lengthwise into thin and long slices)
- ½ cup mushrooms thinly sliced
- 1 cup cottage cheese cut in to long and slightly thick fingers
- ½ cup shredded cabbage

- 1 tbsp. coriander, chopped
- 1 tbsp. vinegar
- 1 tsp. white wine
- A pinch of salt to taste
- ½ tsp. red chili flakes
- 1 tsp. freshly ground peppercorns
- ½ cup pickled jalapenos (Chop them up finely)
- 2 carrots (Cut in to long thin slices)

Salad:
- 1-2 lettuce leaves shredded.
- 1 or 2 spring onions chopped finely. Also cut the greens.
- Take one tomato. Remove the seeds and chop it into small pieces.
- 1 green chili chopped.
- 1 cup of cheddar cheese

Directions:

1. Cook the beans along with the onion and garlic and mash them finely.
2. Now, make the sauce you will need for the burrito. Ensure that you create a slightly thick sauce.
3. For the filling, you will need to cook the ingredients well in a pan and ensure that the vegetables have browned on the outside.
4. To make the salad, toss the ingredients together.
5. Place the tortilla and add a layer of sauce, followed by the beans and the filling at the center. Before you roll it, you will need to place the salad on top of the filling.
6. Pre-heat the Air Fryer for around 5 minutes at 200 Fahrenheit. Open the fry basket and keep the burritos inside. Close the basket properly. Let the Air Fryer remain at 200 Fahrenheit for another 15 minutes or so. Halfway through, remove the basket and turn all the burritos over in order to get a uniform cook

56. Cheese and Bean Enchiladas

Prep.Time: 45 min - **Cooking Time:** 15 min - **Servings:** 2-4

Ingredients:
- Flour tortillas (as many as required)

Red sauce:
- 4 tbsp. of olive oil
- 1 ½ tsp. of garlic that has been chopped
- 1 ½ cups of readymade tomato puree
- 3 medium tomatoes. Puree them in a mixer
- 1 tsp. of sugar
- A pinch of salt or to taste
- A few red chili flakes to sprinkle
- 1 tsp. of oregano

Filling:
- 2 tbsp. oil
- 2 tsp. chopped garlic
- 2 onions chopped finely

- 2 capsicums chopped finely
- 2 cups of readymade baked beans
- A few drops of Tabasco sauce
- 1 cup crumbled or roughly mashed cottage cheese (cottage cheese)
- 1 cup grated cheddar cheese
- A pinch of salt
- 1 tsp. oregano
- ½ tsp. pepper
- 1 ½ tsp. red chili flakes or to taste
- 1 tbsp. of finely chopped jalapenos

To serve:
- 1 cup grated pizza cheese (mix mozzarella and cheddar cheese)

Directions:

1. Prepare the flour tortillas.
2. Now move on to making the red sauce. In a pan, pour around 2 tbsp. of oil and heat. Add some garlic. Add the rest of the ingredients mentioned under the heading "For the sauce". Keep stirring. Cook until the sauce reduces and becomes thick.
3. For the filling, heat one tbsp. of oil in another pan. Add onions and garlic and cook until the onions are caramelized. Add the rest of the ingredients required for the filling and cook for two to three minutes. Take the pan off the flame and grate some cheese over the sauce. Mix it well and let it sit for a while.
4. Let us start assembling the dish. Take a tortilla and spread some of the sauce on the surface. Now place the filling at the center in a line. Roll up the tortilla carefully. Do the same for all the tortillas.
5. Now place all the tortillas in a tray and sprinkle them with grated cheese. Cover this with an aluminum foil.
6. Pre heat the Air fryer at 160° C for 4-5 minutes. Open the basket and place the tray inside. Keep the fryer at the same temperature for another 15 minutes. Turn the tortillas over in between to get a uniform cook.

57. Cottage Cheese Galette

Prep.Time: 10 min - **Cooking Time:** 25 minutes - **Servings:** 2

Ingredients:
- 2 tbsp. garam masala
- 2 cups grated cottage cheese
- 1 ½ cup coarsely crushed peanuts
- 3 tsp. ginger chopped

- 1-2 tbsp. fresh coriander leaves
- 2 or 3 green chilies finely chopped
- 1 ½ tbsp. lemon juice
- Salt and pepper to taste

Directions:

1. Mix the ingredients in a clean bowl.
2. Mold this mixture into round and flat galettes.
3. Wet the galettes slightly with water. Coat each galette with the crushed peanuts.
4. Pre heat the Air Fryer at 160 degrees Fahrenheit for 5 minutes. Place the galettes in the fry basket and let them cook for another 25 minutes at the same temperature. Keep rolling them over to get a uniform cook. Serve either with mint chutney or ketchup.

58. Gourd Galette

Prep.Time: 10 min - **Cooking Time:** 25 min - **Servings:** 2

Ingredients:
- 2 tbsp. garam masala
- 2 cups sliced gourd
- 1 ½ cup coarsely crushed peanuts
- 3 tsp. ginger finely chopped

- 1-2 tbsp. fresh coriander leaves
- 2 or 3 green chilies finely chopped
- 1 ½ tbsp. lemon juice
- Salt and pepper to taste

Directions:

1. Mix the ingredients in a clean bowl.
2. Mold this mixture into round and flat galettes.
3. Wet the galettes slightly with water. Coat each galette with the crushed peanuts.
4. Pre heat the Air Fryer at 160 degrees Fahrenheit for 5 minutes. Place the galettes in the fry basket and let them cook for another 25 minutes at the same temperature. Keep rolling them over to get a uniform cook. Serve either with mint chutney or ketchup.

59. Dal Mint Kebab

Prep.Time: 20 min - **Cooking Time:** 30 min - **Servings:** 2-4

Ingredients:
- ✓ 1 cup chickpeas
- ✓ Half inch ginger grated or one and a half tsp. of ginger-garlic paste
- ✓ 1-2 green chilies chopped finely
- ✓ ¼ tsp. red chili powder
- ✓ A pinch of salt to taste
- ✓ ½ tsp. roasted cumin powder
- ✓ 2 tsp. coriander powder
- ✓ 1 ½ tbsp. chopped coriander
- ✓ ½ tsp. dried mango powder
- ✓ 1 cup dry breadcrumbs
- ✓ ¼ tsp. black salt
- ✓ 1-2 tbsp. all-purpose flour for coating purposes
- ✓ 1-2 tbsp. mint (finely chopped)
- ✓ 1 onion that has been finely chopped
- ✓ ½ cup milk

Directions:
1. Take an open vessel. Boil the chickpeas in the vessel until their texture becomes soft. Make sure that they do not become soggy.
2. Now take this chickpeas into another container. Add the grated ginger and the cut green chilies. Grind this mixture until it becomes a thick paste. Keep adding water as and when required. Now add the onions, mint, the breadcrumbs and all the various masalas required. Mix this well until you get a soft dough. Now take small balls of this mixture (about the size of a lemon) and mold them into the shape of flat and round kebabs.
3. Here is where the milk comes into play. Pour a very small amount of milk onto each kebab to wet it. Now roll the kebab in the dry breadcrumbs.
4. Pre heat the Air Fryer for 5 minutes at 300 Fahrenheit. Take out the basket. Arrange the kebabs in the basket leaving gaps between them so that no two kebabs are touching each other. Keep the fryer at 340 Fahrenheit for around half an hour. Half way through the cooking process, turn the kebabs over so that they can be cooked properly. Recommended sides for this dish are mint chutney, tomato ketchup or yoghurt chutney.

60. Cottage Cheese Croquette

Prep.Time: 20 min - **Cooking Time:** 40 min - **Servings:** 2-4

Ingredients:
- ✓ 2 cups cottage cheese cut into slightly thick and long pieces (similar to French fries)
- ✓ 1 big capsicum (Cut this capsicum into big cubes)
- ✓ 1 onion (Cut it into quarters. Now separate the layers carefully.)
- ✓ 5 tbsp. gram flour
- ✓ A pinch of salt to taste

For chutney:
- ✓ 2 cup fresh green coriander
- ✓ ½ cup mint leaves
- ✓ 4 tsp. fennel
- ✓ 1 small onion
- ✓ 2 tbsp. ginger-garlic paste
- ✓ 6-7 garlic flakes (optional)
- ✓ 3 tbsp. lemon juice
- ✓ Salt

Directions:
1. Take a clean and dry container. Put into it the coriander, mint, fennel, and ginger, onion/garlic, salt and lemon juice. Mix them. Pour the mixture into a grinder and blend until you get a thick paste.
2. Now move on to the cottage cheese pieces. Slit these pieces almost till the end and leave them aside. Now stuff all the pieces with the paste that was obtained from the previous step. Now leave the stuffed cottage cheese aside.
3. Take the chutney and add to it the gram flour and some salt. Mix them together properly. Rub this mixture all over the stuffed cottage cheese pieces. Now leave the cottage cheese aside.
4. Now, to the leftover chutney, add the capsicum and onions. Apply the chutney generously on each of the pieces of capsicum and onion. Now take satay sticks and arrange the cottage cheese pieces and vegetables on separate sticks.
5. Pre heat the Air Fryer at 290 Fahrenheit for around 5 minutes. Open the basket. Arrange the satay sticks properly. Close the basket. Keep the sticks with the cottage cheese at 180 degrees for around half an hour while the sticks with the vegetables are to be kept at the same temperature for only 7 minutes. Turn the sticks in between so that one side does not get burnt and also to provide a uniform cook.

61. Cottage Cheese Fingers

Prep.Time: 12 hours - **Cooking Time:** 15 minutes - **Servings:** 2-4

Ingredients:
- ✓ 2 cups cottage cheese fingers
- ✓ 2 cup dry breadcrumbs
- ✓ 2 tsp. oregano
- ✓ 2 tsp. red chili flakes

Marinade:
- ✓ 1 ½ tbsp. ginger-garlic paste
- ✓ 4 tbsp. lemon juice
- ✓ 2 tsp. salt
- ✓ 1 tsp. pepper powder
- ✓ 1 tsp. red chili powder
- ✓ 6 tbsp. corn flour
- ✓ 4 eggs

Directions:
1. Mix all the ingredients for the marinade and put the chicken fingers inside and let it rest overnight.
2. Mix the breadcrumbs, oregano and red chili flakes well and place the marinated fingers on this mixture. Cover it with plastic wrap and leave it till right before you serve to cook.
3. Pre heat the Air fryer at 160 degrees Fahrenheit for 5 minutes. Place the fingers in the fry basket and close it. Let them cook at the same temperature for another 15 minutes or so. Toss the fingers well so that they are cooked uniformly.

62. Cottage Cheese Gnocchis

Prep.Time: 10 min - **Cooking Time:** 20 min - **Servings:** 2-4

Ingredients:

For dough:
- ✓ 1 ½ cup all-purpose flour
- ✓ ½ tsp. salt
- ✓ 5 tbsp. water

For filling:
- ✓ 2 cups grated cottage cheese
- ✓ 2 tbsp. oil
- ✓ 2 tsp. ginger-garlic paste
- ✓ 2 tsp. soya sauce
- ✓ 2 tsp. vinegar

Directions:
1. Knead the dough and cover it with plastic wrap and set aside. Next, cook the ingredients for the filling and try to ensure that the cottage cheese is covered well with the sauce.
2. Roll the dough and place the filling in the center. Now, wrap the dough to cover the filling and pinch the edges together.
3. Pre heat the Air fryer at 200° F for 5 minutes. Place the gnocchis in the fry basket and close it. Let them cook at the same temperature for another 20 minutes. Recommended sides are chili sauce or ketchup.

63. Honey Chili Potatoes
Prep.Time: 20 min - **Cooking Time:** 20 min - **Servings:** 2-4

Ingredients:

For potato:
- ✓ 3 big potatoes (Cut into strips or cubes)
- ✓ 2 ½ tsp. ginger-garlic paste
- ✓ ¼ tsp. salt
- ✓ 1 tsp. red chili sauce
- ✓ ¼ tsp. red chili powder/black pepper
- ✓ A few drops of edible orange food coloring

For sauce:
- ✓ 1 capsicum, cut into thin and long pieces (lengthwise).
- ✓ 2 tbsp. olive oil
- ✓ 2 onions. Cut them into halves.
- ✓ 1 ½ tbsp. sweet chili sauce
- ✓ 1 ½ tsp. ginger garlic paste
- ✓ ½ tbsp. red chili sauce.
- ✓ 2 tbsp. tomato ketchup
- ✓ 2 tsp. soya sauce
- ✓ 2 tsp. vinegar
- ✓ A pinch of black pepper powder
- ✓ 1-2 tsp. red chili flakes

Directions:
1. Create the mix for the potato fingers and coat the chicken well with it.
2. Pre heat the Air fryer at 250 Fahrenheit for 5 minutes or so. Open the basket of the Fryer. Place the fingers inside the basket. Now let the fryer stay at 290 Fahrenheit for another 20 minutes. Keep tossing the fingers periodically through the cook to get a uniform cook.
3. Add the ingredients to the sauce and cook it with the vegetables till it thickens. Add the fingers to the sauce and cook till the flavors have blended.

64. Baked Chick-Pea Stars
Prep.Time: 20 min - **Cooking Time:** 30 min - **Servings:** 2

Ingredients:
- ✓ 1 cup white chick peas soaked overnight
- ✓ 1 tsp. ginger-garlic paste
- ✓ 4 tbsp. chopped coriander leaves
- ✓ 2 green chili finely chopped
- ✓ 4 tbsp. thick curd
- ✓ Pinches of salt and pepper to taste
- ✓ 1 tsp. dry mint
- ✓ 4 tbsp. roasted sesame seeds
- ✓ 2 small onion finely chopped
- ✓ ½ tsp. coriander powder
- ✓ ½ tsp. cumin powder
- ✓ Use olive oil for greasing purposes

Directions:
1. Since the chickpeas have been soaked you will first have to drain them. Add a pinch of salt and pour water until the chickpeas are submerged. Put this container in a pressure cooker and let the chickpeas cook for around 25 minutes until they turn soft. Remove the cooker from the flame. Now mash the chickpeas.
2. Take another container. Into it add the ginger garlic paste, onions, coriander leaves, coriander powder, cumin powder, green chili, salt and pepper, and 1 tbsp. Use your hands to mix these ingredients
3. Pour this mixture into the container with the mashed chickpeas and mix. Spread this mixture over a flat surface to about a half-inch thickness. Cut star shapes out of this layer. Make a mixture of curd and mint leaves and spread this over the surface of the star shaped cutlets. Coat all the sides with sesame seeds.
4. Pre heat the Air Fryer at 200 degree Fahrenheit for 5 minutes. Open the basket of the Fryer and put the stars inside. Close the basket properly. Continue to cook the stars for around half an hour. Periodically turn over the stars in the basket in order to prevent overcooking one side. Serve either with mint chutney or tomato ketchup.

65. Cauliflower Gnocchis
Prep.Time: 10 min - **Cooking Time:** 20 minutes - **Servings:** 2

Ingredients:

For dough:
- ✓ 1 ½ cup all-purpose flour
- ✓ ½ tsp. salt
- ✓ 5 tbsp. water

For filling:
- ✓ 2 cups grated cauliflower
- ✓ 2 tbsp. oil
- ✓ 2 tsp. ginger-garlic paste
- ✓ 2 tsp. soya sauce
- ✓ 2 tsp. vinegar

Directions:
1. Knead the dough and cover it with plastic wrap and set aside. Next, cook the ingredients for the filling and try to ensure that the cauliflower is covered well with the sauce.
2. Roll the dough and place the filling in the center. Now, wrap the dough to cover the filling and pinch the edges together.
3. Pre heat the Air fryer at 200° F for 5 minutes. Place the gnocchis in the fry basket and close it. Let them cook at the same temperature for another 20 minutes. Recommended sides are chili sauce or ketchup.

66. Cauliflower Relish
Prep.Time: 5 min - **Cooking Time:** 18 min - **Servings:** 4

Ingredients:
- ✓ 1 head cauliflower, cut into small florets
- ✓ 2 teaspoons garlic powder
- ✓ 1 tablespoon butter, melted
- ✓ 1/2 cup chili sauce Olive oil
- ✓ Pinch salt &pepper

Directions:
1. In a bowl, pour oil over cauliflower florets to lightly cover. Season with salt, pepper and garlic powder and toss.
2. Place into Air Fryer at 350°F for 14 minutes and remove. Add together the chili sauce and melted butter then pour over the florets to coat well.
3. Return to the Air Fryer and cook for 3 to 4 minutes longer.

67. Potatoes and Special Tomato Sauce
Prep.Time: 10 min - **Cooking Time:** 16 min - **Servings:** 4

Ingredients:
- ✓ 2 pounds potatoes, cubed
- ✓ 4 garlic cloves, minced
- ✓ 1 yellow onion, chopped
- ✓ 1 cup tomato sauce
- ✓ 2 tablespoons basil, chopped
- ✓ 2 tablespoons olive oil
- ✓ ½ teaspoon oregano, dried
- ✓ ½ teaspoon parsley, dried

Directions:
1. Heat up a pan that fits your air fryer with the oil over medium heat, add onion, stir and cook for 1-2 minutes.
2. Add garlic, potatoes, parsley, tomato sauce and oregano, stir, introduce in your air fryer and cook at 370 degrees F and cook for 16 minutes.
3. Add basil, toss everything, divide among plates and serve.

Nutrition: calories 211 - Fat 6 - Fiber 8 - Carbs 14 - Protein 6

68. Cherry Tomatoes Skewers
Prep.Time: 30 min - **Cooking Time:** 6 min - **Servings:** 4

Ingredients:
- ✓ 3 tbsp. balsamic vinegar
- ✓ 24 cherry tomatoes
- ✓ 2 tablespoons olive oil
- ✓ 3 garlic cloves, minced
- ✓ 1 tbsp. thyme, chopped
- ✓ Salt and black pepper to the taste
- ✓ For the dressing:
- ✓ 2 tbsp. balsamic vinegar
- ✓ Salt and black pepper to the taste
- ✓ 4 tablespoons olive oil

Directions:
1. In a bowl, mix 2 tablespoons oil with 3 tablespoons vinegar, 3 garlic cloves, thyme, salt and black pepper and whisk well.
2. Add tomatoes, toss to coat and leave aside for 30 minutes.
3. Arrange 6 tomatoes on one skewer and repeat with the rest of the tomatoes.
4. Introduce them in your air fryer and cook at 360 degrees F for 6 minutes.
5. In another bowl, mix 2 tablespoons vinegar with salt, pepper and 4 tablespoons oil and whisk well.
6. Arrange tomato skewers on plates and serve with the dressing drizzled on top.

Nutrition: calories 140 - Fat 1 - Fiber 1 - Carbs 2 - Protein 7

69 Mexican Peppers
Prep.Time: 10 min - **Cooking Time:** 25 minutes - **Servings:** 4

Ingredients:
- ✓ 4 bell peppers, tops cut off and seeds removed
- ✓ ½ cup tomato juice
- ✓ 2 tbsp. jarred jalapenos, chopped
- ✓ 4 chicken breasts
- ✓ 1 cup tomatoes, chopped
- ✓ ¼ cup yellow onion, chopped
- ✓ ¼ cup green peppers, chopped
- ✓ 2 cups tomato sauce
- ✓ Salt and black pepper to the taste
- ✓ 2 tsp onion powder
- ✓ ½ tsp red pepper, crushed
- ✓ 1 teaspoon chili powder
- ✓ ½ tsp garlic powder
- ✓ 1 tsp cumin, ground

Directions:
1. In a pan that fits your air fryer, mix chicken breasts with tomato juice, jalapenos, tomatoes, onion, green peppers, salt, pepper, onion powder, red pepper, chili powder, garlic powder, oregano and cumin, stir well, introduce in your air fryer and cook at 350 degrees F for 15 minutes,
2. Shred meat using 2 forks, stir, stuff bell peppers with this mix, place them in your air fryer and cook at 320 degrees F for 10 minutes more.
3. Divide stuffed peppers on plates and serve.

Nutrition: calories 180 - Fat 4 - Fiber 3 - Carbs 7 - Protein 14

70. Green Beans and Tomatoes
Prep.Time: 10 min - **Cooking Time:** 15 min - **Servings:** 4

Ingredients:
- ✓ 1 pint cherry tomatoes
- ✓ 1 pound green beans
- ✓ 2 tablespoons olive oil
- ✓ Salt and black pepper to the taste

Directions:
1. In a bowl, mix cherry tomatoes with green beans, olive oil, salt and pepper, toss, transfer to your air fryer and cook at 400 degrees F for 15 minutes.
2. Divide among plates and serve right away.

Nutrition: calories 162 - Fat 6 - Fiber 5 - Carbs 8 - Protein 9

71. Potatoes and Tomatoes Mix
Prep.Time: 10 min - **Cooking Time:** 16 min - **Servings:** 4

Ingredients:
- ✓ 1 and ½ pounds red potatoes, quartered
- ✓ 2 tablespoons olive oil
- ✓ 1 pint cherry tomatoes
- ✓ 1 teaspoon sweet paprika
- ✓ 1 tbsp. rosemary, chopped
- ✓ Salt and black pepper to the taste
- ✓ 3 garlic cloves, minced

Directions:
1. In a bowl, mix potatoes with tomatoes, oil, paprika, rosemary, garlic, salt and pepper, toss, transfer to your air fryer and cook at 380 degrees F for 16 minutes.
2. Divide among plates and serve.

Nutrition: calories 192 - Fat 4 - Fiber 4 - Carbs 30 - Protein 3

72. Easy Green Beans and Potatoes
Prep.Time: 10 min - **Cooking Time:** 15 min - **Servings:** 5

Ingredients:
- ✓ 2 pounds green beans
- ✓ 6 new potatoes, halved
- ✓ Salt and black pepper to the taste
- ✓ A drizzle of olive oil
- ✓ 6 bacon slices, cooked and chopped

Directions:
1. In a bowl, mix green beans with potatoes, salt, pepper and oil, toss, transfer to your air fryer and cook at 390 degrees F for 15 minutes.
2. Divide among plates and serve with bacon sprinkled on top.

Nutrition: calories 374 - Fat 15 - Fiber 12 - Carbs 28 - Protein 12

73. Flavored Green Beans

Prep.Time: 10 min - **Cooking Time:** 15 min - **Servings:** 4

Ingredients:
- ✓ 1 pound red potatoes, cut into wedges
- ✓ 1 pound green beans
- ✓ 2 garlic cloves, minced
- ✓ 2 tablespoons olive oil
- ✓ Salt and black pepper to the taste
- ✓ ½ teaspoon oregano, dried

Directions:
1. In a pan that fits your air fryer, combine potatoes with green beans, garlic, oil, salt, pepper and oregano, toss, introduce in your air fryer and cook at 380 degrees F for 15 minutes.
2. Divide among plates and serve.

Nutrition: calories 211 - Fat 6 - Fiber 7 - Carbs 8 - Protein 5

74. Potatoes and Special Tomato Sauce

Prep.Time: 10 min - **Cooking Time:** 16 min - **Servings:** 4

Ingredients:
- ✓ 2 pounds potatoes, cubed
- ✓ 4 garlic cloves, minced
- ✓ 1 yellow onion, chopped
- ✓ 1 cup tomato sauce
- ✓ 2 tablespoons basil, chopped
- ✓ 2 tablespoons olive oil
- ✓ ½ teaspoon oregano, dried
- ✓ ½ teaspoon parsley, dried

Directions:
1. Heat up a pan that fits your air fryer with the oil over medium heat, add onion, stir and cook for 1-2 minutes.
2. Add garlic, potatoes, parsley, tomato sauce and oregano, stir, introduce in your air fryer and cook at 370 degrees F and cook for 16 minutes.
3. Add basil, toss everything, divide among plates and serve.

Nutrition: calories 211 - Fat 6 - Fiber 8 - Carbs 14 - Protein 6

75. Baked Zucchini Fries

Prep.Time: 5 min - **Cooking Time:** 15 minutes - **Servings:** 2-4

Ingredients:
- ✓ 3 medium zucchinis, sliced lengthwise
- ✓ 1/2 cup seasoned breadcrumbs
- ✓ 2 egg whites
- ✓ 1/4 teaspoon garlic powder
- ✓ 2 tablespoons parmesan cheese, grated
- ✓ Salt & pepper to taste

Directions:
1. Beat egg whites in a bowl and season with salt and pepper.
2. In a separate bowl, combine garlic powder, breadcrumbs and cheese.
3. Dip the zucchini sticks into the egg, bread crumb and cheese mixture one after the other then place on a single layer in the Air-Fryer tray.
4. Coat lightly with cooking spray and bake for about 15 minutes at 390°F until golden brown.
5. Serve with marinara sauce for dipping.

76. Garam Masala Beans

Prep.Time: 10 min - **Cooking Time:** 7 min - **Servings:** 4

Ingredients:
- ✓ 9 ounce Beans
- ✓ 2 Eggs
- ✓ 1/2 cup breadcrumbs
- ✓ 1/2 cup flour
- ✓ 1/2 teaspoon garam masala
- ✓ 2 teaspoon chili powder
- ✓ Olive Oil
- ✓ Salt to taste

Directions:
1. Preheat the Air Fryer at 350°F. Combine chili powder, garam masala, flour and salt in a bowl, mixing well. Beat the eggs and set to one side.
2. Pour the breadcrumbs on a separate plate then coat the beans with the flour mixture. Now dip beans into the egg mixture and next, into the breadcrumbs. Do this with all the beans.
3. Place the beans into the Air Fryer tray and cook for 4 minutes. Open and coat the beans with oil and cook once more for another 3 minutes.

77. Crisp Potato Wedges

Prep.Time: 15 min - **Cooking Time:** 25 min - **Servings:** 4

Ingredients:
- ✓ 3 teaspoons of olive oil
- ✓ 2 big potatoes
- ✓ ¼ cup of sweet chili sauce
- ✓ ¼ cup of sour cream

Directions:
1. Slice the potatoes lengthwise to create a wedge shape.
2. Heat the air-fryer to 356°F.
3. Place the wedges in a bowl and add the oil. Toss lightly until the potatoes are fully coated with the oil.
4. Put into the cooking basket with the skin side facing down and cook for about 15 minutes. Toss then cook for another 10 minutes until golden brown.
5. Best served while warm with chili source and sour cream.

78. Crispy Onion Rings

Prep.Time: 15 min - **Cooking Time:** 10 min - **Servings:** 2

Ingredients:
- ✓ 1 big sized onion, thinly sliced
- ✓ 8 ounces of milk
- ✓ 1 egg
- ✓ 6 ounces of breadcrumbs
- ✓ 1 teaspoon of baking powder
- ✓ 10 ounces of flour
- ✓ 1 teaspoon of salt

Directions:
1. Heat your air-fryer to 360°F for 10 minutes.
2. Detach the onion slices to separate rings.
3. Mix the baking powder, flour and salt together in a bowl.
4. Put the onion rings into the flour mixture to coat them. Beat the egg and the milk and stir into the flour to form a batter. Dip the flour-coated rings in the batter.
5. Put the breadcrumbs in a small tray, place the onion rings in it and ensure all sides are well coated.
6. Place the rings in the fryer basket and air fry for 10 minutes until crisp.

79. Roasted Heirloom Tomato With Baked Feta

Prep. Time: 15 min - **Cooking Time:** 20 min - **Servings:** 4

Ingredients:

For The Tomato:
- ✓ 2 heirloom tomatoes, sliced thickly into ½ inch circular slices
- ✓ 8-ounce block of feta cheese, sliced thickly into ½ inch circular slices
- ✓ ½ cup red onions, sliced thinly
- ✓ 1 pinch salt
- ✓ 1 tablespoon olive oil

For The Basil Pesto:
- ✓ ½ cup basil, chopped roughly
- ✓ ½ cup parsley, roughly chopped
- ✓ 3 tablespoons pine nuts, toasted
- ✓ ½ cup parmesan cheese, grated
- ✓ 1 garlic clove
- ✓ 1 pinch salt
- ✓ ½ cup olive oil

Directions:

1. Begin by making the pesto. To do this, combine garlic, parmesan, parsley, toasted pine nuts, basil and salt in a food processor.
2. Turn it on and gradually add the olive oil to incorporate into the pesto. Once done, store and put in the refrigerator until ready to use.
3. Preheat the Air-fryer to 390°F. Pat dry tomato with a paper towel. Spread a tablespoon of the pesto on top of each slices of tomato and top with the feta. Add1 tablespoon of olive oil to the red onions and toss; place on top of the feta.
4. Now place the feta/ tomatoes into the cooking basket and cook until the feta is brownish and starts to soften or for 12 to14 minutes.
5. Add a pinch of salt and 1 spoonful of basil pesto. Serve and enjoy.

80. Cheese Lasagna & Pumpkin Sauce

Prep. Time: 10 min - **Cooking Time:** 66 min - **Servings:** 2

Ingredients:
- ✓ 25 ounces of pumpkin, peeled & finely chopped
- ✓ 4 teaspoons of finely chopped rosemary
- ✓ 17½ ounces of beets, cooked and thinly sliced
- ✓ 1 medium sized onion, chopped
- ✓ 1 cup of goat's cheese, grated Grana Padano cheese, grated
- ✓ 28 ounces of tomatoes, cubed
- ✓ 6 teaspoons of olive oil
- ✓ 8½ ounces of lasagna sheets

Directions:

1. Mix the pumpkin, 3 teaspoons of oil and rosemary together in a bowl and air fry for 10 minutes at 347°F.
2. Remove the pumpkin from the air-fryer and use a hand blender to mash into puree with the rosemary, tomatoes and onions. Pour the puree into a saucepan and place over low heat for 5 minutes.
3. Grease a heatproof dish with oil. Put in the pumpkin sauce first and then the lasagna sheets. Divide the sauce in two and the beets and goat cheese in three. Put a portion of the beets and sauce on the lasagna and cover with a portion of the goat cheese. Repeat this until you use up all the ingredients and top with cheese and sauce.
4. Add the grana Padano on the lasagna and air fry for 45 minutes at 300°F. Remove and leave to cool.
5. Use a cookie cutter to cut out round shapes and bake at 390°F for 6 minutes. Garnish with grated goats' cheese and slices of beet.

81. Pasta Wraps

Prep. Time: 15 min - **Cooking Time:** 20 minutes - **Servings:** 4

Ingredients:
- ✓ 8 ounces of flour
- ✓ 2 ounces of pasta
- ✓ 6 teaspoons of olive oil
- ✓ 1 clove of garlic, chopped
- ✓ 1 green chili, chopped
- ✓ 1 small onion, chopped
- ✓ 1 tablespoon of tomato paste
- ✓ ½ teaspoon of garam masala
- ✓ Salt to taste

Directions:

1. Mix the flour with water and salt to make a dough. Add 1 teaspoon of oil mix and set aside.
2. Put the pasta in boiling water and add 3 teaspoons of oil and salt to it. Drain excess water when cooked.
3. Sauté the onions, garlic, chili and add the spices, salt and tomato paste. Lastly, add the cooked pasta and cover with lid and turn down heat to low.
4. Preheat the air-fryer 390°F.
5. Mold the dough into small balls; flatten them using a rolling pin into circle. Put the pasta stuffing on them and fold the opposite edges together. Seal edges with water.
6. Place into the air-fryer and cook for 15 minutes until golden. Remove and serve while hot with a sauce.

82. Mushroom, Onion And Feta Frittata

Prep. Time: 15 min - **Cooking Time:** 30 min - **Servings:** 4

Ingredients:
- ✓ 4 cups button mushrooms, cleaned & cut thinly into ¼ inch
- ✓ 6 eggs
- ✓ 1 red onion, peeled & sliced thinly into ¼ inch
- ✓ 6 tablespoons feta cheese, crumbled
- ✓ 2 tablespoons olive oil
- ✓ 1 pinch salt

Directions:

1. Add olive oil to a sauté pan and swirl the onions and mushrooms around under medium heat until tender. Remove from heat and cool on a dry kitchen towel.
2. Preheat Air-fryer to 330°F. Whisk the eggs thoroughly in a mixing bowl and add a pinch of salt.
3. Coat the inside and bottom of an 8-in. heat resistant baking dish lightly with spray. Pour the whisked eggs into the baking dish; add the onion and mushroom mixture and then add the cheese.
4. Place the dish in the cooking basket and cook 27 to 30 minutes in the Air fryer or until an inserted knife in the center of the frittata comes out clean.

83. Homemade Tater Tots

Prep.Time: 10 min - **Cooking Time:** 13 min - **Servings:** 2

Ingredients:
- ✓ 1 medium sized russet potato, chopped
- ✓ 1 teaspoon of ground onion
- ✓ 1 teaspoon of vegetable oil
- ✓ ½ teaspoon of ground black pepper
- ✓ Salt to taste

Directions:
1. Boil the potatoes until a bit more than al dente. Drain off water, add onions, oil and pepper to it and mash.
2. Preheat the air fryer to 379°F.
3. Mold the mash potatoes into tater tots. Place into the air-fryer and bake for 8 minutes. Shake the tots and bake for 5 minutes longer.

84. Fried Rice In Tomato Bowls

Prep.Time: 15 min - **Cooking Time:** 20 min - **Servings:** 4

Ingredients:
- ✓ 4 large tomatoes
- ✓ 2 cups of cooked rice
- ✓ 8 ounces of frozen peas
- ✓ 1 medium sized carrot, diced
- ✓ 1 medium sized onion, diced
- ✓ 3½ teaspoons of vegetable oil
- ✓ 1 clove of garlic, crushed
- ✓ 3 teaspoons of soy sauce

Directions:
1. Slice off the tops of the tomatoes and clean out the pith and seeds.
2. Heat the oil in a wok over low heat and add the onions, peas, garlic and carrots. Stir fry for 2 minutes, add the soy sauce and rice and then stir.
3. Heat the air fryer to 356°F
4. Stuff the tomatoes with the prepared fried rice and place in the air-fryer for 20 minutes until well cooked.

85. Roasted Bell Pepper Vegetable Salad

Prep.Time: 15 min - **Cooking Time:** 10 minutes - **Servings:** 4

Ingredients:
- ✓ 1½ ounces of yogurt
- ✓ 1 medium sized red bell pepper
- ✓ 2 ounces of rocket leaves
- ✓ 3 teaspoons of lime juice
- ✓ 1 romaine lettuce
- ✓ 1 ounce of olive oil
- ✓ Ground black pepper and salt to taste

Directions:
1. Heat your air-fryer to 392°F and place the bell pepper into it. Roast for 10 minutes until a bit charred. Put the pepper in a bowl, cover and leave for about 15 minutes.
2. Divide the bell pepper into 4, remove skin and seeds and then slice the pepper into thin strips.
3. Mix the lime juice, olive oil and yogurt thoroughly together in a bowl. Add the salt and pepper as required and stir.
4. Add the rocket leaves, lettuce and pepper strips into the yogurt mixture and toss to mix.

86. Crispy Parsley And Garlic Mushrooms

Prep.Time: 10 min - **Cooking Time:** 8 min - **Servings:** 4

Ingredients:
- ✓ 2 slices of white bread
- ✓ 3 teaspoons of finely chopped parsley
- ✓ 16 small mushrooms
- ✓ 4 teaspoons of melted butter
- ✓ 1 clove of garlic, crushed
- ✓ ½ teaspoon of black pepper

Directions:
1. Heat your air-fryer to 390°F.
2. Grind the bread using a food processor into fine crumbs. Add the parsley, garlic and pepper and mix thoroughly. Add the melted butter and stir.
3. Remove all the mushroom stalks and Put the breadcrumbs into the caps. Press to keep breadcrumbs firm in the cap.
4. Put the caps into the fryer basket and cook for 8 minutes until they become crisp and golden brown.

87. Crispy Broccoli Tots

Prep.Time: 40 min - **Cooking Time:** 12 min - **Servings:** 2-4

Ingredients:
- ✓ 2 cups broccoli florets
- ✓ 1¼ cup white cheddar cheese
- ✓ 1¼ cup panko crumbs
- ✓ 1/4 cup parmesan cheese
- ✓ 2 eggs, beaten
- 1 teaspoon kosher salt

Directions:
1. Pulse broccoli with a food processor until finely crumbed.
2. Combine broccoli, cheeses, panko crumbs and salt in a large bowl. Add eggs and mix thoroughly.
3. Roll mixture into small balls and refrigerate for 30 minutes to firm. Preheat Air Fryer to 350°F.
4. Place the broccoli tots into the Air Fryer and then cook until browned and crispy for 12 minutes. Remove and serve.

88. Roasted Winter Vegetables

Prep.Time: 5 min - **Cooking Time:** 20 min - **Servings:** 6

Ingredients:
- ✓ 2 red onions, cut into wedges
- ✓ 11/3 cup parsnips, peeled & cut into 2 cm cubes
- ✓ 11/3 cup butternut squash, halved, seeded & cubed
- ✓ 11/3 cup celery, peeled & cut into 2 cm cubes
- ✓ 1 tablespoon fresh thyme needles
- ✓ 1 tablespoon olive oil
- ✓ Pepper & salt

Directions:
1. Preheat the Air-fryer to 390°F.
2. Combine the cut vegetables with the olive oil and thyme and season well to taste.
3. Place the veggies into the basket and place the basket into the Air-fryer.
4. Roast the vegetables for 20 minutes, stirring once until brown and done.

89. Cheesy Polenta

Prep.Time: 1 hour 5 min - **Cooking Time:** 6 min - **Servings:** 2-4

Ingredients:
- ✓ 2 ½ cups cooked polenta
- ✓ 1 cup marinara sauce
- ✓ 1/4 cup parmesan, shaved
- ✓ 1 tablespoon vegetable oil
- ✓ Salt to taste

Directions:
1. Grease a baking tray with the vegetable oil. Place the polenta into the tray and then refrigerate for 1 hour to firm.
2. Preheat the Air Fryer to 350°F. Remove tray from fridge and cut the polenta into equal slices.
3. Place the slices into the Air Fryer and cook minutes until crispy or for 5-6 minutes.
4. Sprinkle with parmesan, season with salt and serve with marinara on the side.

90. Cajun Shrimp

Prep.Time: 5 min - **Cooking Time:** 5 min - **Servings:** 4

Ingredients:
- ✓ 1¼ pounds tiger shrimp
- ✓ ¼ teaspoon smoked paprika
- ✓ ½ teaspoon old bay seasoning
- ✓ ¼ teaspoon cayenne pepper
- ✓ 1 tablespoon olive oil
- ✓ 1 pinch salt

Directions:
1. Preheat the Air-fryer to 390°F. Combine all ingredients in a mixing bowl; let the shrimp coat well with the oil and spices.
2. Place the shrimp into the cooking basket in the air fryer and cook for 5 minutes.
3. Serve and enjoy over rice.

91. Onion Flowers

Prep.Time: 10 min - **Cooking Time:** 30 minutes - **Servings:** 4

Ingredients:
- ✓ 4 medium sized onions, peeled
- ✓ 4 teaspoons of butter
- ✓ 3 teaspoons of vegetable oil

Directions:
1. Cut off the bottom and top of the onions. Cut 4 slits into the onions but not through to the end, to make 8 segments.
2. Place the onions in salt water for 4 hours to remove the sharp tang.
3. Heat your air-fryer to 356°F.
4. Place the blooming onions in the fryer basket. Add a teaspoon of butter on each and drizzle with oil. Cook for 30 minutes.
5. Remove the charred outer layer and serve.

92. Crunchy Carrots

Prep.Time: 2 min - **Cooking Time:** 12 min - **Servings:** 2

Ingredients:
- ✓ 4 carrots, sliced lengthwise
- ✓ 1 tablespoon of olive oil
- ✓ 2 teaspoons salt

Directions:
1. Add together the salt and olive oil in a bowl. Coat the mixture with the carrots by drizzling over.
2. Heat the Air Fryer to 360 °F.
3. Cook carrots for 12 minutes and serve.

93. Sweet Pepper And Potato Stuffed Bread Rolls

Prep.Time: 15 min - **Cooking Time:** 5 min - **Servings:** 3

Ingredients:
- ✓ 6 medium sized potatoes, boiled
- ✓ 2 teaspoons of flour
- ✓ 6 slices of white bread
- ✓ 1 tablespoon of sesame seed
- ✓ 1 pound of chopped bell peppers (red and green)
- ✓ ½ teaspoon of chaat masala seasoning Salt to taste

Directions:
1. Mash the cooked potatoes in a large bowl and add the seasoning and salt. Stir thoroughly.
2. Add water to the flour to make a thick slurry mixture. Mix sesame seeds and the chopped pepper in a separate bowl.
3. Peel off the brown edges of the bread and use a rolling pin to flatten it. Put the potato stuffing on the edge of the bread and roll it into a cylinder.
4. Seal the rolls by brushing the edge with the flour mixture. Use the mixture to coat the rolls as well. Place the rolls in the mixture of pepper and sesame seeds and allow to coat.
5. Heat your air-fryer to 330°F and place the rolls in it. Bake for 5 minute and remove. Serve hot with ketchup.

94. Mozzarella And Garlic Rice Balls

Prep.Time: 15 min - **Cooking Time:** 15 min - **Servings:** 4

Ingredients:
- ✓ 1 cup of rice, boiled
- ✓ 2 tablespoons of grated carrot
- ✓ 1 medium sized green chili, finely chopped
- ✓ 2 tablespoons of corn flour
- ✓ 8 ounces of paneer cheese, grated
- ✓ 2 tablespoons of sweet corn
- ✓ 2 teaspoons of Mozzarella Cheese Cubes
- ✓ 1 teaspoon of garlic powder
- ✓ 1 teaspoon of Italian seasoning
- ✓ 2 tablespoons of breadcrumbs
- ✓ 4 tablespoons of water
- ✓ Salt to taste

Directions:
1. Mix the rice, seasoning, paneer, garlic, 1 tablespoon of corn flour and salt in a bowl. Mash and make into dough.
2. 2 Add the water to the rest of the corn flour and stir to make a slurry mixture.
3. Mix the cheese cubes, carrots, sweet corn and chili in a separate bowl.
4. Put a small hole into the dough and stuff with the carrot mixture. Roll the dough into a ball. Coat the balls with the corn, slurry and then roll over the breadcrumbs to coat.
5. Place in the air-fryer and cook for 15 minutes at 390°F. Serve while still hot with a tomato sauce.

95. Mozzarella Spinach Rolls

Prep.Time: 10 min - Cooking Time: 15 min - Servings: 2

Ingredients:
- ✓ 10½ ounces of spinach leaves, boiled
- ✓ 1 tablespoon of grated mozzarella cheese
- ✓ 2 tablespoons of breadcrumbs
- ✓ 1 onion, finely chopped
- ✓ 1 clove of garlic, grated
- ✓ 1 tablespoon of vegetable oil
- ✓ 1 teaspoon of ground red chili
- ✓ Salt to taste
- ✓ 2 tablespoons of corn flour

Directions:
1. Mash the spinach to make a puree, add the mozzarella, breadcrumbs, garlic, corn flour and salt. Mix thoroughly and mold into small balls.
2. Mix the onions and red chili with some cheese and mold them into smaller balls. Make a hole into the spinach rolls and insert the cheese rolls into each one. Ensure the rolls are evenly covered on all sides.
3. Brush the rolls with oil and place in an air-fryer at 390°F. Cook for about 15 minutes until crisp, and serve with a tomato sauce.

96. Crispy Eggplant Strips

Prep.Time: 5 min - Cooking Time: 25 min - Servings: 2

Ingredients:
- ✓ 4 tablespoons of cornstarch
- ✓ 1 medium sized eggplant
- ✓ 4 tablespoons of vegetable oil
- ✓ 1 pinch of salt
- ✓ 4 tablespoons of water

Directions:
1. Heat your air-fryer to 390°F.
2. Slice the eggplant to 0.3 x 3 inches strips.
3. Mix the oil, cornstarch and water in a bowl. Add the eggplant strips and mix to coat evenly.
4. Put half of the eggplant strips in the air-fryer and cook for about 14 minutes until they begin to brown. Do same to the next batch of eggplant strips until they are all cooked.
5. Serve while hot with a yogurt dip.

97. Crisp Parmesan-Potato Balls

Prep.Time: 15 min - Cooking Time: 30 minutes - Servings: 4

Ingredients:

For The Filling:
- ✓ 8 ounces of Parmesan, grated
- ✓ 2 egg yolks
- ✓ 6 teaspoons of flour
- ✓ A pinch of nutmeg
- ✓ 4 medium sized potatoes, peeled and chopped
- ✓ 1½ ounce of chopped chives
- ✓ A pinch of ground black pepper
- ✓ A pinch of salt

For The Breading:
- ✓ 6 ounces of breadcrumbs
- ✓ 6 ounces of flour 2 eggs, whisked
- ✓ 3 tablespoons of olive oil

Directions:
1. Cook the potatoes in water with little salt for about 15 minutes and drain.
2. Use a potato masher to mash the potatoes to form a pulp mass and allow to cool.
3. Add the parmesan, egg yolk, chives and flour and mix thoroughly. Add the salt, nutmeg and pepper. Roll the potato fillings into small round balls.
4. Heat your air-fryer to 390°F.
5. Add the oil to the breadcrumbs and mix with fingertips until it becomes crumbly.
6. Roll the balls over the flour, dip into the whisked eggs and lastly coat with the breadcrumbs. Press to ensure coating sticks firmly.
7. Put the potato balls into the air-fryer basket and air fry until golden for about 8 minutes.

98. Potatoes Au Gratin

Prep.Time: 10 min - Cooking Time: 35 min - Servings: 6

Ingredients:
- ✓ 7 medium russet potatoes, peeled & sliced wafer-thin
- ✓ ½ cup cream
- ✓ ½ cup milk
- ✓ 1 teaspoon black pepper
- ✓ ½ teaspoon nutmeg
- ✓ ½ cup gruyere, grated

Directions:
1. Preheat the Air-fryer to 390°F. Combine cream and milk in a bowl and then season with nutmeg, pepper and salt to taste.
2. Coat the thinly sliced potato with the milk mixture and then remove to a baking dish.
3. Pour the remaining cream mixture on top of the potatoes. Put the baking dish in the cooking basket into the Air-fryer. Cook for 25 minutes and then remove.
4. Distribute the cheese uniformly over the potatoes. Bake for 10 minutes until brown.

99. Sweet Potato And Parsnips Crisps

Prep.Time: 5 min - Cooking Time: 20 min - Servings: 2

Ingredients:
- ✓ 1 medium sized sweet potato, peeled
- ✓ 2 medium sized beets
- ✓ 2 medium sized parsnips
- ✓ ½ teaspoon of ground chili
- ✓ 3 teaspoons of vegetable oil

Directions:
1. Preheat your Air-fryer to 460°F.
2. Cut the beets, potato and parsnips into thin slices. Add the oil, chili, salt and pepper and then toss to mix.
3. Put into air-fryer and cook for 10 minutes. Shake the pan and continue cooking until crisp and golden for another 10 minutes.

100. Broccoli Rounds With Cheese

Prep.Time: 2 hours 15 min - Cooking Time: 10 min - Servings: 4

Ingredients:
- ✓ 16 ounce Broccoli, chopped
- ✓ 3 cups cheddar cheese, shredded
- ✓ 3 eggs
- ✓ 1 cup flour
- ✓ 1 cup breadcrumbs
- ✓ Salt and pepper to taste

Directions:
1. Whisk the eggs in a bowl and then add the broccoli, cheese and flour to make a dough. Cover and then put inside the refrigerator for least 2 hours.
2. Use spoonfuls of the mixture to compress into balls then roll into the breadcrumbs to coat.
3. Preheat the Air Fryer to 350°F. Fry the broccoli rounds in batches for 4 to 5 minutes. Serve with ranch dip and enjoy.

101. Tasty Portabella Pepperoni Pizza

Prep.Time: 5 min - **Cooking Time:** 10 min - **Servings:** 3

Ingredients:
- ✓ 3 portabella mushroom caps, cleaned and scooped
- ✓ 3 tablespoons tomato sauce
- ✓ 3 tablespoons olive oil
- ✓ 3 tablespoons shredded mozzarella
- ✓ 12 pepperoni slices
- ✓ 1 pinch dried Italian seasonings
- ✓ 1 pinch salt

Directions:
1. Preheat the Air fryer to 330°F. Drizzle olive oil on the sides of the portabella. Add salt and Italian seasonings inside of the portabella to season it.
2. Spread the tomato sauce over the mushroom, top with cheese. Next, place the portabella into the cooking basket and place into the Air-fryer for 1 minute.
3. Remove the cooking basket and place the sliced pepperoni on top of the portabella pizza.
4. Cook additional 3 to 5 minutes longer. Top with and crushed red pepper flakes and freshly grated parmesan cheese.

102. Air Fryer Cauliflower Rice

Prep.Time: 10 min - **Cooking Time:** 20 min - **Servings:** 2

Ingredients:

Round 1:
- ✓ 1 tsp. turmeric
- ✓ 1 C. diced carrot
- ✓ ½ C. diced onion
- ✓ 2 tbsp. low-sodium soy sauce
- ✓ ½ block of extra firm tofu

Round 2:
- ✓ ½ C. frozen peas
- ✓ 2 minced garlic cloves
- ✓ ½ C. chopped broccoli
- ✓ 1 tbsp. minced ginger
- ✓ 1 tbsp. rice vinegar
- ✓ 1 ½ tsp. toasted sesame oil
- ✓ 2 tbsp. reduced-sodium soy sauce
- ✓ 3 C. riced cauliflower

Directions:
1. Crumble tofu in a large bowl and toss with all the Round one ingredients.
2. Preheat air fryer to 370 degrees and cook 10 minutes, making sure to shake once.
3. In another bowl, toss ingredients from Round 2 together.
4. Add Round 2 mixture to air fryer and cook another 10 minutes, ensuring to shake 5 minutes in.

103. Air Fried Carrots, Yellow Squash & Zucchini

Prep.Time: 15 min - **Cooking Time:** 30 minutes - **Servings:** 2

Ingredients:
- ✓ 1 tbsp. chopped tarragon leaves
- ✓ ½ tsp. white pepper
- ✓ 1 tsp. salt
- ✓ 1 pound yellow squash
- ✓ 1 pound zucchini
- ✓ 6 tsp. olive oil
- ✓ ½ pound carrots

Directions:
1. Stem and root the end of squash and zucchini and cut in ¾-inch half-moons. Peel and cut carrots into 1-inch cubes
2. Combine carrot cubes with 2 teaspoons of olive oil, tossing to combine. Pour into air fryer basket and cook 5 minutes at 400 degrees.
3. As carrots cook, drizzle remaining olive oil over squash and zucchini pieces, then season with pepper and salt. Toss well to coat.
4. Add squash and zucchini when the timer for carrots goes off. Cook 30 minutes, making sure to toss 2-3 times during the cooking process.
5. Once done, take out veggies and toss with tarragon. Serve up warm.

104. Avocado Fries

Prep.Time: 10 min - **Cooking Time:** 5 min - **Servings:** 2

Ingredients:
- ✓ 1 avocado
- ✓ ½ tsp. salt
- ✓ ½ C. panko breadcrumbs
- ✓ Bean liquid (aquafaba) from a 15-ounce can of white or garbanzo beans

Directions:
1. Peel, pit, and slice up avocado.
2. Toss salt and breadcrumbs together in a bowl. Place aquafaba into another bowl.
3. Dredge slices of avocado first in aquafaba and then in panko, making sure you get an even coating.
4. Place coated avocado slices into a single layer in the air fryer.
5. Cook 5 minutes at 390 degrees, shaking at 5 minutes.
6. Serve with your favorite keto dipping sauce.

105. Zucchini Parmesan Chips

Prep.Time: 15 min - **Cooking Time:** 8 min - **Servings:** 2

Ingredients:
- ✓ ½ tsp. paprika
- ✓ ½ C. grated parmesan cheese
- ✓ ½ C. Italian breadcrumbs
- ✓ 1 lightly beaten egg
- ✓ 2 thinly sliced zucchinis

Directions:
1. Use a very sharp knife or mandolin slicer to slice zucchini as thinly as you can. Pat off extra moisture.
2. Beat egg with a pinch of pepper and salt and a bit of water.
3. Combine paprika, cheese, and breadcrumbs in a bowl.
4. Dip slices of zucchini into the egg mixture and then into breadcrumb mixture. Press gently to coat.
5. With olive oil cooking spray, mist coated zucchini slices. Place into your air fryer in a single layer.
6. Cook 8 minutes at 350 degrees.
7. Sprinkle with salt and serve with salsa.

106. Jicama Fries

Prep.Time: 2 hours 15 min - **Cooking Time:** 10 min - **Servings:** 4

Ingredients:
- ✓ 1 tbsp. dried thyme
- ✓ ¾ C. arrowroot flour
- ✓ ½ large Jicama
- ✓ 2 eggs

Directions:
1. Sliced jicama into fries.
2. Whisk eggs together and pour over fries. Toss to coat.
3. Mix a pinch of salt, thyme, and arrowroot flour together. Toss egg-coated jicama into dry mixture, tossing to coat well.
4. Spray air fryer basket with olive oil and add fries. Cook 20 minutes on CHIPS setting.

107. Buffalo Cauliflower

Prep.Time: 10 min - Cooking Time: 15-17 min - Servings: 2

Ingredients:

Cauliflower:
- ✓ 1 C. panko breadcrumbs
- ✓ 1 tsp. salt
- ✓ 4 C. cauliflower florets

Buffalo Coating:
- ✓ ¼ C. Vegan Buffalo sauce
- ✓ ¼ C. melted vegan butter

Directions:

1. Melt butter in microwave and whisk in buffalo sauce.
2. Dip each cauliflower floret into buffalo mixture, ensuring it gets coated well. Hold over a bowl till floret is done dripping.
3. Mix breadcrumbs with salt.
4. Dredge dipped florets into breadcrumbs and place into air fryer.
5. Cook 14-17 minutes at 350 degrees. When slightly browned, they are ready to eat!
6. Serve with your favorite keto dipping sauce.

108. Crispy Roasted Broccoli

Prep.Time: 40 min - Cooking Time: 15 min - Servings: 2

Ingredients:
- ✓ ¼ tsp. Masala
- ✓ ½ tsp. red chili powder
- ✓ ½ tsp. salt
- ✓ ¼ tsp. turmeric powder
- ✓ 1 tbsp. chickpea flour
- ✓ 2 tbsp. yogurt
- ✓ 1 pound broccoli

Directions:

1. Cut broccoli up into florets. Soak in a bowl of water with 2 teaspoons of salt for at least half an hour to remove impurities.
2. Take out broccoli florets from water and let drain. Wipe down thoroughly.
3. Mix all other ingredients together to create a marinade.
4. Toss broccoli florets in the marinade. Cover and chill 15-30 minutes.
5. Preheat air fryer to 390 degrees. Place marinated broccoli florets into the fryer. Cook 10 minutes.
6. 5 minutes into cooking shake the basket. Florets will be crispy when done.

109. Cheesy Cauliflower Fritters

Prep.Time: 15 min - Cooking Time: 15 minutes - Servings: 2

Ingredients:
- ✓ ½ C. chopped parsley
- ✓ 1 C. Italian breadcrumbs
- ✓ 1/3 C. shredded mozzarella cheese
- ✓ 1/3 C. shredded sharp cheddar cheese
- ✓ 1 egg
- ✓ 2 minced garlic cloves
- ✓ 3 chopped scallions
- ✓ 1 head of cauliflower

Directions:

1. Cut cauliflower up into florets. Wash well and pat dry. Place into a food processor and pulse 20-30 seconds till it looks like rice.
2. Place cauliflower rice in a bowl and mix with pepper, salt, egg, cheeses, breadcrumbs, garlic, and scallions.
3. With hands, form 15 patties of the mixture. Add more breadcrumbs if needed.
4. With olive oil, spritz patties, and place into your air fryer in a single layer.
5. Cook 14 minutes at 390 degrees, flipping after 7 minutes.

110. Crispy Jalapeno Coins

Prep.Time: 10 min - Cooking Time: 10 min - Servings: 2

Ingredients:
- ✓ 1 egg
- ✓ 2-3 tbsp. coconut flour
- ✓ 1 sliced and seeded jalapeno
- ✓ Pinch of garlic powder
- ✓ Pinch of onion powder
- ✓ Pinch of Cajun seasoning (optional)
- ✓ Pinch of pepper and salt

Directions:

1. Ensure your air fryer is preheated to 400 degrees.
2. Mix together all dry ingredients.
3. Pat jalapeno slices dry. Dip coins into egg wash and then into dry mixture. Toss to thoroughly coat.
4. Add coated jalapeno slices to air fryer in a singular layer. Spray with olive oil.
5. Cook just till crispy.

111. Air Fryer Asparagus

Prep.Time: 10 min - Cooking Time: 8 min - Servings: 2

Ingredients:
- ✓ Nutritional yeast
- ✓ Olive oil non-stick spray
- ✓ One bunch of asparagus

Directions:

1. Wash asparagus and then trim off thick, woody ends.
2. Spray asparagus with olive oil spray and sprinkle with yeast.
3. In your air fryer, lay asparagus in a singular layer.
4. Cook 8 minutes at 360 degrees.

112. Spicy Sweet Potato Fries

Prep.Time: 10 min - Cooking Time: 27 min - Servings: 2

Ingredients:
- ✓ 2 tbsp. sweet potato fry seasoning mix
- ✓ 2 tbsp. olive oil
- ✓ 2 sweet potatoes

Seasoning Mix:
- ✓ 2 tbsp. salt
- ✓ 1 tbsp. cayenne pepper
- ✓ 1 tbsp. dried oregano
- ✓ 1 tbsp. fennel
- ✓ 2 tbsp. coriander

Directions:

1. Slice both ends off sweet potatoes and peel. Slice lengthwise in half and again crosswise to make four pieces from each potato.
2. Slice each potato piece into 2-3 slices, then slice into fries.
3. Grind together all of seasoning mix ingredients and mix in the salt.
4. Ensure air fryer is preheated to 350 degrees.
5. Toss potato pieces in olive oil, sprinkling with seasoning mix and tossing well to coat thoroughly.
6. Add fries to air fryer basket and set time for 27 minutes. Press start and cook 15 minutes.
7. Take out the basket and turn fries. Turn off air fryer and let cook 10-12 minutes till fries are golden.

113. Cheesy Spinach Toasties

Prep.Time: 15 min - **Cooking Time:** 14-20 min - **Servings:** 1

Ingredients:
- ✓ 2 toasted bread slices cut into triangles
- ✓ 1 tbsp. butter
- ✓ 1 tbsp. all-purpose flour
- ✓ 1 small onion finely chopped
- ✓ 1-2 flakes garlic finely chopped
- ✓ Half a bunch of spinach that has been boiled and crushed (does not have to be crushed finely)
- ✓ 1 tsp. coarsely crushed green chilies
- ✓ 2 tbsp. grated pizza cheese
- ✓ 1 cup milk
- ✓ 1 tbsp. fresh cream
- ✓ Some salt and pepper to taste

Directions:
1. Take a pan and melt some butter in it. Also add some onions and garlic. Now keep roasting them in the butter until the onions are caramelized or attain a golden-brown color.
2. Into this pan add the required amount of all-purpose flour. Continue to roast for 3 minutes or so. Add milk and keep stirring until you bring it to a boil. Add green chilies, cream, spinach and seasoning. Mix the ingredients properly and let it cook until the mixture thickens. Toast some bread. Apply the paste made in the previous step on the bread.
3. Sprinkle some grated cheese on top of the paste.
4. Pre heat the Air Fryer at 290 Fahrenheit for around 4 minutes. Put the toasts in the Fry basket and let it continue to cook for another 10 minutes at the same temperature.

114. Stuffed Eggplant Baskets

Prep.Time: 20 min - **Cooking Time:** 25 min - **Servings:** 4

Ingredients:
For baskets:
- ✓ 6 eggplants
- ✓ ½ tsp. salt
- ✓ ½ tsp. pepper powder

For filling:
- ✓ 1 medium onion finely chopped
- ✓ 1 green chili finely chopped
- ✓ 1 ½ tbsp. chopped coriander leaves
- ✓ 1 tsp. fenugreek
- ✓ 1 tsp. dried mango powder
- ✓ 1 tsp. cumin powder
- ✓ Salt and pepper to taste

For topping:
- ✓ 3 tbsp. grated cheese
- ✓ 1 tsp. red chili flakes
- ✓ ½ tsp. oregano
- ✓ ½ tsp. basil
- ✓ ½ tsp. parsley

Directions:
1. Take all the ingredients under the heading "Filling" and mix them together in a bowl.
2. Remove the stem of the eggplant. Cut off the caps. Remove a little of the flesh as well. Sprinkle some salt and pepper on the inside of the capsicums. Leave them aside for some time.
3. Now fill the eggplant with the filling prepared but leave a small space at the top. Sprinkle grated cheese and also add the seasoning.
4. Pre heat the Air Fryer at 140 degrees Fahrenheit for 5 minutes. Put the capsicums in the fry basket and close it. Let them cook at the same temperature for another 20 minutes. Turn them over in between to prevent over cooking.

115. Fried Up Avocados

Prep.Time: 15 min - **Cooking Time:** 15 min - **Servings:** 2

Ingredients:
- ✓ ½ cup almond meal
- ✓ ½ teaspoon salt
- ✓ 1 Hass avocado, peeled, pitted and sliced
- ✓ Aquafaba from one bean can (bean liquid)

Directions:
1. Take a shallow bowl and add almond meal, salt
2. Pour aquafaba in another bowl, dredge avocado slices in aquafaba and then into the crumbs to get a nice coating
3. Arrange them in a single layer in your Air Fryer cooking basket, don't overlap
4. Cook for 10 minutes at 390 degrees F, give the basket a shake and cook for 5 minutes more. Serve and enjoy!

116. Easy Fried Tomatoes

Prep.Time: 10 min - **Cooking Time:** 5 min - **Servings:** 1

Ingredients:
- ✓ 1 green tomato
- ✓ ¼ tbsp Creole seasoning
- ✓ ¼ cup almond flour
- ✓ ½ cup buttermilk
- ✓ Bread crumbs as needed

Directions:
1. Add flour to your plate and take another plate and add buttermilk
2. Cut tomatoes and season with salt and pepper
3. Make a mix of creole seasoning and crumbs
4. Take tomato slice and cover with flour, place in buttermilk and then into crumbs
5. Repeat with all tomatoes
6. Pre-heat your fryer to 400-degree F
7. Cook the tomato slices for 5 minutes
8. Serve with basil and enjoy!

117. Broccoli and Parmesan Dish

Prep.Time: 15 min - **Cooking Time:** 20 min - **Servings:** 2

Ingredients:
- ✓ 1 head fresh broccoli
- ✓ 1 tablespoon olive oil
- ✓ 1 lemon, juiced
- ✓ Salt and pepper to taste
- ✓ 1-ounce parmesan cheese, grated

Directions:
1. Wash broccoli thoroughly and cut them into florets.
2. Add the listed ingredients to your broccoli and mix well.
3. Pre-heat your fryer to 365-degree F.
4. Air fry broccoli for 20 minutes.
5. Serve and enjoy!

118. Squash and Cumin Chili

Prep.Time: 10 min - **Cooking Time:** 22 min - **Servings:** 2

Ingredients:
- ✓ 1 medium butternut squash
- ✓ 2 teaspoons cumin seeds
- ✓ 1 large pinch chili flakes
- ✓ 1 tablespoon olive oil
- ✓ 1 and ½ ounces pine nuts
- ✓ 1 small bunch fresh coriander, chopped

Directions:
1. Take the squash and slice it
2. Remove seeds and cut into smaller chunks
3. Take a bowl and add chunked squash, spice and oil
4. Mix well. Pre-heat your Fryer to 360 degrees F and add the squash to the cooking basket
5. Roast for 20 minutes, making sure to shake the basket from time to time to avoid burning
6. Take pan and place it over medium heat, add pine nuts to the pan and dry toast for 2 minutes
7. Sprinkle nuts on top of squash and serve

DESSERT RECIPES

1. Bread Pudding

Prep.Time: 10 min - Cooking Time: 1 hour - Servings: 4

Ingredients:
- ✓ 6 glazed doughnuts, crumbled
- ✓ 1 cup cherries
- ✓ 4 egg yolks
- ✓ 1 and ½ cups whipping cream
- ✓ ½ cup raisins
- ✓ ¼ cup sugar
- ✓ ½ cup chocolate chips

Directions:
1. In a bowl, mix cherries with egg yolks and whipping cream and stir well.
2. In another bowl, mix raisins with sugar, chocolate chips and doughnuts and stir.
3. Combine the 2 mixtures, transfer everything to a greased pan that fits your air fryer and cook at 310 degrees F for 1 hour.
4. Chill pudding before cutting and serving it.

Nutrition: calories 302 - Fat 8 - Fiber 2 - Carbs 23 - Protein 10

2. Air Fried Bananas

Prep.Time: 10 min - Cooking Time: 15 min - Servings: 4

Ingredients:
- ✓ 3 tablespoons butter
- ✓ 2 eggs
- ✓ 8 bananas, peeled and halved
- ✓ ½ cup corn flour
- ✓ 3 tablespoons cinnamon sugar
- ✓ 1 cup panko

Directions:
1. Heat up a pan with the butter over medium high heat, add panko, stir and cook for 4 minutes and then transfer to a bowl.
2. Roll each in flour, eggs and panko mix, arrange them in your air fryer's basket, dust with cinnamon sugar and cook at 280 degrees F for 10 minutes.
3. Serve right away.

Nutrition: calories 164 - Fat 1 - Fiber 4 - Carbs 32 - Protein 4

3. Mini Lava Cakes

Prep.Time: 10 min - Cooking Time: 20 minutes - Servings: 3

Ingredients:
- ✓ 1 egg
- ✓ 4 tablespoons sugar
- ✓ 2 tablespoons olive oil
- ✓ 4 tablespoons milk
- ✓ 4 tablespoons flour
- ✓ 1 tablespoon cocoa powder
- ✓ ½ teaspoon baking powder
- ✓ ½ teaspoon orange zest

Directions:
1. In a bowl, mix egg with sugar, oil, milk, flour, salt, cocoa powder, baking powder and orange zest, stir very well and pour this into greased ramekins.
2. Add ramekins to your air fryer and cook at 320 degrees F for 20 minutes.
3. Serve lava cakes warm.

Nutrition: calories 201 - Fat 7 - Fiber 8 - Carbs 23 - Protein 4

4. Chocolate Cookies

Prep.Time: 10 min - Cooking Time: 25 min - Servings: 12

Ingredients:
- ✓ 1 teaspoon vanilla extract
- ✓ ½ cup butter
- ✓ 1 egg
- ✓ 4 tablespoons sugar
- ✓ 2 cups flour
- ✓ ½ cup unsweetened chocolate chips

Directions:
1. Heat up a pan with the butter over medium heat, stir and cook for 1 minute.
2. In a bowl, mix egg with vanilla extract and sugar and stir well.
3. Add melted butter, flour and half of the chocolate chips and stir everything.
4. Transfer this to a pan that fits your air fryer, spread the rest of the chocolate chips on top, introduce in the fryer at 330 degrees F and bake for 25 minutes.
5. Slice when it's cold and serve.

Nutrition: calories 230 - Fat 12 - Fiber 2 - Carbs 4 - Protein 5

5. Crispy Apples

Prep.Time: 10 min - Cooking Time: 10 min - Servings: 4

Ingredients:
- ✓ 2 teaspoons cinnamon powder
- ✓ 5 apples, cored and cut into chunks
- ✓ ½ teaspoon nutmeg powder
- ✓ 1 tablespoon maple syrup
- ✓ ½ cup water
- ✓ 4 tablespoons butter
- ✓ ¼ cup flour
- ✓ ¾ cup old fashioned rolled oats
- ✓ ¼ cup brown sugar

Directions:
1. Put the apples in a pan that fits your air fryer, add cinnamon, nutmeg, maple syrup and water.
2. In a bowl, mix butter with oats, sugar, salt and flour, stir, drop spoonfuls of this mix on top of apples, introduce in your air fryer and cook at 350 degrees F for 10 minutes.
3. Serve warm.

Nutrition: calories 200 - Fat 6 - Fiber 8 - Carbs 29 - Protein 12

6. Apple Bread

Prep.Time: 10 min - Cooking Time: 40 min - Servings: 6

Ingredients:
- ✓ 3 cups apples, cored and cubed
- ✓ 1 cup sugar
- ✓ 1 tablespoon vanilla
- ✓ 2 eggs
- ✓ 1 tablespoon apple pie spice
- ✓ 2 cups white flour
- ✓ 1 tablespoon baking powder
- ✓ 1 stick butter
- ✓ 1 cup water

Directions:
1. In a bowl mix egg with 1 butter stick, apple pie spice and sugar and stir using your mixer.
2. Add apples and stir again well.
3. In another bowl, mix baking powder with flour and stir.
4. Combine the 2 mixtures, stir and pour into a spring form pan.
5. Put spring form pan in your air fryer and cook at 320 degrees F for 40 minutes
6. Slice and serve.

Nutrition: calories 192 - Fat 6 - Fiber 7 - Carbs 14 - Protein 7

7. Simple Cheesecake

Prep.Time: 10 min - **Cooking Time:** 15 min - **Servings:** 15

Ingredients:
- ✓ 1 pound cream cheese
- ✓ ½ teaspoon vanilla extract
- ✓ 2 eggs
- ✓ 4 tablespoons sugar
- ✓ 1 cup graham crackers, crumbled
- ✓ 2 tablespoons butter

Directions:
1. In a bowl, mix crackers with butter.
2. Press crackers mix on the bottom of a lined cake pan, introduce in your air fryer and cook at 350 degrees F for 4 minutes.
3. Meanwhile, in a bowl, mix sugar with cream cheese, eggs and vanilla and whisk well.
4. Spread filling over crackers crust and cook your cheesecake in your air fryer at 310 degrees F for 15 minutes.
5. Leave cake in the fridge for 3 hours, slice and serve.

Nutrition: calories 245 - Fat 12 - Fiber 1 - Carbs 20 - Protein 3

8. Cinnamon Rolls and Cream Cheese Dip

Prep.Time: 2 hours - **Cooking Time:** 15 min - **Servings:** 8

Ingredients:
- ✓ 1 pound bread dough
- ✓ ¾ cup brown sugar
- ✓ 1 and ½ tablespoons cinnamon, ground
- ✓ ¼ cup butter, melted

For the cream cheese dip:
- ✓ 2 tablespoons butter
- ✓ 4 ounces cream cheese
- ✓ 1 and ¼ cups sugar
- ✓ ½ teaspoon vanilla

Directions:
1. Roll dough on a floured working surface, shape a rectangle and brush with ¼ cup butter.
2. In a bowl, mix cinnamon with sugar, stir, sprinkle this over dough, roll dough into a log, seal well and cut into 8 pieces.
3. Leave rolls to rise for 2 hours, place them in your air fryer's basket, cook at 350 degrees F for 5 minutes, flip them, cook for 4 minutes more and transfer to a platter.
4. In a bowl, mix cream cheese with butter, sugar and vanilla and whisk really well.
5. Serve your cinnamon rolls with this cream cheese dip.

Nutrition: calories 200 - Fat 1 - Fiber 0 - Carbs 5 - Protein 6

9. Tasty Banana Cake

Prep.Time: 10 min - **Cooking Time:** 30 minutes - **Servings:** 4

Ingredients:
- ✓ 1 tablespoon butter, soft
- ✓ 1 egg
- ✓ 1/3 cup brown sugar
- ✓ 2 tablespoons honey
- ✓ 1 banana, peeled and mashed
- ✓ 1 cup white flour
- ✓ 1 tsp baking powder
- ✓ ½ tsp cinnamon powder
- ✓ Cooking spray

Directions:
1. Spray a cake pan with some cooking spray and leave aside.
2. In a bowl, mix butter with sugar, banana, honey, egg, cinnamon, baking powder and flour and whisk
3. Pour this into a cake pan greased with cooking spray, introduce in your air fryer and cook at 350 degrees F for 30 minutes.
4. Leave cake to cool down, slice and serve.

Nutrition: calories 232 - Fat 4 - Fiber 1 - Carbs 34 - Protein 4

10. Bread Dough and Amaretto Dessert

Prep.Time: 10 min - **Cooking Time:** 12 min - **Servings:** 12

Ingredients:
- ✓ 1 pound bread dough
- ✓ 1 cup sugar
- ✓ ½ cup butter, melted
- ✓ 1 cup heavy cream
- ✓ 12 ounces chocolate chips
- ✓ 2 tablespoons amaretto liqueur

Directions:
1. Roll dough, cut into 20 slices and then cut each slice in halves.
2. Brush dough pieces with butter, sprinkle sugar, place them in your air fryer's basket after you've brushed it some butter, cook them at 350 degrees F for 5 minutes, flip them, cook for 3 minutes more and transfer to a platter.
3. Heat up a pan with the heavy cream over medium heat, add chocolate chips and stir until they melt.
4. Add liqueur, stir again, transfer to a bowl and serve bread dippers with this sauce.

Nutrition: calories 200 - Fat 1 - Fiber 0 - Carbs 6 - Protein 6

11. Coffee Cheesecakes

Prep.Time: 10 min - **Cooking Time:** 20 min - **Servings:** 6

Ingredients:

For the cheesecakes:
- ✓ 2 tablespoons butter
- ✓ 8 ounces cream cheese
- ✓ 3 tablespoons coffee
- ✓ 3 eggs
- ✓ 1/3 cup sugar
- ✓ 1 tbsp caramel syrup

For the frosting:
- ✓ 3 tbsp caramel syrup
- ✓ 3 tablespoons butter
- ✓ 8 ounces mascarpone cheese, soft
- ✓ 2 tablespoons sugar

Directions:
1. In your blender, mix cream cheese with eggs, 2 tablespoons butter, coffee, 1 tablespoon caramel syrup and 1/3 cup sugar and pulse very well, spoon into a cupcakes pan that fits your air fryer, introduce in the fryer and cook at 320 degrees F and bake for 20 minutes.
2. Leave aside to cool down and then keep in the freezer for 3 hours.
3. Meanwhile, in a bowl, mix 3 tablespoons butter with 3 tablespoons caramel syrup, 2 tablespoons sugar and mascarpone, blend well, spoon this over cheesecakes and serve them.

Nutrition: calories 254 - Fat 23 - Fiber 0 - Carbs 21 - Protein 5

12. Special Brownies

Prep.Time: 10 min - **Cooking Time:** 17 min - **Servings:** 4

Ingredients:
- ✓ 1 egg
- ✓ 1/3 cup cocoa powder
- ✓ 1/3 cup sugar
- ✓ 7 tablespoons butter
- ✓ ½ tsp vanilla extract
- ✓ ¼ cup white flour
- ✓ ¼ cup walnuts, chopped
- ✓ ½ teaspoon baking powder
- ✓ 1 tablespoon peanut butter

Directions:
1. Heat up a pan with 6 tablespoons butter and the sugar over medium heat, stir, cook for 5 minutes, transfer this to a bowl, add salt, vanilla extract, cocoa powder, egg, baking powder, walnuts and flour, stir the whole thing really well and pour into a pan that fits your air fryer.
2. In a bowl, mix 1 tablespoon butter with peanut butter, heat up in your microwave for a few seconds, stir well and drizzle this over brownies mix.
3. Introduce in your air fryer and bake at 320 degrees F and bake for 17 minutes.
4. Leave brownies to cool down, cut and serve.

Nutrition: calories 223 - Fat 32 - Fiber 1 - Carbs 3 - Protein 6

13. Wrapped Pears

Prep.Time: 10 min - **Cooking Time:** 15 min - **Servings:** 4

Ingredients:
- ✓ 4 puff pastry sheets
- ✓ 14 ounces vanilla custard
- ✓ 2 pears, halved
- ✓ 1 egg, whisked
- ✓ ½ teaspoon cinnamon powder
- ✓ 2 tablespoons sugar

Directions:
1. Place puff pastry slices on a working surface, add spoonfuls of vanilla custard in the center of each, top with pear halves and wrap.
2. Brush pears with egg, sprinkle sugar and cinnamon, place them in your air fryer's basket and cook at 320 degrees F for 15 minutes.
3. Divide parcels on plates and serve.

Nutrition: calories 200 - Fat 2 - Fiber 1 - Carbs 14 - Protein 3

14. Cocoa Cake

Prep.Time: 10 min - **Cooking Time:** 17 min - **Servings:** 6

Ingredients:
- ✓ 3.5 ounces butter, melted
- ✓ 3 eggs
- ✓ 3 ounces sugar
- ✓ 1 teaspoon cocoa powder
- ✓ 3 ounces flour
- ✓ ½ teaspoon lemon juice

Directions:
1. In a bowl, mix 1 tablespoon butter with cocoa powder and whisk.
2. In another bowl, mix the rest of the butter with sugar, eggs, flour and lemon juice, whisk well and pour half into a cake pan that fits your air fryer.
3. Add half of the cocoa mix, spread, add the rest of the butter layer and top with the rest of cocoa.
4. Introduce in your air fryer and cook at 360 degrees F for 17 minutes.
5. Cool cake down before slicing and serving.

Nutrition: calories 340- Fat 11 - Fiber 3 - Carbs 25 - Protein 5

15. Strawberry Donuts

Prep.Time: 10 min - **Cooking Time:** 15 minutes - **Servings:** 4

Ingredients:
- ✓ 8 ounces flour
- ✓ 1 tbsp. brown sugar
- ✓ 1 tbsp. white sugar
- ✓ 1 egg
- ✓ 2 and ½ tablespoons butter
- ✓ 4 ounces whole milk
- ✓ 1 tsp baking powder

For the strawberry icing:
- ✓ 2 tablespoons butter
- ✓ 3.5 ounces icing sugar
- ✓ ½ teaspoon pink coloring
- ✓ ¼ cup strawberries, chopped
- ✓ 1 tbsp. whipped cream

Directions:
1. In a bowl, mix butter, 1 tablespoon brown sugar, 1 tablespoon white sugar and flour and stir.
2. In a second bowl, mix egg with 1 and ½ tablespoons butter and milk and stir well.
3. Combine the 2 mixtures, stir, shape donuts from this mix, place them in your air fryer's basket and cook at 360 degrees F for 15 minutes.
4. Put 1 tablespoon butter, icing sugar, food coloring, whipped cream and strawberry puree and whisk well.
5. Arrange donuts on a platter and serve with strawberry icing on top.

Nutrition: calories 250 - Fat 12 - Fiber 1 - Carbs 32 - Protein 4

16. Pumpkin Pie

Prep.Time: 10 min - **Cooking Time:** 15 min - **Servings:** 9

Ingredients:
- ✓ 1 tablespoon sugar
- ✓ 2 tablespoons flour
- ✓ 1 tablespoon butter
- ✓ 2 tablespoons water

For the pumpkin pie filling:
- ✓ 3.5 ounces pumpkin
- ✓ flesh, chopped
- ✓ 1 teaspoon mixed spice
- ✓ 1 teaspoon nutmeg
- ✓ 3 ounces water
- ✓ 1 egg, whisked
- ✓ 1 tablespoon sugar

Directions:
1. Put 3 ounces water in a pot, bring to a boil over medium high heat, add pumpkin, egg, 1 tablespoon sugar, spice and nutmeg, stir, boil for 20 minutes, take off heat and blend using an immersion blender.
2. In a bowl, mix flour with butter, 1 tablespoon sugar and 2 tablespoons water and knead your dough well.
3. Grease a pie pan that fits your air fryer with butter, press dough into the pan, fill with pumpkin pie filling, place in your air fryer's basket and cook at 360 degrees F for 15 minutes.
4. Slice and serve warm.

Nutrition: calories 200 - Fat 5 - Fiber 2 - Carbs 5 - Protein 6

17. Banana Bread

Prep.Time: 10 min - **Cooking Time:** 40 min - **Servings:** 6

Ingredients:
- ✓ ¾ cup sugar
- ✓ 1/3 cup butter
- ✓ 1 teaspoon vanilla extract
- ✓ 1 egg
- ✓ 2 bananas, mashed
- ✓ 1 tsp baking powder
- ✓ 1 and ½ cups flour
- ✓ ½ teaspoons baking soda
- ✓ 1/3 cup milk
- ✓ 1 and ½ tsp cream of tartar
- ✓ Cooking spray

Directions:
1. In a bowl, mix milk with cream of tartar, sugar, butter, egg, vanilla and bananas and stir everything.
2. In another bowl, mix flour with baking powder and baking soda.
3. Combine the 2 mixtures, stir well, pour this into a cake pan greased with some cooking spray, introduce in your air fryer and cook at 320 degrees F for 40 minutes.
4. Take bread out, leave aside to cool down, slice and serve.

Nutrition: calories 292 - Fat 7 - Fiber 8 - Carbs 28 - Protein 4

18. Strawberry Pie

Prep.Time: 10 min - **Cooking Time:** 20 min - **Servings:** 12

Ingredients:
For the crust:
- ✓ 1 cup coconut, shredded
- ✓ 1 cup sunflower seeds
- ✓ ¼ cup butter

For the filling:
- ✓ 1 teaspoon gelatin
- ✓ 8 ounces cream cheese
- ✓ 4 ounces strawberries
- ✓ 2 tablespoons water
- ✓ ½ tablespoon lemon juice
- ✓ ¼ teaspoon stevia
- ✓ ½ cup heavy cream
- ✓ 8 ounces strawberries, chopped for serving

Directions:
1. In your food processor, mix sunflower seeds with coconut, a pinch of salt and butter, pulse and press this on the bottom of a cake pan that fits your air fryer.
2. Heat up a pan with the water over medium heat, add gelatin, stir until it dissolves, leave aside to cool down, add this to your food processor, mix with 4 ounces strawberries, cream cheese, lemon juice and stevia and blend well.
3. Add heavy cream, stir well and spread this over crust.
4. Top with 8 ounces strawberries, introduce in your air fryer and cook at 330 degrees F for 15 minutes.
5. Keep in the fridge until you serve it.

Nutrition: calories 234 - Fat 23 - Fiber 2 - Carbs 6 - Protein 7

19. Cocoa Cookies

Prep.Time: 10 min - **Cooking Time:** 14 min - **Servings:** 12

Ingredients:
- ✓ 6 ounces coconut oil, melted
- ✓ 6 eggs
- ✓ 3 ounces cocoa powder
- ✓ 2 teaspoons vanilla

Ingredients:
- ✓ ½ teaspoon baking powder
- ✓ 4 ounces cream cheese
- ✓ 5 tablespoons sugar

Directions:
1. In a blender, mix eggs with coconut oil, cocoa powder, baking powder, vanilla, cream cheese and swerve and stir using a mixer.
2. Pour this into a lined baking dish that fits your air fryer, introduce in the fryer at 320 degrees F and bake for 14 minutes.
3. Slice cookie sheet into rectangles and serve.

Nutrition: calories 178 - Fat 14 - Fiber 2 - Carbs 3 - Protein 5

20. Blueberry Scones

Prep.Time: 10 min - **Cooking Time:** 10 min - **Servings:** 10

Ingredients:
- ✓ 1 cup white flour
- ✓ 1 cup blueberries
- ✓ 2 eggs
- ✓ ½ cup heavy cream
- ✓ ½ cup butter
- ✓ 5 tablespoons sugar
- ✓ 2 teaspoons vanilla extract
- ✓ 2 teaspoons baking powder

Directions:
1. In a bowl, mix flour, salt, baking powder and blueberries and stir.
2. In another bowl, mix heavy cream with butter, vanilla extract, sugar and eggs and stir well.
3. Combine the 2 mixtures, knead until you obtain your dough, shape 10 triangles from this mix, place them on a lined baking sheet that fits your air fryer and cook them at 320 degrees F for 10 minutes.
4. Serve them cold.

Nutrition: calories 130 - Fat 2 - Fiber 2 - Carbs 4 - Protein 3

21. Lime Cheesecake

Prep.Time: 4 hours 10 min - **Cooking Time:** 4 min - **Servings:** 10

Ingredients:
- ✓ 2 tablespoons butter, melted
- ✓ 2 teaspoons sugar
- ✓ 4 ounces flour
- ✓ ¼ cup coconut, shredded
- ✓ For the filling:
- ✓ 1 pound cream cheese
- ✓ Zest from 1 lime, grated
- ✓ Juice form 1 lime
- ✓ 2 cups hot water
- ✓ 2 sachets lime jelly

Directions:
1. In a bowl, mix coconut with flour, butter and sugar, stir well and press this on the bottom of a pan that fits your air fryer.
2. Meanwhile, put the hot water in a bowl, add jelly sachets and stir until it dissolves.
3. Put cream cheese in a bowl, add jelly, lime juice and zest and whisk really well.
4. Add this over the crust, spread, introduce in the air fryer and cook at 300 degrees F for 4 minutes.
5. Keep in the fridge for 4 hours before serving.

Nutrition: calories 260 - Fat 23 - Fiber 2 - Carbs 5 - Protein 7

22. Strawberry Cobbler

Prep.Time: 10 min - **Cooking Time:** 25 min - **Servings:** 6

Ingredients:
- ✓ ¾ cup sugar
- ✓ 6 cups strawberries, halved
- ✓ 1/8 tsp. baking powder
- ✓ 1 tbsp. lemon juice
- ✓ ½ cup flour
- ✓ A pinch of baking soda
- ✓ ½ cup water
- ✓ 3 and ½ tablespoon olive oil
- ✓ Cooking spray

Directions:
1. In a bowl, mix strawberries with half of sugar, sprinkle some flour, add lemon juice, whisk and pour into the baking dish that fits your air fryer and greased with cooking spray
2. In another bowl, mix flour with the rest of the sugar, baking powder and soda and stir well.
3. Add the olive oil and mix until the whole thing with your hands.
4. Add ½ cup water and spread over strawberries.
5. Introduce in the fryer at 355 degrees F and bake for 25 minutes.
6. Leave cobbler aside to cool down, slice and serve.

Nutrition: calories 221 – Fat 3 - Fiber 3 - Carbs 6 - Protein 9

23. Tasty Orange Cake

Prep.Time: 10 min - **Cooking Time:** 32 min - **Servings:** 12

Ingredients:
- ✓ 6 eggs
- ✓ 1 orange, peeled and cut into quarters
- ✓ 1 teaspoon vanilla extract
- ✓ 1 tsp. baking powder
- ✓ 9 ounces flour
- ✓ 2 ounces sugar+ 2 tablespoons
- ✓ 2 tablespoons orange zest
- ✓ 4 ounces cream cheese
- ✓ 4 ounces yogurt

Directions:
1. In your food processor, pulse orange very well.
2. Add flour, 2 tablespoons sugar, eggs, baking powder, vanilla extract and pulse well again.
3. Transfer this into 2 spring form pans, introduce each in your fryer and cook at 330 degrees F for 16 minutes.
4. Meanwhile, in a bowl, mix cream cheese with orange zest, yogurt and the rest of the sugar and stir well.
5. Place one cake layer on a plate, add half of the cream cheese mix, add the other cake layer and top with the rest of the cream cheese mix.
6. Spread it well, slice and serve.

Nutrition: calories 200 - Fat 13 - Fiber 2 - Carbs 9 - Protein 8

24. Carrot Cake

Prep.Time: 10 min - **Cooking Time:** 45 min - **Servings:** 6

Ingredients:
- ✓ 5 ounces flour
- ✓ ¾ tsp. baking powder
- ✓ ½ teaspoon baking soda
- ✓ ½ tsp. cinnamon powder
- ✓ ¼ tsp. nutmeg, ground
- ✓ ½ teaspoon allspice
- ✓ 1 egg
- ✓ 3 tbsp. yogurt
- ✓ ½ cup sugar
- ✓ ¼ cup pineapple juice
- ✓ 4 tbsp. sunflower oil
- ✓ 1/3 cup carrots, grated
- ✓ 1/3 cup pecans, toasted and chopped
- ✓ 1/3 cup coconut flakes, shredded
- ✓ Cooking spray

Directions:
1. In a bowl, mix flour with baking soda and powder, salt, allspice, cinnamon and nutmeg and stir.
2. In another bowl, mix egg with yogurt, sugar, pineapple juice, oil, carrots, pecans and coconut flakes and stir well.
3. Combine the two mixtures and stir well, pour this into a spring form pan that fits your air fryer which you've greased with some cooking spray, transfer to your air fryer and cook on 320 degrees F for 45 minutes.
4. Leave cake to cool down, then cut and serve it.

Nutrition: calories 200 - Fat 6 - Fiber 20 - Carbs 22 – Protein 4

25. Chocolate Cake

Prep.Time: 10 min - **Cooking Time:** 30 min - **Servings:** 12

Ingredients:
- ¾ cup white flour
- ¾ cup whole wheat flour
- 1 teaspoon baking soda
- ¾ tsp. pumpkin pie spice
- ¾ cup sugar
- 1 banana, mashed
- ½ tsp. baking powder
- 2 tablespoons canola oil
- ½ cup Greek yogurt
- 8 ounces canned pumpkin puree
- Cooking spray
- 1 egg
- ½ tsp. vanilla extract
- 2/3 cup chocolate chips

Directions:
1. In a bowl, mix white flour with whole wheat flour, salt, baking soda and powder and pumpkin spice and stir.
2. In another bowl, mix sugar with oil, banana, yogurt, pumpkin puree, vanilla and egg and stir using a mixer.
3. Combine the 2 mixtures, add chocolate chips, stir, pour this into a greased Bundt pan that fits your air fryer.
4. Introduce in your air fryer and cook at 330 degrees F for 30 minutes.
5. Leave the cake to cool down, before cutting and serving it

Nutrition: calories 232 - Fat 7 - Fiber 7 - Carbs 29 - Protein 4

26. Black Tea Cake

Prep.Time: 10 min - **Cooking Time:** 35 min - **Servings:** 12

Ingredients:
- 2 tsp. vanilla extract
- ½ cup olive oil
- 6 tbsp. black tea powder
- 2 cups milk
- ½ cup butter
- 2 cups sugar
- 4 eggs
- 3 and ½ cups flour
- 1 teaspoon baking soda
- 3 tsp. baking powder

For the cream:
- 6 tablespoons honey
- 4 cups sugar
- 1 cup butter, soft

Directions:
1. Put the milk in a pot, heat up over medium heat, add tea, stir well, take off heat and leave aside to cool down.
2. In a bowl, mix ½ cup butter with 2 cups sugar, eggs, vegetable oil, vanilla extract, baking powder, baking soda and 3 and ½ cups flour and stir everything really well.
3. Pour this into 2 greased round pans, introduce each in the fryer at 330 degrees F and bake for 25 minutes.
4. In a bowl, mix 1 cup butter with honey and 4 cups sugar and stir really well.
5. Arrange one cake on a platter, spread the cream all over, top with the other cake and keep in the fridge until you serve it.

Nutrition: calories 200 - Fat 4 - Fiber 4 - Carbs 6 - Protein 2

27. Easy Granola

Prep.Time: 10 min - **Cooking Time:** 25 minutes - **Servings:** 4

Ingredients:
Ingredients:
- 1 cup coconut, shredded
- ½ cup almonds
- ½ cup pecans, chopped
- 2 tablespoons sugar
- ½ cup pumpkin seeds
- ½ cup sunflower seeds
- 2 tablespoons sunflower oil
- 1 teaspoon nutmeg, ground
- 1 teaspoon apple pie spice mix

Directions:
1. In a bowl, mix almonds and pecans with pumpkin seeds, sunflower seeds, coconut, nutmeg and apple pie spice mix and stir well.
2. Heat up a pan with the oil over medium heat, add sugar and stir well.
3. Pour this over nuts and coconut mix and stir well.
4. Spread this on a lined baking sheet that fits your air fryer, introduce in your air fryer and cook at 300 degrees F and bake for 25 minutes.
5. Leave your granola to cool down, cut and serve

Nutrition: calories 322 - Fat 7 - Fiber 8 - Carbs 12 - Protein 7

28. Plum Cake

Prep.Time: 1 hour and 20 min - **Cooking Time:** 36 min - **Servings:** 8

Ingredients:
- 7 ounces flour
- 1 package dried yeast
- 1 ounce butter, soft
- 1 egg, whisked
- 5 tablespoons sugar
- 3 ounces warm milk
- 1 and ¾ pounds plums, pitted and cut into quarters
- Zest from 1 lemon, grated
- 1 ounce almond flakes

Directions:
1. In a bowl, mix yeast with butter, flour and 3 tablespoons sugar and stir well.
2. Add milk and egg and whisk for 4 minutes until you obtain a dough.
3. Arrange the dough in a spring form pan that fits your air fryer and which you've greased with some butter, cover and leave aside for 1 hour.
4. Arrange plumps on top of the butter, sprinkle the rest of the sugar, introduce in your air fryer at 350 degrees F, bake for 36 minutes, cool down, sprinkle almond flakes and lemon zest on top, slice and serve.

Nutrition: calories 192 - Fat 4 - Fiber 2 - Carbs 6- Protein 7

29. Mandarin Pudding

Prep.Time: 20 min - **Cooking Time:** 40 min - **Servings:** 8

Ingredients:
- 1 mandarin, peeled and sliced
- Juice from 2 mandarins
- 2 tbs. brown sugar
- 4 ounces butter, soft
- 2 eggs, whisked
- ¾ cup sugar
- ¾ cup white flour
- ¾ cup almonds, ground
- Honey for serving

Directions:
1. Grease a loaf pan with some butter, sprinkle brown sugar on the bottom and arrange mandarin slices.
2. In a bowl, mix butter with sugar, eggs, almonds, flour and mandarin juice, stir, spoon this over mandarin slices, place pan in your air fryer and cook at 360 degrees F for 40 minutes.
3. Transfer pudding to a plate and serve with honey on top.

Nutrition: calories 162 - Fat 3 - Fiber 2 - Carbs 3 - Protein 6

30. Lentils and Dates Brownies

Prep.Time: 10 min - **Cooking Time:** 15 min - **Servings:** 8

Ingredients:
- 28 ounces canned lentils, rinsed and drained
- 12 dates
- 1 tablespoon honey
- 1 banana, peeled and chopped
- ½ teaspoon baking soda
- 4 tbsp. almond butter
- 2 tbs. cocoa powder

Directions:
1. In your food processor, mix lentils with butter, banana, cocoa, baking soda and honey and blend really well.
2. Add dates, pulse a few more times, pour this into a greased pan that fits your air fryer, spread evenly, introduce in the fryer at 360 degrees F and bake for 15 minutes.
3. Take brownies mix out of the oven, cut, arrange on a platter and serve.

Nutrition: calories 162 - Fat 4 - Fiber 2 - Carbs 3 - Protein 4

31. Ginger Cheesecake

Prep.Time: 2 hours and 10min - **Cooking Time:** 20 min - **Servings:** 6

Ingredients:
- ✓ 2 teaspoons butter, melted
- ✓ ½ cup ginger cookies, crumbled
- ✓ 16 ounces cream cheese, soft
- ✓ 2 eggs
- ✓ ½ cup sugar
- ✓ 1 teaspoon rum
- ✓ ½ teaspoon vanilla extract
- ✓ ½ teaspoon nutmeg, ground

Directions:
1. Grease a pan with the butter and spread cookie crumbs on the bottom.
2. In a bowl, beat cream cheese with nutmeg, vanilla, rum and eggs, whisk well and spread over the cookie crumbs.
3. Introduce in your air fryer and cook at 340 degrees F for 20 minutes.
4. Leave cheesecake to cool down and keep in the fridge for 2 hours before slicing and serving it.

Nutrition: calories 412 - Fat 12 - Fiber 6 - Carbs 20 - Protein 6

32. Macaroons

Prep.Time: 10 min - **Cooking Time:** 8 min - **Servings:** 4-6

Ingredients:
- ✓ 2 tablespoons sugar
- ✓ 4 egg whites
- ✓ 2 cup coconut, shredded
- ✓ 1 teaspoon vanilla extract

Directions:
1. In a bowl, mix egg whites with stevia and beat using your mixer.
2. Add coconut and vanilla extract, whisk again, shape small balls out of this mix, introduce them in your air fryer and cook at 340 degrees F for 8 minutes.
3. Serve macaroons cold.

Nutrition: calories 55 - Fat 6 - Fiber 1 - Carbs 2 - Protein 1

33. Lentils Cookies

Prep.Time: 10 min - **Cooking Time:** 25 minutes - **Servings:** 4-8

Ingredients:
- ✓ 1 cup water
- ✓ 1 cup canned lentils, drained and mashed
- ✓ 1 cup white flour
- ✓ 1 tsp. cinnamon powder
- ✓ 1 cup whole wheat flour
- ✓ 1 tsp. baking powder
- ✓ ½ tsp. nutmeg, ground
- ✓ 1 cup butter, soft
- ✓ ½ cup brown sugar
- ✓ ½ cup white sugar
- ✓ 1 egg
- ✓ 2 tsp. almond extract
- ✓ 1 cup raisins
- ✓ 1 cup rolled oats
- ✓ 1 cup coconut, unsweetened and shredded

Directions:
1. In a bowl, mix white and whole wheat flour with salt, cinnamon, baking powder and nutmeg and stir.
2. In a bowl, mix butter with white and brown sugar and stir using your kitchen mixer for 2 minutes.
3. Add egg, almond extract, lentils mix, flour mix, oats, raisins and coconut and stir everything well.
4. Scoop tablespoons of dough on a lined baking sheet that fits your air fryer, introduce them in the fryer and cook at 350 degrees F for 15 minutes.
5. Arrange cookies on a serving platter and serve

Nutrition: calories 154 - Fat 2 - Fiber 2 - Carbs 4 - Protein 7

34. Lemon Tart

Prep.Time: 1 hour - **Cooking Time:** 35 min - **Servings:** 6

Ingredients:

For the crust:
- ✓ 2 tablespoons sugar
- ✓ 2 cups white flour
- ✓ A pinch of salt
- ✓ 3 tablespoons ice water
- ✓ 12 tbs. cold butter

For the filling:
- ✓ 2 eggs, whisked
- ✓ 1 and ¼ cup sugar
- ✓ 10 tbsp. melted and chilled butter
- ✓ Juice from 2 lemons
- ✓ Zest from 2 lemons, grated

Directions:
1. In a bowl, mix 2 cups flour with a pinch of salt and 2 tablespoons sugar and whisk.
2. Add 12 tablespoons butter and the water, knead until you obtain a dough, shape a ball, wrap in foil and keep in the fridge for 1 hour.
3. Transfer dough to a floured surface, flatten it, arrange on the bottom of a tart pan, prick with a fork, keep in the fridge for 20 minutes, introduce in your air fryer at 360 degrees F and bake for 15 minutes.
4. In a bowl, mix 1 and ¼ cup sugar with eggs, 10 tablespoons butter, lemon juice and lemon zest and whisk very well.
5. Pour this into pie crust, spread evenly, introduce in the fryer and cook at 360 degrees F for 20 minutes.
6. Cut and serve it.

Nutrition: calories 182 - Fat 4 - Fiber 1 - Carbs 2 - Protein 3

35. Blueberry Pudding

Prep.Time: 10 min - **Cooking Time:** 25 minutes - **Servings:** 6

Ingredients:
- ✓ 2 cups flour
- ✓ 2 cups rolled oats
- ✓ 8 cups blueberries
- ✓ 1 stick butter, melted
- ✓ 1 cup walnuts, chopped
- ✓ 3 tablespoons maple syrup
- ✓ 2 tablespoons rosemary, chopped

Directions:
1. Spread blueberries in a greased baking pan and leave aside.
2. In your food processor, mix rolled oats with flour, walnuts, butter, maple syrup and rosemary, blend well, layer this over blueberries, introduce everything in your air fryer and cook at 350 degrees for 25 minutes.
3. Leave dessert to cool down, cut and serve.

Nutrition: calories 150 - Fat 3 - Fiber 2 - Carbs 17 - Protein 4

36. Tomato Cake

Prep.Time: 10 min - **Cooking Time:** 30 min - **Servings:** 4

Ingredients:
- ✓ 1 and ½ cups flour
- ✓ 1 tsp. cinnamon powder
- ✓ 1 tsp. baking powder
- ✓ 1 teaspoon baking soda
- ✓ ¾ cup maple syrup
- ✓ 1 cup tomatoes chopped
- ✓ ½ cup olive oil
- ✓ 2 tablespoon apple cider vinegar

Directions:
1. In a bowl, mix flour with baking powder, baking soda, cinnamon and maple syrup and stir well.
2. In another bowl, mix tomatoes with olive oil and vinegar and stir well.
3. Combine the 2 mixtures, stir well, pour into a greased round pan that fits your air fryer, introduce in the fryer and cook at 360 degrees F for 30 minutes.
4. Leave cake to cool down, slice and serve.

Nutrition: calories 153 - Fat 2 - Fiber 1 - Carbs 25 - Protein 4

37. Strawberry Shortcakes

Prep.Time: 20 min - **Cooking Time:** 45 min - **Servings:** 6

Ingredients:
- ✓ Cooking spray
- ✓ ¼ cup sugar+ 4 tablespoons
- ✓ 1 and ½ cup flour
- ✓ 1 teaspoon baking powder
- ✓ ¼ teaspoon baking soda
- ✓ 1/3 cup butter
- ✓ 1 tsp. lime zest, grated
- ✓ ½ cup whipping cream
- ✓ 1 cup buttermilk
- ✓ 1 egg, whisked
- ✓ 2 cups strawberries, sliced
- ✓ 1 tablespoon rum
- ✓ 1 tbsp. mint, chopped

Directions:
1. In a bowl, mix flour with ¼ cup sugar, baking powder and baking soda and stir.
2. In another bowl, mix buttermilk with egg, stir, add to flour mix and whisk.
3. Spoon this dough into 6 jars greased with cooking spray, cover with tin foil, arrange them in your air fryer cook at 360 degrees F for 45 minutes.
4. Meanwhile, in a bowl, mix strawberries with 3 tablespoons sugar, rum, mint and lime zest, stir and leave aside in a cold place.
5. In another bowl, mix whipping cream with 1 tablespoon sugar and stir.
6. Take jars out, divide strawberry mix and whipped cream on top and serve.

Nutrition: calories 164 - Fat 2 - Fiber 3 - Carbs 5 - Protein 2

38. Rhubarb Pie

Prep.Time: 30 min - **Cooking Time:** 45 min - **Servings:** 6

For the filling:

Ingredients:
- ✓ 1 and ¼ cups almond flour
- ✓ 8 tablespoons butter
- ✓ 5 tablespoons cold water
- ✓ 1 teaspoon sugar
- ✓ 2 tbsp. low fat milk
- ✓ 3 cups rhubarb, chopped
- ✓ 3 tablespoons flour
- ✓ 1 and ½ cups sugar
- ✓ 2 eggs
- ✓ ½ tsp. nutmeg, ground
- ✓ 1 tablespoon butter

Directions:
1. In a bowl, mix 1 and ¼ cups flour with 1 teaspoon sugar, 8 tablespoons butter and cold water, stir and knead until you obtain a dough.
2. Transfer dough to a floured working surface, shape a disk, flatten, wrap in plastic, keep in the fridge for about 30 minutes, roll and press on the bottom of a pie pan that fits your air fryer.
3. In a bowl, mix rhubarb with 1 and ½ cups sugar, nutmeg, 3 tablespoons flour and whisk.
4. In another bowl, whisk eggs with milk, add to rhubarb mix, pour the whole mix into the pie crust, introduce in your air fryer and cook at 390 degrees F for 45 minutes.
5. Cut and serve it cold.

Nutrition: calories 200 - Fat 2 - Fiber 1 - Carbs 6 - Protein 3

39. Maple Cupcakes

Prep.Time: 10 min - **Cooking Time:** 20 min - **Servings:** 4

Ingredients:
- ✓ 4 tablespoons butter
- ✓ 4 eggs
- ✓ ½ cup pure applesauce
- ✓ 2 tsp cinnamon powder
- ✓ 1 teaspoon vanilla extract
- ✓ ½ apple, cored and chopped
- ✓ 4 teaspoons maple syrup
- ✓ ¾ cup white flour
- ✓ ½ tsp baking powder

Directions:
1. Heat up a pan with the butter over medium heat, add applesauce, vanilla, eggs and maple syrup, stir, take off heat and leave aside to cool down.
2. Add flour, cinnamon, baking powder and apples, whisk, pour in a cupcake pan, introduce in your air fryer at 350 degrees F and bake for 20 minutes.
3. Leave cupcakes them to cool down, transfer to a platter and serve them.

Nutrition: calories 150 - Fat 3 - Fiber 1 - Carbs 5 - Protein 4

40. Ricotta and Lemon Cake

Prep.Time: 10 min - **Cooking Time:** 1 hour and 10 min - **Servings:** 4

Ingredients:
- ✓ 8 eggs, whisked
- ✓ 3 pounds ricotta cheese
- ✓ ½ pound sugar
- ✓ Zest from 1 lemon, grated
- ✓ Zest from 1 orange, grated
- ✓ Butter for the pan

Directions:
1. In a bowl, mix eggs with sugar, cheese, lemon and orange zest and stir very well.
2. Grease a baking pan that fits your air fryer with some batter, spread ricotta mixture, introduce in the fryer at 390 degrees F and bake for 30 minutes.
3. Reduce heat at 380 degrees F and bake for 40 more minutes.
4. Take out of the oven, leave cake to cool down and serve.

Nutrition: calories 110 - Fat 3 - Fiber 2 - Carbs 3 - Protein 4

41. Chocolate and Pomegranate Bars

Prep.Time: 2 hours - **Cooking Time:** 10 min - **Servings:** 6

Ingredients:
- ✓ ½ cup milk
- ✓ 1 teaspoon vanilla extract
- ✓ 1 and ½ cups dark chocolate, chopped
- ✓ ½ cup almonds, chopped
- ✓ ½ cup pomegranate seeds

Directions:
1. Heat up a pan with the milk over medium low heat, add chocolate, stir for 5 minutes, take off heat add vanilla extract, half of the pomegranate seeds and half of the nuts and stir.
2. Pour this into a lined baking pan, spread, sprinkle a pinch of salt, the rest of the pomegranate arils and nuts, introduce in your air fryer and cook at 300 degrees F for 4 minutes.
3. Keep in the fridge for 2 hours before serving.

Nutrition: calories 68 - Fat 1 - Fiber 4 - Carbs 6 - Protein 1

42. Air Fried Apples

Prep.Time: 10 min - **Cooking Time:** 17 min - **Servings:** 4

Ingredients:
- ✓ 4 big apples, cored
- ✓ A handful raisins
- ✓ 1 tablespoon cinnamon, ground
- ✓ Raw honey to the taste

Directions:
1. Fill each apple with raisins, sprinkle cinnamon, drizzle honey, put them in your air fryer and cook at 367 degrees F for 17 minutes.
2. Leave them to cool down and serve.

Nutrition: calories 220 - Fat 3 - Fiber 4 - Carbs 6 - Protein 10

43. Cocoa and Almond Bars

Prep.Time: 30 min - **Cooking Time:** 4 min - **Servings:** 6

Ingredients:
- ¼ cup cocoa nibs
- 1 cup almonds, soaked and drained
- 2 tablespoons cocoa powder
- ¼ cup hemp seeds
- ¼ cup goji berries
- ¼ cup coconut, shredded
- 8 dates, pitted and soaked

Directions:
1. Put almonds in your food processor, blend, add hemp seeds, cocoa nibs, cocoa powder, goji, coconut and blend very well.
2. Add dates, blend well again, spread on a lined baking sheet that fits your air fryer and cook at 320 degrees F for 4 minutes.
3. Cut into equal parts and keep in the fridge for 30 minutes before serving.

Nutrition: calories 140 - Fat 6 - Fiber 3 - Carbs 7 - Protein 19

44. Tangerine Cake

Prep.Time: 10 min - **Cooking Time:** 20 min - **Servings:** 8

Ingredients:
- ¾ cup sugar
- 2 cups flour
- ¼ cup olive oil
- ½ cup milk
- 1 teaspoon cider vinegar
- ½ teaspoon vanilla extract
- Juice and zest from 2 lemons
- Juice and zest from 1 tangerine
- Tangerine segments, for serving

Directions:
1. In a bowl, mix flour with sugar and stir.
2. In another bowl, mix oil with milk, vinegar, vanilla extract, lemon juice and zest and tangerine zest and whisk very well.
3. Add flour, stir well, pour this into a cake pan that fits your air fryer, introduce in the fryer and cook at 360 degrees F for 20 minutes.
4. Serve right away with tangerine segments on top.

Nutrition: calories 190 - Fat 1 - Fiber 1 - Carbs 4 - Protein 4

45. Berries Mix

Prep.Time: 5 min - **Cooking Time:** 6 minutes - **Servings:** 4

Ingredients:
- 2 tablespoons lemon juice
- 1 and ½ tablespoons maple syrup
- 1 and ½ tablespoons champagne vinegar
- 1 tablespoon olive oil
- 1 pound strawberries, halved
- 1 and ½ cups blueberries
- ¼ cup basil leaves, torn

Directions:
1. In a pan that fits your air fryer, mix lemon juice with maple syrup and vinegar, bring to a boil over medium high heat, add oil, blueberries and strawberries, stir, introduce in your air fryer and cook at 310 degrees F for 6 minutes.
2. Sprinkle basil on top and serve.

Nutrition: calories 163 - Fat 4 - Fiber 4 - Carbs 10 - Protein 2.1

46. Pears and Espresso Cream

Prep.Time: 10 min - **Cooking Time:** 30 min - **Servings:** 4

Ingredients:
- 4 pears, halved and cored
- 2 tablespoons lemon juice
- 1 tablespoon sugar
- 2 tablespoons water
- 2 tablespoons butter
- For the cream:
- 1 cup whipping cream
- 1 cup mascarpone
- 1/3 cup sugar
- 2 tablespoons espresso, cold

Directions:
1. In a bowl, mix pears halves with lemon juice, 1 tablespoons sugar, butter and water, toss well, transfer them to your air fryer and cook at 360 degrees F for 30 minutes.
2. Meanwhile, in a bowl, mix whipping cream with mascarpone, 1/3 cup sugar and espresso, whisk really well and keep in the fridge until pears are done.
3. Divide pears on plates, top with espresso cream and serve them.

Nutrition: calories 211 - Fat 5 - Fiber 7 - Carbs 8 - Protein 7

47. Lemon Bars

Prep.Time: 10 min - **Cooking Time:** 25 min - **Servings:** 6

Ingredients:
- 4 eggs
- 2 and ¼ cups flour
- Juice from 2 lemons
- 1 cup butter, soft
- 2 cups sugar

Directions:
1. In a bowl, mix butter with ½ cup sugar and 2 cups flour, stir well, press on the bottom of a pan that fits your air fryer, introduce in the fryer and cook at 350 degrees F for 10 minutes.
2. In another bowl, mix the rest of the sugar with the rest of the flour, eggs and lemon juice, whisk well and spread over crust.
3. Introduce in the fryer at 350 degrees F for 15 minutes more, leave aside to cool down, cut bars and serve them.

Nutrition: calories 125 – Fat 4 - Fiber 4 - Carbs 16 - Protein 2

48. Figs and Coconut Butter Mix

Prep.Time: 6 min - **Cooking Time:** 4 min - **Servings:** 3

Ingredients:
- 2 tablespoons coconut butter
- 12 figs, halved
- ¼ cup sugar
- 1 cup almonds, toasted and chopped

Directions:
1. Put butter in a pan that fits your air fryer and melt over medium high heat.
2. Add figs, sugar and almonds, toss, introduce in your air fryer and cook at 300 degrees F for 4 minutes.
3. Divide into bowls and serve cold.

Nutrition: calories 170 - Fat 4 - Fiber 5 - Carbs 7 - Protein 9

49. Poppyseed Cake

Prep.Time: 10 min - **Cooking Time:** 30 min - **Servings:** 6

Ingredients:
- ✓ 1 and ¼ cups flour
- ✓ 1 tsp. baking powder
- ✓ ¾ cup sugar
- ✓ 1 tbsp. orange zest, grated
- ✓ 2 tsp. lime zest, grated
- ✓ ½ cup butter, soft
- ✓ 2 eggs, whisked
- ✓ ½ tsp. vanilla extract
- ✓ 2 tbsp. poppy seeds
- ✓ 1 cup milk

For the cream:
- ✓ 1 cup sugar
- ✓ ½ cup passion fruit puree
- ✓ 3 tbsp. butter, melted
- ✓ 4 egg yolks

Directions:
1. In a bowl, mix flour with baking powder, ¾ cup sugar, orange zest and lime zest and stir.
2. Add ½ cup butter, eggs, poppy seeds, vanilla and milk, stir using your mixer, pour into a cake pan that fits your air fryer and cook at 350 degrees F for about 30 minutes.
3. Meanwhile, heat up a pan with 3 tablespoons butter over medium heat, add sugar and stir until it dissolves.
4. Take off heat, add passion fruit puree and egg yolks gradually and whisk really well.
5. Take cake out of the fryer, cool it down a bit and cut into halves horizontally.
6. Spread ¼ of passion fruit cream over one half, top with the other cake half and spread ¼ of the cream on top.

Nutrition: calories 211 - Fat 6 - Fiber 7 - Carbs 12 - Protein 6

50. Plum and Currant Tart

Prep.Time: 30 min - **Cooking Time:** 35 min - **Servings:** 6

Ingredients:

For the crumble:
- ✓ ¼ cup almond flour
- ✓ ¼ cup millet flour
- ✓ 1 cup brown rice flour
- ✓ ½ cup cane sugar
- ✓ 10 tbsp. butter, soft
- ✓ 3 tablespoons milk

For the filling:
- ✓ 1 pound small plums, pitted and halved
- ✓ 1 cup white currants
- ✓ 2 tablespoons cornstarch
- ✓ 3 tablespoons sugar
- ✓ ½ tsp. vanilla extract
- ✓ ½ tsp. cinnamon powder
- ✓ ¼ tsp. ginger powder
- ✓ 1 teaspoon lime juice

Directions:
1. In a bowl, mix brown rice flour with ½ cup sugar, millet flour, almond flour, butter and milk and stir until you obtain a sand like dough.
2. Reserve ¼ of the dough, press the rest of the dough into a tart pan that fits your air fryer and keep in the fridge for 30 minutes.
3. Meanwhile, in a bowl, mix plums with currants, 3 tablespoons sugar, cornstarch, vanilla extract, cinnamon, ginger and lime juice and stir well.
4. Pour this over tart crust, crumble reserved dough on top, introduce in your air fryer and cook at 350 degrees F for 35 minutes.
5. Leave tart to cool down, slice and serve.

Nutrition: calories 200 - Fat 5 - Fiber 4 - Carbs 8 - Protein 6

51. Cashew Bars

Prep.Time: 10 min - **Cooking Time:** 15 minutes - **Servings:** 6

Ingredients:
- ✓ 1/3 cup honey
- ✓ ¼ cup almond meal
- ✓ 1 tablespoon almond butter
- ✓ 1 and ½ cups cashews, chopped
- ✓ 4 dates, chopped
- ✓ ¾ cup coconut, shredded
- ✓ 1 tablespoon chia seeds

Directions:
1. In a bowl, mix honey with almond meal and almond butter and stir well.
2. Add cashews, coconut, dates and chia seeds and stir well again.
3. Spread this on a lined baking sheet that fits your air fryer and press well.
4. Introduce in the fryer and cook at 300 degrees F for 15 minutes.
5. Leave mix to cool down, cut into medium bars and serve.

Nutrition: calories 121 - Fat 4 - Fiber 7 - Carbs 5 - Protein 6

52. Tasty Orange Cookies

Prep.Time: 10 min - **Cooking Time:** 12 min - **Servings:** 8

Ingredients:
- ✓ 1 tsp. vanilla extract
- ✓ 2 cups flour
- ✓ 1 tsp. baking powder
- ✓ ½ cup butter, soft
- ✓ ¾ cup sugar
- ✓ 1 egg, whisked
- ✓ 1tbsp orange zest, grated

For the filling:
- ✓ 4 ounces cream cheese, soft
- ✓ ½ cup butter
- ✓ 2 cups powdered sugar

Directions:
1. In a bowl, mix cream cheese with ½ cup butter and 2 cups powdered sugar, stir well using your mixer and leave aside for now.
2. In another bowl, mix flour with baking powder.
3. In a third bowl, mix ½ cup butter with ¾ cup sugar, egg, vanilla extract and orange zest and whisk well.
4. Combine flour with orange mix, stir well and scoop 1 tablespoon of the mix on a lined baking sheet. Repeat with the rest of the orange batter, introduce in the fryer and cook at 340 degrees F for 12 minutes
5. Leave cookies to cool down, spread cream filling on half of them top with the other cookies and serve

Nutrition: calories 124 - Fat 5 - Fiber 6 - Carbs 8 - Protein 4

53. Peach Pie

Prep.Time: 10 min - **Cooking Time:** 35 min - **Servings:** 4

Ingredients:
- ✓ 1 pie dough
- ✓ 2 and ¼ pounds peaches, pitted and chopped
- ✓ 2 tablespoons cornstarch
- ✓ ½ cup sugar
- ✓ 2 tablespoons flour
- ✓ A pinch of nutmeg, ground
- ✓ 1 tablespoon dark rum
- ✓ 1 tablespoon lemon juice
- ✓ 2 tbsp. butter, melted

Directions:
1. Roll pie dough into a pie pan that fits your air fryer and press well.
2. In a bowl, mix peaches with cornstarch, sugar, flour, nutmeg, rum, lemon juice and butter and stir well.
3. Pour and spread this into pie pan, introduce in your air fryer and cook at 350 degrees F for 35 minutes.
4. Serve warm or cold.

Nutrition: calories 231 - Fat 6 - Fiber 7 - Carbs 9 - Protein 5

54. Brown Butter Cookies

Prep.Time: 10 min - **Cooking Time:** 10 min - **Servings:** 6

Ingredients:
- ✓ 1 and ½ cups butter
- ✓ 2 cups brown sugar
- ✓ 2 eggs, whisked
- ✓ 3 cups flour
- ✓ 2/3 cup pecans, chopped
- ✓ 2 tsp. vanilla extract
- ✓ 1 teaspoon baking soda
- ✓ ½ teaspoon baking powder

Directions:
1. Heat up a pan with the butter over medium heat, stir until it melts, add brown sugar and stir. In a bowl, mix flour with pecans, vanilla extract, baking soda, baking powder and eggs and stir well.
2. Add brown butter, stir well and arrange spoonfuls of this mix on a lined baking sheet that fits your air fryer.
3. Introduce in the fryer and cook at 340 F for 10 minutes.
4. Leave cookies to cool down and serve

Nutrition: calories 144 - Fat 5 - Fiber 6 - Carbs 19 - Protein 2

55. Plum Bars

Prep.Time: 10 min - **Cooking Time:** 16 min - **Servings:** 8

Ingredients:
- ✓ 2 cups dried plums
- ✓ 6 tablespoons water
- ✓ 2 cup rolled oats
- ✓ 1 cup brown sugar
- ✓ ½ teaspoon baking soda
- ✓ 1 teaspoon cinnamon powder
- ✓ 2 tablespoons butter, melted
- ✓ 1 egg, whisked
- ✓ Cooking spray

Directions:
1. In your food processor, mix plums with water and blend until you obtain a sticky spread.
2. In a bowl, mix oats with cinnamon, baking soda, sugar, egg and butter and whisk really well.
3. Press half of the oats mix in a baking pan that fits your air fryer sprayed with cooking oil, spread plums mix and top with the other half of the oats mix.
4. Introduce in your air fryer and cook at 350 degrees F for 16 minutes.
5. Leave mix aside to cool down, cut into medium bars and serve.

Nutrition: calories 111 - Fat 5 - Fiber 6 - Carbs 12 - Protein 6

56. Pumpkin Cookies

Prep.Time: 10 min - **Cooking Time:** 15 min - **Servings:** 24

Ingredients:
- ✓ 2 and ½ cups flour
- ✓ ½ teaspoon baking soda
- ✓ 1 tablespoon flax seed, ground
- ✓ 3 tablespoons water
- ✓ ½ cup pumpkin flesh, mashed
- ✓ ¼ cup honey
- ✓ 2 tablespoons butter
- ✓ 1 teaspoon vanilla extract
- ✓ ½ cup dark chocolate chips

Directions:
1. In a bowl, mix flax seed with water, stir and leave aside for a few minutes.
2. In another bowl, mix flour with salt and baking soda.
3. In a third bowl, mix honey with pumpkin puree, butter, vanilla extract and flaxseed.
4. Combine flour with honey mix and chocolate chips and stir.
5. Scoop 1 tablespoon of cookie dough on a lined baking sheet that fits your air fryer, repeat with the rest of the dough, introduce them in your air fryer and cook at 350 degrees F for 15 minutes.
6. Leave cookies to cool down and serve.

Nutrition: calories 140 - Fat 2 - Fiber 2 - Carbs 7 - Protein 10

57. Passion Fruit Pudding

Prep.Time: 10 min - **Cooking Time:** 40 minutes - **Servings:** 6

Ingredients:
- ✓ 1 cup Paleo passion fruit curd
- ✓ 4 passion fruits, pulp and seeds
- ✓ 3 and ½ ounces maple syrup
- ✓ 3 eggs
- ✓ 2 ounces ghee, melted
- ✓ 3 and ½ ounces almond milk
- ✓ ½ cup almond flour
- ✓ ½ tsp. baking powder

Directions:
1. In a bowl, mix the half of the fruit curd with passion fruit seeds and pulp, stir and divide into 6 heat proof ramekins.
2. In a bowl, whisked eggs with maple syrup, ghee, the rest of the curd, baking powder, milk and flour and stir well.
3. Divide this into the ramekins as well, introduce in the fryer and cook at 200 degrees F for 40 minutes.
4. Leave puddings to cool down and serve

Nutrition: calories 430 – Fat 22 - Fiber 3 - Carbs 7 - Protein 8

58. Sweet Squares

Prep.Time: 10 min - **Cooking Time:** 30 min - **Servings:** 6

Ingredients:
- ✓ 1 cup flour
- ✓ ½ cup butter, soft
- ✓ 1 cup sugar
- ✓ ¼ cup powdered sugar
- ✓ 2 teaspoons lemon peel, grated
- ✓ 2 tablespoons lemon juice
- ✓ 2 eggs, whisked
- ✓ ½ teaspoon baking powder

Directions:
1. In a bowl, mix flour with powdered sugar and butter, stir well, press on the bottom of a pan that fits your air fryer, introduce in the fryer and bake at 350 degrees F for 14 minutes.
2. In another bowl, mix sugar with lemon juice, lemon peel, eggs and baking powder, stir using your mixer and spread over baked crust.
3. Bake for 15 minutes more, leave aside to cool down, cut into medium squares and serve cold.

Nutrition: calories 100 - Fat 4 - Fiber 1 - Carbs 12 - Protein 1

59. Sweet Potato Cheesecake

Prep.Time: 10 min - **Cooking Time:** 5 min - **Servings:** 4

Ingredients:
- 4 tablespoons butter, melted
- 6 ounces mascarpone, soft
- 8 ounces cream cheese, soft
- 2/3 cup graham crackers, crumbled
- ¾ cup milk
- 1 teaspoon vanilla extract
- 2/3 cup sweet potato puree
- ¼ teaspoons cinnamon powder

Directions:
1. In a bowl, mix butter with crumbled crackers, stir well, press on the bottom of a cake pan that fits your air fryer and keep in the fridge for now.
2. In another bowl, mix cream cheese with mascarpone, sweet potato puree, milk, cinnamon and vanilla and whisk really well.
3. Spread this over crust, introduce in your air fryer, cook at 300 degrees F for 4 minutes and keep in the fridge for a few hours before serving.

Nutrition: calories 172 - Fat 4 - Fiber 6 - Carbs 8 - Protein 3

60. Sponge Cake

Prep.Time: 10 min - **Cooking Time:** 20 min - **Servings:** 12

Ingredients:
- 3 cups flour
- 3 teaspoons baking powder
- ½ cup cornstarch
- 1 teaspoon baking soda
- 1 cup olive oil
- 1 and ½ cup milk
- 1 and 2/3 cup sugar
- 2 cups water
- ¼ cup lemon juice
- 2 teaspoons vanilla extract

Directions:
1. In a bowl, mix flour with cornstarch, baking powder, baking soda and sugar and whisk well.
2. In another bowl, mix oil with milk, water, vanilla and lemon juice and whisk.
3. Combine the two mixtures, stir, pour in a greased baking dish that fits your air fryer, introduce in the fryer and cook at 350 degrees F for 20 minutes.
4. Leave cake to cool down, cut and serve.

Nutrition: calories 246 - Fat 3 - Fiber 1 - Carbs 6 - Protein 2

61. Strawberry Tart

Prep.Time: 10 min - **Cooking Time:** 15 min - **Servings:** 8

Ingredients:
- 1 ½ cup plain flour
- 3 tbsp. unsalted butter
- 2 tbsp. powdered sugar
- 2 cups cold water

Filling:
- 2 cups sliced strawberries
- 1 cup fresh cream
- 3 tbsp. butter

Directions:
1. In a large bowl, mix the flour, cocoa powder, butter and sugar with your fingers. The mixture should resemble breadcrumbs. Knead the dough using the cold milk and wrap it and leave it to cool for ten minutes. Roll the dough out into the pie and prick the sides of the pie.
2. Mix the ingredients for the filling in a bowl. Make sure that it is a little thick.
3. Preheat the fryer to 300 Fahrenheit for five minutes. You will need to place the tin in the basket and cover it. When the pastry has turned golden brown, you will need to remove the tin and let it cool. Cut into slices and serve with a dollop of cream.

62. Almond Milk

Prep.Time: 10 min - **Cooking Time:** 15 min - **Servings:** 8

Ingredients:
- 2 cups almond powder
- 2 cups milk
- 1 tsp. gelatin
- tbsp. custard powder
- 3 tbsp. powdered sugar
- 3 tbsp. unsalted butter

Directions:
1. Boil the milk and the sugar in a pan and add the custard powder followed by the almond powder and stir till you get a thick mixture. Add the gelatin and mix the ingredients well Combine flour with honey mix and chocolate chips and stir.
2. Preheat the fryer to 300 Fahrenheit for five minutes. Place the dish in the basket and reduce the temperature to 250 Fahrenheit. Cook for ten minutes and set aside to cool.

63. Mini Pancakes

Prep.Time: 10 min - **Cooking Time:** 10 minutes - **Servings:** 6

Ingredients:
- 1 ½ cups almond flour
- 3 eggs
- 2 tsp. dried basil
- 2 tsp. dried parsley
- Salt and Pepper to taste
- 3 tbsp. Butter

Directions:
1. Preheat the air fryer to 250 Fahrenheit.
2. In a small bowl, mix the ingredients together. Ensure that the mixture is smooth and well balanced.
3. Take a pancake mold and grease it with butter. Add the batter to the mold and place it in the air fryer basket. Cook till both the sides of the pancake have browned on both sides and serve with maple syrup

64. Strawberry Pudding

Prep.Time: 10 min - **Cooking Time:** 10 min - **Servings:** 8

Ingredients:
- 1 cup strawberry juice
- 2 cups milk
- 2 tbsp. custard powder
- 3 tbsp. powdered sugar
- 3 tbsp. unsalted butter
- 1 cup strawberry slices

Directions:
1. Boil the milk and the sugar in a pan and add the custard powder followed by the strawberry juice and stir till you get a thick mixture.
2. Preheat the fryer to 300 Fahrenheit for five minutes. Place the dish in the basket and reduce the temperature to 250 Fahrenheit. Cook for ten minutes and set aside to cool. Garnish with strawberry.

65. Bebinca

Prep.Time: 10 min - **Cooking Time:** 15 min - **Servings:** 4

Ingredients:
- ✓ 1 cup coconut milk
- ✓ 1 cup almond flour
- ✓ 2 cups milk
- ✓ 2 tbsp. custard powder
- ✓ 3 tbsp. powdered sugar
- ✓ 3 tbsp. unsalted butter

Directions:
1. Boil the milk and the sugar in a pan and add the custard powder followed by the flour and coconut milk and stir till you get a thick mixture
2. Preheat the fryer to 300 Fahrenheit for five minutes. Place the dish in the basket and reduce the temperature to 250 Fahrenheit. Cook for ten minutes and set aside to cool.

66. Banana Pudding

Prep.Time: 10 min - **Cooking Time:** 15 min - **Servings:** 8

Ingredients:
- ✓ 1 cup banana juice
- ✓ 2 cups milk
- ✓ 2 tbsp. custard powder
- ✓ 3 tbsp. powdered sugar
- ✓ 3 tbsp. unsalted butter
- ✓ 3 tbsp. chopped mixed nuts

Directions:
1. Boil the milk and the sugar in a pan and add the custard powder followed by the banana juice and stir till you get a thick mixture.
2. Preheat the fryer to 300 Fahrenheit for five minutes. Place the dish in the basket and reduce the temperature to 250 Fahrenheit. Cook for ten minutes and set aside to cool. Garnish with nuts

67. Cream caramel

Prep.Time: 10 min - **Cooking Time:** 15 min - **Servings:** 8

Ingredients:
- ✓ 2 cups milk
- ✓ 2 cups custard powder
- ✓ 3 tbsp. powdered sugar
- ✓ 3 tbsp. unsalted butter
- ✓ 4 tbsp. caramel

Directions:
1. Boil the milk and the sugar in a pan and add the custard powder and stir till you get a thick mixture.
2. Preheat the fryer to 300 Fahrenheit for five minutes. Place the dish in the basket and reduce the temperature to 250 Fahrenheit. Cook for ten minutes and set aside to cool.
3. Spread the caramel over the dish and serve warm.

68. Apricot Pudding

Prep.Time: 10 min - **Cooking Time:** 15 min - **Servings:** 8

Ingredients:
- ✓ 2 cups almond flour
- ✓ 2 cups milk
- ✓ 2 tbsp. custard powder
- ✓ 3 tbsp. powdered sugar
- ✓ 3 tbsp. unsalted butter
- ✓ 2 cups apricot

Directions:
1. Boil the milk and the sugar in a pan and add the custard powder followed by the almond powder and stir till you get a thick mixture. Chop the apricot finely and add to the mixture.
2. Preheat the fryer to 300 Fahrenheit for five minutes. Place the dish in the basket and reduce the temperature to 250 Fahrenheit. Cook for ten minutes and set aside to cool. Spread the fruits on the bread and serve.

69. Honey and Orange Pancakes

Prep.Time: 10 min - **Cooking Time:** 10 minutes - **Servings:** 6

Ingredients:
- ✓ 1 orange (zested)
- ✓ 1 ½ cups almond flour
- ✓ 3 eggs
- ✓ 1 tbsp. honey
- ✓ 2 tsp. dried basil
- ✓ 2 tsp. dried parsley
- ✓ Salt and Pepper to taste
- ✓ 3 tbsp. Butter

Directions:
1. Preheat the air fryer to 250 Fahrenheit.
2. In a small bowl, mix the ingredients together. Ensure that the mixture is smooth and well balanced
3. Take a pancake mold and grease it with butter. Add the batter to the mold and place it in the air fryer basket.
4. Cook till both the sides of the pancake have browned on both sides and serve with maple syrup.

70. Baked Cream

Prep.Time: 15 min - **Cooking Time:** 15 min - **Servings:** 8

Ingredients:
- ✓ For the cream:
- ✓ 2 cups condensed milk
- ✓ 2 cups fresh cream
- For garnishing:
- ✓ 1 cup fresh strawberries
- ✓ 1 cup fresh blueberries
- ✓ 1 cup blackberries
- ✓ Handful of mint leaves
- ✓ 3 tsp. sugar
- ✓ 4 tsp. water

Directions:
1. Blend the cream and add the milk to it. Whisk the ingredients well together and transfer this mixture into small baking bowls ensuring you do not overfill the bowls.
2. Preheat the fryer to 300 Fahrenheit for five minutes. You will need to place the bowls in the basket and cover it. Cook it for fifteen minutes. When you shake the bowls, the mixture should just shake but not break.
3. Leave it in the refrigerator to set and then arrange the fruits, garnish and serve.

71. Fig Pudding

Prep.Time: 10 min - **Cooking Time:** 15 min - **Servings:** 8

Ingredients:
- ✓ 2 cups milk
- ✓ 2 cups almond flour
- ✓ 2 tbsp. custard powder
- ✓ 3 tbsp. powdered sugar
- ✓ 3 tbsp. unsalted butter
- ✓ 2 cups figs

Directions:
1. Boil the milk and the sugar in a pan and add the custard powder followed by the almond flour and stir till you get a thick mixture. Chop the figs fine and add it to the mixture.
2. Preheat the fryer to 300 Fahrenheit for five minutes. Place the dish in the basket and reduce the temperature to 250 Fahrenheit. Cook for ten minutes and set aside to cool

72. Pistachio Pudding

Prep.Time: 10 min - **Cooking Time:** 15 min - **Servings:** 8

Ingredients:
- ✓ 2 cups milk
- ✓ 2 cups almond flour
- ✓ 2 tbsp. custard powder
- ✓ 3 tbsp. powdered sugar
- ✓ 3 tbsp. unsalted butter
- ✓ 2 cups finely chopped pistachio

Directions:
1. Boil the milk and the sugar in a pan and add the custard powder followed by the almond flour and stir till you get a thick mixture. Add the pistachio nuts to the mixture.
2. Preheat the fryer to 300 Fahrenheit for five minutes. Place the dish in the basket and reduce the temperature to 250 Fahrenheit. Cook for ten minutes and set aside to cool.

73. Orange Citrus Blend

Prep.Time: 10 min - **Cooking Time:** 15 min - **Servings:** 8

Ingredients:
- ✓ 2 cups milk
- ✓ 2 cups almond flour
- ✓ 2 tbsp. custard powder
- ✓ 3 tbsp. powdered sugar
- ✓ 3 tbsp. unsalted butter
- ✓ 2 oranges (sliced)
- ✓ 2 persimmons (sliced

Directions:
1. Boil the milk and the sugar in a pan and add the custard powder followed by the almond flour and stir till you get a thick mixture. Add the sliced fruits to the mixture
2. Preheat the fryer to 300 Fahrenheit for five minutes. Place the dish in the basket and reduce the temperature to 250 Fahrenheit. Cook for ten minutes and set aside to cool.

74. Po'e

Prep.Time: 10 min - **Cooking Time:** 15 min - **Servings:** 24

Ingredients:
- ✓ 2 cups coconut milk
- ✓ 1 cup fresh cream
- ✓ 2 tbsp. custard powder
- ✓ 3 tbsp. powdered sugar
- ✓ 3 tbsp. unsalted butter
- ✓ 1 cup pineapple slices
- ✓ 1 cup mango slices
- ✓ 1 cup banana slices

Directions:
1. Boil the milk and the sugar in a pan and add the custard powder followed by the coconut milk and fresh cream and stir till you get a thick mixture. Add the sliced fruits to the mixture.
2. Preheat the fryer to 300 Fahrenheit for five minutes. Place the dish in the basket and reduce the temperature to 250 Fahrenheit. Cook for ten minutes and set aside to cool.

75. Blueberry Pudding

Prep.Time: 10 min - **Cooking Time:** 15 minutes - **Servings:** 6

Ingredients:
- ✓ 1 cup blueberry juice
- ✓ 2 cups milk
- ✓ 2 tbsp. custard powder
- ✓ 3 tbsp. powdered sugar
- ✓ 3 tbsp. unsalted butter

Directions:
1. Boil the milk and the sugar in a pan and add the custard powder followed by the blueberry juice and stir till you get a thick mixture.
2. Preheat the fryer to 300 Fahrenheit for five minutes. Place the dish in the basket and reduce the temperature to 250 Fahrenheit. Cook for ten minutes and set aside to cool

76. Cranberry Pancakes

Prep.Time: 10 min - **Cooking Time:** 15 min - **Servings:** 6

Ingredients:
- ✓ 2 cups minced cranberry
- ✓ 1 ½ cups almond flour
- ✓ 3 eggs
- ✓ 2 tsp. dried basil
- ✓ 2 tsp. dried parsley
- ✓ Salt and Pepper to taste
- ✓ 3 tbsp. Butter

Directions:
1. Preheat the air fryer to 250 Fahrenheit
2. In a small bowl, mix the ingredients together. Ensure that the mixture is smooth and well balanced.
3. Take a pancake mold and grease it with butter. Add the batter to the mold and place it in the air fryer basket. Cook till both the sides of the pancake have browned on both sides and serve with maple syrup.

77. Sagu Payasam

Prep.Time: 10 min - **Cooking Time:** 15 min - **Servings:** 8

Ingredients:
- ✓ 2 cups milk
- ✓ 2 cups soaked sagu
- ✓ 2 tbsp. custard powder
- ✓ 3 tbsp. powdered sugar
- ✓ 3 tbsp. unsalted butter

Directions:
1. Boil the milk and the sugar in a pan and add the custard powder followed by the sagu and stir till you get a thick mixture.
2. Preheat the fryer to 300 Fahrenheit for five minutes. Place the dish in the basket and reduce the temperature to 250 Fahrenheit. Cook for ten minutes and set aside to cool.

78. Vanilla Pudding

Prep.Time: 10 min - **Cooking Time:** 15 min - **Servings:** 8

Ingredients:
- ✓ 2 cups milk
- ✓ 2 cups almond flour
- ✓ 1 tbsp. vanilla essence
- ✓ 2 tbsp. custard powder
- ✓ 3 tbsp. powdered sugar
- ✓ 3 tbsp. unsalted butter

Directions:
1. Boil the milk and the sugar in a pan and add the custard powder followed by the almond flour and the vanilla essence and stir till you get a thick mixture.
2. Preheat the fryer to 300 Fahrenheit for five minutes. Place the dish in the basket and reduce the temperature to 250 Fahrenheit. Cook for ten minutes and set aside to cool.

79. Saffron Pudding

Prep.Time: 10 min - **Cooking Time:** 15 min - **Servings:** 8

Ingredients:
- ✓ 2 cups milk
- ✓ 2 tbsp. saffron
- ✓ 2 cups almond flour
- ✓ 2 tbsp. custard powder
- ✓ 3 tbsp. powdered sugar
- ✓ 3 tbsp. unsalted butter

Directions:
1. Boil the milk and the sugar in a pan and add the custard powder followed by the almond flour and stir till you get a thick mixture. Mix the saffron into the mixture and stir till the color has spread well.
2. Preheat the fryer to 300 Fahrenheit for five minutes. Place the dish in the basket and reduce the temperature to 250 Fahrenheit. Cook for ten minutes and set aside to cool

80. Cardamom Cakes

Prep.Time: 10 min - **Cooking Time:** 20 min - **Servings:** 8

Ingredients:
- ✓ 2 cups All-purpose flour
- ✓ 1 ½ cup milk
- ✓ 1 tbsp. cardamom powder
- ✓ ½ tsp. baking powder
- ✓ ½ tsp. baking soda
- ✓ 2 tbsp. butter
- ✓ 2 tbsp. sugar
- ✓ Muffin cups

Directions:
1. Mix the ingredients together and use your fingers to get a crumbly mixture.
2. Add the baking soda and the vinegar to the milk and mix continuously. Add this milk to the mixture and create a batter, which you will need to transfer to the muffin cups.
3. Preheat the fryer to 300 Fahrenheit for five minutes. You will need to place the muffin cups in the basket and cover it. Cook the muffins for fifteen minutes and check whether or not the muffins are cooked using a toothpick. Remove the cups and serve hot.

81. Rice pudding

Prep.Time: 10 min - **Cooking Time:** 15 minutes - **Servings:** 6

Ingredients:
- ✓ 2 cups milk
- ✓ 2 tbsp. custard powder
- ✓ 3 tbsp. powdered sugar
- ✓ 2 tbsp. rice
- ✓ 3 tbsp. unsalted butter

Directions:
1. Boil the milk and the sugar in a pan and add the custard powder and stir till you get a thick mixture. Add the rice to the bowl and ensure that the mixture becomes slightly thicker.
2. Preheat the fryer to 300 Fahrenheit for five minutes. Place the dish in the basket and reduce the temperature to 250 Fahrenheit. Cook for ten minutes and set aside to cool

82. Chocolate Chip Waffles

Prep.Time: 10 min - **Cooking Time:** 15 min - **Servings:** 8

Ingredients:
- ✓ 3 cups cocoa powder
- ✓ 3 eggs
- ✓ 2 tsp. dried basil
- ✓ 2 tsp. dried parsley
- ✓ Salt and Pepper to taste
- ✓ 3 tbsp. Butter
- ✓ 1 cup chocolate chips

Directions:
1. Preheat the air fryer to 250 Fahrenheit.
2. In a small bowl, mix the ingredients, except for the chocolate chips, together. Ensure that the mixture is smooth and well balanced.
3. Take a waffle mold and grease it with butter. Add the batter to the mold and place it in the air fryer basket. Cook till both the sides have browned. Garnish with chips and serve

83. Chocolate Pudding

Prep.Time: 10 min - **Cooking Time:** 15 min - **Servings:** 4

Ingredients:
- ✓ 2 cups cocoa powder
- ✓ 2 cups milk
- ✓ 2 tbsp. custard powder
- ✓ 3 tbsp. powdered sugar
- ✓ 3 tbsp. unsalted butter

Directions:
1. Boil the milk and the sugar in a pan and add the custard powder followed by the chocolate powder and stir till you get a thick mixture.
2. Preheat the fryer to 300 Fahrenheit for five minutes. Place the dish in the basket and reduce the temperature to 250 Fahrenheit. Cook for ten minutes and set aside to cool.

84. Zucchini Pancakes

Prep.Time: 10 min - **Cooking Time:** 10 min - **Servings:** 4

Ingredients:
- ✓ 2 zucchinis (shredded)
- ✓ 1 ½ cups almond flour
- ✓ 3 eggs
- ✓ 2 tsp. dried basil
- ✓ 2 tsp. dried parsley
- ✓ Salt and Pepper to taste
- ✓ 3 tbsp. Butter

Directions:
1. Preheat the air fryer to 250 Fahrenheit.
2. In a small bowl, mix the ingredients together. Ensure that the mixture is smooth and well balanced.
3. Take a pancake mold and grease it with butter. Add the batter to the mold and place it in the air fryer basket.
4. Cook till both the sides of the pancake have browned on both sides and serve with maple syrup

85. Blueberry Cakes

Prep.Time: 15 min - **Cooking Time:** 20 min - **Servings:** 8

Ingredients:
- 2 cups All-purpose flour
- 1 ½ cup milk
- ½ tsp. baking powder
- ½ tsp. baking soda
- 2 tbsp. butter
- 1 cup sugar
- 3 tsp. vinegar
- 2 cups blueberries
- ½ tsp. vanilla essence
- Muffin cups or butter paper cups.

Directions:
1. Mix the ingredients together and use your fingers to get a crumbly mixture.
2. Add the baking soda and the vinegar to the milk and mix continuously. Add this milk to the mixture and create a batter that you will need to transfer to the muffin cups.
3. Preheat the fryer to 300 Fahrenheit for five minutes. You will need to place the muffin cups in the basket and cover it. Cook the muffins for fifteen minutes and check whether or not the muffins are cooked using a toothpick. Remove the cups and serve hot.

86. Cookie Custards

Prep.Time: 10 min - **Cooking Time:** 20 min - **Servings:** 8

Ingredients:
- 1 cup all-purpose flour
- ½ cup icing sugar
- ½ cup custard powder
- 2 tbsp. margarine
- A pinch of baking soda and baking powder

Directions:
1. Cream the margarine and sugar together. Add the remaining ingredients and fold them together.
2. Prepare a baking tray by greasing it with butter. Make balls out of the dough, coat them with flour and place them in the tray.
3. Preheat the fryer to 300 Fahrenheit for five minutes. You will need to place the baking tray in the basket and cover it. Cook till you find that the balls have turned golden brown. Remove the tray and leave it to cool outside for half an hour. Store in an airtight container.

87. Chocolate Tarts

Prep.Time: 10 min - **Cooking Time:** 15 minutes - **Servings:** 8

Ingredients:
- 1 ½ cup plain flour
- ½ cup cocoa powder
- 3 tbsp. unsalted butter
- 2 tbsp. powdered sugar
- 2 cups cold water
- 1 tbsp. sliced cashew

For Truffle filling:
- 1 ½ melted chocolate
- 1 cup fresh cream
- 3 tbsp. butter

Directions:
1. In a large bowl, mix the flour, cocoa powder, butter and sugar with your fingers. The mixture should resemble breadcrumbs. Knead the dough using the cold milk and wrap it and leave it to cool for ten minutes. Roll the dough out into the pie and prick the sides of the pie.
2. Mix the ingredients for the filling in a bowl. Make sure that it is a little thick. Add the filling to the pie and cover it with the second round.
3. Preheat the fryer to 300 Fahrenheit for five minutes. You will need to place the tin in the basket and cover it. When the pastry has turned golden brown, you will need to remove the tin and let it cool. Cut into slices and serve with a dollop of cream

88. Choco – Chip Muffins

Prep.Time: 15 min - **Cooking Time:** 20 min - **Servings:** 8

Ingredients:
- 2 cups All-purpose flour
- 1 ½ cup milk
- ½ tsp. baking powder
- ½ tsp. baking soda
- 2 tbsp. butter
- 1 cup sugar
- 3 tsp. vinegar
- ½ cup chocolate chips
- ½ tsp. vanilla essence
- Muffin cups or butter paper cups

Directions:
1. Mix the ingredients together and use your fingers to get a crumbly mixture.
2. Add the baking soda and the vinegar to the milk and mix continuously. Add this milk to the mixture and create a batter, which you will need to transfer to the muffin cups.
3. Preheat the fryer to 300 Fahrenheit for five minutes. You will need to place the muffin cups in the basket and cover it. Cook the muffins for fifteen minutes and check whether or not the muffins are cooked using a toothpick. Remove the cups and serve hot.

89. Tapioca Pudding

Prep.Time: 10 min - **Cooking Time:** 15 min - **Servings:** 6

Ingredients:
- 2 cups tapioca pearls
- 2 cups milk
- 2 tbsp. custard powder
- 3 tbsp. powdered sugar
- 3 tbsp. unsalted butter

Directions:
1. Boil the milk and the sugar in a pan and add the custard powder followed by the tapioca pearls and stir till you get a thick mixture.
2. Preheat the fryer to 300 Fahrenheit for five minutes. Place the dish in the basket and reduce the temperature to 250 Fahrenheit. Cook for ten minutes and set aside to cool.

90. Brownies

Prep.Time: 15 min - **Cooking Time:** 15 min - **Servings:** 6

Ingredients:
- 1 tbsp. unsalted butter
- 2 tbsp. water
- ½ cup chopped nuts
- 3 tbsp. melted dark chocolate
- 1 cup all-purpose flour
- ½ cup condensed milk

Directions:
1. Add the ingredients together and whisk till you get a smooth mixture.
2. Prepare a tin by greasing it with butter. Transfer the mixture into the tin. Preheat the fryer to 300 Fahrenheit for five minutes. You will need to place the tin in the basket and cover it. Check whether the brownies have been cooked using a knife or a toothpick and remove the tray. When the brownies have cooled, cut them and serve with a dollop of ice cream.

91. An Upside Down Pineapple cake

Prep.Time: 20 min - **Cooking Time:** 20 min - **Servings:** 6

Ingredients:

For the batter:
- ✓ 2 tbsp. butter (Preferably unsalted butter)
- ✓ ¼ cup condensed milk
- ✓ 2 tsp. pineapple essence
- ✓ 2 cups All Purpose Flour (You will need to split the flour into two parts – 1 cup and another ½ cup)
- ✓ ¼ tsp. baking powder
- ✓ ¼ tsp. baking soda
- ✓ Edible yellow food coloring
- ✓ ½ cup drinking soda
- ✓ ½ tbsp. powdered sugar

For the tin preparation:
- ✓ 6 slices pineapple
- ✓ 3 tbsp. sugar (This is to make the caramel)
- ✓ 8 cherries

Directions:
1. You will first need to prepare the tin. Grease the tin with butter and line it on all sides with the butter paper. You will now have to dust the tin with the flour. Add the slices of the pineapple to the base of the tin followed by the cherries. You will need to cut the cherries into halves and place it on the cavities.
2. You will now have to melt the sugar and make it into a caramel. Pour this caramel into the tin and set it aside.
3. Take a large mixing bowl and add the ingredients for the batter. You will need to first sieve the flour, baking soda and powder and then add them to the bowl. Now, add the butter to the bowl and beat the ingredients. Add the sugar and the condensed milk to the bowl and beat till you get a uniform mixture. Add the essence and the yellow coloring followed by the dry ingredients to the bowl. Make sure that there are no lumps in the batter. Transfer the batter into the tin.
4. Preheat the fryer to 300 Fahrenheit for five minutes. You will need to place the tin in the basket and cover it. Cook the cake for fifteen minutes and check whether or not the cake is cooked using a toothpick. Remove the tin and cut the cake into slices and serve.

92. Apple Pie

Prep.Time: 10 min - **Cooking Time:** 15 min - **Servings:** 8

Ingredients:
- ✓ 1 cup plain flour
- ✓ 1 tbsp. unsalted butter
- ✓ 4tsp. powdered sugar
- ✓ 2 cups cold milk

For Apple filling:
- ✓ ½ cup roasted nuts
- ✓ 3 apples (Peel and chop into slices)
- ✓ 2 tbsp. sugar
- ✓ ½ tsp. cinnamon
- ✓ 2 tsp. lemon juice

Directions:
1. Mix the ingredients together to form a crumbly mixture. Knead the mixture with cold milk and wrap it. Roll the dough out into two large circles and press that dough into the pie tin and prick the sides with a fork.
2. Cook the ingredients for the filling on a low flame and pour into the tin.
3. Cover the pie tin with the second round.
4. Preheat the fryer to 300 Fahrenheit for five minutes. You will need to place the tin in the basket and cover it. When the pastry has turned golden brown, you will need to remove the tin and let it cool. Cut into slices and serve with a dollop of cream.

93. Nan Khatai

Prep.Time: 10 min - **Cooking Time:** 15 minutes - **Servings:** 6

Ingredients:
- ✓ 1 ½ cup all-purpose flour
- ✓ 1 cup Gram flour
- ✓ 1 cup +3 tbsp. icing sugar
- ✓ 1 tbsp. Unsalted Butter
- ✓ 1 tsp. baking powder
- ✓ 1 tsp. baking soda
- ✓ 1 tsp. cardamom powder

Directions:
1. Create a crumbly mixture using the ingredients and make small balls of the mixture and flattening them on a prepared baking tray.
2. Preheat the fryer to 300 Fahrenheit for five minutes. Place the baking tray in the basket and reduce the temperature to 250 Fahrenheit. Cook both sides of the ball for five minutes to ensure that they are cooked uniformly. Once the nan khatai has cooled, store them in an airtight container

94. Chocolate Sponge Cake

Prep.Time: 15 min - **Cooking Time:** 20 min - **Servings:** 8

Ingredients:
- ✓ ½ cup condensed milk
- ✓ 1 cup all-purpose flour
- ✓ ½ cup cocoa powder
- ✓ ½ tsp. baking soda
- ✓ ½ tsp. baking powder
- ✓ ½ cup oil
- ✓ 3 tbsp. powdered sugar
- ✓ ½ cup soda
- ✓ 1 tsp. vanilla essence
- ✓ Parchment or butter paper to line the tin

Directions:
1. Mix the ingredients together to create a batter that is smooth and thick.
2. Grease a cake tin with butter and line it with the parchment or butter paper.
3. Transfer the batter into the tin.
4. Preheat the fryer to 300 Fahrenheit for five minutes. You will need to place the tin in the basket and cover it. Cook the cake for fifteen minutes and check whether or not the cake is cooked using a toothpick. Remove the tin and cut the cake into slices and serve.

95. Banana Pancakes

Prep.Time: 10 min - **Cooking Time:** 15 min - **Servings:** 12

Ingredients:
- ✓ 4 ripe bananas (shredded)
- ✓ 1 ½ cups almond flour
- ✓ 3 eggs
- ✓ 2 tsp. dried basil
- ✓ 2 tsp. dried parsley
- ✓ Salt and Pepper to taste
- ✓ 3 tbsp. Butter

Directions:
1. Preheat the air fryer to 250 Fahrenheit.
2. In a small bowl, mix the ingredients together. Ensure that the mixture is smooth and well balanced.
3. Take a pancake mold and grease it with butter. Add the batter to the mold and place it in the air fryer basket.
4. Cook till both the sides of the pancake have browned on both sides and serve with maple syrup.

96. Pumpkin Pancakes

Prep.Time: 15 min - **Cooking Time:** 15 min - **Servings:** 12

Ingredients:
- ✓ 1 large pumpkin (shredded)
- ✓ 1 ½ cups almond flour
- ✓ 3 eggs
- ✓ 2 tsp. dried basil
- ✓ 2 tsp. dried parsley
- ✓ Salt and Pepper to taste
- ✓ 3 tbsp. Butter

Directions:
1. Preheat the air fryer to 250 Fahrenheit.
2. In a small bowl, mix the ingredients together. Ensure that the mixture is smooth and well balanced.
3. Take a pancake mold and grease it with butter. Add the batter to the mold and place it in the air fryer basket.
4. Cook till both the sides of the pancake have browned on both sides and serve with maple syrup.

97. Oats Muffins

Prep.Time: 10 min - **Cooking Time:** 20 min - **Servings:** 12

Ingredients:
- ✓ 2 cups All-purpose flour
- ✓ 1 ½ cup milk
- ✓ ½ tsp. baking powder
- ✓ ½ tsp. baking soda
- ✓ 2 tbsp. butter
- ✓ 1 cup sugar
- ✓ 3 tsp. vinegar
- ✓ 1 cup oats
- ✓ ½ tsp. vanilla essence
- ✓ Muffin cups or butter paper cups

Directions:
1. Mix the ingredients together and use your fingers to get a crumbly mixture.
2. You will need to divide the milk into two parts and add one part to the baking soda and the other to the vinegar. Now, mix both the milk mixtures together and wait till the milk begins to foam. Add this to the crumbly mixture and begin to whisk the ingredients very fast. Once you have obtained a smooth batter, you will need to transfer the mixture into a muffin cup and set aside.
3. Preheat the fryer to 300 Fahrenheit for five minutes. You will need to place the muffin cups in the basket and cover it. Cook the muffins for fifteen minutes and check whether or not the muffins are cooked using a toothpick. Remove the cups and serve hot.

98. Vanilla and Oats Pudding

Prep.Time: 10 min - **Cooking Time:** 15 min - **Servings:** 8

Ingredients:
- ✓ 2 cups vanilla powder
- ✓ 2 cups milk
- ✓ 1 cup oats
- ✓ 2 tbsp. custard powder
- ✓ 3 tbsp. powdered sugar
- ✓ 3 tbsp. unsalted butter

Directions:
1. Boil the milk and the sugar in a pan and add the custard powder followed by the vanilla powder followed by the oats and stir till you get a thick mixture.
2. Preheat the fryer to 300 Fahrenheit for five minutes. Place the dish in the basket and reduce the temperature to 250 Fahrenheit. Cook for ten minutes and set aside to cool.

99. Baked Yoghurt

Prep.Time: 15 min - **Cooking Time:** 20 minutes - **Servings:** 10

Ingredients:
- ✓ 2 cups condensed milk
- ✓ 2 cups yoghurt
- ✓ 2 cups fresh cream

For garnishing:
- ✓ 1 cup fresh strawberries
- ✓ 1 cup fresh blueberries
- ✓ 1 cup blackberries
- ✓ Handful of mint leaves
- ✓ 3 tsp. sugar
- ✓ 4 tsp. water

Directions:
1. Mix the ingredients together and create a thick mixture. Transfer this into baking bowls ensuring that you do not overfill.
2. Preheat the fryer to 300 Fahrenheit for five minutes. You will need to place the bowls in the basket and cover it. Cook it for fifteen minutes. When you shake the bowls, the mixture should just shake but not break.
3. Leave it in the refrigerator to set and then arrange the fruits, garnish and serve.

100. Fruit Tarts

Prep.Time: 15 min - **Cooking Time:** 15 min - **Servings:** 8

Ingredients:
- ✓ 1 ½ cup plain flour
- ✓ ½ cup cocoa powder
- ✓ 3 tbsp. unsalted butter
- ✓ 2 tbsp. powdered sugar
- ✓ 2 cups cold water
- ✓ 1 tbsp. sliced cashew

For Truffle filling:
- ✓ 2 cups mixed sliced fruits
- ✓ 1 cup fresh cream
- ✓ 3 tbsp. butter

Directions:
1. Knead all the ingredients together using milk into dough that is soft.
2. Now, roll the dough out and cut into two circles. Press the dough into the pie tins and prick on all sides using a fork.
3. Mix the ingredients for the filling in a bowl. Make sure that it is a little thick. Add the filling to the pie and cover it with the second round.
4. Preheat the fryer to 300 Fahrenheit for five minutes. You will need to place the tin in the basket and cover it. When the pastry has turned golden brown, you will need to remove the tin and let it cool. Cut into slices and serve with a dollop of cream.

101. Cucumber Pancakes

Prep.Time: 15 min - **Cooking Time:** 10 min - **Servings:** 12

Ingredients:
- ✓ 5 medium cucumbers (shredded)
- ✓ 1 ½ cups almond flour
- ✓ 3 eggs
- ✓ 2 tsp. dried basil
- ✓ 2 tsp. dried parsley
- ✓ Salt and Pepper to taste
- ✓ 3 tbsp. Butter

Directions:
1. Preheat the air fryer to 250 Fahrenheit.
2. In a small bowl, mix the ingredients together. Ensure that the mixture is smooth and well balanced.
3. Take a pancake mold and grease it with butter. Add the batter to the mold and place it in the air fryer basket.
4. Cook till both the sides of the pancake have browned on both sides and serve with maple syrup.

102. Honey and Oats Cookie

Prep.Time: 15 min - **Cooking Time:** 20 min - **Servings:** 8

Ingredients:
- ✓ 1 cup all-purpose flour
- ✓ 1 cups flour
- ✓ ½ cup oats
- ✓ 1 tsp. baking powder
- ✓ 1 tbsp. liquid glucose
- ✓ 2 tbsp. powdered sugar
- ✓ ½ cup milk
- ✓ 1 tbsp. unsalted butter
- ✓ 2 tsp. honey

Directions:
1. Mix the dry ingredients together in a large bowl and warm the glucose with a little water. Mix the glucose, honey and the butter to the bowl followed by the milk. You will need to roll the dough using a pin.
2. Now, create cookies and set them on a prepared baking tray.
3. Preheat the fryer to 300 Fahrenheit for five minutes. Place the baking tray in the basket and reduce the temperature to 250 Fahrenheit. Turn the cookies in the tray to ensure that they are cooked uniformly.
4. When the cookies have cooled, store them in an airtight container.

103. Honey Banana Muffins

Prep.Time: 15 min - **Cooking Time:** 20 min - **Servings:** 12

Ingredients:
- ✓ 2 cups wheat flour
- ✓ 1 ½ cup milk
- ✓ ½ tsp. baking powder
- ✓ ½ tsp. baking soda
- ✓ 2 tbsp. butter
- ✓ 2 cups mashed banana
- ✓ 1 tbsp. honey
- ✓ Muffin cups

Directions:
1. Mix the ingredients together and use your fingers to get a crumbly mixture.
2. Add the baking soda to the milk and mix continuously. Add this milk to the mixture and create a batter, which you will need to transfer to the muffin cups.
3. Preheat the fryer to 300 Fahrenheit for five minutes. You will need to place the muffin cups in the basket and cover it. Cook the muffins for fifteen minutes and check whether or not the muffins are cooked using a toothpick. Remove the cups and serve hot.

104. Chocolate Cake

Prep.Time: 10 min - **Cooking Time:** 15 min - **Servings:** 12

Ingredients:
- ✓ 1 tbsp. unsalted butter
- ✓ 2 tbsp. water
- ✓ 2 tbsp. cocoa powder
- ✓ 3 tbsp. melted dark chocolate
- ✓ 1 cup all-purpose flour
- ✓ ½ cup condensed milk

Directions:
1. Add the ingredients together and whisk till you get a smooth mixture.
2. Prepare a tin by greasing it with butter. Transfer the mixture into the tin. Preheat the fryer to 300 Fahrenheit for five minutes. You will need to place the tin in the basket and cover it. Check whether the cake has risen well. When the cake has cooled, garnish with chocolate chips and serve.

105. Buko Pie

Prep.Time: 15 min - **Cooking Time:** 20 minutes - **Servings:** 12

Ingredients:
- ✓ 1 ½ cup plain flour
- ✓ 3 tbsp. unsalted butter
- ✓ 2 tbsp. powdered sugar
- ✓ 2 cups cold water
- ✓ 1 tbsp. sliced cashew

Filling:
- ✓ 1 cup shredded coconut
- ✓ 2 young coconuts (Remove the flesh)
- ✓ 1 cup fresh cream
- ✓ 3 tbsp. butter

Directions:
1. Mix the ingredients together to form a crumbly mixture. Knead the mixture with cold milk and wrap it. Roll the dough out into two large circles and press that dough into the pie tin and prick the sides with a fork.
2. Cook the ingredients for the filling on a low flame and pour into the tin.
3. Cover the pie tin with the second round.
4. Preheat the fryer to 300 Fahrenheit for five minutes. You will need to place the tin in the basket and cover it. When the pastry has turned golden brown, you will need to remove the tin and let it cool. Cut into slices and serve with a dollop of cream

106. Banoffee Pie

Prep.Time: 15 min - **Cooking Time:** 15 min - **Servings:** 12

Ingredients:
- ✓ 1 ½ cup plain flour
- ✓ 3 tbsp. unsalted butter
- ✓ 2 tbsp. powdered sugar
- ✓ 2 cups cold water
- ✓ 1 tbsp. sliced cashew

Filling:
- ✓ 2 cups sliced banana
- ✓ 1 cup toffee
- ✓ 1 cup fresh cream
- ✓ 3 tbsp. butter

Directions:
1. Mix the ingredients together to form a crumbly mixture. Knead the mixture with cold milk and wrap it. Roll the dough out into two large circles and press that dough into the pie tin and prick the sides with a fork.
2. Cook the ingredients for the filling on a low flame and pour into the tin.
3. Cover the pie tin with the second round.
4. Preheat the fryer to 300 Fahrenheit for five minutes. You will need to place the tin in the basket and cover it. When the pastry has turned golden brown, you will need to remove the tin and let it cool. Cut into slices and serve with a dollop of cream

107. Strawberry Muffins

Prep.Time: 15 min - **Cooking Time:** 20 min - **Servings:** 12

Ingredients:
- ✓ 2 cups All-purpose flour
- ✓ 1 ½ cup milk
- ✓ ½ tsp. baking powder
- ✓ ½ tsp. baking soda
- ✓ 2 tbsp. butter
- ✓ 1 cup sugar
- ✓ 3 tsp. vinegar
- ✓ ½ cup chocolate chips
- ✓ ½ tsp. vanilla essence
- ✓ Muffin cups or butter paper cups

Directions:
1. Mix the ingredients together and use your fingers to get a crumbly mixture.
2. Add the baking soda and the vinegar to the milk and mix continuously. Add this milk to the mixture and create a batter that you will need to transfer to the muffin cups.
3. Preheat the fryer to 300 Fahrenheit for five minutes. You will need to place the muffin cups in the basket and cover it. Cook the muffins for fifteen minutes and check whether or not the muffins are cooked using a toothpick. Remove the cups and serve hot.

108. Vanilla Brownies

Prep.Time: 15 min - **Cooking Time:** 15 min - **Servings:** 12

Ingredients:
- ✓ 1 tbsp. unsalted butter (It is best to have this softened or melted)
- ✓ 2 tbsp. water
- ✓ ½ cup chopped nuts (You could use mixed nuts if you prefer)
- ✓ 3 tbsp. vanilla essence
- ✓ 2 cups all-purpose flour (You will need to split it up as half a cup, two tbsp. and one tsp.)
- ✓ ½ cup condensed milk

Directions:
1. Add the ingredients together and whisk till you get a smooth mixture.
2. Prepare a tin by greasing it with butter. Transfer the mixture into the tin. Preheat the fryer to 300 Fahrenheit for five minutes. You will need to place the tin in the basket and cover it. Check whether the brownies have been cooked using a knife or a toothpick and remove the tray. When the brownies have cooled, cut them and serve with a dollop of ice cream.

109. Bread Pudding

Prep.Time: 10 min - **Cooking Time:** 15 min - **Servings:** 6

Ingredients:
- ✓ 6 slices bread
- ✓ 2 cups milk
- ✓ 2 tbsp. custard powder
- ✓ 3 tbsp. powdered sugar
- ✓ 3 tbsp. unsalted butter

Directions:
1. Spread butter and jam on the slices of bread and cut them into the shapes you would like. Place them in a greased dish.
2. Boil the milk and the sugar in a pan and add the custard powder and stir till you get a thick mixture.
3. Preheat the fryer to 300 Fahrenheit for five minutes. Place the dish in the basket and reduce the temperature to 250 Fahrenheit. Cook for ten minutes and set aside to cool.

110. Muffins and Jam

Prep.Time: 15 min - **Cooking Time:** 15 min - **Servings:** 12

Ingredients:
- ✓ 1 cup + 2 tbsp. powdered sugar
- ✓ 1 ½ cups + 2 tbsp. all-purpose flour
- ✓ 1 tsp. baking powder
- ✓ ½ tsp. baking soda
- ✓ 2 tbsp. jam
- ✓ 1 tbsp. unsalted butter
- ✓ 2 cups buttermilk
- ✓ Parchment paper

Directions:
1. In a bowl, add the flour and the buttermilk. Fold the mixture using a spatula. Add the jam and whisk the ingredients to ensure that the jam has thinned. Add the remaining ingredients to the bowl and continue to mix the ingredients. Do not mix too much.
2. Grease the muffin cups and line them with the parchment paper. Transfer the mixture into the cups and set them aside. Preheat the fryer to 300 Fahrenheit for five minutes. Place the muffin cups in the basket and reduce the temperature to 250 Fahrenheit. Cool in the basket and serve warm.

111. Honey and Nut Pie

Prep.Time: 15 min - **Cooking Time:** 20 minutes - **Servings:** 12

Ingredients:
- ✓ 1 cup plain flour
- ✓ 1 tbsp. unsalted butter
- ✓ 4tsp. powdered sugar
- ✓ 2 cups cold milk

For Honey and Nut filling:
- ✓ 1 cup roasted mixed nuts
- ✓ 3 tbsp. honey
- ✓ 2 tbsp. sugar
- ✓ ½ tsp. cinnamon
- ✓ 2 tsp. lemon juice

Directions:
1. Mix the ingredients together to form a crumbly mixture. Knead the mixture with cold milk and wrap it. Roll the dough out into two large circles and press that dough into the pie tin and prick the sides with a fork.
2. Cook the ingredients for the filling on a low flame and pour into the tin.
3. Cover the pie tin with the second round.
4. Preheat the fryer to 300 Fahrenheit for five minutes. You will need to place the tin in the basket and cover it. When the pastry has turned golden brown, you will need to remove the tin and let it cool. Cut into slices and serve with a dollop of cream

112. Apricot Blackberry Crumble

Prep.Time: 15 min - **Cooking Time:** 25 min - **Servings:** 4

Ingredients:
- ✓ 2 cups fresh apricots
- ✓ 2 cups fresh blackberries
- ✓ 1 cup sugar
- ✓ 3 tsp. lemon juice
- ✓ 1 ½ cups flour
- ✓ 3 tbsp. unsalted butter

Directions:
1. Preheat the fryer to 300 Fahrenheit.
2. Cut the fruits and place them in a bowl along with half the sugar and the lemon juice. Mix the ingredients well and scoop them into an oven dish and spread them out.
3. In another bowl, mix the flour with remaining sugar, followed by the butter and 2 tbsp. water. Make sure that the mixture is crumbly.
4. Put the dish in the basket and bake for twenty minutes until the rings have turned golden brown. Serve warm.

113. Coconut and Plantain Pancakes

Prep.Time: 10 min - **Cooking Time:** 15 min - **Servings:** 8

Ingredients:

- ✓ 2 fresh plantains (shredded)
- ✓ 1 cup shredded coconut
- ✓ 1 ½ cups almond flour
- ✓ 3 eggs
- ✓ 2 tsp. dried basil
- ✓ 2 tsp. dried parsley
- ✓ Salt and Pepper to taste
- ✓ 3 tbsp. Butter

Directions:

1. Preheat the air fryer to 250 Fahrenheit.
2. In a small bowl, mix the ingredients together. Ensure that the mixture is smooth and well balanced.
3. Take a pancake mold and grease it with butter. Add the batter to the mold and place it in the air fryer basket.
4. Cook till both the sides of the pancake have browned on both sides and serve with maple syrup.

114. Bacon and Egg Pie

Prep.Time: 15 min - **Cooking Time:** 15 min - **Servings:** 12

Ingredients:

- ✓ 1 ½ cup plain flour
- ✓ 3 tbsp. unsalted butter
- ✓ 2 tbsp. powdered sugar
- ✓ 2 cups cold water
- ✓ 1 tbsp. sliced cashew

Filling:
- ✓ 1 cup scrambled egg
- ✓ 8 slices bacon
- ✓ 3 tbsp. butter

Directions:

1. Mix the ingredients together to form a crumbly mixture. Knead the mixture with cold milk and wrap it. Roll the dough out into two large circles and press that dough into the pie tin and prick the sides with a fork.
2. Cook the ingredients for the filling on a low flame and pour into the tin.
3. Cover the pie tin with the second round.
4. Preheat the fryer to 300 Fahrenheit for five minutes. You will need to place the tin in the basket and cover it. When the pastry has turned golden brown, you will need to remove the tin and let it cool. Cut into slices and serve with a dollop of cream.

115. Papaya Pancakes

Prep.Time: 10 min - **Cooking Time:** 10 min - **Servings:** 8

Ingredients:

- ✓ 1 cup grated papaya
- ✓ 1 ½ cups almond flour
- ✓ 3 eggs
- ✓ 2 tsp. dried basil
- ✓ 2 tsp. dried parsley
- ✓ Salt and Pepper to taste
- ✓ 3 tbsp. Butter

Directions:

1. Preheat the air fryer to 250 Fahrenheit.
2. In a small bowl, mix the ingredients together. Ensure that the mixture is smooth and well balanced.
3. Take a pancake mold and grease it with butter. Add the batter to the mold and place it in the air fryer basket.
4. Cook till both the sides of the pancake have browned on both sides and serve with maple syrup.

116. Rambutan Cakes

Prep.Time: 15 min - **Cooking Time:** 20 min - **Servings:** 18

Ingredients:

- ✓ 2 cups All-purpose flour
- ✓ 1 ½ cup milk
- ✓ ½ tsp. baking powder
- ✓ ½ tsp. baking soda
- ✓ 2 tbsp. butter
- ✓ 1 cup sugar
- ✓ 1 cup minced rambutan
- ✓ 2 tsp. vinegar
- ✓ Muffin cups or butter paper cups

Directions:

1. Mix the ingredients together and use your fingers to get a crumbly mixture.
2. Add the baking soda and the vinegar to the milk and mix continuously. Add this milk to the mixture and create a batter, which you will need to transfer to the muffin cups.
3. Preheat the fryer to 300 Fahrenheit for five minutes. You will need to place the muffin cups in the basket and cover it. Cook the muffins for fifteen minutes and check whether or not the muffins are cooked using a toothpick. Remove the cups and serve hot

117. Poached pear Waffles

Prep.Time: 15 min - **Cooking Time:** 20 minutes - **Servings:** 24

Ingredients:

- ✓ 3 cups all-purpose powder
- ✓ 3 eggs
- ✓ 3 tbsp. Butter
- ✓ 1 cup sliced poached pear

Directions:

1. Preheat the air fryer to 250 Fahrenheit.
2. In a small bowl, mix the ingredients, except for the poached pear, together.
3. Ensure that the mixture is smooth and well balanced.
4. Take a waffle mold and grease it with butter. Add the batter to the mold and place it in the air fryer basket. Cook till both the sides have browned. Create a cavity and add the poached pears or serve them as a garnish.

118. Jaggery Payasam

Prep.Time: 10 min - **Cooking Time:** 15 min - **Servings:** 8

Ingredients:

- ✓ 2 cups milk
- ✓ 1 cup melted jaggery
- ✓ 2 tbsp. custard powder
- ✓ 3 tbsp. powdered sugar
- ✓ 3 tbsp. unsalted butter

Directions:

1. Boil the milk and the sugar in a pan and add the custard powder followed by the jaggery and stir till you get a thick mixture. You will need to stir continuously.
2. Preheat the fryer to 300 Fahrenheit for five minutes. Place the dish in the basket and reduce the temperature to 250 Fahrenheit. Cook for ten minutes and set aside to cool.

119. Vegetable and Oats Muffins

Prep.Time: 15 min - **Cooking Time:** 20 min - **Servings:** 12

Ingredients:

- 1 cup + 2 tbsp. whole wheat flour
- 1 ½ cup milk
- ½ tsp. baking powder
- ½ tsp. baking soda
- 2 tbsp. butter
- 1 cup + 3 tsp. sugar
- 3 tsp. vinegar
- ½ cup oats
- 1 cup mixed vegetables
- ½ tsp. vanilla essence (This is an optional ingredient.)
- Muffin cups or butter paper cups

Directions:

1. Mix the ingredients together and use your fingers to get a crumbly mixture.
2. Add the baking soda and the vinegar to the milk and mix continuously. Add this milk to the mixture and create a batter, which you will need to transfer to the muffin cups.
3. Preheat the fryer to 300 Fahrenheit for five minutes. You will need to place the muffin cups in the basket and cover it. Cook the muffins for fifteen minutes and check whether or not the muffins are cooked using a toothpick. Remove the cups and serve hot.

120. Banana Cream Pie

Prep.Time: 10 min - **Cooking Time:** 15 min - **Servings:** 12

Ingredients:

- 1 ½ cup plain flour
- 3 tbsp. unsalted butter
- 2 tbsp. powdered sugar
- 2 cups cold water
- 1 tbsp. sliced cashew

Filling:
- 2 cups sliced banana
- 1 cup fresh cream
- 3 tbsp. butter

Directions:

1. Mix the ingredients together to form a crumbly mixture. Knead the mixture with cold milk and wrap it. Roll the dough out into two large circles and press that dough into the pie tin and prick the sides with a fork.
2. Cook the ingredients for the filling on a low flame and pour into the tin.
3. Cover the pie tin with the second round.
4. Preheat the fryer to 300 Fahrenheit for five minutes. You will need to place the tin in the basket and cover it. When the pastry has turned golden brown, you will need to remove the tin and let it cool. Cut into slices and serve with a dollop of cream.

121. Strawberry Pudding (alternative version)

Prep.Time: 10 min - **Cooking Time:** 15 min - **Servings:** 4

Ingredients:

- 2 cups strawberry powder
- 2 cups milk
- 2 tbsp. custard powder
- 3 tbsp. powdered sugar
- 3 tbsp. unsalted butter

Directions:

1. Boil the milk and the sugar in a pan and add the custard powder followed by the strawberry powder and stir till you get a thick mixture.
2. Preheat the fryer to 300 Fahrenheit for five minutes. Place the dish in the basket and reduce the temperature to 250 Fahrenheit. Cook for ten minutes and set aside to cool.

122. Strawberry Pancakes

Prep.Time: 10 min - **Cooking Time:** 15 min - **Servings:** 8

Ingredients:

- 2 cups minced strawberries
- 1 ½ cups almond flour
- 3 eggs
- 2 tsp. dried basil
- 2 tsp. dried parsley
- Salt and Pepper to taste
- 3 tbsp. Butter

Directions:

1. Preheat the air fryer to 250 Fahrenheit.
2. In a small bowl, mix the ingredients together. Ensure that the mixture is smooth and well balanced.
3. Take a pancake mold and grease it with butter. Add the batter to the mold and place it in the air fryer basket. Cook till both the sides of the pancake have browned on both sides and serve with maple syrup.

123. Bougatsa

Prep.Time: 10 min - **Cooking Time:** 20 minutes - **Servings:** 8

Ingredients:

- 1 ½ cup plain flour
- 2 cups cold water
- 1 tbsp. sliced cashew
- 2 tbsp. custard powder
- 3 tbsp. unsalted butter
- 2 tbsp. powdered sugar

Filling:
- 2 cups minced meat
- 1 cup cheddar cheese (melted)
- 1 cup fresh cream
- 3 tbsp. butter

Directions:

1. Mix the ingredients together to form a crumbly mixture. Knead the mixture with cold milk and wrap it. Roll the dough out into two large circles and press that dough into the pie tin and prick the sides with a fork.
2. Cook the ingredients for the filling on a low flame and pour into the tin.
3. Cover the pie tin with the second round.
4. Preheat the fryer to 300 Fahrenheit for five minutes. You will need to place the tin in the basket and cover it. When the pastry has turned golden brown, you will need to remove the tin and let it cool. Cut into slices and serve with a dollop of cream.

124. Bisteeya

Prep.Time: 10 min - **Cooking Time:** 15 min - **Servings:** 8

Ingredients:

- 1 ½ cup almond flour
- 3 tbsp. unsalted butter
- 2 tbsp. powdered sugar
- 2 cups cold water
- 1 tbsp. sliced cashew

Filling:
- 2 cups minced chicken
- 1 cup sliced almonds
- 3 tbsp. butter

Directions:

1. Mix the ingredients together to form a crumbly mixture. Knead the mixture with cold milk and wrap it. Roll the dough out into two large circles and press that dough into the pie tin and prick the sides with a fork.
2. Cook the ingredients for the filling on a low flame and our into the tin.
   Cover the pie tin with the second round.
3. Preheat the fryer to 300 Fahrenheit for five minutes. You will need to place the tin in the basket and cover it. When the pastry has turned golden brown, you will need to remove the tin and let it cool. Cut into slices and serve with a dollop of cream.

125. Blueberry Cake

Prep.Time: 10 min - **Cooking Time:** 20 min - **Servings:** 4

Ingredients:
- ✓ 1 tbsp. unsalted butter
- ✓ 2 tbsp. water
- ✓ 2 cups sliced blueberries
- ✓ 1 cup all-purpose flour
- ✓ ½ cup condensed milk

Directions:
1. Add the ingredients together and whisk till you get a smooth mixture.
2. Prepare a tin by greasing it with butter. Transfer the mixture into the tin. Preheat the fryer to 300 Fahrenheit for five minutes. You will need to place the tin in the basket and cover it. Check whether the cake has risen well. When the cake has cooled, garnish with chocolate chips and serve.

126. Dark chocolate Muffins

Prep.Time: 15 min - **Cooking Time:** 20 min - **Servings:** 12

Ingredients:
- ✓ 2 cups All-purpose flour
- ✓ 1 ½ cup milk
- ✓ 3 tbsp. dark cocoa powder
- ✓ ½ tsp. baking powder
- ✓ ½ tsp. baking soda
- ✓ 2 tbsp. butter
- ✓ 1 tbsp. sugar
- ✓ Muffin cups

Directions:
1. Mix the ingredients together and use your fingers to get a crumbly mixture.
2. Add the baking soda to the milk and mix continuously. Add this milk to the mixture and create a batter, which you will need to transfer to the muffin cups.
3. Preheat the fryer to 300 Fahrenheit for five minutes. You will need to place the muffin cups in the basket and cover it. Cook the muffins for fifteen minutes and check whether or not the muffins are cooked using a toothpick. Remove the cups and serve hot.

127. Cranberry Pudding

Prep.Time: 10 min - **Cooking Time:** 15 min - **Servings:** 8

Ingredients:
- ✓ 1 cup cranberry juice
- ✓ 2 cups milk
- ✓ 2 tbsp. corn flour
- ✓ 3 tbsp. powdered sugar
- ✓ 3 tbsp. unsalted butter

Directions:
1. Boil the milk and the sugar in a pan and add the custard powder followed by the cranberry juice and stir till you get a thick mixture.
2. Preheat the fryer to 300 Fahrenheit for five minutes. Place the dish in the basket and reduce the temperature to 250 Fahrenheit. Cook for ten minutes and set aside to cool.

Nutrition: calories 111 - Fat 5 - Fiber 6 - Carbs 12 - Protein 6

128. Fruit custard

Prep.Time: 10 min - **Cooking Time:** 15 min - **Servings:** 8

Ingredients:
- ✓ 1 cup mixed fruits
- ✓ 2 cups milk
- ✓ 2 tbsp. custard powder
- ✓ 3 tbsp. powdered sugar
- ✓ 3 tbsp. unsalted butter

Directions:
1. Boil the milk and the sugar in a pan and add the custard powder followed by the mixed fruits and stir till you get a thick mixture.
2. Preheat the fryer to 300 Fahrenheit for five minutes. Place the dish in the basket and reduce the temperature to 250 Fahrenheit. Cook for ten minutes and set aside to cool

Nutrition: calories 140 - Fat 2 - Fiber 2 - Carbs 7 - Protein 10

129. Orange Pudding

Prep.Time: 10 min - **Cooking Time:** 15 minutes - **Servings:** 6

Ingredients:
- ✓ 1 cup orange juice
- ✓ 2 cups milk
- ✓ 2 tbsp. custard powder
- ✓ 3 tbsp. powdered sugar
- ✓ 3 tbsp. unsalted butter

Directions:
1. Boil the milk and the sugar in a pan and add the custard powder followed by the orange juice and stir till you get a thick mixture.
2. Preheat the fryer to 300 Fahrenheit for five minutes. Place the dish in the basket and reduce the temperature to 250 Fahrenheit. Cook for ten minutes and set aside to cool.

130. Butterscotch Muffins

Prep.Time: 10 min - **Cooking Time:** 20 min - **Servings:** 8

Ingredients:
- ✓ 2 cups cornstarch
- ✓ 1 ½ cup milk
- ✓ 3 eggs
- ✓ 2 tbsp. butter
- ✓ 2 tbsp. sugar
- ✓ 1 tsp. vanilla extract
- ✓ Muffin cups

Directions:
1. Mix the ingredients together and use your fingers to get a crumbly mixture.
2. Add the baking soda to the milk and mix continuously. Add this milk to the mixture and create a batter, which you will need to transfer to the muffin cups.
3. Preheat the fryer to 300 Fahrenheit for five minutes. You will need to place the muffin cups in the basket and cover it. Cook the muffins for fifteen minutes and check whether or not the muffins are cooked using a toothpick. Remove the cups and serve hot.

131. Cheddar Cheese Muffins

Prep.Time: 10 min - **Cooking Time:** 10 min - **Servings:** 12

Ingredients:
- ✓ 2 cups All-purpose flour
- ✓ 1 ½ cup milk
- ✓ ½ tsp. baking powder
- ✓ ½ tsp. baking soda
- ✓ 2 tbsp. butter
- ✓ 2 cups melted cheddar cheese
- ✓ 1 tbsp. sugar
- ✓ 2 tsp. vinegar
- ✓ Muffin cups

Directions:
3. In a bowl, mix butter with crumbled crackers, stir well, press on the bottom of a cake pan that fits your air fryer and keep in the fridge for now.
4. In another bowl, mix cream cheese with mascarpone, sweet potato puree, milk, cinnamon and vanilla and whisk really well.
5. Spread this over crust, introduce in your air fryer, cook at 300 degrees F for 4 minutes and keep in the fridge for a few hours before serving.

132. Lemon Poppy Cakes

Prep.Time: 15 min - **Cooking Time:** 20 min - **Servings:** 12

Ingredients:
- ✓ 2 cups All-purpose flour
- ✓ 1 ½ cup milk
- ✓ ½ tsp. baking powder
- ✓ ½ tsp. baking soda
- ✓ 2 tbsp. butter
- ✓ 1 tbsp. sugar
- ✓ 2 tbsp. lemon juice
- ✓ 2 tsp. vinegar
- ✓ 1 tbsp. crushed poppy seeds

Directions:
1. Mix the ingredients together and use your fingers to get a crumbly mixture.
2. Add the baking soda and the vinegar to the milk and mix continuously. Add this milk to the mixture and create a batter, which you will need to transfer to the muffin cups.
3. Preheat the fryer to 300 Fahrenheit for five minutes. You will need to place the muffin cups in the basket and cover it. Cook the muffins for fifteen minutes and check whether or not the muffins are cooked using a toothpick. Remove the cups and serve hot.

133. Corn Muffins

Prep.Time: 10 min - **Cooking Time:** 15 min - **Servings:** 12

Ingredients:
- ✓ 2 cups All-purpose flour
- ✓ 1 ½ cup milk
- ✓ ½ tsp. baking powder
- ✓ ½ tsp. baking soda
- ✓ 2 tbsp. butter
- ✓ 1 tbsp. sugar
- ✓ 2 tsp. vinegar
- ✓ 1 cup boiled corn
- ✓ Muffin cups

Directions:
1. Preheat the air fryer to 250 Fahrenheit.
2. In a small bowl, mix the ingredients, except for the jalapenos, together.
3. Ensure that the mixture is smooth and well balanced.
4. Take a waffle mold and grease it with butter. Add the batter to the mold and place it in the air fryer basket. Cook till both the sides have browned. Now, create a cavity and fill it with the jalapenos and serve.

134. Raspberry Buttermilk Cupcakes

Prep.Time: 15 min - **Cooking Time:** 20 min - **Servings:** 12

Ingredients:
- ✓ 2 cups All-purpose flour
- ✓ 1 ½ cup buttermilk
- ✓ ½ tsp. baking powder
- ✓ ½ tsp. baking soda
- ✓ 2 tbsp. butter
- ✓ 2 tbsp. sugar
- ✓ 2 cups sliced raspberries
- ✓ Muffin cups

Directions:
1. Mix the ingredients together and use your fingers to get a crumbly mixture.
2. Add the baking soda to the milk and mix continuously. Add this milk to the mixture and create a batter, which you will need to transfer to the muffin cups.
3. Preheat the fryer to 300 Fahrenheit for five minutes. You will need to place the muffin cups in the basket and cover it. Cook the muffins for fifteen minutes and check whether or not the muffins are cooked using a toothpick. Remove the cups and serve hot.

135. Vanilla Cake

Prep.Time: 10 min - **Cooking Time:** 15 min - **Servings:** 6

Ingredients:
- ✓ 1 tbsp. unsalted butter
- ✓ 2 tbsp. water
- ✓ 2 tsp. vanilla extract
- ✓ 1 cup all-purpose flour
- ✓ ½ cup condensed milk

Directions:
1. Add the ingredients together and whisk till you get a smooth mixture.
2. Prepare a tin by greasing it with butter. Transfer the mixture into the tin. Preheat the fryer to 300 Fahrenheit for five minutes. You will need to place the tin in the basket and cover it. Check whether the cake has risen well. Cool the cake down and serve.

136. Pumpkin Choco – Chip Muffins

Prep.Time: 10 min - **Cooking Time:** 20 min - **Servings:** 12

Ingredients:
- ✓ 2 cups All-purpose flour
- ✓ 1 ½ cup milk
- ✓ ½ tsp. baking powder
- ✓ ½ tsp. baking soda
- ✓ 2 tbsp. butter
- ✓ 2 cups grated pumpkin
- ✓ 1 tbsp. sugar
- ✓ 2 tsp. vinegar
- ✓ ½ cup chocolate chips
- ✓ Muffin cups

Directions:
1. Mix the ingredients together and use your fingers to get a crumbly mixture.
2. Add the baking soda and the vinegar to the milk and mix continuously. Add this milk to the mixture and create a batter, which you will need to transfer to the muffin cups.
3. Preheat the fryer to 300 Fahrenheit for five minutes. You will need to place the muffin cups in the basket and cover it. Cook the muffins for fifteen minutes and check whether or not the muffins are cooked using a toothpick. Remove the cups and serve hot

137. Bacon and Maple Muffins

Prep.Time: 15 min - **Cooking Time:** 20 min - **Servings:** 12

Ingredients:
- ✓ 2 cups All-purpose flour
- ✓ 1 ½ cup buttermilk
- ✓ ½ tsp. baking powder
- ✓ ½ tsp. baking soda
- ✓ 2 tbsp. butter
- ✓ 1 cup finely sliced bacon
- ✓ 2 tbsp. maple syrup
- ✓ Muffin cups

Directions:
1. Mix the ingredients together and use your fingers to get a crumbly mixture.
2. Add the baking soda to the milk and mix continuously. Add this milk to the mixture and create a batter, which you will need to transfer to the muffin cups.
3. Preheat the fryer to 300 Fahrenheit for five minutes. You will need to place the muffin cups in the basket and cover it. Cook the muffins for fifteen minutes and check whether or not the muffins are cooked using a toothpick. Remove the cups and serve hot.

138. Pineapple Pie

Prep.Time: 10 min - **Cooking Time:** 15 min - **Servings:** 8

Ingredients:
- ✓ 1 cup plain flour
- ✓ 1 tbsp. unsalted butter
- ✓ 4tsp. powdered sugar
- ✓ 2 cups cold milk
- ✓ Pineapple filling:
- ✓ ½ cup roasted nuts
- ✓ 1 pineapples (Peel and chop into slices)
- ✓ 2 tbsp. sugar
- ✓ ½ tsp. cinnamon
- ✓ 2 tsp. lemon juice

Directions:
1. Mix the ingredients together to form a crumbly mixture. Knead the mixture with cold milk and wrap it. Roll the dough out into two large circles and press that dough into the pie tin and prick the sides with a fork.
2. Cook the ingredients for the filling on a low flame and pour into the tin.
3. Cover the pie tin with the second round.
4. Preheat the fryer to 300 Fahrenheit for five minutes. You will need to place the tin in the basket and cover it. When the pastry has turned golden brown, you will need to remove the tin and let it cool. Cut into slices and serve with a dollop of cream.

139. The heatwave

Prep.Time: 10 min - **Cooking Time:** 20 minutes - **Servings:** 8

Ingredients:
- ✓ 1 cup plain flour
- ✓ 1 tbsp. unsalted butter
- ✓ 4tsp. powdered sugar
- ✓ 2 cups cold milk
- Filling:
- ✓ 1 cup sliced pineapple
- ✓ 1 cup sliced papaya
- ✓ 2 tbsp. sugar
- ✓ ½ tsp. cinnamon
- ✓ 2 tsp. lemon juice

Directions:
1. Mix the ingredients together to form a crumbly mixture. Knead the mixture with cold milk and wrap it. Roll the dough out into two large circles and press that dough into the pie tin and prick the sides with a fork.
2. Cook the ingredients for the filling on a low flame and pour into the tin
3. Cover the pie tin with the second round.
4. Preheat the fryer to 300 Fahrenheit for five minutes. You will need to place the tin in the basket and cover it. When the pastry has turned golden brown, you will need to remove the tin and let it cool. Cut into slices and serve with a dollop of cream.

140. Mixed fruit cupcake

Prep.Time: 10 min - **Cooking Time:** 15 min - **Servings:** 6

Ingredients:
- ✓ 1 tbsp. unsalted butter
- ✓ 2 tbsp. water
- ✓ 2 cups mixed fruit
- ✓ 1 cup all-purpose flour
- ✓ ½ cup condensed milk

Directions:
1. Add the ingredients together and whisk till you get a smooth mixture.
2. Prepare a tin by greasing it with butter. Transfer the mixture into the tin. Preheat the fryer to 300 Fahrenheit for five minutes. You will need to place the tin in the basket and cover it. Check whether the cake has risen well. Cool the cake down and serve.

141. Vanilla Cupcakes

Prep.Time: 10 min - **Cooking Time:** 20min - **Servings:** 12

Ingredients:
- ✓ 2 cups wheat flour
- ✓ 1 ½ cup milk
- ✓ ½ tsp. baking powder
- ✓ ½ tsp. baking soda
- ✓ 2 tbsp. butter
- ✓ 1 tbsp. honey
- ✓ 3 tbsp. vanilla extract
- ✓ 2 tsp. vinegar
- ✓ Muffin cups

Directions:
1. Mix the ingredients together and use your fingers to get a crumbly mixture.
2. Add the baking soda and the vinegar to the milk and mix continuously. Add this milk to the mixture and create a batter, which you will need to transfer to the muffin cups.
3. Preheat the fryer to 300 Fahrenheit for five minutes. You will need to place the muffin cups in the basket and cover it. Cook the muffins for fifteen minutes and check whether or not the muffins are cooked using a toothpick. Remove the cups and serve hot.

142. Watermelon Pie

Prep.Time: 10 min - **Cooking Time:** 15 min - **Servings:** 8

Ingredients:
- ✓ 1 cup plain flour
- ✓ 1 tbsp. unsalted butter
- ✓ 4tsp. powdered sugar
- ✓ 2 cups cold milk
- Filling:
- ✓ 1 cup frozen cubed pineapple
- ✓ 2 tbsp. sugar
- ✓ ½ tsp. cinnamon
- ✓ 2 tsp. lemon juice

Directions:
1. Mix the ingredients together to form a crumbly mixture. Knead the mixture with cold milk and wrap it. Roll the dough out into two large circles and press that dough into the pie tin and prick the sides with a fork.
2. Cook the ingredients for the filling on a low flame and pour into the tin.
3. Cover the pie tin with the second round.
4. Preheat the fryer to 300 Fahrenheit for five minutes. You will need to place the tin in the basket and cover it. When the pastry has turned golden brown, you will need to remove the tin and let it cool. Cut into slices and serve with a dollop of cream.

143. Pear muffin

Prep.Time: 15 min - **Cooking Time:** 20 min - **Servings:** 12

Ingredients:
- ✓ 2 cups All-purpose flour
- ✓ 1 ½ cup buttermilk
- ✓ ½ tsp. baking powder
- ✓ ½ tsp. baking soda
- ✓ 2 tbsp. butter
- ✓ 2 tbsp. sugar
- ✓ 2 cups sliced pears
- ✓ Muffin cups

Directions:
1. Mix the ingredients together and use your fingers to get a crumbly mixture.
2. Add the baking soda to the milk and mix continuously. Add this milk to the mixture and create a batter, which you will need to transfer to the muffin cups.
3. Preheat the fryer to 300 Fahrenheit for five minutes. You will need to place the muffin cups in the basket and cover it. Cook the muffins for fifteen minutes and check whether or not the muffins are cooked using a toothpick. Remove the cups and serve hot.

144. Corn Waffles

Prep.Time: 15 min - **Cooking Time:** 15 min - **Servings:** 12

Ingredients:
- ✓ 1 ½ cups almond flour
- ✓ 3 eggs
- ✓ 2 tsp. dried basil
- ✓ 2 tsp. dried parsley
- ✓ Salt and Pepper to taste
- ✓ 3 tbsp. Butter
- ✓ 2 cups boiled corn and mayonnaise

Directions:
1. Preheat the air fryer to 250 Fahrenheit.
2. In a small bowl, mix the ingredients, except for the corn and mayonnaise together. Ensure that the mixture is smooth and well balanced.
3. Take a waffle mold and grease it with butter. Add the batter to the mold and place it in the air fryer basket. Cook till both the sides have browned. Now, create a cavity and fill it with the corn and mayonnaise and serve.

Nutrition: calories 140 - Fat 2 - Fiber 2 - Carbs 7 - Protein 10

145. Jackfruit Pudding

Prep.Time: 10 min - **Cooking Time:** 15 minutes - **Servings:** 6

Ingredients:
- ✓ 2 cups grated jackfruit
- ✓ 2 cups milk
- ✓ 2 tbsp. custard powder
- ✓ 3 tbsp. powdered sugar
- ✓ 3 tbsp. unsalted butter

Directions:
1. Boil the milk and the sugar in a pan and add the custard powder followed by the orange juice and stir till you get a thick mixture.
2. Preheat the fryer to 300 Fahrenheit for five minutes. Place the dish in the basket and reduce the temperature to 250 Fahrenheit. Cook for ten minutes and set aside to cool.

146. Vanilla Cake

Prep.Time: 10 min - **Cooking Time:** 15 min - **Servings:** 8

Ingredients:
- ✓ 1 tbsp. unsalted butter
- ✓ 2 tbsp. water
- ✓ 2 tsp. vanilla extract
- ✓ 1 cup all-purpose flour
- ✓ ½ cup condensed milk

Directions:
1. Add the ingredients together and whisk till you get a smooth mixture.
2. Prepare a tin by greasing it with butter. Transfer the mixture into the tin. Preheat the fryer to 300 Fahrenheit for five minutes. You will need to place the tin in the basket and cover it. Check whether the cake has risen well. Cool the cake down and serve.

147. Apricot and Fig Muffins

Prep.Time: 15 min - **Cooking Time:** 20 min - **Servings:** 12

Ingredients:
- ✓ 2 cups wheat flour
- ✓ 1 ½ cup milk
- ✓ ½ tsp. baking powder
- ✓ ½ tsp. baking soda
- ✓ 2 tbsp. butter
- ✓ 1 tbsp. honey
- ✓ 2 cups sliced apricots
- ✓ 2 cups sliced figs
- ✓ 2 tsp. vinegar
- ✓ Muffin cups

Directions:
1. Mix the ingredients together and use your fingers to get a crumbly mixture.
2. Add the baking soda and the vinegar to the milk and mix continuously. Add this milk to the mixture and create a batter, which you will need to transfer to the muffin cups.
3. Preheat the fryer to 300 Fahrenheit for five minutes. You will need to place the muffin cups in the basket and cover it. Cook the muffins for fifteen minutes and check whether or not the muffins are cooked using a toothpick. Remove the cups and serve hot

148. Mango Muffins

Prep.Time: 15 min - **Cooking Time:** 20 min - **Servings:** 12

Ingredients:
- ✓ 2 cups All-purpose flour
- ✓ 1 ½ cup buttermilk
- ✓ ½ tsp. baking powder
- ✓ ½ tsp. baking soda
- ✓ 2 tbsp. butter
- ✓ 2 tbsp. maple syrup
- ✓ 2 cups mango pulp
- ✓ Muffin cups

Directions:
1. Mix the ingredients together and use your fingers to get a crumbly mixture.
2. Add the baking soda to the milk and mix continuously. Add this milk to the mixture and create a batter, which you will need to transfer to the muffin cups.
3. Preheat the fryer to 300 Fahrenheit for five minutes. You will need to place the muffin cups in the basket and cover it. Cook the muffins for fifteen minutes and check whether or not the muffins are cooked using a toothpick. Remove the cups and serve hot.

149. Citrus Custard

Prep.Time: 30 min - **Cooking Time:** 10 min - **Servings:** 8

Ingredients:
- ✓ 1 cup kiwis
- ✓ 1 tsp. lemon zest
- ✓ 1 tsp. orange zest
- ✓ 2 cups milk
- ✓ 2 tbsp. custard powder
- ✓ 3 tbsp. powdered sugar
- ✓ 3 tbsp. unsalted butter

Directions:
1. Boil the milk and the sugar in a pan and add the custard powder followed by the fruits and stir till you get a thick mixture.
2. Preheat the fryer to 300 Fahrenheit for five minutes. Place the dish in the basket and reduce the temperature to 250 Fahrenheit. Cook for ten minutes and set aside to cool

150. Mango Custard

Prep.Time: 30 min - **Cooking Time:** 10 min - **Servings:** 8

Ingredients:
- ✓ 2 cups mango slices
- ✓ 2 cups milk
- ✓ 2 tbsp. custard powder
- ✓ 3 tbsp. powdered sugar
- ✓ 3 tbsp. unsalted butter

Directions:
1. Boil the milk and the sugar in a pan and add the custard powder followed by the mango slices and stir till you get a thick mixture.
2. Preheat the fryer to 300 Fahrenheit for five minutes. Place the dish in the basket and reduce the temperature to 250 Fahrenheit. Cook for ten minutes and set aside to cool.

151. Custard Apple Cake

Prep.Time: 20 min - **Cooking Time:** 15 minutes - **Servings:** 6

Ingredients:
- ✓ 1 tbsp. unsalted butter
- ✓ 2 tbsp. water
- ✓ 2 tsp. vanilla extract
- ✓ 1 cup corn flour
- ✓ 1 cup custard apple juice
- ✓ ½ cup condensed milk

Directions:
1. Add the ingredients together and whisk till you get a smooth mixture.
2. Prepare a tin by greasing it with butter. Transfer the mixture into the tin.
3. Preheat the fryer to 300 Fahrenheit for five minutes. You will need to place the tin in the basket and cover it. Check whether the cake has risen well. Cool the cake down and serve

152. Mangosteen Pudding

Prep.Time: 30 min - **Cooking Time:** 10 min - **Servings:** 8

Ingredients:
- ✓ 1 cup mangosteen pulp
- ✓ 2 cups milk
- ✓ 2 tbsp. corn flour
- ✓ 3 tbsp. powdered sugar
- ✓ 3 tbsp. unsalted butter

Directions:
1. Boil the milk and the sugar in a pan and add the custard powder followed by the mangosteen pulp and stir till you get a thick mixture.
2. Preheat the fryer to 300 Fahrenheit for five minutes. Place the dish in the basket and reduce the temperature to 250 Fahrenheit. Cook for ten minutes and set aside to cool.

153. Apple Pudding

Prep.Time: 30 min - **Cooking Time:** 10 min - **Servings:** 8

Ingredients:
- ✓ 1 cup apple pulp
- ✓ 2 cups milk
- ✓ 2 tbsp. custard powder
- ✓ 3 tbsp. powdered sugar
- ✓ 3 tbsp. unsalted butter
- ✓ 1 cup strawberry slices

Directions:
1. Boil the milk and the sugar in a pan and add the custard powder followed by the apple pulp and stir till you get a thick mixture.
2. Preheat the fryer to 300 Fahrenheit for five minutes. Place the dish in the basket and reduce the temperature to 250 Fahrenheit. Cook for ten minutes and set aside to cool. Garnish with strawberry.

154. Plum Pudding

Prep.Time: 30 min - **Cooking Time:** 10 min - **Servings:** 8

Ingredients:
- ✓ 1 cup plum pulp
- ✓ 2 cups milk
- ✓ 2 tbsp. custard powder
- ✓ 3 tbsp. powdered sugar
- ✓ 3 tbsp. unsalted butter

Directions:
1. Boil the milk and the sugar in a pan and add the custard powder followed by the banana juice and stir till you get a thick mixture.
2. Preheat the fryer to 300 Fahrenheit for five minutes. Place the dish in the basket and reduce the temperature to 250 Fahrenheit. Cook for ten minutes and set aside to cool.

155. Walnut Milk

Prep.Time: 30 min - **Cooking Time:** 10 min - **Servings:** 8

Ingredients:
- ✓ 2 cups walnut powder
- ✓ 2 cups milk
- ✓ 1 tsp. gelatin
- ✓ 2 tbsp. custard powder
- ✓ 3 tbsp. powdered sugar
- ✓ 3 tbsp. unsalted butter

Directions:
1. Boil the milk and the sugar in a pan and add the custard powder followed by the walnut powder and stir till you get a thick mixture. Add the gelatin and mix the ingredients well.
2. Preheat the fryer to 300 Fahrenheit for five minutes. Place the dish in the basket and reduce the temperature to 250 Fahrenheit. Cook for ten minutes and set aside to cool.

156. Barbadine Pudding

Prep.Time: 30 min - **Cooking Time:** 10 min - **Servings:** 8

Ingredients:
- ✓ 1 cup barbadine pulp
- ✓ 2 cups milk
- ✓ 2 tbsp. custard powder
- ✓ 3 tbsp. powdered sugar
- ✓ 3 tbsp. unsalted butter
- ✓ 1 cup strawberry slices

Directions:
1. Boil the milk and the sugar in a pan and add the custard powder followed by the barbadine pulp and stir till you get a thick mixture.
2. Preheat the fryer to 300 Fahrenheit for five minutes. Place the dish in the basket and reduce the temperature to 250 Fahrenheit. Cook for ten minutes and set aside to cool. Garnish with strawberry.

157. Blueberry Caramel

Prep.Time: 30 min - **Cooking Time:** 10 min - **Servings:** 8

Ingredients:
- ✓ 2 cups milk
- ✓ 2 cups custard powder
- ✓ 3 tbsp. powdered sugar
- ✓ 1 cup sliced blueberry
- ✓ 3 tbsp. unsalted butter
- ✓ 4 tbsp. caramel

Directions:
1. Boil the milk and the sugar in a pan and add the custard powder and stir till you get a thick mixture. Add the blueberry slices and mix.
2. Preheat the fryer to 300 Fahrenheit for five minutes. Place the dish in the basket and reduce the temperature to 250 Fahrenheit. Cook for ten minutes and set aside to cool.
3. Spread the caramel over the dish and serve warm.

158. Plum Pancakes

Prep.Time: 10 min - **Cooking Time:** 10 min - **Servings:** 8

Ingredients:
- ✓ 1 cup sliced plums
- ✓ 1 ½ cups almond flour
- ✓ 3 eggs
- ✓ 1 tbsp. honey
- ✓ Salt and Pepper to taste
- ✓ 3 tbsp. Butter

Directions:
1. Preheat the air fryer to 250 Fahrenheit.
2. In a small bowl, mix the ingredients together. Ensure that the mixture is smooth and well balanced.
3. Take a pancake mold and grease it with butter. Add the batter to the mold and place it in the air fryer basket.
4. Cook till both the sides of the pancake have browned on both sides and serve with maple syrup.

159. Blackcurrant Pudding

Prep.Time: 30 min - **Cooking Time:** 10 minutes - **Servings:** 8

Ingredients:
- ✓ 2 cups milk
- ✓ 2 cups almond flour
- ✓ 2 tbsp. custard powder
- ✓ 3 tbsp. powdered sugar
- ✓ 1 cup blackcurrant pulp
- ✓ 3 tbsp. unsalted butter

Directions:
1. Boil the milk and the sugar in a pan and add the custard powder followed by the almond flour and stir till you get a thick mixture. Chop the figs fine and add it to the mixture.
2. Preheat the fryer to 300 Fahrenheit for five minutes. Place the dish in the basket and reduce the temperature to 250 Fahrenheit. Cook for ten minutes and set aside to cool.

160. Passion Fruit Pudding

Prep.Time: 30 min - **Cooking Time:** 10 min - **Servings:** 8

Ingredients:
- ✓ 2 cups almond flour
- ✓ 2 cups milk
- ✓ 2 cups passion fruit pulp
- ✓ 2 tbsp. custard powder
- ✓ 3 tbsp. powdered sugar
- ✓ 3 tbsp. unsalted butter

Directions:
1. Boil the milk and the sugar in a pan and add the custard powder followed by the flour and stir till you get a thick mixture. Chop the apricot finely and add to the mixture.
2. Preheat the fryer to 300 Fahrenheit for five minutes. Place the dish in the basket and reduce the temperature to 250 Fahrenheit. Cook for ten minutes and set aside to cool.
3. Spread the fruits on the bread and serve.

161. Guava Pudding

Prep.Time: 30 min - **Cooking Time:** 10 min - **Servings:** 8

Ingredients:
- ✓ 2 cups milk
- ✓ 2 cups almond flour
- ✓ 2 tbsp. custard powder
- ✓ 3 tbsp. powdered sugar
- ✓ 3 tbsp. unsalted butter
- ✓ 2 cups guava pulp

Directions:
1. Boil the milk and the sugar in a pan and add the custard powder followed by the almond flour and stir till you get a thick mixture. Add the guava pulp to the mixture.
2. Preheat the fryer to 300 Fahrenheit for five minutes. Place the dish in the basket and reduce the temperature to 250 Fahrenheit. Cook for ten minutes and set aside to cool.

162. Mediterranean Blend

Prep.Time: 30 min - **Cooking Time:** 10 min - **Servings:** 8

Ingredients:
- ✓ 2 cups milk
- ✓ 2 cups almond flour
- ✓ 2 tbsp. custard powder
- ✓ 3 tbsp. powdered sugar
- ✓ 3 tbsp. unsalted butter
- ✓ 2 cups Mediterranean fruit mix

Directions:
1. Boil the milk and the sugar in a pan and add the custard powder followed by the almond flour and stir till you get a thick mixture. Add the fruit mix to the bowl.
2. Preheat the fryer to 300 Fahrenheit for five minutes. Place the dish in the basket and reduce the temperature to 250 Fahrenheit. Cook for ten minutes and set aside to cool.

163. Clementine Custard

Prep.Time: 30 min - **Cooking Time:** 10 min - **Servings:** 8

Ingredients:
- ✓ 1 cup clementine pulp
- ✓ 2 cups milk
- ✓ 2 tbsp. custard powder
- ✓ 3 tbsp. powdered sugar
- ✓ 3 tbsp. unsalted butter

Directions:
1. Boil the milk and the sugar in a pan and add the custard powder followed by the clementine pulp and stir till you get a thick mixture.
2. Preheat the fryer to 300 Fahrenheit for five minutes. Place the dish in the basket and reduce the temperature to 250 Fahrenheit. Cook for ten minutes and set aside to cool.

164. Dates Pudding

Prep.Time: 30 min - **Cooking Time:** 10 min - **Servings:** 8

Ingredients:
- ✓ 2 tbsp. custard powder
- ✓ 3 tbsp. powdered sugar
- ✓ 3 tbsp. unsalted butter
- ✓ 1 tbsp. sugar
- ✓ 1 cup pitted and sliced dates

Directions:
1. Boil the milk and the sugar in a pan and add the custard powder followed by the dates and stir till you get a thick mixture. Add the sliced fruits to the mixture.
2. Preheat the fryer to 300 Fahrenheit for five minutes. Place the dish in the basket and reduce the temperature to 250 Fahrenheit. Cook for ten minutes and set aside to cool.

165. Date Cakes

Prep.Time: 15 min - **Cooking Time:** 15 min - **Servings:** 8

Ingredients:
- ✓ 2 cups All-purpose flour
- ✓ 1 ½ cup milk
- ✓ 2 cups pitted and pureed dates
- ✓ ½ tsp. baking powder
- ✓ ½ tsp. baking soda
- ✓ 2 tbsp. butter
- ✓ 2 tbsp. sugar
- ✓ Muffin cups

Directions:
1. Mix the ingredients together and use your fingers to get a crumbly mixture.
2. Add the baking soda to the milk and mix continuously. Add this milk to the mixture and create a batter, which you will need to transfer to the muffin cups.
3. Preheat the fryer to 300 Fahrenheit for five minutes. You will need to place the muffin cups in the basket and cover it. Cook the muffins for fifteen minutes and check whether or not the muffins are cooked using a toothpick. Remove the cups and serve hot.

166. Semolina Pancakes

Prep.Time: 15 min - **Cooking Time:** 10 min - **Servings:** 8

Ingredients:
- ✓ 2 cups semolina pudding
- ✓ 1 ½ cups almond flour
- ✓ 3 eggs
- ✓ 2 tsp. dried basil
- ✓ 2 tsp. dried parsley
- ✓ Salt and Pepper to taste
- ✓ 3 tbsp. Butter

Directions:
1. Preheat the air fryer to 250 Fahrenheit.
2. In a small bowl, mix the ingredients together. Ensure that the mixture is smooth and well balanced.
3. Take a pancake mold and grease it with butter. Add the batter to the mold and place it in the air fryer basket. Cook till both the sides of the pancake have browned on both sides and serve with maple syrup.

167. Grape Pudding

Prep.Time: 10 min - **Cooking Time:** 15 minutes - **Servings:** 8

Ingredients:
- ✓ 2 cups milk
- ✓ 2 cups almond flour
- ✓ 3 tbsp. grape juice
- ✓ 2 tbsp. custard powder
- ✓ 3 tbsp. powdered sugar
- ✓ 3 tbsp. unsalted butter

Directions:
1. Boil the milk and the sugar in a pan and add the custard powder followed by the almond flour and the grape juice and stir till you get a thick mixture.
2. Preheat the fryer to 300 Fahrenheit for five minutes. Place the dish in the basket and reduce the temperature to 250 Fahrenheit. Cook for ten minutes and set aside to cool.

168. Honey and Grapefruit Pudding

Prep.Time: 10 min - **Cooking Time:** 15 min - **Servings:** 8

Ingredients:
- ✓ 2 cups cubed grapefruit
- ✓ 2 cups milk
- ✓ 1 cup honey
- ✓ 2 tbsp. custard powder
- ✓ 3 tbsp. unsalted butter

Directions:
1. Boil the milk and the sugar in a pan and add the custard powder followed by the honey and grapefruit and stir till you get a thick mixture.
2. Preheat the fryer to 300 Fahrenheit for five minutes. Place the dish in the basket and reduce the temperature to 250 Fahrenheit. Cook for ten minutes and set aside to cool.

169. Key Lime Custard

Prep.Time: 10 min - **Cooking Time:** 20 min - **Servings:** 8

Ingredients:
- ✓ 2 cups All-purpose flour
- ✓ 1 ½ cup milk
- ✓ ½ tsp. baking powder
- ✓ ½ tsp. baking soda
- ✓ 2 tbsp. butter
- ✓ 1 cup sugar
- ✓ 1 cup key lime juice
- ✓ Muffin cups or butter paper cups

Directions:
1. Mix the ingredients together and use your fingers to get a crumbly mixture.
2. Add the baking soda to the milk and mix continuously. Add this milk to the mixture and create a batter, which you will need to transfer to the muffin cups.
3. Preheat the fryer to 300 Fahrenheit for five minutes. You will need to place the muffin cups in the basket and cover it. Cook the muffins for fifteen minutes and check whether or not the muffins are cooked using a toothpick. Remove the cups and serve hot

170. Grapefruit Tarts

Prep.Time: 15 min - **Cooking Time:** 15 min - **Servings:** 8

Ingredients:
- ✓ 1 ½ cup plain flour
- ✓ ½ cup almond flour
- ✓ 3 tbsp. unsalted butter
- ✓ 2 tbsp. powdered sugar
- ✓ 2 cups cold water
- ✓ 1 tbsp. sliced cashew

Filling:
- ✓ 1 cup cubed grapefruit
- ✓ 1 cup fresh cream
- ✓ 3 tbsp. butter

Directions:
1. In a large bowl, mix the flour, cocoa powder, butter and sugar with your fingers. The mixture should resemble breadcrumbs. Knead the dough using the cold milk and wrap it and leave it to cool for ten minutes. Roll the dough out into the pie and prick the sides of the pie.
2. Mix the ingredients for the filling in a bowl. Make sure that it is a little thick.
3. Preheat the fryer to 300 Fahrenheit for five minutes. You will need to place the tin in the basket and cover it. When the pastry has turned golden brown, you will need to remove the tin and let it cool. Cut into slices and serve with a dollop of cream

171. Guava Pudding

Prep.Time: 10 min - **Cooking Time:** 15 min - **Servings:** 12

Ingredients:
- ✓ 2 cups milk
- ✓ 2 cups guava pulp
- ✓ 2 cups almond flour
- ✓ 2 tbsp. custard powder
- ✓ 3 tbsp. powdered sugar
- ✓ 3 tbsp. unsalted butter

Directions:
1. Boil the milk and the sugar in a pan and add the custard powder followed by the almond flour and stir till you get a thick mixture. Mix the guava pulp into the mixture and stir till the color has spread well.
2. Preheat the fryer to 300 Fahrenheit for five minutes. Place the dish in the basket and reduce the temperature to 250 Fahrenheit. Cook for ten minutes and set aside to cool

172. Nannyberry cake

Prep.Time: 10 min - **Cooking Time:** 15 min - **Servings:** 8

Ingredients:
- ✓ 1 tbsp. unsalted butter
- ✓ 2 tbsp. water
- ✓ 1 cup nannyberry pulp
- ✓ 1 cup all-purpose flour
- ✓ ½ cup condensed milk

Directions:
1. Add the ingredients together and whisk till you get a smooth mixture.
2. Prepare a tin by greasing it with butter. Transfer the mixture into the tin. Preheat the fryer to 300 Fahrenheit for five minutes. You will need to place the tin in the basket and cover it. Check whether the cake has been cooked using a knife or a toothpick and remove the tray. Serve with a dollop of ice cream.

173. Pistachio Pancakes

Prep.Time: 15 min - **Cooking Time:** 15 min - **Servings:** 8

Ingredients:
- ✓ 2 tbsp. sliced pistachio
- ✓ 1 ½ cups almond flour
- ✓ 3 eggs
- ✓ 2 tsp. dried basil
- ✓ 2 tsp. dried parsley
- ✓ Salt and Pepper to taste
- ✓ 3 tbsp. Butter

Directions:
1. Preheat the air fryer to 250 Fahrenheit.
2. In a small bowl, mix the ingredients together. Ensure that the mixture is smooth and well balanced.
3. Take a pancake mold and grease it with butter. Add the batter to the mold and place it in the air fryer basket.
4. Cook till both the sides of the pancake have browned on both sides and serve with maple syrup

174. Multigrain Cookie

Prep.Time: 15 min - **Cooking Time:** 15 min - **Servings:** 8

Ingredients:
- ✓ 1 cup all-purpose flour
- ✓ 1 cups flour
- ✓ 1 tsp. baking powder
- ✓ 1 tbsp. liquid glucose
- ✓ 1 cup mixed grains
- ✓ ½ cup milk
- ✓ 1 tbsp. unsalted butter
- ✓ 2 tsp. honey

Directions:
1. Mix the dry ingredients together in a large bowl and warm the glucose with a little water. Mix the glucose, honey and the butter to the bowl followed by the milk. You will need to roll the dough using a pin.
2. Now, create cookies and set them on a prepared baking tray.
3. Preheat the fryer to 300 Fahrenheit for five minutes. Place the baking tray in the basket and reduce the temperature to 250 Fahrenheit. Turn the cookies in the tray to ensure that they are cooked uniformly.
4. When the cookies have cooled, store them in an airtight container

175. Mulberry Pudding

Prep.Time: 10 min - **Cooking Time:** 15 minutes - **Servings:** 12

Ingredients:
- ✓ 2 cups almond flour
- ✓ 1 cup milk
- ✓ 2 tbsp. custard powder
- ✓ 3 tbsp. powdered sugar
- ✓ 1 cup mulberry juice
- ✓ 3 tbsp. unsalted butter

Directions:
1. Boil the milk and the sugar in a pan and add the custard powder followed by the almond flour and mulberry juice and stir till you get a thick mixture
2. Preheat the fryer to 300 Fahrenheit for five minutes. Place the dish in the basket and reduce the temperature to 250 Fahrenheit. Cook for ten minutes and set aside to cool.

176. Tangerine Cake

Prep.Time: 10 min - **Cooking Time:** 15 min - **Servings:** 12

Ingredients:
- ✓ 1 tbsp. unsalted butter
- ✓ 2 tbsp. water
- ✓ 2 cups all-purpose flour
- ✓ ½ cup condensed milk
- ✓ 1 cup sliced tangerine

Directions:
1. Add the ingredients together and whisk till you get a smooth mixture.
2. Prepare a tin by greasing it with butter. Transfer the mixture into the tin. Preheat the fryer to 300 Fahrenheit for five minutes. You will need to place the tin in the basket and cover it. Check whether the brownies have been cooked using a knife or a toothpick and remove the tray. When the brownies have cooled, cut them and serve with a dollop of ice cream

177. Cauliflower Pudding

Prep.Time: 10 min - **Cooking Time:** 15 min - **Servings:** 8

Ingredients:
- ✓ 1 cup cauliflower florets
- ✓ 2 cups milk
- ✓ 2 tbsp. custard powder
- ✓ 3 tbsp. powdered sugar
- ✓ 3 tbsp. unsalted butter

Directions:
1. Parboil the cauliflower florets and set on a tray.
2. Boil the milk and the sugar in a pan and add the custard powder and stir till you get a thick mixture. Pour the mixture over the florets.
3. Preheat the fryer to 300 Fahrenheit for five minutes. Place the dish in the basket and reduce the temperature to 250 Fahrenheit. Cook for ten minutes and set aside to cool.

178. Rhubarb Pancakes

Prep.Time: 10 min - **Cooking Time:** 10 min - **Servings:** 8

Ingredients:
- ✓ 1 cup shredded rhubarb
- ✓ 1 ½ cups almond flour
- ✓ 3 eggs
- ✓ 2 tsp. dried basil
- ✓ 2 tsp. dried parsley
- ✓ Salt and Pepper to taste
- ✓ 3 tbsp. Butter

Directions:
1. Preheat the air fryer to 250 Fahrenheit.
2. In a small bowl, mix the ingredients together. Ensure that the mixture is smooth and well balanced.
3. Take a pancake mold and grease it with butter. Add the batter to the mold and place it in the air fryer basket.
4. Cook till both the sides of the pancake have browned on both sides and serve with maple syrup.

179. Key Lime Pie

Prep.Time: 15 min - **Cooking Time:** 15 min - **Servings:** 12

Ingredients:
- ✓ 1 ½ cup plain flour
- ✓ 1 cup almond flour
- ✓ 3 tbsp. unsalted butter
- ✓ 2 tbsp. powdered sugar
- ✓ 2 cups cold water

Filling:
- ✓ 2 cups key lime
- ✓ 1 cup fresh cream
- ✓ 3 tbsp. butter

Directions:
1. Knead all the ingredients together using milk into dough that is soft.
2. Now, roll the dough out and cut into two circles. Press the dough into the pie tins and prick on all sides using a fork.
3. Mix the ingredients for the filling in a bowl. Make sure that it is a little thick. Cover the pie tin with the second round.
4. Preheat the fryer to 300 Fahrenheit for five minutes. You will need to place the tin in the basket and cover it. When the pastry has turned golden brown, you will need to remove the tin and let it cool. Cut into slices and serve with a dollop of cream

180. Dry Fruit Muffins

Prep.Time: 10 min - **Cooking Time:** 20 min - **Servings:** 12

Ingredients:
- ✓ 2 cups All-purpose flour
- ✓ 1 ½ cup milk
- ✓ ½ tsp. baking powder
- ✓ ½ tsp. baking soda
- ✓ 2 tbsp. butter
- ✓ 1 cup mixed nuts
- ✓ 1 cup sugar
- ✓ 1 cup oats
- ✓ Muffin cups or butter paper cups

Directions:
1. Mix the ingredients together and use your fingers to get a crumbly mixture.
2. You will need to divide the milk into two parts and add one part to the baking soda. Now, mix the milk mixture and add this to the crumbly mixture and begin to whisk the ingredients very fast. Once you have obtained a smooth batter, you will need to transfer the mixture into a muffin cup and set aside.
3. Preheat the fryer to 300 Fahrenheit for five minutes. You will need to place the muffin cups in the basket and cover it. Cook the muffins for fifteen minutes and check whether or not the muffins are cooked using a toothpick. Remove the cups and serve hot.

181. Date Cakes

Prep.Time: 15 min - **Cooking Time:** 15 min - **Servings:** 8

Ingredients:
- ✓ 2 cups All-purpose flour
- ✓ 1 ½ cup milk
- ✓ 2 cups pitted and pureed dates
- ✓ ½ tsp. baking powder
- ✓ ½ tsp. baking soda
- ✓ 2 tbsp. butter
- ✓ 2 tbsp. sugar
- ✓ Muffin cups

Directions:
5. Mix the ingredients together and use your fingers to get a crumbly mixture.
6. Add the baking soda to the milk and mix continuously. Add this milk to the mixture and create a batter, which you will need to transfer to the muffin cups.
7. Preheat the fryer to 300 Fahrenheit for five minutes. You will need to place the muffin cups in the basket and cover it. Cook the muffins for fifteen minutes and check whether or not the muffins are cooked using a toothpick. Remove the cups and serve hot.

182. Pear Pudding

Prep.Time: 15 min - **Cooking Time:** 10 min - **Servings:** 8

Ingredients:
- ✓ 2 cups pear pulp
- ✓ 2 cups milk
- ✓ 2 tbsp. custard powder
- ✓ 3 tbsp. powdered sugar
- ✓ 3 tbsp. unsalted butter

Directions:
1. Boil the milk and the sugar in a pan and add the custard powder followed by the pear pulp and stir till you get a thick mixture.
2. Preheat the fryer to 300 Fahrenheit for five minutes. Place the dish in the basket and reduce the temperature to 250 Fahrenheit. Cook for ten minutes and set aside to cool.

183. Banana Sponge Cake

Prep.Time: 10 min - **Cooking Time:** 15 minutes - **Servings:** 6

Ingredients:
- ✓ ½ cup condensed milk
- ✓ 1 cup all-purpose flour
- ✓ 2 cups mashed banana
- ✓ ½ tsp. baking soda
- ✓ ½ tsp. baking powder
- ✓ ½ cup oil
- ✓ 3 tbsp. powdered sugar
- ✓ ½ cup soda
- ✓ Parchment or butter paper to line the tin

Directions:
1. Mix the ingredients together to create a batter that is smooth and thick.
2. Grease a cake tin with butter and line it with the parchment or butter paper.
3. Transfer the batter into the tin.
4. Preheat the fryer to 300 Fahrenheit for five minutes. You will need to place the tin in the basket and cover it. Cook the cake for fifteen minutes and check whether or not the cake is cooked using a toothpick. Remove the tin and cut the cake into slices and serve.

184. Asparagus Pancakes

Prep.Time: 10 min - **Cooking Time:** 10-15 min - **Servings:** 8

Ingredients:
- ✓ 1 asparagus (shredded)
- ✓ 1 ½ cups almond flour
- ✓ 3 eggs
- ✓ 2 tsp. dried basil
- ✓ 2 tsp. dried parsley
- ✓ Salt and Pepper to taste
- ✓ 3 tbsp. Butter

Directions:
1. Preheat the air fryer to 250 Fahrenheit.
2. In a small bowl, mix the ingredients together. Ensure that the mixture is smooth and well balanced.
3. Take a pancake mold and grease it with butter. Add the batter to the mold and place it in the air fryer basket.
4. Cook till both the sides of the pancake have browned on both sides and serve with maple syrup.

185. Plum Cakes

Prep.Time: 15 min - **Cooking Time:** 15 min - **Servings:** 8

Ingredients:
- ✓ 2 cups All-purpose flour
- ✓ 1 ½ cup milk
- ✓ ½ tsp. baking powder
- ✓ ½ tsp. baking soda
- ✓ 2 tbsp. butter
- ✓ 2 tbsp. sugar
- ✓ 2 tsp. vinegar
- ✓ 2 cups grated plums
- ✓ Muffin cups

Directions:
1. Mix the ingredients together and use your fingers to get a crumbly mixture.
2. Add the baking soda and the vinegar to the milk and mix continuously. Add this milk to the mixture and create a batter, which you will need to transfer to the muffin cups.
3. Preheat the fryer to 300 Fahrenheit for five minutes. You will need to place the muffin cups in the basket and cover it. Cook the muffins for fifteen minutes and check whether or not the muffins are cooked using a toothpick. Remove the cups and serve hot.

186. Cherry Muffins

Prep.Time: 15 min - **Cooking Time:** 15 min - **Servings:** 8

Ingredients:
- ✓ 2 cups All-purpose flour
- ✓ 1 ½ cup milk
- ✓ ½ tsp. baking powder
- ✓ ½ tsp. baking soda
- ✓ 2 tbsp. butter
- ✓ 2 tbsp. sugar
- ✓ 2 cups pitted and sliced cherries
- ✓ Muffin cups

Directions:
1. Mix the ingredients together and use your fingers to get a crumbly mixture.
2. Add the baking soda to the milk and mix continuously. Add this milk to the mixture and create a batter that you will need to transfer to the muffin cups. Preheat the fryer to 300 Fahrenheit for five minutes. You will need to place the muffin cups in the basket and cover it. Cook the muffins for fifteen minutes and check whether or not the muffins are cooked using a toothpick. Remove the cups and serve hot.

187. Tapioca Pearl Pie

Prep.Time: 15 min - **Cooking Time:** 15 minutes - **Servings:** 8

Ingredients:
- ✓ 1 ½ cup plain flour
- ✓ 2 tbsp. custard powder
- ✓ 3 tbsp. unsalted butter
- ✓ 2 tbsp. powdered sugar
- ✓ 2 cups cold water
- ✓ 1 tbsp. sliced cashew

Filling:
- ✓ 1 cup tapioca pearls
- ✓ 1 cup cheddar cheese (melted)
- ✓ 1 cup fresh cream
- ✓ 3 tbsp. butter

Directions:
1. Mix the ingredients together to form a crumbly mixture. Knead the mixture with cold milk and wrap it. Roll the dough out into two large circles and press that dough into the pie tin and prick the sides with a fork.
2. Cook the ingredients for the filling on a low flame and pour into the tin.
3. Cover the pie tin with the second round.
4. Preheat the fryer to 300 Fahrenheit for five minutes. You will need to place the tin in the basket and cover it. When the pastry has turned golden brown, you will need to remove the tin and let it cool. Cut into slices and serve with a dollop of cream.

188. Mango and Cream Pie

Prep.Time: 15 min - **Cooking Time:** 15 min - **Servings:** 8

Ingredients:
- ✓ 1 ½ cup plain flour
- ✓ 3 tbsp. unsalted butter
- ✓ 2 tbsp. powdered sugar
- ✓ 2 cups cold water
- ✓ 1 tbsp. sliced cashew

Filling:
- ✓ 2 cups mango pulp
- ✓ 1 cup fresh cream
- ✓ 3 tbsp. butter

Directions:
1. Mix the ingredients together to form a crumbly mixture. Knead the mixture with cold milk and wrap it. Roll the dough out into two large circles and press that dough into the pie tin and prick the sides with a fork.
2. Cook the ingredients for the filling on a low flame and pour into the tin.
3. Cover the pie tin with the second round.
4. Preheat the fryer to 300 Fahrenheit for five minutes. You will need to place the tin in the basket and cover it. When the pastry has turned golden brown, you will need to remove the tin and let it cool. Cut into slices and serve with a dollop of cream.

189. Strawberry Pancakes

Prep.Time: 15 min - **Cooking Time:** 15 min - **Servings:** 8

Ingredients:
- ✓ 2 cups minced strawberries
- ✓ 1 ½ cups almond flour
- ✓ 3 eggs
- ✓ 2 tsp. dried basil
- ✓ 2 tsp. dried parsley
- ✓ Salt and Pepper to taste
- ✓ 3 tbsp. Butter

Directions:
1. Preheat the air fryer to 250 Fahrenheit.
2. In a small bowl, mix the ingredients together. Ensure that the mixture is smooth and well balanced.
3. Take a pancake mold and grease it with butter. Add the batter to the mold and place it in the air fryer basket. Cook till both the sides of the pancake have browned on both sides and serve with maple syrup.

190. Kidney Beans Waffles

Prep.Time: 15 min - **Cooking Time:** 15 min - **Servings:** 8

Ingredients:
- ✓ 1 ½ cups almond flour
- ✓ 3 eggs
- ✓ 2 tsp. dried basil
- ✓ 2 tsp. dried parsley
- ✓ Salt and Pepper to taste
- ✓ 3 tbsp. Butter
- ✓ 1 cup mashed beans

Directions:
1. Preheat the air fryer to 250 Fahrenheit.
2. In a small bowl, mix the ingredients, except for the beans, together. Ensure that the mixture is smooth and well balanced.
3. Take a waffle mold and grease it with butter. Add the batter to the mold and place it in the air fryer basket. Cook till both the sides have browned. Now, create a cavity and fill it with the beans and serve.

191. Persimmons Muffins

Prep.Time: 15 min - **Cooking Time:** 15 min - **Servings:** 8

Ingredients:
- ✓ 2 cups cornstarch
- ✓ 1 ½ cup milk
- ✓ 3 eggs
- ✓ 2 tbsp. butter
- ✓ 2 tbsp. sugar
- ✓ 2 cups persimmons pulp
- ✓ 1 tsp. vanilla extract
- ✓ Muffin cups

Directions:
1. Mix the ingredients together and use your fingers to get a crumbly mixture.
2. Add the baking soda to the milk and mix continuously. Add this milk to the mixture and create a batter, which you will need to transfer to the muffin cups.
3. Preheat the fryer to 300 Fahrenheit for five minutes. You will need to place the muffin cups in the basket and cover it. Cook the muffins for fifteen minutes and check whether or not the muffins are cooked using a toothpick. Remove the cups and serve hot.

192. Blackberry Buttermilk Cupcakes

Prep.Time: 15 min - **Cooking Time:** 15 min - **Servings:** 8

Ingredients:
- ✓ 2 cups All-purpose flour
- ✓ 1 ½ cup buttermilk
- ✓ ½ tsp. baking powder
- ✓ ½ tsp. baking soda
- ✓ 2 tbsp. butter
- ✓ 2 tbsp. sugar
- ✓ 2 cups sliced blackberries
- ✓ Muffin cups

Directions:
1. Mix the ingredients together and use your fingers to get a crumbly mixture.
2. Add the baking soda to the milk and mix continuously. Add this milk to the mixture and create a batter, which you will need to transfer to the muffin cups.
3. Preheat the fryer to 300 Fahrenheit for five minutes. You will need to place the muffin cups in the basket and cover it. Cook the muffins for fifteen minutes and check whether or not the muffins are cooked using a toothpick. Remove the cups and serve hot.

193. Lamb Pie

Prep.Time: 15 min - **Cooking Time:** 15 minutes - **Servings:** 8

Ingredients:
- ✓ 2 cups cornstarch
- ✓ 1 ½ cup milk
- ✓ 3 eggs
- ✓ 2 tbsp. butter
- ✓ 2 tbsp. sugar
- ✓ 2 cups minced lamb
- ✓ Muffin cups

Directions:
1. Mix the ingredients together and use your fingers to get a crumbly mixture.
2. Add the baking soda to the milk and mix continuously. Add this milk to the mixture and create a batter, which you will need to transfer to the muffin cups.
3. Preheat the fryer to 300 Fahrenheit for five minutes. You will need to place the muffin cups in the basket and cover it. Cook the muffins for fifteen minutes and check whether or not the muffins are cooked using a toothpick. Remove the cups and serve hot.

194. Chicken and Honey Muffin

Prep.Time: 15 min - **Cooking Time:** 15 min - **Servings:** 8

Ingredients:
- ✓ 2 cups All-purpose flour
- ✓ 1 ½ cup buttermilk
- ✓ ½ tsp. baking powder
- ✓ ½ tsp. baking soda
- ✓ 2 tbsp. butter
- ✓ 2 cups minced chicken
- ✓ 2 tbsp. honey
- ✓ Muffin cups

Directions:
1. Mix the ingredients together and use your fingers to get a crumbly mixture.
2. Add the baking soda to the milk and mix continuously. Add this milk to the mixture and create a batter, which you will need to transfer to the muffin cups.
3. Preheat the fryer to 300 Fahrenheit for five minutes. You will need to place the muffin cups in the basket and cover it. Cook the muffins for fifteen minutes and check whether or not the muffins are cooked using a toothpick. Remove the cups and serve hot.

195. Mixed Vegetable Muffins

Prep.Time: 15 min - **Cooking Time:** 15 min - **Servings:** 8

Ingredients:
- ✓ 2 cups All-purpose flour
- ✓ 1 ½ cup milk
- ✓ ½ tsp. baking powder
- ✓ ½ tsp. baking soda
- ✓ 2 tbsp. butter
- ✓ 2 cups mixed vegetables
- ✓ 1 tbsp. sugar
- ✓ Muffin cups

Directions:
1. Mix the ingredients together and use your fingers to get a crumbly mixture.
2. Add the baking soda to the milk and mix continuously. Add this milk to the mixture and create a batter, which you will need to transfer to the muffin cups.
3. Preheat the fryer to 300 Fahrenheit for five minutes. You will need to place the muffin cups in the basket and cover it. Cook the muffins for fifteen minutes and check whether or not the muffins are cooked using a toothpick. Remove the cups and serve hot.

196. Mexican Waffles

Prep.Time: 15 min - **Cooking Time:** 15 min - **Servings:** 8

Ingredients:
- ✓ 1 ½ cups almond flour
- ✓ 3 eggs
- ✓ 2 tsp. dried basil
- ✓ 2 tsp. dried parsley
- ✓ Salt and Pepper to taste
- ✓ 3 tbsp. Butter
- ✓ 1 cup pickled jalapenos
- ✓ 1 cup green olives
- ✓ 1 cup black olives
- ✓ 2 tbsp. salsa

Directions:
1. Preheat the air fryer to 250 Fahrenheit.
2. In a small bowl, mix the ingredients, except for the jalapenos, olives and salsa together. Ensure that the mixture is smooth and well balanced.
3. Take a waffle mold and grease it with butter. Add the batter to the mold and place it in the air fryer basket. Cook till both the sides have browned. Now, create a cavity and fill it with the jalapenos, olives and salsa and serve.

197. Honey and Blackberry Cake

Prep.Time: 15 min - **Cooking Time:** 15 min - **Servings:** 8

Ingredients:
- ✓ 2 cups All-purpose flour
- ✓ 1 ½ cup milk
- ✓ ½ tsp. baking powder
- ✓ ½ tsp. baking soda
- ✓ 2 tbsp. butter
- ✓ 2 tbsp. honey
- ✓ 2 cups sliced blackberry
- ✓ 2 tsp. vinegar
- ✓ Muffin cups

Directions:
1. Mix the ingredients together and use your fingers to get a crumbly mixture.
2. Add the baking soda and the vinegar to the milk and mix continuously. Add this milk to the mixture and create a batter, which you will need to transfer to the muffin cups.
3. Preheat the fryer to 300 Fahrenheit for five minutes. You will need to place the muffin cups in the basket and cover it. Cook the muffins for fifteen minutes and check whether or not the muffins are cooked using a toothpick. Remove the cups and serve hot.

198. Cardamom Cheese Cake

Prep.Time: 15 min - **Cooking Time:** 15 min - **Servings:** 8

Ingredients:
- ✓ 2 cups All-purpose flour
- ✓ 1 ½ cup milk
- ✓ 1 tbsp. cardamom powder
- ✓ ½ tsp. baking powder
- ✓ 1 cup cheese
- ✓ ½ tsp. baking soda
- ✓ 2 tbsp. butter
- ✓ 2 tbsp. sugar
- ✓ Muffin cups

Directions:
1. Mix the ingredients together and use your fingers to get a crumbly mixture.
2. Add the baking soda to the milk and mix continuously. Add this milk to the mixture and create a batter, which you will need to transfer to the muffin cups.
3. Preheat the fryer to 300 Fahrenheit for five minutes. You will need to place the muffin cups in the basket and cover it. Cook the muffins for fifteen minutes and check whether or not the muffins are cooked using a toothpick. Remove the cups and serve hot.

199. Butterscotch Cake

Prep.Time: 15 min - **Cooking Time:** 10-15 minutes - **Servings:** 4

Ingredients:
- ✓ 1 tbsp. unsalted butter
- ✓ 2 tbsp. water
- ✓ 2 tsp. vanilla extract
- ✓ 2 tbsp. brown sugar
- ✓ 1 cup corn flour
- ✓ ½ cup condensed milk

Directions:
1. Add the ingredients together and whisk till you get a smooth mixture.
2. Prepare a tin by greasing it with butter. Transfer the mixture into the tin. Preheat the fryer to 300 Fahrenheit for five minutes. You will need to place the tin in the basket and cover it. Check whether the cake has risen well. Cool the cake down and serve.

200. Kiwi Custard

Prep.Time: 15 min - **Cooking Time:** 10 min - **Servings:** 4-6

Ingredients:
- ✓ 1 cup kiwi slices
- ✓ 2 cups milk
- ✓ 2 tbsp. custard powder
- ✓ 3 tbsp. powdered sugar
- ✓ 3 tbsp. unsalted butter

Directions:
1. Boil the milk and the sugar in a pan and add the custard powder followed by the kiwi slices and stir till you get a thick mixture.
2. Preheat the fryer to 300 Fahrenheit for five minutes. Place the dish in the basket and reduce the temperature to 250 Fahrenheit. Cook for ten minutes and set aside to cool.

201. Blackberry Pancakes

Prep.Time: 15 min - **Cooking Time:** 10-12 min - **Servings:** 8

Ingredients:
- ✓ 2 cups minced blackberry
- ✓ 1 ½ cups almond flour
- ✓ 3 eggs
- ✓ 2 tsp. dried basil
- ✓ 2 tsp. dried parsley
- ✓ Salt and Pepper to taste
- ✓ 3 tbsp. Butter

Directions:
1. Preheat the air fryer to 250 Fahrenheit.
2. In a small bowl, mix the ingredients together. Ensure that the mixture is smooth and well balanced.
3. Take a pancake mold and grease it with butter. Add the batter to the mold and place it in the air fryer basket. Cook till both the sides of the pancake have browned on both sides and serve with maple syrup.

202. Green citrus Pie

Prep.Time: 15 min - **Cooking Time:** 10-15 min - **Servings:** 8

Ingredients:
- ✓ 1 cup plain flour
- ✓ 1 tbsp. unsalted butter
- ✓ 4tsp. powdered sugar
- ✓ 2 cups cold milk

Filling:
- ✓ ½ cup roasted nuts
- ✓ 2 tbsp. sugar
- ✓ ½ tsp. cinnamon
- ✓ 2 tsp. lemon juice
- ✓ 4 tsp. lemon zest
- ✓ 1 cup sliced kiwi

Directions:
1. Mix the ingredients together to form a crumbly mixture. Knead the mixture with cold milk and wrap it. Roll the dough out into two large circles and press that dough into the pie tin and prick the sides with a fork.
2. Cook the ingredients for the filling on a low flame and pour into the tin.
3. Cover the pie tin with the second round.
4. Preheat the fryer to 300 Fahrenheit for five minutes. You will need to place the tin in the basket and cover it. When the pastry has turned golden brown, you will need to remove the tin and let it cool. Cut into slices and serve with a dollop of cream.

203. Jalapeno Waffles

Prep.Time: 15 min - **Cooking Time:** 10-15 min - **Servings:** 4-6

Ingredients:
- ✓ 1 ½ cups almond flour
- ✓ 3 eggs
- ✓ 2 tsp. dried basil
- ✓ 2 tsp. dried parsley
- ✓ Salt and Pepper to taste
- ✓ 3 tbsp. Butter
- ✓ 1 cup pickled jalapenos

Directions:
1. Preheat the air fryer to 250 Fahrenheit.
2. In a small bowl, mix the ingredients, except for the jalapenos, together.
3. Ensure that the mixture is smooth and well balanced.
4. Take a waffle mold and grease it with butter. Add the batter to the mold and place it in the air fryer basket. Cook till both the sides have browned. Now, create a cavity and fill it with the jalapenos and serve.

204. Cinnamon Cakes

Prep.Time: 15 min - **Cooking Time:** 15 min - **Servings:** 4

Ingredients:
- ✓ 2 cups All-purpose flour
- ✓ 1 ½ cup milk
- ✓ 1 tbsp. cinnamon powder
- ✓ ½ tsp. baking powder
- ✓ ½ tsp. baking soda
- ✓ 2 tbsp. butter
- ✓ 2 tbsp. sugar
- ✓ Muffin cups

Directions:
1. Mix the ingredients together and use your fingers to get a crumbly mixture.
2. Add the baking soda and the vinegar to the milk and mix continuously. Add this milk to the mixture and create a batter, which you will need to transfer to the muffin cups.
3. Preheat the fryer to 300 Fahrenheit for five minutes. You will need to place the muffin cups in the basket and cover it. Cook the muffins for fifteen minutes and check whether or not the muffins are cooked using a toothpick. Remove the cups and serve hot.

205. Buttermilk and Blueberry Muffins

Prep.Time: 15 min - **Cooking Time:** 15 minutes - **Servings:** 4-6

Ingredients:
- ✓ 2 cups All-purpose flour
- ✓ 1 ½ cup buttermilk
- ✓ ½ tsp. baking powder
- ✓ ½ tsp. baking soda
- ✓ 2 tbsp. butter
- ✓ 2 tbsp. sugar
- ✓ 2 tsp. vinegar
- ✓ 2 cups sliced blueberries
- ✓ Muffin cups

Directions:
1. Mix the ingredients together and use your fingers to get a crumbly mixture.
2. Add the baking soda and the vinegar to the milk and mix continuously. Add this milk to the mixture and create a batter, which you will need to transfer to the muffin cups.
3. Preheat the fryer to 300 Fahrenheit for five minutes. You will need to place the muffin cups in the basket and cover it. Cook the muffins for fifteen minutes and check whether or not the muffins are cooked using a toothpick. Remove the cups and serve hot.

206. Cranberry Cakes

Prep.Time: 15 min - **Cooking Time:** 15 min - **Servings:** 4-6

Ingredients:
- ✓ 2 cups All-purpose flour
- ✓ 1 ½ cup milk
- ✓ ½ tsp. baking powder
- ✓ ½ tsp. baking soda
- ✓ 2 tbsp. butter
- ✓ 2 tbsp. sugar
- ✓ 2 tsp. vinegar
- ✓ 2 cups grated cranberries
- ✓ Muffin cups

Directions:
1. Mix the ingredients together and use your fingers to get a crumbly mixture.
2. Add the baking soda and the vinegar to the milk and mix continuously. Add this milk to the mixture and create a batter, which you will need to transfer to the muffin cups.
3. Preheat the fryer to 300 Fahrenheit for five minutes. You will need to place the muffin cups in the basket and cover it. Cook the muffins for fifteen minutes and check whether or not the muffins are cooked using a toothpick. Remove the cups and serve hot.

207. Orange Muffins

Prep.Time: 15 min - **Cooking Time:** 15 min - **Servings:** 6-8

Ingredients:
- ✓ 2 cups All-purpose flour
- ✓ 1 ½ cup milk
- ✓ ½ tsp. baking powder
- ✓ ½ tsp. baking soda
- ✓ 2 tbsp. butter
- ✓ 2 tbsp. sugar
- ✓ 2 tsp. vinegar
- ✓ 3 tbsp. orange juice and zest
- ✓ Muffin cups

Directions:
1. Mix the ingredients together and use your fingers to get a crumbly mixture.
2. Add the baking soda and the vinegar to the milk and mix continuously. Add this milk to the mixture and create a batter, which you will need to transfer to the muffin cups.
3. Preheat the fryer to 300 Fahrenheit for five minutes. You will need to place the muffin cups in the basket and cover it. Cook the muffins for fifteen minutes and check whether or not the muffins are cooked using a toothpick. Remove the cups and serve hot.

208. Blueberry Tarts

Prep.Time: 15 min - **Cooking Time:** 10-15 min - **Servings:** 6-8

Ingredients:
- ✓ 1 ½ cup plain flour
- ✓ 3 tbsp. unsalted butter
- ✓ 2 tbsp. powdered sugar
- ✓ 2 cups cold water
- ✓ 1 tbsp. sliced cashew

Filling:
- ✓ 1 cup fresh blueberries (Sliced)
- ✓ 1 cup fresh cream
- ✓ 3 tbsp. butter

Directions:
1. Mix the ingredients together to form a crumbly mixture. Knead the mixture with cold milk and wrap it. Roll the dough out into two large circles and press that dough into the pie tin and prick the sides with a fork.
2. Cook the ingredients for the filling on a low flame and pour into the tin.
3. Cover the pie tin with the second round.
4. Preheat the fryer to 300 Fahrenheit for five minutes. You will need to place the tin in the basket and cover it. When the pastry has turned golden brown, you will need to remove the tin and let it cool. Cut into slices and serve with a dollop of cream.

209. Kidney Bean Tart

Prep.Time: 15 min - **Cooking Time:** 10-15 min - **Servings:** 4-6

Ingredients:
- ✓ 1 ½ cup plain flour
- ✓ 3 tbsp. unsalted butter
- ✓ 2 tbsp. powdered sugar
- ✓ 2 cups cold water
- ✓ 1 tbsp. sliced cashew

Filling:
- ✓ 2 cups mashed kidney beans
- ✓ 1 cup fresh cream
- ✓ 3 tbsp. butter

Directions:
1. Mix the ingredients together to form a crumbly mixture. Knead the mixture with cold milk and wrap it. Roll the dough out into two large circles and press that dough into the pie tin and prick the sides with a fork.
2. Cook the ingredients for the filling on a low flame and pour into the tin.
3. Cover the pie tin with the second round.
4. Preheat the fryer to 300 Fahrenheit for five minutes. You will need to place the tin in the basket and cover it. When the pastry has turned golden brown, you will need to remove the tin and let it cool. Cut into slices and serve with a dollop of cream.

210. Pumpkin Choco – Chip Muffins

Prep.Time: 15 min - **Cooking Time:** 15 min - **Servings:** 4

Ingredients:
- ✓ 2 cups All-purpose flour
- ✓ 1 ½ cup milk
- ✓ ½ tsp. baking powder
- ✓ ½ tsp. baking soda
- ✓ 2 tbsp. butter
- ✓ 2 cups grated pumpkin
- ✓ 1 tbsp. sugar
- ✓ 2 tsp. vinegar
- ✓ ½ cup chocolate chips
- ✓ Muffin cups

Directions:
1. Mix the ingredients together and use your fingers to get a crumbly mixture.
2. Add the baking soda and the vinegar to the milk and mix continuously. Add this milk to the mixture and create a batter, which you will need to transfer to the muffin cups.
3. Preheat the fryer to 300 Fahrenheit for five minutes. You will need to place the muffin cups in the basket and cover it. Cook the muffins for fifteen minutes and check whether or not the muffins are cooked using a toothpick. Remove the cups and serve hot.

211. Persimmons Pudding

Prep.Time: 15 min - **Cooking Time:** 10 minutes - **Servings:** 4

Ingredients:
- ✓ 1 cup persimmon slices
- ✓ 2 cups milk
- ✓ 2 tbsp. custard powder
- ✓ 3 tbsp. powdered sugar
- ✓ 3 tbsp. unsalted butter

Directions:
1. Boil the milk and the sugar in a pan and add the custard powder followed by the orange juice and stir till you get a thick mixture.
2. Preheat the fryer to 300 Fahrenheit for five minutes. Place the dish in the basket and reduce the temperature to 250 Fahrenheit. Cook for ten minutes and set aside to cool.

212. Mediterranean Waffles

Prep.Time: 15 min - **Cooking Time:** 10-15 min - **Servings:** 4-6

Ingredients:
- ✓ 1 ½ cups almond flour
- ✓ 3 eggs
- ✓ 2 tsp. dried basil
- ✓ 2 tsp. dried parsley
- ✓ Salt and Pepper to taste
- ✓ 3 tbsp. Butter
- ✓ 1 cup coleslaw

Directions:
1. Preheat the air fryer to 250 Fahrenheit.
2. In a small bowl, mix the ingredients, except for the coleslaw, together.
3. Ensure that the mixture is smooth and well balanced.
4. Take a waffle mold and grease it with butter. Add the batter to the mold and place it in the air fryer basket. Cook till both the sides have browned. Now, create a cavity and fill it with the coleslaw and serve.

213. Raspberry Cake

Prep.Time: 15 min - **Cooking Time:** 10-15 min - **Servings:** 2-4

Ingredients:
- ✓ 1 tbsp. unsalted butter
- ✓ 2 tbsp. water
- ✓ 2 cups sliced raspberries
- ✓ 1 cup all-purpose flour
- ✓ ½ cup condensed milk

Directions:
1. Add the ingredients together and whisk till you get a smooth mixture.
2. Prepare a tin by greasing it with butter. Transfer the mixture into the tin. Preheat the fryer to 300 Fahrenheit for five minutes. You will need to place the tin in the basket and cover it. Check whether the cake has risen well. When the cake has cooled, garnish with chocolate chips and serve.

214. Creamy Fig Pie

Prep.Time: 15 min - **Cooking Time:** 10-15 min - **Servings:** 4-6

Ingredients:
- ✓ 1 ½ cup plain flour
- ✓ 3 tbsp. unsalted butter
- ✓ 2 tbsp. powdered sugar
- ✓ 2 cups cold water
- ✓ 1 tbsp. sliced cashew

Filling:
- ✓ 2 cups sliced figs
- ✓ 1 cup fresh cream
- ✓ 3 tbsp. butter

Directions:
1. Mix the ingredients together to form a crumbly mixture. Knead the mixture with cold milk and wrap it. Roll the dough out into two large circles and press that dough into the pie tin and prick the sides with a fork.
2. Cook the ingredients for the filling on a low flame and pour into the tin.
3. Cover the pie tin with the second round.
4. Preheat the fryer to 300 Fahrenheit for five minutes. You will need to place the tin in the basket and cover it. When the pastry has turned golden brown, you will need to remove the tin and let it cool. Cut into slices and serve with a dollop of cream.

215. Chickpeas Tart

Prep.Time: 15 min - **Cooking Time:** 10-15 min - **Servings:** 4-6
Ingredients:
- ✓ 1 ½ cup plain flour
- ✓ 3 tbsp. unsalted butter
- ✓ 2 tbsp. powdered sugar
- ✓ 2 cups cold water
- ✓ 1 tbsp. sliced cashew

Filling:
- ✓ 2 cups mashed chickpeas
- ✓ 1 cup fresh cream
- ✓ 3 tbsp. butter

Directions:
1. Mix the ingredients together to form a crumbly mixture. Knead the mixture with cold milk and wrap it. Roll the dough out into two large circles and press that dough into the pie tin and prick the sides with a fork.
2. Cook the ingredients for the filling on a low flame and pour into the tin.
3. Cover the pie tin with the second round.
4. Preheat the fryer to 300 Fahrenheit for five minutes. You will need to place the tin in the basket and cover it. When the pastry has turned golden brown, you will need to remove the tin and let it cool. Cut into slices and serve with a dollop of cream.

216. Salmon Tart

Prep.Time: 15 min - **Cooking Time:** 10-15 min - **Servings:** 4-6
Ingredients:
- ✓ 1 ½ cup almond flour
- ✓ 3 tbsp. unsalted butter
- ✓ 2 tbsp. powdered sugar
- ✓ 2 cups cold water
- ✓ 1 tbsp. sliced cashew

Filling:
- ✓ 2 cups fileted salmon
- ✓ 1 cup sliced almonds
- ✓ 3 tbsp. butter

Directions:
1. Mix the ingredients together to form a crumbly mixture. Knead the mixture with cold milk and wrap it. Roll the dough out into two large circles and press that dough into the pie tin and prick the sides with a fork.
2. Cook the ingredients for the filling on a low flame and pour into the tin.
3. Cover the pie tin with the second round.
4. Preheat the fryer to 300 Fahrenheit for five minutes. You will need to place the tin in the basket and cover it. When the pastry has turned golden brown, you will need to remove the tin and let it cool. Cut into slices and serve with a dollop of cream.

217. Mangosteen Tarts

Prep.Time: 15 min - **Cooking Time:** 10-15 minutes - **Servings:** 4
Ingredients:
- ✓ 1 ½ cup plain flour
- ✓ 3 tbsp. unsalted butter
- ✓ 2 tbsp. powdered sugar
- ✓ 2 cups cold water
- ✓ 1 tbsp. sliced cashew

Filling:
- ✓ 1 cup sliced mangosteen
- ✓ 1 cup fresh cream
- ✓ 3 tbsp. butter

Directions:
1. Mix the ingredients together to form a crumbly mixture. Knead the mixture with cold milk and wrap it. Roll the dough out into two large circles and press that dough into the pie tin and prick the sides with a fork.
2. Cook the ingredients for the filling on a low flame and pour into the tin.
3. Cover the pie tin with the second round.
4. Preheat the fryer to 300 Fahrenheit for five minutes. You will need to place the tin in the basket and cover it. When the pastry has turned golden brown, you will need to remove the tin and let it cool. Cut into slices and serve with a dollop of cream.

218. Chestnut Tart

Prep.Time: 15 min - **Cooking Time:** 10-15 min - **Servings:** 4-6
Ingredients:
- ✓ 1 ½ cup plain flour
- ✓ 3 tbsp. unsalted butter
- ✓ 2 tbsp. powdered sugar
- ✓ 2 cups cold water
- ✓ 1 tbsp. sliced cashew

Filling:
- ✓ 2 cups sliced chestnut
- ✓ 1 cup fresh cream
- ✓ 3 tbsp. butter

Directions:
1. In a large bowl, mix the flour, cocoa powder, butter and sugar with your fingers. The mixture should resemble breadcrumbs. Knead the dough using the cold milk and wrap it and leave it to cool for ten minutes. Roll the dough out into the pie and prick the sides of the pie.
2. Mix the ingredients for the filling in a bowl. Make sure that it is a little thick.
3. Preheat the fryer to 300 Fahrenheit for five minutes. You will need to place the tin in the basket and cover it. When the pastry has turned golden brown, you will need to remove the tin and let it cool. Cut into slices and serve with a dollop of cream.

219. Raspberry Cake

Prep.Time: 15 min - **Cooking Time:** 10-15 min - **Servings:** 4-6
Ingredients:
- ✓ 3 cups almond flour
- ✓ 3 eggs
- ✓ 2 tsp. dried basil
- ✓ 2 tsp. dried parsley
- ✓ Salt and Pepper to taste
- ✓ 3 tbsp. Butter
- ✓ 2 cups pitted and sliced dates

Directions:
1. Preheat the air fryer to 250 Fahrenheit.
2. In a small bowl, mix the ingredients, except for the dates, together. Ensure that the mixture is smooth and well balanced.
3. Take a waffle mold and grease it with butter. Add the batter to the mold and place it in the air fryer basket. Cook till both the sides have browned. Create a cavity and fill with dates and serve.

220. Semolina Pudding

Prep.Time: 15 min - **Cooking Time:** 10 min - **Servings:** 4
Ingredients:
- ✓ 2 cups milk
- ✓ 2 tbsp. custard powder
- ✓ 3 tbsp. powdered sugar
- ✓ 2 tbsp. semolina
- ✓ 3 tbsp. unsalted butter

Directions:
1. Boil the milk and the sugar in a pan and add the custard powder and stir till you get a thick mixture. Add the semolina to the bowl and ensure that the mixture becomes slightly thicker.
2. Preheat the fryer to 300 Fahrenheit for five minutes. Place the dish in the basket and reduce the temperature to 250 Fahrenheit. Cook for ten minutes and set aside to cool.

221. Simple & Delicious Spiced Apples

Prep.Time: 10 min - **Cooking Time:** 10 min - **Servings:** 2-4

Ingredients:
- ✓ 4 apples, sliced
- ✓ 1 tsp apple pie spice
- ✓ 2 tbsp sugar
- ✓ 2 tbsp ghee, melted

Directions:
1. Add apple slices into the mixing bowl. Add remaining ingredients on top of apple slices and toss until well coated.
2. Transfer apple slices on instant vortex air fryer oven pan and air fry at 350 F for 10 minutes.
3. Top with ice cream and serve.

222. Delicious Brownies

Prep.Time: 10 min - **Cooking Time:** 33 min - **Servings:** 4-6

Ingredients:
- ✓ 2 eggs
- ✓ ½ cup walnuts, chopped
- ✓ ¼ cup all-purpose flour
- ✓ 1 cup brown sugar
- ✓ 1 ½ tsp vanilla
- ✓ ¼ cup of cocoa powder
- ✓ ½ cup butter
- ✓ Pinch of salt

Directions:
1. Spray air fryer shallow baking dish with cooking spray and set aside.
2. In a microwave-safe bowl, combine together butter and cocoa powder and microwave until butter is melted. Stir to combine and set aside to cool.
3. Once the butter mixture is cool then whisk in eggs and vanilla.
4. Stir in brown sugar, walnuts, flour, and salt.
5. Pour batter into the prepared baking dish and bake in instant vortex air fryer oven at 320 F for 33 minutes.
6. Allow to cool completely then slice and serve.

223. Peanut Butter Cookies

Prep.Time: 10 min - **Cooking Time:** 5 minutes - **Servings:** 4

Ingredients:
- ✓ 1 egg, lightly beaten
- ✓ 1 cup of sugar
- ✓ 1 cup creamy peanut butter

Directions:
1. In a mixing bowl, mix together egg, sugar, and peanut butter until well combined.
2. Spray air fryer oven tray with cooking spray.
3. Using ice cream scooper scoop out cookie onto the tray and flattened them using a fork.
4. Bake cookie at 350 F for 5 minutes.
5. Cook remaining cookie batches using the same temperature. Serve and enjoy.

224. Dried Raspberries

Prep.Time: 10 min - **Cooking Time:** 12-15 hours - **Servings:** 4-6

Ingredients:
- ✓ 4 cups raspberries, wash and dry
- ✓ 1/4 cup fresh lemon juice

Directions:
1. Add raspberries and lemon juice in a bowl and toss well.
2. Arrange raspberries on instant vortex air fryer oven tray and dehydrate at 135 F for 12-15 hours.
3. Store in an air-tight container.

225. Healthy Oatmeal Cookies

Prep.Time: 10 min - **Cooking Time:** 5 min - **Servings:** 4-6

Ingredients:
- ✓ 1 egg, lightly beaten
- ✓ ¾ cup dried cranberries
- ✓ 2 cups old fashioned oats
- ✓ 1 tsp vanilla
- ✓ 1 stick butter
- ✓ 1 ½ cups brown sugar
- ✓ ½ tsp baking soda
- ✓ ½ tsp ground nutmeg
- ✓ 1 tsp cinnamon
- ✓ ½ cup can pumpkin
- ✓ 1 cup flour
- ✓ Pinch of salt

Directions:
1. Add all ingredients into the mixing bowl and mix until well combined.
2. Spray air fryer oven pan with cooking spray.
3. Using scooper scoop cookie dough onto the prepared pan and bake at 350 F for 5 minutes.

226. Sweet Peach Wedges

Prep.Time: 10 min - **Cooking Time:** 6-8 hours - **Servings:** 4

Ingredients:
- ✓ 3 peaches, cut and remove pits and sliced
- ✓ 1/2 cup fresh lemon juice

Directions:
1. Add lemon juice and peach slices into the bowl and toss well.
2. Arrange peach slices on instant vortex air fryer oven rack and dehydrate at 135 F for 6-8 hours.
3. Serve and enjoy.

227. Tangy Mango Slices

Prep.Time: 10 min - **Cooking Time:** 12 hours - **Servings:** 4-6

Ingredients:
- ✓ 4 mangoes, peel and cut into ¼-inch slices
- ✓ 1/4 cup fresh lemon juice
- ✓ 1 tbsp honey

Directions:
1. In a bowl, mix together lemon juice and honey and set aside.
2. Add mango slices in lemon-honey mixture and coat well.
3. Arrange mango slices on instant vortex air fryer rack and dehydrate at 135 F for 12 hours.

228. Grilled Peaches

Prep.Time: 10 min - **Cooking Time:** 10 min - **Servings:** 4

Ingredients:
- ✓ 2 peaches, cut into wedges and remove pits
- ✓ ¼ cup butter, diced into pieces
- ✓ ¼ cup brown sugar
- ✓ ¼ cup graham cracker crumbs

Directions:
1. Arrange peach wedges on air fryer oven rack and air fry at 350 F for 5 minutes.
2. In a bowl, mix together butter, brown sugar, and graham cracker crumbs.
3. Turn peaches skin side down.
4. Spoon butter mixture over top of peaches and air fry for 5 minutes more.
5. Top with whipped cream and serve.

NOTE YOUR FAVORITE RECIPES

PAGE	NUMBER	RECIPE NAME

PAGE	NUMBER	RECIPE NAME